THE
OLD NORTHWEST
PIONEER PERIOD
1815-1840

Volume I

Lefevre J. Cranston

"I loved thee, when first down thy placid wave
And round the bend of hills, myself I gave
To the wide reaching West . . ."

THE
OLD NORTHWEST
PIONEER PERIOD
1815-1840

BY

R. CARLYLE BULEY

VOLUME ONE

INDIANA UNIVERSITY PRESS
BLOOMINGTON
1951

PRINTED IN THE UNITED STATES OF AMERICA
BY THE HADDON CRAFTSMEN, SCRANTON, PA.

To
EVELYN BARNETT BULEY

PREFACE

THE ORDINANCE of 1787 established the first colony of the United States, the Territory of the United States Northwest of the River Ohio. From this territory five states (and part of a sixth—Minnesota east of the Mississippi River) were eventually admitted into the Union on an equal footing with the original states. As the United States moved on to the Pacific and a new northwest developed, the region north of the Ohio came to be known in American history as the Old Northwest.

The Old Northwest, geographically the connecting region between the Great Lakes–St. Lawrence system and the Mississippi, and socially the fusion center of population elements from the Northeast, East, South, and Europe, came in time to control the economic and political balance in the Union; traditionally and culturally it developed and maintained, at least until the close of the Civil War, something of an entity.

In 1829 the Detroit *North-Western Journal* said: "It is a matter of general notoriety, that the history of the North-Western Territory, of which this section of country was once a part, is yet to be written." Although many historians and writers have since worked at some part of the task, a realization of the size and importance of which has grown with the years, no one has yet covered that history comprehensively.

This work presents an outline of the history of the Old Northwest from 1815, the beginning of the "Great Migration," to 1840, the date which roughly marks the end of the pioneer period. In it I have sought to accomplish three things: first, to present a balanced summary of the record, without emphasizing the interesting and dramatic at the expense of the prosaic but important; second, to introduce the reader to the rich contemporary historical literature of the period and region; and third, through this literature to capture something of the attitudes and beliefs, struggles and way of life—what Timothy Flint called the "material of poetry"—of the time and place. If at times I have chosen merely to hurl the chronicle at the reader, it is because there it was and because I believe it worth preserving; if at other times I have drawn freely upon the words of the contemporary actors and writers, it is for the purpose of accomplishing my second and third objectives. To further the last objective I have in many instances used colloquialisms and frequently used expressions of the period, not only in paraphrasing but in the text.

The illustrations have in general been selected from the works of artists of the period.

The most important single sources I have used are the newspapers; the next most important are the contemporary periodicals, pamphlets, books, and the accumulated publications of the historical societies of the states of the Old Northwest. Patience and time only are required to comb from these and other items a considerable content of material; no historian can achieve more than an approximation of the history in the selection and presentation of that content. Naturally I have also utilized special histories, biographies, and monographs for coverage of special topics and have explored numerous collections of manuscripts. In most instances, I have sampled the sources of the secondary works sufficiently to justify their use; in all instances I have sought to make clear where they have been used.

In the early 1830's James Hall expressed his creed: "I have loved the West, and it still claims my preference over all other portions of the earth. Its magnitude, its fertility, the kindness of the climate, the variety and excellence of its productions, are unrivaled in our own country, if not on the globe. In these characters it presents itself to my mind, in the light of a strong and generous parent, whose arms are spread to extend protection, happiness, and life to throngs who seek them from other and less favored climes. . . ."

Two generations later Theodore Roosevelt said: "The states that have grown up around the Great Lakes and in the Valley of the upper Mississippi, [are] the states which are destined to be the greatest, the richest, the most prosperous of all the great, rich, and prosperous commonwealths which go to make up the mightiest republic the world has ever seen. These states . . . form the heart of the country geographically, and they will soon become the heart in population and in political and social importance. . . . I should be sorry to think that before these states there loomed a future of material prosperity merely. I regard this section of the country as the heart of true American sentiment."

And in 1921 W. L. George, the English novelist, wrote: "Without wealth aristocracy cannot survive; without wealth it cannot be born. Wealth does not necessarily create aristocracy, but it can do so. I feel that the aristocracy of America will not be maintained out of the elegancies of Boston or the languors of South Carolina, but is being born, born of the rugged, fierce stock of the Middle West. After all, the early aristocrats, the Normans and the Crusaders, too, were kid gloved neither in their morals nor in their manners."

Feeling with Hall, and hoping with Roosevelt and George, on this, the one hundred and fiftieth anniversary of the appearance of Indiana on the maps of our country, I present this segment of the history of one of the sections which comprise the United States of America. For as John Finley, Indiana editor and poet, said:

> Then who can view the glorious *West*,
> With all her hopes for coming time,
> And hoard his feelings unexpressed
> In poetry or prose, or *rhyme*?

ACKNOWLEDGEMENTS:

My indebtedness to James Hall, Timothy Flint, Daniel Drake, and scores of their contemporaries is obvious; less obvious is that which I owe to Logan Esarey, Frederic Logan Paxson, and other teachers who first introduced me to these men. To the critical scholarship of Milo M. Quaife, who read the manuscript, I am deeply indebted; his interest and encouragement were no less appreciated than his knowledge. Of the many librarians and specialists on the region who have graciously co-operated I wish particularly to thank Paul M. Angle—who also read the manuscript—Jay Monaghan, Ernest T. Wessen, and R. E. Banta; also Frederick Kuhns for valuable help on the tangled problem of religion; Donald F. Carmony, who read parts of the manuscript and supplied additional newspaper items; and Clark Ray for his map-making pen. It is impossible to mention individually the many students and assistants who made contributions and labored at copying and checking; their interest in this history was a major stimulus to its completion.

The Indiana University Library generously permitted reproductions of the Lefevre J. Cranstone originals, the Indiana University Foundation did the same for those of Basil Hall, the Indiana State Library, the Indiana Historical Society Library, and the Wisconsin State Historical Library contributed other illustrations, and Eugene D. Rigney and the Ross County (Ohio) Historical Society reproduced rare prints not available elsewhere. The painting of the "City of Detroit, Michigan," by W. J. Bennett, is reproduced through the courtesy of the Detroit Institute of Art.

I acknowledge with gratitude the financial aid given by Stanley Pargellis and the Newberry Library Committee on Mid-Western Studies which expedited the finishing of the manuscript, and that given by the Graduate School of Indiana University which provided for its processing.

Last but not least I express my sincerest thanks to Howard H. Peckham, who directed the editing and publishing; to the editorial staff of the Society, whose patient, critical, and exacting editing saved me many an error; to Bruce Rogers "Of Indiana," master typographer and designer of books, who shared so freely of his knowledge of bookmaking; and the Lilly Endowment, Incorporated, whose interest made possible the publication of this work in its present form.

BLOOMINGTON, INDIANA   R. C. B.
July 4, 1950

CONTENTS

Volume I

ing—Agriculture—Breaking and plowing—Corn, wheat, reaping, horticulture, and silk culture—Livestock—Agricultural improvements—The agricultural press—The weather —Early clothing—Flax, wool, spinning, weaving, and dyeing—Quilting and coverlet making—Butchering and meat packing—Dairying—Household economy—Cooking, soapmaking, preserving, sugaring, distilling, milling, and smithing—Prairies—Improved homes—Life in country and town

Health—Diseases—Domestic medicine: Home remedies and folk cures—Country doctors—Regular practice—Surgery— Medical education—Medical literature—Dentistry—Irregular practice: Botanics, Eclectics, Homeopaths—Regulation of medical practice—"Patents"—Childbirth—Drugs

Sports—Corn huskings—Play parties—Courtships and weddings—Visiting—Home amusements—Young folks and the woods—Spelling bees and singing schools—City amusements —Dress—Pioneer speech—Western character and manners —Morals—Lotteries—Whiskey—Crime—Criticism of the West—Western reaction to criticism—Estimate of western character

The fur trade in the Old Northwest: under the French, the English, and the United States; methods, personnel, importance of—River transportation—Types of boats—The steamboat and its influence—Steamboats on the Great Lakes —Problems of river navigation—Life of the boatmen—Early roads in the Northwest—The Old National Road—Other roads—Problems of construction—Stage service, teams, wagons, and wagoners—Stock droving on the roads—Taverns and hotels—Movers and travelers—Canals: Ohio, Indiana, Illinois—Passenger and freight lines—Beginning of railroads—Coming of the railroad craze to the West— Railroads vs. canals—Commerce of the Northwest—Products and prices—"Buy-at-home" movements—Relation of the Northwest to the East; to the South—Commercial centers in the West—Salt, coal, iron—Manufacturing in the Northwest—Merchandising and advertising—The peddler —Mercantile centers—Boom times in the 1830's

ILLUSTRATIONS

Volume I

MAPS

1

New Homes in the West

A savage wilderness, resting in primæval solitude, or inhabited only by a race whose practice it is when they migrate, to leave no trace behind, is suddenly opened to an eager multitude, who pour in like the waters of the sea, and cover it with civilized life. The forest falls around them, and is consumed or converted into habitations; the ground is opened by the industrious ploughshare, to the sun; the vapors and the malaria dry up; the fruits of other climes are planted; the comfortable log house is raised, the rude wagon is built, and the spot where "yesterday" all was silent, save the beast and the bird, becomes today the home of the woodsman—the center of human affections—the nucleus perhaps of an intelligent, social, virtuous community—the focus, where, it may be, light shall emanate to other parts of the world.

Western Monthly Magazine, November, 1836

IT WAS spring at Pittsburgh,[1] wet and cold, but nevertheless, spring. The muddy waters of the Monongahela joined the clear and more rapid current of the Allegheny, and westward between the wooded hills stretched the broad Ohio, *La Belle Rivière* of the French, for a thousand miles an open and inviting pathway to the West. The thriving young city of about 5,000 people was stirring with the bustle of commerce and industry, for the western traffic was booming, and Pittsburgh was the gateway to the West.

Between Pittsburgh and Wheeling the river, studded with alluvial islands, wound back and forth between shores which alternately presented almost level bottoms and headlands which rose three to four hundred feet. Said the traveler,

Truly, the waters have here chosen a lovely spot for their meeting, and it was but natural that such a stream as the Ohio should spring from such

[1] The original spelling for the town at the forks of the Ohio, as used by Gen. John Forbes, was "Pittsburgh." This is also the spelling used in the act of incorporation, 1816. The more usual spelling, however, in the early nineteenth century was "Pittsburg." Travelers, newspapers, journals, etc., generally so spelled it. Late in the century the Post Office Department ruled in favor of this spelling, but the decision was reversed in 1908. Any deviations from the "official" spelling in these volumes are in keeping with the sources used.

a union. Looking backward now I could see that river, like a young giant rejoicing in its birth, sweeping suddenly on its course, but turning every moment among its green islands, as if to look back till the last upon the home of its infancy. . . . The windings of the river present, at every turn, some of the most beautiful views in the world; but the regular alternations of "bluff" and "bottom" give such a sameness to the landscape, that unless familiar with the points of the country around, one might be dropped in a dozen different places along the river, and not be aware of a change in his situation. Nature seems to have delighted in repeating again and again the same lovely forms, which she first moulded in this favorite region.

This traveler, who first saw the Ohio at Wheeling in 1833, continued:

The Ohio is beneath your feet. . . . The clear majestic tide, the fertile islands on its bosom, the bold and towering heights opposite, with the green esplanade of alluvion in front, and the forest-crowned headlands above and below, round which the river sweeps away, to bless and gladden the fruitful regions that drink its limpid waters,—these, with the recollections of deeds done upon its banks—the wild incidents and savage encounters of border story, so immediately contrasted with all the luxuries of civilization that now float securely upon that peaceful current,—these make a moral picture whose colours are laid in the heart, never to be effaced:—no man will ever forget his first view of the Ohio.[2]

From the pack-train trails and wilderness roads, by Braddock's Road from Virginia, Forbes's Road from Philadelphia, even by the Genesee Road through New York, came the movers. At Redstone on the Monongahela, Kittanning on the Allegheny, and most of all at Pittsburgh at the forks, they assembled. Some had sent their belongings by the big Conestoga freighters, ridden the stagecoaches and stopped at taverns, but the greater numbers traveled in the light wagons drawn by horses or oxen, hauling

[2] Charles Fenno Hoffman, *A Winter in the West* (2 volumes. New York, 1835), I, 49–50, 57, 59–60.

So much had been written in praise of the Ohio that by 1838 a New England traveler, like the Athenian citizen who tired of hearing of Aristides the Just, was almost prepared to be prejudiced against it. "I had often heard the praises of this majestic river sung, and had curbed my expectations lest I should be disappointed. The Ohio *is* a beautiful river. There are points on the Hudson and Connecticut, and other rivers of the East, which equal any thing I saw on the Ohio; but its peculiarity is that it is *all* beautiful. There are no points bare of beauty; but every mile is as rich in scenery as it was in verdure at the time of my passage down its 'winding way.'" Abner Dumont Jones, *Illinois and the West* . . . (Boston and Philadelphia, 1838), 23.

The scenery on the Upper Ohio was best depicted in colors by the English engraver-artist, Lefevre J. Cranstone, who in 1859 made some 312 pen-and-water-color drawings largely of western Virginia, Ohio, and Indiana. To no subject did he turn more frequently than the Ohio. Originals in Indiana University Library.

their plunder with them, or walked with packs, and in some instances pulled carts or pushed wheelbarrows. At the river towns axmen, carpenters, and boatmakers were ready to supply anything from a light skiff for two up to the elaborate seventy-foot barges with sails and poling platforms, but whether the newcomer got a good job of seasoned wood with well-caulked seams, or a green, heavy, and leaky craft, depended upon his own knowledge and shrewdness. Many secured boats by trading their horses; some built their own. Equipping emigrants was almost a business in itself, and to the stores freighted by wagon over the long haul from Philadelphia and Baltimore, Pittsburgh added the products of her own budding manufacturers—the blacksmiths, cutlers, founders, glassmakers, hatters, saddlers, ropemakers, tanners, chandlers, weavers, and bootmakers.[3]

When the river rose and floating ice no longer threatened, the sundry types of craft were loaded and the tide of humanity headed for the land of promise, the West. Armed with only a copy of Cumings' *Western Pilot* or Cramer's *Navigator*, or depending upon hearsay and his own ability, the emigrant faced the dangers of snags and sawyers, planters, and driftwood islands. Little time had he to notice, and none to record, the beauties of bountifully wooded shores, as yet undenuded by the ax, or the majestic stretches of stream bearing their burden of strange craft,

> As down Ohio's ever ebbing tide,
> Oarless and sailless silently they glide,
> How still the scene, how lifeless, yet how fair,

[3] Among the travelers' descriptions of Pittsburgh in the period from 1800 to 1820 are those in John Melish, *Travels in the United States of America, in the Years 1806, & 1807, and 1809, 1810, & 1811* . . . (2 volumes. Philadelphia, 1812); Morris Birkbeck, *Notes on a Journey in America, from the Coast of Virginia to the Territory of Illinois* . . . (3d ed. London, 1818); Henry Bradshaw Fearon, *Sketches of America* . . . (2d ed. London, 1818); Estwick Evans, *A Pedestrious Tour of Four Thousand Miles, through the Western States and Territories, during the Winter and Spring of 1818* . . . (Concord, N. H., 1819), reprinted in Reuben Gold Thwaites (ed.), *Early Western Travels* . . . (32 volumes. Cleveland, 1904–7), VIII; Elias Pym Fordham, *Personal Narrative of Travels in Virginia, Maryland, Pennsylvania, Ohio, Indiana, Kentucky; and of a Residence in the Illinois Territory: 1817–1818*, edited by Frederic A. Ogg (Cleveland, 1906); James Flint, *Letters from America, containing Observations on the Climate and Agriculture of the Western States, the Manners of the People, the Prospects of Emigrants* . . . (Edinburgh, 1822); John Woods, *Two Years' Residence in the Settlement on the English Prairie, in the Illinois Country* . . . (London, 1822), reprinted in *Early Western Travels*, X; William Tell Harris, *Remarks Made During a Tour through the United States of America, in the Years, 1817, 1818, and 1819* . . . (London, 1821).

Was the lone land that met the strangers there!
No smiling villages, or curling smoke,
The busy haunts of busy men bespoke,
....
Nothing appear'd, but Nature unsubdu'd,
One endless, noiseless, woodland solitude. . . .[4]

The thrill of new ventures in strange lands no doubt was there, but to the man with family it was largely a part of the prosaic day's work. Rather it was the traveler, the Easterner or Englishman with means and education, who was impressed with the pageantry of the scene, the beauties of nature, the manners of the people. To him the collection of floating contrivances was an interesting sight: pirogues, batteaux, barges, schooners, and keelboats; flatboats, broadhorns, arks, and now and then a steamboat.[5] Equally fascinating were the picturesque, hard-spitting and fluently cussing professional rivermen.

Since the Indian shore of the Ohio no longer presented the danger of hostile arrows and bullets, the heavily boarded and enclosed flatboat, or Kentucky boat, was no longer a necessity, and the cumbersome ark began to prove its worth. These craft, shallow and uncovered, ran up to a hundred feet in length and, except for the long sweep at the stern, were largely at the mercy of the current. But for the family or group which wished to take much plunder, the ark had its advantages. In its spacious hulk were packed boxes, bags, and bundles; tools, wagons, chickens, horses, neat cattle, and hogs; dogs, children, and supplies. A shanty in the middle for the family, or several families, if it was a communal affair, offered shelter. A stone- or dirt-filled enclosure housed a fire for domestic purposes. A pillar of smoke by day and of fire by night marked the progress of the crude craft, from which emanated the squalling of infants, the yapping of dogs, and chatter of voices.

The more cautious traveled only by day; but some going far, or fearing the good land would be gone, traveled by night as well, taking turn at the sweeps and on watch. The miles slowly fell behind as the progress varied, dependent upon current and wind, from a few miles a day to forty or fifty. After a sojourn of from ten days to three weeks on the river, the settler, arrived at the

[4] James Kirke Paulding, *The Backwoodsman* (Philadelphia, 1818), 65–66.
[5] For a discussion of river boats and navigation, see Chapter VII.

point of debarkation, could sell his raft for use downstream or
for the timbers in it, or, if he was locating close by, he might
knock it apart himself and use the material for a temporary
shelter.

The poet, in retrospect, paid his tribute to the river, neglected
in sentiment and description by the emigrant:

> O loveliest river of this Western clime!
> Thou shalt not flow unsung, as in the time
> When in the mirror of thy winding waters
> Gazed on their forms, the groups of Indian daughters.
>
> . . . .
> O'er the wide ocean they have borne thy name;
> Thy sons have told thy legends unto fame;
> The enchanted Frank hath fondly lingered here,
> And called thee, in his joy, "La Belle Riviere;"
> The Briton stranger here hath fought and died,
> And then *he* bore thy name o'er ocean's tide;—
> The daring emigrant hath ploughed thy wave,
> And built upon thy shores a hut—a grave;—
> The rudest savage hath his tale to tell,
> What deeds of wonder and of war befel,
> Ere the white robber came and drove him far,
> To hunt his game beneath a setting star.
>
> But not alone to swell the harp of Clio,
> Thou windest in thy beauty—bright Ohio![6]

Not all came by river, for in summer or early fall the low stage
of water made such travel precarious. There were those who
would rather undertake the laborious travel by land. The Cumberland Road was opened to the Ohio at Wheeling in 1817. West
from Pittsburgh ran the road to Steubenville and on to Zanesville
and to Columbus, but horseback mail service between Pittsburgh
and Steubenville did not come until 1818, and it was two years
later before a stage line was in use. Zane's Road from Wheeling
to Limestone, laid out in 1796, was so worn in places that the
ruts were almost deep enough to bury a horse in. From the South
across Kentucky came the streams of emigrants to swell the tide.
"We do not recollect of ever having seen so many families
emigrating to the western country as are this fall," said a Mays-

---

[6] C. P. C., "To the River Ohio," in *The Hesperian*, II (1839), 217.

ville editor.[7] "Old America seems to be breaking up and moving westward," wrote Birkbeck in 1817. Easterners on the move said they were going to Ohio, but when one got to Ohio the people there were going on to Indiana, Missouri, or Alabama. "The American has always something better in his eye, further west; he therefore lives and dies on hope, a mere gypsey in this particular."[8] The final point of settlement receded as the traveler moved west and would continue to do so, thought one observer, until terminated only by the effective barrier of the Pacific Ocean.[9]

§

The peace at the end of the second war with England had come with unexpected suddenness. The joyful elation over Jackson's victory at New Orleans had hardly subsided when the bells, handbills, and excited cries of citizens in New York announced "A peace! A peace!" In spite of the fact that the treaty did not mention the major causes of the war, the terms were more favorable than the military successes of the Americans would in themselves have warranted. Relatively few people, particularly in the West, saw any incongruity in Madison's declaration that the war had "been waged with a success which is the natural result of the wisdom of the Legislative Councils, of the patriotism of the people, of the public spirit of the Militia, and of the valor of the military and naval forces of the country." The spirit of nationalism forged ahead apace; America entered into adolescence. A new era was at hand.

[7] Copied in *Zanesville Express,* December 12, 1816. Ohio roads were described as intolerable, shocking, wretched, and devilish, in fact, the worst in the world. Horses expired on them, axles snapped, and coaches of Kentucky notables upset. *Ibid.,* November 30, 1814. "Emigration to this state is almost immense: The road leading through this town seems to be covered with wagons and carriages of all descriptions." *Ibid.,* October 5, 1815. "We are induced to believe that in no year since the adoption of the Federal Constitution, has the tide of emigration set so strongly westward as the last." Chillicothe *Supporter,* June 24, 1817. From Philadelphia an observer wrote: "I can scarcely walk a square without meeting with Irish, Dutch, English and Scotch emigrants, whose destination is principally Ohio and Indiana." He predicted that in twenty years the bulk of the population would be west of the Allegheny Mountains. Letter in the Mount Pleasant (Ohio) *Philanthropist,* November 14, 1817.
[8] Birkbeck, *Notes on a Journey in America,* 31; William Faux, *Memorable Days in America* . . . (London, 1823), 179.
[9] Fearon, *Sketches of America,* 234.

Since the earliest years of the young republic, problems of foreign affairs had loomed large in its path of development. In 1793 war began between England and the French Republic, to continue with but one interruption to the end of the Napoleonic period in 1815. During the years following the War for Independence hard times had sent the people westward into the trans-Appalachian region, and Kentucky, Tennessee, and a broken fringe along the southern part of the Old Northwest were settled. But with the European wars of the French Revolution came the opening of the French and Dutch West Indies, the demand for American products, and high profits in the carrying trade. Sailors, merchants, farmers, and artisans found attractive markets for their goods and services, and emigration to the West slumped, especially to the region north of the Ohio. Kentucky and Tennessee continued to gain, for the prosperity of wartimes affected less the regions of Virginia and the Carolinas than New England and the Middle States. The Harrison Land Act of 1800, which permitted installment payments over a period of five years, and temporary peace in Europe brought enough settlers into that part of the Northwest Territory still bearing the name to justify the admission of Ohio as a state under Republican auspices in 1803.[10] War again checked the movement, however, and soon blockades, orders in council, decrees, impressment, and rights of neutrals became problems of national concern. Nonimportation, embargo, and nonintercourse produced disastrous effects on American prosperity and threatened ruin to commerce.[11] Napoleonic trickery, English blundering, and Republican indecision combined with the flare-up of national feeling and the desire for expansion to drag the United States into the European struggle.

The second war with England did not involve any great expenditure of life, property, and treasure. As wars go, it was a small war, but in economic effects and nationalistic influences it

[10] Indiana Territory was set off in 1800, and only that part east of the Indiana line from the mouth of the Kentucky River to Fort Recovery and due north to Canada was left as the Territory Northwest of the Ohio. See Chapter II and map, 62.

[11] For views on the comparative results in New England and the South, see Edward Channing, *A History of the United States* (6 volumes. New York, 1905-1925), IV, 387; Henry Adams, *History of the United States* . . . (9 volumes. New York, 1891-1911), IV, 280; James Truslow Adams, *New England in the Republic, 1776-1850* (Boston, 1926), 250.

played a part out of proportion to its size. The Bank of the United States expired by charter limitation in 1811, and for money the country was left to rely upon notes of individuals and corporations, foreign coins which had been recognized as legal tender, cut money, the few United States coins which remained in the country, and state bank notes. From 88 state banks in 1811, mostly located in the West and western sections of the older states, the number increased in two years to 288.[12] With note issues three times capital stock, and often ten times specie held, the business of the country was soon on a paper basis. Trade restrictions and the war served as a protective tariff, and much capital, especially in New England, was turned from trade and shipping into manufacturing. New England goods sold in the South and West far overbalanced purchases, and the ensuing drainage of specie from those regions forced their banks to suspend specie payment. But times were hard everywhere. The war, with the blockade, taxes, and property destruction, was exacting its toll, and by 1814 not only those who had made up their minds before the war but thousands of others turned their faces to the West.

Better times were expected with the peace, but with peace came quite the contrary. Merchants prepared for revival of commerce, ships were overhauled and rigged, and goods were advertised for. Some time was allowed to elapse for the news of the peace to reach warships at sea, but in March, 1815, a great merchant fleet sailed away to Europe, still at war and hungry for American goods. Then came the fleets of English merchantmen, bearing the silks, hardware, wine, molasses, and coffee which Americans after a prolonged period of curtailed consumption were eager to get. Auction sales were held in the leading Atlantic Coast cities from Boston to Charleston, and American buyers scrambled for the importations, often at prices which domestic producers would hardly have dared to charge.[13]

Nor was this the worst. With June came Waterloo and peace in Europe, the closing of many continental markets to England,

[12] John Bach McMaster, *A History of the People of the United States from the Revolution to the Civil War* (8 volumes. New York, 1883–1913), IV, 290.
[13] "New Goods at Peace Prices—Just Received from Philadelphia!" and similar notices were published in Ohio papers as early as May. See Chillicothe *Supporter*, May 30, 1815.

and decreased demand for American goods. At the very time that decreasing profits in the carrying trade and export business made necessary further investment opportunities for Americans in their own manufacturing, England, with no notion of losing a good market to her late offspring, saw the American market as her financial salvation. Gladly would she have sold at or below cost to overwhelm threatening competition, but at first the dumping process was not necessary. When in the autumn cash sales in America began to slacken, business was promoted by liberal credit extensions, and overbuying was the result. Importers, merchants, and manufacturers soon found themselves overstocked with goods which they could neither sell nor pay for. By the end of the year American woolen and cotton industries were in a bad way, and it was evident that neither patriotism nor prices were enough to stop the deluge of English imports.

The tariff of 1816 was supposed to save the day, but English manufacturers and exporters were wise in the ways of the business world. Disbanded armies and unemployment offered a cheap labor market. England was confronted with a colossal national debt. Sales abroad had to be made, and neither tariffs nor fine points of business ethics were permitted to interfere. Shiploads of goods, many of them unordered, were sent to the United States, and the dumping process began with a vengeance. Goods were billed to one agent at prices below cost, and tariff duties paid on false invoices. Once safely through the tariff lines, the goods were sold by the first agent to another, who, knowing the real values, disposed of them at auction. When an American merchant ordered goods, manufacturers would duplicate the order, ship it through on false billing and frequently auction it off in the importing merchant's town before he had his stuff on the shelves.

By the winter of 1816 widespread distress and unemployment were common in American cities. Of the estimated 130,000 spindles in 140 mills near Providence, only those in the old Slater Mill were reported turning in 1816.[14] Shipping, upon which probably one seventh of New England's population was dependent, was almost as hard hit as industry. Ships lay idle and deteriorating, crews wandered away, and artisans and traders dependent upon coasting and foreign trade were thrown out

[14] Adams, *New England in the Republic,* 309.

of employment. Agriculture, too, felt the stress, for not only were the farmers deprived of the wartime markets, but many had been caught in the postwar buying spree and some in land speculation as well. The new factory economy had unsettled conditions in the villages and on the farms. The abnormally cold season of 1816–17 and ensuing crop failures made taxes more burdensome and debtors more numerous.[15]

Besides the economic disorders of the times there were evidences of social and religious discontent. The old restraints weighed heavily on the more individualistic and independent types, and the distant promises of liberal reforms hardly seemed worth waiting for. New England may have been in transition; many New Englanders were in transit, for:

> 'Tis I can delve and plough, love,
> And you can spin and sew;
> And we'll settle on the banks
> Of the pleasant Ohio.[16]

Since the coming of the white man to America there never had been a time when the appeal of the region beyond, whether for precious metals, furs, land speculation, or homes, did not furnish sufficient incentive to a few bold pioneers. Mass migration, the *volkwanderung*, which included many of the older generation as well as the youths starting out in life, came only when the pressure of unsatisfactory conditions back home was combined in the popular mind with a conception of the promised land sufficiently glamorous to break the old ties and overcome natural inertia.[17] In a growing people the problem of finding

[15] In May, 1816, ice froze an inch thick, June brought heavy snows in New England and New York, and ice continued to form in July and August. It was truly a "year without a summer."

[16] "New-England Ballad," in *Edinburgh Review*, LV, 480 (July, 1832).

[17] Lois Kimball Mathews, in *The Expansion of New England* . . . (New York, 1909), gives a general account of the emigration from that section, with maps. Richard J. Purcell, *Connecticut in Transition, 1775–1818* (Washington, D. C., 1918), 139 ff., speaks of the movement in 1815 as "almost a migratory furor." See also passages reprinted in Louis B. Schmidt and Earle D. Ross (eds.), *Readings in the Economic History of American Agriculture* (New York, 1925), 137 ff.
    The thesis that hard times back East stimulated emigration to the West is decisively contested by Murray Kane in "Some Considerations on the Safety Valve Doctrine," in *Mississippi Valley Historical Review*, XXIII (1936–37), 169–88, and by Carter Goodrich and Sol Davison in "The Wage-Earner in the Westward Movement," in *Political Science Quarterly*, L (1935), 161–85, LI (1936), 61–116. On the other side: Leifur Magnusson, *Disposition of the Public Lands of the United States with Particular Reference to Wage-Earning Labor* (U S. Department of Labor, Washington, D. C., 1919); Frederic Logan Paxson, *History of the American*

homes and opportunities for the new generation is a constant one, hence the western movement was ever continuous but not uniform in flow. At times when the negative forces of expulsion operated in maximum conjunction with the positive forces of attraction, then resulted the flood tide.[18]

The West had its own appeal and its own ways of being advertised. There were the writings of the foreign travelers, a great number of whom were attracted by the uniqueness of the American frontier. Some were merely making the customary tour, others were professional writers and travelers, likely to describe only that which would prove interesting and popular. But whether they wrote from curiosity or sincere interest, with their propaganda-filled accounts, good or bad, or with their accurate description and narration, they were advertising the West.

Thomas Hutchins, later geographer of the United States, Gilbert Imlay, Count Volney, and John Melish,[19] among others, had published their accounts and descriptions of the trans-Appalachian region between 1778 and 1812. It was in the years following the War of 1812 that travel books became numerous and easily available. Between 1815 and 1825, more than a dozen travel books on the region north of the Ohio were published either in England or America, put on sale in the bookshops of

---

Frontier, 1763–1893 (Boston, 1924), 187; McMaster, History of the People of the United States, IV, 38; Frederick Jackson Turner, The Frontier in American History (New York, 1920); Channing, History of the United States, V, 40.

Perhaps there is no basic issue here after all. Obviously, westward emigration diminished during the periods of national depression, such as between 1818 and 1825, and 1837 and 1841. Equally apparent, it seems, is the fact that it was increased by economic and social troubles in the Northeast between 1814 and 1818. As for the "safety valve" idea, that is, that the cheap lands offered an escape and mitigated pressing economic and social conditions back East, it all depends on the viewpoint. People who emigrated before and after the depressions helped relieve the pressure in the older regions just as certainly as if they had gone during the depression. On the other hand, it might be well argued that, since the western lands tended to stimulate speculation, build up top-heavy credit structures, encourage flimsy finance and banking, and create pressure groups, they intensified and augmented the very condition which they were supposed to relieve.

[18] This has been true of European movements to America as well. Paxson, History of the American Frontier, Chapter XXI, treats briefly the great migration.

[19] Thomas Hutchins, A Topographical Description of Virginia, Pennsylvania, Maryland, and North Carolina . . . (London, 1778); Gilbert Imlay, A Topographical Description of the Western Territory of North America (New York, 1793); Constantin François Volney, A View of the Soil and Climate of the United States of America (Philadelphia, 1804); Melish, Travels in the United States.

eastern cities, and reviewed in literary and news periodicals.[20]
All were interesting, most were favorable, and some enthusiastic.[21]
Among the most optimistic and rosy hued was Morris Birkbeck's
Notes on a Journey in America, published in 1817, which called
forth letters in refutation from the prolific William Cobbett.
Birkbeck, interested financially in colonization in the Illinois
country, emphasized the opportunities of material gain, but did
not overlook the more abstract but nonetheless important rewards
of independence and "Liberty—the fair enchantress." At his best,
however, he could hardly equal in style and appeal the legislator
in Missouri Territory who, in 1816, wrote that in the states west
of the mountains:

. . . there neither is, nor, in the nature of things can there ever be, any
thing like poverty there. All is ease, tranquility and comfort. Every person,
however poor, may with moderate industry, become in a very short time
a landholder; his substance increases from year to year; his barns are
filled with abundant harvests; his cattle multiply and are sustained by his
attentions rather than the expences bestowed upon them; and his children,
active, vigorous and enterprising, seem destined to sustain and extend the
respectability of their parentage. Truly may it be said of that fortunate and
highly favored country, "A paradise of pleasure is open'd in the wild."[22]

From romantic description to prophecy was but a step:

Looking only a few years through the vista of futurity, what a sublime
spectacle presents itself! Wilderness, once the chosen residence of solitude
or savageness, converted into populous cities, smiling vilages beautiful farms
and plantations! The happy multitude, busy in their daily occupations,
manifests contentment and peace, breathing their gratitude and their
prayers only to the great King of Kings! The wild Indian, taught by mild
persuasion and example is become an enthusiast in the cause of civilization—
behold him cultivating his fields, or at his cabin door studying the Book

---

[20] Fairly complete lists of the travelers who wrote of the West prior to 1840
may be found in Solon J. Buck, *Travel and Description 1765–1865* . . . (*Illinois
Historical Collections,* IX, Springfield, 1914); Ralph Leslie Rusk, *The Literature
of the Middle Western Frontier* (2 volumes. New York, 1925); R. G. Thwaites in
Early Western Travels reprints many of the better-known accounts. Gershom
Flagg, David Thomas, Estwick Evans, Henry Bradshaw Fearon, Morris Birkbeck,
Elias P. Fordham, R. L. Mason, James Flint, William Faux, Thomas Hulme, John
Woods, Richard Flower, Timothy Flint, William Darby, Edouard de Montulé and
others, published journals, descriptions, or letters during the period from 1816 to
1826. See bibliography for titles.

[21] For classification and estimate of the travelers, see Allan Nevins (comp. and
ed.), *American Social History as Recorded by British Travellers* (New York, 1923).

[22] Letters from Rufus Easton, House of Representatives, Missouri Territory, to
Senator William Hunter, Rhode Island. *Niles' Weekly Register* (Baltimore, 1811–
49), X, 428–29 (Aug. 24, 1816).

of Life. The Mississippi rolls her proud waves as before, but her bosom is plowed by thousands of Keels, and her surface whitened by thousands of sails, bearing the produce of millions of industrious citizens, to its destined mart! What a scene—how beautiful, how grand!—yet not ideal: another century will realize it. Yes—this fine country is destined to become the finest foothold of the Genius of American Liberty—and should he ever be driven from the Atlantic shores, he will take his stand on the loftiest peak of the Alleghany and shout to his votaries—"Here is my hold—here have I erected an empire beyond the reach of despots, which will endure when the stream of time shall have been drained into the ocean of eternity."[23]

As powerful in advertising value as the fair words of the travelers and prophets, and certainly more definite, were the military campaigns in the West. From the time of the Revolution, during the Confederation period and the Indian wars in the Northwest, down through the campaigns of the second war with England, each and every expedition into the Indian country was in effect an officially conducted land-looking tour. The expeditions of Bouquet, Clark, Harmar, St. Clair, Wayne, and Harrison all led within a few years to settlements in the regions penetrated. At times officers and men seemed more interested in the land and prospective speculation or settlement than in the defeat of the Indians. The horrors incidental to Indian warfare always checked further settlement for the time, and frequently brought about a recession of the frontier, but the frontiersman was essentially an optimist. The loss was always more than regained in the reaction following peace.

By the time military campaigns had practically ceased and the western country was no longer possessed of the mystery and romance which interested the literary traveler, the newspapers of the region took over the task of advertising. The western journalist, like the speculator, businessman, or politician, profited directly by the growth of his community. Nor was all newspaper stuff mere "puffing" or optimistic promotion. Land sales, commodity price lists, new building, new trade opportunities, crop reports, notices of the need for artisans, doctors, and teachers— the serious news of the day—were the most effective advertising. And much of such material was republished in the "exchange

[23] Quoted from the *National Intelligencer,* in the Chillicothe *Supporter,* June 24, 1817.

clippings" of the papers in the very region which suffered most from the westward migration.

Last, and probably most effective of all, was the advertising done by word of mouth and the written communications of those who had gone before. True, means of communication were not easy, and facilities neither frequent nor cheap, yet people did return to tell of the new lands and possibilities of the West, and letters did find their way back to the settled regions to be passed around until worn out or printed and copied in newspapers and read with interest. Reports of relatives and friends could be trusted, and often the settlement of whole communities was the result of the pioneering efforts and favorable reports of one or two pioneers.

Naturally the seaboard states were alarmed over the unprecedented emigration of their people. New England was particularly sensitive on the subject, and her newspapers, in their eagerness to warn of the hardships and low prices of produce in the West, frequently went so far that they were accused by western papers of propagating known falsehoods in the interests of the "mercantile nobility" of their section.[24] The governors and legislators of Massachusetts and Connecticut hinted that the "unsettled population" of their states, tempted so much by seductive tales of milder climes and richer lands, would better stay where it was than make new settlements in distant wildernesses. It was proposed that New England taxes be lightened, and the editor of the *Boston Gazette* thought that wide distribution of attractive maps of their own country would help acquaint the people with its advantages and keep them at home. To this a western editor

[24] Cincinnati *Liberty Hall,* July 31, 1815, and *Liberty Hall and Cincinnati Gazette,* September 29, October 20, 1817. The Portland (Me.) *Eastern Argus* said that wheat was selling at 33 cents in Ohio and $1.25 in the Maine district. The Hamilton (Ohio) *Miami Intelligencer,* November 19, 1815, copied a long extract from the *Worcester* (Mass.) *Gazette* of October 11, 1815, which regretted that so many had emigrated. The *Gazette* thought the western climate was overrated and the absence of luxuries a hardship, and stated that many had returned to acknowledge the superiority of the character of New England, its well administered laws, civil liberty, security, and happiness. When the Bridgeport (Conn.) *Republican Farmer* cautioned against smallpox in the Ohio country, the editor of the *Columbus* (Ohio) *Gazette,* May 21, 1818, gave notice to all from 9 months to 999 years in the poor hills of Connecticut not to pay any attention. And when the Hartford (Conn.) *American Mercury* published what seemed "plain and unaffected simple truth" in criticism of western land speculation, the unhealthy prairies of Illinois, and the western country which was like "a great muddy hogyard," and said that western pride and distance prevented the East hearing its groans, the editor of the *Gazette* gave it vigorous and derisive treatment.

replied that it was land and not maps that counted. "The march of power is to the west—let our eastern brethren think of this, and cease their unworthy efforts to retard what they cannot prevent."[25] Articles on English emigration were likewise eagerly copied from the English magazines by the western editors, for young America was elated to think she could worry the old enemy by taking away her people.

§ §

To the north of the Ohio, stretching from Pennsylvania on the east to the Mississippi River, and bounded on the north by the Great Lakes, lies a region known in American history as the Old Northwest. Its area of 265,878 square miles constitutes a domain larger than France or Germany before 1918 and about twice as large as the British Isles.[26] Physiographically this section of the United States falls within the large expanse of rolling country classified as the prairie plains or Central Lowlands.[27] Climatically or zoogeographically, all except the narrow strip which borders the two northernmost lakes, lies in the upper part of the austral or southern zone.[28] For the most part, the climate

[25] *Western Herald and Steubenville Gazette,* edited by James Wilson, August 1, 1817.

[26] Thomas Donaldson, *The Public Domain* ... (Washington, 1884), 161, lists the area of the states established from the Territory Northwest of the Ohio River as follows: Ohio 39,964; Indiana 33,809; Illinois 55,414; Michigan 56,451; Wisconsin 53,924; Minnesota east of the Mississippi and international boundary of 1776, 26,000 (estimated); and Erie purchase in Pennsylvania 316—total 265,878 square miles. Later surveys have increased the figures for the region, although current statistics vary somewhat. For instance, the area of the five states, plus the 26,316 square miles of the Northwest not now included in these states, is listed in the *Statesman's Year Book,* 1936, at 271,880, but in the *Rand McNally Atlas,* 1936, at 274,421. Nor will inclusion or omission of water area account for the difference. Modern surveys are constantly changing the figures. The land area of Indiana, for instance, was listed in the 1930 census as 36,045 square miles, but later official recalculations list it at 36,205 square miles. Land areas of the five states as given by the *Sixteenth Census of the United States: 1940* are Ohio 41,122; Indiana 36,205; Illinois 55,947; Michigan 57,022; and Wisconsin 54,715.

[27] Of the portion of the region which is classified as Central Lowlands, the largest part (western Ohio, Indiana, Illinois) lies in the Till Plains. Eastern Ohio attaches to the Appalachian Plateau region, northern Wisconsin to the Superior Upland, and part of southern Indiana to the Interior Low Plateau region. Most of Michigan falls within the East Lake Section of the Central Plateau. Nevin W. Fenneman, "Physiographic Divisions of the United States," in *Annals of the Association of American Geographers,* XVIII, No. 4 (Dec., 1928).

[28] The northern parts of what are now Michigan and Wisconsin lie in the southern zone of the Boreal region; most of Wisconsin and southern Michigan in the transition zone of the Austral region. The rest of the area falls within the upper Austral. Isaiah Bowman, *Forest Physiography* (New York, 1911), map, 122.

is temperate, summers hot. Except for the Lower Ohio Valley, mean annual precipitation runs from thirty to forty inches. The old Ohio-Mississippi drainage systems serve the southern and western portions of the area, but the successive glacial invasions which at one time or another covered all but small portions of what are now southeastern Ohio, southern Indiana and Illinois, and southwestern Wisconsin, established new drainage systems for the northern regions, and modified the old. Not only did glaciation account to a large extent for physical features, but also for the soil distribution, and this fact, as well as the determination of lake locations and watercourses, profoundly affected the economic history of the region. From the extensive tracts of rich organic till of the corn belt of Indiana and Illinois to the sandy and infertile pine barrens of Michigan, the glacier left its mark. It accounted for the sand dunes and the swamps, for the lake plains and beach lines, the wandering boulders and the sparkling lakes.

Over all, except the grand prairie of Illinois and other openings, stretched the great forests, somber and almost unbroken. In the region south of the lakes prevailed the deciduous trees or hardwoods—elm, beech, hickory, oak, poplar; to the north were the conifers—pine, fir, and spruce. In these forests wandered and lived bands of Indians, mostly of the Algonquin group.

> The unshorn forest o'er them waved
> Dark, dense as at Creation's birth,—
> The free winds round them wildly rav'd—
> Their tents the boughs—their couch the earth.[29]

Into the Great Lakes–Upper Mississippi country in the seventeenth century had penetrated the French explorers, fur traders, and missionaries—the pioneers of New France in America. But both La Salle's vision of western empire and the Jesuit dream of a Christian nation of Indians were destined to give way before English conquest and the westward expansion of the English colonies. The two colonial empires came together in the final struggle over the valley of the Upper Ohio, and the compact and numerous English took the heart of the continent from the more highly militarized but more widely scattered French and their Indian allies. France withdrew almost completely from

---

[29] Mrs. Hentz, in *Western Monthly Magazine,* II (1834), 147.

North America; the French had left little of the mark of empire on the Northwest.

Under the English from 1763 to 1783, the inhabitants of the Northwest felt but lightly the rule of the mother country; a few hundred French *habitants*, a few thousand Indians, neither was much disturbed. Colonial plans and British politics, however, were influenced by the problems of this vast area to the west of the settled colonies.[30] When, in 1774, for administrative purposes the region north of the Ohio was annexed to Quebec, Virginia, who claimed the land by charter grant, as well as other colonies who felt they were being cut off from westward expansion, regarded the act as one of the "Intolerable Acts." During the Revolution, George Rogers Clark, acting under the authority of the Commonwealth of Virginia, seized the southern part of the territory and broke up British military plans in the West. At the peace in 1783 the western boundary of the United States was fixed at the Mississippi River.

The ratification of the Articles of Confederation had been held up by the states without western land claims and by land company speculation and politics until 1781, when New York offered to cede her uncertain claims to the United States. Virginia generously gave over her lands north of the Ohio to the General Government on condition that when settled they should be organized into new states and admitted into the Union on an equal footing with the old. By the Ordinance of 1785 a Congressional land survey was provided for; the Ordinance of 1787 set up a territorial government, and established a colonial policy not only for the Northwest, but for all of the public domain of the future.

Aggressive Pennsylvania and Virginia squatters, largely Scotch-Irish, had pushed over into the lands north of the Ohio during the Revolution, but were ordered out by United States troops when the land was surveyed. Revolutionary soldiers who had accompanied George Rogers Clark on his campaign of 1778–79 were awarded Virginia lands north of the Ohio at the Falls in 1784, where Clarksville was founded. A still larger American settlement in the Northwest Territory was made in

[30] See Clarence W. Alvord, *The Mississippi Valley in British Politics* (2 volumes. Cleveland, 1917); Clarence E. Carter, *Great Britain and the Illinois Country, 1763–1774* (Washington, D. C., 1910).

1788 by New Englanders of the Ohio Company of Associates at Marietta, on their land grant along the Muskingum.[31] The closely related Scioto Company of speculators inveigled some settlers, among them some Frenchmen who had believed the attractive descriptions of Joel Barlow, on to their lands immediately to the west. Judge Symmes and his associates speculated and promoted settlements, largely of Middle States men, in the region between the Miami rivers, and people from the South infiltrated into the Virginia military lands just to the east of the Miami Purchase. With the addition of Pennsylvania Germans and Carolina Quakers, the population of this section of the Northwest presented from the beginning a mixed make-up, a fact which was destined to play an important part in the political and social history of the future state of Ohio.

The Indian problem was imminent during the early years of the Territory. Generals Harmar and St. Clair struggled unsuccessfully with it, but after Gen. Anthony Wayne's victory over the confederated tribes at Fallen Timbers in August, 1794, peace and a boundary line were agreed upon. By the Treaty of Greenville in 1795 the Indians were restrained to the region north and west of a line running from the mouth of the Cuyahoga River through Fort Recovery to the mouth of the Kentucky River. The following year Moses Cleaveland and more New Englanders settled on the Connecticut Reserve up in the northeast corner of the Territory. A zone of settlement fifty to seventy-five miles wide now paralleled the Ohio River from Pennsylvania on past Cincinnati, with scattered settlements to the west. People continued to come in. In 1800 Indiana Territory was set off by the line running from the mouth of the Kentucky River to Fort Recovery and thence due north to the international boundary. The eastern part of the region, which still bore the name of Territory of the United States Northwest of the Ohio, was expecting redivision and early admission into the Union as the state of Ohio. William Henry Harrison, governor of Indiana Territory, by a series of treaties between 1803 and 1809, cleared the lands well back from the Ohio and up the Wabash and Mississippi valleys from any Indian claim, and the eve of the War of 1812 found the frontier line of settlement

[31] For the scattered but important settlements already made, see Chapter III.

moved north and west in Ohio, looping up the Whitewater, Wabash, and Mississippi valleys, but swinging back near the Ohio River in between.[32]

Settlement did not cease during the war. In February, 1812, the Ohio legislature located the new capital site on the Scioto, on "the East High Bank, opposite the town of Franklinton."[33] On the day that Congress was declaring war the sale of town lots in the thick woods took place, and in the autumn of 1816 the government was moved to Columbus.[34] Land sales fell off, but two new counties were organized during the war, and from a population of 230,000 in 1810 Ohio had grown to about 400,000 by 1815. In Indiana Territory settlements advanced deeper into the forests as danger of Indian hostilities lessened, and the border settlements in modern Lawrence, Monroe, and Jackson counties were consolidated, while the eastern wing of advance crept up the Whitewater and into present-day Fayette, Ripley, and Jennings counties. After a temporary setback, the Wabash-White River Valley advance swept on to Spencer and Gosport. Land sales at the Jeffersonville and Vincennes offices showed a decided increase in 1813 over the preceding year. "Indiana, notwithstanding the war, is peopling very fast. Its settlements are bursting forth on the right hand and on the left. . . . Settlers will now begin to flock in, especially if the war should soon terminate."[35] The population of 24,520 in 1810 had increased to 63,897 in 1815.[36] The outposts of the invading army of settlers, mostly from Kentucky and the South, had pushed northward almost to the limits of the Indian cessions.

Across the Wabash from Vincennes were the prairies. These rich lands were at first not desirable in the eyes of the pioneers. Land which would not grow tall trees was considered infertile; besides the settlers were dependent upon the timber for homes

[32] See map of Indian Land Cessions, 111, and Land Surveys and Land Offices, 117.
[33] E. O. Randall, "Location of Site of Ohio Capital," in *Ohio Archaeological and Historical Society Publications*, XXV (1916), 210–34.
[34] *Columbus Intelligencer* in *Liberty Hall and Cincinnati Gazette*, October 21, 1816.
[35] Samuel J. Mills and Daniel Smith, *Report of a Missionary Tour Through that Part of the United States Which Lies West of the Alleghany Mountains* . . . (Andover, Mass., 1815), 15.
[36] *Executive Journal of Indiana Territory, 1800–1816* (Indiana Historical Society Publications, III, No. 3, Indianapolis, 1895), 82. Charles Kettleborough (ed.), *Constitution Making in Indiana* . . . (3 volumes. *Indiana Historical Collections*, I, II, XVII, Indianapolis, 1916, 1930), I, 69.

and outbuildings, for fires and fences. Malaria and other lowland ailments also acted as deterrents. By 1809, when Illinois Territory was organized, the people were on the edge of the prairies and they did not push back from the river valley and into the open until 1814. The Indian troubles and the impossibility of getting legal land titles to any but the lands in the hands of the French settlers held down immigration into the Illinois country, and only about 3,000 people were added during the war years.[37]

In the Great Lakes—Upper Mississippi country were the old French settlements of Detroit, Mackinac, Green Bay, and Prairie du Chien. Of this country the Americans knew little. James Monroe in 1786 had written that most of it was miserably poor, "especially that near lakes Michigan and Erie and that upon the Mississippi and the Illinois consists of extensive plains which have not had from appearances and will not have a single bush on them, for ages." At the close of the war, when Edward Tiffin was sent to survey two million acres of Congressional military lands, he reported that the whole tract in Michigan Territory did not contain one hundredth of that amount in tillable land, and was not worth the expense of surveying. He said the land was low and wet, covered with swamp grass, bush, and slime. "Taking the country altogether . . . there would be not more than one acre in a hundred, if there were one out of a thousand, that would in any case admit of cultivation."[38] As for the Upper Mississippi country, the account of Zebulon Montgomery Pike's expedition of 1806 and vague reports of hunters and boatmen constituted about all the information available. It was thought to be a wild region, filled with savages—and it was.

§ § §

"Should peace be restored," reported two missionaries in 1814, "the region west of the Alleghany mountains will fill up with unexampled rapidity."[39] Into the Northwest during the

[37] Clarence W. Alvord, *The Illinois Country, 1673–1818* (*Centennial History of Illinois,* Volume I, Springfield, 1920), 454.

[38] Until 1839 Morse's school geography printed across the interior of Michigan, "interminable swamp." Carl E. Pray, "A Historic Michigan Road," in *Michigan History Magazine,* XI (1927), 326.

[39] John F. Schermerhorn and Samuel J. Mills, *A Correct View of that Part of the United States which Lies West of the Allegany Mountains, with Regard to Religion and Morals* (Hartford, 1814), 11.

years following the second war with England poured successive
waves of the great migration. From thriving little cities along
the Ohio to the Indian frontier in remote regions of northern
Indiana and Illinois, the country felt its effect. Into the Ohio
flowed the Muskingum, the Scioto, and the Great Miami, navigable from one to two hundred miles, and which for small boats
constituted highways which connected by portages of a few miles
with the Cuyahoga, Sandusky, and Maumee of the Great Lakes.
Marietta, at the mouth of the Muskingum, was losing out in the
boat-building business and declining in importance, in spite of
stone, coal, and salt springs near the banks of the river.

While Steubenville and Zanesville engaged in verbal combat
over the location of the western end of the Cumberland Road
and boasted of their manufactories, Cincinnati was becoming
the first city of the West.[40] It had grown from 2,300 people in
1810 to 6,500 in 1815, and become a thriving place with "hundreds of commodious, well finished brick houses, the spacious
and busy markets, the substantial public buildings, the thousands
of prosperous, well dressed, industrious inhabitants, the numerous wagons and drays, the gay carriages and elegant females . . .
the shoals of craft on the river, the busy stir prevailing everywhere, house building, boat building, paving and levelling streets,
the numbers of country people, constantly coming and going,
with the spacious taverns, crowded with travellers from a distance." There were about 1,100 buildings, 20 of which were
stone and 250 brick, and 60 mercantile houses. There were
blacksmiths, coopers, glassmakers, stonecutters and cabinetmakers; there were also a cotton manufactory and a $130,000
steam mill with gas lights. A subscription library, a Lancasterian
seminary, a theater—which some said was to cultivate dissolute
practices and deterioration of all principles of morality and
decorum—a college, a museum, and two newspapers were among

---

[40] *Zanesville Express,* February 22, August 11, December 6, 1816; *Pittsburg
Navigator,* 1818; for descriptions of these towns, see W. H. Hunter, "The Pioneers
of Jefferson County," in *Ohio Archaeological and Historical Society Publications,*
VI (1898), 235 ff.; Daniel Drake, *Natural and Statistical View, or Picture of
Cincinnati and the Miami Country . . .* (Cincinnati, 1815); Fordham, *Personal
Narrative;* Fearon, *Sketches of America;* Flint, *Letters from America;* "Pioneer
Letters of Gershom Flagg," edited by Solon J. Buck, in *Transactions of the Illinois
State Historical Society,* 1910, pp. 139–83; *Narrative of Richard Lee Mason in the
Pioneer West, 1819* (Heartman's Historical Series No. 6, New York [1915]).
Steubenville in 1810 had 800 population; in 1820, 2,479.

the cultural attractions of the town which was so frequently chided by its neighbors for calling itself a city. Good unimproved land within a few miles of the city sold at $50 to $150 per acre, and up to twelve miles at $10 to $30, while fertile land in the settled portions of the Miami country averaged around $8.00. This country, including southeastern Indiana, was contributory to Cincinnati, and helped swell its commerce and industry. By adding about seven hundred people a year the young city was able to surpass Pittsburgh by a big margin in 1820.

Columbus, the new Ohio capital, with 156 houses, 816 persons, 7 stores, and 5 licensed inns, was beginning to feel its importance. Dayton claimed 130 houses and Hamilton about half as many. Chillicothe was approaching 2,000 population; Springfield was almost half as large; Cleveland at the end of the war was just being incorporated as a village and contained fewer than 150 inhabitants. Speculation was abroad in the realm and notices of town platting, lot sales, promotion schemes, and lotteries were appearing regularly in the Cincinnati and Columbus papers during these boom years.

Yet it was not in the towns that the most significant Ohio growth took place, for life in the state, destined shortly to be the first in commerce and industry in the Northwest, was chiefly rural. Once away from the river towns and the waterways, the problem of communications loomed large. Over on the eastern side of the state[41] a traveler described the country in 1819: "Roads extremely rough. Country fertile, but hilly. Log cabins, ugly women and tall timber." Many ragged and ignorant children were about, and there was but little appearance of industry.[42] Land was priced at $2.00 to $30 an acre; with improvements at $15 to $30. Near St. Clairsville: "all fine land in grain, corn, and pasture, with a beautiful clover face, white as with a shower of sleet; and abundance of flourishing orchards full, above and below, of excellent fruit, although sixteen years ago all was wild, and a complete forest."[43] The idea of extensive cultivation prevailed. The question was not how much corn or potatoes could be raised per acre, but per man, for the cost of land was low in comparison to that of labor.

Over on the western side, in Champaign County, another

41 In Columbiana and Harrison counties.
42 Mason, *Narrative*, 22.
43 Faux, *Memorable Days*, 171.

traveler listed among the good things plenty of grain, fat horses, rich land, whiskey and abundance of feed, plums, peaches, deer, wild turkeys, and small game. Less desirable were the lack of stone and building timber, overflowing streams, bad roads, ignorant people, sick milk, sick wheat, ague, and the pioneer hogs, the meanest he had ever seen. "There is no regulation for educating the youth by common schools. The inhabitants are from all parts north and east of Kentucky and are the most ignorant people I ever saw."[44] Land was priced at $4.00 to $25, a plow cost $20, and salt was $9.00 a barrel at the works. Around the Upper Scioto in the centrally located counties of Franklin, Licking, Delaware, and Madison, lay 2,500 square miles of excellent land, but the population was only 24,000 instead of the 100,000 which resident promoters and patriots thought it should have been. The settlement of this country was retarded, not because the ball of empire had ceased to roll westward, for the number who annually entered the state was incredible and not ascertainable, but because of lack of roads.[45]

Northwestern Ohio, the land bounded by the Western Reserve –Greenville Treaty line, and in part by the Maumee River, a tract 102 by 96 miles, was not cleared of Indian title until 1817.[46] Sales in the Piqua district—land along the St. Marys, Auglaize, and on to Lake Erie—lagged in spite of the fact that "the lake country in a few years must possess advantages superior to any portion of North America."[47] Most of the land, largely timbered, but also prairies and bottoms around Fort Meigs, Defiance, Upper and Lower Sandusky, and the Black Swamp, was surveyed and ready for sale by 1821. Orleans, Maumee, and Port Miami were towns already projected.[48] Between the Sandusky and Miami of the Lakes (Maumee) lay the Black Swamp,

[44] Buck (ed.), "Pioneer Letters of Gershom Flagg," in *Transactions of the Illinois State Historical Society*, 1910, pp. 143–48.

[45] Columbus *Ohio Monitor*, November 28, 1816.

[46] See Chapter III and map, 111. An excellent description of the country from Delaware northwest to Fort Meigs is given by William Woodbridge, newly appointed secretary of the Michigan Territory, who made the trip to Detroit in January, 1815. He predicted that Sandusky would eventually become a great city. His "great terour, the Black Swamp," did not prove so bad, since the ground was frozen. "From Marietta to Detroit in 1815," edited by Milo M. Quaife, in The Historical Society of Northwestern Ohio *Quarterly Bulletin*, XIV, No. 4 (Oct. 1942), 135–55. A four-page letter in *Niles' Weekly Register*, XI, 321–24 (Jan. 11, 1817), described the Sandusky-Maumee region in considerable detail—the land, resources, fisheries.

[47] *Piqua Gazette*, August 2, 1821.

[48] *Hamilton Intelligencer and Advertiser*, December 15, 1821.

roughly 40 by 120 miles, through which a road had been surveyed from the Western Reserve to the foot of the Maumee rapids. Near the rivers and their tributaries were large tracts of rich land, partly prairie but mostly covered with heavy growth of hardwood timber. At the rapids in both the Maumee and Sandusky prodigious quantities of lake fish were taken which marketed for as high as $25 per barrel. New Orleans was a distant and unprofitable market for northern Ohio, and New York's plans for a canal to the lakes were eagerly discussed.

Game was still plentiful in all parts of the state, except in the vicinity of the towns and older settlements. The wild pigeons, which at times darkened the sky for hours as untold numbers went to and from feeding grounds, had not as yet felt the effects of advancing settlement. Near Zanesville, as late as 1819, one observer wrote: "they fly and alight around you on every tree, in immense flocks, and loving to be shot. . . . They breed in the woods, and seem to court death by the gun, the sound of which appears to call them together, instead of scaring them away; a fowling-piece well charged with dust shot might bring down a bushel of these willing game dead at your feet."[49] Near Columbus the bears, wolves, deer, and turkeys were still numerous in 1817, and a hunting party headed by James Kilbourne in its official report listed 3 bears, 2 wolves, 33 deer, and 117 turkeys. On the Reserve and to the west were numerous flocks of geese and turkeys, and the deer ranged from 150 to 200 pounds.[50]

During the five years following the war eighteen new counties were organized in Ohio, nine in one group lying in the south-central part of the state, four on the west side just south of the new Indian cession (see map, 111), and four around the south-western shore of Lake Erie. The state, now well along in its second decade, had sixty-one organized counties and a population of 581,295 by 1820.

§ § § §

"Indiana is a vast forest, larger than England," said Fordham, "just penetrated in places, by the back-wood settlers, who are half hunters, half farmers."

[49] Faux, *Memorable Days,* 174.
[50] Columbus *Ohio Monitor,* November 21, 1816; Estwick Evans, *Pedestrious Tour,* in Thwaites (ed.), *Early Western Travels,* VIII, 195.

The forests of Indiana, the mountains of Kentucky, the wilds of the Illinois, if they are not so beautiful [as England], yet their grandeur calls forth deeper, more sublime emotions. They are the fields of enterprise, the cradle of freedom, the land of rest to the weary, the place of refuge to the oppressed. Every sound that issues from the woods, from the crashing tornado which rushes across entire regions, clothed in sheets of fire and shaking the hills to their foundations,—to the soft murmur of an autumnal breeze,—all excites the most profound sentiments of adoration for the divine author of Nature,—all call to man the uncertain duration of his existence; but these thoughts are unmixed with aught that can debase his worth or circumscribe his powers. These wildernesses are given to him alone: in them he is free; owning no master but his God, and no authority but that of reason and truth.

> "And sovereign man scarce condescends to see
> A nation's laws more sovereign still than he."[51]

The Indian boundary had not been changed since 1809, but the squatters reckoned little of legal rights. President Madison's order[52] for unlawful occupants and "uninformed or evil disposed" persons to remove from the Indian lands was little heeded. These people reasoned that they had held in check the savage foe and they intended to reap some of the benefits. In 1816 the Jeffersonville Land Office sales increased 30 per cent but those at Vincennes increased 425 per cent. It was estimated that 42,000 people came into the state in that year. The cheaper lands of Indiana influenced many emigrants to pass up Ohio, and many who had first settled there sold out and moved, or else forfeited their lands and started anew farther west. From the uplands of North Carolina came movers, among them many Quakers, disgruntled with drought, slave competition, the institution of slavery, and expansion of the plantation system. To these thrifty souls the richer lands in Indiana and Illinois were probably more of an incentive than antislavery sentiments. Kentucky was in commotion over its cheap-money struggle, and those in favor of more paper money and relief laws were winning in the battle against the courts. Inflation and speculation were rampant; land took on fictitious values. Getting into debt was the one alternative to ruin, and the creditor class was largely bankrupt. When the bubble burst, one of the ways out led across

[51] Fordham, *Personal Narrative*, 96, 187–88.
[52] December 21, 1815.

the river into Indiana and Illinois, or to Missouri, or the Far South.

Southern Indiana, unlike Ohio, had few streams of navigable size which reached back farther than forty miles from the Ohio. The Whitewater and Wabash valleys had represented the tips of the crescent of settlement, but in the years following the war the interior of the segment filled and by 1820 had a population greater in density than the Whitewater Valley, and equal to the Lower Wabash. This at first thought seems peculiar, for it is this triangle with its base on the Ohio between Clark County and southern Illinois, and its blunt apex near the West Fork of White River, that comprises the unglaciated or driftless area. Cutting north and south through it is the Knobstone Escarpment with rugged hills rising four to six hundred feet above the valleys, while just to the west lies the belt of sinkholes of the Mitchell Plain and the rough topography of the Crawford Upland.

That this area, which today with its thin clays, shales, and outcrops of rock, and thousands of acres idle or for sale for taxes, should have proved attractive to the earlier settlers is not after all so strange. To them it appeared distinctly the best land. It was well drained, had an abundance of springs, and thousands of years of forest decay had added to the weathered bedrock a coat of humus which had not yet been washed away. The woods supplied game and forage for the stock, the small valleys acreage enough for hand cultivation. The higher levels were freer from the mosquito and the ague, and in spite of the roughness of the country, travel on horseback was easier than in the low marshy regions which today, changed by modern drainage and transportation facilities, are regarded as the rich and desirable agricultural areas.[53]

Sparsely settled as the country was, town booming was anyone's business, and with true frontier optimism, each promoter proclaimed his townsite destined to be a metropolis of industry and culture. Many of these towns were never discovered by sufficient numbers of potential inhabitants to be brought out of the

[53] For topographical description and maps, see *Handbook of Indiana Geology*, by William N. Logan, *et al.* (Department of Conservation, Indianapolis, 1922); Stephen S. Visher, *Economic Geography of Indiana* (New York, 1923).

wilderness. One traveler was in part justified when he said that Americans planted their towns in the dirtiest puddles they could find. Lot sale advertisements for Paoli appeared in the spring of 1816.[54] In October Terre Haute sales began,[55] and the following spring Evansville and Washington sales were advertised.[56] In May of 1818 lots were advertised at Bloomington, Fredonia, Rockport, and Portersville; in the autumn at Sprinklesburg, Palestine, Concord, Clinton, and other points.[57] Perhaps the settlers did plant their towns in the dirtiest puddles they could find, but the creek or river was a necessity not easily dispensed with.

The people of southern Indiana and Illinois have been variously described. Although they may have developed some local characteristics, most of them were essentially no different from the upland South folk who filled Kentucky and Tennessee, southern Illinois, Missouri, or Arkansas. The description of one type by James Hall is as good as any:

Behind the rest, some distance in the rear, comes the lonesome looking couple from *old North Carolina*. They had evidently, from their appearance, ventured their all, such as it was, upon the enterprise. An old one horse tumbril, with two high creaking wheels, and an old store box for a body— drawn by a lean pony of the preceding generation, constituted their mode of conveyance. A bed, a spinning wheel, a pair of cards, a bag of dye stuff, and a few hanks of copperas colored cotton, with six sickly looking children, made up their stock in trade. As they moved slowly along, the man walking before, and the wife behind, the tumbril, their lean pony occasionally stopping to crop the tall grass which stood by the way, it was evident to all who saw them, that they had long since arrived at that term of life which the magistrate alluded to, who married them, when he said *"better for worse."*[58]

As elsewhere on the frontier the people might be roughly classed into three types. First had prevailed the daring and hardy hunter, content with the rudest of shelters, a corn and pumpkin

[54] *Liberty Hall and Cincinnati Gazette,* March 25, 1816.
[55] *Niles' Weekly Register,* XII, 96 (Apr. 5, 1817); Vincennes *Western Sun and General Advertiser,* May 9, 1818.
[56] *Western Sun,* April 19, 1817; *Liberty Hall and Cincinnati Gazette,* June 9, 1817.
[57] *Western Sun and General Advertiser,* May 16, 30, August 1, 1818; Madison *Indiana Republican,* October 17, 1818.
[58] Quoted in *Congressional Globe,* 26 Congress, 1 session, Appendix, 65. For fuller description of the people of southern Indiana and Illinois, see Chapter VI.

patch, a few hogs of the same bold disposition as himself, sometimes possessed of a cow. Expert with the rifle, vindictive against the Indians, often mild mannered withal, honest, inclined to move often and heeding little the trappings of land titles or the refinements of civilization, these men of the "long knife" stock were not tenderfeet, for back of them was usually more than one generation of pioneers.

Speaking of the hunters in the Illinois country, Fordham wrote:

The hunters live rather worse [than the farmers], but are more entertaining and interesting companions. Clothed in *dressed* not *tanned* buckskins:— a home-made, homespun hunting shirt outside;—belted to his waist with a broad belt, to which is appended a knife with a blade a foot long: a tomohawk, or powder horn, in the belt of which is sometimes a smaller knife to cut the patch of the bullet; a bullet-pouch; moccasins on his feet; a blanket on his saddle; and a loaf of Indian Corn. Thus equipped and accoutered he enters the trackless woods, without a compass, or a guide, but what appears a kind of instinct. He is fearless of every thing, attacks everything that comes in his way, and thinks himself the happiest and noblest being in the world. These men have kindly feelings. I should expect to receive more sympathy from them in real distress, such as they could understand, than from more enlightened, and more civilized men. They never swear. Their women never sit at table with them; at least, I have never seen them. I cannot speak in high terms of the manners or of the virtue of their squaws and daughters. Their houses contain but one room, and that used as a sleeping room as well by strangers as by the men of the family, they lose all feminine delicacy, and hold their virtue cheap.[59]

Hardly distinguishable from the hunters were the first settlers, half hunter, half farmer. These possessed more of the utensils for civilized life, but on the whole constituted a transition class who were equally likely to retrograde into the more primitive life by selling out their few improvements and moving on, or to enter their land and join the permanent settlers.

The permanent settlers conformed to no type. Among them were hunters and squatters of another day, men from the older settled regions with money enough to start anew, enterprising young lawyers, storekeepers, and mechanics, many of whom were to become the well-to-do farmers and businessmen of the community. There were men from the Middle States, western Penn-

[59] Fordham, *Personal Narrative*, 181–82.

sylvania, Ohio, Kentucky, and Tennessee, but in southern Indiana and Illinois few from New England.[60]

Contrasting with the "lonesome looking couple from *old North Carolina*" were two families from the same state who were bound for the country around Jacksonville, Illinois, in 1838. They disembarked from the steamboat

> with every appurtenance of necessity and comfort. . . . There were two noble, spirited bays, one of which fell overboard in landing him, and which could only be accomplished by backing him over the planks. Then there were a neat barouche, a buggy, a light wagon, and four farm wagons; each for two horses. Besides, there was a full compliment of "household stuff" among which I discovered a piano. Add to this, a year's stock of groceries, and other nicnacs of luxury, and a very vivid idea of comfort in their wilderness home was presented to one's mind. They appeared to be in high spirits, and an air of genteel breeding and intelligence gave the impression that the true *otium cum dignitate* was in store for these fortunate emigrants in this land of milk and honey—of fair skies and a balmy atmosphere.[61]

Few are the descriptions of these people recorded by themselves. They were not literary; many were illiterate. To the outsider, however, they were interesting studies, and from the abundance of observations may be gathered, as from case material, a fairly accurate estimate. To nearly all the travelers the Hoosier appeared different, and at times he fared none too gently at their hands. To those who had recently left the beautiful Bluegrass region of Kentucky, with its proud society and appearance of culture, Indiana seemed a decided change for the worse. The country was different, and so seemed the people. Kentucky politeness and hospitality gave way to impudence, ignorance, and laziness.[62] The Hoosier dialect, the nasal twang, and provincial expressions became more noticeable in the speech.[63] We are "now

[60] Mathews in *Expansion of New England*, 254, explains the paucity of New Englanders as follows: "Indiana was never a favorite stopping-place for New Englanders, for the Southern element was strong here, and the Virginian or Kentuckian was apt to confuse the shrewd, unscrupulous 'Yankee' peddler of cheap clocks with the substantial Connecticut farmer, and to treat the two alike." On the basis of reasoning such as this New Englanders should not have settled in Ohio or Illinois either, for the same Virginians and Kentuckians got there first. Besides, the treatment given peddlers was not likely to scare away anybody, let alone serious-minded settlers.

[61] A. D. Jones, *Illinois and the West*, 64–65.

[62] Mason, *Narrative*, 34. Yet Faux, on quitting Kentucky was "well pleased to turn . . . [his] back on all the spitting, gouging, dirking, duelling, swearing and staring, of old Kentucky."

[63] For frontier speech, see Chapter VI, 350–58.

quite out of society; every thing and every body, with some few exceptions, looks wild, and half savage."[64] Such was the reputation of the Hoosiers—lawless, semibarbarous vagabonds, dangerous to live among.[65]

At the end of a long day's travel in the deep shade of giant poplars, walnuts, and oaks, which, notwithstanding the lack of underbrush in the virgin timber, seldom offered a view of two hundred yards in any direction, the traveler was glad to avail himself of whatever food and shelter was offered. Most likely it would be stewed pumpkin and cabbage, rye or parched-corn coffee, a bit of salt pork and hominy, or venison bones and corn bread, with sleeping privileges in the single room in the cabin or in the loft, frequently shared with eight to twelve members of the family, numerous dogs, and sometimes a calf or two.[66] Or now and then the stranger might run into the more prosperous farmer, an important man in his community, by whom he would be given excellent shelter and regaled with a breakfast of venison, fowls, ham and bacon, hot johnnycakes, honey or maple syrup, and a dram of whiskey to keep the cold off his stomach. Also oats for the horse, all gratis, or at a nominal price.[67]

The small cabin in the clearing, with its one room and perhaps a loft, its floor of dirt or puncheons, and windows covered with greased paper or deerskins, was often the domicile for more than one family. It was necessary to shelter the newcomers until they could erect their own homes, and half a dozen mouths more or less seemed to make little difference, though in 1816 the inrush of newcomers was so great that at times the corn meal gave out and food became a problem. But there was always the forest with

[64] Faux, *Memorable Days*, 206, speaking of the country west of New Albany.

[65] Birkbeck, contrary to most, rated the Ohio people as indigent and those of Indiana as superior in character, with their neat cabins and gardens. They were law respecting, kind and gentle. And David B. Warden in his account of Indiana in 1819 said: "Indiana is but recently settled; but many of the settlers are of a respectable class, and their manners are more refined than could be expected in a place where society is but in its infancy. They are sober and industrious; drunkenness is rare, and quarrelling rare in proportion." *A Statistical, Political, and Historical Account of the United States of North America* . . . (3 volumes. Edinburgh, 1819), II, 310. Naturally much depended on the people with whom the traveler came in contact as well as his own predilections and prejudices, or, at times, self-interest. For comment on the travel writers, see Chapter VI, 366–67, 378 ff.

[66] Mason, *Narrative*, 34, 38. The poorer farmers were usually hospitable according to their means, but in the absence of taverns, food and lodging were often demanded by the traveler rather than accepted as a favor, and those who lived near the frequented path expected payment.

[67] Fordham had such a breakfast near Corydon, Indiana, for 37½ cents. *Personal Narrative*, 155.

its abundance of game, and in a pinch the breasts of turkeys and dried venison could be regarded as bread. Split-log tables, benches, and bunks, a few wooden bowls and spoons, an iron spider or skillet, and an iron or copper kettle or boiling pot constituted the furnishings and equipment of the average family. Whatever agricultural implements were needed were of the same homemade construction as the furniture.[68]

The backwoods people were admirably adapted by nature and training to the surroundings in which they lived. Lean and sallow, curious, inquisitive, independent, as likely to be indolent and shiftless as industrious, crude in speech and as naïvely unaware of his picturesque profanity as he was innocent of underwear or a daily bath, the frontiersman was a product of his environment. "Lax morals; few principles, but those deeply impressed on the mind; a careless haughtiness of manner, without any affectation, or consequential airs; and a quick perception of the ridiculous—these are some of the characteristics of a man born and raised in the backwoods."[69] There were few weak or effeminate men in the West. Physical and military courage were taken for granted, and little affection or respect was held for Easterners or those too dressed up or finicky in their tastes, yet everywhere was readiness to accept the newcomer when he conformed to the ways of the frontier. Social comforts counted less than friendship and neighborliness. Equality was not a theory or creed; it was merely a natural circumstance. Nature is a great leveler and no respecter of persons. Before her the individual pioneer was just as good as his right arm, keen-sighting eye, and constitutional resistance to her vapors and pests. The pioneer realized this fact; on the one hand it led to effective informal co-operation, on the other to almost unrestrained individualism. But into all activities was carried the practice of democracy, whether politics, law, military or religious life. The judge could leave his bench, shake hands, and retire to his plow; the preacher go from pulpit to stable work; the lawyer serve as private or lieutenant under his client who was a colonel in the militia. No one worked willingly as "hired man" and servants were out of the question.

William Faux, the most critical of the English travelers of the

---

[68] For a fuller description of pioneer homes, see Chapter IV.
[69] Fordham, *Personal Narrative*, 222–23.

period, as a rule was overfinicky and too often showed peevishness, yet beneath some of his most biting comments was an aptitude for shrewd observation which sometimes reached beneath the surface of dirt and lack of refinement to delineate character and characteristics. Wrote Faux: "The American, considered as an animal, is filthy, bordering on the beastly; as a man, he seems a being of superior capabilities; his attention to his teeth,[70] which are generally very white, is a fine exception to his general habits. All his vices and imperfections seem natural; those of a semibarbarian. He is ashamed of none of them." Yet ". . . however mean may be the exterior of a citizen of this free, equal country, there is a spirit and an intelligence, and often sprightliness about him, which decorate any thing and make even rags respectable." Politeness in manner and address Faux commented upon, and was partly correct in his conclusion that it was more necessary, especially among strangers, on the frontier than on Bond Street.[71]

It was a land of early marriages, for the teamwork of man and woman was almost necessary in the primitive economy of the early settlements. Young people married first, then looked around for the means of livelihood with little fear, for there was land in plenty—if not at home, a little farther on—and most necessities for life could be had for the labor. Little thought was given at first to such things as medical facilities or education. The expectation of life was probably shorter than in the older regions of the East, for exposure, disregard of personal hygiene, bad teeth, rheumatism, diseases of swamp and shade—such as chills, malaria, and ague—too frequent childbearing, infant mortality, lack of medical attention, and the universal use of spirituous liquors, exacted their toll. One observer thought that the excitement of the strenuous existence and the violent religious enthusiasms were contributory to short life.[72]

Two miles below the Falls of the Ohio was New Albany, but recently settled. Of it Isaac Reed, the traveling preacher, said

[70] Probably none beyond the common and constant use of chewing tobacco.

[71] *Memorable Days*, 202, 231. Faux has been described as "an English farmer, so credulous, coarse, and ill natured as to excite the ridicule of the very magazines whose prejudice against the republic equalled his own." *Blackwood's* called him "a simpleton of the first water, a capital specimen of a village John Bull, for the first time roaming far away from his native valley—staring at everything and grumbling at most." Nevins (comp. and ed.), *American Social History as Recorded by British Travellers*, 17.

[72] For pioneer health and medical practices, see Chapter V.

in 1818: "I have come to this town; why it is I know not; but Divine Providence has so ordered it. O that I may be submissive! heartily inclined to do my duty whilst I stay." Most of the town-site lay thickly covered with the trunks of large trees which had been felled but not cleared away. Its several hundred inhabitants included people from New England, New Jersey, Pennsylvania, Kentucky, and Ireland. Houses were crude and too few for the growing population. The village had a sawmill, several stores and mechanics' shops, and a yard for building steamboats.[73] From New Albany north and west to Vincennes stretched a road which followed the buffalo trail of an earlier day. The eastern end, over the "knobs," was rough and bad, even in midsummer. As the traveler approached the White River–Wabash low-lands, he noted a distinct change in topography and soil. The knobs and rock outcrops covered with clay gave way to deep, sandy loam. At the present site of Washington, David Thomas, American pomologist and writer, noted three houses and many Kentuckians round about in 1816.

Vincennes was "an old dirty French settlement," "small, ugly and meanly built, though beautifully situated." The water was bad and the situation generally sickly along the Wabash. Faux called the settlement "an antique lump of deformity" and thought it would be much benefited by a fire. The refuse of the East seemed to be there and excessive drinking was the "all pervading, easily besetting sin" of this wild country. French, Americans, and a few Indians comprised the population of 1,000 to 1,500. There were 250 houses, 18 merchandise stores, 6 taverns, a couple dozen shops, 2 newspaper and printing offices, a Roman Catholic cathedral, and an academy.[74]

The old French inhabitants were an easy-going and life-loving lot. Thrift and enterprise were not in their rule of life. To money-making, improvements, and American speculation and politics, they were charmingly indifferent; a fiddle, some wine or liquor,

---

[73] Isaac Reed, *The Christian Traveller, . . . including Nine Years and Eighteen Thousand Miles* (New York, 1828), 79, 86.

[74] "Asahel North—Biographical Sketch and Diary," in *Journal of the Illinois State Historical Society,* XV (1922–23), 682; Faux, *Memorable Days,* 214–15. The country around Vincennes and to the south is described in an unsigned letter of September 8, 1817, to Nathan Guilford, corresponding secretary of the Western Emigrant Society, published in the Mount Pleasant (Ohio) *Philanthropist,* March 14, 1818.

the dance and social intercourse constituted an important part of their existence. Intermarriage with the Indians had combined in many the wild roving disposition of the savage with the politeness and poise of the Frenchman. With cotton handkerchiefs bound around their heads and the hooded blanketlike "capot" thrown over their shoulders, these villagers were alike ready for the sustained hardships of hunting, fur trade, weeks of travel upstream on short rations, or the ballroom. Their horses and cattle were of scrawny stock but tough. Outside the town remained vestiges of the medieval three-field system in the commons and woodland pasture. With the abundant game and some Indian corn, the easy-going *habitant* lived a simple life and an enjoyable one, though accused of primitive indolence by the better-class Americans.[75]

Twenty-five miles to the south was the new village of Princeton (founded in 1813), with its eighty log houses, three brick, and ten frame. The forests still hemmed in the settlement, and only the sound of falling trees, undermined by fires or severed by the ax, relieved the dreary silence of the wilds. The country between Vincennes and Princeton was sprinkled with cabins, and the "indolent, dirty, sickly, wild-looking inhabitants" seemed almost to have arrived at the choice of work or starving. Perhaps Faux's estimate was somewhat affected by personal discomforts, such as having hunks of wet clay falling from between the logs and onto his face on rainy nights. In some of the homes soft soap, candles, maple sugar, yarns, and homespun clothes were produced by the exertions of the women. Mills were as yet few in number and widely scattered, and a twenty-mile ride or walk with a bushel of corn to be ground was not exceptional.

About the same distance southwest of Princeton, and about equidistant from the mouth of the Wabash, was the Harmony settlement of the Rappites, established in 1815. George Rapp, a German peasant, had led his group of 125 families to America,

---

[75] Descriptions of Vincennes may be found in Volney, *View of the Soil and Climate;* Melish, *Travels;* Jervis Cutler, *A Topographical Description of the State of Ohio, Indiana Territory, and Louisiana* (Boston, 1812) ; Faux, *Memorable Days;* David Thomas, *Travels through the Western Country in the Summer of 1816* (Auburn, N. Y., 1819), etc.; also in the *Gazetteers* such as Samuel R. Brown's (1817), E. Dana's (1819). The description of the life of the Illinois *habitants* by Thomas Ford in his *A History of Illinois* . . . (Chicago, 1854) applies to the French at Vincennes as well.

and after developing a thriving community in Pennsylvania, purchased 20,000 acres of rich land and moved to the Wabash. The settlement soon became a busy center of agriculture and industry. Within three years 6,000 bushels of wheat were being raised on 150 acres, or 40 bushels to the acre. One year's crop would thus pay for the land twenty times, whereas in England it took twenty to thirty crops to pay for it once.[76] Orchards, vineyards, manufactories—some run by steam—a silk plant, distillery, woolen mill, brickyard, oil well, boats, and a clean inn were among the early improvements. Rapp was high priest and chief executive by "divine right."

Simplicity, humility, persevering industry, prayer, and celibacy were fundamental points of the Rappite creed. Some maintain that complete celibacy was not practiced, but that regulations permitted augmentation of the population at stated intervals, so arranged that when the children came, they came "in little flocks, all within the same month perhaps like farmers' lambs." The toll by malaria was heavy in the first years, but later, under the management of Frederick Rapp, adopted son of the leader, conditions were improved and the settlement became a beauty spot in the woods. Many admired the success of the rather unimaginative German peasants, but few imitated them. Communism and celibacy were too contradictory to the individualistic spirit of the frontier to make much of an appeal.[77]

A few miles north of Vincennes began the prairies. The contrast with the forested areas was remarkable. Those unaccustomed to the woods always felt shut in and depressed by the mass and somberness of their surroundings. The everlasting gloom and inability to see out, together with the quietness and awesome size of the trees, tinged their mood with a spirit of melancholy, sometimes of morbidness. Not so with the open or broken country of the prairies, where the mind became more

[76] *Niles' Weekly Register,* XIV, 440 (Aug. 22, 1818), from the *National Intelligencer.*

[77] For accounts of the Harmony settlement, see George B. Lockwood, *The New Harmony Movement* (New York, 1905); John S. Duss, *The Harmonists, A Personal History* (Harrisburg, Pa., 1943); and the travels and journals of Birkbeck, Faux, Hulme, Thomas, and Woods. The Rappites sold out to Robert Owen in 1824. The reasons are not clear, whether it was owing to poor health conditions, lack of close markets, or the attractiveness of Owen's offer. Their property increased much more rapidly in value after they left than before. The Harmony settlements are discussed more fully in Chapter XV.

cheerful. Along the river bottoms grew the tall pecans, hickories, and cottonwoods, and among them hung giant grapevines. Then came the wide treeless expanses of grass, horseback high. Along the edges, when fires ceased their annual ravage, grew the plum, persimmon, and crab apple. Hazelnuts were abundant, as were pussy willows, and in the shorter grasses or meadows in season were cowslips, marsh marigolds, johnny-jump-ups, early sweet william, cyclamen, Indian paint brushes, and buttercups; also the pernicious ironweed. Besides the great variety of rabbits, squirrels, foxes, raccoons, opossums, turkeys, and the like, there were prairie chickens, deer, elk, and wolves. The deep black soils capable of forty bushels of wheat or a hundred of corn to the acre excited the admiration of those not subject to the fears of untimbered land, and a vision was had of an easier, more productive agriculture than that of the forest clearings.

In traversing such delightful regions, the mind acquires a degree of cheerfulness that rarely attends it in the deep gloom of the forest. But on reverting to the long toils and privations that beset the inhabitant of the wilderness,—and on contrasting the lightness of labour to possess these ancient abodes—a feeling more intense must pervade the patriot. The dark days of the country are past. In fancy, must he view the current of population breaking from the mountains, full, broad, resistless; and the vast and long deserted plains of the Mississippi, fill with life, with intellect, and with elegance.[78]

Among the extensive prairies north of Vincennes were the Shakertown, Gill, and *terre haute* prairies. There were a few settlers with cabins and corn patches, an occasional sawmill, and a coal mine. At Terre Haute stood Fort Harrison, built in the autumn of 1811. A few miles beyond were the "limits of the civilized world; and no white settlers of any description . . . [were] known beyond Fort Harrison."[79]

By treaties made with the Potawatomi and Miami nations in October, 1818, the Indian title to the land lying south of the Wabash-Maumee line (with certain reservations) and also to a strip north of the Wabash lying between the Tippecanoe and Vermilion rivers was extinguished.[80] Shortly thereafter there

[78] Thomas, *Travels,* 187.
[79] *Ibid.,* 197. Thomas' description of the scenery, soils, and flora of this region is excellent. When he speaks of being within the "New Purchase," he refers to the land ceded by Harrison's treaty of 1809, and not the New Purchase of 1818.
[80] See below, Chapter III and map, 111.

was opened to settlement an area almost equal to that portion of Indiana purchased from the Indians by all the treaties made since 1795, a broad rolling expanse of glaciated land, with deep soil, forested for the most part, but interspersed with prairies. This tract was called "The New Purchase." By 1820 squatters from the settlements around Spencer and Gosport on the West Fork of White River were penetrating northward to Greencastle and within a few years reached Sugar Creek and Crawfordsville. By the same year others from around Vallonia and Brownstown on the East Fork or Driftwood, followed the river northward and established settlements in Bartholomew County, where lots were sold in Columbus in 1821. From the Whitewater country settlers came by Whetzel's Trace across to the West Fork of White River in Morgan County, and from the older settlements along the Ohio they came by the old Indian trail or Three Notch Road, which divided on the Driftwood, the one branch leading from the Madison-Vevay region, the other from the settlements around the Falls with connections to Corydon, the territorial capital.

Now that the New Purchase was opened to settlement, the location of a more centrally located capital was attended to by a commission appointed by the legislature. Their choice of a site at the mouth of Fall Creek on the West Fork of White River was ratified by the legislature in January, 1821, and the name chosen was Indianapolis.[81] A planning commission designed the circle and avenue plan for this city that was to spring up in the

[81] The legislature's choice of a name brought forth ridicule as keen, though not as effective, as met Filson's attempt to name Cincinnati "Losantiville." Said the Vincennes *Indiana Centinel,* January 13, 1821: "One of the most ludicrous acts, however, of the sojourners at Corydon, was their naming the new seat of government. Such a name, kind readers, you would never find by searching from Dan to Beersheba; nor in all the libraries, museums, and patent-offices in the world. It is like nothing in heaven nor on earth, nor in the waters under the earth. It is not a name for a man, woman or child; for empire, city, mountain or morass; for bird, beast, fish, nor creeping thing; and nothing mortal or immortal could have thought of it, except the wise men of the East who were congregated at Corydon. It is composed of the following letters: I-N-D-I-A-N-A-P-O-L-I-S!

"Pronounce it as you please, gentle readers—you can do it as you wish—there is no danger of violating any system or rule, either in accent, cadence, or emphasis —suit your own convenience, and be thankful you are enabled to do it, by this rare effect of the scholastic genius of the age. For this title your future capital will be greatly indebted, either to some learned *Hebraist,* some venerable *Grecian,* some sage and sentimental *Brahmin,* or some profound and academic *Pauttowattimie.*"

woods, and in October more than three hundred lots were sold at an average price of $113. Axes were busy and cabins rose as if by magic; some persons even pretended to frame houses. By late winter forty dwellings and several shops had been erected, as well as a gristmill and two sawmills. Carpenters, blacksmiths, masons, tanners, four physicians, and seven innkeepers served the community. Before long neighbors were enjoying dinner parties, teas, and quiltings; and politics, in which "Whitewater" men and "Kentucky" men contended for the local offices, was brewing merrily.

At the upper northeast corner of the New Purchase, on a six-mile square ceded by the Treaty of Greenville in 1795, stood Fort Wayne. Here at the headwaters of the Maumee, General Wayne had built a stockaded fort, and the United States kept a garrison until 1819. After the withdrawal of the military command only the Indians and a few traders and settlers remained. Located at the portage between the Wabash and Maumee over which came a considerable traffic in furs from the Wabash and Illinois country, the outpost possessed a strategic position.

Besides the water communications, Fort Wayne could be reached by horse trail from Fort Recovery, and trails which paralleled the Maumee to Lake Erie. Another ran westward to Fort Dearborn on Lake Michigan. The country round about was wooded with oak, hickory, maple, and other hardwoods commonly found farther south, but scattered among the timber were beautiful prairies of waving grass. A wholesale house to supply traders was established in the town in 1820. The following year Thomas Teas found thirty log cabins and two frame houses, a barracks occupied by the Indian agent, a Baptist missionary (Isaac McCoy), and a Lancasterian school for the Indians. The families were mostly of French-Canadian descent.[82] The Indians were debauched on whiskey supplied by the traders, who hid it in the woods away from the agency. Dozens at a time could be

[82] Thomas Scattergood Teas, "Journal of a tour to Fort Wayne and the adjacent country, in the year 1821," published in Harlow Lindley (ed.), *Indiana as Seen by Early Travelers* (*Indiana Historical Collections*, Indianapolis, 1916), 250. Fort Wayne and the Maumee country are described in a letter to Nathan Guilford, published in the Mount Pleasant (Ohio) *Philanthropist*, March 28, April 4, 1818.

found drunk and about thirty were said to have been killed in drunken quarrels in two months.

Of Indiana in 1818 it was said: "There are few countries in the world can much exceed this part of the banks of the Ohio. . . . It may be doubted whether any state of the United States, all things duly considered, can present more advantages than Indiana."[83]

§ § § § §

The Illinois country was named after the once proud tribe who had boldly fought with the Winnebago and even the Iroquois, but who, vitiated by white man's liquor and diseases, had degenerated into lazy vagrants and cowards, and finally became extinct. When Illinois Territory was set off in 1809 by the line of the Wabash-Vincennes meridian, it included the region which extended north to the international boundary.[84] Along the east and south sides ran the Wabash and Ohio, and on the west the Mississippi. From the Wabash and Ohio reached back the Embarrass, Little Wabash, and Saline rivers, but the longer drainage slope lay to the west, and the Kaskaskia, Illinois, Rock, and Wisconsin rivers reached back from the Mississippi almost to the eastern edge of the territory. These westward-flowing streams had been the highways of the French between the St. Lawrence and Mississippi countries, and the older settlements were those of the old traders at Kaskaskia, Cahokia, Prairie du Rocher, and Peoria. Farther to the north, in the region destined later to be separated from Illinois, were Green Bay and Prairie du Chien.

That part of Illinois which lay south of a line from Kaskaskia to opposite the mouth of White River was much like southern Indiana. It was but in part glaciated, largely rough and forested.[85] The rest of the area later included in the state of Illinois was mostly prairie, dissected by woods along the bottoms and

---

[83] William Darby, *The Emigrant's Guide to the Western and Southwestern States and Territories* . . . (New York, 1818), 214–15.

[84] See map, 63.

[85] Among the trees were white, black, Spanish, chinquapin, and burr oak, white and black walnut, basswood, cherry, buttonwood, ash, elm, sassafras, sumac, honey locust, elder, mulberry, crab apple, pecan, hackberry, maple, cottonwood, and pawpaw.

stream valleys.[86] At the end of the War of 1812 the crescent of settlements extended along the Wabash from a little above Vincennes, down along the Ohio and up the Mississippi Valley to the mouth of the Illinois. The region between the Kaskaskia and the Mississippi rivers was most thickly settled. This rich "American bottom," occupied by the French a century before, had long been under cultivation. The strip of land, two to seven miles wide and more than a hundred long, had a light, black soil eight to ten feet deep, but the pale faces and bilious fevers of the settlers marked it as none too healthful.[87] There were fields of corn with stalks fifteen feet tall, and the same crop had been grown thirty years without fertilizer. The river here was fringed with forests, and east of the valley was a ridge of steep, rocky bluffs covered with grass and trees.[88] Kaskaskia had lost many of its inhabitants after the English occupation in 1765, but in 1804 it was made a land-office seat, and in 1809 became the capital of Illinois Territory. In 1817 the town contained about 160 houses of characteristic French appearance, most of them with spacious picketed gardens in the rear. The inhabitants, more than half of whom were French, raised horned cattle, horses, hogs, and poultry. Besides the land office there was a post office and a printing office from which was issued the *Illinois Herald*.[89] In the latter were advertisements of nine general stores, a hat shop, and three tailor shops. The one tavern was frequently unable to handle the patronage. Prairie du Rocher, fifteen miles on up the bottom, was a village of about forty families. Cahokia, almost directly opposite St. Louis, was another old French village which had declined in importance.

Over on the Ohio, between the Saline and Little Wabash, was Shawneetown, the chief port of entry, a village of thirty

[86] Earlier descriptions of Illinois topography may be found in Samuel R. Brown, *The Western Gazetteer or Emigrant's Directory* . . . (Auburn, N. Y., 1817); Timothy Flint, *The History and Geography of the Mississippi Valley* . . . (2 volumes. Cincinnati, 1832); Jones, *Illinois and the West*. Chapter I in Alvord, *The Illinois Country,* is an excellent summary, and very helpful are the physiographic maps assembled in Edith M. Poggi, *The Prairie Province of Illinois* (*University of Illinois Studies in the Social Sciences*, XIX, No. 3, Urbana, 1934). Douglas C. Ridgley, *The Geography of Illinois* (University of Chicago Press, 1921), has a useful bibliography of items on geology, geography, etc.

[87] Mason, *Narrative*, 51.

[88] Ferdinand Ernst, "Travels in Illinois in 1819" (extracts from Ernst's *Observations* . . . [1823]), in *Transactions of the Illinois State Historical Society*, 1903, p. 151.

[89] Samuel R. Brown, *Western Gazetteer*, 10; Fearon, *Sketches*, 258.

or forty log buildings. The development of this place had been impeded by the United States saline reserve near by, which was not open to entry. Lots had been sold at Shawneetown at good prices in 1814, when the wartime price of salt was high. The ensuing slump in salt prices, combined with mismanagement of the works, left many purchasers badly pinched, but their petitions to Congress to be relieved of further payments were not granted. In pre-steamboat days the town had been overrun periodically by bargers and keelboatmen, a rough and lawless crowd. Though these incidents decreased, the outrages of the *mosquitoes* continued; though it was not proved that these varmints could bite through the sole of a boot, unacclimated visitors swore that they could. Muscular, sprightly, and dissipated, they preferred human blood to that of brutes. Shawneetown illustrated, said Birkbeck, the "pertinacious adhesion of the human animal to the spot where it has once fixed itself."

From Shawneetown to Kaskaskia and St. Louis ran the "Great Western Road" from which, near Muddy Creek, branched southward the road to Fort Massac on the Ohio. Over the prairies from Vincennes to St. Louis, through lands not yet surveyed, ran a newly located road, along which a few taverns had been established. From just east of the Kaskaskia River near Carlyle a branch led southeast to Shawneetown, and about half way between Vincennes and St. Louis branched off the Kaskaskia post road. Near Johnson's settlement the road to Edwardsville, also a land-office town, curved off to the northwest. Other roads led from Edwardsville to St. Louis, Cahokia, and down the river valley to Kaskaskia.

Town projecting and site promoting abounded on all sides during the years following the war, and by 1818, fourteen of the fifteen counties had county seats, but most of these places represented merely a location for courthouse, jail, tavern, and general store. Many county-seat locations were changed after a few years, and often the prospective towns never survived after the removal of the county government.[90] "Every man makes his own town," said Mason. The lives of many were short, but the guileful speculators could do much mischief to a community. In

[90] Solon J. Buck, *Illinois in 1818* (*Illinois Centennial Publications,* Introductory volume, Springfield, 1917), 60.

1816 Carmi was laid out on the Little Wabash, a ferry was established, and it soon became the second in size of the towns along the Wabash. In 1818 Jonesboro emerged from among the paper towns down in the triangle between the Ohio and Mississippi rivers. "Waterloo" on the Ohio, and "Hamburg" on the Mississippi failed to take. "The City and Bank of Cairo" was chartered in 1818 by the territorial legislature, and the promoter who entered 1,800 acres expected to sell 2,000 lots, construct levees, make improvements, and use the remainder of the proceeds for capital for the bank, but the plans failed to create a city at this time.

Most of the settlers who came into Illinois following the war entered either by Shawneetown or Vincennes. A ferry was built on the site of Russellville in 1818. But few newcomers had gone back far from the streams upon which they were at first so dependent,[91] and comparatively few settled along the Ohio. The prairies which in summer sunlight presented a beautiful picture with splotches of contrasting colors of wild flowers and tall grass billowing in the breeze, were at first of more interest to the traveler than to the settler. Of them Edmund Flagg wrote in 1837:

The touching, delicate loveliness of the lesser prairies, so resplendent in brilliancy of hue and beauty of outline, I have often dwelt upon with delight. The graceful undulation of slope and swell; the exquisite richness and freshness of the verdure flashing in native magnificence; the gorgeous dies of the matchless and many-coloured flowers dallying with the winds; the beautiful woodland points and promontories shooting forth into the mimic sea; the far-retreating, shadowy *coves*, going back in long vistas into the green wood; the curved outline of the dim, distant horizon, caught at intervals through the openings of the forest; and the whole gloriously lighted up by the early radiance of morning, as with rosy footsteps she came dancing over the dew-gemmed landscape; all these constituted a scene in which beauty unrivalled was the sole ingredient. And then those bright enamelled clumps of living emerald, sleeping upon the wavy surface like the golden Hesperides of classic fiction, or, like another cluster of Fortunate Isles in the dark-blue waters, breathing a fragrance as from oriental bowers; the wild-deer bounding in startled beauty from his bed, and the merry note of the skylark, whistling, with speckled vest and dew-wet wing, upon the resin-weed, lent the last touchings to Nature's *chef d'oeuvre*.

[91] For settlement map showing location of people, see Buck, *Illinois in 1818*, 58, and Theodore C. Pease, *The Frontier State, 1818–1848* (*Centennial History of Illinois,* Volume II, Springfield, 1918), 4.

"Oh, beautiful, still beautiful,
Though long and lone the way."[92]

And again some years later the newcomer saw this picture: "The whole glowing landscape about and around us far as eye could command, gave hint that the stars of night when eclipsed by the transcendent glories of dawn had slipped from their high places in the cerulean dome down to the green flowered earth, kindling it to 'rival the constellations.' The sunny, fragrant atmosphere palpitated with glad songs of mocking birds, thrush and meadow-larks, soaring on wing or swaying in the tall white-bloomed milkweed."[93] If at times the larger prairies strikingly resembled the solitary grandeur of the ocean, they could also, treeless, silent and lonesome, be remindful of the African desert. The eagle and buzzard might soar lazily overhead, but conspicuously absent were the smaller singing birds.[94] But in 1817 many thought that the prairie lands would be returned to the General Land Office as unfit for cultivation.[95]

The people of Illinois were much like their Hoosier neighbors, but, as the country was more recently settled, they presented an even more homogeneous picture of pioneer life. Still mostly in the hunting, squatter, half-farming classes, they provided enough peculiarities to fascinate the traveler, whose descriptions are at best unconsciously filled with half truths.[96] Across the river from Vincennes one found cutthroats, murderers, and travelers, said Mason. The inhabitants were impolite, lazy, and disobliging. Illinois was the hiding place for villains from every part of the United States. It was easy to make a living, and laziness and idleness were owing to this fact as well as to the fevers and ague

[92] *The Far West: or A Tour Beyond the Mountains* . . . (New York, 1838), reprinted in Thwaites (ed.), *Early Western Travels*, XXVI, 340–41.

[93] James Haines, "Social Life and Scenes in the Early Settlement of Central Illinois," in *Transactions of the Illinois State Historical Society*, 1905, p. 48.

[94] A description of the more stern aspects of the prairie may be found in the Springfield *Sangamo Journal*, August 25, 1832.

[95] Buck (ed.), "Pioneer Letters of Gershom Flagg," in *Transactions of the Illinois State Historical Society*, 1910, p. 153.

[96] William Oliver, fair-minded British traveler of 1841–42, soundly observed: "Your true hunter is often a simple-minded, unaffected child of nature; true he is ignorant, but this ignorance includes the follies and very many of the vices of civilized life. The worst example of his tribe is he who has not fled before the influx of population, and who, impatient of the restraint of industrious habits, has generally reaped nothing from civilization beyond its vices and its scorn." *Eight Months in Illinois* . . . (Newcastle upon Tyne, 1843, reprinted by W. M. Hill, Chicago, 1924), 155–56.

from which the people suffered.[97] "The people of the territory are from all parts of the United States and do the least work I believe of any people in the world. Their principal business is hunting deer, horses, hogs and cattle, and raising corn."[98] The farmer's horses and cattle roamed in the prairie grass that was taller than a man on horseback, and often were found a half-dozen miles away from home. Dirks were carried by many persons and duels were frequent. No one was called master, and yet there was no coarse familiarity or vulgarity.[99]

Upon entering Illinois the traveler left behind all the refinements of civilization. It was a beautiful country, but the inhabitants, with some exceptions, were semi-Indian in character, ruder and less civilized.[100] They looked with disfavor upon the land hunter, forgetting that many of their own class were intruding on Indian lands or squatting on government domain. The hunters were as persevering as the Indians in the pursuit of game; otherwise they cultivated indolence as a privilege with the attitude that it was a mark of freedom. Idleness was a malady prevalent among all classes and the people existed in yawning indifference, surrounded by nuisances and petty wants. Cabins were of rough bark logs, frequently without floors and chimneys, with only holes in the roofs for the smoke. The scanty wardrobes were carelessly hung over strings of buffalo hide, and a few pots and pans, some old rifles, perhaps a fiddle, constituted the furnishings and utensils. One settler near the Little Wabash had built three such cabins in a period of a year. In one, Birkbeck found the man, his pregnant wife, eldest son, three big rude daughters, and "a squalling tribe of dirty brats of both sexes—all pale yellow without a bit of healthful bloom." Their color indicated their place of residence.

Scientific and cultural pursuits were practically unknown, notwithstanding the common use among the people of the word "elegant." There were "elegant" cabins of rude logs, "elegant" mills, "elegant" tanneries, and "elegant" roads, in the last instance meaning passable. Deficiencies in science and taste were not the result of lack of energy, for in politics the usual American zest was

[97] Mason, *Narrative*, 38, 51; *Wisconsin Historical Collections*, II, 327.
[98] Buck (ed.), "Pioneer Letters of Gershom Flagg," in *Transactions of the Illinois State Historical Society*, 1910, p. 162.
[99] Fearon, *Sketches of America*, 262.
[100] Birkbeck, *Notes on a Journey in America*, 117, 120.

shown, probably because through political activity Americans had made themselves free. Nature had done much for these frontiersmen and they left much to nature. "What yawning and stretching, and painful restlessness they would be spared, if their time were occupied in the acquisition of useful knowledge!"[101] Yet if the traveler did not prove too superior, he would find these folks generous and hospitable.[102]

In this country and among these people was planted a settlement important not for its size but for the leadership and influence of some of the founders and as an illustration of the conflict between two types of agricultural economy.

Morris Birkbeck was an English tenant farmer of means, who, disgusted with his lack of political status in England, oppressed with taxes, and discouraged by the poor opportunities for economic advancement, fled "the approaching crisis of anarchy and despotism" and sought to establish careers of enterprise for himself and children in America. There was also an element of philanthropy involved, unless Birkbeck was merely a shrewd advertiser. He would rejoice "to transplant, into these boundless regions of freedom, the millions whom he has left behind him, grovelling in ignorance and want." Limited by distaste for the climate in the East and slavery in the South, the choice of location was the Northwest.

Birkbeck and family were joined in America by George Flower, and though these men had no love for the frontier, attracted by the prairies and cheapness of land, in 1817–18 they entered 26,400 acres of prairie land between the Little Wabash and Bon Pas Creek. A petition was presented to Congress for the right to purchase on an extended payment plan a large tract of land in the unsurveyed areas just to the north of the base line, but it was not granted. Flower returned to England to get settlers and Birkbeck endeavored to get the land and cabins ready. Several

---

[101] Birkbeck, *Notes on a Journey in America,* 133–34. Birkbeck was well aware of the dangers lurking in the making of comparisons by those not qualified to form fair judgments. He reminded himself that conditions were as bad or worse in England off the main roads, and that to be fair the frontiersman would have to be compared to the lowest social and economic group of England, the peasantry or those just emerging from peasantry. The interests of the travelers were centered largely in this class in America. The always thinly scattered minority of people of culture and means was much the same whether found on the frontier, back in the older settlements, or in Europe, and called forth a proportionately less amount of attention.

[102] For analysis of such estimates of the frontier settlers, see Chapter VI.

parties, mostly farmers and a few mechanics recruited largely in the United States, joined Birkbeck and his group, and by October, 1818, about two hundred Englishmen were in the settlement.[103] Much was to be done; few seemed to know just how to go about doing it. The plan of the leaders was to apply capital, machinery, and the most approved methods to agriculture and stock raising, and in effect to establish a group of manors. The labor and servant problem was hard to solve, for Americans hired out only intermittently as farm laborers, and those imported frequently got the notion of becoming landowners themselves. A split developed between Birkbeck and George Flower, partly over the affections of a young lady friend of Birkbeck's daughters. Instead of the one big project, the two families parted company, Wanborough becoming the seat of the Birkbeck settlement, and Albion of the Flower. By 1819 there were about 1,100 people in the settlements, 400 of them English. The venture did not work out as expected, partly because of labor problems and the quality of the soil in the region selected, and partly because of the bearing of the English gentleman, who, try as he would to live as an American, became known as "the Emperor of the Prairie."[104]

This venture, because of its size and attendant publicity, brought Illinois and the prairies into public notice both at home and abroad. Birkbeck's *Notes* went through eleven editions in America, England, and Ireland, his *Letters* through seven, and were translated into French and German. The writings of Richard Flower, Hulme, Woods, Faux, Fordham, and others, all widely circulated, also gave excellent publicity to this settlement on the prairies.[105]

[103] The *Pittsburgh Gazette,* September 29, 1818, stated that the river shores presented the most animated scenes ever witnessed. The beaches of the Monongahela were lined with flatboats for Illinois and other parts, and among the movers were many English, who came full handed, probably as a result of Birkbeck's advertising.

[104] "They of the Prairie were proud and wanted only high bred English." Faux, *Memorable Days,* 258. Faux was particularly critical of the Birkbeck-Flower plans. He accused Birkbeck of being impractical, careless, improvident, and felt that English laborers were worth nothing, "hewing, splitting, clearing, grubbing and plowing among roots being a business which they do not understand, and wish not to understand." *Ibid.,* 223. The western country he thought fit only for the hardworking farmer and small capitalist; agriculture to succeed on the frontier must be a retail and not a wholesale business.

[105] Ernst considered Birkbeck's *Notes* to be in conformity with the truth, but did not think that the *Letters from Illinois* (1818) were so well founded. *Transactions of the Illinois State Historical Society,* 1903, p. 150. Brief descriptions of

Southerners comprised by far the largest element of the early settlers of Illinois, yet there were probably more "Yankees" than is commonly realized. Most of those who left New England for the Northwest in this period no doubt headed for Ohio, yet Brother Jonathan was usually well informed on land prices, and removals from Ohio to Illinois were numerous. James Hall, describing the emigrants, was no less aware of the Yankee than of the somewhat more picturesque and "lonesome looking couple from old North Carolina":

First in order, as he is always first when speculation is concerned, comes the hardy, enterprising New Englander. Of all the emigrants to the West, Brother Jonathan alone knows where he is going to—the cheapest mode of travel, and what he is going to do when he gets there; he alone has read the preemption laws, and knows what sum he must take with him, or notions in the way of trade, to secure a home in the wilderness. Already, before he gets there, he converses fluently about ranges, townships, and sections, has ascertained the number of acres in each subdivision, the amount reserved for schools, and is ready on his arrival to avail himself of his new position.[106]

The contrast in types and manners between the southern folk and the New Englanders was striking. They differed in speech, in manners and attitudes, often in politics. Yankee food and recipes and household methods were different. The ideas of thrift and shrewdness and addiction to notes, bonds, bookkeeping, and mechanical contraptions were frequently irritating to the easier-going and neighborly Southerner who would lend his oxen but seldom think of renting them. Yankee feelings of superiority were not easily concealed, and at least one pioneer records they became "objects of the deepest animosity to the settlers in Southern

the English settlements may be found in Buck, *Illinois in 1818;* Pease, *The Frontier State;* and George Flower, *History of the English Settlement in Edwards County Illinois . . . (Chicago Historical Society's Collection,* I, Chicago, 1882). Birkbeck's *Notes on a Journey in America* and his *Letters from Illinois* give his own account. Richard Flower's *Letters from the Illinois* are reprinted in Edwin E. Sparks (ed.), *The English Settlement in Illinois* (Cedar Rapids, Ia., 1907), and in Thwaites (ed.), *Early Western Travels,* X. Thomas Hulme's *Journal of a Tour in the Western Countries of America—September 30, 1818—August 8, 1819,* and John Woods's *Two Years' Residence in the Settlement on the English Prairie* are also in *Early Western Travels,* X. The subject is well covered in Jane Rodman, "The English Settlement in Southern Illinois as Viewed by English Travellers, 1815–1825," MS. thesis, Indiana University, 1947, and printed in *Indiana Magazine of History,* XLIII (1947), 329–62, and XLIV (1948), 37–68.

[106] Quoted in *Congressional Globe,* 26 Congress, 2 session, Appendix, 65.

Illinois, Indiana, and the South-western States."[107] In all probability there was no serious clash of elements. Each type made
fun of the other yet the two lived peaceably side by side, intermarried as did Irish, English, and Germans on an earlier frontier,
and elected each other to office. After all, their differences were
more marked in the domesticities than in the publicities. In the
hardships and necessary co-operations of frontier life the good
qualities were brought out as well as the bad, and "narrow nosed
Yankee" and "shiftless Kaintuck" learned to recognize the useful
traits of each other.

In 1815 the northern two thirds of the present state of Illinois
was still Indian country.[108] The boundary line ran east from the
mouth of the Illinois River to within ten miles of the Wabash
and then veered north and east to the Vermilion. The war had
ended with England in possession of the region around Rock
Island and as far south as the present Quincy. None knew whether
there would be lasting peace with the Indians. The Sacs and
Foxes had hunting and living privileges on the land north of the
Illinois River, ceded by them in 1804. The Potawatomi, Kickapoo,
and other tribes claimed large areas in central Illinois. By estimate of the Secretary of War the Indians numbered more than
13,000 with upwards of 3,000 warriors, and the need for their
pacification was pressing. Two million acres of the land between
the Illinois and Mississippi rivers had been set aside by Congress
in 1812 for military bounties. Although the Chippewa, Potawatomi, and others having claim to the territory did not cede it
until 1816, the surveys were in progress in the summer of 1815
and were completed in September, 1817. During the next sixteen

---

[107] Joseph Gillespie, *Recollections of Early Illinois and her Noted Men* (*Fergus'
Historical Series*, No. 13, Chicago, 1880), 6. Estwick Evans felt the people of
Pittsburgh and points west to be suspicious of Yankees. "The Yankees are every
where considered an intelligent, hardy, bold, active, and enterprising people; but
they are supposed to be excessively fond of money, and frequently to obtain it by
fraudulent means." *Pedestrious Tour*, in Thwaites (ed.), *Early Western Travels*,
VIII, 253.

The *Edwardsville* (Ill.) *Spectator*, June 26, 1821, had the following on sectional
prejudices: "The southern emigrants consider the eastern to be all cheats; the
eastern man imagines the southern to be all savages. The white man damns the
yankee, and the yankee the white man—the one term synonymous with rascal, and
the other with outlaw, with those who reproachfully use them; and when they
come together, the one expects swindling, the other personal abuse. . . . The *one*
associates with an eastern name, ideas of intelligence and industry; with a southern,
ignorance and laziness. The *other* considers avaricious meanness for the former,
and careless independence for the latter, to be more appropriate terms."

[108] See map, 111.

View of the Ohio from Shipping port near Louisville in Kentucky. Looking down the River. 14th May 1828

From original sketch by Basil Hall

Dessiné par Tardieu l'aine

French Habitation in the Country of the Illinois.

months, about 18,000 warrants were exchanged for quarter sections.[109] Many of the titles were transferred, and, as much of the land fell into speculators' hands, no settlement took place until after 1818. In July, 1819, the Kickapoo ceded their claim to the lands south and east of the Illinois and Kankakee rivers. Squatters were north of the survey line before 1818, even on the military lands,[110] and the best lands in the three land-office districts were entered by settlers or speculators.[111]

In the three and one-half years following the war the population of Illinois increased one and three-fifths times, and the census for statehood purposes listed about 35,000 people by July, 1818. Many overbought land, and relief acts were necessary to enable them to save a part of their entries. Land sales slumped after 1819 for a period of years. The constitutional convention, influenced by land speculation, imposed upon the legislature the duty of removing the capital as soon as it should get a land grant from Congress. A site was selected outside of the proposed localities about eighty miles northeast of Kaskaskia, and squatters were in the vicinity of Vandalia, the new capital, by 1819.[112] More than two hundred lots were sold in September. The same year Gershom Flagg wrote that two hundred families had settled north of Edwardsville, some as far as one hundred and twenty miles. A squatter or two had built cabins in the rich and beautiful Sangamon country by 1817, and by 1819 not only had numerous settlers arrived but people of means were looking over this much-talked-of region. Within two years the legislature organized Sangamon County. Schoolcraft in 1821 referred to the fertility of the region as proverbial, and a few years later Timothy Flint described it as follows:

The Sangamon, in particular, is an Arcadian region, in which nature has delighted to bring together her happiest combinations of landscape. It is generally a level country. The prairies are not so extensive, as to be

[109] Buck, *Illinois in 1818*, 43.
[110] *Ibid.*, 39, 44, 46–47.
[111] See land entry map in *ibid.*, 52.
[112] Ernst, "Travels in Illinois in 1819," in *Transactions of the Illinois State Historical Society*, 1903, p. 159. A disgruntled Edwardsville citizen said, apropos the action of the legislature which ratified the site, that it was aptly named, i.e., after the Vandals. His story was that one of the commissioners selected to locate the capital, "a good kind of man but better known as a bear hunter," had heard of La Salle, but mistook the name for "Vandal." *Edwardsville Spectator*, November 14, 1820.

incapable of settlement from want of timber. The Sangamon itself is a fine boatable water of the Illinois. . . . All the waters that enter this beautiful river, have sandy and pebbly bottoms, and pure and transparent waters. There is a happy proportion of timbered and prairie lands. The soil is of great fertility. The climate is not very different from that of New York, and the latitude about the same. The summer range for cattle is inexhaustible. . . . The proportion of locust, black walnut, and peccan trees, that indicate the richest soils, is great. Iron and copper ore, salt springs, gypsum, and stone coal are abundant.[113]

At the site of Chicago in 1821 there were but two families outside of the fort, while at Galena, soon to be a center of lead mining, but one cabin had been built by 1822. A new survey of Lake Michigan found the Mississippi to be one hundred and sixty-one miles to the west instead of two hundred and fifty as heretofore supposed, and later maps reduced the width of Illinois accordingly. Already there was talk of a canal to unite the Lake with the Mississippi, and thus open the only internal waterway of its kind in the world. The prospects of the young state were exceedingly fair. "In short," said Ernst in 1819, "I do not believe that any one State in all America is so highly favored by nature, in every respect, as the State of Illinois."[114] When the lands of the Sangamon region were put on the market in 1823, emigration was so noticeable that the *Intelligencer* believed that the state would soon be able to take rank in population among her sister states.[115]

§ § § § §

The settlement in Michigan Territory by those seeking to establish permanent homes and develop the land, as contrasted with the earlier inhabitants who were engaged in missionary work, fur trade, or military occupation, dates from about the close of the War of 1812. Detroit, founded by Cadillac in 1701, was incorporated as a city by the Governor and Judges of Michigan Territory in 1815. Its population five years before had been about 800, but many families left during the war. The town was walled in with high pickets, over each of the three gates stood a sentry, and the fort was full of soldiers. The old market stood in

[113] *History and Geography of the Mississippi Valley,* I, 321.
[114] *Travels in Illinois,* 162.
[115] Vandalia *Illinois Intelligencer,* November 22, 1823.

the center of Woodward Avenue, and at the southeast corner
was a whipping post where petty criminals were punished. The
two-wheeled French carts plowed through the muddy streets,
hauling water from the river in barrels, or carrying passengers
on business or social calls. Business was concerned largely with
the maple-sugar and fur trade with the Indians.[116]

The war had seriously affected settlement, but was not without
its compensations. Many soldiers from Ohio, Kentucky, Pennsylvania, and Virginia who had been on duty in Michigan Territory remained as settlers, and those who returned to their homes
advertised the opportunities of the region. Surveyors sent to the
interior in 1815 to survey the military bounty lands found the
Indians still hostile, so gave up and returned.[117] Lewis Cass was
appointed governor of the Territory in 1813 and his life and
labors became intimately associated with the development of
Michigan. In August, 1817, Detroit celebrated the unexpected
visit of President Monroe with an illumination, and the newspapers were soon utilizing this event to advertise Michigan
Territory. The *Detroit Gazette* asked its readers for contributions on the soil, climate, and products of the region, to satisfy
the interest in Michigan on the part of the people of the East.[118]
Immigration into Michigan was stimulated somewhat by the
opening of lands to public sale. Advertisements appeared in
eastern newspapers in June, 1818; sales were to take place in
July. With the return of some former residents and the addition
of new ones, Detroit grew to about 1,100 population by the end
of 1818.

William Darby, who visited the city in this year, wrote:
"Detroit . . . remains . . . an isolated moral mass, having few
sympathies in common, and but a slight tie of interest to unite
it to the sovereignty of which it forms a part." Its extensive currents of business, mixture of peoples, and direct contact with the
Indians and wilderness reminded him of Natchitoches on the Red

---

[116] A detailed description of Detroit in 1815–16, building by building, may be
found in the *Detroit Journal and Michigan Advertiser*, August 1, 1834; in 1820
in Henry R. Schoolcraft, *Narrative Journal of Travels Through the Northwestern
Regions of the United States* . . . (Albany, 1821), 51. Early life in Detroit is well
sketched in Bela Hubbard, "The Early Colonization of Detroit," in *Michigan Pioneer and Historical Collections*, I (1877), 347–71.

[117] Chillicothe (Ohio) *Supporter*, July 13, 1815.

[118] July 25, August 16, 29, 1817.

River. "In each place, you behold at one glance the extremes of human improvement, costume, and manners. You behold the inhabitants in habiliments that would suit the walks of New-York, Philadelphia, London or Paris, and you also behold the bushy, bare-headed savage, almost in primæval nudity. In the same storehouse, you see placed upon the same shelf, objects to supply the first and last wants of human nature."[119] Estwick Evans noted the city's prospects for farmers, artisans, and merchants,[120] and Schoolcraft emphasized its strategic situation for future commerce.

A meeting was held to encourage securing of information on the interior, a region less known than any other part of the country so close to settlements. In a way Edward Tiffin's report on the wretchedness of the region was an advantage rather than a handicap, as military bounty lands were located elsewhere, and southeastern Michigan, cleared of Indian title by the treaty of 1807, when settled, received actual farmers rather than speculators. The Monroe and Tiffin views, aided and abetted somewhat by those interested in the fur trade, were shortly overcome by actual observation. In the early autumn of 1818 a party of several persons struck north along the Indian trail which led toward Saginaw Bay, crossed the Clinton River at Pontiac, and explored and selected land. When they returned and reported that the interior of Michigan was not a vast impenetrable and uninhabitable wilderness morass as supposed, the people of Detroit were awakened to its possibilities.[121] A team and wagon got through to Pontiac in three days and a cabin was built in the winter of 1818–19.

Emigrants did not come in very fast, however. The greatest obstacle was the "universal pressure of hard times on almost all classes of people in the United States."[122] The advantages of geography and the possible effects of the Clinton [Erie] and the Illinois canals were discussed by one who saw Detroit "exhibiting the faint, yet imposing outlines of a great commercial city."[123]

[119] *A Tour from the City of New-York, to Detroit, in the Michigan Territory* . . . (New York, 1819), 188, 190.
[120] *Pedestrious Tour*, in Thwaites (ed.), *Early Western Travels*, VIII, 219–20.
[121] *Detroit Gazette*, May 8, 22, October 30, November 13, 1818.
[122] *Ibid.*, June 25, 1819.
[123] In a two-column article by one who had not seen the city since 1805, in *ibid.*, January 7, 1820.

Knowledge of the interior increased slowly also. Description of the oak openings, against which had been exhibited some prejudice, the lakes, fish, soil, and timber began to appear in the *Gazette*, to be copied in Ohio and eastern papers.[124] Pontiac was something more than a "paper town" in 1821, for it had a mill and another building or two. Fifty or sixty lots were sold in the summer of 1821 at from $20 to $70.[125] In October of that year the "Sciawassa Company" organized an exploring party further to investigate the interior (the Saginaw country), and after a four-weeks' trip it reported that though there was some rough land, there was also some fine land, many fine lakes, and timber of oak, ash, hickory, and maple.[126] Another report by "Traveller" stated that the Saginaw country was not flooded by the river but that the fur traders were fostering that idea to keep the settlers out.[127] By the summer of 1822 the stream of emigrants began to trickle. One schooner brought forty-five, mostly from New York, but Vermont, Massachusetts, Pennsylvania, and Ohio were also represented.

Pioneer life in Michigan combined features of that in the woods of southern Indiana and the prairie regions of Illinois. Timber was at hand in abundance for the shake-covered cabins, yet the ground of oak openings required three or four yokes of heavy oxen for the first plowing. Winters were mild during the early years of settlement and breaking of land was common from December to March, when the only considerable snow came. Among the hardships and evils were the woods flies, mosquitoes, snakes, fever, agues, and the Indians. The latter, although nearly always friendly, were often a nuisance, frequently became drunk, and begged or intimidated women and children in the absence of the men. They traded maple sugar, usually not too clean, wax, skins, and furs to the early settlers, who in turn sold these articles to aid in getting necessary tools, seeds, and supplies. Wild game was everywhere. Deer could be killed just out of sight of the

[124] For instance, that by "Stranger," who was "most agreeably surprised," in *ibid.*, September 1, 1820; two long articles in issues of February 15, 22, 1822; and the long article printed in the *Onondaga* (N. Y.) *Journal*, June 28, 1822.

[125] *Detroit Gazette*, July 20, 1821.

[126] *Ibid.*, October 5, November 9, 16, 23, 1821. Further descriptions appeared in the issues of February 15, 22, and March 1, 1822.

[127] *Ibid.*, June 7, 1822.

cabins, and could at times be seen grazing like sheep in flocks in the oak openings.[128]

In 1819 the Chippewa, by the Treaty of Saginaw, ceded the land in the central and northeastern part of the Lower Peninsula, and two years later, at Chicago, a treaty with the Ottawa, Chippewa, and Potawatomi nations cleared the land title to the southwestern part.[129]

The only road to Michigan led through the Black Swamp of northwestern Ohio—a heavily timbered, blind trail over land treacherous enough in summertime, seemingly bottomless at other seasons. About halfway through from Cleveland stood a half-breed's cabin where travelers might get shelter and wildcat soup to strengthen them for further efforts. Game was plentiful along the way, as were bilious fevers and ague. Governor Lewis Cass had called the attention of the United States Government to this road in the winter of 1814–15. The war had made clear the need of roads from the Ohio Valley and westward to Chicago. In 1818 the government established a road from Detroit through Monroe to the rapids of the Maumee, and Cass's road north to Saginaw was passable to wagons as far as Pontiac the same year. The arrival of the *Walk-in-the-Water*, the first steamboat to navigate the upper lakes, with her 330 tons and low pressure boilers, constituted an event, not only in the lives of the Indians but of the people of Michigan Territory.[130] No matter if it did have to be helped up the Niagara rapids by oxen, and could average only about five miles an hour, it was a promise for the future, and a link between Michigan and Buffalo and the East.

Far to the north at the extreme point of the southern peninsula was Michilimackinac or Mackinac. The old town had been on the mainland, but following George Rogers Clark's capture of Vincennes in 1779 the new town and fort had been built on the island, which rose several hundred feet above the lake. There the Giant's Arch, the Natural Pyramid, and Skull Rock offered specimens of natural curiosities. The town of several hundred population was situated on the little bay which offered a safe harbor and towering above it was the fort taken over by the

---

[128] For a reminiscence of early settlement in Oakland County, see *Michigan Pioneer and Historical Collections*, VIII (1884), 238–39.

[129] See map, 111.

[130] For this event, see Chapter VII.

Americans in 1796, after Jay's Treaty. The people were mostly French Canadians and half-breeds; trading with the Indians, fishing, and the cultivation of a few potatoes, cabbages, and beets were the chief occupations. When the traders and Indians of the American or South West fur companies came in to sell and reoutfit, the town sometimes contained 2,000 people; vast quantities of beaver, fox, otter, martin, and less valuable skins passed through the settlement. Fish existed in variety and abundance: white fish, trout, bass, pike, perch, and "musquenonge."[131] At Sault Ste. Marie, forty-five miles to the north, were a number of buildings inhabited by a half-dozen English and French families. At the foot of the rapids the Indians speared and netted the fish, and a skillful fisherman could land hundreds of fish for winter drying in a few hours.

The only settlements in what later became Wisconsin were at Green Bay and Prairie du Chien. Here the population, before the coming of the Americans, was made up of natives, French Canadians, and "breeds," and the genial easy-going life of the French, a blend of civilization and primitive simplicity, marked the tone of society. The people were polite, lively, hospitable, and improvident. They danced, drank, took sleigh rides, and conducted horse races on the ice. Maple-sugar making, which with a month or so of preparation and a considerable period of sap running, was both a labor and an occasion, was so perfected that the crude runs of Indian sugar could be refined and added to the output. The Easter festivities and post-Lenten celebrations were held in the woods, where the chickens and game were roasted among the *sucreries*.[132]

The War of 1812 separated this happy carefree existence from the period of American colonization. The economic basis of the French settlements had been the trade with the natives, particularly in furs, but there had developed also the beginnings of agriculture.[133] The little river farms of worn-out *voyageurs*

[131] Schoolcraft, *Narrative Journal*, 118; "Journal of Gurdon S. Hubbard," in *Michigan Pioneer and Historical Collections*, III (1879–80), 125.

[132] Descriptions of life in the old French settlements of Wisconsin may be found in *Wisconsin Historical Collections*, II (1855), 104; IV (1857–58), 205; VII (1873–76), 219–20; *Wisconsin State Historical Society Proceedings*, 1899, pp. 123, 136, 178; 1905, p. 269; 1913, p. 110, etc.; Louise P. Kellogg, *The French Régime in Wisconsin and the Northwest* (Madison, 1925), Chapter XVIII.

[133] For the fur trade, see Chapter VII.

produced enough vegetables for local use, and at times potatoes were added to exports of furs, pelts, deer tallow, cattle, and maple sugar. There was an abundance of horses, cattle, hogs, and fowls. At the beginning of the war the Green Bay settlement could count about 250 people, two trading stores, three black-smiths, a tailor, and a carpenter. From the end of the Revolution to the close of the War of 1812 there was little evidence that the Wisconsin country had come into the possession of the United States, for the British traders still controlled the trade with the Indians.

The first American Indian agent arrived during the summer of 1815; the next year Fort Howard was founded and an American garrison established. Most of the Indians, the English, and some of the French were antagonistic to American rule, but it did not prove so disastrous as anticipated. The Green Bay loyalists, who by a legal fiction were considered to have been forced to yield to English tyranny in the absence of American protection, soon became reconciled, and the private land grants along the Fox River were confirmed. The population of the settlement had doubled by 1820. The Americans brought in fruit trees, John Jacob Astor extended credit, gave presents and whiskey, and the presence of the garrison with attendant parties and sports served to enliven the tedium of long winter months when the settlement was isolated from the adjoining posts at Mackinac, Prairie du Chien, and Chicago. In summer came the "grasshoppers" (dragon flies), called mosquito hawks by the French. These pests "shed their skins daily and dying by the millions every hour," infected the atmosphere. Cattle, hogs, and Indians ate and fattened on them.[134]

A few French resided at the portage of the Fox-Wisconsin rivers, and engaged in freighting boats and cargoes between the two rivers, while at Prairie du Chien at the mouth of the Wisconsin resided a number of French families. Fort Crawford was established in 1816 and early friction between the troops and the natives was soon replaced by agreeable relations. In 1818 at the time jurisdiction over this region passed from Illinois to Michigan Territory, Governor Cass, by executive proclamation,

---

[134] Letter in the Chillicothe *Supporter,* September 27, 1819, copied from *Detroit Gazette.* See also Mrs. John H. Kinzie [Juliette A.], *Wau-Bun; The "Early Day" in the North-West* (New York, 1856), 433–34.

established three new counties west of Lake Michigan: Brown, with seat at Green Bay; Crawford, with seat at Prairie du Chien; and Michilimackinac, which included the Upper Peninsula and extended from Lake Huron to the Mississippi.

"Michigan Territory to the Front," was the title of a notice in Zanesville and Cincinnati papers in 1821, which concerned the rising importance of this region formerly so little known.[135] With the development of Detroit trade, the copper mines of the Northwest, the increase of sail on the lake, and the prospects of the Great Western Canal [Erie], the territory bade fair to equal and surpass some of the eastern states.

In 1817 a man familiar with the western country had written:

The western states are yet in their infancy, as well in agriculture and commerce as in population; but, in each of these respects, they are steadily and rapidly advancing to manhood. Possessing, as they do, a mild and salubrious climate, and a rich and fertile soil, with so great an extent of territory, the western states must shortly become the most wealthy and populous in the union. The centre of population and wealth is rapidly inclining *westward; and within a very* [few] *years hence it will "cross the mountains."* The tide of emigration to the westward this season, principally to the states of Ohio and Indiana, has exceeded all example! These two states contain, I believe, a greater body of good land, in proportion to their extent, than any other two states or territories in the union. Towns, villages and settlements are rising where, a few months ago, there was nothing but a trackless forest—and I look forward to the time, as at no great distance, when the great western rivers and lakes shall be covered with hundreds of steam boats, performing regular voyages between New-Orleans and the numerous ports on the Mississippi and its great tributaries —between New-York and the upper lakes, through the grand canal; and even the great inland voyage *from New-York to New-Orleans*! and when we shall be regularly supplied with *"ship news"* from numerous great and flourishing *"ports"* on the lakes and great western rivers! These "notions" may to many seem extravagant, but I verily believe that the event will justify them.[136]

[135] *Liberty Hall and Cincinnati Gazette,* October 27, 1821.
[136] Letter of Samuel Williams of Chillicothe to Samuel W. Young, Esq., of Hillsboro, Virginia, in *Niles' Weekly Register,* XI, 324 (Jan. 11, 1817). This letter is an unemotional report on the soil, streams, markets, land sales, etc., of the region from Ohio to Missouri.

Two New States: Indiana and Illinois

They came, a long and dangerous journey then,
Through paths that had not known of civil men;
With wives and children looking back, and still
Returning long in dreams confusing will,
They came, and in the panther-startled shade
The deep foundations of a State were laid.

John James Piatt, "The Lost Farm"

BY ACT of Congress approved May 7, 1800, the Territory Northwest of the Ohio was divided by a line drawn from opposite the mouth of the Kentucky River to Fort Recovery and thence due north to Canada.[1] The area to the east retained the title "Territory of the United States Northwest of the River Ohio," and anticipated early admission to statehood. The remainder of the Northwest Territory became Indiana Territory, Vincennes the seat of government, and William Henry Harrison was appointed governor. The Ohio enabling act of April 30, 1802, established the northern boundary of that state on a line east from the southern tip of Lake Michigan and added the territory to the north to Indiana Territory, as well as the triangular strip or "gore" lying between the Kentucky River–Fort Recovery line and a line drawn from the mouth of the Big Miami to Fort Recovery.

The people of Indiana Territory were exempted from that part of the Ordinance of 1787 which required 5,000 free adult males for second-grade territorial status and the privilege of electing a legislature.[2] Within a year malcontents and office

---

[1] Governor Arthur St. Clair, believing that there were 5,000 adult freemen in the Territory had, by proclamation in 1798, taken the Territory into the second stage. Since legislative salaries and other added expenses necessitated increased taxes, and the inhabitants of the more remote areas were reluctant to pay for a government which they felt but little benefited them, they had petitioned for a division of the Territory so as to return the western part to the less expensive first stage. For the petitions of the Knox County people and the Illinois inhabitants, see Clarence E. Carter (ed.), *The Territorial Papers of the United States* (Volumes 1—. Washington, D. C., 1934—), VII, 3–4; III, 76–78.

[2] *Annals of Congress*, 6 Congress, 1 session, 1498; U. S. *Statutes at Large*, II, 58; Kettleborough (ed.), *Constitution Making in Indiana*, I, 41–43.

seekers, who feared a cleanup by Governor William Henry Harrison, were seeking to arouse sentiment for representative government. Slavery as well as personal politics may have played a part. Harrison opposed the advance to second grade at this time and called attention to the heavier taxes which would result, but by 1804 the Governor was willing to put the matter before the voters. In the election in September a majority of 138 (of the 400 who voted in the Territory) favored the advance. The counties nearest the seat of government gave the largest affirmative vote, the more remote voted against the change. Harrison's proclamation of December 4 proclaimed Indiana Territory to have passed into the second grade and called for an election on January 3, 1805,[3] to choose the nine members of the House of Representatives.

The proclamation for the September election had not reached the northern portion of the Territory (Wayne County) in time for a vote. Detroit inhabitants, separated from Vincennes by several hundred miles of wilderness, claiming the need of better protection against the English and Indians for almost 4,000 people in their section, and opposing further tax burdens, had petitioned for a separate government.[4] Congress established Michigan Territory by law of January 11, 1805, with boundaries to include that part of Indiana Territory north of a line drawn east through the southern tip of Lake Michigan until it should intersect Lake Erie, and east of a line through the middle of Lake Michigan and thence north to Canada.[5]

More than one hundred and fifty miles to the west from Vincennes, separated by prairies, forests, and swamps, and connected only by a lonesome trail, "through a dreary and inhospitable wilderness," lay the most important settlements of the Illinois country. The commercial and religious ties of the old French settlers were closer to the Spanish to the west and south than to the Americans. The question of land titles had alienated many

[3] The discussions may be followed in Elihu Stout's Vincennes *Indiana Gazette* in the summer of 1804. See also Dorothy Burne Goebel, *William Henry Harrison* (*Indiana Historical Collections*, XIV, Indianapolis, 1926); Carter (ed.), *Territorial Papers*, VII, 81n-82n. Harrison's proclamation is in the Territorial *Executive Journal*, 124.

[4] Carter (ed.), *Territorial Papers*, VII, 99 ff. and 118 ff.

[5] U. S. *Statutes at Large*, II, 309-10; Kettleborough (ed.), *Constitution Making in Indiana*, I, 44-47.

Frenchmen, while territorial taxes, especially the poll tax, furnished further grounds for discontent.

Among the Americans two factions developed; both were proslavery, but differed in the methods to be used to achieve their object. One group was favorable to Governor Harrison and his administration policies, the other opposed the Governor and demanded the separation of the Illinois counties from Indiana Territory. When Michael Jones, Harrison's friend in the Kaskaskia Land Office, won the enmity of this latter group through his exposé of fraudulent land claims on the part of some of the leaders, his ouster also became an issue. With the co-operation of the antislavery men of Dearborn County in the eastern part of Indiana Territory, this anti-Harrison group in the legislature elected Jesse B. Thomas, of Dearborn, as delegate to Congress in 1808 on the issue of division of the Territory and the establishment of Illinois as a separate territory. Petitions to Congress were referred to a committee with Thomas as chairman, and on February 3, 1809, Thomas Jefferson signed the law to go into effect March 1 which set off Illinois Territory by the Wabash River and a line due north from Vincennes to the international boundary. From March 1, 1809, until Indiana's admission as a state in 1816, Indiana Territory included what is now the present state of Indiana, but with a northern boundary ten miles farther south, that portion of the northern peninsula of Michigan lying due north of Indiana, and the tip of the Green Bay Peninsula.[6]

§

Although Harrison was one of the best territorial governors ever to serve the United States, there was a certain amount of discontent with territorial status in Indiana. In its reply to the Governor's address of July, 1805, the Council, or upper legislative house, composed of Harrison's own appointees, regretted

---

[6] See map, 63. The petitions from the Illinois country as well as those in opposition may be found in *Annals of Congress*, 8 Congress, 1 session, 489; 9 Congress, 1 session, 297, 467–68; Carter (ed.), *Territorial Papers*, VII, 129 ff., 140 ff., 544 ff., 627 ff. The law is in U. S. *Statutes at Large*, II, 514–16, and Kettleborough (ed.), *Constitution Making in Indiana*, I, 54–56. See also Francis S. Philbrick (ed.), *The Laws of Indiana Territory, 1801–1809* (*Illinois Historical Collections*, XXI, Springfield, 1930, and reprinted [Indianapolis, 1931] by the Indiana Historical Bureau), xxv–xxix.

that such powers had been lodged in the hands of anyone as rested in the hands of a territorial governor, and hoped that the time was not far distant when the people would "burst the trammels of a territorial government, and . . . assume a character more consonant to republicanism."[7] In October, 1808, the House of Representatives passed resolutions which requested Congress to permit the election of the territorial delegate to Congress and the members of the Council, and to repeal "that part of the Ordinance which vests in the Govenor of this Territory an absolute negative on all acts; and also that part which confers on him the power of proroguing and dissolving the General Assembly."[8] Congress, by law approved February 27, 1809, gave the qualified electors of Indiana Territory the right to elect the delegate to Congress and the members of the Legislative Council. After the separation of Illinois Territory, the Whitewater and Ohio River settlements sought to move the territorial capital from Vincennes and bring it closer home. When the 1810 session of the legislature appointed a committee to select a more central location, the rivalry among advocates of Madison, Lawrenceburg, Vevay, Jeffersonville, and Corydon became keen. A bill of 1811 to locate the capital at Madison was vetoed by Governor Harrison, a property holder in Vincennes and in Harrison County. Thereupon Jonathan Jennings, delegate in Congress and leader of "the people" as against the "Virginia aristocrats," presented a "representation of sundry inhabitants" which complained of the arbitrary conduct of the Governor and prayed for redress.

The War of 1812 and the problem of Indian defense augmented the desire for statehood. Although Harrison, as representative of the General Government, had negotiated the Indians out of their lands, opened the southern third of the Territory to settlement, and had foiled Tecumseh's plans in 1811, never-

[7] Quoted in Moses Dawson, *A Historical Narrative of the civil and military services of Major-General William H. Harrison* . . . (Cincinnati, 1824), 76–77. The wording is different from the text as printed in the Vincennes *Indiana Gazette*, August 7, 1805. Under the Northwest Ordinance the appointments to the Council were to be made by the President from persons nominated by the lower house. The lower house nominated ten men for the Council; Jefferson referred the list to Harrison for a selection of five, but since two were excluded as being from Michigan Territory, the Governor had a choice of five out of eight.

[8] House Files, 10 Congress, 2 session, printed in Carter (ed.), *Territorial Papers*, VII, 600; similar resolutions of the Council are in *ibid.*, VII, 608.

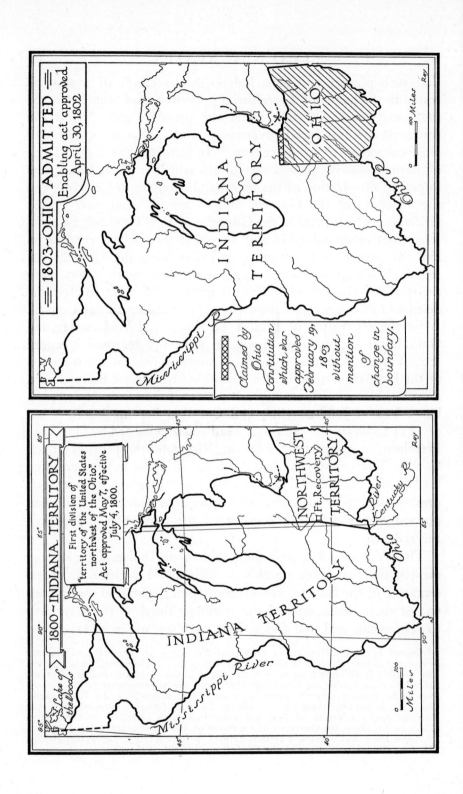

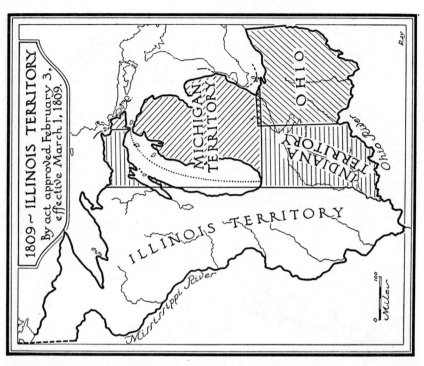

1809 ~ ILLINOIS TERRITORY
By act approved February 3,
effective March 1, 1809.

OHIO

MICHIGAN TERRITORY

INDIANA TERRITORY

Ohio River

ILLINOIS TERRITORY

Mississippi River

Roy

0   100
Miles

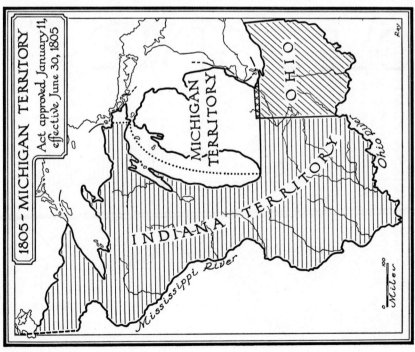

1805 ~ MICHIGAN TERRITORY
Act approved January 11,
effective June 30, 1805.

OHIO

MICHIGAN TERRITORY

INDIANA TERRITORY

Ohio River

Mississippi River

Roy

0   100
Miles

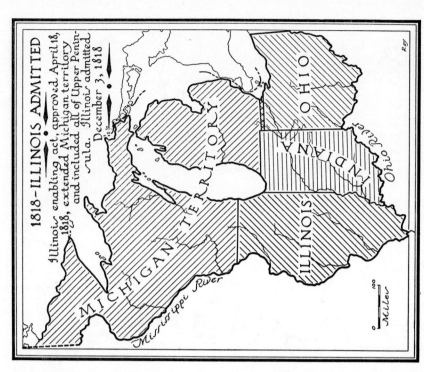

1818–ILLINOIS ADMITTED

Illinois enabling act, approved April 18, 1818, extended Michigan territory and included all of Upper Peninsula. Illinois admitted December 3, 1818

MICHIGAN TERRITORY

ILLINOIS

INDIANA

OHIO

Mississippi River

Ohio River

0   100
Miles

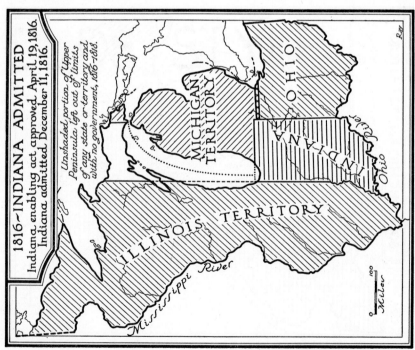

1816–INDIANA ADMITTED

Indiana enabling act approved April 19, 1816. Indiana admitted December 11, 1816.

Unshaded portion of Upper Peninsula left out of limits of any state or territory and with no government, 1816–1818.

MICHIGAN TERRITORY

ILLINOIS TERRITORY

INDIANA

OHIO

Mississippi River

Ohio River

0   100
Miles

theless, there was a feeling that a state government could better handle the Indian problem.

Political considerations also played a part. The democracy of the frontier was already seeking freer expression and more direct control. Congress and the territorial legislature had widened the suffrage in 1811 and qualified as voters all taxpaying men over twenty-one who had a year's residence. Control of elections was taken from the hands of the sheriff and put in charge of the common pleas judges, yet sheriffs, judges, and tavernkeepers worked hand in hand and largely controlled the politics and elections in the Territory. Political leaders expected more offices and higher salaries with statehood.

In December, 1811, the House of Representatives of Indiana Territory passed a resolution favoring statehood, the Council concurred, and this memorial, together with one praying that the people be given the right to elect county sheriffs, was presented in the Senate of the United States on December 31, and in the House of Representatives by Jonathan Jennings, January 1, 1812. "Born and educated in different states of the Union in the enjoyment of civil and political rights, They think it hard to be in a degree, disfranchised as a people when they have done no crime . . . and pray that they may have the liberty of framing a constitution. . . . It is principle and not men or measures that we complain of." The memorial was referred to select committees, with Thomas Worthington, of Ohio, chairman of the Senate, Jonathan Jennings, of the House committee. A protest against the petition, signed by James Dill and Peter Jones, members of the Indiana House of Representatives and friends of Governor Harrison, was referred to Jennings' committee. After three months the House committee reported that complete emancipation from territorial government was not only desirable but should be granted as soon as compatible with the interest of the United States and the Territory, and submitted a resolution to the effect that a law for the admission of Indiana be provided when by territorial census the population should reach 35,000.[9]

The Indiana territorial assembly did not meet in 1812 because

[9] Louis B. Ewbank and Dorothy Riker (eds.), *The Laws of Indiana Territory, 1809–1816* (*Indiana Historical Collections*, XX, Indianapolis, 1934), 787–88; *Annals of Congress*, 12 Congress, 1 session, part II, 1247; Kettleborough (ed.), *Constitution Making in Indiana*, I, 66–67.

of the war. The 1813 assembly compromised on Corydon as the new capital, and two sessions later, August, 1814, authorized the tax listers to take a census of the white adult males and of the total number of free inhabitants the following year.[10]

Statehood was one of the objectives prayed for in a petition from sundry inhabitants of Indiana Territory, presented February 1, 1815, in the national House of Representatives. The petition was laid on the table without discussion. Discussion continued, however, among the people. Evidences of growth were everywhere at hand; land sales at Vincennes and Jeffersonville, Ohio River traffic of emigrants, town lot sales, the advancing of the line of squatters up to the Indian boundary, all led many to believe that even the 60,000 specified in the Ordinance of 1787 already resided within the boundaries. The Lexington (Ind.) *Western Eagle* estimated the population as of November, 1815, at 68,084.[11]

The General Assembly which met in December prepared another petition for statehood, and it was presented in the House of Representatives, December 28, and in the Senate, January 2, 1816.[12] Since the people had made great sacrifices in settling the exposed frontiers and thereby enhanced the value of the public lands, the petitioners felt confident that Congress would be disposed to grant the new state 7 per cent of the receipts from land sales received after April, 1816, to confirm the grant of the township given the Territory for an academy and the sections 16 for schools, to give an additional township for a college and one for a capital site, and to give the new state the coal mines and salt licks which had been reserved for the United States. On January 5 Jennings, as chairman of the House committee

[10] *Acts of the General Assembly, Indiana Territory*, 1814, pp. 92–93; reprinted in Ewbank and Riker (eds.), *Laws, 1809–16*, 587–88.

[11] Carter (ed.), *Territorial Papers*, VIII, 331–35; Lexington *Western Eagle*, October 7, 1815; *Niles' Weekly Register*, IX, 171, 186 (Nov. 4, 11, 1815). "Again the vast augmenting population of the West is about to burst into new evidence upon the eyes of the nation; another manly link is about to be added to the bright chain of our glorious republics, in the territory of Indiana, which it will be seen, . . . is entitled to demand her admission into the union, 'upon an equal footing with the original states in all respects whatever.'" Frankfort (Ky.) *Western Argus*, quoted in *ibid*.

[12] Journal of the House of Representatives of Indiana Territory, December 11, 12, 1815, printed in *Journals of the General Assembly of Indiana Territory* (*Indiana Historical Collections*, XXXII, Indianapolis, 1950). Also in the *Western Eagle*, December 23, 1815; Vincennes *Western Sun*, January 27, 1816; *Niles' Weekly Register*, IX, 352–53 (Jan. 20, 1816); Ewbank and Riker (eds.), *Laws, 1809–16*, 811–14; Kettleborough (ed.), *Constitution Making in Indiana*, I, 69–72.

to which the petition was referred, reported, and introduced a bill for an enabling act.

The report mentioned as the northern boundary for the new state, the Ordinance of 1787 line—"an east and west line drawn through the southerly bend or extreme of Lake Michigan." Just what amendments were made in the House are not clear, but the bill passed the House March 30, by a vote of 108 to 3. When the Senate committee under the chairmanship of Senator Jeremiah Morrow, of Ohio, reported the bill back to the Senate, the northern boundary was defined as "an east and west line drawn through a point ten miles north of the southern extreme of Lake Michigan." The bill passed without division April 13, the Senate amendments were concurred in by the House, and the bill was approved by the President on April 19.[13] The enabling act moved the northern boundary of the new state ten miles to the north of the southern tip of Lake Michigan, authorized the election of delegates to a constitutional convention on May 13, and the meeting of the convention on June 10. Five propositions were offered for the acceptance of the convention: (1) section 16 in each township, or its equivalent, to be granted the inhabitants of the township for the use of schools; (2) the salt springs and lands, not exceeding thirty-six sections in area, to be granted to the state; (3) 5 per cent of the net proceeds from the sale of lands in the Territory after December 1, 1816, to be reserved for making roads and canals (three fifths for improvements within the state, two fifths for those leading to it); (4) one township, in addition to the one given the Territory, to be vested in the legislature for a seminary of learning; (5) four sections of land to be given for a seat of government. These five propositions were contingent upon provision by the convention "by ordinance irrevocable," that public land sold on or after December 1, not be taxed for five years.

Announcement of the passage of the enabling act appeared in

[13] See *Annals of Congress*, 14 Congress, 1 session, 459–60, for Jennings' committee report; *ibid.*, 1841–44, and U. S. *Statutes at Large*, III, 289–91, for the enabling act. Both the committee report and act are reprinted in Kettleborough (ed.), *Constitution Making in Indiana*, I, 72–77. See *Annals*, 408, 1293, 1300, 1367, 1373, etc., for progress through Congress.

The northern boundary line is thoroughly covered in Mrs. Frank J. Sheehan, *The Northern Boundary of Indiana* (*Indiana Historical Society Publications*, VIII, No. 6, Indianapolis, 1930). For further discussion of the Indiana-Michigan boundary, see Chapter XI, 191, 194.

the Vincennes *Western Sun,* May 4. This left only ten days before the election of delegates. Jennings, no doubt anticipating
criticism for the brief interval allowed, wrote a letter to his constituents on April 16, but it did not appear in the *Sun* until May
11. In it he explained that the dates selected were the best, all
things considered, which he was able to fix. He neglected to state
that he had not anticipated that the enabling act would be held
up so long because of opposition to the Mississippi act with
which it was linked in Congress. Many pro- and anti-Jennings
letters appeared in the columns of the *Sun.* Madison's squatter
edict, Jennings' neglect to do anything, attacks upon office-seek-
ing politicians, and the question of statehood all were aired over
signatures such as "A Settler," and "Farmers and Patriots
Rights."[14]

Prior to the announcement of the election for delegates, some
electioneering had been going on in a quiet way, for the passage
of the act had been anticipated. Editor Stout nominated five men
for Knox County but said they had not been consulted. Aside
from the files of the *Sun* little or no material remains to throw
light on the election. In general the communications were in
opposition to statehood. The stand of the four or five other
papers then published in the state is not known. It probably
made little difference, for relatively few people read them. There
must have been some rivalry over seats, for two contests
reached the convention. It is probable that the people, as usual,
left the matter to the few who had the time and inclination for
politics, and trusted their abilities and judgment to accomplish
the task in hand. The slavery question occupied a place of importance in the minds of some. After the election the Cincinnati
Western Spy reported that "A gentleman of respectability from
Indiana informs us that from the sentiments of the members
elected to the convention, as far as they are known, he has no
doubt that a constitution will be formed which will exclude involuntary slavery from that rising state. We sincerely hope this
expectation will be realized."[15] The *Sun,* on June 1 in an extra,
opposed the formation of a state government because it would

14 Vincennes *Western Sun,* February 10, 24, April 20, 1816.
15 Quoted in *Liberty Hall and Cincinnati Gazette,* May 27, 1816.

result in increased expense of government and a considerable loss of taxes because of the five-year exemption of public lands.

The 43 elected delegates met at Corydon on June 10, 1816. The advent of so many outsiders severely taxed the accommodations of the small southern Indiana town, since 1813 the territorial capital. The new stone courthouse, forty feet square with walls more than two feet thick, had been intended for use by the territorial legislature. Final cost was about $3,000. Here sat the constitutional convention, but since the weather was hot, the shade of a great elm, a furlong distant on the banks of Big Indian Creek, probably was the scene of more than one committee session.

The personnel of the convention was respectable, if not distinguished. More than half of the preceding territorial legislature were members. The majority were farmers but there were about a dozen preachers and somewhat fewer lawyers. Among the more distinguished members were Jonathan Jennings, native of New Jersey, delegate in Congress from Indiana Territory, and leader of the Clark County delegation; James Noble, of Kentucky-Virginia ancestry, prominent speaker and jury persuader from Brookville; John Badollet, of Knox, a Swiss friend of Albert Gallatin; John De Pauw, son of a companion of Lafayette; Frederick Rapp, the adopted son of the leader of the Harmony group; Dennis Pennington, Virginia born stonemason and one of Corydon's leading citizens; and David H. Maxwell, pioneer physician and later to be the father of Indiana University. Hugh Cull was a Methodist circuit rider, Charles and William Polke, and Ezra Ferris were Baptist preachers and church founders. William Hendricks, of Madison, son of a Pennsylvania politician, a product of Washington and Jefferson College, teacher, editor, and lawyer, was chosen secretary of the convention though not a delegate. Of the delegates twenty-three later served in the Indiana Senate, seventeen in the House, one as governor, two as representatives in Congress, two as United States senators, three became distinguished judges, and a number filled other important Federal and state offices.[16] As to politics,

[16] Logan Esarey, *A History of Indiana* (3d ed. 2 volumes. Fort Wayne, 1924), I, 248.

the old Federalist-Republican strife never reached Indiana and there is no evidence to indicate that a majority of the delegates were even partisan to the personal politics of territorial days.

The convention organized on June 10, elected Jennings president, Hendricks secretary, and examined credentials. The question of expediency of statehood, as provided for decision in the enabling act, was framed. The following day rules were adopted and the convention, in committee of the whole, voted for statehood. There were eight dissenting votes. The responsibilities of the task aroused no fear of inability or inadequacy in the minds of these men. Two centuries of experience in colonial self-government, in state making in Revolutionary days, in the framing of two constitutions for the Union, in the making of new states, had created such confidence that one of the easiest things which Americans did, even on the frontier, was to make a constitution. The rules and principles were simple and well established, models for style were at hand. The theories of Locke, Montesquieu, Madison, and Jefferson were known. Representative constitutions of the states were available. The editor of the *Louisville Correspondent* was duly impressed with the convention, "this momentous preliminary in the glorious system of government with which the freemen of our republic are blessed," and never was he more delighted than by "the *solemn decorum, the high sense of manly freedom, and the accuteness of political discussion,* which animated the assembly in this infantine state of society."[17] Questions of complicated taxation systems, corporations, representation of economic interests, home rule, urban versus rural interests, government by commissions—administrative, legislative and judicial in function—government by science, government in business, business in government, socialism, despotism, religion, race—that multiplicity of problems which gives the framing of a modern state constitution the importance of a major operation on the body politic, did not exist for these men.

On the third day twelve committees were appointed and went to work, to report when ready, and by June 14, five had re-

[17] Quoted in Hamilton (Ohio) *Philanthropist,* June 28, 1816. As Tocqueville said: "True information is mainly derived from experience; and if the Americans had not been gradually accustomed to govern themselves, their book-learning would not help them much at the present day."

ported.[18] The sessions were businesslike, and there is no evidence of groups, blocs, or partisan politics, though some warm discussions seem to have developed over slavery, as well as over the judiciary and suffrage sections.

The preamble and Article I, comprising twenty-four items of the Bill of Rights, was reported June 14. The social compact idea is presented in the preamble: "and do mutually agree with each other to form ourselves into a free and independent state." The Ohio constitution furnished the bulk of Article I, which, with the exception of seven sections which were changed, was copied almost verbatim. Minor amendments and changes were made and the article passed June 27.[19]

Because of territorial experience the committee on distribution of powers sought a very definite separation, and finding none in the constitutions of Ohio, Pennsylvania, or Virginia, modeled one upon the article in the Kentucky constitution on the legislative department. Article II was also accepted on June 27. Article III on the legislative department was likewise copied largely from the corresponding article (Article I) of the Ohio constitution, which in turn was copied in part from the constitution of Pennsylvania. A change was made, however, in the section of the Ohio article which provided that legislators should not be holders of other offices, Federal or state, to exempt the delegates to the convention from such provision. The convention was thus enabled to take care of its members in state and Federal elections to follow. Representatives were to be chosen annually, senators for three years, and the age requirements were twenty-one and twenty-five years, respectively.

The committee on the executive department found most nearly

[18] On bill of rights and preamble; distribution of powers; legislative department; executive; judiciary; impeachments; general provisions; revision; schedule; education; militia; franchise and elections. Convention Journal, 152–53, 154, 155, 156, as published in the *Report of the Sixteenth Annual Meeting of the State Bar Association of Indiana* (Indianapolis, 1912). A copy of the 1816 printing of the constitution as finally adopted is in the Indiana State Library. The Journal, kept by Hendricks, records the proceedings day by day, but discussions, debates, and committee workings are not reported. The *Bar Report* has an article on the convention by W. W. Thornton. The most detailed analysis of the convention, its personnel and work, is a MS. thesis (Indiana University, 1929) by Miss Ruth E. Brayton. Kettleborough (ed.), *Constitution Making in Indiana*, Volume I, contains all the essential documents.

[19] For comparison of the Indiana Constitution of 1816 with previous state constitutions, see the documentary compilation in John D. Barnhart's "Sources of Indiana's First Constitution," in *Indiana Magazine of History*, XXXIX (1943), 55–94.

what it wanted in the Kentucky constitution, and as reported June 15, Article IV of the Indiana constitution was almost identical with Article III of the Kentucky constitution. Between June 19 and 25 various amendments were made, borrowed in part from Pennsylvania and Ohio. The governor was to serve three years. A lieutenant governor was also to be elected, but the secretary of state, treasurer, and auditor were to be selected by joint ballot of the two houses of the General Assembly. The governor was given a suspensive veto, which a majority of each house could override, and some appointive power, the latter to be exercised with the advice and approval of the Senate.

The article on the judiciary, which drew heavily from the Ohio and Kentucky constitutions, was reported June 17, but was referred later to a select committee and redrafted, to be accepted finally June 27. The judiciary power of the state was invested in a supreme court of three members, in circuit courts, and such other inferior courts as the General Assembly might establish. Supreme court judges were to be appointed by the governor with the advice and consent of the Senate. Presidents of the circuit courts were to be elected by joint ballot of the houses of the General Assembly, and the associate judges elected by the voters in the counties. The terms were for seven years; township justices of the peace were to be elected for five years.

The franchise was given to white males twenty-one years of age and with one year's residence in the state. All elections were to be by ballot, but the legislature of 1821 might change the method to *viva voce,* after which time it was to remain unalterable.

Article VII provided for a militia of all free able-bodied white males of eighteen to forty-five years of age, but granted exemption to conscientious objectors on payment of a fine equivalent to that assessed on a private who neglected or refused to perform militia duty. Subalterns, captains, majors, and colonels were to be elected by those subject to militia duty; brigadier generals and major generals by the commissioned officers.

The provision on changing the constitution—Article VIII—as originally reported provided for a poll on the question of calling a new constitutional convention at each election for governor, but as amended and accepted by the convention provided that every twelfth year a poll should be opened on the question, and if a majority voted in the affirmative, the governor was to inform the legislature which would make provision for a convention. This article was to be the subject of some interesting discussion at a later time.

In no part of its work did the convention do so much constructive thinking or show more vision than in that part of the constitution which dealt with education. In this the constitutions of neighboring states offered little help; here the convention was clearing new ground. Article IX, which was both comprehensive and specific, entitled Indiana to the distinction of being the first to recognize the duties of the state in the education of its citizens and to provide powers to achieve this end. It became the duty of the General Assembly to take care of the government lands reserved to the state, and the funds derived therefrom were to be used exclusively for the "purpose of promoting the interest of Literature, and the sciences, and for the support of seminaries and public schools." Laws should be passed for the encouragement of "intellectual, Scientifical, and agricultural improvement" and "the promotion and improvement of arts, sciences, commerce, manufactures, and natural history." As soon as circumstances would permit, laws should be passed to provide for "a general system of education, ascending in a regular gradation, from township schools to a state university, wherein tuition [should] be gratis, and equally open to all." A penal code, "founded on the principles of reformation, and not of vindictive Justice," and farms and asylums for the aged, infirm, and otherwise misfortunate, were to be provided. And from the proceeds of the sales of town lots in county seats 10 per cent was to be set aside for the support of public libraries.

Slavery was prohibited by section 7 of Article XI, but indentures of persons as apprentices, excepting those of Negroes executed outside the state, were not mentioned. The Journal records no debates or discussions on the slavery provision, which is included among the seventeen miscellaneous items of the general article.[20]

Again, in writing the article on banking, the convention was wrestling with a matter on which the model constitutions helped

[20] There is apparently no justification for making this section the culmination of a century of struggle for freedom, as did Jacob Piatt Dunn in his *Indiana, A Redemption from Slavery* (Boston and New York, 1905).

little. The provisions as accepted by the convention on June 28 forbade the establishment in Indiana of any bank or moneyed institution for the purpose of issuing bills of credit or bills payable to the bearer. This was not to apply to a state bank established by the General Assembly, nor to the bank at Vincennes and the Farmers' and Mechanics' Bank of Indiana (Madison).

The schedule called for the election on the first Monday in August, of the governor, lieutenant governor, congressman, members of the General Assembly, sheriffs and coroners. Official notice of the election was issued by the convention on the last day of its meeting. The convention adjourned June 29, having, in eighteen working days and at a cost of $3,076.21, not only made a constitution but, assisted by the politicians of the Territory, planned the framework for the political machinery which would, under that constitution, inaugurate the new government and run it.

The Indiana Constitution of 1816 was of the type then prevalent among the states of the Union. It was concise, for the most part clear in style, though lacking somewhat in organization, and, for its day, advanced in representative theory. The electoral franchise provided was generous, elections were frequent, terms of office short, and the number of elective offices few. The government setup was simple and inexpensive; salaries were modest. The separation of powers was made clear and definite, although the greatest power was placed in the hands of the General Assembly. The provisions for education, a penal code, libraries, and asylums were progressive and liberal beyond their day. Political ideas of the period had not yet made mandatory the submission of constitutions to the people for ratification, and Indiana's new instrument of government was declared in effect on June 29, the date the convention finished its labors.

The official notice of Indiana's first state election appeared in the few newspapers of the day, and, in spite of lack of important issues, some of the canvasses were sharply contested.[21] The voters of Indiana were Republicans (Jeffersonian Democrats) and supported Monroe.[22] Jonathan Jennings was elected gover-

[21] In the *Western Sun* of July 20 there were ten columns of letters from candidates and voters.
[22] See Chapter IX.

nor, William Hendricks to Congress, and the General Assembly which met November 4 elected James Noble and Waller Taylor to the United States Senate.

The process of attaining statehood was completed for Indiana by passage of the resolution for admission into the Union in the United States Senate on December 6, and in the House of Representatives on December 9. It was approved by the President on December 11. Hendricks was admitted to his seat in the House on December 2, the day Congress convened, and Taylor and Noble were seated in the Senate on the twelfth. On February 12, 1817, the votes of the Indiana electors, selected by the legislature on November 13, were counted for Monroe and Tompkins, and on March 3 a law was approved providing for the execution of the laws of the United States in the new state.[23]

The work of the convention of 1816 apparently received the approval of the people of the state. In the files of the *Western Sun,* which constitute about the only available source for opinion in the few years following, constitutional discussions are few and brief. Sporadic criticisms were made for about five years. These had to do with the constitutional establishment of the capital at Corydon until 1825, the prohibition of amendment for twelve years, fixing of salaries, limiting terms of judges, failure to provide for an attorney general and state's attorneys, and the existence of ambiguous provisions.[24] Some of those who opposed statehood in 1816 continued to grumble and refer to the "premature offspring" and the "puny child, taken from nurse too soon." Since the politicians were frustrated by territorial rule, "we were therefore hurried into the *State Form* to gratify a group of demagogues, who have since managed and manacled us. . . ."[25]

By the constitution the General Assembly was permitted to

[23] The *London Morning Chronicle* of May 6, noted the admission of Indiana as follows: "The bill for adding a *new Province, Indiana,* to the union, has passed. . . . The DESIGNS of the States upon the *great rivers Mississippi and Missouri,* are BECOMING EVERY DAY MORE APPARENT." William Cobbett took up his pen and lashed the editor for his use of *province,* and his ignorance of geography. What if Americans should accuse the English of having designs upon the Severn? Niles admitted that we had designs on the rivers: to people their banks, build ships and cities, and drive out the deer and the bear with the hum of commerce. *Niles' Weekly Register,* X, 366 (July 27, 1816).
[24] Kettleborough (ed.), *Constitution Making in Indiana,* I, xxiii-xxiv.
[25] Letters from voters in Vincennes *Western Sun,* July 27, 1816, June 23, 30, July 21, August 4, 1821.

remove the capital from Corydon at the session of 1825 or thereafter, and at the session of 1821 to change the method of voting
at elections from ballot to *viva voce*. The fixing of the capital at
Corydon was apparently the result of an understanding between
the delegates and the citizens of the town. Sectional rivalries
and geographical considerations made the decision unpopular;
consequently, at the second session of the General Assembly, in
1817, a resolution to submit the question to the people was seriously considered but finally postponed. By act of January, 1820,
ten commissioners were appointed to select a site for the permanent seat of government. The site selected on White River was
designated as such by law a year later, and by law of January 28,
1824, Indianapolis was selected and established as the permanent capital from and after the second Monday in January, 1825.

On the question of *viva voce* voting, the General Assembly,
by joint resolution of December 23, 1820, called for a referendum at the next August elections. The *Western Sun* called it "a
consideration of the utmost importance with the people,"[26] but
returns seem to have reached the Secretary of State from only
fifteen of the thirty-nine counties.[27] The vote was fairly evenly
divided, and the General Assembly was undecided as to what
action to take. Finally, when a bill was introduced in December
to change to *viva voce* voting, opponents of the measure argued
that a majority of the voters were against the change, that it
would destroy freedom of elections, promote personal contro-
versies, and keep peaceable citizens from the polls. The bill was
lost in the Senate, but the advocates of the change continued the
agitation by attempting to get a constitutional convention called
and another referendum on the method of voting.[28]

The provision for amendment of the constitution called forth
considerable discussion. Article VIII read: "Every twelfth year
. . . at the general election held for Governor there shall be a
poll opened in which the qualified Electors of the State shall express, by vote, whether they are in favour of calling a convention,
or not. . . ." The question was whether the General Assembly
was restricted to each twelfth year for submission of the question
to a vote, or might it constitutionally do so at any time sooner

[26] May 12, 1821.
[27] Indiana *House Journal*, 1821–22, pp. 325–27.
[28] In 1826, 1833, 1844.

than, or in addition to, 1828, 1840, etc. At first, opinion supported the contention that elections might be held on the subject only every twelfth year.[29] The *Sun* at first concurred in this view, but by 1823, when the question of a convention was first submitted to the people, it was favorably inclined towards calling a convention. The Corydon *Indiana Gazette* was opposed. Members of the General Assembly were divided in opinion as to the meaning of Article VIII, but submitted the calling of a convention to the voters in 1823, 1828, 1840, 1846, and 1849, and Indiana finally made and put into operation a new constitution before the third twelfth year came around.[30]

The organization of local government for the new state was left largely to the General Assembly. Beyond providing for the election of the sheriff and coroner, and a recorder if the work was too much for the clerk of the circuit court, the county received but scant notice. Powers of the General Assembly to organize counties were implied in Section 12, Article XI ("when they lay off any new county . . .") and it was forbidden to reduce the size of any county below four hundred square miles. The county board of commissioners of three members was provided for by the First General Assembly. Taxes, finance, roads, and other affairs were given into its hands; it appointed a treasurer, fence viewers, pound keepers, selected superintendents of school sections, election inspectors, and overseers of the poor. The clerk of the circuit court was clerk of the board, and the sheriff its administrative officer.[31]

Township government was constitutionally recognized in the provision for justices of the peace and the appointment of township officers in such manner as might be provided by law. The county board of commissioners was to divide each county into a suitable number of townships and hold elections for justices. A constable for each township was appointed annually by the county boards.

The judicial department of the new state government was perhaps the best constituted. In the territorial period the judiciary

[29] Letters of "Hortensius" and "A New-Comer," in Vincennes *Western Sun,* July 20, 1816, August 1, 1818.

[30] Unsuccessful attempts were made in 1820, 1821, 1826, 1827, 1829, 1830, 1831, 1833, 1835, 1836, 1841, 1843, 1844, 1845, 1847. Kettleborough (ed.), *Constitution Making in Indiana,* I, xxv.

[31] *Laws of Indiana,* 1816–17, Chapter XV.

establishment had become considerably involved, and the results somewhat incongruous. The three territorial judges on circuit at times sat together and made decisions which one of them, as a quorum, sitting as supreme court on appeal, might and sometimes did reverse or overrule. Under the constitution this possibility was obviated by requiring two of the supreme court judges for a quorum and granting the supreme court appellate jurisdiction only, excepting that original jurisdiction might be given by law in capital cases and cases in chancery, where the president of the circuit court might be interested or prejudiced.[32] The state was divided into three circuits, and the circuit courts consisted of a president judge appointed by the General Assembly, and two associate judges, elected in each county. The president alone, or the president and one associate judge, was competent to hold court, or the two associate judges except in capital cases or cases in chancery. By giving the circuit courts common law and chancery jurisdiction as well as criminal, it was possible to eliminate the common law and special courts of the territorial period such as quarter sessions, chancery, and probate. The General Assembly was authorized to create such other inferior courts as might be necessary, but at first there was no machinery set up between the circuit courts and the justices of peace in the townships, who were shortly given county-wide jurisdiction over petty crimes and misdemeanors, and township jurisdiction over civil cases involving $50 or less.[33] The Second General Assembly outlined the civil code of the state as essentially followed for the next century, and adopted a criminal code which, excepting for punishments, remained basically unchanged under the constitution of 1816. Whipping posts and other primitive methods of punishment were abandoned in 1821.

§ §

When Illinois Territory was set off by the act of February 3, 1809,[34] the people of that area were for the third time placed under the rule of the Governor and Judges as provided by the Ordinance of 1787. Judge Ninian Edwards, of Kentucky, was

[32] Constitution of Indiana, 1816, Article V, section 2.
[33] Laws of Indiana, 1816-17, Chapter IV.
[34] To take effect March 1.

appointed governor and Nathaniel Pope of the same state became secretary; by affiliation with part of the old Harrison following and recruiting from newcomers, these leaders were able to lay the foundation for a political party. Illinois Territory, as had been Indiana, was exempted from the requirement of having 5,000 free males before advancing into the second grade. When Governor Edwards called an election for April, 1812, the people voted for second-grade status and the privilege of having a legislature. Suffrage limited by the 50-acre freehold provision of the Ordinance as applied to Indiana Territory in 1805 would have been particularly distasteful because of the great number of squatters in Illinois. To obviate this difficulty, Governor Edwards presented petitions to Congress, and that body by law[35] gave the right to vote to all adult free white males who paid any county or territorial tax and had resided one year in the territory, and permitted the electors to elect their delegate to Congress and the Council members. This was the most liberal territorial establishment yet granted by Congress, but it hardly satisfied the growing democracy and its politicians. In the General Assembly of 1814 a memorial prayed for the abolition of the absolute veto of the governor. "To freemen this clause wears the aspect of slavery—vesting our Executive with a Despotism that can frustate the most deliberate and well digested measures of our Council and House of Representatives. . . ."[36] When Congress failed to yield, "Aristides" in the *Intelligencer* wrote:

The colonial and degraded status of this country under the government of the Ordinance, that accursed badge of despotism, which withholds from the people, the only true source of all power, a participation in those rights, guaranteed by the constitution of every state in the Union, seems to have the effect of chilling every spark of political disquisition, and to have sunk man beneath the dignity of his nature, a poor fallen creature from that proud station, the destiny of freemen.

The present rapid influx of population, the growing and prosperous state of the country, justifies the belief that it will not be more than three or four years before we will burst the chains of despotism, by which we are now bound, and stand a sovereign and independent State.

It therefore becomes necessary that the public mind should be prepared

---

[35] Approved May 20, 1812.
[36] Miscellaneous Assembly Papers, December 19, 1814, in Secretary of State's Office, Springfield, quoted in Buck, *Illinois in 1818*, 207.

for the event. It is high time to begin to think and talk about the form of State government that so soon must take place.[37]

The movement for statehood received its first real impetus, however, with the return to Illinois of Daniel Pope Cook, son-in-law of Governor Edwards, in November, 1817. Prospects for a political career in Washington having failed, Cook, who had taken over the Kaskaskia *Illinois Herald* and renamed it the *Western Intelligencer,* began to create prospects in Illinois. Serious consideration was given in editorials to the disadvantages of "territorial or semi-monarchial" government and the advantage of statehood. It was thought unlikely that admission as a state would be withheld until the population reached 60,000, and with the slavery question settled, immigration would increase. In his message to the Assembly in December Governor Edwards referred to the flattering prospects for statehood and suggested making provision for taking a census. Cook, as clerk of the House, saw no need for delay and helped put through a memorial for statehood in which the territorial governor was referred to as "a species of despotism in direct hostility with the principles of a republican government." Since the representatives were unanimously agreed on statehood, and the population was estimated at "not less than 40,000," Congress was asked to pass an enabling act and to make the usual grants such as had been made to Ohio and Indiana, including the lead mines as well as the salt springs.

One of the reasons for the haste in the sudden promotion of statehood seems to have been the desire on the part of the slavery opponents, who had increased in numbers as the newer counties filled up following the war, to settle the question before Missouri, which would no doubt be a slave state, should be admitted to the Union. Illinois had continued the Indiana Territory indenture act, and if Missouri, a competitor for immigrants, was opened to slavery, it would be much more difficult to exclude the institution. At the same time that the memorial for statehood was being passed, the Illinois territorial legislature was passing a bill for the repeal of the indenture system and declaring it contrary to the Ordinance. Governor Edwards vetoed the bill, not because

---

[37] Kaskaskia *Western Intelligencer,* August 21, 1816, quoted in *Transactions of the Illinois State Historical Society,* 1903, p. 187.

Urbana, Ohio

Burning Trees in a Girdled Clearing. *George Harvey*, 1841

he opposed its object but on other grounds, and the slavery issue
became the leading one in the convention campaign. Before ad-
journing, the Assembly provided for a census to be taken in
April and May, 1818, the returns to be filed with the secretary of
the Territory by June 1; to reap full advantage of the summer's
immigration, a supplementary census as of December 1, was to
be filed later.

In Congress the memorial was ably handled by Nathaniel
Pope, the Illinois territorial delegate. It was brought before the
House on January 16, 1818, and one week later a bill for an
enabling act was reported by his committee. This bill, modeled
upon the enabling act for Indiana, reduced the residence requirement for voting for convention delegates to six months, fixed the
election for the first Monday in July, and enabled the convention
which was to meet the first Monday in August, to form a state
government, or, after deciding in favor of it, to provide for
another convention to make a constitution. The population requirement was left blank and the boundaries of the new state
fixed as at present excepting the northern boundary which was
to be a line ten miles north of the southern tip of Lake Michigan,
the same as Indiana's. The propositions offered for acceptance
or rejection were the same as they had been for Indiana with the
addition of the lead mines and the omission of four sections for
a capital site.

In April the bill was considered in the House of Representatives, where Pope introduced an amendment to fix the northern
boundary at 42° 30′ north latitude, thus moving the boundary
line about forty miles farther north than Indiana's. The geographical advantages of the proposal were obvious; whether Pope had
in mind the future influence of this change on slavery politics is
not certain. Another amendment provided that 3 of the 5 per cent
of proceeds from the sale of Federal lands be used "for the
encouragement of learning, of which one-sixth part . . . [should]
be exclusively bestowed upon a college or university." The lead-
mine grant was removed from the measure, and the population
requirement fixed at 40,000. The bill passed the House on April
6. The Senate questioned the diversion of the 3 per cent fund to
education, as well as the moving north of the boundary, added
some amendments, and passed the bill on April 14. The House

concurred in the Senate amendments and the Illinois enabling act
was approved April 18, 1818.

The movement for statehood in Illinois was not as spontaneous as that in Indiana; rather it seems to have been carefully
cultivated by a few interested parties. But once under way, the
question of statehood, election of convention delegates, and the
framing of a constitution aroused greater interest and intensity
of discussion than had been the case in the neighboring state to
the east. This was the result largely of the presence of the slavery
issue and its injection into the convention campaign. Another
factor, which at this distance from the event may account in part
for this apparent greater interest in Illinois, is the relative amount
of material preserved which bears on the history of the corresponding events in the two territories. Whereas in Indiana the
Vincennes *Western Sun* under the editorship of Elihu Stout, an
adherent of the Harrison faction which had lost in the attempt
to keep the capital at Vincennes, was indifferent or lukewarm
towards the movement and pretty well isolated from the center
of news while the convention was in session,[38] the Kaskaskia
Intelligencer[39] was edited by men keenly interested in the movement and was in the midst of the activity while the convention
was in session.

Just why the slavery question should have become so important in Illinois, less than two years after Indiana conducted her
convention campaign with slavery so little discussed as to leave
no evidence of it ever having been an issue, is not clear. The
population of Illinois was surely no more southern in origin than
that of Indiana. Competition with Missouri for immigration no
doubt played a part, but Indiana also was seeking settlers. The
more settlers, the higher the land values and the better the
chances of booming town sites. The nearness of Illinois to her
rival probably brought the realization closer home. There is a
possibility that Illinois had received a greater number of the
western Kentucky people, more favorably inclined towards slavery, while Indiana claimed a larger portion of the eastern Kentucky and upland South folk. After all, the explanation seems

[38] The printing of the Journal and Constitution was later awarded to Mann
Butler, of Louisville, by the First General Assembly.
[39] For a sketch of this important early Illinois paper, see Chapter XV.

to lie largely in the men involved; in 1816 Indiana had no slavery advocates prominent in territorial affairs, while Illinois in 1818 did have.

When news of the passage of Pope's bill was received, the event was celebrated by the *Western Intelligencer* changing its name to the *Illinois Intelligencer*. The names of convention candidates and Congressional aspirants were announced. The people had been advised previously to put aside party and private feeling in the interest of the public, and, as in Indiana, territorial political divisions seem to have given way before the immediate issues.

The amount of proslavery sentiment in Illinois can only be surmised from the number and vigor of the arguments published against admitting the institution. Cook attacked the argument that the admission of slavery would fill the state and convert the forests into cultivated habitations in a letter published in the *Intelligencer* April 1. The editors sought to maintain an unprejudiced attitude and stated that whatever the people should decide, after proper investigation and thought, would be all right. Some of the antislavery men thought that the bait of statehood was being held out in order to get a decision on slavery before the antislavery sentiment, aided by more immigration from the northern states, should become preponderant.[40] To any delay the editors of the *Intelligencer* were opposed. Other writers warned against the danger of the people being lulled to sleep by the theory that the slave question need not be settled by the convention, as it was forbidden by the Ordinance.[41]

Outstanding among the many communications published in the *Intelligencer* were those signed "Agis," the product of the pen of an educated and observing man.[42] To those who thought slavery would settle the country, build the mills, manufactories and bridges, and make the country wear a new appearance, he replied: "I would rather see our rich meadows and fertile woodlands inhabited alone by the wild beasts and birds of the air, than that they should ever echo the sound of the slave driver's scourge, or resound with the cries of the oppressed African. I would

[40] Kaskaskia *Western Intelligencer*, April 1, 15, 1818.
[41] "Candor," in *ibid.*, April 22, May 6, 1818.
[42] Probably Edward Coles, Virginian, formery secretary to President Madison, commissioner to Russia, later governor of Illinois. Buck, *Illinois in 1818*, 242.

rather that our citizens should live fearlessly and contentedly in their peaceful and modest cabins, than that, surrounded by a host of slaves, and inhabiting splendid palaces and gilded domes, they should live in constant apprehension of an attack from those who are, and who ought to be, their mortal enemies." He warned against the insidious possibilities of indenturing and called for the election of men who were friends to liberty, in practice as well as in theory. To the people of Illinois belonged the decision of "whether all its inhabitants shall live in simple and happy freedom, or one half of them shall be reduced to abject and cruel servitude to support the splendid misery and sickly pomp of the other half."[43]

The June census returns, although somewhat padded, showed the Territory still lacking by more than 5,000 the necessary 40,000 required by the enabling act.[44] Should the people go ahead and elect a convention and would any action of the convention be valid when later the population would have reached 40,000? Pope thought the election should be held, and then, if the population had not reached the required number, the first convention could pass an ordinance calling for the election of another convention, after sufficient returns should be received. By the latter part of July the *Intelligencer* was optimistic about the returns, and reported the probable discovery of 800 additional persons in Franklin, 1,000 in Gallatin, and many more in the eastern counties. The census commissioners were urged to be industrious and to get the totals in by the first Monday in August.

A series of letters from the pen of "A Friend to Inquiry" disagreed with Pope's opinion and stated that any action which the people might take would be invalid unless within the law passed by Congress for their guidance, and argued against the exclusion policy of "Agis." The writer would provide for the introduction of slavery and for eventual emancipation, thus to extend and weaken the institution and provide an example for others to follow.[45] On the question of delay the *Intelligencer* disagreed, but with reference to slavery thought that this writer's proposal breathed "the language of philanthropy . . . and must flash con-

---

[43] Kaskaskia *Illinois Intelligencer*, July 1, 1818, quoted in Buck, *Illinois in 1818*, 244.
[44] The original and supplementary returns are in *ibid.*, 318.
[45] Kaskaskia *Illinois Intelligencer*, July 22, 1818.

viction upon the mind of every person who feels a disposition to palliate the condition of the oppressed African. . . . It would reflect much to the honor and humanity of the generous sons of Illinois, when the *grand object of universal emancipation* shall be effected, to hear it sounded from abroad, that this godlike and benevolent act of humanity originated with them."[46] Replies came to "A Friend to Inquiry," calling his proposal the last resort of that party, which, realizing that slavery would not prove acceptable, was trying to coat it over with the form of general humanity.

In addition to the slavery issue the question of the type of men to be elected and the nature of the constitution to be made brought forth discussions. Some thought that "men of talents," with wide experience and an understanding of the science of government, should be selected, regardless of their attitude on slavery. Others distrusted "men of talents" and were afraid that they would look after their own interests rather than those of the average man. The older generation of earlier settlers, many now well-established landholders, speculators, and traders, distrusted the younger group of lawyers and politicians, whom they felt had not yet sufficient stake in the community to be trusted with constitution making, regardless of education and talents. Among the provisions advocated for the new constitution was one for suffrage for all widows and unmarried females over twenty-one years of age; economic and political reasons were advanced for the same.[47] Some emphasized principles, and believed that, these agreed upon, the men should be selected accordingly, but in the elections personal popularity, here as elsewhere where representative government is practiced, probably played the important part.

Little direct evidence remains of the canvass in the different counties. In some counties the candidates declared themselves on the slavery question, in others they did not. Outstanding men were sometimes selected on their personal strength and their colleagues from the same county on the issues. Again, two delegates from the same county sometimes stood in opposition on the slavery issue. The salt works in Gallatin County, with its need

[46] *Ibid.*, quoted in Buck, *Illinois in 1818*, 246–47.
[47] *Ibid.*, May 27, June 10, 1818.

for slave labor, was a local influence. Personal contacts and the usual frontier campaigning tactics were practiced. The election lasted three days, July 6, 7, 8, the voting, by *viva voce,* being possible only at the county seats. The list of successful candidates was available, excepting for Bond, Edwards, and Crawford counties, by July 22.

On the first Monday in August (August 3), the thirty-three delegates to the convention met in the old French village of Kaskaskia, where local tavern facilities were even more taxed by the influx of delegates and visitors than those of Corydon had been two years earlier. Among the more prominent members were Jesse B. Thomas, from St. Clair County, native of Maryland and former delegate in Congress, and Elias Kent Kane, native of New York, Yale trained, and a promising young lawyer of Kaskaskia. Kane, as well as Thomas, had been one of the leaders of the anti-Edwards group in territorial days. He was probably the most influential delegate in the convention. Abraham Prickett, born near Lexington, Kentucky, druggist and merchant of Edwardsville, and Benjamin Stephenson, also of Kentucky birth, were two of Madison County's delegates. John Messinger, pioneer surveyor, teacher, and mapmaker, Massachusetts born, who reached Illinois by way of Kentucky, also represented St. Clair County.[48]

Jesse B. Thomas was elected president and William C. Greenup, secretary. There is no evidence of contest between the political factions of territorial days. On the second day a committee headed by Kane was appointed to examine the census returns. The supplementary returns had added 5,638 to the first canvass, for a total of 40,258. Outlying districts had been combed, transients counted, and the population of Prairie du Chien, outside the boundaries of the proposed state, included. The convention promptly voted that the population was upwards of 40,000 and that it was expedient to form a constitution, and without reference to any second convention proceeded to that end. A committee of fifteen, one from each county, was selected

[48] For brief notes on the personnel of the convention, see Richard V. Carpenter, "The Illinois Constitutional Convention of 1818," in *Journal of the Illinois State Historical Society,* VI (1913–14), 327–53. James Hall, of Vandalia, editor and writer, is here listed as having been a member from Jackson County; he did not arrive in Illinois until 1820.

to frame and report to the convention a constitution for the Territory of Illinois.

During the week in which the committee was at work the convention adopted rules of procedure and considered resolutions and received petitions, among others one from Randolph County, asking that the constitution declare the Scriptures the word of God and that the constitution be founded thereon.

The committee on the constitution, with Leonard White as chairman, but Elias Kent Kane apparently the leading figure, reported on August 12 a draft composed of the preamble and eight articles, together with an ordinance accepting the proposition of the enabling act, which later was adopted by the convention.

At the end of two and a half days of consideration the draft was referred to a committee of five for additional consideration and improvement, and for completion of a schedule. On the seventeenth the second reading of the constitution began, and during the following day the schedule was considered, as well as the report on the permanent seat of government. With the consideration of the sections relating to slavery, division of sentiment became more marked, and roll calls frequent. The third reading of the amended and engrossed draft began on the nineteenth and three days later a committee of revision of three members, including Kane, was appointed to examine the constitution as amended and passed, and to make corrections. The report of this committee was accepted, but some changes were made later. The resolution with reference to a permanent seat of government was passed on the twenty-fourth, and on the twenty-sixth, after a session of twenty-one working days, the constitution was signed and the convention adjourned.[49] Many of the delegates returned to their farms and businesses, worthy pioneers who had accomplished the chore assigned them by their neighbors, sometimes to hold local or state offices, but for the most part to play

[49] The Journal of the convention is published in the *Journal of the Illinois State Historical Society*, VI (1913–14), 355–424, being a reprint of a copy presented to the Secretary of State of Illinois in 1905. The convention provided for the printing of five hundred copies but these were never bound, and only the one copy is known to be in existence. The files of the *Intelligencer* give a perfunctory and incomplete record of the proceedings. The best brief account of the convention and its work is in Buck, *Illinois in 1818*, Chapter X. The older histories of Illinois such as those of Thomas Ford and John Reynolds have little of value on the campaign for statehood or the convention.

no further important part in the public life of their state. A few figured prominently in the later history of their state and in national affairs.

The Illinois convention, in conciseness of its product, did even better than that of Indiana.[50] The Illinois constitution also conformed to the type of the period, and, excepting for a New York influence by way of Kane, was based largely on the constitutions of Kentucky, Ohio, and Indiana. It was not submitted to the people for ratification. The legislature was the strongest branch of the government, and short ballot principles were followed.

The preamble set forth the agreement of the people to form a free and independent state and ratified the boundaries provided by Congress. Article I established three separate departments of government, and the second, on the legislature, followed the Ohio constitution, excepting representatives were elected for two years, senators for four, and sessions were to be biennial. The first election was set for the third Thursday in September. Section 18, which fixed salaries of governor and lieutenant governor, was sharply debated; the governor's salary was finally set at $1,000, the same as that of the supreme court justices. The right to vote was given all white males over twenty-one with six months' residence; the method of voting was to be *viva voce* until it should be altered by the General Assembly. The section [26] of the first draft, which made ministers of the gospel ineligible for membership in the legislature, did not survive, and found no place in the finished constitution.

Article III, on the executive, followed the Ohio constitution, but provided a four-year term for governor, and made him ineligible for more than four years out of any period of eight. Qualifications and the term for lieutenant governor were the same as for governor. As for veto powers, the first draft provided for a council of revision, as did the New York constitution. On first reading this provision was amended and the veto given the governor,[51] but on second reading Mr. Kane's idea was again incorporated,[52] and a council of revision, consisting of the gov-

[50] Thirteen pages as compared to sixteen as printed in Francis N. Thorpe (comp.), *The Federal and State Constitutions, Colonial Charters, and Other Organic Laws of the States, Territories and Colonies* ... (7 volumes. Washington, D. C., 1909), Volume II.

[51] *Journal*, 38 (*Journal of the Illinois State Historical Society*, VI, 390).

[52] *Journal*, 46, in *ibid*, VI, 398.

ernor and the judges of the supreme court, was constituted to
revise and return all bills to the legislature. Bills objected to
could be enacted by a majority vote of each house of the General
Assembly. The governor was given the appointment of the secretary of state, with the approval of the Senate, but the treasurer
and the public printer were to be selected by joint ballot of the
legislature. Section 10 of the schedule gave to the General Assembly the appointment and fixing of duties of an auditor of public
accounts, attorney general, and such other officers for the state
as might be deemed necessary.

The judicial power of the state was vested in a supreme court
and such inferior courts as the legislature might create (Article
IV). Justices were to be appointed by joint ballot of the General
Assembly, to hold office until 1824, but appointments thereafter
were to be for good behavior. The supreme court jurisdiction
was appellate only, excepting in cases relating to revenue, man-
damus, and impeachment. The manner of appointment of justices of the peace was left to the legislature.

Article V on the militia differed in no essential from the corresponding provision in the Indiana constitution, from which apparently it was copied.

The provisions regarding slavery, instead of being included in
the bill of rights as in the Ohio constitution (Article VIII), or
inserted as a section among the miscellanies as in the Indiana
constitution (Article XI), were made the subject of Article VI.
The discussion of slavery in the *Intelligencer* continued right up
to the time of final action by the convention. On second reading
(August 18) the article prohibiting introduction of slavery or
involuntary servitude was modified by the words "under any indenture hereafter made." Ohio had gone practically the whole
way in keeping out slavery and admitting only indentures made
by parties in a state of perfect freedom and on condition of a
bona fide consideration. Indiana had made no mention of indentures executed in the state. Illinois accepted the bona fide consideration type of indenture but went further and added a section
(3) which provided that those indentures executed without fraud
or collusion, should be served out, but children born of inden-
tured parents were to be free at the ages of twenty-one and
eighteen respectively for men and women. Bound laborers were

permitted at the saline for one-year terms up to 1825. The apparent intention was to prevent both slavery and indenture for the future, but to recognize the property rights in slaves and servants existing at the time. The enactment represented a solution midway between the hopes of the extreme anti- and proslavery men. Since Illinois did not, as did Ohio and Indiana, incorporate a provision against amendment of the slavery section, and the acceptance by Congress had to be kept in mind, it seems that many of the proslavery delegates, as well as those who took middle ground, favored the provision.[53]

Amendment to the constitution was provided for as follows: The General Assembly, by a two-thirds vote, might call for a vote of the electors for or against holding a convention, and if a majority of those who voted for representatives voted favorably, the next General Assembly was to call a convention to consider amendment.

The usual guarantee of individual rights and liberties was incorporated in Article VIII. A provision against any banks or moneyed institutions, excepting a state bank and those already provided for, was herein included as a section similar to Article X of the Indiana constitution. Another section (20) provided that taxes should be levied by valuation, so that every person should pay a tax in proportion to the value of property held.

The references to local government were brief and scattered. In each county a sheriff and a coroner were to be elected for a term of two years. A board of three county commissioners, to transact the business of the county, was to be elected, powers and duties to be defined by law. Judges of such inferior courts as the legislature might create were to be appointed by the legislature, and a competent number of justices of the peace for each county were to be appointed in such manner as the assembly might direct, as well as inspectors, collectors, surveyors, constables, and such inferior officers whose jurisdiction might be confined to the counties. No provision was made for the creation

---

[53] N. Dwight Harris in *The History of Negro Servitude in Illinois, and of the Slavery Agitation in That State, 1719–1864* (Chicago, 1904), 21, writing before the discovery of the *Journal*, considered Article VI a victory of the "compromisists." The votes of those members known to have favored slavery, however, were cast on the winning side on the three roll calls recorded. Kane was a slaveholder, but as a politician sought to keep the favor of both sides, and was one of the strongest advocates of the middle-ground solution.

of new counties nor was township or town government mentioned in the constitution.

The schedule provided for issuance of a general election writ by the president of the convention to the sheriffs for an election on the third Thursday of September, to be conducted according to territorial election laws. The seat of government was fixed at Kaskaskia until otherwise provided for by the General Assembly. This question of the location of the capital had stirred up interest second only to the slavery issue, and the old territorial factional divisions seem to have flared up, with a number of the old Edwards faction being defeated by Kane, Thomas, Michael Jones, and others of the anti-Edwards men.[54] Pope's Bluff, Hill's Ferry, and Covington, all on the Kaskaskia River, had presented propositions and offered donations of land, and the speculative interests were aroused. Only Covington was a town, but prospects of the others were being boomed and notices of developments published. Since none of these offers received sufficient support to get the seat of government of the new state, it was finally agreed to have the first legislature petition Congress for a grant of from one to four sections on the Kaskaskia River east of the third principal meridian and as near to it as possible. This would locate the capital in unsurveyed lands and any speculative profits would accrue to the state rather than to individuals. If the grant was made, the legislature was to appoint a commission of five to select the land and provide for laying out a town, which would be the capital for twenty years. If the state failed to get the grant, then the legislature might fix the permanent seat of government wherever it thought best.

At the end of the schedule a provision was attached stipulating that anyone who was thirty years of age, a citizen of the United States, and two years a resident within the limits of Illinois, might be eligible for lieutenant governor, regardless of the qualifications prescribed in Article III. This was to make possible the election of Pierre Menard, who had been naturalized but a short time.[55]

The completion of the work of the convention was celebrated by the inhabitants of Kaskaskia; salutes were fired, pledges of

---

[54] Buck, *Illinois in 1818*, 291.
[55] Ford, *History of Illinois*, 26.

support were made, and the constitution approved as wise, republican, and equitable in distribution of just rights to all classes. This opinion was no doubt concurred in by the majority of the people of Illinois.

The election campaign for the new state offices was limited to three weeks. Daniel Pope Cook, an Edwards man, and John McLean, of Shawneetown, an anti-Edwards man, had announced earlier as representative to Congress, as did Shadrach Bond, Jr., a farmer of the older generation of citizens, who had been prominent in territorial offices, but not a member of either of the political groups. When statehood appeared probable, Bond withdrew and offered for the governorship. Cook and McLean were known to have different views on the slavery question, but with this issue decided by the convention, the contest became largely one of sectional support based on popular acquaintance. McLean carried the eastern counties and Cook those of the northwest; McLean won by fourteen votes. Bond was unopposed for governor by either of the old political factions, and in but one county were votes cast against him. Menard won the lieutenant governorship over two opponents. Of the thirteen members of the convention who ran for the General Assembly, twelve were elected, but only two of the successful legislative candidates had been members of the territorial legislature.

The First General Assembly met at Kaskaskia on Monday, October 5. Governor Bond, after qualifying, delivered a message in which he counseled against party strife, but his appointment of Kane as secretary of state aroused the distrust of the Edwards men. From a list of six candidates the legislature elected Ninian Edwards and Jesse B. Thomas as U. S. Senators. Election of supreme court judges followed, then on October 9, Daniel Pope Cook was elected attorney general, and the offices of auditor, treasurer, and public printer were filled. A petition to Congress for the grant of a capital site was prepared and on the thirteenth, pending recognition of statehood, the General Assembly adjourned until the first Monday in January.

Congress did not meet until November 16. The constitution of Illinois was referred to a select committee in the House and on November 20 a resolution for admission was presented. Some question was raised concerning the population, and James Tall-

madge of New York, soon to lead the fight against the admission
of Missouri as a slave state, questioned whether the principle
of slavery had been sufficiently prohibited. He believed that
Article VI contravened the provisions of the Ordinance, in letter
or spirit, in each of its three sections. Congress, he thought, was
bound to reject the constitution or at least the part concerning
slavery. George Poindexter, of Mississippi, a member of the
select committee, argued that the provision in the Illinois constitution was practically copied from that of Ohio, and furthermore that it would be found difficult, after admitting the
independence of a state, to prevent it fixing its constitution in
any way it saw fit. Richard C. Anderson, Jr., of Kentucky, also
on the committee, thought that there was nothing binding about
the compact feature of the Ordinance, since the people were
neither represented nor consulted on the subject at the time.
This was an inadmissible doctrine to Tallmadge, who believed
that should a state change its constitution in this respect after
admission, it would thereby cease to be a competent part of
the Union. William Henry Harrison, speaking for Ohio, stated
that the people had entered into no compact which had shorn
them of their sovereign authority. This seemed to be the sentiment of the western states. On the question of admission the
vote stood 117 to 34, all but one of the minority being from
New England, New York, New Jersey, and Pennsylvania. The
resolution for admission was introduced in the Senate on November 25 and passed December 1 without division. On December
3, 1818, the act admitting Illinois was approved by President
Monroe, and the next day John McLean was seated in the House
as representative for Illinois, and Ninian Edwards and Jesse
B. Thomas took their seats in the Senate.[56]

[56] *Annals of Congress*, 15 Congress, 2 session, 23, 26, 31, 32, 38, 296, 297–98, 305–
11. For the struggle for another convention to change the slavery provision, see
Chapter IX.

III

The Settler and the Land

They do not come to lead a life of inglorious ease—to live without honest labor—to exempt themselves from those manly toils which invigorate both body and mind—but they come imbued with the spirit of independence, determined to acquire for themselves, and for those near and dear to them, that happiness and comfort which reward the labors of freemen in a land exhaustless in the bounties of nature.

Madison *Wisconsin Enquirer*, March 16, 1839

IN THE early decades of the nineteenth century the great majority of the people in the United States lived on farms, and a considerable number of those living in the towns engaged in some farming. The people lived on the land, and from it they made their living. Land was the chief source of wealth and the most generally accepted measure of wealth, as well as the chief medium for speculation. Its possession offered economic security and determined social status; it fulfilled in the eyes of parents the hopes for the coming generation. Absence of good land at reasonable prices in the older settled regions was the most important factor in turning the faces of the people towards the West; its abundance in the West was the most powerful factor in drawing them thither. Above all things the settler came West for land.

When, between 1781 and 1802, the states with western land claims surrendered their lands to the United States, there came into possession of the Federal Government a public domain of 404,955 square miles, or almost 260,000,000 acres, an area greater in size than the thirteen original states.[1] Of this domain

---

[1] This does not include Kentucky, which was never a public-land state, but does include Tennessee, which, though ceded by North Carolina, was so covered with claims as not to constitute an addition to the public domain. Donaldson, *The Public Domain*, 11, 83. Donaldson's 1,300-page compilation contains the essential documents, maps, and statistics on the history of the public lands from the colonial charters to 1880, and, together with *American State Papers, Public Lands; American State Papers, Finance;* and the *House* and *Senate Documents,* constitutes the core material for any study of the subject in the early period. Payson J. Treat, *The National Land System 1785–1820* (New York, 1910); Roy M. Robbins, *Our Landed Heritage. The Public Domain 1776–1936* (Princeton University Press, 1942); and Benjamin H. Hibbard, *A History of the Public Land Policies* (New York, 1924), are the standard works on the public lands.

more than 265,000 square miles or about 170,000,000 acres lay within the boundaries of the Territory Northwest of the Ohio.

The first public-land policy of the United States was laid down in the Land Ordinance of 1785, which provided that the land ceded by the states should, as soon as the Indian title was cleared, be surveyed into townships six miles square and disposed of to purchasers. The survey was to begin at the junction of the western boundary of Pennsylvania and the Ohio River, and as soon as seven ranges (tiers of townships) should be completed, advertised public sales were to be held. Excepting the one seventh drawn for Continental Army bounties, the land was to be sold, alternate townships intact, and the intervening ones in lots (sections) of 640 acres. The land was to be sold at public sale for not less than "one dollar the acre, to be paid in specie or loan office certificates reduced to specie value by scale of depreciation or certificates of liquidated debts of the United States including interest, besides the expence of the survey and other charges thereon, which are hereby rated at thirty-six dollars the township. . . ." When the terms were complied with, the loan office commissioners under the Board of the Treasury were authorized to give deed for the purchase in the name of the United States.

In this ordinance, the leading provisions of which have continued in operation throughout the history of the public domain, the New England plan of prior survey, township planting, and the granting of a deed in fee simple, was adopted in preference to the Virginia system of indiscriminate locations with its clumsy machinery of warrants, certificates, caveats, and grants. Western emigration prior to 1795 was confined largely to the region south of the Ohio. The Indian troubles in the Northwest which held up the surveys also in large part kept out the settlers, and since the same authority which was to dispose of the Indians was also to dispose of the land, it became possible, in spite of the ubiquitous squatter, to establish the system.

Throughout the history of the public domain the squatter constituted an interesting problem. In fact he antedated the public lands, for the colonies from New Hampshire to Georgia had been confronted with troubles arising from his presence.

Squatters had settled in the vicinity of Boston as early as 1625.[2] In 1773 squatters were on George Washington's western lands, and warnings to vacate were ignored by them. In 1776 it was estimated that there were 25,000 on the lands around the Upper Ohio claimed by Virginia and Pennsylvania. They proclaimed themselves "a rational and Social people," who having emigrated from almost every province and imbibed the most extensive ideas of liberty, refused to be "annexed or Subjugated" by any province, or suffer themselves to be enslaved or "arbitrarily deprived and robbed" of the lands to which, as first occupants, they were entitled by the "Laws of Nature & of Nations." They maintained they had served as an effective barrier against the savages and fought for Liberty while the rest of their countrymen were "softened by Ease, enervated by Affluence & Luxurious Plenty, & unaccustomed to Fatigues, Hardships, Difficulties or dangers."[3]

Virginia and Pennsylvania found the problem so difficult that they threatened emigrants to their lands with the death penalty. Prior to the passage of the Ordinance of 1785 Washington advocated that the government purchase from the Indians land enough for two states, and provide that settlers who would squat on these lands or go beyond should "not only be considered as outlaws, but fit subjects for Indian vengeance." Ensign John Armstrong, when sent to clear out the lands north of the Ohio under Congressional proclamation of 1785, reported that unless some speedy method was adopted to keep the settlers out, that country would soon be inhabited by a banditti whose actions were a disgrace to human nature. Some resisted removal at this time, and neither Armstrong nor Gen. Josiah Harmar, four years later, accomplished more than temporary eviction.[4] Governor St. Clair realized the seriousness of attempting to dispossess the 2,000 there, whose numbers were being augmented daily.

From Confederation times to the Civil War the squatter was often discussed in Congress. In the land discussion of 1789 Rep-

---

[2] Justin Winsor, *Memorial History of Boston, 1630–1880* (4 volumes. Boston, 1880–81), I, 80.

[3] Quoted in George Henry Alden, *New Governments West of the Alleghanies before 1780* (*Bulletin of the University of Wisconsin, Historical Series*, II, No. 1, Madison, 1897), 65–66.

[4] *Annals of Congress*, 1 Congress, 1 session, 412.

resentative Andrew Scott, of Pennsylvania, noted that it was practically impossible to prevent unlawful settlements and that if the people were not accommodated in western lands, they would occupy them without payment, law or no law.

The squatter as a type no more conformed to pattern than the rest of the frontiersmen, and he differed from them in no particular, excepting possibly in being possessed of fewer worldly goods. Was he more bold, restless, lawless? According to Timothy Pickering, of Massachusetts, all frontiersmen were savage and unworthy subjects. Some reasoned that when the squatter settled on lands he did not own in the hope of selling his improvements to the legal purchaser, he was but speculating with his endurance and labor as the purchaser or speculator did with his money. Lawless and bad men there were among them; also the meek and passive failures, who could battle nature and the Indian more successfully than the realities of economic life. The squatter has been variously described. Washington at times thought those on his own lands not only unjust but "pitifully mean," and feared reprisals in burned buildings if they were legally ousted. Eastern papers spoke of "these poor miserable preemptioners," "violators of all law," "these vagabond squatters on the rights of others," "these ignorant and illiterate settlers." Sometimes they were referred to as suspicious, inquisitive, savage and dangerous as Indians, fugitives of justice, thieves and banditti; a lazy, thriftless, ornery, dirty, and trashy lot.

The Westerner was, on the whole, more considerate of, and patient with the squatter, than the Easterner. In contrast to Judge Hall's sympathetic description of the "lonesome looking couple from old North Carolina,"[5] was a picture of the squatters, attributed to Senator Willie P. Mangum: "A sort of North Carolina blue beards, who are ragged, dirty, brawling, browbeating monsters, six feet high, whose vocation is robbing, drinking, fighting, and terrifying every peaceable man in the community."[6] On the other hand the squatter was referred to as "the best part of the population of all the new States," inoffensive, harmless, and patient, who bore vexations from the government uncomplainingly lest he be denounced as unmannerly,

[5] See Chapter I, 27.
[6] *Congressional Globe,* 26 Congress, 2 session, Appendix, 65.

impudent, or lawless.[7] He was characterized as a person of justice, honesty, patriotism, hospitality and enterprise.[8] Capt. Basil Hall, the English traveler, spoke of ". . . honest Squatters —free-and-easy settlers, who are their own law-makers and law-breakers, as the case may be."

As these people, after all, do great good to the countries in which they settle, their operations are not discouraged. In process of time, many of them become useful citizens of thickly peopled territories, of which but a few years before they were the only inhabitants, while the idlers and rovers proceed to the westward.

It is the fashion to speak slightly of these Pioneers, Squatters, Crackers, or by whatever name it pleases them most to be called by, but I must own that I was well satisfied with almost every one of them whom I encountered. In general, I thought they had less of that frigid, uninviting formality, which characterises the Americans further to the eastward. They were somewhat gruff, indeed, at times; but they seemed to trust themselves and us with more readiness, and sometimes understood a joke, which I hardly ever saw exemplified on this side of the Mississippi.[9]

Daniel Webster thought the squatter possessed the general character of frontiersmen—hardy, adventurous, and enterprising, and felt it unjust that people should slander him. A western paper considered these people, often misunderstood and mis-represented, equal to any of the farmers of the East, and a group of which any state might be proud:

In Wisconsin they will compare with any portion of the farmers in the Eastern States. Indeed, as a body, they are men of whom any State might be proud. They are most of them men of intelligence, industry, and integrity, who have come with their families to avail themselves of the advantage offered by a fertile soil and salubrious climate—by the healthful breezes and pure waters of the lovely west. They do not come to lead a life of inglorious ease—to live without honest labor—to exempt themselves from those manly toils which invigorate both body and mind—but they come imbued with the spirit of independence, determined to acquire for themselves, and for those near and dear to them, that happiness and com-fort which reward the labors of freemen in a land exhaustless in the bounties of nature. Among them are those who hold seats in the Legislature—those who have been reared in the colleges of the East—those who have been accustomed to all the elegancies of society—those who have been educated for the learned professions, and whose attainments qualify them for the most exalted sphere in life.

[7] Senator Ambrose H. Sevier, of Arkansas, 1841, *ibid.*
[8] Senator Oliver H. Smith, of Indiana, 1841, *ibid.*, 69.
[9] Capt. Basil Hall, *Travels in North America in the Years 1827 and 1828* (3 volumes. Edinburgh, 1829), III, 355.

Let not then, the claim of the honest settlers of the West be either disparaged or disregarded. By developing the riches of the soil in the remote interior, they enhance the wealth of the seaboard, and swell the sails of commerce.[10]

The *Milwaukee Sentinel* said that "a more hardy industrious, enlightened, enterprising and worthy people does not exist, than these same squatters."[11] Even the New York *Evening Post* wrote: "We have known among these squatters some of the best and purest men it has ever been our fortune to be acquainted with."[12] Among the squatters, as elsewhere on the frontier, the evangelistic sects found faithful followers and Methodists and Baptists made many zealous converts. Only one thing was certain about the squatter: he was everywhere to be found on the frontier. If on government land he was in conflict with the sovereignty of the United States, if on Indian lands, with that of the tribes as well.

The policy of the United States with reference to the American Indian and the land which he occupied was essentially the same as that of the English government in the later colonial period. Some writers have indicated a distinct difference in the policies of England and France in the period of struggle for the interior of North America.

The French asserted possession against the heathen, but cared little for the territory except to preserve it for the fur trade. They were not, consequently, dispoilers of the savages' hunting-grounds. . . . But, nevertheless, they seized such points as they wished, without thought of recompensing the savage owners. . . . On the other hand, the English pioneers, by their charters and patents, got a jurisdiction over, but not a fee in, the lands conveyed. In the practice which England established, or professed to establish, occupation could follow only upon the extinguishment by purchase or treaty of the native title.[13]

[10] Madison *Wisconsin Enquirer,* March 16, 1839.
[11] March 6, 1838.
[12] Quoted in Allan Nevins, *American Press Opinion, Washington to Coolidge* . . . (Boston, 1928), 129.
[13] Justin Winsor, *The Mississippi Basin* (New York, 1895), 323. Since the Indian had no concept of private property in land, it was easy to argue that he could have no title to the land; he merely inhabited or overran it, a right not to be transferred but extinguished, not to be regulated by deeds of conveyance but by treaties, not by municipal law but by the law of nations. Vattel, Montesquieu, Adam Smith, John Quincy Adams, and others so held. The lands held by the Indians, then, were in the same state that all lands were originally, and the title to them was to be acquired as all first titles were, that is, by occupancy. "Occupancy," said Blackstone, "is the true ground and foundation of property, or of holding those things in severalty, which, by the law of nature, unqualified by that of society, were common to all mankind." See also Grotius, Puffendorf, Locke, Rutherford.

This, in general, was true, yet clear-cut policies with such an easy distinction are hard to locate. In their dealings with the Indians the French were never very specific on the question of the title in the land, and whatever their policy, it does not seem to have been set forth in legal enactments or other documentary material, but brought out only in presentation of claims against rival powers in the struggle for territory. Then they assumed that tribal agreements which brought the Indians under French dominion carried with them the ownership of the lands.[14]

English policy until the later colonial period was equally indefinite. As far as the Indian's possession of the land was concerned, Parkman's statement that "English civilization scorned and neglected the Indian" seems to be justified. The Indian was as a rule ignored by England in the granting of colonial charters, but the colonies were not always in a position to do likewise.

In their contest with the French the English produced a treaty made in 1701 by Lieutenant Governor John Nanfan with the Iroquois, in which the latter "freely and voluntarily surrendered delivered up and for ever quit claimed, unto our great Lord and Master the King of England . . . for ever all the right title and interest and all the claime and demand whatsoever which wee . . . now have or which wee ever had . . . in or to all that vast Tract of land . . . " north of the Ohio and stretching to the Illinois and Mississippi rivers.[15] Attempts were later made to regard the title to the lands as transferred, and grants were made within the territory.

During the last war of the long struggle with France, the Indian problem became so important that the British government had finally to adopt some kind of a policy. Instructions were issued to colonial governors against any further grants of lands "within or adjacent to the Territories possessed or occupied by the said Indians or the Property Possession of which has at any time been reserved to or claimed by them." At the end of the

[14] For summary of policy and citations of treaties, see *Indian Land Cessions in the United States*, compiled by Charles C. Royce (U. S. Bureau of American Ethnology, *Annual Report*, 1896–97, part II, 521–997. Washington, D. C., 1899), 545–49.

[15] "Deed from the Five Nations to the King, of their Beaver Hunting Ground," in Edmund B. O'Callaghan (ed.), *Documents Relative to the Colonial History of the State of New-York* . . . (15 volumes. Albany, 1856–87), IV, 909. There is some question as to whether this treaty might not have been manufactured at a later date to antedate French claims.

war, with France out of North America, the Indian problem was considered so difficult that the government, to pacify the tribes, sought by the Proclamation of 1763 to confine settlement by the colonists to the region east of the watershed line separating the streams flowing into the Atlantic from those flowing into the Ohio, Mississippi, and Gulf. The lands to the west were reserved for the use of the Indians, under the sovereignty, protection, and dominion of the King. Thus went into imperial hands the handling of a problem which had been variously handled by the different colonies. A more definite boundary line in the northern region was fixed in 1768 by the Treaty of Fort Stanwix with the Six Nations, and the land east of the Ohio and south of an irregular line across Pennsylvania was opened to settlement.[16]

The Articles of Confederation gave Congress the sole and exclusive right to regulate trade and manage all affairs with the Indians not members of any of the states, and in 1783, by act of Congress, all persons were prohibited from making settlements on lands claimed by the Indians outside of the jurisdiction of any state, and from purchasing or receiving any such lands "without the express authority and direction of the United States in Congress Assembled." The Constitution of the United States gave no specific authority to the Federal Government for treating with the Indians, but by the treaty clause and general powers granted to it such right was assumed, and in spite of Chief Justice Marshall's famous opinion of 1831 to the effect that since the Indians had acknowledged themselves to be under the protection of the United States, they were not then foreign nations but "domestic dependent nations in a state of pupilage," the United States until 1871 maintained the legal fiction that the tribes were independent nations. From its first treaty in 1778 to its last, 370 all told, the United States, with one exception, maintained the policy that the Indian title could be extinguished only with the consent, in treaty, of the tribes recognized as having claim to the soil.[17]

[16] Map in Justin Winsor, *The Westward Movement* (Boston, 1897), 18–19. Treaty in O'Callaghan (ed.) *New-York Colonial Documents*, VIII, 135–37.

[17] At a total cost for title, etc., to 1880 of more than $275,000,000 plus $46,000,000 for surveys. Total receipts from the public domain to 1880 were more than $120,000,000 less than the above expenditures. Donaldson, *The Public Domain*, 21.

The authority of the government of the United States was first recognized by the Indian in the second Treaty of Fort Stanwix, 1784, whereby the Six Nations yielded to the United States all claims west of the New York–western Pennsylvania boundary. In order to carry out the surveys under the Ordinance of 1785 it was necessary to enlarge the territory open to settlement, and United States commissioners met representatives of the Wyandot, Delaware, and other tribes at Fort McIntosh; there it was agreed that for a consideration the Indians should surrender claim to land south of a Lake Erie–Cuyahoga–Maumee River line. At Fort Harmar in 1789 these same tribes reaffirmed this boundary, and the Six Nations renewed and confirmed the Stanwix treaty, but the validity of these treaties was not accepted by the rest of the western tribes, who insisted on maintaining their title to all land north of the Ohio.

The desire for revenue was no doubt uppermost in the minds of those who formulated the land policy of 1785, and this to a large extent accounts for the land deals made with the Ohio Company and Judge Symmes; but probably the desirability of buffer colonies to bear the brunt of Indian strife and connect outlying settlements in Kentucky and Tennessee with the East played its part. The five years following 1789 were spent breaking the power of the Miami confederation, and after Wayne's victory the Greenville Treaty of 1795 cleared the Indian title south and east of the Cuyahoga–Tuscarawas–Fort Recovery–Kentucky River line.[18]

The essentials of the Ordinance of 1785 withstood the efforts of Alexander Hamilton, who with the financial needs of the day in mind, favored a modified system of indiscriminate locations.[19] The clearance of title to approximately 25,000 square miles by the Greenville Treaty and the British promise of abandonment of the western posts in Jay's Treaty, brought the land question again before Congress in 1796. "To raise revenue, and to sell the land in such lots as would be most convenient to purchasers,"

[18] Made with the Delaware, Shawnee, Ottawa, Chippewa, Potawatomi, Miami, Eel River, Wea, Kickapoo, Piankashaw, and Kaskaskia. For line see map, 111.
[19] Congress by law in 1795 provided that the net proceeds of land sales in the western territory should go into the sinking fund of the United States for the extinction of the public debt.

were the twin considerations to be kept in mind.[20] The questions
of size of lots, auction system, prior survey in rectangular townships or indiscriminate locations, were subjected to debate, but
the act approved May 18, providing for the sale of lands in the
Territory Northwest of the Ohio and above the mouth of the
Kentucky River, made no basic changes in the law of 1785. The
six-mile townships were retained, one half of which were to be
sold in quarters (three miles square), and the remainder subdivided into sections and sold in 640-acre lots. The quarter townships were to be sold at Philadelphia, the sections at Pittsburgh
and Cincinnati. The minimum price of $2.00 an acre was to
include cost of survey; terms were one twentieth down payment,
half to be paid in thirty days, balance in one year. The government reserved the salt springs and four sections at the center of
each township. By the extension of the credit feature the law of
1796 was made to conform more to the western or frontier
ideas. Only 48,556 acres were sold under this law prior to May,
1800.

In December, 1799, William Henry Harrison came to Congress as delegate from the Northwest Territory. He was
shortly appointed chairman of the House committee to inquire
into necessary changes in the public-land law, and largely under
his sponsorship was introduced the land act of 1800. For the
first time the interests and desires of the settlers on the frontier
were paramount to the revenue motive and the wishes of eastern
speculators and conservatives who were not very eager to encourage emigration to the West. Lands east of the Muskingum
were to be divided into sections, those west of that river half in
sections and half in 320-acre lots. Land offices with a receiver
and register were to be opened at Chillicothe, Marietta, Steubenville, and Cincinnati. After public auction of three weeks, lands
were to go on private sale, minimum price $2.00 an acre plus
$6.00 a section for survey, the purchaser to pay one twentieth
down, one fourth in forty days, another fourth in two years,
another in three, and the last in four years from the date of
sale. A year of grace was allowed after the last payment was due
before forfeiture would result. Interest at 6 per cent was calcu-

[20] Statement of chairman of the Land Office Committee of the House, in *Annals of Congress,* 4 Congress, 1 session, 331.

lated on the deferred payments but a discount of 8 per cent was allowed for prepayment of any of the last three payments.

In 1804 further concession was made to popular demand: the size of tract purchasable was reduced to a quarter section (160 acres), interest was not charged until after payment was due, thus reducing cash price from $1.84 to $1.64 an acre, fees were abolished, and additional land offices were established at Detroit, Vincennes, and Kaskaskia.[21] Definite concessions though these were, reduction of price and pre-emption were not yet accomplished.

Between the passage of the Harrison Land Act in 1800 and the opening of the War of 1812 no less than a dozen treaties involving important land cessions in the Northwest were made with the Indian tribes. Beginning with the Treaty of Fort Wayne in 1803 and ending with the Treaty of Fort Wayne in 1809, the process of surrender had cleared wholly or in part the Indian title to a broad crescent-shaped area of about 29,000,000 acres.

This area stretched from the west side of the Greenville Treaty line across Indiana Territory to the Vermilion River and on to the Mississippi so as to include about four-fifths of the present state of Illinois.[22] It also included a large tract in Ohio north of the Greenville Treaty line between the Cuyahoga River and the Put-in-Bay meridian, and the southeastern corner of Michigan Territory. The Indians, realizing the fact that they were rapidly losing their lands, and encouraged and aided by the British, organized their last important resistance in the Northwest against the advancing army of white settlers.[23] Tecumseh's war broke prematurely in his absence, and Harrison's Tippecanoe campaign of 1811 and the campaigns of the War of 1812 broke the power of the Indians. Just as the Creeks in the South were help-

[21] In acts of 1801 and 1802, Congress had exempted from interest on deferred payments until they were due, those who purchased land from John Cleves Symmes which lay outside his grant, thus making possible a cash price on these lands of $1.64 per acre.

[22] A large part of the area in northern Illinois was ceded in 1804 by Harrison's treaty with some of the Sac and Fox chiefs, but claims to the same land on the part of other tribes were not settled until later. See Chapter X, 57 ff.

[23] It must be kept in mind that as a rule the Indian, who had no concept of private property in land, at first did not understand the significance of treaty cessions. But the effects of settlement on his hunting grounds he did understand. Furthermore, the tribes rarely possessed adequately authorized agencies for making treaties, and treaties made by representatives of a tribe were frequently repudiated by the younger and bolder elements, as well as by other tribes using the same land.

less after their defeat at the hands of Andrew Jackson, so were the Indians of the Northwest rendered more or less helpless before armed forces, treaty commissioners, surveyors, and settlers.

By the end of the first year under the act of 1800, 398,646 acres of land had been sold in the Northwest at a price of $834,887, of which $586,426 represented balance unpaid. Excepting 1803, sales increased annually to a maximum of 619,266 acres at a price of $1,235,953 in 1805, in which year unpaid balances amounted to more than $2,000,000. From then until the War of 1812 sales fell off irregularly.[24] The war affected sales but little. Indian campaigns were nothing new to the frontier, and, unless directly on the outskirts of settlement, were not particularly detrimental to home seeking and the business of the day. In fact the halting or even driving back of the outposts to a certain extent may have stimulated land sales, for the squatter frequently found it more advantageous to buy and dig in until the way was again open. Sales for 1813 showed a decrease from the preceding year but 1814 registered a jump to 823,264 acres.

Congress had watched the effects of the credit system with some misgivings. In 1806 the House Committee of Ways and Means advised against any further extension of credit, and feared that if existing regulations were in any way relaxed, "that important branch of our public resources should be altogether dried up and lost." The viewpoint of this committee was reactionary in that it was determined largely by the revenue idea rather than desire for encouragement of settlement. The same year, however, the recently created House Committee on the Public Lands, having noted the doubling in two years of the amount of balances due from purchasers, recommended the abolition of the credit system.[25] It was apparent that a great many forfeitures were shortly to take place, and with the reluctance of neighbors to bid against the delinquents, or of speculators or outsiders to come in and buy them out in opposition to the hostile spirit and sometimes direct action of the community, the government would

---

[24] 1806—473,212 acres; 1807—284,180 acres; 1808—195,579; 1809—143,409; 1810 —158,844; 1811—207,017; 1812—391,665; 1813—239,981; 1814—823,264; 1815— 1,092,980; 1816—1,131,956. *American State Papers, Public Lands* (8 volumes. Washington, D. C., 1834–61), III, 420.

[25] *Ibid.,* I, 265–66.

be placed in an embarrassing position. As a party to differences, rather than arbiter, its dignity would suffer compromise.[26] In his letter which accompanied the report, Secretary of the Treasury Gallatin pointed out the danger of the development of a powerful interest hostile to the Federal Government, which might adversely affect both the public debt and land sales.

Instead of tackling the problem at this time and either enforcing the credit provisions or else abandoning them, Congress passed a law on April 15, 1806, which suspended the forfeiture provision of the act of 1800 for actual residents in Ohio and Indiana Territory until October 1. This was the first of the relief acts, of which a dozen were enacted before the final breakdown of the credit system. The law of the following year made settlement on United States land illegal and gave the president power to use, if necessary, the military establishment against squatters. This act, as well as others, was ignored. The population was headed West; it outran the surveyors, land offices, even the Indian frontier line, and in its accumulated momentum paused not to read or heed the United States *Statutes at Large.*

The War of 1812 and the attendant financial and monetary difficulties made worse the predicament not only of those who, under the law of 1800, bought more land than they could pay for, but also of those who stayed within their means. The frontiersman was, as far as land was concerned, an incorrigible optimist. Tall tales of western projects fell upon eager ears, and facts regarding rapid population increases and appreciation of land values five- to tenfold in a few years were abundant and comforting. Each land buyer assumed that such conditions would continue and that he would gain as had the most favorably situated. He discounted the future accordingly. As in most speculative booms, potential factors which might determine a different ending from that conceived in the mind of the adventurer were either unthought of or else ignored.

The exceptionally high prices for American produce as a result of European demand during the years of the earlier Napoleonic

[26] Under the law of 1800 forfeiture on no payment, except the down one twentieth, was not to take place until one year after the last payment was due. Until 1806 then, only the one twentieth was subject to forfeiture. Beginning in 1806 many stood to forfeit from one to three of the quarterly payments as well, compensation for which they could recover only after the government had sold the land and recovered its claims.

wars came to an abrupt end with the embargo policy. Exports of agricultural products fell from an approximate $30,000,000 annual average to $5,000,000 in 1808, and the effect was immediate on land values and land sales, as well as on the payment of the installments on lands purchased. Ostensibly to meet this situation, but in reality to save the credit system, Congress passed the law of 1809 which extended for two years the time for payment of purchase money due. The Ohio legislature in 1811 instructed the state's senators and requested its representatives in Congress to make it possible for a purchaser, on forfeiting his first installment, to have pre-emption rights until the time of sale; and Indiana Territory in 1810 petitioned for repeal and remission of back interest on payments and for a two-year extension of time before forfeiture. Chairman Jeremiah Morrow of the House Committee on Public Lands reported adversely on the Indiana memorial,[27] but stated that the existing system could not be rigidly enforced without working hardship and injury on some.

It is believed that a Government founded on the general sentiment of the community cannot, with safety to itself, hold as debtors the citizens of any considerable portion of the country. Such a state of things will engender disaffection of the most dangerous kind—disaffection nerved by the powerful motives of interest. And as it regards purchasers, the credit at present allowed often induces individuals to make purchases beyond their means. To remove the day of payment two years further from the time of purchase would be adding to those inducements, whilst it still more admits of the intervention of unforeseen circumstances to defeat their hopes.

Reduction of price to $1.25 per acre, sale of eighty-acre tracts, extension of time two years further, and repeal of the credit provisions were recommended. The Senate committee's recommendations were similar, with $1.00 as the price:

A sale on long credit of any property never fails to induce many, from false calculations, to become purchasers. There can scarcely be imagined a situation better calculated to rouse the feelings or mislead the mind of an individual whose hopes have been blasted in a purchase of land. He has made his purchase, and with difficulty paid his first instalment. The fascinating prospect of five years' credit to pay the other instalments induces him to take his family on to the lands to begin improvements and cultivation for their comfort and support. The time taken to effect this ought to have been employed in earning the money he owes, which becomes due, and finds him

[27] See *Annals of Congress*, 11 Congress, 3 session, 672, 748; *American State Papers, Public Lands*, II, 256.

unprepared to pay it. Perhaps he has relied on the payments due him by others, and has been disappointed; or, if he has received them, losses, sickness, (which not infrequently attacks the new settler,) and the wants of his family, plead his excuse for appropriating it to their use. The credit allowed by law (five years) expires; his land is advertised for sale; he is threatened with the loss of all he has paid, whether one, two, or three instalments. But this is not all; his labor for five years, which has put his land in a state of cultivation, and placed around him the comforts of life where a wilderness existed before, is also to be lost, and his family turned out of a home to seek some new situation. It is very true, that, from the very nature of the contract, the purchaser ought to expect such a result from failure of payment; yet there is strong reason to believe that there will be an association of individuals, under the same circumstances, to relieve themselves by some means. Indeed, it is quite probable such has been the case, and that few, if any, persons appear to bid at the public sales of lands, or to re-enter the lands in opposition to the original purchase, after a forfeiture to the public has taken place for want of bidders.[28]

Again Congress failed to act according to recommendations and passed a relief law. The law of 1812 applied to the lands northwest of the Ohio. Purchasers of a section or less prior to April 1, 1808, were allowed three years from January 1, 1813, the balance to be paid in four annual installments, beginning on that date.

Naturally the war of 1812–14 did not improve conditions. Enlistments, uncertainties of trade and transportation, Indian troubles on the frontier, and above all the disordered state of the currency contributed to further delinquency and embarrassment. In 1811, on the eve of the war, the Bank of the United States expired by charter limitation, and Congress refused a renewal. Ample war revenues were not provided and the Treasury Department—after Gallatin's tenure inefficiently administered— had to sell government bonds at a discount of $12 to $20 on the hundred and frequently take its pay in paper depreciated from 20 to 30 per cent.[29] Beginning in June, 1812, Congress provided for an issue of treasury notes, to be issued at par, payable in one year, acceptable for duties, taxes, and payments for land. But these too depreciated, and to keep them in circulation the Treas-

[28] *American State Papers, Public Lands,* II, 440.
[29] For brief discussion of war finance and currency problems, see Davis Rich Dewey, *Financial History of the United States* (New York, 1903), Chapter IV; McMaster, *History of the People of the United States,* IV; Ralph C. H. Catterall, *The Second Bank of the United States* (Chicago, 1903).

ury Department agreed to accept the notes of state banks in the South and West for land dues, provided the latter would receive and reissue treasury notes.

The amount of specie available for use in the United States was small, and transaction of business was dependent largely upon the credit supplied by state banks, private banks, unchartered associations, and individual concerns. Eighty-eight state banks were doing business when the Bank of the United States closed, but in two years there were 208, and in 1816, 246. Pennsylvania chartered 41 over the Governor's veto in 1813, of which 37 opened; Massachusetts added 20, New Jersey 6, and the western states followed in line. Regulations were lax or non-existent, specie was drained to New England, notes so depreciated as to be unacceptable even in the community where issued, and the Treasury, unauthorized to make allowance for discounts, could not use the notes of one state in another. After the capture of Washington in 1814, specie payment was impossible at banks from New York to Georgia and panic ensued. New England banks even refused to pay out specie on United States treasury drafts.

In 1813[30] receipts from land sales in the Northwest were $643,055 from purchase money, $63,262 from forfeitures, and the unpaid balance totaled $1,483,861. During the next year, when sales jumped to 823,000 acres, the unpaid balance had grown to $2,134,898.[31] In spite of the habit of some purchasers of anticipating an annual relief law, none applying to the Northwest was passed until 1814, and this did not apply to purchases made prior to 1809.[32]

§

At the close of the War of 1812 the United States was still at war with some of the Indian tribes of the Northwest, but by the ninth article of the treaty signed between England and the

---

[30] September 30, 1812—September 30, 1813.
[31] *American State Papers, Public Lands,* III, 420.
[32] When President Madison issued his proclamation against squatters in December, 1815, there were those who argued that squatters' occupation was no more illegal than pre-emption acts were; that purchasers were frequently made into squatters when Indian hostilities made payment impossible. Vincennes *Western Sun,* January 27, February 23, 1816.

United States both parties promised to put an end to their Indian wars. At Greenville, Ohio, in 1814, peace had been negotiated with the tribes which inhabited Ohio, and Indiana and Michigan territories,[33] and at the end of the war Secretary of War Dallas requested the commissioners to make clear to the Indians that no grant or cession of lands was wanted, only peace.[34] The Harrison campaign of 1811 and the campaigns of the war of 1812–14 had so broken the power of the Indians of the Northwest as to render impossible further serious opposition to settlement, even though some remained insolent and hostile. Followed then more treaties until by the early 1830's practically all the lands of the Northwest, excepting northwest Michigan and what is now Wisconsin, were cleared of Indian title, and, under the policy established by the United States in 1825, early removal of the tribes to permanent location west of the Mississippi was anticipated.[35]

Governors William Clark, of Missouri Territory, and Ninian Edwards, of Illinois Territory, who were commissioned to deal with the tribes of the Upper Mississippi, found the Sac of the Rock River still belligerent and they considered the attainment of a permanent peace doubtful.[36] Nevertheless, at Portage des Sioux, in 1815, the Missouri River Sac and the Foxes assented to the Sac cession of 1804, north and west of the Illinois River; the temporizing Rock River Sac concurred in the following year; and the Ottawa, Chippewa, and Potawatomi surrendered their claims to much the same area. At the foot of the Maumee Rapids Governor Lewis Cass, of Michigan Territory, and Gen. Duncan McArthur, of Ohio, met the representatives of the Wyandot, Delaware, Shawnee, and other tribes in 1817 and cleared the Indian title to several million acres in Ohio north of the Greenville Treaty line and west of the line drawn south through Put-in-Bay. This cession opened to settlement the area which connected

---

[33] Wyandot, Delaware, Shawnee, Seneca, and Miami.

[34] Dallas to Harrison, Duncan McArthur, and John Graham, in *American State Papers, Indian Affairs* (2 volumes. Washington, D. C., 1832, 1834), II, 13–14.

[35] The subject has received special treatment in George Dewey Harmon, *Sixty Years of Indian Affairs, Political, Economic, and Diplomatic, 1789–1850* (Chapel Hill, N. C., 1941); the treaties are in Charles J. Kappler (ed.) *Indian Affairs. Laws and Treaties* (2 volumes. Washington, D. C., 1904); the maps and treaty descriptions are in Royce (comp.), *Indian Land Cessions in the United States.*

[36] *American State Papers, Indian Affairs*, II, 9. A part of this tribe was later to furnish, in Black Hawk's raid, the last important Indian trouble in the Old Northwest. See Chapter X.

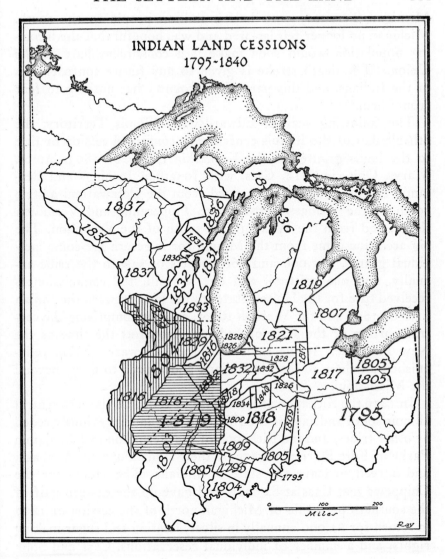

INDIAN LAND CESSIONS
1795-1840

Michigan Territory with half a million people to the south. Michigan no longer felt isolated and was hopeful that the incoming population would soon make it a constituent part of the Union. "The death stroke is given to any future confederacies of the Indians, and this part of the country has nothing to fear from them."[37]

The following year at Edwardsville, Illinois Territory, the other tribes of the Illinois confederacy confirmed cession of title to the lands granted in the Kaskaskia treaty of 1803. At St. Marys, Ohio, in 1818, Cass, with Jonathan Jennings and Benjamin Parke, of Indiana, received from the Potawatomi a strip north of the Wabash between the Tippecanoe and Vermilion rivers, and from the Wea an area south of the Vermilion. The big accession came from the Miami, for in return for some individual grants, $15,000 and 160 bushels of salt to the tribe annually, and one gristmill and one sawmill, the commissioners received title for the United States to the land between the Indian lines of 1809 and the Wabash River, an area comprising the central portion of the state of Indiana, known at the time as the New Purchase. At the same time the Delaware Nation relinquished all claim to land in Indiana and agreed to move beyond the Mississippi.

In 1819 the Kickapoo at Edwardsville ceded all claim to central Illinois south and east of the Illinois River, land previously ceded by other tribes, and the Kickapoo of the Vermilion met Benjamin Parke at Fort Harrison, gave up their lands along the Wabash, and agreed to leave the state of Indiana. The same year the Chippewa met Cass at Saginaw and gave up the eastern half of the southern peninsula of Michigan north of the cession of 1807 in return for $1,000 annually in silver, hunting and sugar-making rights, and a number of individual reservations. Cass and Solomon Sibley met representatives of the Ottawa, Chippewa, and Potawatomi at Chicago in 1821 and acquired cession of the land west of the above tract and south of the Grand River—the southwest corner of the present state of Michigan—and a strip of

[37] *Detroit Gazette*, October 3, 1817. The *Gazette* estimated the cession at 6,000,000 acres, but Ohio papers estimated about 3,862,000. Chillicothe *Supporter* in *Niles' Weekly Register*, XIII, 151 (Nov. 1, 1817). A few years later, so rapid was the inrush into this region, the Columbus *Ohio Monitor*, April 13, 1822, thought it possible that within twenty years it would be the most popular part of the state.

northern Indiana. The government gave in return to the Ottawa an annuity of $1,000 in specie, and $1,500 annually in support of a blacksmith, a teacher, and an agricultural instructor, and for cattle and utensils; and to the Potawatomi $5,000 annuity for twenty years and $1,000 for fifteen years for a blacksmith and a teacher. In 1826 Cass, James B. Ray, and John Tipton, the latter two from Indiana, secured from the Potawatomi at the mouth of the Mississinewa the rest of the strip ten miles wide across the northern Indiana border and a strip ten to twenty miles wide just north of the Wabash and reaching from the Tippecanoe River to the Ohio line. Two years later the Potawatomi surrendered another considerable tract in northeastern Indiana. In 1829 at Prairie du Chien, the Chippewa, Ottawa, and Winnebago gave up the southwest corner of present Wisconsin and a large tract in northern Illinois.

These were the more important of the treaties for cessions of Indian lands between the end of the war and 1830. Others dealt with overlapping claims and were ratifications by other tribes which claimed ownership. In addition many treaties were required to obtain title to the scores of reservations granted to the tribes within previous cessions.

By 1825 it had become evident that some general policy with reference to the Indians was expedient. Early in that year President Monroe submitted to the Senate his recommendations for the removal of the tribes from lands which they then occupied within the limits of the several states and territories, "to the country lying westward and northward thereof, within our acknowledged boundaries."[38]

Removal should be brought about only in such a way as to promote the interest and happiness of the tribes as well as the honor of the United States, that is, by conveying to each tribe title to an adequate allotment of land to which it might consent to remove. Since the Indians had already treated away title to so much of their land, this policy appeared not only practicable, but possessed of advantages both to the tribes and the United States. The government would then seek to connect the tribes in amicable relations, preserve order, prevent intrusions on their property, eliminate conflicting interests between red man and frontier,

[38] *American State Papers, Indian Affairs,* II, 541–42.

teach him the arts of civilized society, and wield in general a beneficent influence.

Accompanying Monroe's communication was the report of John C. Calhoun, secretary of war, on the number of Indians, amount of land held, the possibilities and expenses of removal. The number of Indians in the states and territories of the United States was placed at 97,000, not counting those residing in Michigan Territory west of Lake Michigan (Wisconsin); they occupied about 77,000,000 acres of land. The number in the Old Northwest was placed at 42,345; at the time they held an estimated 22,885,981 acres of land, not including that west of Lake Michigan.[39] Calhoun did not think the Indians residing in the northern parts of Ohio, Indiana, Illinois, and Michigan should be removed west of the Mississippi, but to the region west of Lake Michigan where the climate and nature of the country were much more favorable to their habits. He, too, emphasized the protection of the interests of the tribes, assurance of permanency for the arrangement, and the training of the Indians for civilized life.[40]

Pursuant to this policy treaties were made with the Osage and Kaw (Kansa) for admission of the tribes to their lands in the Far West. The tribes west of Lake Michigan which were still engaged in bloody wars among themselves were met by Governors Clark and Lewis Cass in grand conference at Prairie du Chien August 19, 1825, and there boundaries were agreed upon between Sac and Foxes and the Sioux, Sioux and Chippewa, Chippewa and Winnebago, Winnebago and Sioux, and so on. A "firm and perpetual peace" was to exist between Sioux and Chippewa, Sioux and Sac and Foxes, Sioux and Iowas. No tribe was to hunt on the land of another, and if trouble resulted it was agreed that the government of the United States might take such measures as it considered proper. This action, at the time, seemed to be a dis-

[39] Ohio, 2,350 Indians and 409,501 acres; Michigan Territory, 28,316 Indians and 7,057,920 acres (in the lower peninsula only); Indiana and Illinois, 11,579 Indians and 15,418,560 acres. Practically all the land included in the present limits of Wisconsin, part of Minnesota, and the northern peninsula of Michigan is not included in these figures. Calhoun's report, *American State Papers, Indian Affairs*, II, 542–47.

[40] Agent John Johnston, already in 1826 engaged in removing some of the tribes, expressed the idea in a letter to the *Piqua Gazette:* "The frequent removal of the Natives of the soil to make way for our population, and the consequent distress and misery entailed upon their race, calls loudly upon Congress to provide for them a country, from which they will not again have to be removed."

tinct step towards the solution of the Indian problem in the Northwest, but the arrangements at Prairie du Chien had hardly been made before the advance pickets of the squatter invaders were penetrating the Indian country.[41]

Into these lands, ahead of the squatters if possible, came the surveyors:

> Strange men with chain and compass came at last
> Among the hills, across the valley pass'd;
> Through field and woodland, pasture, orchard, they
> Turn'd not aside, but kept straight on their way.[42]

Extinguishment of Indian title, surveying, land sale—these were the steps necessary to take the public domain from the hands of the Indian into those of the settlers. It was impossible for the surveying to keep ahead of, or even up with, settlement, for the surveyors had to survey all the land, much of which was often of no interest to the buyer, while the settler, keen on the best location, hitch-hopped on past in irregular waves of advance. Furthermore, as a result of the Indian cessions not being contiguous, the surveys were made piecemeal, and in units of various sizes and shapes.

The direction of the surveys under the Land Ordinance of 1785 was given to the geographer of the United States—after 1796 the surveyor-general—who was empowered to form regulations and issue instructions.[43] Starting at the point of intersection of the Pennsylvania boundary and the Ohio River the "geographer's line" was run forty-two miles west, and this together with a north and south line running through the same point, constituted the basis for survey of the first seven ranges. Working from these lines, ranges of townships were laid off, and the townships subdivided into lots (sections) one mile square. Sections were numbered from south to north in each row, starting in the southeast corner. All lines were to be run by the true

---

[41] For later cessions and settlement of this region, see Chapter X. The invasion of the permanent Indian country by traders, immigrants, and settlers, the breakdown of this policy, the wars which followed, the last battle between white man and red for the continent—constitute a later chapter in the history of our country.

[42] Piatt, *Idyls and Lyrics of the Ohio Valley*, 80.

[43] By law in 1812 the General Land Office, headed by a commissioner, was established in the Treasury Department and all matters concerning the public lands were assigned to it. In 1849, the office was transferred to the newly created Department of the Interior.

meridian, and the variation of the magnetic needle noted, but difficulties soon brought a modification in the rule, and magnetic bearings were used.[44] All lines were to be measured by chain,[45] marked by chops on the trees, described on a plot; notes were to be made in the field notebooks of mines, salt licks, mill seats, and the nature of the land. Correction for convergence of the meridians was not provided for. This omission was to be supplied and the scheme of numbering sections in the townships to be changed for later surveys.[46] Only the seven ranges were surveyed under the Ordinance of 1785.

Lying along the Ohio to the west of the seven ranges was the Ohio Company grant. Although Congress had provided that the land should be laid out according to the Ordinance of 1785, the company used a system of survey which it thought would better provide for division of its tract into 822 shares of 1,173 acres each, each share to consist of six lots varying in size from 37/100 of an acre to 640 acres. The result naturally was a very confusing modification of the rectangular survey system as applied to the seven ranges.[47]

Bounding the Ohio Company grant on the north and west were the Congress lands, added by the Treaty of Greenville in 1795. Here the rectangular survey of 1785 was followed but the numbering system was quite irregular. The new scheme for numbering sections as provided for in the law of 1796 was followed.

[44] Christopher E. Sherman, *Original Ohio Land Subdivisions* (*Ohio Topographic Survey, Final Report*, III, Ohio State Reformatory, 1925), 42. Resolution of May 12, 1786, in *Journals of the Continental Congress, 1774–1789* (34 volumes. Library of Congress ed., Washington, D. C., 1904–37), XXX, 262. The history, instructions, and methods of surveys are best covered in Lowell O. Stewart, *Public Land Surveys; History, Instruction, Methods* (Ames, Iowa, 1935). The use of the compass led to many difficulties and errors in the early surveys. As a result of an accident to a magnetic compass, William Austin Burt, of Michigan, invented the solar compass about 1836. George H. Cannon, "The Life and Times of William A. Burt," in *Michigan Pioneer and Historical Collections*, V (1882), 118. Although not called to the attention of surveyors by the surveyor-general at Cincinnati until 1841, it was used prior to that date.

[45] First chains were by law two-perch chains (16½ feet to the perch), but by regulation of 1815 measurements were reckoned in four-perch chains of 66 feet, or 80 to the mile. See Stewart, *Public Land Surveys,* 115 ff., for changes in regulations regarding measurements.

[46] See map, 117. The convergence of two meridians six miles apart in 60 miles (10 townships) at latitude 40° is about 400 feet. The Ohio surveys were completed before provision for correction for convergence was made. The modern system of correction lines every four townships—"twenty-four mile tracts"—was set forth in the instructions of 1855.

[47] William E. Peters, *Ohio Lands and Their Subdivisions* (2d ed., Athens, Ohio, 1918), 251.

I. The Seven Ranges II. Ohio Company Purchase III. Congress
Lands by Greenville Treaty IV. United States Military District
V. Virginia Military District VI. Symmes Purchase VII. Connecti-
cut Western Reserve VIII. Clark's Grant IX. Old French Grants

To the north of the Ohio grant and the Congress tract lay the United States military lands, reserved for Continental soldiers by the law of June 1, 1796. The law provided for survey into townships five miles square, and ranges were numbered westward from the seven ranges.

Along the west side of the Scioto lay the Virginia military district, reserved by Virginia for her own soldiers, when she ceded her lands north of the Ohio. Here the system of indiscriminate surveys constituted a crazy patchwork.[48] Symmes' grant between the Miamis was surveyed with a system not duplicated elsewhere in the United States.[49] It had "two crooked rivers as its initial lines, one from which the ranges are numbered north, and the other from which the townships are numbered east." Fractional ranges were also provided for. Symmes started the scheme and government surveyors continued it on north between the Miami rivers.

West of Symmes' lands the meridian through the mouth of the Miami was used, and the same line was extended northward for surveys in the areas in Ohio acquired after 1817, but with the 41st degree as base line. All told in Ohio six different survey districts were used in addition to the private surveys in the Ohio Company and Symmes' grants, Connecticut reserve, and irregular surveys in the Virginia military reserve.[50]

When survey of the Indian cession of 1803 around Vincennes was contemplated, uncertainty of the lines corresponding to the surveys east of the Greenville line led to the laying out of a new meridian and base line. For later surveys of the Northwest three more principal meridians and another base line were added (Michigan-Wisconsin).[51] Thus was begun the system of great lines used not only for the Northwest but, excepting Texas, for the rest of the United States thereafter surveyed.

As the various survey districts were laid off, the surveyor-

[48] See, for instance, plates five and six in Sherman, *Ohio Land Subdivisions.*
[49] *Ibid.,* 69.
[50] As a result of the irregular shapes and sizes of the five-mile townships in the Western Reserve (and in the United States military lands), there was no regular method of subdividing the townships into sections. For details of this complicated business, see Sherman, *Ohio Land Subdivisions.* Maps of each section, a large sectional map of Ohio, survey methods, instructions, and records are here assembled. See also Charles Whittlesey, *Ohio Surveys (Western Reserve Historical Society Tracts,* II, No. 59, Cleveland, September, 1883), and *Surveys of the Public Lands in Ohio,* in *ibid.,* II, No. 61, July, 1884.
[51] See map, 117.

general awarded the contracts to deputies and Congress fixed the compensation. By the law of 1796 the whole expense of surveying was not to exceed $3.00 per acre. The surveyor-general laid down the instructions, administered the oaths, and had the power of removal for negligence or misconduct.

With base line and meridian established for a given district, the crew of deputy surveyors, chainmen, and axmen, working from the intersection, began the survey. The surveyor ran the north and south line with his instrument, the axmen cleared a path for vision, blazed trees on the line, and the chainmen followed to measure the distance. On hilly ground care had to be taken to measure horizontal length and not surface length, and if the stretch was very steep, the chain had to be doubled and half length used to keep the downhill end within reach of the chainman. When ponds, swamps, rivers, and other obstacles presented, it was necessary to take offsets or work by traverse or trigonometry, to ascertain the distance on any line not run. At the end of 40 chains or a half mile, the quarter-section stake was set and located in the field notebook by distance and directions from two witness trees which were properly notched. At the end of a mile the section stake was set, four corners to the cardinal points of the compass, and notches cut on north and south sides to indicate number of miles from the township line; it was located by two witness trees properly marked and described in the field book, or in prairie land by mounds of earth. At the end of the sixth mile the township stake was witnessed by four trees, one in each section, with proper description thereon.

The crew then returned to the starting point, worked west on the east and west line, and ran the line as before. At the end of six miles the survey turned north and ran the western boundary of the township, endeavoring the while to keep it parallel with the meridian. At the end of another six miles it remained only to run the fourth side of the township, which, after 1800 would properly be done by going back to the east-side boundary and running the line west. Only by accident would the end of the fourth line fall at the stake at the northern end of the west boundary, for by convergence of meridians, two range lines six miles apart at the beginning would be more than forty feet closer together six miles farther north. The surveyor probably ran a random line, noted the amount of error in his notebook, then set the stakes so as to close the line at the northwest post, in this way complying with the law of 1800, which required that the excess or deficiency, especially noted, should be added to or deducted from the western and northern sections or half sections of the township.[52]

In this way the Congressional township was laid out. North and south rows of townships were known as ranges, and an individual township was located by meridian and base line, as, for example, T 2 N, R 1 W. In the first surveys interior lines of the section were not run but were later provided for by the laws of 1796 and 1800. The system of numbering of sections in a township from the northeast corner to the west and back east on the second row was adopted in 1796. Detailed instructions for subdividing townships were provided for by Edward Tiffin, surveyor-general for lands north of the Ohio from 1814 to 1829. Courses of navigable streams were to be surveyed, and the plot of the township accurately protracted on durable paper on a scale of two inches to the mile, with a compass showing the true magnetic meridian in one corner.

Notwithstanding laws and instructions, the surveys were of necessity often very inaccurate. Surveyors were not always competent and occasionally, in spite of their oaths, did hasty or poor work, or even none at all, with the result that land had to be resurveyed when the fraud was discovered.[53] At times the

[52] This description of method is a general or composite one. Methods varied according to the different laws from 1785 on, and the instructions issued. For description of general method, see *Niles' Weekly Register*, XII, 97–101 (Apr. 12, 1817), part of which is reproduced in Treat, *National Land System*, 91–94; Jerome S. Higgins, *Subdivisions of the Public Lands* . . . (St. Louis, 1894); Sherman, *Ohio Land Subdivisions*, in which are the various land laws applying to the surveys, instructions, diagrams, and descriptions of present system of survey; Stewart, *Public Land Surveys;* "The Public Domain and Its Survey," in Report of the Land Department, Indiana *Documentary Journal*, 1892, part I, 270–86. C. S. Woodard, "The Public Domain, Its Surveys and Surveyors," in *Michigan Pioneer and Historical Collections*, XXVII (1896), 306–23, gives the methods and life of the crews.

[53] An example of nepotism and profiteering is the case of William Rector, surveyor-general of Illinois, Missouri, and Arkansas, 1814 to 1824. He was accused of giving the best contracts to relatives who sublet the contracts to surveyors and pocketed the difference. He was investigated by Congress, accused openly by Joshua Barton, attorney general of Missouri, in the St. Louis *Missouri Republican* and indicted for murder after he killed his accuser in a duel. *American State Papers, Public Lands*, III, 618–20, IV, 19–25; *Illinois Historical Collections*, IX, 56–57; John Reynolds, *Pioneer History of Illinois, Containing the Discovery, in 1673, and the History of the Country to the Year Eighteen Hundred and Eighteen* . . . (Belleville, 1852), 353–54; Buck (ed.), "Pioneer Letters," in *Transactions of the Illinois State Historical Society*, 1910, p. 160, note 66.

compensation was entirely too low, but government accountants showed little appreciation of local difficulties and were reluctant to allow additional compensation. Townships were not always six miles square nor did sections always contain 640 acres, but it was impossible for the buyer who got the small-sized lots to secure rebates for land lost as a result of errors.[54] Records of plots were at first transmitted to the Board of Treasury, but by the law of 1796 copies were kept for public information in the surveyor-general's office and at the places of sale. Later the General Land Office took charge of all records and many were distributed to the governments of the states in which the land lay.

In addition to the practical and administrative difficulties of the survey there was the problem of confirmation of foreign titles. Around Vincennes, Detroit, and Kaskaskia were French settlers who claimed lands by various sorts of titles, some granted by the King, some by French governors, some by local commandants, others by Indian cession.[55] Records were imperfect or nonexistent, scraps of paper were lost, and oral testimony had frequently to be accepted in lieu of documents. Around Vincennes matters were further complicated by the illegal granting of lands, mostly to its own members, by the Virginia court which was in charge of civil and military affairs between 1779 and 1783. Congress by various laws made provision for review of titles, and grants to those who had what seemed to be reasonably valid French or British titles. In cases where the original lands were not available, reserves were laid aside.[56] Until these various claims were disposed of, it was impossible to survey and offer for sale lands adjacent to the regions concerned. Other trouble resulted from the uncertainty of boundaries of the grants to individuals or companies, such as the Symmes tract, between the Little and Big Miami rivers.

Life of the surveying gangs while on field work was of necessity

[54] By the law of 1800 the western and northern rows of sections were recognized to be short or over, but other sections were to be sold as of 640 acres; by the law of 1805, tracts were to be sold as of the area specified in the surveyors' returns.

[55] In Michigan Territory the Governor and Judges were constituted a land board by law of 1806, to handle the tangled land claims there. See M. Agnes Burton (ed.), *Proceedings of the Land Board of Detroit* (Detroit, 1915).

[56] Treat, *The National Land System*, Chapter IX, gives a brief review of this complicated problem. See also Leonard Lux, *The Vincennes Donation Lands* (*Indiana Historical Society Publications*, XV, No. 4, Indianapolis, 1949).

hard and primitive. In some respects it was worse than that of scout, hunter, or trapper, for whereas these advance pickets utilized the streams and trails and avoided the swamps, hills, and tangled growths, the surveyor had to traverse all. A rude lean-to camp or tent provided shelter, and barrels of flour, salt pork, beans, some dried fruit, coffee, sugar, saleratus, tea, and such items, supplemented by game in the woods, constituted the usual food. Equipment was necessary for months of living in the woods, and blankets, axes, frying pans, eating utensils, soap, pails, and other paraphernalia were as necessary as chains, instruments, compasses, notebooks, pens, and ink. A general depot once located, from which supplies might be packed by horse or boat, the temporary camp moved with the party. Grass or evergreen boughs made bunks to which tired muscles retired early. Camp cooking was of the cruder sort, and confined to early morning and late evening hours, while midday refreshment would probably consist of a piece of salt pork cooked on a stick, some bread, and a hot drink.[57]

By law of 1830 Congress sought to protect the surveyor against interference or interruption by any individual. Any obstructionary tactic was made a misdemeanor punishable by a fine of from $50 to $300 and imprisonment of at least three years. If necessary, Federal marshals were to provide sufficient force to protect the surveyor.

Surveying was a profession much respected, probably more so than school teaching. The surveyor's work directly concerned more people, and the elementary mathematics required put it beyond the reach of most and provided it with an element of mystery. Even though few were so fortunate as was George Washington in their fees, it was a career which fathers held up as an incentive when their sons fought their arithmetic. In 1824 when Baynard Hall met his first class in the embryonic academy in the woods—later to become Indiana University—the little group of more or less barefoot boys were frankly disappointed that it was Latin and Greek rather than "surveyin' and book-

[57] Capt. Hervey Parke, "Reminiscences," in *Michigan Pioneer and Historical Collections*, III (1879-80), 572-90; Cannon, "The Life and Times of William A. Burt, of Mt. Vernon, Michigan," in *ibid.*, V, 115-23; and Woodard, "The Public Domain," in *ibid.*, XXVIII, 306-23, give accounts of the surveyor's life and work.

keepin' " which they were to master. In the absence of technical schools or even applied science courses the surveyor learned his job by manuals and experience. Most surveyors were self-educated or, like the doctors, served for a while with someone already practicing the art. Among the manuals which were widely used at one time or another were Robert Gibson, *A Treatise on Practical Surveying . . .*, which went through various American editions from 1803 to 1835; Abel Flint, *A System of Geometry and Trigonometry: together with a treatise on surveying . . .* (Hartford, various editions, 1804–35); John Gummere, *A Treatise on Surveying . . . to which is affixed a perspicuous system of plane trigonometry* (Philadelphia, various editions, 1817–53); and Frederic Walter Simms, *A Treatise on the Principles and Practice of Levelling . . .* (Baltimore, 1837, etc.).

§ §

Following the hard times and economic troubles of embargo days and the war years came one of the periodic waves of inflation, speculation, and prosperity which in alternation with periods of depression and readjustment, have paraded across our economic history. Foreign commerce of the United States which in the year ending September 30, 1814, had totaled less than $20,000,000, increased the next year to $152,000,000, and in 1816 to $194,000,000, with imports being about twice the value of exports. Though specie was scarce, money became plentiful. The second Bank of the United States, by questionable practice, permitted stock-jobbing, speculation and manipulation, and extended its circulation beyond sound limits.[58] State banks, which in 1816 numbered 246, by 1818 had increased to 392, and their notes flooded the country.[59] Bank-note circulation in 1812 was $45,000,000, in 1817, $100,000,000.[60] Calhoun, supporting the establishment of a United States Bank in 1816, violently attacked

[58] Note circulation, 1817, $1,911,000; 1818, $8,339,000. See Chapter VIII.
[59] See McMaster, *History of the People of the United States,* IV, 485, for list by states.
[60] Dewey, *Financial History of the United States,* 144; William Graham Sumner, *A History of American Currency . . .* (New York, 1874), 80.

the state banks and accused them of circulating $170,000,000 of bank notes with not more than $15,000,000 of specie on hand. ". . . banks have been incorporated, not because there was capital seeking investment," said William H. Crawford, secretary of the treasury, "not because the places where they were established had commerce and manufactures which required their fostering aid; but because men without active capital wanted the means of obtaining loans, which their standing in the community would not command from banks or individuals having real capital and established credit."[61] In addition were the issues of scrip, "shinplasters," and "tickets" by business firms, contractors, and even counties.[62]

In this state of inflation and apparent prosperity, fictitious values were placed on everything, and town booming, improvements, commerce, and land speculation were naturally encouraged. The western farmer, as well as the mechanic and the merchant, shared in the profits.

In Ohio where improved land near Cincinnati was spoken of as worth $50 an acre, $30 was asked for unimproved, while in Illinois some of the land but recently put under cultivation was priced at $5.00 to $12 and was expected to reach $30 shortly. Even the seasons and unfavorable weather helped contribute to the high prices of produce. From 1816 to 1818 corn sold around 50 cents, wheat $1.00 to $1.50, oats 50 cents, flour $6.50 to $12, depending on transportation, potatoes 50 cents to $1.00, beef $3.50 to $5.00 per hundred, pork $4.00 to $7.00, bacon 10 cents to 12 cents, butter 25 cents to 50 cents, and whiskey 50 to 60 cents a gallon.[63]

These were the years of the unprecedented rush of settlers into the Northwest, and "a land office business" became enough of a reality in the minds of Americans to linger as a descriptive phrase long after the average citizen ceased to know what a

[61] *American State Papers, Finance* (5 volumes. Washington, D. C., 1832–59), III, 494.

[62] See Chapter VIII.

[63] *Niles' Weekly Register*, XII, 144 (Apr. 26, 1817); Fearon, *Sketches of America*, 260; Buck (ed.), "Pioneer Letters of Gershom Flagg," in *Transactions of the Illinois State Historical Society*, 1910, p. 162; *Western Herald and Steubenville Gazette*, May 16, 1818; Chillicothe *Scioto Gazette*, November 28, 1816. For more extended treatment of prices, trade, etc., see Chapter VIII.

land office was.[64] Although sales at the Steubenville office, 1816–17, fell off about 100 per cent from the preceding year, and those at Marietta and Zanesville declined, those at Shawneetown registered a gain, at Jeffersonville and Kaskaskia doubled, and at Vincennes rose from 53,000 to 325,000 acres. The office at Edwardsville, Illinois, just opened, sold 104,000 acres. Total annual sales north of the Ohio, which in 1814 were 823,264 acres, in 1816 were 1,131,956, in 1817, 1,414,952, and by 1819 were 2,064,177 acres. Unpaid balances in 1814 were $2,134,989 but the next year were more than $3,163,936, in 1817 more than $5,627,797, and in 1819 had run up to $9,868,295. By the last-named year the average sale price had risen to $3.16 an acre. It was now that the hard times came, the makeshift relief policy of Congress proved inadequate, and burdens began to weigh so heavily on the West that finally the United States government, both in the interest of its own fiscal policy and the welfare of its citizens, was brought to effect a major change in its land policy.

The price to be paid for inflation, speculation, high prices, and abnormal profits is depression, stagnation, and hard times, and the effects are seemingly as bad whether the country be preponderantly agricultural or industrial in its interests. In 1819 came our first major financial and economic depression.[65] The causes, as always, were varied and complex, and easier seen and understood in retrospect than at the time. Manufacturing, in spite of the inflation, had not shared appreciably in the wider prosperity of postwar days, and had been unable to recover the position gained under stimulus of the embargo and war. Pittsburgh, intimately connected financially and economically with the West, had felt depression to a certain extent ever since the

[64] Total sales of the public domain in 1814 were 864,536 acres, more than a fourth more than any year since 1796. In 1819, 4,342,222 acres were sold, an amount not surpassed until 1834. As a result of bidding up of price, purchase-money receipts increased even more rapidly. From 1800 to 1813 the annual average receipts were $735,392, in 1814 they were $1,784,560—a 44 per cent increase over any other year —and, after twice doubling in the next four years, reached $14,645,547 in 1819. *American State Papers, Public Lands*, III, 420; *Finance*, III, 431; "Report from the Commissioner of the General Land Office showing the operations of that office during parts of the years 1839 and 1840," in *Senate Documents*, 26 Congress, 2 session, No. 61, p. 31.

[65] For an excellent brief discussion, see Samuel Rezneck, "The Depression of 1819–22, a Social History," in *American Historical Review*, XXXIX (1933–34), 28–47.

war. Tradesmen complained because ocean trade, which they
had almost monopolized during the war, was being thrown to
New Orleans.

The second Bank of the United States, chartered by law in
1816 to go into operation by April, 1817, had tried to restore
specie payment on the part of the state banks, but failed, and
instead entered into an agreement whereby it was forced to
make large loans whether justified or not, and which prevented
it from securing specie from the state banks, while the latter,
by presenting the notes of the Bank, could get specie from
it. In regions where there was no branch of the Bank of the
United States, the Treasury Department permitted state banks
to be used as "intermediate" places for deposit of government
funds collected by land-office agents. By the agreement between
Treasury and Bank, April, 1817, the Treasury did not designate
what kinds of money (notes) were acceptable but left this to
the Bank. The Bank apparently did not realize the extent of
its responsibility or liability in this matter until Secretary Crawford informed William Jones, president of the Bank, that the
Bank was responsible for all money deposited in the appointed
state banks. The Bank thereupon, to protect itself, abandoned
the agreement.

President Jones's successor, Langdon Cheeves, believed the
Treasury, rather than the Bank, should risk the odium of select-
ing what currency (bank notes) was acceptable,[66] but was unable
to get it to do so. State banks were permitted to over trade and
inflate the currency by the extension of loans up to midsummer
of 1818. Within a few months, however, the Bank was called
upon to pay the price of its mismanagement, stock manipulation,
speculation, and fraud, and was struggling to save itself, with
$22,372,000 of demand liabilities and $2,357,000 of specie on
hand. Drastic measures were necessary. The Bank declared that
its agreement with the state banks would terminate on June 30,
1818, and ordered its cashier to receive nothing as cash except

[66] For fuller discussion of the Bank's relation to western banks see below, Chapter VIII. Good brief summary of the subject may be found in John T. Holdsworth
and Davis Rich Dewey, *The First and Second Banks of the United States* (*Publications of Monetary Commission*, IV, Washington, D. C., 1910) and Catterall,
Second Bank of the United States. Most of the documents may be found in *American State Papers, Finance*, IV.

specie and its own notes.[67] The Bank's policy of curtailment of issues, refusal to accept state bank notes as before, and calling of loans, brought the enmity of the state banks and the wrath of the people down upon its head. The effect was almost immediate. Deflation and hard times were at hand.

Inseparable from the currency troubles was the government's arrangement concerning payment on the land purchases. Early in 1818 when the Senate inquired into the expediency of further extending the time for making payments, the Secretary of the Treasury replied that delinquency was due to the inundation of the country by a paper currency which did not possess the essential properties of a circulating medium. For more than a year the paper of all incorporated banks which ostensibly discharged their notes in specie had been accepted by the receivers of public money, until more than a million of bills not current had piled up in the treasury. The hope that in time the banks would redeem their promises was not realized; the receivers of public moneys were instructed to receive in payment of taxes and for lands nothing but current specie, bills of the Bank of the United States and its branches, of state and local banks used as depositories, "and the bills of such other banks as will be received by them and credited as specie for the use of the United States." Secretary Crawford estimated that these other specie-paying banks numbered about one hundred, and that no hardship would be inflicted on land purchasers except in those sections where the unsound local banks had driven out the notes of specie-paying banks.[68]

But these sections included the very regions where the land purchases had been heaviest. At the Steubenville Land Office, with the bulk of the bank notes not acceptable, little or no money was being received even as early as 1817.[69] Bank delegates from Ohio, Indiana, and Kentucky had met at Cincinnati in March and promised to resume specie payments within a few weeks, but

[67] *American State Papers, Finance,* V, 69.
[68] Crawford's report to the Senate Committee on Finance, in *ibid.,* III, 263.
[69] *Western Herald and Steubenville Gazette,* February 28, 1817. "More Oppression," cried the *Gazette,* when the land-office receiver had orders from the Treasury Department to accept only money which the Bank of the United States would accept. It called this discrimination against Ohio banks. March 17, 1818, February 27, 1819.

as banks called in loans, trade declined, agriculture suffered, and markets became deserted. Farmers would rather keep their produce than accept wildcat notes, and tradesmen protested against the condemnation of unchartered banks, as well as oppression on the part of the government which showed partiality in receiving some paper but refusing other. "All men are created equal," said they, and now the government was taking away the means of livelihood; the colonies had revolted from England for such reasons.

The contraction of loans and deflation undertaken in the latter half of 1818 resulted in general bankruptcy in the South and West. Probably at no other time in our history was the fall in commodity prices and real estate so precipitate as in 1818–19.[70] At Pittsburgh manufactories which employed 1,960 persons and produced $2,617,000 worth of goods in 1815, declined to 672 employees and $832,000 value in 1820. The iron foundries and glass works were in a bad way. No money was to be seen and there was little credit or business. Only the auctioneer had plenty to do. "God send us better times."[71] At Cincinnati, where in July, 1818, the Bank ordered its branch to collect 20 per cent of the balances due from the state banks each month, conditions became precarious, and the banks suspended specie payment.[72] Other Ohio banks followed suit and by January, 1819, only two or three banks in Ohio were still on a specie basis. It was a case of "save himself who can." Credit was at an end and universal distress prevailed.[73] It was said that more than half of the business property of the city, now near 10,000 in population, would have been foreclosed at the block had there offered any buyers.

[70] Theodore Elijah Burton, *Financial Crises and Periods of Industrial and Commercial Depressions* (New York, 1902), 276. The decline in stocks, real estate, and commodity prices, following the crash of 1929, lasted three years. The stock decline during the last half of 1937 may have been as great as the price decline of the latter part of 1818, but the decline in commodity prices was slight.

[71] In addition to newspapers, Fearon (1817), Evans (1818), Adlard Welby (1819), and other travelers commented upon the decline at Pittsburgh.

[72] *Liberty Hall and Cincinnati Gazette*, November 11, 1818; *Western Herald and Steubenville Gazette*, November 28, 1818.

[73] Flint, *History and Geography of the Mississippi Valley*, I, 180; Charles Theodore Greve, *Centennial History of Cincinnati and Representative Citizens* (Chicago, 1904), 570 ff.; G. A. Worth (cashier of Cincinnati Branch) to Thomas Sloo, in *Quarterly Publications of the Historical and Philosophical Society of Ohio*, VI, No. 2 (April–June, 1911), 32.

By September the notes of sixteen Ohio banks were refused in payment of state taxes; two months later the land office at Cincinnati was ordered to accept nothing but specie and United States notes in payment for land, and the sale of land practically ceased.[74] When the legislative committee on banking reported, it largely exonerated the state banks and blamed rather the Bank of the United States and branches for drainage of specie to the East and resulting stringency.[75] Speculators often were able to get out from under in time, leaving the farmer and mechanic in possession of bank notes which at the end of the year were not even listed in the discount table in Grotjans' *Price Current*, or acceptable at Philadelphia on any terms whatsoever. The notes of Steubenville, Marietta, Zanesville, Cincinnati, and Chillicothe banks were quoted at 15 to 20 per cent discount.[76] The legislature made discounting of bank notes a misdemeanor finable to the extent of $500.[77]

The effects on trade were disastrous. A trader, short of capital, desiring to ship produce to New Orleans, drew a bill for sixty or ninety days on the New Orleans trading house in anticipation of sale and discounted it at his local bank. Then he bought up the goods and flatboated them down the river. But his bill having preceded him and being already in the hands of his buyer, he was offered but half price for his produce, under the assumption that he had to sell. Consequently, the honest trader as well as the speculator was seriously hurt. "This is how the operation, so much praised, of branch bank facilities, works out."[78] Specie had been drained from the West. Two wagon-loads started from the United States branch at Chillicothe to Philadelphia in November, all drawn from Ohio and neighboring banks.[79] In February, 1819, the steamboat *Perseverance* left Cincinnati with $400,000 in specie and thirty passengers. It was

---

[74] *Niles' Weekly Register*, XV, 59 (Sep. 19, 1818); *Liberty Hall and Cincinnati Gazette*, November 17, 1818; *Western Herald and Steubenville Gazette*, September 26, November 28, 1818. "Uncle Sam of course stands a good chance of having a fine crop of forfeited land coming to him in a short time." *Ibid.*, December 5, 1818.

[75] *Western Herald and Steubenville Gazette*, February 18, 1819.

[76] *Ibid.*, January 9, 30, 1819.

[77] Chillicothe *Supporter*, February 14, 1819.

[78] Frankfort *Argus* quoted in *ibid.*, April 28, 1819.

[79] *Liberty Hall and Cincinnati Gazette*, November 24, 1818; *Niles' Weekly Register*, XVI, 256 (June 5, 1819).

estimated that $800,000 was drawn from Ohio for the Bank of the United States from midsummer of 1818 to June, 1819.[80]

As a result of the scarcity of specie, small notes issued by traders in denominations of 25 cents, redeemable in dry goods or drinks, and cut money were eagerly accepted. Spanish pistareens worth about 18 cents, cut into six pieces, circulated at twice that value, and Spanish dollars were cut, like a pie, into halves, quarters, bits, and fips. Wheat, which had been $1.00 to $1.50 in 1816, was quoted locally at 20 cents to 75 cents; flour dropped to $2.50 to $3.00 per barrel; corn to 12 cents per bushel, whiskey to 12½ cents; beef sold at $1.00 to $3.00 per hundred, eggs 3 to 5 cents per dozen, chickens 37½ to 75 cents per dozen, pork $1.25 to $1.75 per hundred, butter 6 cents, and other things in proportion.[81] Bargains were available for those fortunate enough to have a little money, for at auctions anything from a "very handsome gig and valuable horse," to imported carpets might go at $3.00 to $4.00. "All things are changed, the rich have become poor, and the poor distrust, one universal state of embarrassment exists; tis want, and fear and prosecution and suspicion and terror and dismay and bankruptcy and pauperism on all sides and on all hands," wrote Gorham A. Worth, cashier of the Cincinnati branch of the Bank.[82] Real estate had had its day, he thought, and those who had built upon that foundation had built on sand. As for his Illinois lands, "if there is a prospect of selling those land lots, etc., for Godsake *sell* them!"

But to sell anything meant a sacrifice, for half value was the best one could hope to get. The newspapers from all parts of the Union gave evidence of the most unexampled pressure and commercial embarrassment. "Never within the recollection of our oldest citizens has the aspect of the times, as it respects property and money, been so alarming." "The western country at the present moment exhibits a feature truly gloomy to those who

[80] *Niles' Weekly Register,* XVI, 298 (June 26, 1819).
[81] Chillicothe *Supporter,* autumn, 1818, 1819; *Liberty Hall and Cincinnati Gazette;* Cincinnati *Western Spy;* Vincennes *Western Sun;* William Faux, *Memorable Days,* 315, 339; Perret Dufour, "Early Vevay," in *Indiana Magazine of History,* XX (1924), 312; Buck (ed.), "Pioneer Letters of Gershom Flagg," in *Transactions of the Illinois State Historical Society,* 1910, p. 162.
[82] Worth to Thomas Sloo, Jr., August 2, 1820, in *Quarterly Publications of the Historical and Philosophical Society of Ohio,* VI, No. 2, p. 32.

were acquainted with her in the halcyon days of 1813–14."[83]
In fact, conditions were so bad that even the General Assembly
of the Presbyterian Church felt it necessary to take a stand and
publish its views. It believed that the times were the result of
the spirit of cupidity, of adventurous and unjustifiable speculation, of extravagance and luxury, which prevailed in the land,
as well as of the want of that kind of education which is calculated to prepare youth for solid usefulness in the church and
civil society. The remedy was a return, under God, to the principles of Holy Religion.[84] About the only redeeming feature
in the whole state of affairs was the hope that the country would
be saved from a general breaking up as a result of the desire to
go still farther west and to speculate.[85]

Others were not so sure, however. The reversions of land to
the United States in 1819 totaled 365,000 acres, of which
153,000 acres lay in the Northwest, an amount more than double
that of any year excepting the first two years of the war.[86] The
money paid into the Treasury, including previous installments
due, fell $1,146,000 short of the legal minimum due on land
sold that year. By December 31, 1820, the balances due had
risen to $21,213,350, a sum equal to more than one fifth of
the national debt.[87] Of this amount $6,610,924 was for land
in the Northwest. A series of articles which appeared over the
name of "Dion" in the *Liberty Hall and Cincinnati Gazette*[88]
not only attacked the "Great Mammoth of the East," the Bank,
but blamed most of the ills of the western country upon the
unwise and ungenerous policy of the General Government towards
the West, a policy the result either of unpardonable ignorance
or willful neglect. By counting in land payments as revenue, the
author showed how much higher the West was taxed than the
East, and stated that most of the revenue was spent in the East—

[83] Chillicothe *Supporter*, July 30, 1819; *Western Herald and Steubenville Gazette*,
May 15, 1819, July 22, 1820, and extracts from *Alexandria Herald, Pittsburg
Gazette*, Frankfort *Argus*, etc., quoted therein.
[84] Chillicothe *Supporter*, July 7, 1819; *Western Herald and Steubenville Gazette*,
July 3, 1819.
[85] *Liberty Hall and Cincinnati Gazette*, September 10, 1819.
[86] *American State Papers, Public Lands*, III, 420. These figures do not agree with
those given in *American State Papers, Finance*, III, 431. See table I at end of
this chapter.
[87] *American State Papers, Public Lands*, IV, 795. Total sales to June 30, 1820,
were estimated at $45,811,842. *American State Papers, Finance*, III, 561–62.
[88] May, 1819. Copied widely in other papers.

in 1818 not one million of $26,000,000 income being spent elsewhere. The writer in the *London Quarterly Review* who had predicted a division of the United States at the line of the Alleghenies was criticized for British enmity; nevertheless, the West had every right to expect reasonable treatment at the hands of the government.

Another article from the western viewpoint rated speculation as the one big cause of the sad state of things and said that "the banks had conspired with the government to promote it; the former by lending money to the speculators, and the latter by its wretched system of selling the land on credit." Most of the money paid went over the mountains and this evil would continue to operate, with increasing force, as long as the credit system continued. But in addition to the debts, bankruptcies, and temporary economic setbacks, there was a larger danger behind the credit system: it threatened the dissolution of the Union. Debts would continue to accumulate year after year. No motive was a more powerful influence on the human mind than that of interest. A government owing its people money was certain of their support. Reverse the status and the effect would be reversed also. Let numberless individuals, of all classes, be deeply indebted to the government of the Union, will they not very naturally become disaffected? The writer continued:

Let nine tenths of these persons reside in a particular section of the union; let that section be pre-eminently well situated for the formation of a separate government; let the existence of the debt depend on the continuance of the union; let the doctrine be advanced and enforced by every press and every orator in that quarter, that the other states had no just and natural right to the property for which the debt was incurred, while those states insist rigidly on an enforcement of the collection; and where will the bonds be found sufficiently strong to hold us together? They do not exist! No people are more patriotic and firmly attached to the government of the union than those of the west; the idea of a separation has never been indulged; it is literally abhorred; but their patriotism and fidelity are not invincible. When it becomes their interest to separate, the plausible arguments and motives by which it may be enforced are numerous and powerful, and will render its influence irresistible. Let not, therefore, the general government credit the people of the west to the amount of fifty or a hundred millions of dollars, if it would not foolishly drive them into a declaration of independence; for that will inevitably be the result—The Rubicon is not yet passed; but we now stand upon the shore, and it depends on the measures to be adopted by the next congress, whether we shall remain a peaceful, happy and united people, or advance, with a steady and certain pace, to civil war and a dissolution of the union.[89]

Congress could no longer ignore the situation. A relief law of 1815 applied only to those who had purchased land between April 1, 1810, and April 1, 1811. No further action was taken until 1818, when time was extended, and laws of 1819 and 1820 moved the forfeiture date up to March 31, 1821. As these laws often applied to different purchasers, they had by no means prevented considerable forfeiture. The Senate in 1819 passed Senator Morrow's bill which provided for cash sales in parcels of eighty acres, minimum price $1.50, but the bill died in the House. In December the subject was again brought before Congress by resolutions to abolish the credit system, and the committee reported a bill. Amendments to permit the purchaser to turn in his lands for resale and get back the proceeds above the minimum price, and to give squatters pre-emption or first purchase rights to 160 acres, were voted down. Although Senator James Noble, of Indiana, presented a petition from the legislature of his state "praying that no law may be passed changing the terms of sale of public lands, and representing the injurious effects that such a law would have on the western States," a bill to abolish the credit system passed the Senate 31 to 7. Senators Benjamin Ruggles and William Trimble, of Ohio, and Waller Taylor, of Indiana, voted with the majority, but Noble, of Indiana, and Ninian Edwards, of Illinois, voted against the bill. No serious changes were made in the House, where the bill passed 133 to 23. Two-thirds of the negative votes were from western representatives. President Monroe signed the bill April 24, 1820.

Sentiment in the Northwest was divided as to the change. Besides Indiana's petition against the measure, Senator Edwards and Representative Daniel Pope Cook, of Illinois, both heartily in favor of the law which suspended forfeiture for nonpayment, opposed the cash law as detrimental to the settlement of the western country.[90] The Chillicothe *Supporter*[91] regretted that the method requiring cash payment had not been adopted sooner, as

[89] "Franklin," in the *Kentucky Reporter*, quoted in *Niles' Weekly Register*, XVII, 11 (Sep. 4, 1819).
[90] Letters of Edwards and Cook in *Edwardsville Spectator*, April 25, 1820.
[91] June 21, 1820.

the effects would certainly be salutary on the western country as well as on the Treasury. The Cincinnati *Western Spy* said the law affected somewhat the recent purchasers and that they would seem to be entitled to some sort of relief, ". . . and a relief can be granted, which, whilst it benefits, will also forever free Congress from that tiresome, constant, annual petition for procrastination of payments as they become due, both from real settlers and speculators, whether actuated by necessity or other motives."[92]

The land law of 1820, entitled "An act making further provision for the sale of Public Lands," was brief, but it constituted the most important piece of land legislation since the Ordinance of 1785. By its provisions the credit system was abolished, the price reduced to $1.25 per acre, and the size of the purchasable tract to eighty acres, or one-eighth section. No reverted lands were to be subject to private entry until they had first been offered at public sale.[93] About the only objection to the change was that it would check emigration and retard the growth of the western country. But with the reduction in price, only $100 in cash was required to get clear title to 80 acres, whereas under the credit system $80 was required to make merely one-fourth payment on a doubtful 160 acres. The essential object, a sure and permanent home, was still within reach of the poor man. The auction sale was still retained, as the practicability of a fixed price for all land, good and bad, as well as a system of local valuation, was doubted. Speculators and settlers with ready money could still get the best land, but as Senator Morrow said in 1819, "The idea of providing equal facility to the poor and to the rich by any regulation is incompatible with that of disposing of the land for a valuable consideration," and he might have added, impossible in any case.[94]

Discontinuance of credit sales put a stop to the piling up of the debt to the government, but there still remained the accumulated debt and the problem of its liquidation. Congress in a way was

---

[92] Quoted in *Edwardsville Spectator*, October 17, 1820.

[93] *Annals of Congress*, 16 Congress, 1 session, part II, 2578; U. S. *Statutes at Large*, III, 566; Treat, *National Land System*, 140–41.

[94] When states, by taxes, sought to force the speculator to sell his lands to settlers, complaints were made that said taxes were too hard on the "poor man." See argument between "Farmer" and "Rustic" in *Edwardsville Spectator*, August, 1820.

responsible, for the credit system, bank policy, embargo, and war were largely the products of Democratic Republican Congresses, and incidentally it was from the Republican areas that demands for relief were most insistent. One solution was to offer the purchaser title to the amount of land covered by payments made, providing he relinquish the remainder purchased. Many petitions came to Congress from the West in favor of this plan. The main objection was that the great number of purchasers of 1818–19 would have had to give up three fourths of their lands.

The law of March, 1821, offered three plans of relief: (1) Relinquishment of part of the purchase and application of payments made on that retained; (2) Payment of amount due, less 37½ per cent, thus putting the debtors on even footing with those buying at $1.25 per acre; (3) Further extension of credit.[95] The Illinois senators, Edwards and Thomas, were largely instrumental in getting the 37½ per cent discount, for they argued that relief of suffering should take precedence over "narrow considerations of interest [and] nice calculations of pecuniary profit."

The results were encouraging. Within seven months the balance due on all lands diminished by almost one half,[96] and on those north of the Ohio by more than a third. Progress continued during the following year, but slowed up perceptibly in 1823–24. The provisions of the law of 1821 were re-enacted in 1822 and 1823 for the benefit of those who had failed to take advantage of them. Those who had taken the further credit plan accounted for more than 3,588,588 acres on which $6,740,358 were due at the beginning of 1823, 2,189,573 acres and $3,037,629 being from the region north of the Ohio. Since nine tenths of the balance due was on land on which but one payment had been made, heavy forfeitures were certain. The acts of 1824 and 1826,

[95] U.S. *Statutes at Large,* III, 612. Five columns on the land relief law of 1821 were published in the *Liberty Hall and Cincinnati Gazette,* July 7, 1821, under the heading "Notice to Debtors to the United States on Public Lands." Western papers generally gave prominent space to the relief laws. As the deadlines approached on the period in which it was possible to discharge a $160 debt with $100, the warnings became frequent. See Columbus and Cincinnati papers, for instance, for August, 1822. Government notices of relinquished land sales also began to appear frequently.

[96] From $21,173,489 to $11,957,430. In the Northwest from $6,610,924 to $4,139,755. *American State Papers, Public Lands,* III, 645. The purchasers in the Northwest took advantage of the cash discount plan in greater numbers than in the Southwest, thus getting their land at or near the $1.25 price. Prices had never been bid up so high in this region, and there was probably more cash available than in Alabama.

in order to take care of this situation, permitted those who had tried the further credit plan to complete payment by one of the other plans of the law of 1821. More than $4,000,000 of unpaid balances were outstanding by the end of 1827. Eight years after the relief law of 1821, 687,000 acres further credited had reverted and $741,000 were forfeited, but only about 20 per cent of this amount was in the Northwest. To finish the liquidation, Congress by law in 1830 permitted pre-emption to those who had forfeited and completion of title on payment of $1.25 per acre in addition to what was already paid; in 1831 it gave patents to purchasers at less than $14, who had paid or would pay $1.25 an acre. Seventy per cent of the debt was taken care of by the relinquishment of 4,602,000 acres of land; about 15 per cent by cash and discounts; more than 6 per cent by abatement under the 1830 law; and the rest by reversions and other means.

Land sales fell off noticeably in 1820 and the years immediately following. Hard times were the principal cause, although the cash payment requirements of the law of 1820 no doubt played a part. In 1821 sales north of the Ohio totaled only 437,351 acres, and they hovered around the half million mark until 1829 when sales rose to 787,000 acres.[97] In 1830 the total was again near the one million mark. Within a few years the cycle was inclining towards another crest with its booming land sales and speculative fever.[98]

After 1820 the relief question ceased to have the importance it had held for almost a quarter of a century. The people had the land, the government had some money, and with returning prosperity both were hopeful of getting more. Pre-emption and cheap money then began to replace relief as questions foremost in the minds of people and politicians.

[97] The Brookville (Ind.) Land Office entered 200,000 acres in 1821 and the Delaware (Ohio) office 60,000. By 1829 the Crawfordsville (Ind.) office was far in the lead with sales of 203,000 acres.

A comparison of Tables II and III below indicates that sales just about balanced forfeitures between 1820 and 1825.

[98] See Chapter VIII.

TABLE I[99]
Table of Land Sales Northwest of the Ohio, 1800–1820*

	Acres	Dollars**	Acres Reverted
1800 and 1801	398,646	$ 834,887	
1802	340,009	680,019	
1803	181,068	398,161	
1804	373,611	772,851	
1805	619,266	1,235,953	
1806	473,211	1,001,358	
1807	284,180	588,610	
1808	195,579	423,444	
	2,865,573	$5,981,310	
1809	143,409	355,783	
1810	158,843	344,256	
1811	207,017	449,502	
1812	391,664	849,632	94,075
1813	239,980	560,810***	123,571
1814	823,264	1,702,016	33,648
	4,829,753	$10,210,310	
1815 (Oct., 1814— Sep., 1815)	1,092,979	2,285,680	42,435
1816	1,131,956	2,464,792	54,008
1817 (Oct., 1816— Sep., 1817)	1,414,952	3,090,868	79,287
1817 (Oct.–Dec.)	460,889	922,907	22,491
1818 (Jan.–Sep.)	1,245,106	2,571,336	46,221
1819 Oct., 1818— Sep., 1819)	2,064,178	4,939,659	153,309
	11,106,391	$23,446,016	575,527
1820 (to June)	68,268	$ 138,477	14,013

* The figures in general may show slight discrepancies because of the omission of fractions and cents.

** The amount in dollars is not listed for the years 1800-8 in *American State Papers, Finance*, III, 24, but is given in *Public Lands*, III, 420.

*** This amount is the adjusted figure found in *Public Lands*, III, 420, and throws off slightly the total as given in *Finance*, III, 24.

TABLE II[100]

Under the Credit System, 1800 to 1820, were sold:

	Acres	Dollars
In Ohio	8,848,152	$17,226,187
Indiana	2,490,736	5,137,350
Illinois	1,593,247	3,227,805
Michigan Territory	67,362	178,400

TABLE III[101]

Net amount of lands sold after deducting lands reverted and relinquished from 1787 to the end of 1825.

	Acres	Dollars	Remaining unsold
Ohio	8,778,715	$16,235,123	6,191,927
Indiana	3,068,868	5,611,197	12,131,461
Illinois	1,222,442	1,729,145	24,161,662
Michigan Territory	291,839	416,096	16,600,554

[99] *American State Papers, Finance*, III, 24, 39, 224, 284–85, 431, 561; *Public Lands*, III, 420.

[100] Donaldson, *The Public Domain*, 203.

[101] From Register's Office, Treasury Department, report of February 14, 1827, U. S. *Senate Documents*, 19 Congress, 2 session, No. 63.

IV

Pioneer Life—the Material Side

Amidst those forest shades that proudly rear'd
Their unshorn beauty toward the favoring skies,
An axe rang sharply. There, with vigorous arm
Wrought a bold emigrant.

PORTRAYAL of the life of a people at any time and in any place is a difficult task, one not easily performed by the skilled contemporary observer, more difficult still for the historian viewing at second hand and from a distance. One might list a thousand sample histories of the lives of representative pioneers; the result would be a tedious document. One might write an interesting composite description or generalization and the result not be accurate. Perhaps by a combination of specific material and the general description, it may be possible to approximate the actual, though the result be not exactly applicable to any large group or area over any length of time.

The materials for a study of home life among the early settlers are, in spite of their abundance, entirely inadequate. Family letters are few, and often disappointing when found; diaries and journals were seldom kept and less often preserved. Newspapers were scarce in the earlier period, and contained little or no local news or descriptive material aside from advertisements; magazines and contemporary descriptive literature were rare and libraries almost nonexistent. By far the bulkiest of the literature on pioneer life consists of the reminiscences of participants, written years later, or preserved from interviews with the authors and compilers of the older county and local histories. The accounts of earlier days as given in these reminiscences constitute an invaluable storehouse of materials on the everyday life of the settlers, but for the purposes of history they must be used with care. Like modern accounts in fiction and picture, they are usually subject to one of two tendencies. On the one hand will be the harsher or ultrarealistic viewpoint of pioneer life described in all its primitiveness, with its animal-like existence, its ills, diseases, ignorance, superstition; its narrowness, hardness, vulgarity, and crass sordidness. On the other is the slant so often created by time and distance which expresses itself in romanticism and over-idealization of the good old days, and glosses over with a rich patina the raw edges and defects of life as it was.

I recall my pioneer days as the happiest of my life. Coarse food and rough diet were the regimen of those days, but every cabin was a tent of refuge and relief from want. There were no instances of heaped up wealth, or pauper tramps. There existed social reciprocity, a general spirit of charity and free giving, which prevented the extreme poverty of more affluent times. The condition of oppression and want was but the occasional tares in a general harvest of sweet anticipations, ever existing pleasure and happiness.[1]

It appears to me that the people lived happier and had more real enjoyment then, than they do at the present time (1842), with their luxuries, fine dress, pride, vanity, pomp and show.[2]

In all gatherings of both sexes of this people while there was levity, jollity, frankness and liberal affection manifested—there were few or no sallies or attempts at flirting with the true, pure feelings of the heart, now called *flirting.* . . . So simple and domestic were all the ways and wants of that early country life. Loafing was yet unknown. That came with earliest saloons for sale of intoxicating liquors, in small towns. . . . For offices of all kinds . . . the best, wisest and most competent men were always sought and selected. . . . And the value of liberty, newly and blood-bought, seemed greater to them than to us. Hence the revolutionary war and the war of 1812 that demonstrated our ability to defend and maintain our dearly bought rights were the leading and constant themes of thought and discussion. Nobler and more patriotic themes than now absorb and control the whole thought, aim and struggle of our active, strenuous, commercial, money-grabbing voting population.[3]

It is probably only human nature to sublimate the hardships of youth and bygone days, and to read into them vital forces for the building of character, morals, and culture; to see in the drab struggle for existence of the pioneer, a conscious evolution and sacrifice of self for the reward of higher things for posterity. The pioneer's own concept of his world, as well as the truth, will lie somewhere between these extremes.

So long as America had a frontier it was possible to get a cross-

[1] John M. Norton, "Early Pioneer Life in Oakland County," in *Michigan Pioneer and Historical Collections,* XXVI (1894–95), 262–63.
[2] Spencer Records, "Pioneer Experiences in Pennsylvania, Kentucky, Ohio and Indiana, 1766–1836," in *Indiana Magazine of History,* XV (1919), 202.
[3] Haines, "Social Life and Scenes in the Early Settlement of Central Illinois," in *Transactions of the Illinois State Historical Society,* 1905, pp. 39–40.

section view of social evolution by traveling along a line drawn from the frontier back toward the Atlantic Coast. By picking a spot on the frontier and waiting for the various stages of development from fur trade to the urban-industrial system to file by, the same view might have been obtained. In the development of the United States the progress of the frontier was from east to west; in the Old Northwest, while the same trend still prevailed, the more important direction of progress was from south to north. At any given date between 1815 and 1840, a more significant cross-section view could be obtained, not by following a line from Pittsburgh west to St. Louis, but one drawn north from Cincinnati to the Upper Peninsula of Michigan or Wisconsin—from the city with steamboats, newspapers, banks, schools, and a theater, to the outpost or camp of the fur trader living among the Indians in the wilderness.

Pioneer life, from one viewpoint, was much more simple than that in the complicated industrial order of the twentieth century, with its many interdependent relationships and delicate balances. But to one who might be transferred from the modern farm of central Indiana or the average town of southern Illinois to the same scene of a century ago, the process of getting the mere essentials of existence—food, shelter, clothes, medicines—to say nothing of conveniences, travel, and amusements, would no doubt make life seem infinitely complex.

Nor were all of the people of pioneer days of the same economic status and given to the same type of life, regardless of the general leveling influences of the frontier. In many respects the contrasts in homes and manner of living between the pioneer aristocracy and the log-cabin dweller in the woods were more striking in their day than those between the millionaire on Lake Shore Drive and the wage earner a scant mile to the west, or the agricultural lord and his tenant farmer, in our own day. Only a few years were required in any community for the few, with ability and capital, transplanted or acquired, to establish social and economic gaps between themselves and the lesser folk. The homes of the Flowers, Harrisons, Ewbanks, Roberts, Wylies, Laniers, Baums, and many others, often built of imported brick, finished in carved woodwork and furnished with mahoganies, rosewoods, fine china, and tapestries, were built and occupied by those who had their own coaches and pews,[4] while within a short distance were those settlers barely past the open-faced-camp stage, who hauled their stuff on a forked-stick drag in lieu of a vehicle with wheels.

As the earlier settlers came into the region north of the Ohio, they were confronted with two sets of problems; the one concerned with shelter, food, health, and protection—things vital and immediate to the individual and his family; the other with ownership of land, transportation, and currency—things necessary for his economic advancement. Without the successful solution of the first, there was little need to worry about the second; with the beginning of progress on the second it became possible to think of schools, churches, cultural societies, humanitarian reform, and the development of institutions which mark social accomplishment.

The newcomer on the frontier, whether squatter or recent purchaser of government land, was likely to find his new home some distance from a settlement or even from friends and neighbors. If the move to the new site was a short one, the settler sometimes spent a season getting a cabin started, some trees deadened, and a little corn planted, then returned to the old home for the winter, to come again with the family in the spring. More often, however, the family with its plunder pushed into the wilderness and started the new life all at once. The facility with which this could be done depended upon the equipment possessed, location with respect to established trails and streams, nearness of friends and neighbors, and above all upon the experience and ability of the settler and his wife, who constituted the economic and social unit which conquered the frontier.

[4] These homes usually required two to three years to build. There were no architects, but plans were copied and modified by the stonemason and master carpenter in consultation with the owner. Bricks were often made on the job, as were the window frames, stairs, moldings, and carvings. Walls were from eighteen inches to three feet in thickness and interior walls solid. Expert masons built dry houses by permitting no stones to reach all the way through the exterior walls; bonding and joining were done in such a way as to leave an air barrier. Fancy wrought-iron balconies were not uncommon. Descriptions of some of the fine homes of the period are preserved in the Historic American Buildings Survey, Library of Congress; see also Lee Burns, *Early Architects and Builders of Indiana* (*Indiana Historical Society Publications*, XI, No. 3, Indianapolis, 1935), and Ihna T. Frary, *Early Homes of Ohio* (Richmond, Va., 1936); John Drury, *Historic Midwest Houses* (Minneapolis, University of Minnesota Press, 1947), and *Old Illinois Houses* (*Occasional Publications of the Illinois State Historical Society*, Springfield, 1948).

The location of the new home, were the settler a squatter or familiar with the land before purchase, was determined largely by availability of water, timber, streams, and quality of land. Springs were more plentiful among the hills, the timber furnished mast for the hogs as well as wood for buildings and fuel, and streams means of access in absence of roads. These considerations as well as those of health, accounted for early settlement of lands now among the roughest and poorest in the region. The hostile Indian was no longer a serious threat after 1814, and concentration of settlements around stations or blockhouses and stockades, so long the practice in the Kentucky settlements, was no longer necessary.

Since the need for labor in girdling trees, planting, and clearing was pressing, a temporary shelter, or open-faced camp or lean-to, sometimes sufficed for the family for the first year. Two forked posts or trees supported a cross timber, and sloping down from this to a large log were laid poles or saplings for a roof. Logs, brush, and clay mud were piled against the sides, brush and soil on the roof, and bearskins, wolf and cat pelts, or buffalo hides lined the interior and served as mattresses and covers. In front of the open side which usually faced south or was protected from the winds, a large log fire furnished warmth in winter and protection from woods varmints at night. It was in such a home as this near Little Pigeon Creek, in Spencer County, that the Lincoln family spent their first winter in southern Indiana.

A better home was offered by one of the more primitive types of log cabins. Logs of nearly uniform size, ash, beech, maple, or poplar, were cut to length and dragged to the cabin site. Here they were probably notched and saddled in one of the several approved methods, or they might even be hewn slightly on two sides, and piled to await the day when neighbors would arrive for the cabin raising. Until then, additional labor could be spent riving oak or chestnut clapboards, splitting and hewing puncheons, timbers for door and window frames, roof poles, and chimney slats. Although many an isolated settler was forced by laborious methods to roll up the logs into place and erect his small cabin by his own efforts, as a rule the cabin raising was accomplished by the co-operative efforts of the neighbors, and the heavy work rushed to completion, under the inspiration of liberal drafts of hard liquor and anticipation of sporting and gastronomic feats to come.

> His lusty arm, well skill'd to wield
> The axe, and make the forest yield,
> Soon bow'd the slender trees, and cut
> The rude materials of his hut.
> Each log, with hasty mortise scarr'd
> At either end, is soon prepar'd,
> And pil'd aloft, until they rise
> In square and superincumbent guise,
> Forming a box, compact and tight,
> As yet with neither door nor light.[5]

When the workers assembled, the ground was leveled and the first logs laid. At each corner was placed an axman who fitted the notches, and as the walls rose the logs were skidded up with forks and hand spikes. The width of space between the logs depended upon straightness and uniformity of size as well as upon the skill of the notchers; the greater the latter, not only the narrower the cracks but the stronger the corner joints. The rectangular frame of a 10- by 16- or 20-foot cabin was soon erected; some more time was taken to slope the ends and bind in the shorter logs for the gable ends, a few longitudinal roof poles were pegged on, or rafters set, and the job left to be finished by the owner. There remained the labor of sawing or chopping out openings for the door, window, and fireplace—since these were usually not built in as the cabin was raised—fitting of frames, hanging of the door, and laying of the roof. The door, constructed of wide slabs pegged to heavy cross battens, the projecting ends of which were inserted into "heads" attached to the logs or door frame with a heavy wooden pin dropped in for a hinge, was provided with a heavy wooden drop latch fitted into a notch on the opposite side and controlled by the latchstring which passed through a hole and hung outside. A strong crossbar which dropped into notches reinforced the door at night. Shutters for the windows, necessary in earliest days, were similarly constructed.

The clapboards or shakes[6] for the roof were split from bolts

---

[5] Henry Whiting, *The Emigrant* . . . (Detroit, 1819).
[6] Called "shakes" by the Michigan and Wisconsin pioneers from New England and New York. In the Lower Wabash Valley the cypress made easily worked and long-lasting clapboards.

of oak or ash three or four feet long; they were tapered slightly in the process by turning the slab over and guiding the split with the frow. They were laid on the roof poles in courses like shingles and held in place by long poles placed over the lapping rows and tied down at the end to the roof poles, or held apart by blocks and down by weights. The wide opening for the fireplace was usually cut in one of the end walls and around it was built a pen of small split logs, notched at the corners and pegged to the cabin walls. For best results an inner pen would be built, and the foot or more of space between the two filled with clay to the height of four or five feet; as the inner wall was removed or burned away, the firebox remained. In simpler construction the first pen was plastered with mud and the famous "cat and clay"[7] fireplace tapered off above into a chimney of similar pattern. Before cold or rainy weather set in the cracks between the cabin logs would be chinked with wedge strips and plastered over with mud, and as time offered, the logs could be rough hewn or scutched, as they lay. An earthen floor might suffice for a while, and thin skins or greased paper in the windows would have to do until a few panes of glass could be imported.

These primitive dwellings, the cabins of unfinished logs which frequently sprouted and covered the exterior with a growth of foliage, floorless and loftless, with one door and window, constructed without a nail, became the "Hoosier Nests"[8] of poetry, and the "rude tenements, taunted and jeered at by an aristocratic party—yet still the citadels of our young republic—the low but mighty towers of our nation—the home of the free unfettered souls."

In time, as the family grew and the supply of labor increased, as produce was marketed, stores and blacksmith shops came closer, and tools and equipment were more easily acquired, improvements and refinements were developed and added until the simple log house became an abode of some comfort and convenience. Hewn logs replaced the round bark-covered timbers. One of the first additions, if not originally included, would be the puncheon floor, made at first by splitting small logs in half and laying the slabs round side down, either on the ground or

[7] So called from the mixture of "cattail" down in the clay to give it cohesion.
[8] John Finley, "The Hoosier's Nest." See Chapter XV 521–22, 561.

Cabin in Southern Indiana. *Basil Hall*, 1828

Log Cabin in Ohio. *Lefevre J. Cranstone*

Near Wheeling. October 2d. 183[?].

Houses along the Upper Ohio. *Lefevre J. Cranstone*

better still into notches cut in the lower logs of the walls. The easily worked yellow poplar, black walnut, or cottonwood were preferred for this purpose, but oak was also used.

As more labor became available and saw pits—later mills— were set up, the puncheons became boards, the floor smoother, and cracks narrower. A loft could be added and the capacity of the one room almost doubled. Sometimes a lean-to or annex would be built on one end or side, to serve as kitchen, or else the original cabin became the annex when a more commodious dwelling was joined to one side or end.

A slight variation from the usual design was the cabin built with a ten-foot front wall of larger logs, and a seven-foot rear wall of smaller logs, with the roof on the low side built on out to cover a porch or additional room. Second cabins or dwellings of the more permanent sort were usually made of hewn logs with the ends cut off even at the corners, provided with lofts, perhaps a small cellar underneath, a porch under the projected roof of one side, rain troughs at the eaves, two doors, several windows, fireplaces with stone or brick hearths and walls, and roof of dressed clapboards or shingles fastened with nails. Hollowed half logs, laid tile fashion, the lower layer cupped up, the top placed cup surface down over the joints of the lower were sometimes used for roofs. The double or two-shanty dwelling was constructed by placing two cabins, square or rectangular in shape, a few yards apart, and roofing both units and the open court between with one roof. The doors in this type usually opened on the court. The dwellings of the average settler varied in type, size, and elegance with the individual and the location. Whereas the simple cabin of unfinished logs prevailed in new settlements, and the improved cabins were more common in regions longer settled, the houses of sawed lumber and even of brick predominated in the villages and towns.[9]

The furnishings of these early homes depended upon the means, tastes, and abilities of the settler.[10] Some arrived with

[9] The restoration of the pioneer village at New Salem, Illinois, gives an excellent idea of the earlier type cabins; that at Spring Mill State Park, Indiana, is a fine reproduction of the more improved hewn-log, two-story and double-cabin type village.

[10] Among the better articles on early home life are: H. B. Curtis, "Pioneer Days in Central Ohio," in *Ohio Archaeological and Historical Society Publications*, I (1887–88), 243–54; Martin Welker, *Farm Life in Central Ohio Sixty Years Ago*

only an ax, rifle, iron pot, a few tools, scraps of metal, packets of seeds, a bit of bedclothing, and the clothes on their backs. Others came with plunder enough to start housekeeping in decent shape. A skilled pioneer, even though possessed of little to start on, soon found time to make the most necessary furniture from materials at hand. Beds were built in the cabin corners by driving crotched posts into the ground or holes in the floor and running rails to the cabin walls. Across this crude frame could be stretched thongs of deer hide or twisted elm bark which would serve as springs for the bear-hide mattresses or grass ticks. Or an eight-foot length would be cut from the butt end of an easy-splitting oak, and from this posts and rails would be split, later to be dressed down with the ax and finished with the drawknife. Slats were made from a shorter length, holes were bored in the posts for the two side rails and three end rails, and holes in the side rails for the slats. When the whole was joined up the posts were held together at the top by thongs or rods from which curtains might be hung, and the result was a rough but strong and practicable bedstead.[11] For tables thin splits of poplar, two feet or more in width, were dressed down and pegged to crosspieces, into which were fitted strong legs; the dining table was literally a board. Three-legged stools, benches, and sturdy chairs were of similar construction, or of half logs. The first corner cupboards were clapboards set on wooden pins driven into the log walls; early cradles were troughs hollowed from poplar logs.

From these crude products and simple beginnings, skilled

(*Western Reserve Historical Society Tracts*, IV, No. 86, Cleveland, 1895); George S. Cottman, "The Pioneer Fourth of July," in *Indiana Magazine of History*, VIII (1912), 65–69; James B. Lewis, "Pioneers of Jefferson County," in *ibid.*, XII (1916), 214–27; Logan Esarey, "The Pioneer Aristocracy," in *ibid.*, XIII (1917), 270–87; Benjamin S. Parker, "Pioneer Life," in *ibid.*, III (1907), 1–11, 51–57, 125–31, 182–88; "Reminiscences of Judge Finch," in *ibid.*, VII (1911), 155–65; Robert B. Duncan, "*Old Settlers*" (*Indiana Historical Society Publications*, II, No. 10, Indianapolis, 1894); Noah J. Major, *Pioneers of Morgan County* (*ibid.*, V, No. 5, Indianapolis, 1915); Logan Esarey, *The Indiana Home* (Crawfordsville, Ind., 1943, and New York, 1947); "Memoir of Alvan Stone," in *Journal of the Illinois State Historical Society*, III, No. 4 (Jan., 1911), 85–97; William Nowlin, "The Bark-Covered House or Pioneer Life in Michigan," in *Michigan Pioneer and Historical Collections*, IV (1881), 480–541, and reprinted as *Back in the Woods Again* (Chicago, 1937); Melvin D. Osband, "My Recollections of Pioneers and Pioneer Life in Nankin," in *Michigan Pioneer and Historical Collections*, XIV (1890), 431–83; William James Beal, "Pioneer Life in Southern Michigan in the Thirties," in *ibid.*, XXXII (1903), 236–46; Edward W. Barber, "Recollections and Lessons of Pioneer Boyhood," in *ibid.*, XXXI (1902), 178–227; Gen. B. M. Cutcheon, "Log Cabin Times and Log Cabin People," in *ibid.*, XXIX (1899–1900), 609–24.
[11] Duncan, "*Old Settlers*," 24–25.

artisans, either itinerant or local, later evolved furniture copied
after the best of colonial types. From the split-oak bedstead
came the carved and turned four-poster with rope springs tightened with keys, to support enormous featherbeds, the pride of
the housewife.[12] Rough benches grew into settees, stools into
slat-back chairs with woven cornhusk, hemp, or split-hickory
bottoms, and more comfortable than many of their store counter-
parts of today; shelves in the corner became artistic corner
cupboards of cherry, maple, and walnut. Pegs on the wall gave
way to great clothes cupboards or presses, boxes and barrels to
classic-designed chests and chests of drawers. The trough cradle
took on rockers, as did some of the chairs, the latter to be viewed
with suspicion by many a pioneer housewife or mother of the
older generation as a lazy person's refuge.

Among household utensils, the most important were the cooking irons.[13] Were the pioneer housewife possessed of a bulbous
iron pot with a flare at the top to hold the lid, a heavy iron frying
pan with three legs, usually known as a spider, another deeper
pan, or oven, often with rounded bottom and a lid with curled
up edges to hold the hot coals on top, she was well equipped.
A reflector oven would have been a luxury. A few knives were
the only other implements absolutely necessary. Serviceable
bowls, piggins, firkins, and keelers could, in the absence of
coopers or woodenware makers, be made by hollowing out cuts
of maple with fire and tools; trenchers and platters were made
from poplar, buckeye, or basswood; spoons, paddles, and forks
from various hardwoods. The gourd, of many sizes and shapes,
was a boon to the woods dweller and played a conspicuous part
in domestic life.

Of many sizes and shapes, it served, when properly scraped out and
cleansed, a variety of purposes. It hung as a dipper beside the spring or
well with its long sweep, and in the same capacity it was a companion to the
cider barrel and whisky jug; it was used at the table, at the lye kettle or at
the sugar camp for soup, soap or sap; a large one properly halved made a
wash pan or a milk pan, or, cut with an opening, it became a receptacle for

[12] Cabinetmakers had beds which were set up without mortices, tendons, or
screws but with drop-down iron fastenings, and were offering these for sale at
Cincinnati in the 1830's. *Cincinnati Daily Gazette*, October 27, 1834.
[13] Household articles from lamps and spinning wheels to heavier furniture and
vehicles are well described and illustrated in a series of articles on the Henry
Ford collection at Dearborn in the *Michigan History Magazine*, volumes I to VI.

the storing of divers things; a small one was used by the grandmother to darn the family socks over; the boy used one to carry his bait in when he went fishing and the baby used another for a rattle. A veritable treasure was the gourd, and it should be celebrated in song.[14]

Gourd seeds were usually among the items most cherished by the housewife going into a new country. Hard-shelled squashes often served the same purpose, and knots with hollow centers also could be made into noggins and cups. Brooms of husks and bristles were not uncommon, but the old stand-by in the early pioneer home was the hickory broom. A sapling several inches in diameter was cut to length, the lower end carefully slivered until the heart was reached and removed, the slivers fluffed out, sometimes spread over a centerpiece, bound into place, and the handle cut to size. Crockery of home manufacture supplemented the woodenware or few store pieces, especially where good clay was available, but being unglazed was soon saturated with grease, and when used for cooking was likely to take fire on the outside. The necessary fireplace furnishings were few: a lug pole of green wood with double-prong pothooks of the same material, some stones to hold the logs in place, a thong or string for a spit. These served their purposes until iron lugs, cranes, firedogs, and turning spits replaced them.

§

The problem of food assumed serious proportions in the affairs of the first settlers in any region. But little stuff could be brought along; there was no surplus round about from which to purchase, even though money or barterable articles were in hand; settlements were at a distance and communications bad. It was only the hunter's skill that carried the family through the first year or two, and it was called upon to supplement the larder for years to come. Wild game was to be found on all sides while the country was new, and to one living near urban areas of today —from which the last few sticks of timber have been stripped

[14] Parker, "Pioneer Life," in *Indiana Magazine of History*, III, 130. "Gourds were used for carrying water until 'nuggins' were made. A nuggin was made like our wooden buckets, with one stave, double length for handle. They did not have bails." John F. Edgar, *Pioneer Life in Dayton and Vicinity* (Dayton, Ohio, 1896), 53.

for fence posts or railroad ties, and through which, behind bill-
boards, flow polluted streams, or streams which go dry in summer—the accounts of the great abundance of animal life, and
the ensuing destruction thereof, furnish stuff for dreams and
tragic contemplation.

Bear, deer, wild turkeys, pigeons, opossums, ducks, geese,
brant, partridges, quail, prairie chickens, parakeets, and squirrels
and lesser game in such numbers as to constitute a nuisance were
to be found in the woods and prairies of the region north of the
Ohio. Fish abounded in the streams.[15] Even along the Ohio River
in the first quarter of the nineteenth century bear, deer, and
turkeys were so plentiful that there was no fear of lack of meat.
As late as 1831 in the cane brakes around the mouth of the Ohio,
deer, bear, wolves, turkeys, and wild honey were abundant.[16]
At times wild turkeys were so numerous and tame that they had
to be kept away from the corn when the hogs were fed, and if
one was wanted, a fat specimen was selected and hit on the head
with a club.[17] "Bears, deer, squirrels and wild turkeys made sad
inroads on grain fields and the deer helped the settlers to dispose
of the tobacco crop, eating the green leaves, to the last vestige,
they being curiously enough, the only animal that will eat the
'weed.' "[18] In parts of southern Indiana in 1815 flocks of five
hundred wild turkeys were not uncommon, in the winter herds of
10 to 20 deer could be seen, and there were shoals of fish in the
Driftwood River which covered half an acre. A week's supply
of game could be killed in a half day.[19]

Fish were abundant in White river, even beyond what I shall be able to
make any one believe now. I have stood on the bluff bank of the river,
fifty or sixty feet above the water in "the deep hole," on the prairie, and
seen the surface of the water as far as the eye could reach, so literally

[15] Descriptions of animal life are to be found in the accounts of such travelers as
Fordham, Fearon, Woods, Faux, Flint, Evans, Thomas, etc.; in the reminiscences,
journals, and the letters of early settlers, such as William Owen's diary and
Gershom Flagg's letters, and in many others printed in the *Michigan Pioneer and
Historical Collections, Wisconsin Historical Collections, Journal of the Illinois State
Historical Society*, early county histories, and newspapers. Quite a few otter and
some beaver were still to be found in the Ohio River Valley as late as the 1820's.
[16] "Memoir of Alvan Stone," in *Journal of the Illinois State Historical Society*,
III, No. 4, p. 85.
[17] Perret Dufour, "Early Vevay," in *Indiana Magazine of History*, XX, 6–7.
[18] Robert and Alexander Miller, "Pioneers of Jefferson County," in *ibid.*, XII
(1916), 232.
[19] Josiah Shewmaker, in *Brownstown* (Ind.) *Banner*, August 26, 1874.

covered with fish—about six inches below the surface—that they appeared to touch each other and in many instances did touch; and this of all kinds of fish, from the monster muskalonge to the hated gar, large and small—but mostly large—lying together, a happy family, "sunning themselves," as it was called[20]

Fishing with hook and line was considered too slow work; the gig and seine were favored for large catches.

My brother and I fished at Maumee, in the rapids, in 1830, and a number of years afterwards. We usually calculated to fill about 800 barrels with wall-eyed pike, that being the desired amount; some seasons leaving off when the last haul would bring in 50 or 60 barrels of wall-eyed pike, and about half as many of other varieties which were allowed to escape. . . . It was then quite common to catch 50 barrels of bass at one haul.[21]

Next to the fish stories the most impressive accounts of wild life deal with the flocks of pigeons, which at certain seasons in the years when the mast crop was heavy, darkened the skies.

A pigeon roost is a singular sight in thinly settled states. . . . The screaming noise they make when thus roosting is heard at a distance of six miles; and when the beech nuts are ripe, they fly 200 miles to dinner, in immense flocks, hiding the sun and darkening the air like a thick passing cloud. They thus travel 400 miles daily. They roost on the high forest trees, which they cover in the same manner as bees in swarms cover a bush, being piled one on the other, from the lowest to the topmost boughs, which so laden, are seen continually bending and falling with their crashing weight, and presenting a scene of confusion and destruction, too strange to describe, and too dangerous to be approached by either man or beast. While the living birds are gone to their distant dinner, it is common for man and animals to gather or devour the dead, then found in cartloads. When the roost is among the saplings, on which the pigeons alight without breaking them down, only bending them to the ground, the self slaughter is not so great; and at night, men, with lanterns and poles, approach and beat them to death without much personal danger. But the grand mode of taking them is by setting fire to the high dead grass, leaves, and shrubs underneath, in a wide blazing circle, fired at different parts, at the same time, so as soon to meet. Then down rush the pigeons in immense numbers,

[20] "Reminiscences of Judge Finch," in *Indiana Magazine of History*, VII, 161. David Thomas reported the Wabash well supplied with gar, catfish—Mississippi, mud, and bull-head—pond pike, white perch, black perch or bass, buffalo fish and red horse of the sucker kind, rock mullet, and jack pike or pickerel. Some of the catfish ran to more than 100 pounds, perch and buffalo to 30 pounds, and pike to 20. Sturgeon and river pike, also large fish, were scarcer. Eels and crawfish were common, and mussels so plentiful that the shells were burned for lime. *Travels,* 211–12.

[21] George Clark, "Recollections," in *Michigan Pioneer and Historical Collections,* I (1877), 506.

and indescribable confusion, to be roasted alive, and gathered up dead next day from heaps two feet deep.[22]

An educated Easterner with ministerial leanings reported on pigeons firsthand:

With a friend, I stood in an open space in the woods, two miles east of Woodville [Bloomington, Indiana], from 10 o'clock A. M. to 3 o'clock P. M.—five hours—during which, with scarcely thirty seconds intermission, a stream of pigeons, about two hundred yards wide, and averaging two layers, flowed above us, and with the rapidity of thought! It was an endless hurricane on wings, rushing innoxious, yet with such an uproar as seemed to be prostrating the forests: and the deep reverberating thunder, in the distant wilds, seemed to announce the fall of their ponderous and ancient trees! Never had I felt the awe and solemnity of sound thus; even in beholding the wind-tempest pass over the same wilds, blowing the submissive woods, and bearing onward their wide tops, as if mown off with an angel's scythe![23]

In the mild December weather of 1828 multitudes of pigeons passed through Ohio with a noise like the strong rush of wind. Witnesses calculated that the flocks were thirty miles long, and the numbers equal to the dollars lost in the Adams-Jackson bet.[24]

Abundance such as this could not last long after settlement, for not only was game needed for food but these creatures were frequently destructive of crops and livestock. The bear and deer were among the first to become scarce, for these animals were sought for their hides, grease, and sinews, which were much used in the home, as well as for food. Log traps or deadfalls helped the dog and rifle soon to thin out bruin's ranks; and the deer which at first could be found on a before-breakfast hunt in southern Indiana and Illinois, or seen in flocks like sheep in the prairie openings in Michigan Territory, soon had to be patiently stalked at watering places and licks, or hunted with torches from canoes. While turkeys were still to be found in flocks of hundreds, a shot into their midst would scatter them; then "turkey calls"

[22] Faux, Memorable Days, 248–49. Faux does not claim to have seen a pigeon roost.
[23] Robert Carlton [Baynard Rush Hall], The New Purchase . . . (reprinted 1916, Princeton University Press), 466–67. The 1843 edition reads "bowing the submissive woods." A description of a pigeon hunt follows. The long-titled article by Samuel P. Hildreth in American Journal of Science and Arts (New Haven, Conn., 1819–1879), XXIV, 132 ff. (July, 1833), gives a good account of the wild pigeons in the West.
[24] Piqua Gazette, January 3, 1829. The bet was one cent for the first elector Jackson got over 143, two cents for the second, four for the third, etc., and ran into billions.

of bone in the mouth of the hunter imitated the calls of the older
birds which always sought to assemble the flock, and the fowls
were led to their fate by the dozens. Turkeys were also led into
rail traps by trains of corn grains, but once in, seldom thought to
lower their heads and crawl out again. If anyone ate wildcats and
rattlesnakes, which were found to be as "sweet and white as an
eel," they did so from choice and not from necessity.[25]

The pioneer's gun was his pet, and in his mind was something
more than a shooting tool. It was or had been the guardian of
his home and provider for his wants; it symbolized liberty and
life. It received at his hands more care than any other of his
possessions, ofttimes not excepting children, and on it were bestowed names of affection. Many United States muskets and
yagers (German Jaegers) loaded with an ounce ball and three
buckshot were in use, but the "Old Betsey" or "Long Tom" of
the better hunter was more likely the old smoothbore or a rifle
with round or octagonal barrel from four to five feet long,
loaded with a single bullet.

From 1728 to about 1760 skilled gunsmiths among the German
settlers around Lancaster, Pennsylvania, had evolved a rifle
which came to be known in American history as the Kentucky
rifle. It was a gun manufactured to fit the needs of the frontier
where powder and lead were precious and the loud reports of
.50- to .75-caliber muskets were often dangerous. As the barrel
lengthened, caliber was reduced. Rifles for use against Indians
or big game were usually about .45 caliber, whereas "turkey"
rifles would run about .30. These guns might weigh from eight
to twelve pounds and the bullets run from approximately 37
to a pound for a .50 caliber gun to 175 for a .30 caliber. For
accurate shooting the rifle ball was loaded with a greased patch
of cloth.

The flintlock and single trigger prevailed until the early 1820's,
when they began to be replaced by the double trigger and the
percussion cap. Good hunters were sparing of powder and lead,
and as a rule were reluctant to adopt newfangled devices. Many
of the gun barrels were made by skilled "blacksmiths," who
hammered out the barrel from bar iron, bored and rifled it,

[25] Faux, *Memorable Days*, 249, reported that Birkbeck ate the snakes.

tempered it, made the flintlocks and the double triggers, set a segment of a slick quarter for front sight and rounded out and set the hindsight, made the bullet molds, stocked the gun with curly maple or black walnut, tested it on their own proving grounds and then staked their reputations upon the job.[26] Less sterling barrels were apparently turned out by bringing the edges of a piece of strap iron together and welding them. When this was poorly done, barrels were inclined to burst. Even coarser guns of this type with crude locks made of iron usually cost from $25 to $40.[27]

Hunting, which at first was almost the sole means of support for the family, remained in pioneer life as a sport long after the pressing need of wild game for food disappeared, and so deeply ingrained in the natures of certain types of men was the love of the woods and the chase, that they could never decide to adapt themselves to the more prosaic but less strenuous life of farming. Even the farmers, at certain seasons, felt a peculiar restlessness.

As soon as the leaves were pretty well down and the weather became rainy, accompanied with light snows, these men, after acting the part of husbandmen . . . soon began to feel that they were hunters. They became uneasy at home. Everything about them became disagreeable. The house was too warm. The feather bed too soft, and even the good wife was not thought for the time being a proper companion. The mind of the hunter was wholly occupied with the camp and the chase.

Autumn hunting expeditions lasted for weeks and trapping in winter returned hides and furs equivalent to ready cash for many years after the clearings became as numerous as the woods.[28]

[26] For boring of guns see below, 227; for use in shooting matches, see Chapter VI. For the history of the rifle, see John G. W. Dillin, *The Kentucky Rifle* (Washington, D. C., 1924) with its many fine plates.

[27] For an interesting but not very illuminating discussion of the rifle, see Oliver, *Eight Months in Illinois*, 159–66. Oliver argued against the long barrels and large calibers.

[28] Tales of bear, "painters," and wolves, rather than knights, dragons, fair maids, and heroic exploits in pursuit thereof, constituted the diet of romance and adventure upon which more than one generation of youth was reared in the days before the Civil War. The adventures of the Nimrods of the period, though never crystallized into a folklore or literature such as has perpetuated the names of Mike Fink, Paul Bunyan, or Jinglebob, were told and retold, until overshadowed by the exploits and deeds of the scouts, hunters, Indian fighters, bad men, and cowboys of the Far West. Examples of hunting yarns may be found in Emanuel Inman, *Stories of Hatfield the Pioneer* (New Albany, 1890). For a tale of the superstition of the bewitching of a rifle, see Esarey, *The Indiana Home*, 94–102. As late as 1842 at Indianapolis, saddles of venison sold at 25 to 50 cents, turkeys at 10 to 12 cents, and a bushel of pigeons for 25 cents.

A diet of game is not as attractive as it might seem, more particularly if eaten without salt, and the illusion that turkey breasts and venison were bread, could with difficulty be maintained over a period of months. Unless too far away, the first settlers usually depended upon outside sources for breadstuffs for the first year. Many in eastern Indiana made three- or four-day trips to Ohio for grain and meal. Pumpkin was often mixed with meal in such quantities that the product was hardly distinguishable from dried pumpkin. Even among the older settlements, during the years of heavy immigration, the corn meal supply frequently ran out long before summer, and the growth of the young corn shoots was eagerly watched not only by the children but by grown-ups as well. Many a corn nubbin never lived to be a roasting ear, but was grated into shavings over a "jack plane" and made into a green corn mush or cakes. Even potatoes that had been planted were dug up to be eaten.

When the grain matured, it was pounded into samp in the mortar made of a log burned out at one end, grated into meal by rubbing over a strip of "tin" punched full of rough-edged holes, or ground by hand between two stones. From the meal, sifted through a stretched deerskin punched full of holes by a hot point, came the corn dodger, pone, and "johnnycake." The dodger was merely meal, water, and salt mixed into a stiff dough ball and baked in the oven—the iron utensil with the lid—buried in hot ashes and coals. The pone was somewhat richer in mixture, having milk and yeast added to the basic ingredients, and when baked rose to make an oven-sized loaf. The "johnnycake" or "hoecake" which was made of meal with shortening—bear grease, lard, or butter—and baked flat on a board, was considered by many the best of the corn breads. Meal slowly boiled in water and salted made mush, a nourishing dish when eaten with milk, and in the absence of the latter acceptable with sweetened water, bear's oil, or meat gravy. Cold mush fried and eaten with syrup or honey constituted a dish not to be sneered at in any home. Whole corn grains soaked in water and pounded free of the outer shells in a wooden mortar, or, better still, treated in lye water made from wood ashes, produced hominy, which boiled or fried took its place as a staple of diet.

With the coming of corn the immediate danger of famine was past.

Until such time as the new settler could depend upon his own produce, the woods which furnished the wild game could be counted upon for some things with which to vary the diet. Varieties of hickory nuts and black walnuts, chestnuts and beechnuts, were usually plentiful in the hardwood belt, the hazelnut and pecan in some regions, and the paw paw, wild cherry, persimmon, black and red haw, wild grape, plum and crab apple were widely distributed. Wild strawberries, raspberries, and blackberries, the latter much larger than the domesticated berry, varied in quantity with different locations and seasons. In addition there were hops, herbs, and roots, some of which were called upon for emergency rations, others used for teas, medicines, and seasoning.

The honey of the wild bee was almost as valuable to the settlers as ambrosia and nectar to the gods. The honey bee was not a native but came into the woods from domestic hives. Unlike the housefly and rat, however, which followed settlement, the bee, by reason of its swarming and migrating tendencies, was usually a hundred or more miles in advance of the frontier, and the product of its labors, found on all sides, was one of the most sought after treasures which the woods could yield.[29] Woods near prairie regions were especially well provided with honey because of the great variety of flowers. Flagg said that Illinois had more honey than any other place in the world.[30] Bee trees were as much hunted as big game, and more valuable. On sunny winter days when snow covered the ground, frozen fallen bees

[29] It is thought that the maximum distance of travel of a new swarm is about four or five miles. With two swarms a year, and assuming that some always traveled away from settlement, the bee could easily have covered most of the Northwest by 1820. Blackbirds, crows, and red squirrels, as well as the rat, were apparently latecomers into the western woods.

[30] Buck (ed.), "Pioneer Letters," in *Transactions of the Illinois State Historical Society*, 1910, p. 58. " 'It appears that the time has been, when the bee was not known in our country. The old French settlers saw none; and toward the Mississippi, it has not been more than twenty or twenty-five years since it was first discovered. J. M'Donald informs me, that in the Military bounty lands above the junction of the Illinois with the Mississippi, which he surveyed last winter, the bee has not been seen more than fifteen years.'

"Another correspondent says, 'Bees are very plenty in the woods; and as the Indians here call them "white people's flies," it is believed they are not natives.'

" 'Great quantities of honey have been found in the woods above Fort Harrison. One man found twelve bee-trees in less than half a day.' " Quoted by David Thomas in notes at end of his *Travels*, 206.

gave a certain clue; in warm weather the buzzing sound of the hive revealed the location. A more scientific method of location called for a little box, glass if available, and a bit of honey or sweet. Bees gathered their cargo from it and their flight home was noted, then the box and a few captive bees were carried some distance to one side and as the bees were released another line was established. Somewhere near the intersection of the lines of flight was likely to be the bee tree, upon which the discoverer was entitled to place his mark, and by the law of the woods it became his property.

> Another sport the woods present,
> When brown October's frost has lent
> Its chill to hive the sylvan bee,
> That stores its sweets in hollow tree.
> Then forth he hies, when sunny day
> Has lur'd the insect 'round to play,
> Kindles a fire amid the grove
> Where'er he sees a wanderer move,
> Two stones within its furnace heats,
> Then throws between the honied sweets,
> Which, fuming upwards, odors spread
> Through all the forest o'er his head.
> Attracted by the fragrant air,
> The vagrant bees assemble there,
> Circling awhile in dubious flight,
> Then darting swiftly out of sight.
> He sees them as they eddying rise,
> And marks the course each insect flies.
> With hapless instinct sure they dart,
> And all the fatal truth impart.
> Pursuing on, with eye upturn'd,
> The index tree is soon discern'd,
> Where, basking in the noon-tide ray,
> The hovering bees their hive betray.
> He plies the axe, whose frequent blow
> Soon lays their lofty refuge low.
> As it descends, the branches rive,
> And ope the treasures of the hive,
> While left on high, the buzzing swarm
> Flies 'round and 'round in wild alarm,
> Nor thinks to trace the ruin down,
> Till sweets and robber, all are flown.[31]

[31] Henry Whiting, *The Emigrant.*

It was not unusual to gather hundreds of pounds of honey from one hollow tree, and the sweetening properties of such a find opened new culinary possibilities to the housewife. The only other sweetening available was syrup and sugar from the sap of the sweet maple, but the preparation in quantity required equipment and labor which the settler at first could ill afford.[32] The beeswax was as valuable as the honey. Often the bee was redomesticated and the settler housed a dozen or more hives or bee gums. With cattle range and bees both available it was truly "a land of milk and honey."[33]

More difficult to obtain than sugar and more important in the primitive domestic economy was salt, needed not only for flavoring but in quantity for preserving meats. Salt was obtainable from the licks, or salines, of which there were a number in Kentucky, southern Indiana, and Illinois. At these places a hundred gallons of water boiled down produced about a bushel of salt, but not everyone lived near a saline, and salt was heavy and difficult to transport.[34] At times families went for months without a grain of salt in the house. In regions away from the rivers the price sometimes rose to $20 a barrel. Salt was among the most important of the staples handled by the stores, and the arrival of a new shipment was heralded abroad in the locality.

Coffee and tea were rare and expensive luxuries for the table. Makeshift beverages were made from the materials at hand— tea from a kind of wild bohea plant,[35] sassafras roots, and various herbs; a kind of coffee was brewed from parched corn, wheat, barley, rye, or even browned bread crumbs.

Into the little corn patch in the clearing went some pumpkin seeds, and a vegetable patch close by the cabin was given to potatoes, cucumbers, cabbages, and other common vegetables. The tomato, when grown, was used only to garnish the platter,

[32] Loaf sugar sold at 40 cents per pound at Cincinnati in May, 1816, at 50 cents at Zanesville in 1818, and moist sugar at 31 cents at Albion, Illinois, in 1819. After steamboat service reduced prices, New Orleans sugar sold at Cincinnati at 14 to 16 cents in 1826. *Niles' Weekly Register*, XXIX, 363 (Feb. 4, 1826); XXXV, 387 (Feb. 7, 1829).

[33] *Detroit Gazette*, August 2, 1822.

[34] For salt production and prices, see Chapter VII, 543–46.

[35] The *Ceanothus americanus*, or Jersey tea plant, was plentiful on the prairies and, adapting itself to frequent burnings, blossomed at a height of six or eight inches. Thomas, *Travels*, 222. The China leaf was cultivated from imported seed in gardens at Princeton and New Harmony prior to 1820. Faux, *Memorable Days*, 228.

for few considered it edible, and many thought it poisonous. The bolder spirited were beginning to eat this valuable vegetable by the early 1830's. A little orchard of apple, plum, peach, and pear trees was set out by the more provident as soon as possible, but the fruit was not available during the years when the food problem was most acute.

If possible the early settlers brought at least one cow; if not they sought to acquire one soon. Cows pastured in the woods, and although the milk might taste of leeks or other wild odors, and cause at times the mysterious "milk sickness,"[36] it was almost indispensable. Butter and cheese added to meat and vegetables gave variety and stability to the food supply and soon became a source of ready profit as well. Abundance or scarcity of these articles depended partly upon the locality of settlement, but also upon the thrift and industry of the settler and his wife. A few domestic fowls were probably included in the original inventory, chickens for eggs and geese for feathers, until numerous enough to be eaten. Hogs of the "razorback" variety could be brought along, obtained from the Indians, or sometimes be found wild in the woods. These long-legged, long-bodied, long-nosed creatures with short, straight-up ears, were often known as "elm peelers," "wind splitters" or "tonawandas"; they could do almost anything except climb trees. They were adapted to their environment, and ordinarily were left to forage for themselves. In years of poor mast they lived on roots—particularly of the slippery elm—snakes, and other provender. Hogs were not always easily raised in the early years, and frequently there was a scarcity of pork. Woods-ranging hogs became quite wild, hard to brand or mark; it was not unusual for the owner to have to hunt his hogs with the rifle in order to have pork. Such "critters" never grew fat or very tender, but in good mast years the lean meat had a splendid flavor. Hog cholera was unknown. The wolves were so bad near Evansville, Indiana, in the 1820's that the settlers could not raise pigs enough to supply pork and lard, and sheep not at all.[37] As late as the 1840's pork and lard were

[36] See Chapter V, 248.

[37] *History of Vanderburgh County* (Brant & Fuller, Madison, Wis., 1889), 355–56. Fordham, writing of Princeton, Indiana, in 1817, said: "The woods around us are inhabited by Indians, bears, deer, opossums and racoons. We hear the howling of the wolves every evening, as they are driven back from the farmyards by the dogs, who flock together to repel the invaders." *Personal Narrative,* 109.

often so scarce in Wisconsin that a grease mark on the floor was viewed with pride by the women, for it was a mark of affluence and gave social prestige.[38] Semiwild sows with broods at times banded together and protected their offspring against smaller bears and marauding wolves, but the poor sheep, unless housed, were a total loss. Hence the scarcity of wool among the earlier settlers in the woods.

§ §

The pioneer was of necessity a woodsman before he could be an agriculturist. Excepting for the prairies of Illinois and limited areas in Michigan and Indiana, vast forests of virgin timber covered the region of the Northwest. In the bottom land and along stream margins grew the black and white walnut (butternut), ash, hackberry, elm (white, red, and slippery), sugar maple, honey locust, buckeye, catalpa, sycamore, cottonwood, hickory, mulberry, pecan, and various oaks—such as the water oak, burr oak, white oak, and red oak. The white oak, black oak, post oak, hickory, walnut, cherry, beech, and others covered the ridges, hills, and uplands. Not until the settler reached a line midway up in Michigan and Wisconsin did he begin to find a preponderance of pine, spruce, and hemlock.

For thousands of years generations of trees had seeded, grown, fallen, and rotted to add a layer of humus to the subsoil. Into these almost unbroken forests, somber and gloomy, came the American frontiersman, puny in size and at first few in numbers, but skilled by generations of practice in the use of two tools, the first of which, the long rifle, enabled him to protect his life, overcome his enemies, and feed his body, and the second, the woodsman's ax, to build his home, conquer the forest, and provide for his maintenance from the soil. The story of the long rifle, favorite weapon of the pioneer in war and the hunt, has been told in poetry and prose; and the plowshare, mightier than the sword, symbolic of the art of agriculture, has received full treatment at the hands of historians, economic and scientific; but the epic of the ax remains to be written. The Indian had his tomahawk and scalping knife, the white man his woodsman's ax, tools fitted to the purposes of life which each sought to pur-

---

[38] *Wisconsin Magazine of History,* IX (1925–26), 14.

sue. It was said that it took civilization two hundred years to
develop the ax, and in the hands of a skilled wielder it was capable of deeds mightier than those attributed to the colossal broad-
sword of Richard I, or the keen and delicate scimitar of Saladin.

To hand forge a good ax of bar iron and cast steel, give it the
proper shape in relation to its weight so as properly to place
the center of gravity, temper the metal just so to achieve the
right degree of toughness and still keep edge, and to hang the
same correctly on the helve, was an art which many practiced
but few mastered. That which can now be done with modern
metallurgy, electricity, high temperature thermometers, chemistry, and precision tools was accomplished by practice and "in-
tuition." No one could tell just how hot to heat the metal; the
expert knew.[39] And his reputation spread far and wide. Men in
the settlements would ride a hundred miles on horseback to get
such an ax, or to have their favorites upset and resteeled. One
to two days' time was required to make an ax; the price was from
$3.00 to $5.00.[40] Other artisans specialized in helves, but many
woodsmen preferred to split out and finish their own ax handles
from second-growth hickory.

The light chopping ax was a wonderful tool, and adeptness in
its use was a matter of pride surpassed only by skill in marksman-
ship. "Whether 'Baltimore pattern,' 'Yankee,' single- or double-
bitted, concave or ridged, 'jumped,' new-patent or homemade,
double-portioned, light or heavy, the tool was essentially the
same."[41] The English farmer-traveler, William Oliver, appreciated the American ax.

But what would the American be without his axe of the true Yankee cut?
He would be dexterous, no doubt, in the use of any axe, according to its
capabilities; but I very much doubt if he could do half of the chopping
and splitting with any axe I ever saw in Britain. The Yankee axe, with its
handle, is a scientific implement—much more so, indeed, than many who
use it are aware of—and it is most beautifully made of the very best

---

[39] "He had many journeymen who made axes in his shop, but of all he would
yield the palm to but one man, a dissolute, drunken genius, named Richardson,
who worked for him for years and whose presence was only tolerated by reason
of his great and peculiar skill. . . . 'Nobody could equal Seward in making an
ax, but Richardson; he could beat him.' " H. C. Duncan, "Austin Seward," pioneer
gunsmith and toolmaker of southern Indiana, in *Indiana Magazine of History*,
IV (1908), 108.
[40] "Reminiscences of Judge Finch," in *ibid.*, VII, 104.
[41] *History of Clark County, Ohio* . . . (W. H. Beers & Co., Chicago, 1881), 253.

materials, cast steel of the finest quality being used. Among the best and handsomest I saw were of the brand Collin's and Co., Hartford, (Connecticut).[42]

Among a random group of pioneers the subject of ax helves and the proper weight of ax for most effective service would normally be more frequently and fully discussed than politics or religion. Weight varied from three to six pounds, and best results were by no means proportioned to the size of the ax or its wielder. A medium-sized wiry man, who developed the proper co-ordination of muscle to apply through a moving fulcrum the power which results from rhythm and constantly increasing acceleration at the end of the swing, with the delicate twist at the end to clear the bit and lightly lift out the chips, who could strike within a hair's breadth of where he aimed—that man was a chopper and could outcut and outlast some of the strongest and heaviest.[43] A man such as this had "larned the sling o' the axe." Singlehanded he tackled the trees, 3, 6, even 10 feet in diameter[44] and 50 to 80 feet to the first limbs, felled them cleanly within a yard of the line selected, trimmed and cut the logs into lengths capable of being handled. When possible, teamwork was used on the larger trees, and as many as six axes, beating a rhythmic tat-

[42] *Eight Months in Illinois*, 83.
[43] Hall, *The New Purchase*, 161. The technique of chopping bears a striking resemblance to that of certain modern athletic sports, in which timing, "whip," centering of weight of bat or club to produce sound or "sweet" blows are of greater importance than mere strength.

William Oliver was duly impressed by the dexterity and speed with which Westerners accomplished their chopping. He said it was necessary for one to learn the art when young, "a person past middle age very rarely becoming proficient." *Eight Months in Illinois*, 83.

Pride in the woodsman's craft grew with the lumber industry of a later day and led to the development of the Paul Bunyan myths, one of America's original contributions to folklore.

[44] Poplars (tulip trees) at times reached a diameter of 8 to 10 feet and often sycamores, sometimes hollow, however, a diameter of 12 or 14 feet. Some of these trees would hold ("comfortably lodge") 20 to 30 standing men. Wild cherries of 4 to 5 feet were not uncommon. "The land was covered with heavy forests, many of the large poplar, oak, and walnut trees having trunks from ten to fifteen feet in diameter." Mrs. Lucina O. Hamilton, "Ephraim Samuel Frazee, 1824–1896," in *Indiana Magazine of History*, XXIV (1928), 187, and correction, 327–28.

François A. Michaux, the French botanist, reported plane (sycamore) trees along the Ohio 44 and 47 feet in circumference. Much more remarkable, however, was his statement that poplars sometimes were 15 to 18 feet in diameter. *Travels to the Westward of the Allegany Mountains . . . in 1802* (London, 1805), 42.

One of the last remnants of the fine hardwood forests of the Ohio Valley stands two miles south of Paoli, Indiana. Here remain a few black walnuts 130 feet high with trunks 5 feet in diameter, 70 feet high to the first limbs; oaks, poplars, etc., in proportion. Andrew H. Hepburn, "Joe Cox's Trees Live On," in *Saturday Evening Post*, CCXIV, 18 ff. (Jan. 31, 1942).

too like unto the staccato blows of the sledges of oldtime circus Negro stake-driver gangs, brought these patriarchs of the forest trembling to earth midst the crashing of lesser neighbors and the roar and reverberation of the impact.[45] No power ribbon saws for this work, nor even the crosscut man-powered backbreakers; just the woodsman's ax.

> The axe, in stalwart hands, with steadfast stroke,
> The savage echoes of the forest woke,
> And, one by one, breaking the world-old spell,
> The hardy trees, long-crashing, with thunder fell.
> The log-house rose, within the solitude,
> And civilized the tenants of the wood.
> It was not long before the shadow'd mold
> Open'd to take the sunshine's gift of gold;
> In the dark furrow dropp'd the trusted seed,
> And the first harvest bless'd the sower's need.[46]

Trees to be cleared for the cabin site, trees to be cleared for fields, trees to be cleared for roads; timber to be cut for cabins and outbuildings, split for rails, ricked for fuel. The labor of clearing appeared stupendous, and in the earlier years it was a tedious and laborious task, but cumulative in results as time went by. The settler might "cut smack smooth" and have the job done once for all, or he might clear extensively, start his crops, and finish the job later.[47] As a rule the underbrush and trees under 18 or 20 inches were cut, and the larger ones girdled. Walnut, hickory, elm, and beech never put out leaves again after being girdled while in full leaf, but hackberry, sugar, and ash had to be piled around with brush and burned deeply, or they would shade the crops.[48] Some farmers set fire to the dead trees the winter following, and a several-acre "deadnin' " spouting flames heaven-

---

[45] A description of the felling of a nine-foot bee tree is given in Hall, *The New Purchase*, 190–92.

[46] Piatt, *Idyls and Lyrics of the Ohio Valley*, 76.

[47] As late as 1840 in Ohio many fields were cleared only of underbrush, stubble, and small trees, the trees more than a foot through being merely girdled. These trees offered some shade; as they died twigs and limbs fell, only half crops were raised, and eventually a second clearing as extensive as the first had to be undertaken. The best way was to clear only 5 acres per year and get a full crop, rather than 15 and have half a crop. *Western Farmer* (Cincinnati, 1839–40, continued as *Western Farmer and Gardener*, 1840–45), I, 231–32 (Apr., 1840).

[48] Some farmers maintained that oak, hickory, poplar, and sugar maple trees were the ones which gave up easiest. Some girdled deep, others just through the bark (cambium layer), leaving an upturned edge to catch water and start decay. Perhaps the only sure way was to girdle "in the dark of the moon in August when the sign was in the heart"; then nothing could survive.

ward at night was a sight to behold. If not fired, dead beech and sugar maples would begin to fall about the third year, but oak, poplar, and walnut would stand for several years. Once down, the trees had to be trimmed, cut into sections, rolled into piles, and burned. If felled so as to form rough windrows, labor of handling slashings could be saved by firing as the trees lay, and, by "niggering off" or burning the logs into sections, further chopping be obviated. Early plowing would be made easier by cutting off the larger roots near the surface with the ax; German settlers as well as some Yankees went after them conscientiously with the mattock.

Timber to be used for fence rails, buildings, and the like was best cut in full sap. It seasoned quicker and resisted weather and worms better.[49] That the process of clearing could be carried too far was realized by some settlers. The advantage of keeping a part of each farm in timber was pointed out, and it was recommended that legislatures encourage this practice.[50]

After the winter's chopping came the log rolling in the spring or following autumn, with neighbors giving freely of their time and labor, and no reckoning made.

Up in the morning and busy among their own burning heaps by cock-crowing, and off to a distant neighbor's, often four or five miles away, by sun-up, and then with handspike put forth such muscular effort and strength among the green logs, as happily laborers are seldom called upon to give nowadays, and at sunset off for home, where the smoldering heaps must again be stirred together before the wearied man could find rest in sleep. And it was not for one day, or two, or three, but for weeks this wearisome work went on.[51]

There was an art to piling the logs so that the pile would burn down completely with one firing; he who had not mastered that art was likely to be the recipient of blunt jibes. Men attended a dozen or more log rollings a spring, and if aspirants for office, two or three times as many. Fields were cleared a few acres at a time; for years the pungent, eye-stinging, but hunger-provoking smoke of burning wood piles permeated the settlements; and

---

[49] *Western Tiller* (Cincinnati, 1826–31 [?]), March 2, 1827.
[50] See, for example, one column "communicated" in Springfield *Illinois State Register,* December 25, 1839.
[51] David D. Banta, *A Historical Sketch of Johnson County, Indiana* (Chicago, 1881), 60.

neighbors assembled to work, drink, exchange gossip, talk politics, "wrastle," gouge, shoot, and play practical jokes.

Log rollings took care of the logs, and burning piles of wood and brush accounted for some of the stumps, but fire could not rid the soil of roots or take care of the underbrush and briars of the slashings. In bottom lands the paw paw, spicewood, grapevine, and leatherwood grew so thickly as to frighten any but the stoutest hearts. Months and years of backbreaking work with brush hooks, briar scythes, mattocks, and other grubbing tools had still to be spent.

The first clearings brought the problem of fencing, as the woods were a communal foraging ground for the stock of the neighborhood. To save time temporary fences of brush, logs, and poles were built. Trees felled in rows with limbs partially cut through, bent and interlaced and reinforced with poles or saplings would turn cattle. Pole fences could be built as a rail fence, as a post and rail fence, or the poles laid in the crotches of standing saplings. Even log fences were built. But the fence which was constructed as soon as possible by the more ambitious settler was the Virginia or "worm" rail fence.

Splitting was an important branch of woodcraft in the days before sawmills. For splitting rails and other coarser work the necessary tools were a couple of iron wedges, several wood wedges or gluts of dogwood or other hard tough material, and a maul.[52] The simplest maul was made by cutting a six- or eight-inch second growth hickory down to handle size for three or four feet, and leaving a cylinder of full size at the bottom for the maul head. Better still was the mallet maul, with handle inserted in the side of the head and iron rims to keep the faces from shattering.

For rails white ash, oak, chestnut, poplar, or walnut was felled by most settlers in winter when the sap was down; it was the only season they had the time. Cuts of ten or twelve feet in length were halved by starting the iron wedges in one end and inserting the gluts in the crack as it ran the length of the log. The halves in turn were split, the heartwood split out and perhaps laid aside for ground rails, and the rest worked into as many rails as the material allowed. Skill was required to get fairly

[52] Usually called a beetle by the settlers from New York and New England.

uniform size, reasonable straightness, and to waste no material. A common hand could cut and split a hundred rails a day, a good man twice as many. The usual pay was a dollar a day or per hundred, or fifty cents and found.

Rail splitting continued as a part of farm labor long after pioneer days had passed, for fences decayed, new fields were cleared, and road and railway right of ways had to be enclosed. The "snake" or "worm" fences were laid from seven to ten rails high, and often the panel joints were reinforced by leaning cross stakes, along the intersecting angles of which a pole or rider was laid. This was one form of the stake and rider fence. Simple and effective gates were provided by bars, which were let down at one end for stock or slid back out of the way for wagons. Such a fence lasted from fifteen to fifty years, sometimes longer. The rail fence was a product of its environment. It was wasteful of land, its angles were conducive to briars and brush, or convenient dumping spots for stones and trash, but properly aged, covered with moss and vines, weathered and fitted into its surroundings, it became possessed of beauty and historical atmosphere which it would share with its contemporary, the rubble stone fence, but never with its more practical and efficient successor, the barbed wire.

Clearing and fencing were followed by other demands upon the woodworking talents of the settler. In the early rush to get a cabin and clearing, little time or labor was spent on outbuildings. For the cow and horse, or the few head of stock not left at large, shedlike lean-to structures of poles and grass provided shelter, but as clearings were enlarged, crops raised, and stock multiplied, these were replaced by stables and barns of rough or hewn logs. Sections of hollow sycamore, given a bottom, were used as grain bins, or inverted as out- or well houses. Split and supplied with ends they provided water troughs. Hay barns, corncribs, smoke- and springhouses, enlarging the cabin or building of a new, necessitated further woodworking. In addition there were the dozens of implements and devices used around house and farm.

A man of average skill made gates, carts, barrows, plow frames, single- and doubletrees, ox yokes, wooden shovels, hay forks, troughs, benches, woodhorses, tool handles, stirring paddles, rakes, well sweeps, mortars, flails, cradles for mowing, swingling knives, flax brakes, and many other articles. The more skillful needed not the local or traveling artisans but made wagons—spokes, felly, hub, frame and body—spinning wheels, chests, clock cabinets, beds, chairs, carved butter molds, and did cooperage work—buckets, tubs, firkins, churns, barrels, and casks. Hoop-pole barrel hoops split from saplings and notched at the ends could be made by all. "The pioneer who forges ahead and makes the improvements from year to year, is of a naturally hopeful temperament, and in doing rather than dreaming, finds many of life's satisfactions."

Tools needed for the more common work were not numerous. What the woodsman's ax was to the cutter, the broadax was to the dresser of wood. With this tool, with its broad crescent-edged battle-ax blade and a handle curved out of the plane of the blade, a rough log could be squared and hewn to a smoothness dependent only upon the skill of the workman.[53] Skilled hewers scorned the use of the adz[54] for finishing a flat surface; with the broadax they flaked off the last layer of chips in sections of six to ten inches so neatly that hardly a line remained to mark the scoring. For splitting of clapboards the frow, a long thin iron wedge with a handle on one end, was used. The bolt of wood, hewn to size, was placed on the woodhorse or vise and held in place by a foot lever. When the frow was entered at one end, the split was run by prying upon the handle, and guided by turning the wood over from time to time. The secret of good riving lay in knowledge of woods and their qualities.

Next in importance to the ax was that universal backwoods tool, the drawing knife, a double-handled pulling implement for shaving and dressing down everything from heavy frames, wagon tongues, and ox yokes, to ax handles, staves, spokes, and smaller pieces. Augers, reaming tools, saws, and other tools were added as they became available, and could be afforded. Crosscut wood saws were a rarity on the frontier until about 1815.[55] With their introduction, sawpits were dug, or the side of a steep hill used, and with one man above and one below the log, boards of some uniformity in thickness were laboriously cut off. The more enter-

[53] The handle of the broadax was curved so as to permit hewing parallel to the surface without barking of knuckles.
[54] A tool built somewhat like a short handled hoe, with a curved, axlike blade.
[55] Lewis, "Pioneers of Jefferson County," in *Indiana Magazine of History,* XII, 218.

prising folks could then replace the puncheon floors with a smoother surface. The next step was the sawmill, with its vertical saws run by water wheels, which produced boards and dressed timbers and made possible better houses.

§ § §

The most important business of the pioneer was living. Speculation, money-making, accumulation of capital, were matters of concern to the few; making a living, to all. Yet ideas as to what constituted a living varied. To the hunting farmer, or rather the farming hunter, agriculture was reduced to the barest minimum necessary to furnish sufficient food to supplement that supplied by the rifle. He had time to hunt and kill deer, but not to fence his cornfields, with which the cows and horses played havoc. His cows and calves ran loose for lack of enclosures, yet his family might eat five pounds of butter a day three days a week, though butter sold at 25 cents a pound.[56] Many, shiftless and unenterprising, went for years without barn or outbuildings, except perhaps for a corncrib of sorts and a stable, and lived in homes without windows or floors and with a platform covered with husks for a bed. "His family is compelled to live on 'hog and hominy,' and often pays the penalty of fever and ague, bilious fever, scrofula and the like. Where the strawberry bed should be, you will perhaps find a tobacco patch, and the hog pen had usurped the place of the currant bush."[57] Farmers such as these raised no surplus and would not have done so had there been transportation facilities and markets. Either their wants were simple and easily satisfied, or they had not the acumen and ambition to satisfy them. Other settlers, true husbandmen, by heritage and experience, knew how to locate the best land and to use it.

> His skillful eye rov'd o'er the ground,
> And soon the fittest section found.
> For taught from youth with skill to know
> Where best each grain and seed would grow,
> His judgement soon discern'd the soil
> Most fitted to reward his toil.[58]

[56] Faux, *Memorable Days,* 250.
[57] Eliza W. Farnham, *Life in Prairie Lands* (New York, 1846), 64 ff.; Springfield *Illinois State Register,* January 17, March 13, 1850.
[58] Whiting, *The Emigrant.*

A society in process of establishment in a new region seeks to develop the most available resources of that region, at first for itself, then as communications and markets develop, for exchange with other parts. Sometimes this process necessitates the learning of new occupations and skills, as when an agricultural people go into mining areas; at others it merely means meeting a new set of problems in a familiar method of life. With the people of the Old Northwest the latter was generally the case. This was pre-eminently an agricultural region, soon to be the granary not only of America, but to a large extent of Europe as well.

Pioneer agriculture in the Old Northwest developed as two general types, which, though they had much in common, arose under different conditions and called for different methods. First came the forest-clearing, small-field farming, much of it on the hilly, nonglaciated, relatively thin-soiled areas of southern Ohio, Indiana, and Illinois. Then, as settlement expanded and fears of the treeless areas diminished, came the agricultural development of the openings and prairies of northern Indiana, Illinois, and parts of Michigan and Wisconsin.

Farming in the wooded lands presented no new problems. Since the earliest settlements along the Atlantic Coast, Americans had been clearing the land and raising crops. In learning and adopting Indian methods they had reverted to the practices of their primitive ancestors. It was a natural husbandry—loose and extensive cultivation, with no serious attempt at cropping and resting or soil building. As fields diminished in productivity or played out, more land was cleared, and the system continued. But in time it became necessary to give some attention to improved methods. Cropping and resting was one of the first evidences; then at various places prior to 1800 the naked-fallow practice came into use—that is, cultivation of the idle field to rid it of weeds and fungi and to restore the soil. Then followed experiments in legume rotation—peas, clover and the like—and in field-grass husbandry, with such rotation as corn, wheat, pasture, but neither system achieved great success. By the end of the eighteenth century knowledge of more scientific crop rotation and soil fertilization was spreading in the United States. Washington, Jefferson, Randolph, Jared Eliot, John Taylor, and others did noble pioneering work and during the first quarter of the nineteenth century the idea of scientific rotation began to take root.[59] Such advanced ideas, however, little concerned the mass of American farmers until a much later date. Land was plentiful and cheap in relation to labor. Excepting for a few favored regions there were no markets and hence no incentive to produce a surplus. Tools and implements were of the simplest sort, in fact had not been considerably improved upon since ancient times. Further, there was the lack of root crops and the great emphasis upon Indian corn or maize.

As the settlers worked west they naturally reverted to primitive methods. Corn was usually the first crop and in many regions occupied first importance for years. Methods of cultivation as well as use of this grain were borrowed from the Indian, and the maize complex became as important a culture trait among the pioneers as it had been among the red men.[60] Corn, cultivated with the hoe, did well even on partially cleared land. New land, with the rich accumulation of humus and the addition of phosphate and other elements from the ashes of brush heaps, produced excellent yields.

This soil, however, was not so good for wheat; seven to ten years were required for "new soil" to produce a good flour grain.

[59] For a brief review of stages in American agriculture, see Norman S. B. Gras, *A History of Agriculture in Europe and America* (New York, 1925), Chapter XII; Schmidt and Ross (eds.), *Readings in Economic History of American Agriculture*, Chapters III, V, X; and Joseph Schafer, *The Social History of American Agriculture* (New York, 1936). A more compendious treatment is the compilation by Percy W. Bidwell and John I. Falconer, *History of Agriculture in the Northern United States 1620–1860* (Carnegie Institution, Washington, D. C., 1925). The bibliographies in these histories should be supplemented by the *Bibliography of the History of Agriculture in the United States*, by Everett E. Edwards (U. S. Department of Agriculture, 1930). The files of *Agricultural History* (1927–   ) and the article by its first editor, Everett E. Edwards, "Middle Western Agricultural History as a Field for Research," in *Mississippi Valley Historical Review*, XXIV (1937–38), 315–28, are useful for additional references. Of the states in the Northwest, Ohio, Indiana, and Wisconsin have histories devoted exclusively to agriculture: Charles W. Burkett, *History of Ohio Agriculture* (Concord, N. H., 1900); William A. Lloyd, J. I. Falconer, and Charles E. Thorne, *The Agriculture of Ohio* (*Bulletin 326* of the Ohio Agricultural Experiment Station, Wooster, Ohio, 1918); W. C. Latta, *History of Indiana Agriculture* (Lafayette, Ind., 1938); and Joseph Schafer, *A History of Agriculture in Wisconsin* (Madison, 1922).

[60] The Indian deadened trees, planted corn in hills, beans and squashes among the corn, used a husking pin, built corncribs on posts to keep out mice, and even knew how to test seed by warm-water germination. Hominy, succotash, and mush were Indian dishes; braiding the husks of seed ears, weaving husk mats, and making lye hominy were Indian practices. Clark Wissler, "Aboriginal Maize Culture as a Typical Culture-Complex," in *American Journal of Sociology*, XXI (1915–16), 657. See also Arthur C. Parker, *Iroquois Uses of Maize and Other Food Plants* (Albany, N. Y., 1925).

Wheat sowed on new land produced lots of straw but the grain was shriveled and musty; rust and smut were too much for it. Sometimes "sick wheat" resulted, which seemingly matured and looked sound, but when baked into bread very potently affected the stomach. Even hogs, whose stomachs were arsenic proof, would not give such grain a second trial.[61] Corn sickness, too, might result from using meal made from corn not properly ripened, or, if the unsound grain was distilled into whiskey, it materially aided the cause of temperance.[62] Besides rust, the Hessian fly and the army worm were vigilant enemies to be faced by the farmer. Many of the weeds which later became troublesome, such as thistle, pigweed, and pigeon grass, were not in evidence in the early years.

Breaking new land was a stubborn task, equally hard on man and beast. Plows, although somewhat improved over the forked stick, were far from satisfactory. The plow of colonial days was a heavy affair made of wood and wrought iron, had a 10-foot beam and cost $40 or $50. The moldboard[63] was of wood fitted crudely to the irons, the landside was four feet long, and the point or share was of steel, which had to be frequently sharpened by the blacksmith at some considerable cost. The handles were so vertically set as to give little leverage or control. The action of this plow might be illustrated by turning a sharp-pointed shovel upside down and pushing it through the soil;[64] it made the

[61] George Branson, "Early Flour Mills in Indiana," in *Indiana Magazine of History*, XXII (1928), 20; Major, *Pioneers of Morgan County*, 299.

[62] Springfield *Sangamo Journal*, March 1, 1832.

[63] The broad flaring part of the plow which turns over the soil after it has been cut by the point or share. The straight piece which runs a vertical inside wall to the furrow is the landside.

[64] A. B. Allen described the method of making a plow: "A winding tree was cut down, and a moldboard hewed from it, with the grain of the timber so nearly along its shape as it could well be obtained. On to this moldboard, to prevent its wearing out too rapidly, was nailed the blade of an old hoe, thin strips of iron or worn-out horseshoes. The land-side was wood, its base and sides shod with thin plates of iron. The share was of wood with a hardened steel point. The coulter was tolerably well made of iron steel-edged and locked into the share nearly as it does in the lock coulter plow of the present day. The beam was usually a straight stick. The handles, like the moldboard, were split from the crooked trunk of a tree, or as often from its branches. The crooked roots of the white ash were the most favored timber for plowhandles in the northern states. The beam (frequently 10 feet long) was set at any pitch fancy might dictate, with the handles fastened on at almost right angles with it, thus leaving the plowman with little control over his implement, which did the work in very slow and most imperfect manner." Quoted in Lloyd, Falconer, and Thorne, *Agriculture of Ohio*, 78, from *Report* of the Ohio State Board of Agriculture, 1856.

"furrows stand up like the ribs of a lean horse in the month of March."[65]

About 1796 Charles Newbold had patented a plow of solid cast iron, consisting of bar, sheath, and moldplate, and spent $30,000 trying to get it introduced. It worked far better than any previously used, but farmers were prejudiced against it because it was supposed to poison the land and stimulate the growth of weeds. Jethro Wood's plow of 1817 had a cast iron share as well as moldboard and landside, and interchangeable parts. Pessimistic predictions of what would happen to this "pot metal" affair were not borne out in practice. The implement held up, could be pulled with less effort, and be produced in quantity at a cost of $7.00 or $8.00. These patent plows were on sale at Columbus, Ohio, and probably elsewhere, in 1825.[66]

Although these improvements met with success and the farm implement industry became established, the typical plow in use in the West for years was either the plain shovel or jump plow, or the old bar-share or bull plow, which made no pretense of scouring.[67] Blacksmiths and "inventors" tried their hands, and

[65] U. S. Department of Agriculture, *Yearbook* (1899), 315.
[66] *Delaware* (Ohio) *Patron,* March 24, 1825.
[67] Albert D. Richardson, *Garnered Sheaves* (Hartford, Conn., 1871), 325.
"The plow was the common shovel plow mostly, though a few called the bar-share were used. This was a bar on the land side, with a broad flat share running to a point at the forward end, attached to a colter, with a steel nose in front. The colter extended up through the wooden beam of the plow; two wooden handles, one attached to the beam and to the bar of the land side of the plow, the other handle connected with a wooden moldboard, which pressed out the dirt and partially turned it. It was connected with the other handle by wooden pins or rounds. To the plow horses were attached often without an iron clevis. The double-tree was connected with a wooden fixture not unlike a clevis; the single tree fastened to the double-tree with a hickory withe; sometimes with a kind of wooden clevis. The horses were mostly geared for plowing with a collar made of corn-shucks; hames, made from the roots of the ash or oak, fashioned, as best they could be, with a drawing knife, a hole, top and bottom, so as to fasten with a cord, or a thong made from some raw hide; not uncommonly, a hole was made with an augur, near the middle of the hame, to take in the trace, which was made from hemp or flax tow, and spun and made on a rude ropewalk. The trace was run through the hole in the hame, and secured by a knot, and looped over the end of the single-tree, on which there was a notch at the back part to keep it in place. For a back-band a strong piece of tow cloth, doubled, was used. The horses were guided by a bridle, with iron bits, a rope headstall, and rope line; mostly driven with one line. . . . Even a four-horse team was driven with a single line attached to the near forward horse." Philip Mason, *A Legacy to My Children, including Family History, Autobiography, and Original Essays* (Cincinnati, 1868), 105–6.
The French settlers in Illinois in 1812 were using plows made of wood with a small iron point on the front part, with a beam which rested on an axle supported by small wooden wheels. Their carts had no iron in them. Reynolds, *History of Illinois,* 49–50. As late as 1850 the old cast iron plows were in general use. *Twelfth Census of the United States . . . 1900. Agriculture,* I, xxix.

the "Clark," the "Diamond," the "Tobey and Anderson," the "Carey" with its upright iron projection above the flat wrought-iron bar and small wooden moldboard, the "Jewett," the "Peacock," the "Daniel Webster," and many others were used at one time or another.[68]

Into the light woodland soils, probably cleared "in the green," went the plowman with the implement with which he was familiar. Beneath the surface was a mass of roots and grubs interwoven and interlaced: long slender elm roots served as warp, white and blue ash, hackberry, beech, and sugar the woof, spicewood and paw paw the finer filling, while oak and other tough giants supplied reinforcement. The Southerner, more philosophic perhaps, or just not so work-brittle, used the shovel plow,[69] jumped the big roots, and in the end stirred up the soil just as effectively as the eastern man or "Yankee" who, with the massive old cast iron bar share, with a man on the beam to keep it in the ground, and power enough often to cut through a four-inch solid oak root, sought to do the job right. Such an implement suited both the New England temperament and conscience.

Holding a breaker drawn by seven yokes of oxen was no sinecure. It needed a quick judgment to decide on which side of a big oak grub the plow should go to be the most effective, and then a strong and supple action to accomplish the purpose. Sometimes the coulter point of the plow would strike the center of a big oak root, split it, and march on triumphantly; but woe to him who made the rash attempt and failed. Upon this failure hinged multiplied catastrophes—the breaking of chains being the least. When the plow became stuck fast, and the impetus of the moving face was stopped, a second attempt was useless. Then came a tug at the handles to loosen the wedge-shaped coulter, and all hands and sometimes the leading team were required to free the plow.[70]

In either case this jerking, wracking, shin-cracking labor was not usually accomplished without an accompaniment of language

[68] Webster in 1836 devised a plow to clear new land. It was 12 feet from handles to beam end, had a landside 4 feet long and a moldboard of strap iron with 27-inch spread. The "Diamond" appeared about 1835. John Reynolds, *My Own Times* . . . (Belleville, Ill., 1855), 90. Pulverization was not regarded as important and the first patent for twisting and breaking the furrow slice was not issued until 1839. "Jewett's newly invented Cary plow," with a one-fourth inch wrought-iron moldboard, and share of wrought iron or steel, both polished smooth, was manufactured and sold by the Springfield, Illinois, Foundry by 1840. Advertisement and cut in *Sangamo Journal*, January, 1840.

[69] Major, *Pioneers of Morgan County*, 297; Mason, *Autobiography*, 105.

[70] A. C. Glidden, "Pioneer Farming," in *Michigan Pioneer and Historical Collections*, XVIII (1891), 419–20.

in addition to the necessary "gee!" "haw!" and "giddap!" A crude harrow consisting of a tree fork with proper angle of trunk for a tongue and branch stubs for teeth, could serve as clod breaker until a crossbar or a harrow of hewed oak and heavy wooden or iron pins could be constructed. Harrowing was no play task either, for the best of breaking left one or more live grubs to the square rod. These grubs were the result of accumulation of sprouts which, cut or burned off for years, developed just underground around the tap root into giant toadstool shapes which could be removed only by direct attack with an eight-pound grubbing hoe. Those not dug out were cropped above the surface when the ground was frozen, to facilitate mowing of the grain.

The difficulties of breaking prairie land were for the average pioneer even greater than those encountered in new clearings. The heavy prairie grass had roots as large as a man's finger which extended twelve to fifteen inches under ground, and formed a heavy tough sod which had to be cut through on the bottom of the furrow as well as turned over. Plowing was delayed until the grass was quite green, otherwise it would turn and spring up again. Sod plows were broader and more shallow than ordinary breaking plows, with the beam framed on an axle with wheels, one of which ran in the furrow and the other on the uncut surface. They broke a furrow about eighteen inches wide and three or four inches deep. Since at that depth they cut through the toughest part of the sod, it required from five to ten yoke of oxen to pull them.[71] This plow was supposed to require little guiding or holding, but as a matter of fact it was often out of the ground as much as in. Since the thin slice of sod was not completely inverted, the result was that the heavy prairie grasses frequently sprouted up again.[72] Nor did the problem end with first breaking; once the grass roots and fibers were rotted the nonfriable soil stuck to the

[71] The beam of these prairie plows was rather upright and the handles on some of them nearly perpendicular. "The share, sole, and breast, are made of malleable iron, and generally all in one piece. The share is made as broad as the furrow intended to be cut, and is laid with steel beaten very thin, filed sharp on the outer edge, and tempered hard, in order to cut the tough roots of the grasses and weeds. The coulter, which is used only in the prairie plough, is also sharpened and tempered, and has on the under edge, near its point, a small socket, which fits on to a corresponding plug at the point of the share. The mould board is of wood." Oliver, *Eight Months in Illinois*, 98–99.

[72] William Oliver, an English farmer, stated that "the slightest displacement of the soil destroys the prairie grasses." *Ibid.*, 98. Had he stayed longer than his one season in the prairie country, he would have learned differently.

plow like soft snow to a boot sole. The implement had to be removed and cleaned every few rods. It was not until 1837 that a satisfactory prairie plow was made by John Deere, pioneer blacksmith of Grand Detour, Illinois. This plow, made of a mill-saw blade, was light, self-scouring, and turned over the sticky black soil in good shape and kept on turning it over; being at first a handmade affair, and the saw steel a German product, it was expensive and scarce. It was a number of years before this type of plow was available in quantities, and the prairies finally conquered. Whereas good unimproved prairie land could still be obtained in Illinois for $2.00 or $3.00 per acre, the first breaking cost $2.50.[73]

Proper preparation of soil for crops was not only difficult in new ground, but its importance little appreciated in fields longer under cultivation. Plowing was shallow and pulverizing incomplete. The bull plow simply broke the ground and edged it up, and the shovel plow did little better. "The fields are rudely tilled, yet yield an abundant harvest,"[74] was true only of a soil laden with the accumulated humus of the ages. The proper time for corn planting was when the oak or maple leaves were as large as squirrel ears or when the dogwood blossoms were fully expanded. In the smaller fields of the valley bottoms, hillsides, or forest clearings, corn was dropped by hand and cultivated one or more times with the hoe or light shovel plow, and "hilled up," Indian fashion, at the time it was "laid by."

Cultivation was often neglected and weeds and burrs grew as tall as the corn. When they viewed their neighbors' fields, farmers sometimes remarked that they could take hold of the wild cucumber vines at one corner and shake all the corn in the field. Corn would grow very well in new ground, but if wheat were

[73] In Michigan as much as $5.00 per acre. *Michigan Pioneer and Historical Collections*, V (1882), 296 ff. Descriptions of prairie breaking may be found in *Western Farmer*, I, 132–33, 148 (Jan., 1840); *Transactions of the Illinois State Historical Society*, 1923, p. 203; *Journal of the Illinois State Historical Society*, XIX (1926–27), 107; Henry W. Ellsworth, *Valley of the Upper Wabash* . . . (New York, 1838), 50 ff.; Oliver, *Eight Months in Illinois*, 97–100; Jones, *Illinois and the West*, 160–61. The numerous emigrant guidebooks usually contained estimates for clearing, breaking, fencing, and building for farms from 160 to 640 acres in size. The cost of breaking and fencing of prairie land was approximately three times the cost of the land itself, provided it was purchased at the minimum price of $1.25 per acre.

[74] Hall, *Statistics of the West*, . . . (Cincinnati, 1836), 62.

attempted before several years of corn, rye, and buckwheat, the product would be worthless. On prairie land, since a year or more was required for the turf to rot, if a corn crop was desired the first year, grains were dropped in holes made with an ax, or in the landside edge of about every third furrow, so the plant could come through the cracks. A yield of 10 to 30 bushels was thus possible without cultivation. The second year the land was cross plowed and a yield of 30 bushels could be expected; or oats, rye, or spring wheat might be put in as a sod crop and some kind of a yield had, unless the season proved too dry. A more methodical start might be made by plowing the sod in the spring and letting it lie for a year, by which time if the plowing was well done, the green grass would be rotted and a regular plowing possible. Corn planted then and cultivated would produce 50 or 60 bushels per acre. By the 1830's some of the rich prairie or bottom lands were raising 100 to 120 bushels to the acre, with many of the stalks 12 to 15 feet in height. Plowing was not necessary for seeding of tame grass, as the prairie grass could be burned over, then harrowed a few times to break up the roots, and the domestic grass broadcast.

Experiments in deeper plowing were carried on in Ohio by Christopher Leaming who, by plowing two or three inches deeper and keeping out the weeds, harvested 104 bushels of corn to the acre as contrasted to the usual 50 bushels.[75] Although plows for subsoil plowing were on the market in the 1830's they were not widely used.[76]

Slight attention was paid to seed selection and little was understood about soil composition and the value of fertilizers. "Squaw" corn was the type commonly grown in the early period, but improved types such as Hackberry and Gourdseed were soon offering more rows to the ear and more quarts of whiskey to the bushel.[77] Some white flint corn was grown, especially in the

[75] Lloyd, Falconer, and Thorne, *Agriculture in Ohio,* 48–49, quoting J. S. Leaming's account of corn culture in 1826.

[76] For example, Smith's improved subsoil plow.

[77] In Illinois the farmers claimed that the commonly used "Little Yellow" had come from the Indians. In 1846 Robert Reid, of Ohio, moved to Tazewell County, Illinois, and planted Gordon Hopkins corn which he brought along. When many hills failed to germinate, neighbors supplied Little Yellow for replanting. From this mixture eventually came Reid's Yellow Dent, a favorite of the corn country until the advent of hybrid corn.

Western Reserve and in Illinois. In the 1830's other new types were being introduced, among them the Baden, the white dented corn with 12 to 20 rows to the cob. Its advocates claimed as high as 120 bushels to the acre and up to 8 ears to the stalk.[78] The Tuscarora, an early type, was also being tried and from the mid-April planting some farmers reported roasting ears the last of June, ripe corn by August 1, and corn bread from the meal by August 7.[79] In Wisconsin Territory, where corn was an uncertain crop, many favored the Dutton. To avoid the possibility of killing September frosts farmers were advised to select their seed from first-ripening ears of corn grown in middle and northern states.[80] In harvesting in the earlier period the corn was usually stripped from the stalks in the field and the fodder not used. Shocking the corn, a Virginia practice indulged in by the settlers from the South, later came into general use.

Besides corn, which was food and bread for man as well as provender for animals, and in the form of whiskey almost equivalent to currency, wheat, rye, oats, and some hay and coarser grasses were more or less widely raised. Wheat sown broadcast in cleared ground and harrowed in with a brush harrow would produce some kind of a crop, provided the ground was not too new. Some farmers sowed as much as two bushels of wheat to the acre on raw sandy soil and got a fuzzy product which in vain tried to head. In prairie land winter wheat sown six months after sod-breaking usually did fairly well, but as Governor Coles, of Illinois, pointed out, wheat was the worst crop. He recommended better preparation of the soil, earlier and heavier seeding, and reaping before ripe.[81] In land which had been cultivated for some time wheat was usually sown after a summer fallow (land left idle and preferably kept clear of weeds), but later progressive farmers substituted a clover crop. Among the early varieties of wheat were Red-chaff Bearded (Old Red Chaff), Red Blue Stem, and Mediterranean, which, under the name of Black Sea

[78] *Hennepin* (Ill.) *Journal,* in *Cincinnati Daily Gazette,* August 24, 1838; *St. Louis Republican* in *Sangamo Journal,* November 10, 1838.
[79] Vandalia *Illinois Advocate and State Register,* August 10, 1833.
[80] William Rudolph Smith, *Observations on the Wisconsin Territory* . . . (Philadelphia, 1838), 9.
[81] Address to the Illinois Agricultural Society, in Vandalia *Illinois Intelligencer,* December 24, 1824.

Hamer's Mill, Spring Mill State Park in Southern Indiana
(Restoration)

Original Wooden Gears in Hamer's Mill

Pottery Kiln, Indianapolis. *Christian Schrader*

Tumbles near present Military Park, Indianapolis
Christian Schrader

wheat, was widely grown in Ohio. Wheat yields varied widely. The industrious Rappites got 25 to 30 bushels per acre on the Lower Wabash, whereas farmers across the river in Illinois got 15. Near Milwaukee the yield ran as high as 40 bushels.[82]

In the woods clearings bears, deer, wild turkeys, birds, and squirrels made such inroads on crops, particularly corn, that unless constant vigilance was exercised no part of the crop would be left. Boys, girls, and the women folk often patrolled the fields three or four times a day when the grain was first sprouting, and again when maturing, and with the aid of dogs and "bull fiddles" drove away the marauders. "The squirrels and birds stole by day, the coons and bears by night, and so they kept the first settler anxious until his corn was safely cribbed out of their reach."[83] In addition there was always the roaming livestock. On prairie lands fencing was a serious problem. Rails cost $3.00 to $4.00 per hundred, when they were to be had, as contrasted to one third that amount in timbered areas. At this price it cost $100 to $150 to fence a 10-acre lot, or $200 to $300 for a 40-acre field. Some writers thought hedges would solve the problem, as in England, but the hot dry summers were not conducive to hedge growth. Others advocated ditches and dikes as a substitute for fences; a few discouraged individuals thought the only solution was training shepherds to herd the stock.[84] Hessian fly, rust, the army worm, and the seventeen-year locust came and went, but corn borers and Japanese and Mexican beetles had, of course, not yet arrived. Thus often subject to attack, early and late, from land and air, as well as by disease, crops were bound to suffer.

Grain and grass were ordinarily sown by hand or by a broad-

[82] *Diary of William Owen,* 1824–25, edited by Joel W. Hiatt (*Indiana Historical Society Publications,* IV, No. 1, Indianapolis, 1906), 88; Madison *Wisconsin Enquirer,* May 27, 1840.

[83] Major, *Pioneers of Morgan County,* 298; Robert and Alexander Miller, "Pioneers of Jefferson County," in *Indiana Magazine of History,* XII, 232. In Ohio in 1817 "an act to encourage the killing of squirrels" was passed. Each taxpayer was to be given a quota, and was supposed to be fined three cents for each scalp under his quota. Organized squirrel hunts were held. Near Columbus, Ohio, in 1822 some 20,000 scalps were collected in one big hunt, and near Lancaster five years later two hunts collected about 1,000 each. *Columbus Gazette* item in *Hamilton Intelligencer and Advertiser,* September 23, 1822; *Lancaster Gazette* in *Hamilton Advertiser,* April 27, 1827. Wolf-bounty laws were passed in different states. In Ohio in 1822 the bounty was $3.00.

[84] *Sangamo Journal,* July 19, 1839; *Western Farmer,* I, 121 (Dec., 1839). Many articles appeared on this subject in the agricultural papers.

cast seeder.[85] Wheat and rye were still cut in 1830 as they had
been for five thousand years, with the smooth-bladed reaping
hook or the long narrow-bladed sickle with its fine saw-tooth
edge; oats, buckwheat, and grasses were usually cut with the
scythe. Bands of sicklers sometimes followed the harvest and
worked for 37½ cents per day each, or a bushel of wheat. Around
the fields they followed each other, perhaps enlivening the work
with song and jest, to the end of the round. If the reaper bound
back his sheaves as he reaped, he would harvest about half an acre
per day, but if followed by one or more binders, might more than
double this amount. Only extreme heat or fatigue would force
a worker to rest up in a fence corner and admit that "his hide was
hung on the fence." By the 1830's the cradle—the big scythe
with the wood fingers above it which held the grain until laid
neatly in rows on the back stroke—had come into more general
use. The cradle cut a deeper and wider swath than the sickle, consequently cradling was easier—at least on the legs—and faster
work, since it was done standing up instead of from a squatting
position. The snaths of cradles were crudely shaped—often quite
straight in fact—and the whole contraption was poorly balanced
and awkward to handle; there was not the same pleasure to be
derived from cradling as from the rhythmic swish of the unencumbered scythe in a hay field. Nevertheless, to the onlooker
cradling appeared easy and beautiful.[86]

Two men, one cradling, the other assembling and binding
the bundles with bands of the grain, could harvest and shock two
or more acres a day. Few cradlers practiced the awkward and
slow method of "gripping" or assembling their own sheaves by
turning up the cradle fingers at the end of the stroke and grabbing
the grain in the left hand before dropping it in sheaves.

> All day the reapers through the wheat
> Have wrought amid the sultry heat,
> Reaping the harvest wide and fleet.
>
> All day the binders' stooping train
> Have swelter'd through the sweating grain,
> Binding the bearded sheaves amain:

[85] The manufacture of grain drills in the United States began about the end of
our period (1840). Two-horse planters and straddle-row sulky cultivators came
in in the 1850's.

[86] Mrs. Caroline M. Kirkland, *Western Clearings* (New York, 1845), 58.

With shouted jest, with breaks of song,
Lightening their heavy toil along,
A merry-hearted, boisterous throng!

· · · · · · ·

Tramping a steady tramp, they moved like soldiers
    that march to the beat
Of music that seems, a part of themselves, to rise
    and fall with their feet;

Tramping a steady tramp, they came with flashes of
    silver that shone,
Every step, from their scythes that rang as if they
    needed the stone—[87]

Wheat harvest was the leading harvest of the year; for much of the country corn was just as important, but its harvesting could be carried on at leisure. Not so with the wheat harvest:

When it comes, as we have said, all is activity and bustle. All energies are concentrated upon it, and every thing gives way to it. Politics for a time let go their hold upon the rustic partisan. He cares not for vetoes, nor even for tariffs; bad legislation stays not the ripening of corn; (fortunately for us all.) When the beneficent Sun has done his work, and wheat nods its brown head and sways languidly in the faint breath of the morning; when corn flings its silken banners abroad, and the earth seems every where burdened with Heaven's bounty; at this glorious season the farmer, with his heart and his arm nerved by hope, goes forth to put the finishing stroke to the year's labours. No fear of the sun's fervours deters or disheartens him. He fears only the delicious cooling shower which would drive his "hands" to the barn, and perhaps detain his grain on the ground long enough materially to injure its quality.

To be early in the field is the farmer's maxim. He waits only for light enough to work by, before calling up his men, who are apt to be up before he calls them, so contagious is the enthusiasm of the hour. No one likes to be a laggard in harvest. And then the early morning air is so fresh and so inspiriting; the brightening hues of the pearly East so irresistibly glorious, the rising of the sun so majestic, that even the dull soul feels, and the dull eye gazes, with an admiration not unmixed with awe. Two hours' labour before the six o'clock breakfast lays bare a wide space in the field, for very numerous are the strong arms brought up to the work. This season is the test of the husbandman's capabilities, whether as master or man.

The harvest efforts of "Neighbour Feckless," who depended upon luck rather than his own preparation, were contrasted with

[87] Piatt, *Idyls and Lyrics of the Ohio Valley*, 31, 93.

those of "Neighbour Thrifty," who had everything and everybody lined up. The blacksmith could shoe no horses; the carpenter could drive no nails; and none but the smaller children remained in school; even lawsuits were suspended for the justice, too, was in the field. Everyone was bespoke in advance by "Neighbour Thrifty," who himself led rather than commanded his help. "It is proverbial in the country that 'Come, boys!' is always better than 'Go, boys!' . . ."[88]

From the early years of the Christian era man had been seeking a way to harvest grain with horsepower, but it was not until 1831 that Cyrus Hall McCormick produced a machine which combined the seven essential parts into a working and practicable unit.[89] This machine with eight men and two horses could harvest ten acres per day—no better than a similar number of cradlers could do. McCormick did not secure a patent until 1834. It was four years before he was ready to market his reaper, and fifteen years from its introduction before it was perfected, produced in quantity, and ready to affect seriously agriculture in the West. Meanwhile dozens of others were inventing and advertising their reapers, while a few sought to combine a reaper and threshing machine. In 1833 Obed Hussey, of Ohio, demonstrated a reaper at the Hamilton County Agricultural Society Fair near Cincinnati.[90] The same year he secured a patent, and news of the event was recorded in eastern agricultural periodicals, although the editors were not inclined to become enthusiastic. Since Hussey's patent antedated McCormick's by some months, he claimed to be the inventor of the reaper, and the long war of the reapers began. Few machines were put on the market prior to 1839 by either McCormick or Hussey, and those mostly in the

[88] Kirkland, *Western Clearings*, 60–61.

[89] From the time of the industrial revolution, the idea of a reaping machine had developed in both England and the United States. The first patent granted was to an Englishman in 1799; the first in the United States was granted in 1803. For the history of the development of the reaper and the dispute over priority, the best work to date is William T. Hutchinson, *Cyrus Hall McCormick* (2 volumes. New York, 1930, 1935).

[90] Note in *Farmer's Reporter and United States Agriculturist* (Cincinnati, 1830–37; title varies; called *Western Farmer*, 1835–37), July, 1833, p. 38. The machine, using two horses, cut a swath five feet wide, and required a boy to drive and a man to lay in bundles. For illustrations and descriptions of the Hussey and McCormick reapers, see Bidwell, *History of Agriculture in the Northern United States*, 286–90.

East. Interest was developing rapidly in the West, however, by 1840.[91]

Farmers who produced but little grain threshed with the flail, a beating instrument consisting of a hickory or white ash stick three or four feet long, bound with thongs to a handle about twice as long. When more than one flail operated at a time, it was necessary to time the strokes, and the rhythm of the beat might be interrupted only at the risk of a blow from a rebounding flail. The grain was cleaned by letting it fall in the wind or before a sheet fanned by two persons. Two men could flail and winnow a dozen bushels of wheat, or two or three times that amount of oats, barley, or buckwheat per day.

Threshing and cleaning the crop of a ten-acre field was nearly an all-winter job for the singlehanded farmer. Fanning mills came in time, and progressive or lazy farmers who purchased them were sometimes criticized by devout neighbors for creating a "wind contrary to nater," and hence offensive in the sight of the Lord.[92] Those who produced more than a few acres of grain threshed on the treading floor or barn floor, where the grain was spread in a circle and cattle or horses driven over it until it was tramped out, at the rate of 20 to 200 bushels per day.

Improved horsepower and treadmill threshers came into use in the 1830's; they were first introduced into the West along the line of the National Road. The early models of these crude heavy wooden affairs required four to six strong horses to revolve the gears, and had a capacity of 30 to 60 bushels per day. The grain had to be fanned separately.

In 1828 Peter Barker, of Worthington, Ohio, submitted testimonials to the effect that his machine, run by one horse and two men, could thresh 250 to 300 bushels.[93] Soon the sellers of Fox and Borland's patent offered to stake $1,000 on the superiority of their machine.[94] Benjamin Maltby's new and improved machine promised to thresh 20 bushels of wheat or 30 of oats per

---

[91] Ellsworth, in *The Valley of the Upper Wabash,* a combination of emigrants' guide, land-sales prospectus, and treatise on agriculture, gives several pages to description and testimonials of the Hussey machine, and includes a very good cut of it, but does not mention McCormick's.

[92] Fans were made at Alton, Illinois, and sold in southern Illinois in the early 1820's. Reynolds, *My Own Times,* 90.

[93] Columbus *Ohio State Journal,* April 10, 1828.

[94] *Ibid.,* January 1, 1832.

hour;[95] and near Springfield, Illinois, was displayed a two-horse-power machine with fan mill attachment, with capacity of 200 to 300 bushels per day.[96] The next advance was a traveling thresher. When this affair, pulled by six strong horses,

driven by a rollicking country Jehu, and fed by an expert—the bundles being thrown upon the band-cutter's table from a wagon driven beside the thresher—came rattling and rumbling along the great road on a display trip, scattering straw and chaff to the disgust of the townspeople and the great delight of the pigs, chickens, and little children, and closely followed by the inevitable fanning mill peddler with his newly painted wind-raisers, the rural heart beat high and happily, and the agricultural statisticians figured out big profits for those who should thereafter cultivate cereals in the wheat belt of Ohio and Indiana.

Previous to the improvements in implements toward the end of the period, it required twenty-four long days of work for one man to plow, seed, and harvest ten acres of wheat, and forty-four days to plow, plant, cultivate, and harvest ten acres of corn.[97]

Rich native grasses furnished excellent pasturage. Buffalo grass and buffalo clover grew on the prairies and in the woods openings, and cane in the brakes along the Ohio. As clearings and cultivation progressed, the native grasses disappeared, but white clover and Kentucky bluegrass "volunteered" and spread. A few experiments had been made in the cultivation of timothy and red clover in Indiana and Illinois before 1840.[98] Some interest was also being shown in "Florin" or bent grass, which propagated from roots or runners.[99]

Root crops, good alike for cattle and soil, were on the whole neglected or raised only for household use. Early Wisconsin settlers found it possible to raise 300 to 500 bushels of potatoes per acre, but ready markets were not available. Flax was widely raised in patches for domestic consumption largely, while hemp,

---

[95] Columbus *Ohio State Journal,* October 3, 1832.

[96] *Sangamo Journal,* November 3, 1832

[97] William Henry Smith, *History of the State of Indiana* (2 volumes. Indianapolis, 1903), I, 353.

[98] Hall, *Statistics of the West,* 26, 74; Caleb Atwater, *History of the State of Ohio* (Cincinnati, 1838), 92; Birkbeck, *Letters,* 38; Ellsworth, *Valley of the Upper Wabash,* 38.

[99] See for example two-column article by Samuel L. Mitchell in Chillicothe *Weekly Recorder,* February 2, 1815. The Lawrenceburg *Indiana Palladium,* March 25, 1825, said that western farmers were discovering that they could raise not only corn and hogs but timothy and clover as good as that raised in the East, and at pumpkins, potatoes, turnips, etc., they could beat the East "all to smash."

which required the richest of soils and was a soil-exhausting crop, was frequently cultivated for export. Hemp required no cultivation, but the labor of handling and retting was heavy. It could be retted by being left out in the field over winter; by "dew retting" and constant turning over, in six or eight weeks; or by "pond retting," weighted under water, in less time. Some calculated on 800 pounds to the acre or a net profit of $24 as compared with one fourth as much for corn.[100] There were scattered mills, mostly in Ohio, for converting flaxseed into linseed oil. The seed sold at about 90 cents per bushel, and the oil at about $1.25 per gallon. Some tobacco was cultivated in southern Ohio, Indiana, and Illinois, some of it very fair in quality.[101] Castor beans were raised here and there for local use and the New Orleans market. David Dale Owen had a press at New Harmony, Indiana, in 1835 and advertised for beans at one dollar per bushel.[102]

The culture of the vine was introduced by the Swiss settlers in southeastern Indiana, where, as early as 1808, 800 gallons of wine were produced. By 1818, 7,000 gallons were produced and later the output reached 12,000 gallons, but as the older settlers retired, the vines were neglected and their children turned to corn and potatoes.[103] Nicholas Longworth, of Cincinnati, became interested in vine culture and about 1818 planted his first vineyard. He tried the Schuylkill and various European varieties but finally settled upon the Catawba as the best wine grape for the region. When in the autumn of 1837 his wine production was estimated at one hundred barrels, the editor of the *Ohio Farmer*

---

[100] *Western Tiller,* June 15, 1827; articles by Ruricola in *Hamilton Intelligencer,* December, 1831—January, 1832.

[101] Cultivation of a light, yellow leaf Maryland tobacco centered around Licking, Fairfield, Perry, and Muskingum counties in Ohio. This plant was ripened on the stalk and cured over fire. William C. Howells, *Recollections of Life in Ohio, from 1813 to 1840* (Cincinnati, 1895), 131; Caleb Atwater, *History of Ohio,* 50. A letter in the *St. Clairsville Gazette* stated that the Hollanders preferred Ohio tobacco to any other, and that in quality some thought it superior to the Maryland product. Quoted in *Liberty Hall and Cincinnati Gazette,* December 13, 1825. In 1825 Congressman Whittlesey sent seeds of the yellow leaf tobacco plant, together with instructions for cultivation, to the Portage County Agricultural Society. The instructions were published in the Ravenna (Ohio) *Western Courier,* March 25, 1825.

[102] Walter B. Hendrickson, *David Dale Owen . . .* (*Indiana Historical Collections,* XXVII, Indianapolis, 1943), 21–22.

[103] Dufour, "Early Vevay," in *Indiana Magazine of History,* XX (1924), 21. John James Dufour published at Cincinnati in 1826, *The American Vine Dressers' Guide; being a treatise on the cultivation of the vine and the process of wine-making, adapted to the soil and climate of the U. S.*

predicted that the day was not far distant when the banks of the
Ohio would rival the rivers of France and Germany in the quantity and quality of their wines.[104]

Some orchards, the work of "Johnny Appleseed," were already
at hand in Ohio and Indiana by the time the early settlers came,
but development of fruit culture came slowly.[105] This interesting
character believed grafting to be "against Nature," consequently
most of the fruit from these seedling trees was of poor quality.
About two dozen varieties of apples were introduced by the
Marietta settlers in the 1790's. One of the early nurseries on the
Muskingum was offering these as well as some twenty other New
England varieties.[106] Quite by accident a seedling tree from this
nursery gave the Middle West the Rome Beauty apple. Other
nurseries in northeastern Ohio and around Cincinnati were introducing new varieties not only of apples, but of cherries and pears
as well. Since nursery work was not widely understood, trees were
relatively expensive.[107] Various notions in the popular mind illustrate the lack of knowledge of pomology: to force a tree to bear,
a ring one fourth of an inch wide was cut through the bark and
the bark removed. If done during the bud-swelling season, more
and better fruit was supposed to result.[108] Another method was
to drive the trunk full of old rusty nails.

There was no wide market for fruit, and local consumption
was satisfied with the produce of a few trees of indifferent
quality. Attention was called by the *Detroit Gazette* in 1819 to
the dead and decaying fruit trees along the "Strait." Neglect
had permitted the sod to sap their strength.[109] Twenty years later
the situation was much the same. "Hard green apples of an
ordinary variety are hawked about at one cent a piece," said the

[104] *Ohio Farmer and Western Horticulturist* (Batavia and Columbus, 1834–39),
November 15, 1837. Longworth had published an article on vine culture in the
Cincinnati Republican in October. Not so well known is the fact that Longworth
also published the secret of sex distinction in strawberry plants. This apparently
was not an original discovery but gained from a Cincinnati gardener. Needless
to say it made possible greater production of this expensive luxury.
[105] See Henry A. Pershing, *Johnny Appleseed and His Time* (Strasburg, Va.,
1930), for a semihistorical account of this famous pioneer.
[106] For names of these early varieties, see Lloyd, Falconer, and Thorne, *The
Agriculture of Ohio*, 56.
[107] The *Milwaukee Advertiser*, April 21, 1838, called attention to the feasibility
of farmers grafting apple, pear, and quince scions on to the numerous wild apple
and plum stocks, and described the process.
[108] *Western Tiller*, March 2, 1827.
[109] *Detroit Gazette*, November 5, 1819.

Advertiser in 1836; it was hard to believe that a region so long settled should thus have neglected horticulture.[110] Nursery advertisements appeared more frequently in the 1830's and articles on grafting, pruning, and feeding were copied in the newspapers. Many of our modern fruit pests and diseases were not prevalent a century ago; advice on spraying, fungicides, and the like was conspicuously absent from the agricultural papers.[111]

A few of the common vegetables were often planted by the early settlers almost as soon as the corn crop in the clearing, but unless the good housewife was interested in its maintenance, the vegetable area was likely to remain a patch rather than become a garden. The western farmer seldom developed intensive cultivation of vegetables, or truck farming, as did the German settlers of the 1850's. Lack of city markets and the fact that canning had not yet come into use left no incentive to raise beyond the immediate needs of the family. That there was considerable interest in products other than pumpkins and potatoes is evidenced by the very frequent notices of large vegetables. Someone would bring in an exceptionally large specimen, others would seek to beat the record, and sometimes whole communities or states would wage a big vegetable war (or else a liars' tournament, it is difficult to determine which). Detroit in 1818 offered a 12-inch turnip, a 23-pound turnip, and a 25-pounder.[112] Cleveland papers in the 1820's noted 4-inch tomatoes in Ohio, a 131-pound pumpkin, 2 cucumbers 4½ feet long and a radish 5½ feet long.[113] Vandalia, Illinois, entered the lists in 1835 with a beet 19¼ inches in circumference, 31 inches long and weighing 9¾ pounds.[114] Alton countered with a 143-pound pumpkin, a 40-pound muskmelon ("seen by the editor"), and a patch of Rohan potatoes which yielded at the rate of 512 bushels to the acre.[115] Milwaukee challenged both hemispheres with turnips 44 and 45 inches in cir-

---

[110] *Detroit Daily Advertiser*, September 14, 1836.

[111] One of the few insecticides mentioned was a paint compounded from urine, soapsuds, and cow dung. *Farmer's Reporter and United States Agriculturist*, October, 1831.

[112] *Detroit Gazette*, July 10, 1818.

[113] *Cleaveland Herald*, September 9, 1825, October 13, 1826. "The World's Biggest Radish" was the caption under a photograph in the *Indianapolis Sunday Star* of February 6, 1938, of a white radish from Wisconsin which was 27½ inches long and weighed 25¼ pounds.

[114] Vandalia *Illinois Advocate and State Register*, November 25, 1835.

[115] *Alton Telegraph*, August 29, 1838, October 12, 19, 1839.

cumference,[116] but Green Bay challenged Milwaukee with a whole list of ponderosities which included a merino potato 2 feet 7½ inches in circumference and a turnip 11 inches in diameter, which weighed almost 10 pounds long before mature. Green Bay refused even to notice the puny specimens submitted by Mineral Point. It was "Green Bay against Wisconsin, and Wisconsin against the World."[117] When in 1836 Editor Byron Kilbourn of the *Milwaukee Advertiser* offered $3.00 prizes for the largest rutabaga, turnip, potato, beet, etc., interest proved so great that it was decided to call a meeting to organize an agricultural society.[118] In 1840 the *Quincy Whig* remarked that it was a year of large melons, peaches, Whig majorities, and long cucumbers.[119]

The tomato is worthy of special mention. This fruit or vegetable, sometimes called "the love apple," was either regarded as poisonous or was used only to garnish the meat platter in the 1820's. A few brave souls began to eat it in the early 1830's,[120] and from then on its rise was rapid. Soon it was a universal favorite and recipes for every conceivable use were appearing, including omelets, soup, with ham, dried, and as "katchup." Physicians proclaimed that it was not obnoxious, but useful and healthful.[121] After a brief career as a panacea, the tomato settled down to a less glamorous existence, and after the rise of the tin can, began to produce for midwestern farmers a part of the income which was promised by the silk advocates of a century ago.

The silk craze swept the country in the late 1820's. Silk was a useful and valuable product. Silk came from cocoons of the silkworm. Silkworms lived on the mulberry leaf. The mulberry tree grew abundantly in the South and West. "Wherever the mulberry finds a congenial climate and soil, there also, the silkworm will flourish. Such a climate and soil, and such a country is ours, throughout its whole extent, from its Eastern to its Western shores."[122] Therefore farmers could always be sure of one big cash crop. "How long will it be before the old fields of the

---

[116] *Milwaukee Advertiser*, October 27, 1836; *Milwaukee Sentinel*, November 6, 1838.
[117] Green Bay *Wisconsin Democrat*, October 1, 15, 29, November 5, 1839.
[118] *Milwaukee Advertiser*, December 24, 31, 1836.
[119] *Quincy* (Ill.) *Whig*, September 12, 1840.
[120] *Transactions of the Illinois State Historical Society*, 1906, p. 78.
[121] See Chapter V, 304–5.
[122] *The American Silk Grower's Guide* (Boston, 1839), 25.

middle and southern states will be converted into mulberry orchards, and the United States into an exporter instead of an importer of silk.—We answer, not twenty years!"[123] Every agricultural periodical printed dozens of articles annually on the culture and profits of silk. By 1839 there were at least five periodicals in the country devoted mainly or exclusively to silk growing,[124] besides numerous manuals on the subject. From these publications the newspapers regularly copied long extracts on silk and often added enthusiastic editorials and letters.[125] When the Ohio legislature appointed a committee to find a staple crop to enhance the state's wealth, the committee felt it could make no better recommendation than silk and sugar beets.[126] Apparently the great silk boom existed on paper rather than in reality, and the Midwest never became a serious competitor with the Orient.

Areas of land reduced to cultivation and the amount of crops produced were limited not only by lack of transport facilities and markets, but by the scarcity of labor. Frontier life did not supply an abundance of "hired hands" or even of tenant farmers. Government land was within reach of most, and squatting privileges open to all. Outside the family there was no certain labor supply. Neighbors co-operated in harvest, cornhusking, threshing, butchering, but when the need was most urgent, as in harvest, they were most likely to be needed at home.

Stock raising was as important as agriculture. Horses and cattle for transportation and power as well as milk and meat for domestic consumption, sheep for wool, and cattle and hogs for export, on hoof to the East, or down river in barrels, were produced by most farmers. Little attention was paid to breeds. The

---

[123] *Cleveland Herald*, March 26, 1833, quoting the Baltimore *American Farmer*.
[124] *Ohio Farmer and American Horticulturist*, July 15, 1839. These were the *Journal of the American Silk Society and Rural Economist*, Baltimore; *The Southern Silk Grower*, Baltimore; the *American Silk Grower*, Philadelphia; the *Silk Culturist*, Hartford, Connecticut; and one at Keene, New Hampshire.
   In 1826 silk was taken up seriously by Congress. The Secretary of the Treasury was ordered to prepare a manual on the growth and manufacture of silk, and in 1828 six thousand copies were printed. (U. S. *House Executive Documents*, 20 Congress, 1 session, No. 158.) In 1830 a national school was proposed by Congress with M. D'Homergue, of France, as instructor in sericulture. The House of Representatives Committee on Agriculture issued a report on silk culture in 1830 (U. S. *House Reports*, 21 Congress, 1 session, No. 289), which included D'Homergue's directions. Reviewed by James Hall in *Illinois Monthly Magazine*, I (1830–31), 145–58.
[125] For instance the *Hamilton* (Ohio) *Advertiser*, May 4, 1827, ran a two-and-one-half-column editorial on silk culture.
[126] *Cincinnati Daily Gazette*, February 20, 1837.

"razorbacks," "tonawandas," "land sharks," and other hogs of such breeding, or lack of breeding, which when fattened never averaged over two hundred pounds gross weight, held their own long after the merits of improved breeds were demonstrated. "They are long-nosed, thin creatures, with legs like greyhounds, and, like the greyhound among dogs, seem to be the kind formed for speed and agility among swine, as they think nothing of galloping a mile at a heat, or of clearing fences which a more civilized hog would never attempt. Still, as the hog of a pioneer settler has, at some seasons, need for all the activity he can exert to procure a subsistence, he may after all be the best fitted for the backwoods."[127] Shaker farmers in Warren County, Ohio, in 1816 crossed these "natives" with some white Big Chinas from Pennsylvania, and thus began the Miami Valley hog, also known as the Shaker hog.[128] This hog became the ancestor of the Poland China breed. Other improved types such as Irish Graziers, Woburns, and Berkshires were introduced, but most farmers could not afford them at first.[129] It was not always the factors of

[127] Oliver, *Eight Months in Illinois,* 80–81.

[128] Illustrated in *Western Farmer and Gardener,* III, 6 (Oct., 1841).

[129] A committee of Sangamon County, Illinois, farmers in 1840 estimated that the 2,000 farmers of that county were losing $18,000 per year by marketing an average of 15 hogs each of the long-nosed variety instead of improved types. The former at 15 to 16 months weighed 150 pounds as contrasted to the 300 pounds of the newer breeds. *Western Prairie Farmer, Journal of Agriculture, Rural Economy and Education* (Springfield, Ill., 1839–40), July 8, 1840.

On the merits of the "land sharks" see Solon Robinson's article in the Albany *Cultivator,* May, 1840, and reprinted in *Solon Robinson. Pioneer and Agriculturist* (2 volumes. *Indiana Historical Collections,* XXI, XXII, 1936), I, 129–31. Robinson's wild hogs multiplied all right, but after catching and penning up a few, and feeding fifty bushels of corn to each, he seemed to have less hog than before. When, a few months later, he got a pair of Berkshires, they attracted as much attention as would have African lions. Berkshires six to eight weeks old were advertised in Ohio in 1837 at $20 a pair.

Many of the Berkshires of the western country originated in the pens of Mr. A. B. Allen, of Buffalo. He personally purchased in Europe "South Downs, York, Kenilworth, and Berkshire pigs; Shepherd's Dogs, Dorking Fowls, English Pheasants, &c. . . . Many of our citizens have also commenced improving their stock hogs in particular, which need it bad enough in all conscience." *Fort Wayne Sentinel,* November 6, 1841. Four years later an Indiana farmer had in the same pen "a genuine *Indiana Land-pike,* only three weeks younger than the improved hogs, and whose lean, lank appearance, long snout and legs, and diminutive proportions contrast so ludicrously with his portly neighbors, that it is difficult to suppress a smile on beholding him. The poor fellow himself seems fairly ashamed of his miserable looks, and can scarcely look a visitor in the face. We should guess he might weigh about one-third as much as the others. We trust those of our farmers who have been in the habit of raising the long-legged breed will call and see this proof of the relative value of the different breeds, and we think they cannot but be convinced that it would be both economy and wisdom on their parts to procure better hogs. The old breed are now pretty well used up in this part of the country, and the present would be a favorable time to introduce a better

size, food consumption, and rapidity of maturing which determined the practicability of a breed, for ability to take care of themselves in the woods or to travel to market on the hoof was just as important.[130]

Neat cattle of the common stock were predominant. These were a mixture of every breed, "small, shortbodied, thin and coarse-haired, steep-rumped, slab-sided, having little aptitude to fatten, or to lay the fat on the right place." Types developed locally and names never became standardized. In Ohio, for instance, there were "brindles" and "yellows" on the Reserve, Hocking or "hill cattle," Brush Creek cattle, Pattons, and so forth.[131] Some were good milkers as for quantity, but could not produce more than three pounds of butter per week. Calves were small and of slow growth, averaging about 700 to 900 pounds at five years. Long- and spreading-horned English cattle of a large, slow-maturing, rough type came into Ohio from Kentucky about 1800 and when crossed with the native stock, resulted in considerable improvement. English cattle of the "shorthorn" breed were raised in Kentucky by 1820 but the farmers across the river generally regarded them as too fancy for their purposes.[132]

In 1833 a group of Ross County, Ohio, farmers which included Governor Allen Trimble, Gen. Duncan McArthur, and others, organized the Ohio Importing Company and subscribed $9,200 for cattle improvement. Three men were sent to England where they bought nineteen head from the herds of the Duke of Leeds, Earl of Carlisle, and other noted breeders of English Shorthorns or Durhams. The animals crossed the ocean and were driven across the mountains in time to be exhibited at the Ross County fair in October, 1834. Among them were two bulls of

---

breed of stock hogs. Such a step would add much to the wealth of the country." *Ibid.*, December 6, 1845.

The *Quincy Whig*, January 2, 1841, called attention to a 650-pound hog received at that place, as what could be expected with the improved stock. When it came to "going the whole hog," however, a specimen from Warren County, Ohio, was shipped to Cleveland in 1833 which measured 3 feet 11 inches in height, 8 feet plus in circumference, and weighed 1,400 pounds. *Cleveland Herald*, June 15, 1833.

[130] See Chapter VII, 478–81, for droving to markets.

[131] A picture of the Patton breed may be found in *Western Farmer and Gardener*, II, following 72.

[132] *Agriculture of the United States in 1860; compiled from the Original Returns of the Eighth Census . . .* (Washington, D. C., 1864), cxxii; Smith, *History of Indiana*, I, 356.

2,000 to 2,100 pounds each and "ten to twelve feet long not including their tails."[133] Two years later a big sale was held at which one cow and calf brought $2,225.[134] By this time progressive farmers were becoming interested in improved cattle which could be brought to 1,400 to 1,600 pounds in the same period of time it took to bring native cattle to half that weight, but despite the importation of Durhams, Devons, Herefords, Ayrshires, and the rest, the average farmer was either indifferent or too poor to take advantage of breeding facilities. In Illinois when a state law with severe penalty was passed to prevent small bulls of scrub stock running at large, a howl of protest arose from the common folk who upheld the rights of the small bulls. The measure was regarded as class legislation in favor of the rich who were seeking to profit from the breeding services of their large bulls. Besides, "there was a generous feeling in the hearts of the people in favor of an equality of privileges, even among bulls."[135]

In the prairie country when much grazing land was still open to all settlers, cattle were allowed to range and breed naturally and more or less irregularly. As a result calves frequently arrived during severe winter weather and sometimes failed to survive, or, if they did, had their ears frozen. The survivors when rounded up and put in pens served as inducements for the cows to come home at night, at which times the calf and the milkers were likely to work simultaneously on the same cow, provided her wildness did not prevent. Some farmers depended upon the range forage to sustain their cattle in large part; others threw them some fodder now and then, especially in severe weather. Under this system of natural husbandry the animals became hardy, but neither very large nor fat.

Sheep breeding seems not to have encountered quite the same indifference. Probably the difference in quality of wool and prices attainable was more obvious than corresponding advantages in

---

[133] *Farmer's Reporter and United States Agriculturist*, August, 1834, p. 107. The herd apparently included various kinds of blooded English shorthorns (Holderness, Teeswater, Yorkshire, Durham) but were often referred to simply as Durhams.

[134] In 1836 C. S. Clarkson, of Ohio, imported several Durham bulls and heifers from the East. Two years later he sold "Mina" and her calf "Colossus" for $1,700 and other head at $500 to $1,000 each. *Cincinnati Daily Gazette*, July 12, 1836, July 2, 1838; *Ohio Farmer and Western Horticulturist*, August 1, 1838.

[135] Ford, *History of Illinois*, 107.

improved cattle. Much interest was shown in the Spanish Merino breed in the 1820's. There were a few Merinos in Ohio in the early 1800's. W. R. Dickinson, of Steubenville, had a flock of 2,500 Merinos by 1825 and was issuing challenges to breeders throughout the country.[136] It was said that one could expect to market annually from Merinos 3½ pounds of washed wool at $1.00 per pound, plus one lamb for each ewe, and net $4.00 per year from each sheep.[137] George Flower, of Albion, Illinois, had several hundred Merino and Saxony sheep and crosses for sale by 1834.[138] By the early 1830's the advocates of the Cotswold, Southdown, New Leicester, and other mutton breeds were advertising the merits of their favorites.

Pioneer horses were of inferior quality—small, scrawny, and ungainly looking. New England stock, mostly degenerate English breeds, was particularly poor. Around Detroit and elsewhere in Michigan were the French ponies, tough and possessed of great endurance. They were said to resemble Balkan ponies rather than English or Arabian horses. Descendants of the horses of early French settlers in Illinois ran wild, later to be roped, broken, and sold to farmers at $20 to $30 a head. Horses with a strain of thoroughbred blood brought in from Virginia and Kentucky were

[136] W. H. Hunter, "The Pathfinders of Jefferson County," in *Ohio Archaeological and Historical Society Publications,* VI (1898), 236–37; *New York Statesman,* March 28, 1826; *Western Herald and Steubenville Gazette,* April 22, 1826; Columbus *Ohio State Journal,* June 22, 1826.

[137] *Edwardsville Spectator,* November 28, 1820. Some were not so conservative. A writer in Cincinnati *Liberty Hall* (August 28, 1815) was so certain that one could raise 2,200 sheep on 220 acres at a net profit of $6.00 each or $13,200, that he ended by saying, "There is no getting over this calculation." Native wool usually sold at about 25 cents a pound. Some local mills would pay 50 cents for a quarter blood, 75 for half, and $1.00 for full blood.

[138] *Illinois Advocate and State Register,* May 17, 1834. The Saxony wool was finer than that of the Spanish Merino, but the sheep did not produce so much wool, was not so hardy, nor did it have so heavy a carcass. Saxony wool sold at $1.70 in eastern markets in the middle 1820's, but the price difference between it and the Spanish Merino wool was slight ten years later.

Flower's father in England purchased 2,000 Merinos which came from the Spanish royal flock. Flower brought with him to Illinois in 1817 six rams and six ewes. By 1834 his flock had increased to 400, which contained five breeds of fine wool sheep. Besides the Merino and Saxony, he had the Illinois Grazier, a stout short-legged thrifty animal with a long-staple soft wool and good meat; the "Prairie Down," similar to the "South Down" of England, hornless, and with fine wool; and a Moorish ram, derived from his Merinos, with very fine black and white wool. On a neighboring farm Mr. William Pickering was breeding Lincoln and Leicester sheep which produced from 8 to 12 pounds of heavy combing wool. Flower thought it possible that as fine wool could be raised in the interior of North America as in Spain or Saxony. Letter to *Western Monthly Magazine,* II (1834), 389–90.

somewhat better, particularly for saddle purposes. Since much of the heavy work was done by oxen or even cows, no great interest was shown in the development of draft animals. Pennsylvania German settlers brought the Conestoga horse into east-central Ohio. Shakespeare, of Maryland ancestry, was brought to Butler County, Ohio, about 1816, the first "blooded" horse of record in the state. Shortly his numerous progeny were widely known in southwestern Ohio, where a "Shakespeare" was rated as top class in horse quality. Other blooded stallions were introduced about 1825, including the Messenger and imported Diomede stock. French settlers in Stark County introduced the Norman horse in the late 1820's. Descendants of Norman, Conestoga, and Flemish stock of the Dunkard, Mennonite, and Amish settlers were crossed with other blooded stock descended from Selim, Post Boy, Timoleon, Eclipse, and Florizel. The great Percheron stallions which influenced horse breeding widely in the Middle West were not brought in until 1851. Many local breeds, sometimes famous over several counties, were developed for all-around purposes, for light wagons and buggies, or as "riding critters." A traveler described the horse turnout at a steamboat launching at Monroe, Michigan Territory, in 1833: "There was the bull-necked French pony and his scraggy looking Indian cousin, the sleek spongy-looking Ohio horse, and the clean-limbed quickly-gathering Kentuckian, galloping between the swift but shuffling Illinois pacer, and the high-actioned tight-looking New-York trotter."[139]

Improvement of horses came slowly. In Ohio, for example, in the 1820's, although many horses were driven to eastern and southern markets, little attention was paid to the raising of good horses. Prices received hardly covered costs and charges. The number of horses in the state in 1826 was estimated at 120,000 and the value at $4,000,000. The tax on stallions did much to discourage better breeding.[140]

Veterinary practice was on a parity with medical practice of the period but on the whole not so vicious. Since mad staggers were supposed to be caused by too much blood, the horse was

[139] Hoffman, *A Winter in the West*, I, 131.
[140] *Ohio State Journal*, September 21, 1826; *Western Tiller*, January 12, 1827.

bled until he fainted, then purged with Croton oil. Tetanus was considered an affection of the nerves, and called for blistering of the spine. Botanic doctors and home-remedy books prescribed many herb and root remedies for horses and other animals as well as for humans. Boneset, tansy, and wormwood were recommended for hollow horn; pine buds, black snakeroot, and whiskey for heaves; bloodroot and vinegar for windgall, etc. Bots called for drenching the horse with sweet milk and molasses —whether internal or external was not specified.

Agriculture, horticulture, and stockbreeding, although of almost universal interest, were conducted mainly by rule of thumb, the almanac (the moon was regarded as particularly important), or folk tradition. "The people are not given to experiments; [they] continue to farm in the beaten way. Agriculture improvement comes at a slow pace."[141] Not that there was a lack of leaders who recognized the need for improvement, but the western farmer, either because of lack of initiative, inertia, poverty, or distrust, never seemed to turn to new ideas with reference to seed, soil, and fertilizers with the same readiness with which he took up mechanical improvements. Men such as Morris Birkbeck, who was regarded as a "gentleman farmer," saw the farmer's doubt. In his address to the Agricultural Society of Illinois at its third annual meeting in 1822 he advocated working from solid foundations. "We are not amateur professors of agriculture, taking it up for our amusement, but plain, hard working farmers. Refinements are for Society in its advanced stage." Much of the time of agricultural improvers in the older states was taken up in seeking to repair the errors of former days, to abolish injurious practices, and to restore the fertility of exhausted soils. Farmers of the West must profit by their example, and "avoid that system which, if it replenished the purse at first, and gives a temporary show of prosperity, impoverishes the land, and leaves a barren inheritance for our children." Birkbeck thought the most certain and durable profits would come from increase and improvement of livestock; the main difficulties to be overcome in the West were wolves and a

---

[141] Timothy Flint, *A Condensed Geography and History of the Western States* . . . (1833 ed.), 398.

lack of salt.[142] He called attention to cotton, hemp, flax, fruit trees, and the vine, as other possibilities for the farmer.[143]

Ten years later, in Ohio, an agricultural editor wrote: "We have not yet attained a very great degree of perfection in the arts of agriculture." Farmers came from exhausted farms in the East to exhaust their farms in Ohio, then expected to go to Indiana and Illinois. When warned of their neglect of manure, they would reply, "When my land needs manure I will sell it and remove to the new country."[144] He listed the pressing needs as (1) manure [fertilization], (2) rotation of crops, (3) diffusion of knowledge. The only rotation practiced was alternation of wheat and corn. Yet Increase Allen Lapham, of Ohio, was even then explaining the modern doctrine on rotation and renovation of soil by fertilizers in the *Genesee Farmer*.[145]

Solon Robinson, of Indiana, soon to be the most important agricultural writer in the North, was even more perturbed:

WHAT CAN, WHAT MUST, WHAT SHALL WE DO, to elevate the standing of the cultivators of the soil? There is "something rotten in Denmark," that needs ALL the energy of ALL the friends of agriculture, to eradicate from the community. A false pride pervades the land, and a false estimate is placed upon the value of that class of community, who are the very creators of, not only all wealth, but are the very basis and only foundation of all real wealth. What shall we do to bring about that happy state of society, that once pervaded the Roman empire, when he who cultivated the soil took the first rank among all trades and occupations? One of the very best things that the friends of this whole country can do, is to make the science of agriculture take that rank that shall induce merchants and professional men to seek to make *their* sons farmers, instead of that worst of all manias that now pervades the farming community, and which

[142] The Illinois wolf-bounty law was passed within a few weeks of this address. It provided a $200 state prize for the person who destroyed the greatest number, not under sixty, between April 15 and November 15, 1824, and a $20 prize in each county, provided the number was not less than ten. Vandalia *Illinois Intelligencer*, February 1, 1823. As for salt, Birkbeck pointed out that as New Orleans meat prices were governed by the quality of salt used, inferior salt, which was about all that was available, came high. If one bushel cured 600 pounds, which sold at $1.00 less per hundred because of poor salt, it added $6.00 per bushel to the original price of the salt.

[143] *Illinois Intelligencer*, December 14, 1822.

[144] *Farmer's Reporter and United States Agriculturist*, September, 1833. Yet in 1814 (November 14), quoting *Silliman's Journal*, the Chillicothe *Weekly Recorder* pointed out the results of the farmers' failure to follow the English practice of using compost made from barnyard offal, vegetable tops, etc.

[145] *Wisconsin Magazine of History*, I (1917–18), 6.

induces the annual ruin of thousands of young men, by seeking to be what nature never intended them for.[146]

Robinson's remedy was education through agricultural periodicals and the founding of an American Society of Agriculture, with branches to reach into every county in the Union.

Henry L. Ellsworth, a heavy investor in Wabash River lands who became Commissioner of Patents in 1835, wrote: "For commerce and manufactures, much has been done; for agriculture . . . much remains to be done. Husbandry seems to be viewed as a natural blessing, that needs no aid from legislation. Like the air we breathe, and the element of water, which sustain life, the productions of the soil are regarded by too many as common bounties of Providence, to be gratefully enjoyed, but without further thought or reflection." He advocated use of some of the Smithson funds for vocational education for farmers, and Congressional appropriations for the dissemination of agricultural knowledge.[147]

Agricultural periodicals were not lacking, but their influence developed slowly. The first American farm journal was the *American Farmer*, published by John Skinner at Baltimore (1819–34). Other early publications were the *New England Farmer* (Boston, 1822–46), the *New York Farmer* (1828–39), the *Genesee Farmer* (Rochester, N. Y., 1831–39), and *The Cultivator* (Albany, N. Y., 1834–65). One of the earliest in the West was the *Western Tiller*, a five-column, four-page weekly published at Cincinnati by J. W. Gazlay (1826–31). In addition to agriculture this paper devoted much attention to markets, morals, and taxes. At Cincinnati in 1830 was begun the *Farmer's Reporter and United States Agriculturist*, a small, book-sized monthly publication, which four years later became a four-column paper. In 1834 at Batavia, Ohio, appeared the *Ohio Farmer and Western Horticulturist*, under the editorship of Samuel Medary, later famous Democratic editor and politician. At Lexington,

[146] *Solon Robinson*, I, 87. As expressed by some, the genius of American liberty would delight to reside where the cultivation of the soil was the basic interest of the people. *Zanesville Express*, December 5, 1816.

[147] Annual Report of Commissioner of Patents, 1837, in U. S. *House Reports*, 25 Congress, 2 session, No. 112, p. 5. As a result of Ellsworth's efforts, the Patent Office began issuing an annual publication; another result was the free distribution of seeds. Ellsworth has been called the "father of the United States Department of Agriculture." *Dictionary of American Biography* (20 volumes and index. New York, 1928–36), VI, 110–11.

Kentucky, was begun the *Franklin Farmer* in 1837; about the same time the *Indiana Farmer* was started at Indianapolis, and in the forties the *Wisconsin Farmer and Northwestern Cultivator* and the *Michigan Farmer* were launched. At Springfield, Illinois, in 1839–40 the *Western Farmer: Journal of Agriculture and Rural Economy* was published, and in Chicago in October, 1840, appeared the first issue of John S. Wright's *The Union Agriculturist* which in January, 1841, added *Western Prairie Farmer* to its title. There were others besides these, but many were short lived.[148]

The farm publications copied generously from one another.[149] Since the circulation of the farm journals was limited, their widest influence came from the diffusion of their material by way of the newspapers. They were on the exchange list of most of the important newspapers, and whole articles were regularly lifted with the scissors and reprinted, sometimes with, but often without, acknowledgment. Western papers such as the *Cincinnati Gazette, Ohio State Journal, Cleveland Herald*, Ravenna *Western Courier, Hamilton Intelligencer*, Indianapolis *Indiana Journal, Madison Courier, Sangamo Journal, Illinois Advocate and State Register, Detroit Gazette, Detroit Daily Advertiser, Wisconsin Enquirer, Milwaukee Advertiser* and a dozen others, either maintained a regular column on agriculture (frequently a page) or else intermittently devoted much space to the subject. It is possible, through a careful study of the general newspapers, to know practically all there was to know about the science of

---

[148] *The Cultivator*, II, 51 (June, 1835), listed 15 agricultural periodicals. Of these 1 was quarterly, 7 were monthly, and 7 were weekly papers. There were also two horticultural and one sericultural (silk) papers. Geographically the distribution was: New England 4, New York 6, the South 4, west of Appalachians 1. The *Genesee Farmer* in 1839 stated that there were 32 agricultural periodicals, of which nearly half were but recently started. Besides farm journals there were many books, pamphlets, and tracts on agriculture. These were frequently advertised in the newspapers and noted in the general periodicals. See for instance the *American Quarterly Review*'s (XXI, 13–15, March, 1837) list of recommended books, by English and American authors, for the farmer's library. Albert Lowther Demaree, *The American Agricultural Press 1819–1860* (Columbia University Press, 1941) covers the subject well, though it is not at all complete in its listing of agricultural papers. Richard Bardolph, *Agricultural Literature and the Early Illinois Farmer* (*University of Illinois Studies in the Social Sciences*, XXIX, Nos. 1–2, Urbana, 1948), is the only study of the agricultural press of any of the states of the Old Northwest.

[149] In the *Ohio Farmer* in 1835, for example, were extracts from the *Tennessee Farmer*, the *Maine Farmer*, the *Genesee Farmer*, *The Cultivator*, the *Farmer and Gardener*, *Silliman's Journal*, the *New England Farmer*, and English and Scottish publications.

agriculture. The treatments varied from brief paragraphic recipes to four- and five-column serials. Everything was covered,
from killing flies and vermin to farriery, fruit-tree grafting,
fences, cellars and dyeing; from ashes and asparagus to silk
and thistles.

For example: in one issue of the *Sangamo Journal* one could
have read the latest on horses, fruit trees, and sheep; in a single
copy of the *Illinois Advocate*, on "the Duration of Vegetable
Species," proper building and use of cellars, and how to work
cows and oxen. Page one of the *Ohio State Journal,* June 14,
1827, contained information on bottling cider, killing flies and
bugs, cultivation of apples, parsnips, and peas, and treating sore
backs in horses. Consecutive issues of the *Milwaukee Advertiser*
in 1838 dealt with gardening, hogs, husbandry improvement,
asparagus, celery, agricultural chemistry, rhubarb, and clover
seed. The *Hamilton Intelligencer* in a series of fourteen articles
in 1831–32, covered, among other things, hemp culture and
profits, wheat, barley, forests for timber, fuel and fences, hedges,
and the black locust. Other articles dealt with fruit-tree pests,
culture of the vine, plaster, lime, ashes, pumpkins, caterpillars,
farm machinery, millet, alfalfa, retting of flax, bees, fowls,
buttermaking, zoology, the stomach, spring flowers, female
loveliness, curing of beef and pork, silk, toothache, cockroaches,
the army worm, the Hessian fly, and a multitude of household
activities. There were maps of the western states, descriptions
of land and prospects, and cuts of improved tools. Also now and
then appeared interesting bits on the old stand-by, the sea
serpent or multiheaded calves.

"Agriculture requires a constant recurrence to science and the
economy of nature, in order to secure its best products," said
the *Western Tiller.* Yet old habits were hard to overcome, and
inertia or indifference prevented some from reading for information, while others had a positive distrust of "book larnin' "
or newspaper farming. "I reckon I know as much about farming
as the printers do."[150] An Illinois farmer wrote that he had
interviewed hundreds of farmers and lent dozens of copies of
the *Ohio Farmer*, but had not won one subscriber. "Unfortunately, I find a large portion of our farmers prejudiced against

[150] *Farmer's Reporter and United States Agriculturist,* September, 1833.

every variety of improvement, particularly where the knowledge of that improvement is to be acquired from books." He saw but few changes in agricultural methods.[151] The editor of the *Western Prairie Farmer* thought that the reason the American people improved so fast was because they were a reading people. This habit would have to be extended to agriculture. He reasoned with a progressive farmer who tried improvements which he learned about from other men but who was prejudiced against "book farming" and asked him if he would believe in and try some of his own (the editor's) improvements and successes if he told him of them. The answer was yes. If the ideas were put in writing would he still believe? Certainly. Then if they were put in a book or paper so hundreds could benefit, would there be any difference? The farmer seemed confused but not convinced.[152] It was to require another generation for the farmer generally to begin to respect science as distributed by way of the printed page.

Next in importance to the farm journals and agricultural articles in the newspapers in promoting improvement, were the agricultural societies and fairs.[153] The societies, usually promoted and run by a few progressive farmers, seldom gained the active interest of the representative farmer; they devoted much of their time to papers and addresses, but the fairs which they promoted offered visual and effective argument to the average farmer. A few samples will illustrate the development of societies and fairs. The first agricultural society in the Northwest was organized at Vincennes in 1809; it held several local fairs in ensuing years and in 1817 sought, but did not get, a charter. The *Detroit Gazette*, which in the early period was constantly pointing out the backwardness of agriculture in Michigan Territory, in November, 1817, stated that agricultural societies were being organized everywhere, and advocated founding one for Michigan. A meeting was held, a society organized, and resolu-

[151] *Ohio Farmer*, cited in *Western Farmer* (Cincinnati), May, 1835.
[152] *Western Prairie Farmer*, June 3, 1840.
[153] On agricultural societies and fairs, see Bidwell and Falconer, *History of Agriculture in the Northern United States;* Rodney C. True, "The Early Development of Agricultural Societies in the United States," in American Historical Association, *Annual Report*, 1920, pp. 293–306; Earle D. Ross, "The Evolution of the Agricultural Fair in the Northwest," in *Iowa Journal of History and Politics*, XXIV (1926), 445 ff.; G. Sprague, "Agricultural Associations of Ohio," in *Transactions of the Illinois State Agricultural Society*, 1853–54, pp. 34–37.

tions passed the same month.[154] Local societies or "Agricultural Associations" were recommended in later issues.

A few attempts at fairs were made in the 1830's, but the first state fair in the Old Northwest was not held until 1849 when the Michigan State Society held one near Detroit. One of the first local fairs in Ohio was the Scioto Agricultural Society Cattle Show held "on a handsome lot" south of Chillicothe in November, 1819. The Agricultural Society of Illinois was organized by Birkbeck and others in 1819, and its early meetings seem to have been unusually well supplied with good papers which combined theoretical and practical treatments. The effort proved too great, however, and in 1823 the members, having become tired of keeping up their organization, turned over their funds to the Sunday School agent and disbanded. A Madison County society was organized in 1822 at Edwardsville and continued for three years; nine northern counties organized in 1839 and held a few fairs until 1846, but it was not until 1853 that a permanent state organization was made.[155]

The Cuyahoga County (Ohio) society was organized in 1823;[156] the Portage County society was giving prizes of from $1.00 to $4.00 at its fair and cattle show in 1825.[157] That year the Marion County (Indiana) society was formed.[158] The Hamilton County (Ohio) society drew up its constitution in 1827, and dedicated itself to the interests of agriculture, domestic manufactures, and rural affairs.[159] The Butler County society in 1831 listened to a six-column address by William Bebb, who sought to arouse public interest in a "more scientific, thorough and consequently more profitable mode of husbandry," with study of the nature of soils, manures, climate, rotation of crops, and the cultivation of neglected items, notably silk.[160] Prizes for stock and produce were offered at the county fair. Indiana, by act of the legislature in 1835, provided for organization of county societies, for a state board of agriculture of

[154] *Detroit Gazette*, November 14, 28, 1817.
[155] Chillicothe *Supporter*, November 10, 1819; Ross, "The Evolution of the Agricultural Fair," in *Iowa Journal of History and Politics*, XXIV, 447–51.
[156] *Cleaveland Herald*, May 8, 1823. Its first fair was not held until 1839.
[157] Ravenna *Western Courier*, October 22, 1825.
[158] The constitution is given in the Indianapolis *Gazette*, September 13, 1825.
[159] *Western Tiller*, May 18, June 15, 1827.
[160] *Hamilton* (Ohio) *Intelligencer*, November 12, 1831.

five members, and a state agricultural society composed of the board and delegates from the county societies. Ohio passed a similar law in 1839.[161] The Milwaukee County Agricultural Society was organized in January, 1837; Byron Kilbourn was president, Solomon Juneau was vice-president. A county fair in October marked the first annual meeting of the society; prizes from $5.00 to $50 were offered for the best-blooded sow, "yew," ram, cow, bull, and stallion; prizes were also offered for winter and spring wheat, oats, and corn.[162] Henry Ward Beecher and others organized the Indiana Horticultural Society in 1840. State fairs in all five states began in the early 1850's.

Perhaps a word about the weather would be in order in connection with agriculture. Obviously the weather was of great importance to people in early days, and often affected communications, transportation, even politics, but no one else was so constantly affected as the farmer. Although the weather was much discussed, few continuous records over any considerable period were kept. Jefferson had been interested in the climate of the West; Count Volney in his travels in the 1790's had paid special attention to the subject. Daniel Drake, of Cincinnati, aided by his friend Col. Jared Mansfield, of Ludlow Station, kept meteorological records, from 1807 to 1813, and Dr. Samuel P. Hildreth, the historian, assembled and studied weather data on the period 1818 to 1859. Dr. Lyman Foote, stationed with the army garrison at Sault Ste. Marie, recorded observations between 1823 and 1825; Henry R. Schoolcraft also kept records on his trip to the source of the Mississippi in 1820. Newspapers noted the exceptional weather and now and then one such as the *Illinois Advocate* or the *Alton Telegraph* in the 1830's made regular comments. The editor of the *Advocate*, John York Sawyer, had formerly conducted the *Plough Boy* (Greencastle, Indiana), and never lost interest in rains, crops, temperatures, and even the arrival of the birds.

Two or three observations may safely be made. First, the weather varied. Second, weather prognostications based on the

---

[161] *Laws of Indiana,* 1834–35 (general), 87, 90–91; Indianapolis *Indiana Journal,* May 22, 1835; *Cincinnati Daily Gazette,* April 4, 1839.
[162] *Milwaukee Advertiser,* February 4, 1837.

"Indian sign" or the wise one's rheumatism were not, on the whole, as reliable as are modern weather bureau predictions. Third, the "old fashioned winter" was as likely to be a mild and open one, as a period of deep snow and subzero blasts.

The unusual summer of 1816— "the year without a summer," "the year of 18—and everybody froze"—gave frost and sometimes ice, during June, July, and August. Corn was generally ruined, and eastern prices went as high as $4.00 to $5.00 per bushel. A similar summer was experienced in Michigan Territory in 1835.[163] In 1819 the winter was so mild that boats continued their regular trips at Detroit in February. In 1824–25 ice houses remained empty and the geese were going north in midwinter. At Cleveland the bees swarmed in March, rather than June, and vegetables were a month early.[164] In Ohio tender vegetation was not killed and lettuce, cabbage, and other vegetables were standing green in the gardens in March.[165] Again in 1828 there was no ice to impede navigation in Lake Erie and beets, carrots, onions, and lettuce planted in December were up by the middle of February and flourishing in March.[166] In January, 1833, frogs were singing along the Sangamon River in Illinois, and when two years later frogs and grasshoppers were seen in the river bottoms, the editor of the *Illinois Advocate* asked, "Was the like ever seen."[167] In Michigan in 1839–40 boys played ball at intervals all winter and plowing was done each month.

On the other hand in February, 1826, temperature reached 10° below zero at Indianapolis and 12° below at Detroit, where there were five weeks of sleighing. Perhaps the hardest winter in the period was that of 1830–31. It caught the people of southern Indiana and Illinois particularly unprepared. For weeks snow lay, sometimes 3 to 4 feet deep. It snowed 15 inches at one time. Stock, turkeys, and deer died in numbers and travelers perished on the road. Such a winter had not been known in

---

[163] *Wisconsin Historical Collections*, VII (1876), 338; *Michigan Pioneer and Historical Collections*, XXXVIII (1912), 643.
[164] *Detroit Gazette*, February 25, 1825; *Cleaveland Herald*, April 8, 1825; Vandalia *Illinois Intelligencer*, May 27, 1825.
[165] *Portsmouth* (Ohio) *Gazette*, March 18, 1825.
[166] *Cleaveland Herald*, February 22, March 7, 1828.
[167] *Sangamo Journal*, January 5, 1833; *Illinois Advocate and State Register*, January 28, 1835.

the memory of the oldest inhabitant.[168] Floods in the spring helped complete the destruction of food. The spring of 1834 gave killing frosts in southern Ohio, Indiana, and Illinois in April and May and at places hailstones large enough to kill hogs and even calves.[169]

Fluctuating almost as much as the temperature was the rainfall. Rainfall at Marietta for instance was 51 inches in 1818, 36 inches in 1819. The average rainfall for that place was 42 inches. Ten inches of variation from one year to the next was not unusual. The average temperature was 55.22 F. (1828), the lowest 50.13 F. (1856); the average was 52.46 F.[170]

November, 1833, witnessed the grand meteor shower, doubtless the finest display recorded in our history. From midnight until dawn they fell, thousands per hour, a blinding maze of streaks and exploding fire balls. The contemporary descriptions made no effort to do justice to this natural phenomenon.

§ § § §

Poor transportation facilities and the resultant high costs left the western communities isolated to a certain extent not only from the East, but from each other as well. Scarcity of markets and money further contributed to the practice of a self-sufficient domestic economy which in many regions by 1840 reached a high degree of development. Pioneer life centered around the home; in and around the home were cultivated those arts of husbandry and domestic crafts which, supplemented by the trades and stores of the towns, made it possible for the skilled and enterprising settler to achieve a standard of living high in proportion to his wealth as measured in cash values.

[168] Vandalia *Illinois Intelligencer,* February 2, 1831; Eleanor Atkinson, "The Winter of the Deep Snow," and newspaper extracts therein, in *Transactions of the Illinois State Historical Society,* 1909, pp. 47–62. For record low temperatures or sustained subzero weather, this winter would apparently fail by a wide margin to equal 1918, 1936, or the cold week of February, 1899, when the minus 20 line reached from St. Louis to Cleveland, and the zero line ran along the Gulf coast. Similarly, no sustained high temperatures were recorded comparable to those of the summers of 1931, 1934, and 1936.

[169] *Illinois Advocate and State Register,* May 3, 8, 1834.

[170] Later (1856 and 1858), rainfall in Washington County, Ohio, was 32.4 and 61.8 inches. Joseph Wood, land register at Marietta, kept records in the early years. A summary of the Wood-Foote-Hildreth data may be found in the *American Journal of Science and Arts,* IX (1825), 171, X, 303, and XII, 206–13.

As essential as food and shelter was clothing. Original settlers brought along as much substantial wearing apparel, or materials for making their own clothing, as convenient or as they could afford, but the rough life of the open soon necessitated replacement, and in the absence of wool and flax, reversion to the more primitive dress of the Indian or hunter was common. Moccasins of tanned buckskin, breeches and shirts of dressed skin worked soft and thin by hand, sewed with sinews or "whang" strips, and caps of coonskin met the needs of the men in woods or fields.[171] This clothing of dressed skin stood the wear and tear of briars and brush, was impervious to snake bite and cold winds, but if wet and then dried without constant rubbing, it became hard and set in the shape last held.[172] For material for women's clothing various expedients were resorted to. Buffalo wool and even bear's wool was experimented with on the wheels, but was too coarse and stiff to twist well. When combined with the down of wild nettles or milkweed to give it consistency, a coarse yarn was possible from which was made a cloth probably as good as some of the shoddy of a later date. Hemp with its coarse wiry fiber was also used.

The blue flowers of the thickly sown flax plant were waving in the sunshine before the corn crop was tasseling. It was supposed to be sown on Good Friday and a small patch was ample for the needs of the largest family. In late summer or early autumn the

[171] Moccasins were often worn by both sexes, especially the younger folks, in summer months, for years after shoes were available. They were no good for wet weather and then were merely "a decent way of going barefooted." Deer hair or other stuffing helped insulate the feet in cold weather.

[172] These loose-fitting garments also proved surprisingly warm when the wearer, after standing in front of the open fire, decided to sit down. Methods of dressing deerskins varied in detail, but were essentially those of the Indians. The main steps were: (1) If not skinned in summer, when hide was thickest, and fleshed and grained when warm, soak until slippery in a weak lye (water and ashes) solution; (2) Flesh the skin with a knife, preferably a narrow blade set lengthwise in a rounded piece of wood at a 15° angle; (3) With the hair side up grain the hide, i.e., "bark off" the top skin, being careful not to scalp the white skin underneath; (4) Soften by rubbing in on flesh side a preparation of buck (or calf or beef) brains simmered in water and grease; by soaking several days in a solution of soft soap, then greasing and rolling the hide for several days; or treat with neat's foot oil; (5) Wash in soapsuds and wring out; (6) Stretch by hand, lace onto drying frame, rub with paddle and smoke in oak-chip smudge for one day.

On hide dressing, see Isaac Lippincott, "Industry among the French in the Illinois Country," in *Journal of Political Economy*, XVIII (1910), 123–24; Reynolds, *Pioneer History of Illinois*, 52; Sidney Breese, *The Early History of Illinois* (Chicago, 1884), 173 ff.; *Western Reserve Historical Society Tracts*, No. 50 (Cleveland, n. d.), 107; *Outdoor Life*, XCII, No. 5 (Nov., 1943).

ripened plant was pulled and left on the ground a month or more to rot out or ret the woody stalks. During the winter the men folk applied the flax brake to crimp the stalks, and the process of "scutching" was completed with the swingling knife.[173] The roughage cleared away, the strikes, bound in bundles, were soaked in the water trough and pounded with pestles until soft and pliable. A particularly soft dressing could be had by boiling the flax in strong lye or lime, wood ashes, and water, then chilling with cold water, and repeating. In the hands of the women the fibers were drawn across the long sharp iron teeth of the hackle or hatchel, and the shorter fibers, or tow, were removed. Many combings, sometimes over different sets of hackles, left a fine long fiber, which on the little spinning wheel was twisted into a strong thread.[174] With this thread as warp and the tow spinnings as filling, the hand loom turned out a coarse cloth called tow linen, used for towels, ticking, men's shirts and summer pants, and women's and children's everyday dresses. Tow was widely used for gun wadding, spun into twine and rope, and the coarsest woven into sacking. Finer linen was spun with most of the long fiber threads. Repeated wetting and drying in the sun gave the linen its light color, worn natural by the men, frequently dyed for women's clothes.[175]

Sheep shearing in the spring started another home-manufacturing process. The fleece was washed, scoured to rid it of yolk and natural feltings, hand picked for dirt, straws, and burrs, greased, then carded on a pair of hand cards,[176] and made into

[173] A sort of wooden knife or paddle for scraping the broken stalks.

[174] Drawing over sharp edges, scraping, beating, scrubbing, and boiling in potash between hacklings, would further improve texture and impart softness and gloss to finer linens, laces, etc.

[175] In finer linens for dress-up shirts as many as forty bleachings were made in the cloth, in addition to the thread or yarn bleachings. These latter required several days of warm-water bath with frequent changing of water and wringing of skeins, rinsing, repeated treatment with ashes and hot water, a week's clear water bath, seething, rinsing, beating, washing, and drying. Slaked lime or buttermilk also were used as bleaches.

[176] One of the most effective scouring agents was a one-third solution of ammonia obtained from old urine, which left the wool soft and full of life. Hand cards were blocks of curved wood about five by eleven inches covered with leather in which were set rows of slanting or curved fine wire teeth. With their side handles they resembled currycombs. The wool was placed on one card and the other was gently drawn over it until the wool was torn open and blended, then by reversing the upper card and carrying out a shuffling movement it was stripped and collected into a roll or card. The purpose of carding of wool is not to lay the fibers parallel but to break up previous arrangement and prepare them for a new arrangement.

small rolls or cards for spinning. The carding process was the first to leave the home, for as soon as carding mills came into a community the wool was usually turned over to them to prepare for spinning. Spinning wheels were a necessary part of household equipment and serviceable hardwood machines could be obtained from the wheelwright's shop for a dollar or two. The small wheel, about twenty inches in diameter and run by foot pedal, was used for flax; the type most generally used was the Saxony wheel, which took the rove through the hole in the spindle end, twisted it with the rotating flyer, and wound it on the more rapidly rotating bobbin. The large wool-spinning wheels, rotated by hand, were more primitive in type; spinning on them necessitated walking to and fro as the rove was drawn and twisted by the horizontal spindle and wound on the same when slack was given and the spinner brought her hand quickly in towards it.[177] The hum of the spinning wheel was more or less continuous as the housewife and daughters, when not engaged in more pressing tasks, utilized the winter months for production of stuff for summer clothing, and those of summer for winter clothing.

Yarn removed from the bobbins was wound into knots and skeins (forty threads to the knot, seven knots to the skein) on the hands of impatient children, who had to sit still and hold arms a certain distance apart, or better still on the clock reel which measured the skein by emitting a loud popping noise at the end of forty turns. This contraption was destined to become a favorite plaything of children of later generations when they discovered it in the attic. After bleaching or dyeing in the skein, the yarn, if intended for weaving, was wound by hand or wheel upon quills for the shuttles.

Home looms were much less common than spinning wheels, but prior to the advent of the itinerant or professional weaver, the better class homes were often provided with at least one

---

[177] Descriptions of wheels and spinning may be found in Alice Morse Earle, *Home Life in Colonial Days* (New York, 1913), Chapters VIII and IX; Albert S. Bolles, *Industrial History of the United States* (Norwich, Conn., 1881), 421; Ella Shannon Bowles, *Homespun Handicrafts* (Philadelphia, 1931), 64; Luther Hooper, "The Loom and Spindle: Past, Present and Future," in *Annual Report* of the Smithsonian Institution (Washington, D. C., 1914), 629–78, and in numerous texts on spinning, but the act of spinning cannot be understood without seeing it carried out on a wheel.

loom made by a skilled woodmaker, which with its bulky frame of hewn oak was probably the largest piece of furniture in the house, but being put together without nails, was easily knocked down and stored when not in use. People of means built separate loom houses, or used the first cabin for this purpose when the larger house was built. Stringing the loom, tripping the treadles to raise and lower the heddles for alternate threads, throwing or jerking a fast shuttle, and pounding the cross thread evenly into place with the batten, called for no mean order of muscular co-ordination for skillful operation, and produced the while a series of rattles and clickings. This racket combined with the hum of a spinning wheel and, on rainy days or winter evenings, the noises of some fireside cobbling or repair work on the part of the men, gave the home all the earmarks of a true manufactory.[178]

Patterns and design were simple and the cloth as a rule coarse. The looser homespun wool yarns when woven as weft or filler on a linen warp resulted in linsey-woolsey, a durable, warm cloth much used for women's apparel. Woven with a cotton warp it produced "jean," much used for men's clothing. Stripes and checks of browns and blues predominated. Sometimes wool of black sheep was woven into yarn and mixed in weaving to save dyeing. The output of some of these home looms, considering the multifarious duties of the housewife, was truly prodigious.

She [mother] was my father's equal in every respect; in energy, ambition and perseverence. We children were destitute of foot-wear and my mother took some wool of Lewis Cass . . . and carded, spun and knit one-half, for the other half, which she knit into stockings, the first we had in Michigan. Mother was a woman of great ambition and besides doing her own work she did considerable for others and in 1835 she wove over 700 yards of woolen cloth for her neighbors. She lived to a good old age, eighty-eight years.[179]

And again:

In the early years of married life, my mother not only helped in the farm work, but took in spinning on shares, and in this way her family were

---

[178] Brief but adequate descriptions, with illustrations, of the setup and operation of the home loom may be found in Earle, *Home Life in Colonial Days*, Chapter X; Mary Lois Kissell, *Yarn and Cloth Making* . . . (New York, 1918), Chapter IX.
[179] P. S. Richards, "Eighty Years in Michigan," in *Michigan Pioneer and Historical Collections*, XXXVIII (1912), 369.

supplied with all the necessary woolen garments for winter wear, from the woolen socks and stockings, to the dresses, coats and pants, besides the all wool home-made blankets and sheets for the beds. In 1842 her brother-in-law, being a carpenter, made her a loom, and with this for more than twenty years she provided many comforts for her family of four daughters and a son; besides, in this way laid up money to help build the new house, never from the beginning falling short of weaving upwards of 1,000 yards, and going as high as 1,800 or 2,000 yards in some few years, taking it in all, averaging the first 18 years, 1,400 yards per year.[180]

Homespun and home-loomed cloths were coarse, scratchy, and more or less uncomfortable, hence required shrinking and softening for use. This fulling process involved soaking in warm suds and beating with wooden mallets or sticks, or the neighbors might be called in for a "kicking party" at which the men were asked to remove their boots and work the suds with their bare feet. Fulling, as well as carding, left the home when mills for the purpose became available.

Although many yarns and cloths were made up in the natural color, desire for variety and ornamentation led to development of a number of home dyeing practices. Sometimes the raw fiber was colored, more often the yarn or cloth. Early dyestuff came almost entirely from the woods. Hulls of the black walnut gave a dark brown, those of the white walnut or butternut a dull yellow or tawny shade; sumac berries produced a warm red, hickory bark or smartweed, yellow; peach leaves, green; oak and maple, purple; black oak, chestnut, and other barks, various colors. Combinations of these colors were possible, and these vegetable dyes, relatively fast and not injurious to the fibers, faded but did not run or disappear.

Some home-grown indigo was produced, but its preparation was a tedious and delicate work, and it was not until peddlers and stores made commercial indigo and madder available that the best of the home dyeing developed. By the use of different mordants with these primary colors new color combinations were offered and a faster dye resulted.[181] Goldenrod flowers with in-

[180] Mrs. Sarah E. Soper, "Reminiscence of Pioneer Life in Oakland County," in *Michigan Pioneer and Historical Collections*, XXVIII (1897-98), 405.

[181] A mordant is a chemical agent such as alum, tartar, copperas, etc., which unites two materials without chemical affinity. Animal fibers take most dyes more readily than vegetable fibers, hence wool dyeing was easier than flax. The chemistry of dyeing was treated now and then in the agricultural press and the newspapers. See, for example, the two long discussions in the *Ohio Farmer and Western Horticulturist*, August 1, 15, 1835.

digo and alum gave a brighter green, sassafras with the alum made yellow, pokeberry and alum a crimson, while sorrel combined with logwood and copperas produced black. Indigo was the most satisfactory of all and the "blue pot" with its mixture of dye and old urine, kept near the hearth or chimney corner to ripen, constituted an evil-smelling but necessary accessory. The several colors could be modified by mixing and clouding. Two tints of raw wool carded together gave a yarn of the color of neither, while yarns of different colors spun together gave still different effects. Clouding was produced by wrapping yarn skeins with strings in such a way that the dye reached them unevenly.[182]

With wool and flax yarns and cloths of various mixtures provided, the task of making clothes could be undertaken. Feminine hands were seldom idle; in spare moments or while a person was "resting," knitting needles flew to provide stockings, caps, mittens, and mufflers for young and grownups. Although boys and girls, and some men and women, went barefoot from spring to autumn, an abundance of woolen stockings was needed for winter, as well as some linen stockings for women for dress-up occasions.

The fringed deerskin hunting shirt gave way to the wamus or loose-fitting blouse of linsey-woolsey, with its narrow band in place of collar; it reached the hips when loose, or the waist when tied at the corners. For boys the tailless coat served the same general purpose, while small children as a rule were considered sufficiently clothed in the warmer months with a tow shirt which hung straight from shoulders to heels. Pantaloons for the men were ordinarily of jean, but in summer work pants might be of cotton or tow linen. Boys' pantaloons were made full length also,

---

[182] For brief treatment of pioneer dyeing, recipes, etc., see M. C. Williams, "The Homespun Age," in *Magazine of American History*, XXV (1891), 241; Daniel Drake, *Pioneer Life in Kentucky* (Cincinnati, 1870), 100; Kate Milner Rabb, *Indiana Coverlets and Coverlet Weavers* (*Indiana Historical Society Publications*, VIII, No. 8, Indianapolis, 1928). Tried and proved recipes as well as new ones appeared by the hundreds in the newspapers and the agricultural papers. A few sample wool-dye recipes: For yellow, boil the yarn one hour in one sixth its weight of alum, then plunge in a bath of boiled black oak bark. For blue plunge into solution of one ounce of indigo, one ounce of pearlash, and four ounces of oil of vitriol. To get green add some of the blue solution to the yellow. Black could be had by boiling first in a solution of black oak bark, then two hours more in a solution of one part copperas and two parts logwood. Dyeing shops in the towns frequently advertised but their prices were high and consequently did not compete as seriously with domestic processing as did the wool-carding mills. For example blue dyeing of cotton and linen, etc., at Chillicothe cost 62½ cents per pound. Chillicothe *Weekly Recorder*, December 13, 1814.

Indianapolis Market House. *Christian Schrader*

Farms and Fences in Ohio. *Lefevre J. Cranstone*

but with sufficient room to allow for considerable growth. This was especially likely to be true of the Sunday best suit, of carefully woven brown or blue jean. "The trousers dragged and folded over his cowhide shoes, bagged at the knees and in the seat, and, in common with the vest, had sufficient girth for two boys, while the coat hung loose at the shoulders and elbows and was turned up at the wrists. A round-crowned, stiff rimmed wool hat completed a picture of discomfort, self consciousness, awkwardness and greenness."[183]

Clothes were durable so there was much cutting down and remaking of suits for the youngsters from clothes of parents or older children. In winter men commonly wore a wool hat with low broad brim of style similar to that worn by the Quakers, and in summer straw hats homewoven from rye straw. Boots and shoes were at first produced in the home from home-tanned hides.[184] Rights and lefts were made from the same last. Soon came the traveling cobbler who spent some days each year with the family and took care of its needs for the following season, then the resident cobbler whose shop became a popular place in which to loaf and settle the problems of the day. Among poorer folk shoes were an article to be cherished and saved. For reasons of economy, comfort, and appearance it was not unusual for men and women as well as children, to carry them on Sundays to the last bushes short of the church before putting them on. Tough cowhide tight-fitting boots, sometimes copper tipped, and well dressed with bear's grease, were not only a necessity for outdoor work in winter, but usually the article of apparel in which the male took most pride; pants' legs were worn either in or out, sometimes both. The better the fit of the boot the more necessary the bootjack.

Common work dresses worn by women about the house were one piece cotton, linen, or woolen garments of "rainy day length" which slipped over the head and fastened at the neck with a drawstring. Ordinarily pins or hooks and eyes served as fastenings, but for a better dress a collar, buttons, and probably a draw-

---

[183] Parker, "Pioneer Life," in *Indiana Magazine of History*, III, 184.
[184] Home-tanned hides were serviceable but usually coarse. Ashes or ash lye were used to remove the hair, and finely shaved bark (oak, etc.) pounded in to let the tannin do its work. Bear's oil, lard, and tallow were at hand, and an inverted drawing knife served as currying knife. Soot and hog lard made blacking. For tanneries see below, 228.

string at the waist would be added. A straw bonnet or sunbonnet of colored calico stretched over stiff cardboard or split-hickory backing and puckered at the back protected head, face, and neck in summer. Underclothing was not worn by ordinary folks prior to 1840; it was too expensive to buy, too troublesome to make, and besides it was not considered necessary.[185] Socks were rarely worn by men about the farm in warmer months.

By the late 1830's ready-made clothing could be purchased not only in Cincinnati and other important towns, but in smaller communities as well.[186] By 1840 when a lanky pioneer appeared at a sale or other public meeting in woolen or coonskin cap, walnut jean shirt, and fringed pants held up by a drawstring, moccasins, and his long deer rifle, he was conspicuous enough to attract attention.[187]

In addition to sheets, ticking, blankets, towels, tablecloths, sacking, and such household articles, some of which were to be found in the most barren of homes, energetic housewives wove or made rugs, carpets, and coverlets. The successor to the bear-skin and buffalo hide was the rag rug. For this purpose durable rags of every description were saved, cut into strips, sewed end to end, and wound into balls. When sufficient balls accumulated, the home loom or near-by weaver was put to work; on a warp of hard yarn the strips were woven either come-as-may or into a previously conceived pattern, depending upon whether the rags had been dyed or left in their original colors. Rag rugs were also made by plaiting and sewing together of strips into elliptical or circular shapes, and by crocheting with heavy hook needles. Heavier wool yarns woven on cotton or linen warp made rugs of finer quality, and the hooked rug, in which yarn or strips of cloth were looped through a coarse cloth as a base and the loops cut to form the pile, gave ample opportunity for artistic expres-

---

[185] Wilson Daniels, "Steamboating on the Ohio and Mississippi before the Civil War," in *Indiana Magazine of History*, XI (1915), 101; Haines, "Social Life and Scenes in the Early Settlement of Central Illinois," in *Transactions of the Illinois State Historical Society*, 1905 p. 39. For descriptions of dress see also Parker, "Pioneer Life," in *Indiana Magazine of History*, III, 182–88; Duncan, "*Old Settlers.*"

[186] For example, see advertisement for ready-made clothing by John D. Coons at Belmont, Wisconsin Territory, in Mineral Point *Miners' Free Press*, October 20, 1837.

[187] Dr. H. Rutherford, "John Richman, a Typical Backwoodsman," in *Transactions of the Illinois State Historical Society*, 1907, p. 293.

sion. These rugs might present formal patterns or tell the story of sugar making, cabin raising, or other familiar tasks.

Quilts of many designs, standard, original, and crazy patch, began in hundreds of small squares and triangles, were pieced into blocks, and these took shape in quilts, which later got their cross-stitching or quilting in long hours of solitary labor or in quilting parties. Among the common patterns were the log cabin, fan, basket, Irish chains, windmill, fox and geese, oak leaf, peony, tulip, and pine tree. There were also appliquéd quilts, built up of superimposed materials, sometimes stuffed or padded to make the patterns of fruit or whatever, stand out. Expert quilters lined up their stitching by eye. There were straight-line patterns, single-, double- and triple-diagonal, single-line diamond, hanging-diamond, broken-plaid. At quilting parties the young ladies eagerly raced to complete the last lap of stitching so as to shake out the quilt and wrap it around them.

Heavier than the quilts were the comforts of cloth quilted over wool or cotton, which did duty when temperature hardly warranted the feather-bed covering. But the highest development of handicraft of the pioneer women was evidenced in the coverlet (usually pronounced "coverlid" or "kiverlid"). Beds were conspicuous objects, in many homes in the main or living room; the coverlet was a sightly display by day and a warm protector by night.

The art of coverlet weaving came to America in early colonial times and was practiced by New Englanders, Huguenots, Virginians, Carolinians, Dutch, and Germans; it came west with the settlers.[188] Coverlets were among the most prized household possessions. There were four main types of weaves distinguishable in the West: the overshot, double-cloth, "summer and winter," and the Jacquard. The overshot weave, which was one of the earliest in point of time, was geometric in design, and the wool instead of being interwoven with the linen or cotton was "floated

---

[188] Two important contemporary weaving books were J. and R. Bronson, *The Domestic Manufacturers Assistant and Family Directory in the Arts of Weaving and Dyeing* . . . (Utica, N. Y., 1817), and Joseph France, *The Weavers Complete Guide, or the Web Analyzed* (1814). A general introduction to coverlets may be had from Elisa Calvert Hall, *Book of Handwoven Coverlets* (Boston, 1912), or Mary Meigs Atwater, *The Shuttle-Craft Book of American Hand Weaving* (New York, 1940). See also Rabb, *Indiana Coverlets and Coverlet Weavers*, and Irma Pilling Anderson, "Ohio Coverlets," in *Antiques*, XLIX, 56–57 (Jan., 1946).

or skipped over the background." In the double-cloth weave two fabric webs were interwoven at the edges of the figures; both geometric and floral figures were used in this type. Webs of dark-blue wool and light-colored cotton or flax were usual combinations; the pattern of dark blue showed against a light background on one side and in light against a dark background on the other side. The "summer and winter or double-face" weave, probably an American contribution, was more difficult and hence less commonly used. As in the overshot, a pattern of wool was underlaid and overlaid in a warp of flax or cotton, not by long skips, however, but by binding in the weft with every fourth warp thread. The result was a closely woven durable fabric of a pleasing subdued effect, with the pattern, as in the double-cloth weave, showing light on one side and dark on the other.

Most of the homemade coverlets were of the overshot weave, woven in two strips and sewn together; the double weave required a more elaborate loom and complicated threading draft, and, though sometimes made in the home, were usually the work of professional weavers. The drafts were written on scraps of paper, on old letters, bills, or notes, and passed around as were favorite "receipts." Most of them were for patterns of geometric figures, but the combinations were varied and pleasing. There were "dainty, feminine patterns, patterns whose solid logic is clearly masculine, irrational patterns, stern and solemn patterns, prim patterns and exuberant patterns—each with its quaint name and its place in history. Curiously, they are like music. They are like little melodies of four notes, full of runs, trills and returns."[189]

With the soft-spun and home-dyed yarns in which indigo blues, madder reds, bronze-blacks, and whites predominated, the weaver dressed the loom and set to work on "Puritan Maiden," "Tennessee Trouble," "Indian War," "Cat Trace," "Snail Trail," "Whig Rose," "Hoosier Beauty," "Gentleman's Fancy," or any of dozens of other patterns. The skillful or practiced weaver possessed a rhythm and touch which was individual. The resulting piece, if not as perfect as the mechanically loomed product, was just as durable and far more charming and satisfying in character; many of these homemade coverlets have re-

[189] Atwater, *Shuttle-Craft Book*, 45.

mained true in color and intact in fabric, after three generations of use.

The Jacquard loom came to the United States in the middle 1820's. Soon the professional weavers, largely Scots, Irish, or English, began to establish their shops in the West and to advertise their work. Many women, like their descendants a century later who suddenly found their old four-poster beds and heavy "bureaus" looking drab in comparison to the shiny brass beds and "chiffoniers" of the latest advertisements, became fascinated with the elegant combinations of flowers, eagles, scrolls, and mottoes in these Jacquard weaves. Besides it saved a lot of work: with numerous daughters each to be supplied with at least one coverlet, it was easier to furnish the materials, select a pattern, and pay the weaver $5.00 or $10. So "they took down their old looms and stored them away in haylofts and garrets to lie forgotten for the next hundred years, and carried their beautifully dyed homespun yarns to the weave shop to be turned into an 'E Pluribus Unum' coverlet with name and date woven into the corner."[190] The weaver was often deluged under "backlogs" of orders which contracted for his time for a year or more in advance.

The preparation and preserving of meat figured prominently in the pioneer scheme of domestic economy. The pioneer was, in the earlier days, a meat eater by necessity. As wild game gave way to the domestic animal, he remained a heavy meat eater from choice. Hogs could not always find a market or bring a profit if they reached it, but the comparatively lean mast-fed animal, or the not too fat farm product would always fill the jars and barrels with sausage, headcheese, and pickled pork, and the rafters and beams with hams, bacon, and side meat.

Butchering was one of the big events in farm life. Woods-ranging porkers in their second or third year were rounded up and fed a month or more on corn to bring them to around two hundred pounds if possible. Some time around Thanksgiving or before Christmas, when the temperature was freezing or below, neighbors were notified, and preparations completed. Wood was assembled for the big open fire, kettles prepared, knives, hooks, and axes were sharpened, scrapers and gambrels laid out, barrels

[190] *Ibid.,* 13–14.

tested, jars and kegs cleaned. A dozen or more hogs would suffice for family purposes, and could be taken care of at one time, but if pork were shipped, there would be other butcherings. The animals were either shot or stunned with an ax, then cut in the throat to bleed; or for best bleeding stuck alive. The last method called for some strength and skill, but many a pioneer woman could turn the trick. After bleeding, the hog was hoisted by hand or block and tackle, dipped into a slanting barrel of scalding water,[191] laid on the table of boards, and scraped with the blade of an old corn knife or the bell-shaped bottom of a metal candlestick. Gambrel sticks were inserted under the tendons of the hind legs, the carcass was hung, and after the entrails were removed, was split lengthwise by cutting the ribs on either side of the backbone with an ax.[192] Leaf fat was loosened, and the whole hung to cool but not to freeze.

Meanwhile division of labor had begun, and the women and children were working on the "innards." Heart and liver were washed and hung to cool;[193] stomach and small intestine cleaned and scraped for sausage casings; gut fat removed for soap; the bladder, if not used as casing, was cleaned, dried, and given to the children to inflate and use as a football; and the remains probably cooked for chicken feed.

Properly cooled, the carcass went onto the cutting table, where head, shoulders, middle, and hams were separated. Large hams and shoulders were trimmed of part of the fat and hide, and butted, to insure better curing. Back and belly were carved apart, fat layers removed, loin cut from the back, spareribs from the belly, and the sides squared up for bacon.

There was no lack of meat during the weeks required for curing. Loin chunks, spareribs, backbone, chitlins, and fresh sausage found their way into the kitchen and were exchanged

[191] Just hot enough to burn the finger the third time it was dipped in rapid succession. Many of the pioneers, particularly in Michigan and Wisconsin, heated the water in the approved New England method by heating stones and dropping them into the barrels. This was the only method when large kettles were not available.

[192] The modern method of splitting down the middle of the backbone was seldom used.

[193] Among New Englanders the "pluck"—heart, liver, and lungs or "lights"—was eagerly awaited in the kitchen, where it was stewed and browned for the big meal of butchering day. Southerners as a rule threw the "lights" to the hounds. On the other hand, the Southerners regarded chitlins, or fresh intestines fried in meal, as a great delicacy.

with neighbors. Scraps went into the sausage grinder,[194] and mixed with salt, pepper, and sage were ready for the skillet or the hand-operated stuffer, by which the sausage was impounded in the casings, twisted, linked, or coiled in one piece and smoked. The liver was either fried fresh, used for liver sausage, or boiled for scrapple[195] or headcheese, and the heart pickled or scrappled. Feet were cleaned and pickled, and the meat from heads, tails, tongues, feet, and scraps cooked, chopped, boiled down, molded, and cooled under weights. Headcheese or souse was then ready for slicing and serving. Lard rendering or "trying out" followed as one of the by-processes of butchering; the big kettles simmered, presses creaked, and jars and firkins were filled. Even the crisp cracklings which remained were not wasted; ground and mixed with meal and baked into a rich bread, they were much relished by the southern folk.

Curing the meat took time and skill and was an art more successfully practiced by some than others. The brine cure was probably easiest and most economical. Salt remained an expensive article until the coming of the railroads and better highways, and brine could be used more than once. Some saltpeter and perhaps sugar were added, and the hams, shoulders, and other pieces weighted down in the brine for varying periods of time, roughly three days for each pound in the piece.[196] Repacking was necessary at intervals and the possibility of the souring of the brine had to be guarded against.

In the dry cure the salt and other ingredients were rubbed evenly on the outside of each piece, the process repeated in about a week, and the meat packed. Since brine formed in the cask bottom, bottom and top pieces were reversed from time to time. The time required was about the same. Meat souring, which usually began at the center, was caused by faulty bleeding, bruised flesh, or decomposition before the salt reached the center; it marked poorly cured meat.

After the cure, meat not to be used during cold weather was

[194] At first they were chopped. Later homemade grinders, some all wood, others with rows of iron pins set spirally on a roller, were used.

[195] Same procedure as headcheese except that three parts of meal were added to one part of meat. After cooling scrapple was served cold or fried in fat.

[196] A common pickle recipe called for eight gallons of water, one-half pound of saltpeter, one pound brown sugar, one quart of molasses, and enough fine salt to float a light egg.

smoked, in the smokehouse if the household establishment afforded one, or in the fireplace or chimney recesses for small-scale operations. Green hickory was the choice of woods, but sugar maple, apple, other hardwoods, or even corncobs were satisfactory. Thirty or forty hours of smoke, supplemented by a few hours smoking on following days, usually produced the desired color; the hams, shoulders, and sides were then either wrapped in cloth, whitewashed or painted, and hung in the dry dark smokehouse, or stored in ashes or elsewhere to protect them from bugs and worms. The bulk of the pork shipped South during flatboat days was smoked, yet a considerable amount of pickled meat was put up as well, and the old pork barrel was an essential part of the commissary.

Butchering of neat cattle and sheep was not such a big event as hog butchering. Neighbors were solicited as to the amount they could use and the meat largely consumed fresh, although a portion was sometimes cured or packed down in lard. By staggering the butchering in a community, a reasonable supply of beef and mutton could be made available in all except the hottest months.

Dairying was not a developed industry in pioneer times, but constituted an integral part of domestic economy. Breeding had not given the farmer the specialized milk producers of our day, nor was scientific feeding commonly understood or practiced, but the poorest farmer or richest landowner maintained from one to a dozen milk cows, fed on pasturage in summer, and on hay, straw, fodder, or possibly some root crop in winter.

Milking, that all too regular chore, frequently fell to the lot of the women and boys, and was often performed in the open. Care of the milk was one of the women's duties. Cooling facilities were provided by the springs or dugout cellars. Springs were much more numerous before deforestation than now, and varied from a shallowed-out pool in a framework of wood or stone, to elaborate stone springhouses with basins hollowed out of solid stone, through which running water trickled. They were often a hundred yards or more from the house, and milk pails were carried to and water fetched from them at least twice daily. Here the milk cooled, cream was skimmed, and butter stored. Churning came at least twice a week. Perhaps one of the boys could be commandeered to officiate at that so necessary article, "big at the bottom, little at the top, with something in the middle that goes flippety flop," until the butter came, but if so, he took no pride in his work. Working the butter with wooden paddles in the large wooden bowl, molding it, and cleaning the pails and utensils was as much a part of women's work as washing dishes.

Butter was consumed in large quantities by the vigorous farmer folk, and in the making of good butter the farmer's wife took great pride. Butter molds were frequently works of art, and as official guarantee for the product, which was marketed locally, as jealously guarded against imitation as trade-marks of manufacturers. Cheese making was not so common, but was engaged in regularly by the Germans and Swiss, and frequently by all, for butter shortage often developed in winter, and a half dozen big cheeses on the shelves helped tide over. A little water in which a piece of rennet[197] had been soaked, was added to the milk to start the curdling. As the curds rose, a cheesecloth was pressed down upon them so that they flowed up through the cloth. After draining, pressure was applied for several days in the press, and the cheese was ready to take out of its hoop, to be rubbed with salt and shelved to ripen. Much soft cheese—"smearcase" or modern cottage cheese—was consumed.[198]

Feeding as well as clothing the large families of pioneer days necessitated planning at least a year ahead and the practice of a diversified cultivation and nicety of balance. Scarcity and lack of variety of food need not exist after the first few years in a new community. Corn, pumpkins, beans, and potatoes were supplemented by cabbages, cucumbers, asparagus, rhubarb, radishes, lettuce, tomatoes, peas, turnips, melons, barley, rye, and buckwheat. As the wild crab apples, grapes, cherries, plums, strawberries, blackberries, and gooseberries became more difficult of access, the domestic products took their place. In addition the garden had to provide those accessories, not foodstuffs in themselves, but necessary to the preserving and seasoning of food—

[197] Contents of the stomach of an unweaned calf, or the lining of the stomach. See Rufus W. Adams, *A dissertation . . . the best method of making butter and cheese . . .* (Marietta, Ohio, 1813), for a contemporary manual.

[198] The *schmierkase* of the Germans.

sage, peppers, thyme, mints, mustard, horse-radish, tansy, and other herbs. In fact the herb garden was often planted nearest the kitchen. As Henry Whiting noted, these gardens were practical rather than ornamental:

Beside his hut a garden lay,
Not fill'd with shrubs and flowrets gay,
—Those trancient fopperies of taste,
That but adorn an useless waste,—
But every esculent and root,
That simple appetite could suit,
And vary farmers' healthy fare,
Was thriving in abundance there.
The current bush and gooseberry too,
In every corner met the view;
Nurs'd by the wife—well skill'd to make
The simple wine and dainty cake.

Were the family not to be restricted to a monotonous diet of meal and meat in the winter, it was as necessary to store and keep fruits and vegetables as pork, and the perfection attained in this phase of domestic economy was the result of an accumulation of knowledge gained by trial and error and handed down through the generations of pioneers. Canning was as yet an undeveloped art; in the absence of glass jars and self-sealers, tin cans, and chemical preservatives, other ways and means were used to preserve the food for the heavy meals so well liked by all and available to all but the most thriftless.

In the garden, choice plants were carefully guarded and certain rows were reserved for special seed; a screen of cloth served to protect young shoots from birds and insects. Later, drying in the attic, hanging from the beams or stored in gourds, were to be found the seeds for pepper plants and cucumbers, sunflowers and pumpkins, sweet corn and cabbage, rhubarb and melons. As cultivation proceeded and the fruits and vegetables ripened, there began a routine of laying away which lasted from June to late autumn. Busy were these days of summer and fall, with the men harvesting and plowing, big meals to cook, and visiting and entertaining to be done. Earliest vegetables were hardly ready for eager appetites before strawberries and cherries were ripe, to be picked and preserved or sun-dried. There were berries and currants to be put into jellies and preserves; cucumbers into the brine or vinegar barrels; cabbages to be cut fine, salted down under weights in big stone jars, stuffed into mango peppers or let sour into kraut; hops to pick; peppers and horse-radish to dry and grind. Then the fruits: quinces for jelly and preserves; apples and pears to be picked, peeled, cored, and dried carefully on the racks prepared; plums and wild grapes for jellies; domestic grapes for jellies and wines; pumpkins and squashes to be dried and mixed with crab apples or saved for stews, butter, and pies.[199]

By the time the "frost was on the pumpkin and the fodder in the shock," cider and apple butter-making time had arrived. The homemade press was sufficient, or the apples might be taken to the neighborhood horse mill. Cider making was almost a religious rite with New Englanders, but they had no monopoly on either its production or use. Beverage needs satisfied, a quantity was laid away to turn to vinegar; the rest went into the apple butter.

Apple butter making as an event in the year's routine ranked second only to butchering and maple sugaring, and in many respects was a more enjoyable occasion than either, for the weather was at its best and the labor less irksome. The big copper kettles were cleaned and scoured, paddles scrubbed and scalded, and the firewood piled handy. The womenfolk got a day's start in peeling and coring, the cider was boiled down, and bright and early the next morning apples began to cook in two or three kettles. Back and forth across the bottom and around the edges went the perforated paddle, steadily and monotonously, pushed and pulled by the long handle which kept the stirrer away from the heat. From white apple color to yellowish pink, then to pink, finally to a reddish brown the thickening contents turned. By midafternoon bubbles were bursting thickly, leaving momentary craters in the surface, and as the mixture boiled down, the exposed sides became coated with dark leatherlike layers of baked and scorched apple. Perhaps the contents of two kettles were now emptied into one. The butter grew thicker and darker. If sugar were added, the butter thinned. More hours of boiling, sometimes in the moonlight late into the evening, until it was pronounced done. Mixed heavily with spices and poured into jars, this dark cider

[199] Calves' feet were boiled for gelatin sometimes used in making jellies and other sweets.

product required no sealing to keep. But there were those who believed that the best apple butter of all was that made without cider.[200]

Other apples were barreled, some choice ones perhaps were shelved individually, and the rest, with cabbages, potatoes, and turnips were buried to prevent freezing. The fruits of the woods were gathered—paw paws to be eaten fresh, persimmons to be dried for puddings, walnuts, hickory nuts, pecans, and chestnuts to be hulled and stored.

> Thus autumn gainful pastime lends,
> And thus the mingled season ends,
> With toil and sport alternate crown'd,
> Till winter close the annual round.

Needless to say, the kitchen was the center of activity in the home. Like its colonial predecessor it was the cooking head-quarters, living room, and manufacturing center. In the substantial homes of dressed lumber, stone or brick, it was perhaps larger than the original cabin. True to southern practice, many of the better-class homes of the Ohio Valley had the kitchens, fireplace and all, built separate from the house; others merely had a "summer kitchen." "Cat and clay" fireplaces were replaced by spacious works of stone or brick; iron cranes and long poles, mechanical spits, roasters, waffle irons, reflectors, or built-in ovens came into more general use, and culinary processes became easier. Corn pone and the lye pot for hominy still held their place, and saleratus biscuits could always be stirred up in little or no time, but glistening fat loaves of white bread leavened with homemade yeast began to grace the fireside. Best of all the bakers was the outdoor oven of bricks, clay, and stone. On baking days the fire was built therein, and when bread, light bread biscuits, coffee cakes, and pies were ready, the fire was raked out, the loaves inserted on clean leaves, and the oven sealed to perform its work silently and effectively. Cookstoves were introduced in some of the cities in the 1820's, but were not

---

[200] The Pennsylvania German method is described in an article from the *Maine Cultivator* in the *Cincinnati Daily Gazette*, October 22, 1840. The division of opinion on this important subject was almost as sharp as that between the two schools of thought on the making of mint juleps.

numerous until the late 1830's,[201] and not common in the country then.

A prodigious amount of cooking was carried on in the pioneer homes. Appetites were large, food was abundant, and the out-door life made it possible to digest the heavy meals; besides there existed a cooking tradition. Southerners had their hot biscuits and salt pork, ham, eggs, mush, grits, molasses, potatoes, and gravy for breakfast; Yankees were known to eat beans and pie, and persons of German antecedents, sauerkraut. Three heavy meals a day was the rule, among the Germans four, plus lunches. At least two kinds of meat, three or four vegetables, gravy, two kinds of bread, eggs, cheese, several kinds of jellies and pre-serves, relishes, pies and cake, with milk, coffee, or tea, was not an uncommon menu in the country home. Harvest meals, or meals served for company, reunions, weddings, and picnics would appear as vulgar displays of superabundance and examples of waste to one unfamiliar with gastronomic capacities and the competition for cooking laurels among the women. On such occa-sions the long tables were loaded with wild game, fowl, beef, and pork—hot and cold—pot pies, vegetables, dressings, sauces, pies, cakes, and other pastries in quadruplicate, pickles, preserves, and puddings galore.[202]

Around Thanksgiving and Christmas the regular commissary was supplemented with mincemeats and fruit cakes, rich, spicy and flavored with whiskey. Young and old enjoyed their food; poor teeth were permitted to be no handicap. The reasons for

---

[201] One of the first advertisements noted in the West was that of "C. Postley's Patent Cooking Stoves, or Portable Kitchens," in the *Liberty Hall and Cincinnati Gazette*, August 25, 1821. Franklin and cooking stoves were for sale in Cleveland in the middle 1820's. See cuts in *Cleaveland Herald*, October 6, 1826. ". . . up to 1828 there was no such thing known as a cast stove. John Sheets brought a seven-plate stove from the east to town [Madison, Indiana] for his stove, but there were no cook stoves until 1835 or '36. It was stipulated when I got my wife that I was to furnish a cooking stove for our kitchen." Lewis, "Pioneers of Jefferson County," in *Indiana Magazine of History*, XII, 218. Cooking stoves were manufactured at St. Louis in 1834. *Sangamo Journal*, July 5, 1834. The following year Nott's "summer baker" was advertised in Cincinnati, as well as H. B. Ward's Improve-ment, a full-bodied octagonal contrivance with boiler and ovens on either side of the firebox. *Cincinnati Daily Gazette*, October, 1835. Stanley's Patent Rotary (the circular top was turned by a crank so as to bring different pots over the fire) was advertised for sale at Cincinnati in 1834. *Ibid.*, December 1, 1834. Also a cookstove with oven and boiler, which was convertible into an open Franklin or fireplace front. *Ibid.*, March 10, 1835. By 1837 cooking, Franklin, and ten-plate stoves were advertised in Galena, Illinois. By this time they were becoming gen-erally available. Mineral Point (Wis.) *Miners' Free Press*, November 3, 1837.

[202] For samples of big dinners, see Chapter VI, 330-31.

the existence of large numbers of rawboned, hollow-chested but pot-bellied youth, in spite of the outdoor life and physical exercise, are not hard to find. Dr. Daniel Drake was probably right: "As a general fact, the people of the valley eat too much. . . . I cannot attempt to enumerate the vicious modes of cooking."[203]

While most of the domestic economy was left largely to the women, there was one process they could not be trusted with, namely, the preparation of "eatin' tobaccy," otherwise known as plug. Men dependent upon the weed in this form would procure a section of green sugar maple, bore two-inch auger holes in it lengthwise, then stuff the holes with a mixture of syrup, honey, rum, maple sugar, or other favorite flavor, and long green leaves when "in case." Wooden plugs rammed in tight with the aid of the cider press completed the operation, and the block was set away in the smokehouse to age. In time a "hole" could be split off as needed, and the round "plugs" sliced off.

Candlemaking was a household chore with most of the pioneers. Bits of tallow were scrupulously saved, and homemade wicks or bought cotton twist were repeatedly dipped and cooled until of size. A heavy candle or "slut" was made of a wooden rod wrapped with strips of linen, and covered with tallow pressed on by hand. These would burn for several nights. Neater results were obtained in the metal molds made for six to two dozen candles. Finer products with a delicately perfumed flavor were made from "candle berries" or the wax melted from the bayberry or wax myrtle, or from tallow and powdered gum camphor. These candles, unless refined, had a greenish color, and possessed more backbone against the heat in warm weather. Fancy stripe effects could be had from the red of pokeberry juice, green of wild nettles, and logwood or alder bark. Candle boxes hung on the walls at convenient points in the house, while lighters and snuffers were close by.

The fireplace or pine torches still provided the chief lighting

[203] *Diseases of the Interior Valley of North America* (2 volumes. Cincinnati, 1850, 1854), I, 654 ff. Said the *Medical Repository* (New York, 1797–1824), XIX (1818), Preface, iii. "The inhabitants are almost constantly in a state of repletion, by stuffing and cramming, and by the use of stimulating drink. The consumption of animal food is probably much greater in Fredonia than in any other civilized nation." Yet George Flower, the Englishman, said that in contrast to the English, the Americans ate a heavy breakfast and often only one other meal. "What will board one German or Englishman will satisfy two Americans." *The Errors of Emigrants* (London, 1841), 34.

facilities in the poorer homes, while grease lamps were supplementing or replacing candles in the better. Almost any sort of shallow vessel, a gourd, or a scraped-out turnip with a spout or stick to hold a twisted wick of cotton or tow linen, would pass as a lamp. Lard or deer tallow supplied the oil. Sperm oil, of course, was best, but not so widely used because of its cost.[204] By the light of these smoking, smelly lamps the women spun and the men worked or read during the comparatively brief interval between dusk and bedtime.

Soft soap making was another regular chore, usually performed in spring time, which remained as a domestic industry long after the passing of pioneer days. Good wood ashes were leached in water and the lye percolated through the loose wood container to be collected in a kettle below. Lye strong enough to float a potato or egg, to which—unless maple ashes were used—was added some unslaked lime, was mixed with old grease and boiled to produce soft soap. By another method the grease was mixed with warm lye and left to stand in the sun with daily stirring, for about a week. If soap had not come by that time, a little hot lye or more grease was added until it did. This unrefined and unperfumed article was a dirt and grease cutter and was believed by most farm wives to be easier on the clothes than the later store product. The well known odor given to clothing washed in soft soap was regarded as a sort of hallmark of cleanliness.[205] The laundering of heavy clothes and bedding was accomplished by the "rub and bile" method. Washing machines, some of the compression type, were advertised and demonstrated at Cincinnati in the 1820's, but never came into general use.

Wood-ashes lye was often utilized on a large scale during the years of clearing, particularly in Michigan and northern Ohio, in the manufacture of black salts. The lye water was boiled until the matter in solution took solid form. It was usually sold in this form to traders or potash makers for $3.00 or $4.00 per

[204] Manufacture of illuminating oil from corn was regarded as a possibility also. Corn oil at the rate of one-half gallon from the bushel was advertised at Norwalk, Ohio, as a substitute for sperm oil. *Cincinnati Daily Gazette*, February 2, 1837. Modern portable gas service was anticipated by a promoter who sold local rights to manufacture gas from a concoction of whiskey, ether, camphor, turpentine, and pearlash. Springfield *Sangamo Journal*, June 1, 1833.

[205] Typical soft soap recipes may be found in *Ohio Farmer and Western Horticulturist*, May 15, 1839; *Western Prairie Farmer*, September 23, 1840.

hundred pounds. Sometimes the process was carried a step further on the farm, the salts being subjected to a red heat for several hours to burn out combustible matter, broken up, and packed in casks.[206] It was not unusual for the cash profits thus derived to be sufficient to pay for the land. The black salts or pot- and pearlash production seems to have been little practiced by the settlers from the South.

Few pioneers in the hardwood belt did not, at some time or other, participate in maple sugar making. Not everyone had a sugar camp, yet sugar trees were common in the neighborhood. Sugar making came in early spring with the rising of the sap, at a time when farm labor was not otherwise in demand. After a late January or early February thaw, the notches were cut, holes were bored, spouts or spiles inserted, and wooden troughs or buckets fixed in place. The quantity of sap varied from season to season and from tree to tree; a good tree would yield three to five gallons of sap per day, depending upon the number of spiles. The boys came around with the barrel on the sled or drag to collect the sweet water and haul it to the shed where the kettles, or better still the large shallow pans, were kept merrily boiling by those in charge. When evaporated to about one tenth in volume, the liquid was permitted to cool and settle, then poured off from the sediment, heated with the addition of some skimmed milk, whites of eggs, or a bit of saleratus, skimmed of risen impurities, and boiled down to proper consistency. The amount of "sugar molasses" derived from sap depended upon the sweetness of the sap and the thickness of the syrup wanted. Roughly speaking, thirty to forty gallons of sap were required for a gallon of syrup. When the syrup was poured into a tub to cool, a layer of sugar crystallized on top, and the molasses was drained out from the bottom. Stirring while cooling produced more sugar. Sugar brought three to six cents, sometimes more, at the country stores, or, when molded into little circles, hearts, and shamrocks, was a much sought-after confection.

[206] "The black-salts were sold to merchants in Charlotte, who had them made into potash, then drawn to Marshall and shipped to Buffalo, where they were made into saleratus, ready to be shipped back to the merchants and sold to the same families who had cut the timber and burned the logs that made the ashes they had raked up to make the black salts that made the saleratus that raised our pancakes." Theodore E. Potter, "A Boy's Story of Pioneer Life in Michigan," in *Michigan Pioneer and Historical Collections*, XXXV (1907), 406.

Those who were not so fortunately located as to have maple sugar and syrup were dependent upon store sugar which was expensive. By the time the forests were thinning out, the steamboat had made New Orleans sugar and molasses generally available. It was not until the 1850's that the introduction of Chinese cane gave the midwestern settler a substitute for the mild New Orleans molasses in the form of the strong sorghum or "black strap" molasses. Molasses was not only an important article of diet, but in the form of "long sweetening" was widely used in cooking.

Stills were frequently run by enterprising farmers who sought to supplement their income by exchange of a product so universally used and readily marketed as almost to serve as money. Sprouted corn mash, if kept warm, soon fermented into a beer which when once distilled gave watery raw singlings. A restill through the copper worm covered with cold spring water took out most of the water and left a clear but potent corn whiskey, which if aged in charred green white oak casks at proper temperatures took on color and some mellowness. Proof of authority was judged by the "bead" or number of bubbles when shaken. Manuals such as Samuel M'Harry's *The Practical Distiller* (Harrisburg, Pa., 1809) were available; agricultural papers also gave directions for stilling and wine making. Although the average distiller knew nothing of vatting and blending, or the finer points of distilling, his liquor was an honest product. There was no reason for haste or dilution, hence no need for lye or tobacco, to give it bite, or soap to give it "bead." A bushel of corn was good for about two gallons of whiskey. Sometimes the argument for stilling ran as follows: The land would produce nothing but corn. There was no market for the corn so they made it into whiskey. The whiskey market was glutted and the price low, so they drank the whiskey. Since all the apples and peaches could not be used in the kitchen, the surplus was made into applejack and brandy.

Among the first of the operations to leave the farm was the grinding of grain. Corn meal could be made successfully in small quantities by hand, but the same was not true of flour. Mills always followed the settlements, but for years a trip to the mill twenty or more miles away was a matter of three or four days. The cost of milling a bushel of grain was equal to the price of two or three bushels. Horse mills were simple affairs. In one type the horse turned an upright shaft which had a large pulley some six feet above the ground from which a rawhide belt extended to a smaller pulley at the same height on another upright post or shaft. Above the latter were the platform and grinding stones.

Damsites were much sought after and exploited in early days.[207] Dams of logs, stone, brush and clay, hewn timbers, or stone impounded the waters in the pond. The millrace was usually of hewn or sawed timber, closed at the lower end by a water gate. The turbine wheel sat on end and the shaft extended through the floor to the mill room above. For the overshot wheel the water was directed over the top and the burrs geared to the horizontal shaft. The undershot wheel was similar except the water was directed against the lower edge, and the top of the wheel turned toward the current. Homemade burrs were chiseled out of granite erratics or niggerheads, or even sandstone. The best of millstones in the United States came from New York, Pennsylvania, and western Virginia, but superior to these were the French stones with surface ridges hard and sharp.[208] Imported burrs usually came in sections and were banded together with iron hoops.

In grinding, the lower stone remained stationary while only the upper turned, but it was the lower which had to have its ridges reset now and then. Grist was fed through the hole in the upper stone and the meal or flour found its way out around the edges of the lower. The fineness of the product was regulated by the space between the stones. Flour was bolted in a reel covered with silk or bolting cloth, set at a slant so that the bran worked out the lower end. The miller took his toll in kind, usually from a fourth to an eighth, depending upon location, competition, or legal regulation; he was frequently the most prosperous citizen of local parts. A good millsite sometimes boasted a sawmill

[207] Roger Butterfield, in "Wherever Water Blooms," in *Saturday Evening Post*, July 26, 1941, states that there are no real millsites between the Appalachians and the Rockies. This certainly was not the case a century and a quarter ago, when the forests conserved the water and streams were more dependable.
[208] Branson, "Early Flour Mills in Indiana," in *Indiana Magazine of History*, XII, 25. Millstones were made by the French settlers in the Illinois country from stones found at the rapids of the Illinois River about 270 miles from its mouth. Warden, *A Statistical, Political and Historical Account of the United States*, III, 53.

also; round about would spring up a blacksmith shop, general store, and probably a village. In times of water shortage or rush seasons, when there was more business than could be taken care of promptly, by rigid custom and the law of democracy each person had to wait his turn. Waits of two or three days were common; the time was spent in general repairs, trading, politics, and gossip.

The blacksmith was gunsmith, farrier, coppersmith, millwright, machinist, and surgeon general to all broken tools and implements. His forge was a center of social as well as industrial activity. From soft bar iron, nails as well as horseshoes were forged as needed. Tires were hammered out, measured, welded, heated, and shrunk on the felly. Chains, reaping hooks, bullet molds, yoke rings, axles, bear and wolf traps, hoes, augers, bells, files, shears, locks, keys, adzes, plowshares, hackle teeth, bits, saws, and the metal parts of looms, spinning wheels, sausage grinders, presses, and agricultural implements were a few of the items either manufactured or repaired in his shop. In addition the master smiths created axes and rifles,[209] and, if provided with foundry and machine facilities, stoves, skillets, kettles, pots, mills, threshing machines, and plows. Some smiths were so adept that they were said to be able to discern the slightest deviation in the bore or alignment of a rifle barrel without measurements. Many were able to cut the rifling in a gun barrel to precision with only a cutting edge fastened to a rod and directed in its progress by a handcut spiral groove on a wooden stick about the length of the barrel.[210] Bar iron and cast steel of various types came from Pittsburgh or Europe, and were expensive.

[209] See above, 159–61.
[210] This process has been hazily explained, but not demonstrated, by "old timers" who have seen it done. Others apparently have had the same trouble in forming a clear understanding of it: "The actual cutting is done by working the wooden cylinder back and forth by hand, the barrel being clamped in a vise, and the movements of the cylinder are somehow regulated by the so-called head-block, a contrivance of wood and leather, the operation of which I have never been able completely to understand." Randolph, *The Ozarks*, 244. It is very simple when seen or diagramed. See Dillin, *The Kentucky Rifle*, plates 31, 59, 61, 62, or diagrams reproduced in Roger Burlingame, *March of the Iron Men* . . . (New York, 1938).

Since the rifling was usually shallow, barrels had to be rebored periodically. Catching the pitch of the rifling and getting a clean, square regrooving was even more complicated than the original boring. One way of doing this was to insert a hickory rod in the barrel and pour around it about a foot of melted lead. When cool, the lead plug was driven out, a steel cutting tooth about half an inch long and slanted to conform to the rifling, was fixed onto one of the relief parts of the

Tanneries were never as numerous as blacksmith shops or mills, but when available were distinct assets to the community. Sometimes hides of fur-bearing animals were tanned, as well as those of horses, neat cattle, sheep, and deer. After soaking in water the hides were put on the breaking beam (probably a hollow log split in half) and scraped with the breaking knife. Several weeks more in limewater would loosen the hair which was then scraped off. After another prolonged soaking in "rotted" water (water treated with manure) vats known as the "bates," the glue and lime were scraped away with a piece of sandstone or soapstone. Next the hides went into vats filled with water and ground chestnut or oak bark. After two months in this ooze hides were usually packed between layers of bark in a storage tank for several months. Then followed drying and dressing, treatment with tallow and fish oil, further drying, whitening, and scraping to uniform thickness with razor-edged knives. This last operation required great skill. All told, the tanning operation took about a year. Hides were sold down river, to the local cobbler and harness maker, and carried in the general store for household use.

§ § § § §

Pioneer life in the prairie regions was of the same general pattern as described above, modified, however, by the topography and environment, particularly by the lack of forests and drainage, and exposure to winds and prairie fires. The few bold spirits who pushed into the treeless areas, filled with cattail sloughs or covered with tall coarse grass, were sometimes viewed with suspicion as having isolated themselves for cause. Timber for cabins, outbuildings, and fences could be had along the stream bottoms, or from the groves or isolated woods, but often had to be hauled for miles. Settlers in the prairie regions, particularly in Illinois, found the lumber problem a serious one. In the late 1830's, prior to the opening of the Illinois and Michigan Canal

---

plug, and the plug reinserted into the barrel and worked back and forth until each rifle was deepened in turn. A slightly different method of accomplishing the same thing is described in Herbert Best, *Young 'Un* (New York, 1944), 258.

A partial checklist of gunsmiths may be found in Rhea Mansfield Knittle and Stuart M. Martin, "Early Ohio Gunsmiths," in *Antiques*, XLIII, 214–17 (May, 1943).

or railroads, ordinary building lumber from the timbered bottoms and the prairie groves sold at $25 to $35 per thousand feet, plus hauling charges, a price probably not again reached until the war years of the twentieth century. Pine lumber, mostly shipped from the Allegheny above Pittsburgh, was scarce and costly; at Peoria it sold for from $60 to $70 and in the Rock River country up to $90, which made its use prohibitive to any but persons of means. Settlers were advised, if feasible, to bring their glazed window frames, finished doors, and interior finishing stuff with them or purchase them at Pittsburgh or Cincinnati. A few houses were built altogether at these places and shipped in parts around to Wisconsin Territory.[211] Comfortable log houses of the better type cost even more than a frame house of the same size.[212] A few years later, with more numerous local sawmills and improved transportation, prices fell about half, but streams of water with sufficient fall for mill seats were scarce, as were year-round springs.

Roads in prairie country were often more impassable than in the rough and forested sections. Devastating hot winds from the west or miasmatic humidity and heat alternated in summer months and the usual malarial diseases were worse than in upland regions. In autumn when the rank prairie grass had been killed by frost and dried by Indian summer suns, prairie fires seemed to burst forth spontaneously. Driven by high winds, banks of billowy smoke clouds advanced swiftly with the ominous roar of the tornado, to lift skyward and explode into flame which at night lighted the country for miles around. As birds and beasts fled before the withering blasts, their cries contributed to the atmosphere of eerieness. Frequently they were surrounded and devoured by the flames. For days afterwards the light charred remains of grass hung over the landscape like a pall, until the winds and rain of autumn dissipated and pounded in the black debris—all that remained of the summer's crop of lush grass and sparkling flowers. Prairie settlers early learned to plow wide furrows to protect fences, crops, and buildings against the smaller fires, and to build backfires; but many a heroic battle was waged, not merely to save homes, but life itself.

[211] W. R. Smith, *Observations on the Wisconsin Territory*, 7.
[212] A. D. Jones, *Illinois and the West*, 207–9.

Descriptions of life in the prairie regions as received back East were contradictory; it was represented as most desirable and as the worst on the frontier.

I have been frequently at loss to know how to reconcile these contradictions; but it is now perfectly obvious. Imagine yourself trudging along a dusty prairie road in the middle of a hot summer's day, with the heat of an almost vertical sun pouring on you. Not a shade near; not a breath of wind to move the sultry air, which seems close enough to stifle you. You come to a little low log hut, which you can see through between the logs in a dozen places, without a tree to shelter it from the hot sun, which darts its beams upon it with sufficient power to nearly set it on fire. Perhaps a rickety fence surrounds a patch of ground where the tall weeds have the mastery of whatsoever may have been planted. In the house you will see a parcel of pale dirty children some of them shaking in the rags with the ague; the wife a half naked disconsolate skeleton of a woman, and the husband stretched on a miserable bunk scorching with fever. You need travel but three or four such days, and make but a few such calls, before you are prepared to represent death and destruction as reigning triumphant in the land.

On the other hand, conceive a road winding among the trees, and yourself riding along it, towards the close of a pleasant day in autumn; the wild plums or the grape bending the trees over your head beneath them. You come to a house situated in a grove skirting the margin of a rich prairie. You call, are made welcome, and feel yourself at home. You see acres of the stoutest corn, a granary with hundreds of bushels of wheat, and cattle almost without number. You may at such a time and place see all that is desirable in a country, without seeing any of its evils; and you would be led from this to conclude it was in fact the promised land. Even when seen under certain circumstances and at some seasons, in its natural state, it presents attractions superior perhaps, to any other country.[213]

As the years passed the bark-covered cabin became rarer except on the edge of a settlement; it was supplanted by the substantial houses of hewn logs with two or more rooms and loft. These sturdy dwellings were seldom replaced during the pioneer period, but they were often used as a nucleus around which to build more commodious houses. A story would be added, a wing built on, porches attached, clapboards replaced by shingles, and weatherboards or siding nailed over the logs to give the appearance of a new house. After sawed lumber became available, boxlike

---

[213] "Memoir of Alvan Stone," at Ridge Prairie, Illinois, 1831, in *Journal of the Illinois State Historical Society*, III, No. 4, pp. 89–90. There is perhaps no better description of the prairies and estimate of the advantages and disadvantages of life thereon than A. D. Jones, *Illinois and the West*, 92–94, 161, 173, 189, etc.

frame structures predominated, and like their more flimsy successors of today, were usually left unpainted. Although more
comfortable than the log houses, they were hardly as attractive
in appearance. There were exceptions, of course; here and there
the landscape was dotted with rambling frame houses of pleasing
lines, set on sills and joists of eighteen-inch yellow poplar or oak,
plastered with a mixture of lime and horsehair good for a century, roofed with red-cedar shingles, and given an air of stability
by the three to five huge stone fireplace chimneys which buttressed
them. Or at the end of a drive of "cedars" or in a grove of oaks
or maples, one might find the large rectangular house of homemade brick, which had eight or ten rooms with ten- to twelve-
foot ceilings, many long narrow windows of innumerable panes
with handmade glass and heavy shutters, random width quarter-
sawed oak floors, hand-finished casings, solid hand-carved panel
doors, stately stairs, and a fireplace in every room. Sometimes
wings were added in "L" form with porches or galleries on two
levels. Fine homes as well as broad acres proclaimed the economic
status of those who had succeeded on the frontier.

Ohio with its diverse population origins presented the greatest
variety of architecture. Marietta had as early as 1803 one home
"architecturally pretentious enough to be labeled Georgian." A
fine example of the Early Republican or Federal architecture was
the Taft house built in Cincinnati about 1820. Examples of this
type of architecture are not uncommon in Ohio, and scattered
samples may be found in southern Indiana and Illinois. The
Greek and Roman revivals came to the West in the 1830's and
left their mark not only upon such towns as Hudson and Granville
in Ohio but also on many others. Local builders followed the
eastern handbooks and, to the best of their ability, reproduced,
usually in wood, the classic proportions in their courthouses,
banks, and sometimes residences. Fortunately, the fad for the
classic architecture took no general hold; it hardly fitted the
environment or the needs of the West. Equally incongruous was
the Elizabethan-Romantic-Victorian style which followed; but
relatively few buildings in this style, however, appeared in the
region prior to 1840.[214]

[214] Some of the early homes of the better type were described by a series of
articles in the *Indianapolis Sunday Star* in 1931 by Agnes McCulloch Hanna and
in 1937 by Allen White. See also I. T. Frary, *Early Homes of Ohio*, and Frank J.

Yet whether one lived in log house or mansion, there were certain features of home life common to both. The fireplace remained practically the sole means of heating, and keeping its capacious maw satisfied in winter months was a man-sized job. A good fire required a six- or seven-foot backlog eighteen inches or two feet in diameter, preferably of buckeye or other slow-burning wood, and a couple of lesser logs for feeders, as well as numerous smaller chunks for coals for cooking. Every day or two a new backlog was dragged to the door with a horse and skidded or rolled into place. An abundant supply of resinous knots, dry splints, and hickory bark was kept available to throw on at night for good illumination. In spite of the vast quantities of wood consumed and its cheering influences, the fireplace was not very satisfactory as a heat provider. Cabins were hardly airtight, and a draft always bore toward the fire and up the chimney, whence went most of the heat. Near a roaring fire one might toast in front and be chilled in back. In zero temperatures water would often freeze on the other side of the room.

Needless to say, most of the numerous fireplaces in the finer homes were seldom used. Sleeping quarters, whether loft or elegant bedroom, were left unheated, though the delicate might be permitted a bed warmer or a position near the warm chimney end. Floors and walls were cold and though the night air was regarded as peculiarly dangerous and all windows kept closed, certainly there was no lack of fresh air either in the log house or its successor, as wintry blasts howled within as well as without. Hence the featherbed was used both for foundation and covering for those who were not warm-blooded. Fires were carefully tended, for they were hard to start with flint and steel, and firing a gun into some tow was a waste of good powder. Unless neighbors lived too far away it was usually quicker to send a boy to borrow fire. Matches did not come into use until about 1835; the earliest lucifers or sulphur sticks had to be dipped into a vial

---

Roos, "Ohio's Early Architecture," in *Antiques*, XLIX (Jan., 1946), and *Writings on Early American Architecture . . . before 1860* (Columbus, Ohio, 1943). An article in the *North American Review*, XLIII (1836), 383, criticized Americans for trying to copy pretentious and ornate architectural forms in their small homes, rather than building homes for interior comfort and livability. It recommended consideration of plans of the English cottage type. The editor of the *Chicago American*, November 19, 1836, anticipating much building in Chicago, agreed that people should quit "multiplying the abortive temples with which the land groans."

of prepared liquid to ignite. Since these "loco-focos," although not always dependable when wanted, had a habit of igniting spontaneously, they had to be kept in an earthen or metal container. Resinous splinters or rolled paper tapers were kept on the fireboard for candle lighters; also perhaps tongs for the tender-handed pipe lighter who could not handle a live coal in his hands. The little sheet- or wrought-iron fire carrier, shaped like an enclosed corn popper, was a common article in many homes, as were the foot and bed warmers.

Ordinary toilets were performed just outside or inside the kitchen door, where the wooden or tin basin, a battered mirror, and a comb on a string were kept. For bathing there was always the "crick" in warm weather, and in winter the full bath was not lightly undertaken. Particular housekeepers insisted that men and boys wash their feet each evening, especially in plowing time. Small outhouses were situated at some distance for the convenience of women and children, but were frequently disdained by the male contingent who with true pioneer contempt of log cabin days viewed them as too restrictive or effeminate.[215]

Screens were lacking, manure piles were plentiful, and soon after settlements developed in any region, the housefly became a pest to be taken for granted. Swarms of them infested the cow barn or milk house, got into the milk and cream and even the butter. They overran the kitchen and filled the house. Dried fruit was frequently so bespecked as to be almost black. At mealtimes a fly switch of branches and leaves or a duster of narrow-cut paper strips was kept at hand to enable one of the children to "mind the flies." Babies slept with clusters of flies parading over their mouths. A few fastidious persons used cheesecloth or netting for protection, but flies were commonly accepted and regarded as much less dangerous than the night air. As a traveler described the situation during the summer:

The house is no sooner entered than you hear a continued hum, and the room is almost darkened by myriads of house-flies, which, in Illinois, are never seen out of doors, and which, when there are sick people in bed, require the constant attention of some assistant to drive them off, otherwise, if the patient were a child, or very weak, I believe they would soon suffo-

[215] "It is a fact that very few of the old-time Ozark cabins have any sort of toilet facilities, and even a rough outdoor privy is sometimes regarded as an indication that the owner is 'puttin' on airs.'" Randolph, *The Ozarks*, 39.

cate him. Molasses, sugar, preserved fruit, bread, everything on the table, is loaded with them, and the very operation of fanning them off drives numbers of them into the molasses and other things of an adhesive nature. It is not safe to open your mouth. It is evident, too, on examining the molasses, that the small red ant has been purloining it, and has left a number of his unfortunate companions enveloped in its mass; whilst ever and anon a cockroach makes a dash at the table, and in nine cases out of ten, succeeds in scampering across over meat dishes and everything that comes in the way, and that too in spite of the bitter blows aimed at him with knife and spoon, he is "so t'nation spry."[216]

Less dangerous but more obvious filth was provided by the numerous chickens, ducks, and geese which had the freedom of the yard and porches, if not of the house, and by numerous dogs or barnyard animals. Paths of gravel or walks of solid material were rare, drains were few, and in the wet months, house surroundings as well as the barnyard, were apt to be a muddy combination of soil, dung, and dishwater.

Beyond the vicinity of Cincinnati, Madison, St. Louis, Detroit, and other river or lake ports, the village or country store was the chief reliance for those goods necessary to supplement the products of the farm.[217] Supplies were bought in Pittsburgh, Buffalo, St. Louis, or New Orleans and brought to the merchants in the towns by river, pack horse, or wagon over all but impassable roads. Village and country stores bought from the town stores.

If you entered one of the little stores then, you would see on the right hand about ten feet of counter and shelves covered with very plain, cheap dry goods. The next ten feet covered with leather of various kinds, and back of that the shoemakers bench with the cobbler at his post ready to make or to mend according to circumstances. Opposite the dry goods you would find about ten feet of groceries and back of that the hardware, which consisted of nails and bars of iron, while back of all was a table upon which was a barrel of pure corn whisky. Every person who traded with the merchant was expected to step back and take a drink. The price of this article was two shillings per gallon or one bushel of corn.[218]

Here was a rude counter; there were a few shelves fixed up to the log wall. On these were seen packages of Barlow knives, with a sample knife outside for a sign; sheep shears done up in the same manner; also gimlets, augers, etc. There were sickles wherewith to cut the first crops of wheat,

[216] Oliver, *Eight Months in Illinois,* 149–50.
[217] For the part played by the stores in general trade, see Chapter VII, 554–58.
[218] Harvey Haynes, "Reminiscences of Early Days in Coldwater and Vicinity," in *Michigan Pioneer and Historical Collections,* XXVII (1897), 287.

hair sieves, trace chains, blind bridles, currycombs, and numerous other necessaries for the farmers. Nor were the wants of their wives and daughters forgotten. There were found calico, fine cambric, cap stuff, pins, needles, etc. Here were sold some of the first wedding garments for the settler's daughters, and here was kept also a small stock of imported broadcloth, but rather too fine for many to wear. Occasionally a young man who wished to appear in a coat of blue cloth, with yellow metal buttons, a high and rolling collar, and a forked tail, after the fashion of those days, got his outfit here.[219]

At such stores the settlers did their trading, exchanging meat, butter, eggs, grain, whiskey, maple sugar, and ginseng for tools, powder, glass, dyes, iron utensils, crockery, store cloth for dress-up clothes, and coffee, tea, or other luxury foodstuffs. The storekeeper fixed the price of the farmer's produce and that of his own stock. Muslin frequently sold at 50 cents a yard or 2 bushels of wheat, calico at 8 bushels of corn. Silk or broadcloth required 80 to 100 bushels per yard. As "cross roads" changed into villages, and villages into towns, and barter gave way with the advent of money, many of the general stores abandoned certain items of their stock and specialization began. Sugar, coffee, and similar articles, together with liquor, were handled by grocery stores; supplying cloth, needles, caps, and ribbons became the function of the dry goods store, while harness, leather, utensils, and tools fell to the hardware store or seed and implement establishments.

Life in the villages and country towns differed but little from that in the country; neighbors were somewhat closer and contacts more frequent, but the essentials of life were the same. A group of houses sprawling at intervals along a road or street full of stumps and seasonal mud holes, weeds, dust and garbage, flanked by a rail fence, paralleled by cow paths for sidewalks, with a few rods of wooden sidewalks and hitching racks in front of the "business section" of store, post office, tavern, and blacksmith shop; a couple of churches, a schoolhouse, a doctor's and lawyer's office, a few shops of local tradesmen such as the cooper, tanner, cobbler, or tailor—such was the country town. Glass fronts and window exhibits did not display any of the fly-bespecked stock of goods; only the sign of the horse, pestle and mortar, boot,

---

[219] Andrew W. Young, *History of Wayne County, Indiana* . . . (Cincinnati, 1872), 63.

hide, or wooden Indian labeled the establishment. The atmosphere within the room was flavored with raw humanity—whiskey, horses, perspiration, and tobacco—combined with the distinctive smell of the shop[220] and the doggy odor of drying wool or scorching leather. Inside in summer, flies and perspiration; outside, flies, dust, horse manure, and odor of outhouses.

Town dwellers had gardens and probably fields close by, kept pigs and chickens, and let the cow graze in the open lots or led her to and from the pasture. Some had log houses, many possessed unpainted frame houses, while a few lived in painted frames with picket fences; there were always a few substantial bricks for the local aristocrats. The old rain barrel, town spring or pump, in some instances cisterns and wells, furnished the water supply. Hogs, dogs, and surface drainage took care of garbage and rainfall; little shanties with crescent-shaped ventilating holes constituted the sanitary disposal facilities. A few buckets and water barrels were the fire department. The constable or marshal was the "law."

The county-seat town had more houses, larger stores, a longer hitching rack, and the advantage of the courthouse, jail, a newspaper, and stagecoach service. One way of following the development of western towns from a cluster of houses along a road or stream through the village-town stage, and sometimes into a city, is by way of the town's ordinances. Among the first problems faced was that of animals running at large. Cleveland in 1820 forbade cattle and swine to run at large and required its officers to register "every dog, hound, cur or spaniel."[221] Ten years later the corporation was forbidding shooting, dumping of dead carcasses, and building of fires in the streets. Licenses were being required for wandering shows.[222] Hamilton, Ohio, got around to a dog ordinance in 1831 after a hydrophobia scare.[223] Cincinnati in the early 1830's was still worrying with hogs at large and trying to regulate the driving of hackney coaches, carts, drays, and other vehicles, as well as the observation of the Sabbath. Detroit hogs were forbidden the freedom of the streets in

---

[220] Perhaps the only difference between the aroma of the general store of the pioneer period and that of a generation later was that the former contained a greater portion of raw hides and drying herbs and less of the ubiquitous kerosene.
[221] Cleaveland Herald, August 22, 1820.
[222] Ibid., November 18, 1830.
[223] Hamilton (Ohio) Intelligencer, July 19, 1831.

1821, but the city had not solved the problem of filth in the streets by 1833.[224] In 1824 Delaware, Ohio, provided a fine of $1.00 to $5.00 for leaving dead animals in town,[225] and Piqua did the same for running horses, shooting guns (except on training days or the Fourth of July), or breeding mares in the town limits in 1835.[226] Springfield, Illinois, was trying to eliminate stagnant pools, ponds, and filth as well as to prevent noisemaking with horns and kettles in 1832; four years later it published a set of ordinances which required three newspaper columns. These covered everything from driving on the sidewalk, leaving cellar doors open, hitching to shade trees, disposing of garbage, locating slaughter houses, breeding animals, and playing at long bullets, to blowing horns, beating drums, and otherwise disturbing the peace. When the corporation got a charter in 1840, a still more elaborate set of ordinances was provided.[227]

Sidewalks and streets, lighting, fire protection, and water supply were never-ending problems. The first sidewalks were paths. These were replaced by board walks in front of hotels or the more pretentious business buildings. Town streets were as bad as country roads, sometimes worse—axle-deep in mud in winter and spring, equally deep in dust in summer. Indianapolis, for example, in 1835, was using the argument that paved sidewalks would promote health and sociability, improve school attendance, increase business, as well as improve the looks of the town.[228] Streets sometimes were given a few rods of cobblestones, wood boards, or blocks in the business section. Lighting was, of course, poor, the few lamps provided by hotels or individuals being oil burners, although gas was used now and then. Louisville was providing street lights at the very end of the period (1839), but neither Cincinnati nor St. Louis had city lights.

As towns grew in size and needed water for fire protection as well as other purposes, they were confronted with the task of building reservoirs and providing pipe lines. Early pipe lines were of wood, some of which outlasted iron pipe of a later day. One of the advantages of Indianapolis, Indiana's new capital, was

[224] *Detroit Gazette*, June 15, 1821; *Detroit Journal and Advertiser*, June 28, 1833.
[225] *Delaware* (Ohio) *Patron*, April 8, 1824.
[226] Ravenna (Ohio) *Western Courier*, May 23, 1835.
[227] *Sangamo Journal*, April 26, 1832, January 30, 1836, May 1, 1840.
[228] Indianapolis *Indiana Journal*, February 27, 1835.

that "good wholesome water . . . [might] be found at a depth of 20 feet in any part of it in a sandy stratum."[229] Yet in 1833 a town ordinance declared it unlawful for any person to wash himself, or any other thing, to water stock, or to commit any act of indecency in or near the public spring. Brookville, Indiana, built a pipe line of green sycamore saplings (3-inch bore) from Amos Butler's spring and an oak-plank reservoir, in 1820. Sewage disposal became a more complicated affair after the hogs were run off the streets.

Fire departments were still in the bucket-brigade stage, but the larger towns were buying engines in the 1830's. These hand-manipulated contraptions usually "worked hard on the handle" and cost about $1,000. Many volunteers rushed to the fire but few helped pull the engine or pump it after they got there.

Aside from labor at home on the farm various opportunities were open to young men. Clearing, splitting, and hewing for neighbors offered some cash return. Working permanently as a hired hand was not relished; those who did such labor expected to be treated as one of the family. The same was true of the girls who hired out, many of whom demanded social privileges and sometimes put on condescending airs.[230] It was possible for a handy man to pick up the rudiments of several manual arts on the farm, while a likely lad could often earn his keep in or around the towns where in informal apprenticeship he learned lime making, sawmilling, cabinetwork, flour grinding, soap manufacture, tanning, cobbling, fulling, coopering, or blacksmithing. Bright boys were sought for printers' devils and in a few years developed into journeymen printers, who, if they remained sober enough, might print their own papers.

The professions were easily entered: prerequisites were a few months of clerking and "reading law" in an office for bar and bench, of pill rolling for medicine, and ability to read, write, and cipher to the rule of three for teaching or business. The ministry in most denominations required only the call. When none of these possibilities appealed, there was always the lure of easy land

---

[229] Vincennes *Indiana Centinel*, August 11, 1821.

[230] Edna M. Twamley, "The Western Sketches of Caroline Mathilda (Stansbury) Kirkland," in *Michigan Pioneer and Historical Collections*, XXXIX (1915), 99; Caroline M. Kirkland, *A New Home, Who'll Follow . . .* (Boston and New York, 1840), *passim*. See also Birkbeck, Flower, and other commentators of the period.

and new chances just a little farther on. As for the girls, they worked at home or "helped" in the homes of neighbors, while waiting for marriage, the only recognized occupation for them.

§ § § § § §

From bearskins and dirt floors to homemade coverlets and woven rugs; from jerked venison and corn dodger to the well-filled larder of pork, beef, fowl, and fruit, with meals of such size and frequency as to stand out in the memories of those of the older generation a half century later; from dressed buckskins to homespun, cotton prints, even silk and broadcloth—such progress was possible with labor, luck, and management. The duration of the period of hardship and uncertainty in which the settler came to grips with nature in an elemental struggle, depended upon location, circumstances, and the individual concerned. In the earlier settlements along the Ohio this phase of pioneer life had passed for most people, while it still prevailed in northern Ohio, central Indiana and Illinois, and was just beginning in Michigan and Wisconsin.[231] But within the older regions there always remained those who never seemed to get beyond this first stage, marginal workers by temperament and nature, incapable of the energy, judgment, and technical skill necessary for success. Idleness, shiftlessness, and general "orneriness" were common then as now, and not peculiar to any particular strain of immigration based on racial or geographic origins. Sometimes it was the Pennsylvania German or Yankee who led the way into the pioneer aristocracy and the Southern Uplander who remained in the "hog and hominy" stage; just as likely the "Scotch-Irisher" from Carolina became a cattle lord and a leading citizen while Brother Jonathan, in spite of his bookkeeping propensities and New England conscience, got involved in land deals and left only a heritage of children and mortgages.

[231] Yet in 1840 Buckingham found primitive log cabins being erected between Zanesville and Columbus, Ohio. James Silk Buckingham, *The Eastern and Western States of America* (3 volumes. London, 1842), III, 293. And in southern Indiana and Illinois, as well as in the more sparsely settled parts of Wisconsin and Michigan, the same was true a hundred years later.

V

Ills, Cures, and Doctors

The dawn will break upon us, and bright day shall go forth and shine; when we may hope to live with the dear objects of our love, until ripe and full of years, we shall be gathered to our fathers.

Dr. Samuel Robinson, Lecture IX, Cincinnati, 1829

NOTHING was more vital in the conquest of the wilderness than health, but over none of the factors involved did the settlers seemingly have less control. Active life in the open did not suffice to counteract the effects of exposure, decaying vegetation, swamps, poor food habits, lack of sanitation and hygiene, and inadequate knowledge and facilities for prevention and cure. The sallow complexions and jaundiced looks of the firstcomers, so often noted by the travelers, bore ample witness to the fact that all was not well within, and for a generation or longer sickness was a thing certainly to be expected. The reputation of the West for unhealthfulness was the one important factor to be weighed in the balance against the powerful appeals of fortune and freedom.[1]

"The principal objection I have to this country is its unhealthiness the months of August and September are generally very sickly," wrote Gershom Flagg in 1819 from Edwardsville, Illinois, after he had been ill of fever and ague for two months, and he decided if another season did not bring improvement, to sell out and leave the country.[2] The *Spectator* announced that its hands had been so disabled by the influenza, that it could issue

---

[1] Judge James Hall, in an address delivered at the organization of the Illinois Antiquarian and Historical Society in 1826, argued that the western country was not unhealthful, but that it was rather the habits of the people—exposure, food (all meat at first), spirituous liquors, and lack of attention to simple diseases. *Western Monthly Review* (Cincinnati, 1827–30), I, 563–65.

The materials on health and medicine in this chapter were published in expanded form in Madge E. Pickard and R. Carlyle Buley, *The Midwest Pioneer: His Ills, Cures, and Doctors* (Crawfordsville, Ind., 1945, New York, 1946).

[2] *Transactions of the Illinois State Historical Society*, 1910, p. 163; Fordham, *Personal Narrative*, 227.

only half a sheet.[3] Conditions remained much the same for years. Fifteen years later, during the exceptionally dry, hot summer of 1834, there was much sickness in this same region.[4] "It ought not to be concealed that . . . there are many sick people; and we believe that there are many situations, some of which have been noticed, that may properly be denominated sickly . . . ," wrote Thomas of the Wabash country in 1816.[5] He listed the prevailing ills as bilious, intermittent, and remittent fevers, with some liver complaints.

Around the new settlement at Indianapolis toward the end of the summer and during the fall of 1821 epidemic intermittent and remittent fevers and agues assailed the people to such an extent that the few unafflicted were employed night and day ministering to the sufferers, and one eighth of the population was swept away.[6] "Out of one thousand souls in town on the donation and the farms surrounding the town, at least 900 sickened during the prevailing epidemic."[7] At Vevay, where rapid influx of settlers resulted in congestion and two or three families to the house, one in six died of bilious fevers during the summer and fall of 1820.[8] The next autumn the sluggish, green, putrid waters of the Wabash and White rivers affected towns in Indiana and Illinois. "The situation of this town is at present truly deplorable," wrote the Vincennes *Western Sun*.[9] "Nearly one-third of the population appears to be confined on beds of sickness, while the houses of the humane farmers in the vicinity are crowded with our fugitive convalescents." "Last season has been unprecedented in the annals of the Western States for malignant diseases," wrote Dr. Asahel Clapp of New Albany in January, 1823.[10]

In the middle 1830's the people of Elkhart County had an

[3] *Edwardsville Spectator*, December 19, 1820. See also the long letter to the president of the medical society on the "most fatal endemic" fevers in *ibid.*, January 23, 1820.
[4] Vandalia *Illinois Advocate*, September 3, 1834.
[5] Thomas, *Travels*, 213.
[6] Berry R. Sulgrove, *History of Indianapolis and Marion County, Indiana* (Philadelphia, 1884), 30; Dr. Samuel G. Mitchell, "A History of the Malignant Intermittent Bilious Fever . . . in Indianapolis . . . in 1821," in *Western Journal of the Medical and Physical Sciences* (Cincinnati, 1827–38), II (1829), 443.
[7] *Indianapolis Gazette*, March 6, 1822. Note by Dr. Samuel G. Mitchell.
[8] Dufour, "Early Vevay," in *Indiana Magazine of History*, XX, 311.
[9] Quoted in *Detroit Gazette*, November 10, 1820.
[10] Diary of Dr. Clapp, 1819–1862. Photostat in Indiana State Library.

epidemic of typhoid and pneumonia and in 1838 almost half the population was affected with bilious disorders. The wave of erysipelas which enveloped the whole Northwest in the early 1840's struck this county with unusual severity; also Evansville and southern Indiana. Dysentery, scarlatina, phthisis, pneumonia, bronchitis, occasionally yellow and spotted fevers, whooping cough, and diphtheria appeared in many parts of the state. The year 1845 was a "disastrous and melancholy sickly season" in the Wabash country; the South Bend *St. Joseph Valley Register* noted that it was the seventh year from the last bad outbreak, as if that explained it.[11]

In Michigan as soon as the land was plowed "and the malarial gases set free, . . . the country became very sickly. . . . There were ten all down at once, my mother, the only one able to minister the cup of cold water and care for the sick. Crops went back into the ground, animals suffered for food, and if the people had not been too sick to need much to eat they, too, must have gone hungry. The pale, sallow, bloated faces of that period were the rule; there were no healthy faces except of persons just arrived."[12] Bilious diseases were very prevalent in Detroit in the autumns of 1819, 1823, and 1826. Filth in the streets and filthy drinking water scooped up from the river shore were partly blamed.[13] As late as 1839 whole villages were laid out temporarily, but after a few days people would crawl about like yellow ghosts, fortunate if they got enough to eat, for appetites were ravenous, but food digested little easier than stones.[14]

> Don't go to Michigan, that land of ills;
> The word means ague, fever, and chills.

Even in Ohio the most distressing sickness generally prevailed and great mortality, particularly from bilious fevers and cholera morbus. Said James Kilbourne, prominent journalist and

[11] More detailed information on prevailing health conditions in Indiana may be obtained from the *Transactions of the Indiana State Medical Society* (1850–1909), of which the only known complete set is in the Indianapolis Public Library. See particularly III (1852), IV (1853), VII (1856), XXIV (1874), XXV (1875), XXIX (1879), XXXV (1885).

[12] Ruth Hoppin, "Personal Recollections of Pioneer Days," in *Michigan Pioneer and Historical Collections*, XXXVIII (1912), 414.

[13] *Detroit Gazette,* September 10, 1819; September 8, October 8, 1823; September 19, 1826.

[14] *Michigan Pioneer and Historical Collections*, V (1882), 131.

legislator: "Respecting the healthfulness of this country, I have
to repeat that it is in fact sickly in a considerable degree." He
reported the presence of bilious fever:

Almost all were sick, both in towns and country, so that it became difficult, in many instances, to get tenderers for the sick. In many instances
whole families were down at a time and many died. . . . What seems
strange to me is that the Indians who were natives of the country are as
subject to the disorder as the whites. Of the few who remain in the territory some are now sick with it and they say it has always been so, and that
they have often been obliged to move back from the meadows and bottoms
where they always lived, into the woods and uplands during the sickly
season to escape it.

The autumn of 1819 was bad along the Scioto bottoms,
"whence deleterious exhalations arise." "The angel of disease
and death, ascending from his oozy bed, along the marshy margin of the bottom grounds . . . floats in his aerial chariot, and
in seasons favorable to his prowess, spreads mortal desolation
as he flies."[15] In 1821 "even in the memory of the oldest Indian,
so unhealthy a season was never known here before," said the
Piqua Gazette.[16] Of the 165,000 people in the seventeen counties within a radius of fifty miles of Columbus, more than one
half were sick in September, 1823. "The most extravagant
imagination can hardly picture desolation greater than the reality." Actual conditions substantiated political desires when the
Steubenville Gazette and the *Muskingum Messenger* called for
removal of the capital to Zanesville.[17] At Cleveland in 1827
there was perhaps more fever and ague than at any time since
the first settlement.[18]

On the whole newspapers were reluctant to report sickness
in their own localities; it was usually somewhere else. Land-sale
promotions and local pride required rather the "puffing" of that
particular climate for "healthiness"—ordinarily quite "salubrious." In 1802, when reporting to the Scioto Land Company,

---

[15] *Scioto Telegraph*, March 11, 1820. "Philo" in a rather sensible letter said that
these "Azotic" diseases which came from the poisonous effluvia of the bottoms could
be avoided by erecting houses at a distance from such sites.
[16] October 18, 1821.
[17] Columbus *Ohio Monitor*, September 29, 1821; November 23, 1822; *Western
Herald and Steubenville Gazette*, November 1, 1823; August, 1833, *passim*.
[18] *Cleaveland Herald*, August 17, November 28, 1827. There had been forty-five
deaths out of a population of about twelve hundred. The *Herald* said it was
trying to give facts to refute the many unfounded reports which were circulating.

James Kilbourne had spoken of the "healthfulness of the country." The *Illinois Intelligencer* stated that "the clamor which exists abroad about the sickliness of Illinois is entirely unfounded. Prejudices have arose against our town [Vandalia] even by the citizens of the state on account of its health, but we have no hesitation in saying, that it is entirely unjustifiable."[19] The *Milwaukee Sentinel* in 1838 said that notwithstanding the fact that the season had been bad in most sections, Wisconsin had no prevailing diseases. "Physicians say that our *Territory* is *distressingly* healthy."[20] Both the *Sentinel* and the Green Bay *Wisconsin Democrat* attacked the *Chicago Democrat* for including Wisconsin in the sick belt. They reported that canal work had been suspended in Illinois and Indiana, that there people were much too sick to harvest crops, and there was nothing that looked like life, even in the populous towns. The *Daily Chicago American* declared that "the whole West was unusually sickly" the preceding fall, but that Michigan, Ohio, and Indiana suffered most, and Illinois only among the Irish laborers along the canal lines.[21]

Of all the ills to which the new country was heir, the ague was the most common. So inescapable was it that many refused to regard it as a disease but, like hard work, a concomitant of the frontier. "He ain't sick, he's only got the ager," was the usual view. The symptoms were unmistakable: yawnings and stretching, a feeling of lassitude, blueness of the fingernails, then little cold sensations which increased until the victim's teeth chattered in his jaws and he "felt like a harp with a thousand strings." After an hour or so warmth returned, then came raging heat with racking head pains and aching back. The spell ended with copious sweating and a return to normality, when the world looked bright and happy again.

> And on every day there, as sure as day would break,
> Their neighbor "Ager" came that way, inviting them to shake.[22]

In 1836 members of one family of the Illinois country shook so severely that workmen were frightened from their task of

[19] September 2, 1825.
[20] October 9, 1838.
[21] May 2, 1839.
[22] A. D. P. Van Buren, "The Fever and Ague—'Michigan Rash'—Mosquitoes—The Old Pioneers' Foes," in *Michigan Pioneer and Historical Collections*, V (1882), 300.

shingling the cabin roof.[23] A Wisconsin pioneer frankly admitted that when he went to that place he "had a wholesome fear of two things: fever and ague, and rattlesnakes."[24] An early settler in the Michigan Territory "shook so that the dishes rattled on the shelves against the log wall."[25] There it was even reported that an Indian dog had the malady, the cattle were said to lean against the fence and shake, and children were "born with it."[26]

There were varieties of ague—dumb ague, shaking ague, chill fever, and so forth. Some had the combined chills and fever each day, or on alternate days, or even every third day; others had the chills one day and the fever the next.[27] Which ever brand was favored, it was regular, but, like the moon, it appeared somewhat later each day; it often came back in season for years, until a sort of immunity was established. Work schedules were planned to accommodate the fits. The justice arranged the docket to avoid the sick day of the litigant, the minister made his appointments in keeping with his shakes, the housewife and traveler planned accordingly, and even the sparking swain reckoned the "ager" schedule of self and intended.

Although seldom fatal, the ague often served as a prelude to more serious maladies, and no doubt left many with weakened bodies and malarial systems which were susceptible to other ailments in later life. Quinine was not generally available, and

[23] J. H. Walsh, "Early Medical Practice in the Illinois Country," in *Illinois Medical Journal*, XLVI (1924), 200.

[24] David F. Sayre, "Early Life in Southern Wisconsin," in *Wisconsin Magazine of History*, III (1919–20), 424.

[25] Van Buren, "Pioneers' Foes," 301.

[26] C. B. Burr, *Medical History of Michigan* (2 volumes. Minneapolis and St. Paul, 1930), I, 682.

[27] Ague and malaria were usually classified by the doctors as autumnal fevers. Dr. Daniel Drake under that heading in *Diseases of the Interior Valley* listed: intermittent fever, simple, and inflammatory; malignant intermittent fever; remittent fever; malignant remittent fever; and protracted, relapsing, and vernal intermittent fevers. Together with the geography, causes, and consequences he gave 11 chapters and 182 pages of this treatise to the subject. Dr. William Daily, Indian doctor of Louisville, in *The Indian Doctor's Practice of Medicine, or Daily's Family Physician* (Louisville, 1848), in a more complex manner classified fevers as: continued; remitting; intermitting; quotidian; tertian—simple and double; tertiana duplicata; haemitritoeus; tertiana triplex; anticipating; postponing; and attypic, or erratic.

The most recent study of malarial diseases is Erwin H. Ackerknecht's *Malaria in the Upper Mississippi Valley 1760–1900*, supplement to *The Bulletin of the History of Medicine*, No. 4 (Johns Hopkins Press, Baltimore, 1945). The "dumb ague," or cerebral malaria, may result from repeated infections. In the tropics it frequently causes persons to run amuck.

the mosquito, from which the person had little protection, and in some regions and at certain seasons so numerous and vicious as to thwart man and beast alike in their regular activities, was not suspected in connection with the disease: the marsh miasma or swamp "paludal" influence was generally recognized.[28]

Many home remedies were used in treatment, among them two teaspoons of strong tea of inside fir balsam bark and yellow birch in equal part of wine,[29] and "a strong decoction of white ash bark drank plentifully on the first symptoms." A brew of mullen and sassafras roots, or better still three large pills made of cobwebs to be taken on the approach of a shake was the remedy prescribed by one prominent doctor. He also recommended a mixture of calomel, saltpeter, Jesuit bark, pulverized columbo, elixir of vitriol, spirits of niter, and a pill of steel dust. At the same time blister plasters should be applied to the patient's wrists and ankles and an opened young pullet to the

[28] See John Macculloch, *Malaria; an Essay on the Production and Propagation of this Poison* . . . (Philadelphia, 1829), and *Western Journal of Physical and Medical Sciences*, III (1830), 500 ff., for discussion of malaria, causes, cures, etc. Cinchona (Peruvian bark or Jesuit bark) seems to have been used for the treatment of fevers since 1600, but not until 1820 was the extract quinine isolated from the bark (Pelletier and Caventou of Paris). Three years later a Philadelphia chemist set up the first quinine production plant in America. In 1824 C. and J. Bates of Cincinnati were advertising "Genuine Sulphate Quinine. A few ounces just received and for sale." In 1826 Dr. Henry Perrine, botanist and doctor who had practiced at Ripley, Illinois, from 1819 to 1824, was advocating by means of the *Philadelphia Journal of the Medical and Physical Sciences* the use of quinine during the febrile stages of malaria. When Dr. John Sappington, of Arrow Rock, Saline County, Missouri, who apparently adopted the extract soon after its introduction, met with opposition from the regular doctors, he concocted "Anti-Fever Pills" containing quinine, and advertised them to the public as blatantly—and successfully—as any "patent" medicine dispenser. He later revealed his secret in *Theory and Treatment of Fevers* (Philadelphia, 1844). Not until the 1840's was the drug widely used. In addition to the general prejudice prevailing, the cost prohibited its use. "The first I used cost at the rate of thirty dollars per ounce," wrote Dr. Joel Pennington, in *Transactions of the Indiana State Medical Society*, 1873, p. 12. As late as 1846, Dr. J. W. Hervey drove fat cattle to Indianapolis and sold them at $7.50 per head to buy quinine at $6.00 to $8.00 per ounce. "Reminiscences of Western Hancock County," in *ibid.*, 1874, pp. 74–75. Dr. D. L. Porter in his *Letters* (*Journal of the Michigan Medical Society*, 1927) listed quinine at $7.00 and opium at $8.00 in Detroit in 1828. For further discussion of the adoption of quinine, see Dr. William Wishard, "President's Address," in *Transactions of the Indiana State Medical Society*, 1889.

The general agreement that effluvia in the atmosphere from putrid and stagnant waters caused common bilious fevers led to consideration of drainage of mill ponds during the late summer months. When the *Edwardsville Spectator* advocated a law to that end, it provoked some discussion. Birkbeck thought the mud would give rise to more effluvia than water, and that real drainage was the solution. *Edwardsville Spectator*, September 19, 1820, October, 1820, *passim*.

[29] *Farmer's Reporter and United States Agriculturist* (Cincinnati), October, 1833, p. 63.

soles of the feet.[30] A double handful of bloodwort or boneset tops boiled down in water and drunk each morning was prescribed for bilious and intermittent fevers.[31] When Peruvian bark became available, one-half ounce with salts of tartar, red senic, Venice treacle, and port wine in three doses was recommended.[32]

Bilious fevers, cholera morbus, and other seasonal maladies usually made the months of later summer and early autumn a period of terror. "Hot weather with copious showers of rain in the last of July brought us face to face with cholera morbus, diarrhea, flux, and various forms of fever, all born of and nourished by miasma. One would have bilious fever, another remittent fever, while still another intermittent fever, while a fourth would have ague—a sort of miniature earthquake—in the chimney corner."[33] Typhoid epidemics came and went, and took their toll; but since nothing was known concerning the cause or spread of this disease, little attention was paid to it by physicians prior to about 1845.[34] Benezet listed this disease as typhus fever, and Gunn as nervous fever, while many of the pioneers called it brain fever. Causes were generally supposed to be night air, putrid vegetable and animal matter in the air, grief, fear, unripe fruit, want of sleep, and intense thought. Dr. Drake recommended bloodletting in the early stages to prevent the autumnal fevers turning into typhoid, while others thought the use of the lancet in this disease would be certain death.[35] It is probable that a great many of the cases and fatalities listed under bilious fevers, autumnal fevers, and the like, were typhoid. Living conditions with reference to disposal of offal, absence of screens, uncertain water supply, lack of cleanliness in handling

[30] Dr. Richard Carter, *A Valuable, Vegetable, Medical Prescription*, Chapter 23, Part I. For full title and description of this work see below, 262–63.
[31] *Delaware* (Ohio) *Patron and Franklin Chronicle*, August 21, 1822.
[32] From *Toledo Blade* in *Cleveland Advertiser*, July 28, 1836.
[33] Major, *Pioneers of Morgan County*, 304.
[34] M. H. Harding, "Diseases of Eastern Indiana," in *Transactions of Indiana State Medical Society*, 1853, pp. 27–28.
[35] Anthony A. Benezet, *The Family Physician; . . . calculated particularly for the inhabitants of the Western Country* . . . (Cincinnati, 1826), 123 ff.; John C. Gunn, *Domestic Medicine* . . . (Springfield, Ohio, 1835), 194 ff.; Daniel Drake, "Practical Observations in the Typhoid Stage of Autumnal Fever," in *Western Medical and Physical Journal*, I (1827–28), 381 ff.

of milk, and ignorance of method of transfer, were conducive to the development of this scourge.[36]

Milk sickness, or "*morbo loacteo*," was also encountered in many localities. Pioneers called it the milk sick; it was also known as sick stomach, the trembles, the slows, and puking fever. First came weakness and prostration of the voluntary muscles, then nausea, and last a comatose condition with periods of agonizing pain—"ungovernable thirst, great prostration, hiccup, stupor, etc., etc., death."[37] Not much was known about this disease. It had first been noticed by travelers in the West in the early 1800's. Dr. Drake was studying it in the period 1810–15. The chairman of a Kentucky Senate committee appointed to study it in 1827 sent out a questionnaire of twenty-four items concerning its prevalence—who got it, causes, cures if any, and percentage of deaths—and editors were requested to copy and circulate.[38]

The disease affected both cattle and persons and was endemic rather than epidemic. Chickens which ate the flesh of milk-sick animals also became affected. "Buzzards eating the diseased flesh often die and some of them lose the power of flying for some days. One of my dogs having partaken of diseased beef, run after a rabbit across the field, and then fell down and died; another dog died in the same way, whilst in pursuit of a hog," wrote one pioneer.[39] Since the symptoms of milk sick were so similar to arsenic poisoning, one explanation was that spring water absorbed the poison from arsenical iron pyrites. Other theories laid the trouble on vegetable poisons conveyed through milk or flesh of domestic animals. Dr. Drake was rather inclined to blame the

[36] Typhoid and typhus fevers were not differentiated until about 1840. Dr. William W. Gerhard of Philadelphia, who published his observations in the *American Journal of the Medical Sciences* in 1837, perhaps deserves the credit. "Homo" took one and a half columns of space in the *Edwardsville Spectator*, October 16, 1821, to distinguish between piles, colic, looseness with intermittent fever, and flux. The dysentery or bloody flux treatment recommended was large doses of calomel with opium, followed by castor oil, and repeat. Then ipecacuanha to nauseate, and if the ailment proved stubborn, calomel again. "The affection of the mouth will generally mark the decline of the disease."

[37] James S. McClelland, "Report on Milk Sickness," in *Transactions of Indiana State Medical Society*, 1854, p. 43; Dr. Benedict in *Medical Investigator* (Bloomington, Ind.), 1847, pp. 142–44. For a more recent treatment of this subject, see Dr. Leon Zerfas, "Milksickness and the Lincoln Family," in *Journal of the Indiana State Medical Association*, XXIX (1936), 88–89, and Philip D. Jordan, "The Death of Nancy Hanks Lincoln," in *Indiana Magazine of History*, XL (1944), 103–10.

[38] *Cincinnati Daily Gazette*, December 21, 1827.

[39] *Western Journal of the Medical and Physical Sciences*, III (1830), 477.

marsh exhalations.[40] Indian doctors, folk curists, regular physicians, and Botanics alike were helpless in the face of the milk
sickness. Calomel and bleeding proved as futile as Lobelia No. 6
or the powerful dilutions of the homeopaths. At times whole
communities were so seriously depleted that the remaining inhabitants contemplated moving on to safer regions.

The usual contagious diseases such as scarlet fever, diphtheria,
measles, mumps, and smallpox came and went in varying degrees
of severity, but were probably not worse in the West than in
older communities.[41] It was a common belief that measles, whooping cough, diphtheria, and the like, were inevitable and unavoidable, and that to try to escape would be to defy Providence.
Hence, when the weather was seasonable and the blood in good
condition, children were deliberately exposed to them.

Knowledge of vaccination for smallpox spread in the early
years of the nineteenth century, but it was staunchly opposed by
many as contrary to the will of the Almighty. Vaccination was
introduced into the United States in 1800. A year later Dr.
William Goforth, of Cincinnati, was using this new discovery,
and by 1803 Dr. Samuel Brown, of Lexington, had vaccinated
five hundred persons.[42] In 1809 Dr. Saugrain gave notice in the
Missouri Gazette of the vaccine matter brought to St. Louis and

[40] Indianapolis *Indiana State Journal*, September 10, 1845. Guy W. Wright,
"Observations on the Atmospheric Origin of the Endemic Sick Stomach . . . ,"
in *Western Medical and Physical Journal*, I (1827–28), 369. The cause, we know
today is tremetol, a poisonous substance found in white snakeroot and jimmyweed
or rayless goldenrod. The disease has been confined largely to the Ohio Valley.
For its history, description, and cure, see James Fitton Couch, *Trembles (or Milk
Sickness)* (U. S. Department of Agriculture, Circular 306, Washington, D. C.,
1933 and 1938).

[41] Dr. Nathaniel Potter, one of the editors of the *Maryland Medical and Surgical
Journal*, writing of the western country, reported pleurisies, rheumatisms, and
inflammations as generally prevalent during the winter months. "Catarrah," too,
was common and often terminated in consumption which he called the endemic of
the region, serious enough in many districts and seasons to account for one fourth
of the mortality. Quinsy in various forms, inflammation of internal parts of the
body, scarlet fever, and measles came in cycles at three-or four-year intervals.
Nettle rash, asthma, and cholera afflicted the children, particularly in summer
months. Apoplexy and palsy were not endemic so much as the frequent result of
intemperance. Asthma, epilepsy, dropsy, and St. Vitus dance were no more peculiar
to the new country than elsewhere. Rickets were rare, scrofula more common.
From one affliction he felt the West suffered less: the active habits of the people
left little time for hypochondria.

[42] For an excellent survey of the introduction of Dr. Edward Jenner's discovery,
and the pioneering of Dr. Benjamin Waterhouse, of Cambridge, Massachusetts,
see Reginald Fitz, " 'Something Curious in the Medical Line,' " in *Bulletin of the
History of Medicine* (Baltimore, 1933–), XI (1942), 239–64, and Morris C. Leikind,
"The Introduction of Vaccination into the United States," in *Ciba Symposia* (Ciba
Pharmaceutical Products, Summit, N. J., 1939–), III (1942). Dr. Goforth's initial
vaccination is said to have been of his pupil, young Daniel Drake.

promised to vaccinate "indigent persons, paupers and Indians" gratuitously. Notices appeared in some of the western papers in 1814 that James Smith, of Baltimore, recently appointed vaccination agent by the President of the United States, would furnish vaccine matter to any physician or other citizen of the country who might apply.[43] Ten years later when smallpox appeared in the West, the Cincinnati City Council located a doctor in the council chamber to vaccinate all who came at a fee of 50 cents if able to pay, otherwise free.[44] The doctor expected "to be enabled soon to supply upon the ordinary conditions country physicians and others with the genuine vaccine matter" through "an agency or connexion with the agent at Philadelphia." Later this same year it was announced that "County Physicians can be supplied with genuine Matter at all times, at moderate prices," and that for an additional charge of 50 cents each person desiring vaccination might be attended at his own dwelling.[45]

Erysipelas, otherwise known as "St. Anthony's Fire" (one type as Black Tongue), was epidemic at different times, as was influenza. Skin eruptions of a severe nature were not uncommon, and spread to whole communities, respecting neither age, sex, nor creed. In Michigan the disorder was dignified by the name "Michigan rash," but when an outsider noted the naturalness of the motions and suggested brimstone and lard, some were unkind enough to call it the "seven-year itch."[46]

Pneumonia or "lung fever" was often prevalent in winter, but apparently milder in form during the days of cabins and fireplaces than later when tight houses and stoves were more generally used. Many children died from the croup or "bold hives." Rheumatism and attendant troubles were, of course, common, due to exposure in all kinds of weather, the practice of drying heavy, wet clothing on the body, and perhaps to neglected teeth; but tuberculosis, or consumption as it was then called, seemed to be no more in evidence in the West than elsewhere. Cancer, diseases of the heart, and other diseases mostly affecting older persons, attracted little attention. Their incidence was not so high rela-

[43] Hamilton (Ohio) *Miami Intelligencer*, November 14, 1814.
[44] Cincinnati *National Republican*, February 20, 1824.
[45] *Ibid.*, March 26, 1824.
[46] Van Buren, "The Pioneers' Foes," in *Michigan Pioneer and Historical Collections*, V, 303.

tively as today; most people did not live long enough to develop them.

In addition to its own maladies the West was subjected to the attacks of a strange invader in 1832. Since 1816 the Asiatic cholera had been creeping westward from India, leaving its path of destruction. By 1830 it had reached Moscow and the Near East, and within twelve months had spread to western Europe, England, and Ireland. Early in the next year an emigrant ship which landed at Quebec bore this deadly passenger. The disease ascended the St. Lawrence to Montreal, thence traveled to Albany and New York. By July death reports were emanating from New York, Philadelphia, and Erie with alarming frequency.[47]

General Scott's troops on the way from Buffalo to the Black Hawk uprising landed at Detroit on July 4 with the disease, and death and panic followed. The upper story of the capitol was used as a hospital. Fifty-eight cases were reported, twenty-eight deaths resulted in two weeks, and the tolling of bells was discontinued because of the obvious effect.[48] The death cart passed day and night with the cry, "Bring out the dead."[49] The wasted remnant of the troops was taken on to Fort Dearborn to spread the disease in Chicago and the West.[50] The troops arrived July 10, and it was reported that eighteen died within thirty hours. Soon there were thirty or more cases in Chicago and those who could leave did so. "Every family has left Chicago, and gone in

[47] *Liberty Hall and Cincinnati Gazette*, August 26, 1831; Columbus *Ohio State Journal*, July 7, 28, 1832; *New York Mercury*, June 20, November 21 ff., 1832; Albany (N. Y.) *Evening Journal*, June 15, 1832; *Albany Argus* in Hamilton (Ohio) *Intelligencer*, June 23, 1832; *Cleveland Herald*, June 27, 1832; Indianapolis *Indiana Journal*, June 30, July 14, 1832, August 9, 1834; Springfield *Sangamo Journal*, July 5, 12, 19, 26 ff., 1832. The progress of the plague can be followed in *Niles' Weekly Register*, XLII (1832) or in any of the more important newspapers. See also *Western Journal of the Medical and Physical Sciences*, VI (1833), 78–120, 321–64; VII (1834), 43–104, 161–81, 341–49, for discussion of the disease with particular emphasis upon its appearance in certain parts of Ohio. Perhaps the best recent treatment of the subject is John Sharpe Chambers, *The Conquest of Cholera, America's Greatest Scourge* (New York, 1938).

[48] C. M. Burton, "Detroit in the Year 1832," in *Michigan Pioneer and Historical Collections*, XXVIII (1897–98), 168.

[49] "Autobiography of an Octogenarian (Miss Emily V. Mason)," in *Michigan Pioneer and Historical Collections*, XXXV (1907), 251.

[50] General Scott to General Orr of Indiana Volunteer Rangers, in *Indiana Journal*, July 21, 1832. One hundred fifty cases and fifty deaths were reported from Chicago in the *Journal* of July 28, whereas James N. Hyde, *Early Medical Chicago* . . . (Chicago, 1879), gave a total of fifty-eight deaths in one week from the two hundred cases in the Fort Dearborn hospital. Milo M. Quaife, *Chicago and the Old Northwest, 1673–1835* . . . (Chicago, 1913), 332.

different directions to escape from this malignant disease."[51] Apparently nothing could stop the progress of this plague as it spread around the lakes to the Wisconsin country, across Illinois to the Mississippi, thence up the Ohio to Cincinnati, and down the river to localize in New Orleans.

In August the dreaded plague was at Cleveland; by October it hit Louisville, St. Louis, and Cincinnati.[52] Cincinnati was almost demoralized as the deaths mounted to 351 in about three weeks.[53] People fled to the country to escape, business was disrupted, newspaper carriers were gone, and no one knew their routes.[54] From Cincinnati the disease passed down the road toward Lexington and on into the South. Only five cases were reported at Lexington and a few more at Louisville. Madison, Indiana, had forty-two cases and twenty-two deaths by November 8.[55]

Henry Clay introduced a joint resolution in Congress for a day of prayer. Governor Noah Noble of Indiana proclaimed a day "for fasting and prayer to an overruling Providence, beseeching Him to arrest the progress of the disease, with its train of calamities," and urged all who believed in the efficacy of prayer to attend.

With the coming of cold weather the ravages diminished, only to return in the summer of 1833 with greater severity and over a wider range. Cincinnati suffered even worse than the previous year;[56] the disease spread to Columbus and the state penitentiary; to Aurora and Salem, Indiana, where one hundred out of eight hundred inhabitants were said to have died within a week;

---

[51] Letter of Thomas J. V. Owen, Indian agent at Chicago, to Mr. Lamb, of Springfield, July 16, in *Sangamo Journal*, July 26, 1832. General Scott wrote Governor Reynolds, July 15, reporting fifty soldiers dead to date and most families fleeing the place. *Ibid.*, August 2, 1832.

[52] *Ohio State Journal*, July 28, October 10, 1832; *Liberty Hall and Cincinnati Gazette*, July, October, 1832; *Cleveland Advertiser*, August 30, October 6, 1832; *Louisville Herald*, October 30, 1832; *St. Louis Republican* in *Sangamo Journal*, October 20, 1832.

[53] *Cincinnati Chronicle*, October 27, 1832; *Niles' Weekly Register*, XLIII, 148–49 (Nov. 3, 1832). Daily and weekly reports by the Board of Health appeared in the *Gazette*, *Advertiser*, etc. By late autumn it was estimated that Philadelphia and Baltimore had lost one thousand each, New York even more. New Orleans was rumored to be losing three hundred per day from the cholera and yellow fever, burying the dead in trenches, if at all. *Lawrenceburg Palladium* in Indianapolis *Indiana Journal*, November 22, 1832.

[54] *Commercial Daily Advertiser*, October 24, 1832.

[55] *Indiana Journal*, November 10, 22, 1832.

[56] Total cholera deaths in Cincinnati for the year ending September 18, 1833, were 813, or 1 in 40. This included most of the 351 deaths of 1832. *Western Monthly Magazine*, I (1833), 483. For the four years preceding the death rate from all causes was 1 in 34.

made its way north to Bloomington where the Indiana College had to be closed; and to Indianapolis where sixty-two deaths occurred in a month.[57] Apparently the Wabash towns were not affected. Louisville, Lexington, Wheeling, and Alton were also visited. The Michigan legislature authorized the towns to establish a quarantine against travelers, and even Governor Mason was arrested when he tried to get through Ypsilanti. By autumn southern Illinois papers repeatedly announced that there were no cholera cases. It returned, however, to visit Rushville, Pekin, Springfield, and St. Louis in 1834.[58] Madison, Indiana, was revisited in 1835, when thirty-two deaths were reported up to June 24, fifteen having died in one day.[59] Not until 1849 did an epidemic of national scope again appear.

It was not so much the number of cases and high fatality of the disease, but the mysteriousness and suddenness with which it struck that filled people with dread and fear which often reached panic. Persons in excellent health were suddenly stricken with a feeling of uneasiness, shortly were consumed with inward burnings and a craving for cold drinks, then came vomiting, intestinal spasms almost as severe as in tetanus cases, and finally general debility, slow circulation, sunken eyes, cold lifeless skin, and collapse.[60] The fate of many was decided within a few hours. As Dr. Thomas D. Mitchell of the Medical College of Ohio described it:

> The pestilence stalks in the midnight gloom
> And mantles the gay with the pall of the tomb
> Nor beauty nor youth from its clutch can flee
> It kills on the land, it blasts on the sea.

Much speculation as to causes and keen interest as to treatment were aroused. As in earlier yellow fever epidemics, various theories were advanced. Bad air, exhalations from the bowels of the earth, insensible changes in the atmosphere, comets, and animalculae—insects too small to see—in the air, were offered as explanations. Dr. David M. Reese, of New York, listed among

[57] *Transactions of the Indiana State Medical Society*, 1885, p. 105; Madison *Indiana Republican*, July 25, 1833; Madison *Republican and Banner*, August 29, 1833; Terre Haute *Wabash Courier*, July 11, 1833.
[58] *Sangamo Journal*, May 11, September 7, 1833; July 12, September 6, 20, 1834.
[59] *Republican and Banner*, June 18 and 25, 1835.
[60] One of the most vivid descriptions of the symptoms and actions of the cholera is in the *Sangamo Journal*, July 19, 1832.

the exciting causes indigestible vegetables, ardent spirits, beer, ale, and wine; pork, lobsters, and crabs; green corn, clams, and oysters; watermelons, cucumbers, strawberries, peaches, and pears; cabbage and greens; cheese, opium in any form, jalap, and other drastic cathartics; and nostrums of all kinds.[61] Others merely said it was contagious and let it go at that.

Dr. Daniel Drake, of Cincinnati, the best known medical man in the West, whose writings on cholera were copied widely in the newspapers, inclined to the animalculae hypothesis—a rather close approach to the later germ theory. He called attention to the city filth,[62] neglected vaults, lack of personal cleanliness, ventilation, and proper diet, and advised normal diet, continuance of one's normal habits regarding liquor, a calm and hopeful mind, and the wearing of thin flannel over the trunk of the body if one could afford it. Quarantine was considered futile, as well as embarrassing to commerce.[63]

When it came to treatment, Dr. Drake's ideas hardly seem so sensible and modern. He thought calomel, jalap, rhubarb, opium, mercury, weak lye, and mustard might possess some efficacy, but most startling was his recommendation of the old stand-by, bleeding:

To bleed a patient who cannot be raised from his pillow without fainting, whose pulse is nearly imperceptible, whose skin is cold, and extremities shrunk up to half their ordinary size, would at first view, seem rash and unwarrantable. But experience, which in medicine can grant warrants for any procedure, has sanctioned the use of the lancet even when all these and other symptoms of extreme prostration, are present. . . . The quantity taken must vary with the effect. It generally flows with difficulty . . . and sometimes not at all, though large veins be opened. In every desperate case, recourse should be had to the juglars, from which blood will flow when it cannot be elicited from the arms; and, flowing, must contribute more to the relief of the oppressed brain, than when drawn from the extremities.[64]

Other advice called for cleaning streets, alleys, and privies; avoidance of excessive exertion, eating and drinking, or sitting in the sun or a current of air; and recommended airy and clean

[61] *A Plain and Practical Treatise on the Epidemic Cholera* . . . (New York, 1833), quoted in *Piqua* (Ohio) *Gazette*, July 13, 1833.
[62] There were those who thought that Cincinnati's new hog ordinance was calculated to do more harm than good. *Liberty Hall and Cincinnati Gazette*, July 3, 1832.
[63] Series of articles in *ibid.*, July 26, 1832, and following.
[64] Daniel Drake, "Epidemic Cholera:—Its Pathology and Treatment," in *Western Journal of the Medical and Physical Sciences*, V (1832), 612.

rooms, and a daily bath.[65] Warnings were issued against the "infallible" quack remedies. All one could do was to keep in good health and to take prompt care of bowel and stomach disorders by putting the feet in hot ashes and water, taking ten grains of calomel and one of opium, covering up in bed with hot bricks and boiled ears of corn, and using warm mint tea inside, and mustard poultice outside the stomach.[66]

The Botanics, of course, had slightly different ideas. One widely copied recipe called for a mixture of one gallon of fourth-proof West India rum, one gallon of molasses, one quart of Number 6 (Thomson's Lobelia, etc.), and two ounces of cayenne pepper; three doses daily for prevention, one-half glass every half hour for cure. In the 1849 epidemic Dr. Herrick, of Chicago, published an article in the *Northwest Medical Journal* in which he claimed sulphur was an effective specific. Soon thereafter a Dr. Bird was advocating sulphur and charcoal pills, with testimonials. This popular remedy faded with the discovery that morphine was the main ingredient of the pills.

Hardly classifying as diseases but certainly as ubiquitous and sometimes as deleterious in effect were the pests and varmints of the woods and swamps. Although house flies were not present when the first settlers arrived, the stock flies and mosquitoes were. From the woods and lowlands they swarmed by the millions in season to bleed man and beast. Often cows could be milked only under the protection of a rotten wood smudge. Fleas and other vermin emerged from the cracks and crevices of cabin and house to irritate and consume. Despite a relatively late arrival, the house fly soon made up for lost time. In the absence of screens or sprays this insect had the freedom of barn and home. Although regarded as a minor nuisance, it played its part as an arbiter of health. Two generations of science and education and the crusading spirit of Dr. John N. Hurty and others were

---

[65] From seven physicians of the vicinity, in *Hamilton Intelligencer*, July 21, 1832.

[66] Dr. Rigdon in *ibid.*, November 3, 1832. The editor of the *Intelligencer* had had some faith in the Thomsonian system (see below), but when Dr. Horton Howard, one of the Ohio fathers of the lobelia-steam system, and his family died of cholera, he expressed his doubts. Whereupon he got a set of resolutions and a hot reply from what he called the "Friendly Botanic-anti-any-thing-else-than-Lobelia-No.-6-and Hot Brick Branch Society of Hamilton and Rossville." *Ibid.*, August 31, 1833.

required to make the people conscious of the disease-spreading propensities of the fly.

Other dangers lurked in the form of venomous snakes which frequently disputed the white man's occupation of the land as effectively as did the Indian. The spreading viper put up a vicious front, but he was something of a 'possum at heart and more fearful than dangerous. It was the rattlesnake and copperhead which caused the trouble. Although the former was supposed to declare his hostile intent before striking, he had an unpleasant habit of lying on the other side of log or rock to be stepped upon by the unwary. The copperhead was entirely oblivious of the rules of war. Snake drives, as well as wolf and squirrel drives, were participated in by neighbors during off-season on the farm. Statistical summaries of these hunts are astonishing to a person familiar with the country a century later. Sometimes several hundred rattlesnakes, "from three to ten feet in length," would be killed.

In a period of active life in the open, when women as well as men chopped wood, handled horses, and worked around open fires, when men plowed without socks and children went barefoot, cuts, bruises, sprains, and broken bones were regular occurrences. Soiled clothing, infrequent bathing, and intimate contact with germ-infected soil often resulted in serious consequences. "Blood poisoning" and "lockjaw" were all too often fatal.

§

Much of the medical treatment in pioneer days was domestic and primitive. Provided a doctor were available, it required time and money to get his services; he was, generally speaking, called only for serious cases. Even then home remedies or folk cures were likely to have been used before the doctor was called. Besides being responsible for the domestic economy of the home— everything from food and clothing to spelling and courting— the mother, wife, or woman of the house was by prerogative and default the custodian of medicines and administratrix of treatments. If home resources did not suffice, there was usually someone in each community who was "handy" in caring for the sick and steeped in his or her lore or system of cures—a combination of homemade science, empiricism, and superstition.

Naturally, Indian influences were strong, and many relied upon the "yarb and root" doctors who worked largely with remedies obtained from forest and garden. For a century French *voyageurs* and *coureurs de bois* had preferred the Indian treatment of wounds and chronic sores with poultices and herbs to that of the whites. Native medicine men and "jugglers" also doctored many other ills with concoctions of herbs, drinks, sweatings, and rubbings, usually accompanied with ceremonials, incantations, ghost shooting in the night, and other aids. They even sucked out "manitous" or evil spirits. In some western communities in the earlier years there were Indian doctors who were held in quite as high repute as regular white doctors.[67] "Yarb and root" cures were legion, but not all were of Indian origin. Some may be traced to ancient Egypt, China, India, and eastern Europe.[68]

Herb recipes in the Middle West were not confined to the herbals and formal medical works; they were passed along from person to person, copied down in odd places, recorded in household remedy books, and published in almanacs and newspapers.

[67] T. J. Luster, of Springfield, Illinois, advertised as an Indian and German root doctor. He offered numerous testimonials of his success in curing "sciatic, weak lungs, fits, inward weakness, and nervous affections; liver complaints, fever and ague, pleurisy, asthma, coughs, colds, dyspepsia, rheumatism, cancers, rickets, fever sores, piles, worms and tape worms and many other diseases that affect the human system." *Sangamo Journal*, April 9, 1836. See Oliver H. Smith, *Early Indiana Trials and Sketches* (Cincinnati, 1858), 12–13, for accounts of two early Indiana root doctors.

[68] The literature of herbals is extensive. A good brief introduction to the subject is a series of three articles by Arturo Castiglioni, "Magic Plants in Primitive Medicine," "Herbs in the Medicine of Eastern Peoples and of the American Indians," and "Herbals from Antiquity to the Renaissance," in *Ciba Symposia*, V, Nos. 5 and 6 (Aug.—Sep., 1943). The first English book devoted exclusively to herbs was Banckes' *Herbal* (1525), apparently compiled from various earlier sources and containing no American plants, which went through about twenty editions. American plants became known in England half a century later, when, 1577–80, John Frampton "Englished" the works of Dr. Nicholas Monardus (1493–1558), physician of Seville and one of the first Europeans to collect medical lore from the New World and make it available to physicians of his time. The first known American medical work, the Badianus Manuscript of "An Aztec Herbal," was written and probably illustrated by an Aztec Indian, Martin de la Cruz, in 1552, and translated into Latin by a mission colleague, Badianus. In 1929 the manuscript was found in the Vatican Library. Translated and annotated by Emily Walcott Emmart, it was published with 118 color plates by the Johns Hopkins Press, 1940. For a more complete discussion of origins of herb medicines, see Pickard and Buley, *The Midwest Pioneer: His Ills, Cures, and Doctors*, 36–44, 315–16.

Many of them were later taken over by the various botanic medical schools. Some sixty of the drugs used by the American Indian may be found today in the modern materia medica and among the formulas manufactured by standard pharmaceutical houses. Of thousands of recipes used originally a few will suffice for samples. Some were administered for specific ills; others were taken on general principles.

For fevers sweating and snakeroot were recommended with a purge of white walnut bark peeled upward,[69] sassafras, dogwood, willow, or a glass of pearlash and water. The breaking out in eruptive fevers, such as measles, was hastened by the use of sheep dung tea, popularly known as "nanny tea." For pleurisy, if no bleeder was at hand, catnip, or pennyroyal, or butterfly weed tea, and applications of boiled hot nettles, or brimstone, sulphur, and eggs. For indigestion, rhubarb bitters, or cayenne pepper in spirits applied to the stomach outside, and water and good old spirituous liquor within.[70] For "summer complaint" or dysentery a poultice of peppermint and tansy leaves, syrup of rhubarb with niter, or slippery elm would be prescribed. If a child so afflicted wished to indulge in ripe blackberries, old cheese, or fresh ham and eggs he was allowed to do so.[71] Bloodroot was also good for dysentery,[72] or a strong decoction of mullen mixed and simmered in new milk would promote immediate improvement.[73]

If baby had a fit, it was due to worms, and "pink and senna" were quickly administered, or else a dose of twenty to forty grains of scrapings from pewter spoons. Green copperas or sugar and turpentine had their advocates. A tapeworm was not treated so roughly, for pumpkin-seed tea was the proper remedy. For cold and sore throat: a piece of fat meat with pepper tied around the neck, grease from the Christmas goose, mustard and onion poultices, bloodroot or cherry bark, and rock candy

[69] Contrast with Pennsylvania German theory: the leaves of boneset stripped upward act as emetic, downward as a purgative. Edwin Miller Fogel, *Beliefs and Superstitions of the Pennsylvania Germans* (Philadelphia, 1915), 278.

[70] Indianapolis *Indiana Journal*, August 30, 1825.

[71] Dr. S. H. Selman, *The Indian Guide to Health, or A Valuable Vegetable Medical Prescription, for the Cure of All Disorders Incident to this Climate. Designed as a Guide to Families and Young Practitioners* (Columbus, Ind., 1836), 14.

[72] Vincennes *Western Sun and General Advertiser*, August 21, 1819.

[73] *Detroit Gazette*, September 17, 1819.

and whiskey. For croup and asthma, alum, Indian turnip root in molasses, or onion and garlic juice sometimes proved helpful. Garlic rubbed on the spine was a good whooping cough cure. A cold might properly be treated with a mixture of flaxseed, licorice, raisins, sugar candy, and white vinegar.[74]

Rheumatism was treated externally with rattlesnake-, goose-, or bear-oil, and internally with a mixture of calomel, tartarized antimony, cayenne pepper, and gum camphor, or a tincture of butterfly weed roots or ripe pokeberries in French brandy. If fever were present, one might add bleeding. Too, rheumatism might be cured by oil of the "cajipul" [cajuput?] tree, which was also good for sciatica, lumbago, epilepsy, stings, and snake bite.[75] Strong tea of pokeberry leaves or rattleweed was recommended for smallpox patients.[76] Saffron tea would bring out the measles, a bag of pounded slippery elm bark over the eye of the measles sufferer would draw out the fever, while a poultice of scraped raw potato was supposed to cure headache. A wash of diluted essence of sassafras would cure "the most inveterate case" of sore eyes in a few days.[77] The itch cure was hot water and soft soap applied with a corncob, followed by a lotion of sulphur and lard, or gunpowder and lard. Erysipelas called for a mixture of bitter root, yellow root, and slippery elm to be taken internally.

Consumption, having various causes, deserved various remedies. Among them were: drink only water and eat only water gruel; eat only buttermilk and white bread; spring water, new milk and two ounces of sugar candy; one glass before each meal of a handful of sorrel boiled in a pint of whey; twenty ivy leaves and three sprigs of hyssop boiled in one pint of skim milk and one-half pint of small beer ("has cured a desperate case"); take a cow heel, two quarts of milk, nine ounces of hartshorn

---

[74] *Detroit Daily Advertiser*, February 1, 1837.
[75] Chillicothe *Weekly Recorder*, November 8, 1814.
[76] A more comprehensive treatment prescribed snakeroot and "nanny tea" as long as the skin kept its natural color. To raise the pock add saffron and milk punch. If this failed, give sage tea every quarter hour. When pocks were three days old, the "growing medicine" was to be crowded on, but if shrinking, the sage and nanny tea. If fever ran too low, saffron, snakeroot and rum; if too high, a little balm tea. If none of the above worked, give bohea tea, sugar, and rum. If all failed give a teaspoon of paregoric hourly. If that failed, give the barks once per hour, etc. *Piqua Gazette*, June 22, 1831. A few years later the more enlightened said "be vaccinated." *Detroit Daily Advertiser*, April 15, 1837.
[77] *Cleaveland Herald*, April 2, 1822.

shavings, two ounces of isinglass, one-fourth pound of sugar candy and a trace of ginger, set in pot in oven, let cool, and let the patient live on this; cut up a hole in the turf, lie down and breathe in it a quarter hour each morning ("deep cases been cured so"); inhale burning frankincense; inhale steam of white rosin and beeswax. For last stages suck a healthy woman, eat apples and milk, water gruel with fine flour, cider whey, barley water, or apple water sharpened with lemon juice.[78]

Snake bite offered a wide choice of remedies, from white plantain boiled in milk, ash bark tea, alum water, or whiskey internally applied, to incision and application of salt and gunpowder, black ash leaves, crushed garlic juice or salt and tobacco. To cuts and burns were applied crushed horse-radish leaves in vinegar, a salve of pokeberry leaves boiled in flour, honey, eggs, and sweet oil, or poultices of slippery elm or flaxseed. Jimson-leaf salve was recommended for infection, Indian turnip or bog onion for carbuncles, and, of course, the camphor bottle was usually available. Smoke of burning honeycomb was supposed to be efficacious in drawing out the poison from a rusty nail wound; a compound of tar, feathers, and brimstone on hickory coals was considered wonderful for mortifying flesh. Dropsy could be cured by steeping two handfuls of inner bark of white elder in two quarts of Lisbon wine for twenty-four hours and taking a gill each morning on an empty stomach.[79] One cancer cure called for the application of a teaspoonful of scrapings from a brass kettle mixed with mutton suet, applied to the affected part, and not removed until the patient got well.[80] Boiled or bruised root of the narrow leaf dock applied over the sore, with tea of the same taken internally was also recommended.[81] Fluor volatile alkali was known to have cured apoplexy, and a mixture of ivory comb scrapings and honey was considered effective for yellow jaundice, typhus, and putrid diseases.[82] For mad dog bite take one teaspoonful per day of a mixture of one ounce of burned pulverized jawbone of a dog, dried pulverized false tongue of a newborn colt, one scruple of

[78] Dr. Tissot in Hamilton (Ohio) *Miami Herald*, January 29, 1818.
[79] *Piqua Gazette*, July 18, 1828.
[80] *Western Sun and General Advertiser*, August 26, 1820.
[81] Chillicothe *Weekly Recorder*, December 6, 1814.
[82] *Ibid.*, November 8, 1814; January 26, 1815.

old "verdigrease," mixed with calomel.[83] Regular physicians
warned against such cures, as well as lobelia and the like. They
prescribed bathing the wound in thick lye of wood ashes and
vinegar, but believed the best cure was prevention.

Home remedies and botanic medicines were esteemed in proportion to their potency or bitterness. The old reliable for general
purposes was the bottle of bitters, concocted according to various
favorite recipes from dewberry, crane's-bill, wild cherry, yellow
poplar, or sarsaparilla—stewed, crushed, distilled, and combined
with witch hazel leaves, cider, whiskey, or brandy, and sumac or
bitter roots. A favorite of the Botanics was bruised lobelia and
red pepper pods covered with good whiskey. These bitters were
good for cholera infantum, "yaller janders," phthisic (tuberculosis), croup, whooping cough, colds, coughs, and catarrh. Each
spring the mixture was taken as a tonic to drive the humors out
of the system and purify the blood. (After a winter of corn
bread and pork the blood and "jint water" had to be thinned for
more active existence. Teas or bitters taken in the autumn might
have disastrous results; if the blood was too thin in winter, one
ran a chance of freezing to death.) "The buds of the sweet
Apple Tree, infused in rum or cider, are excellent for correcting
the humors, and sweetening the blood and juices, especially in
the spring of the year."[84] Those whose faith in the vegetable
remedies was weak might obviate the necessity of spring purification by wearing a bag of camphor on the chest during winter,
or, if this had not been done, by drinking the waters from the
last snow in March or eating a few hailstones from the first
good storm in spring. Then there was always goose grease, in
and out, good for almost anything which the forthcoming season
might bring.

All told there were between two and three hundred of these
simples which constituted the materia medica of the pioneers.[85]

---

[83] Recommended by one whose son was cured. Ravenna (Ohio) *Western Courier*,
April 2, 1835. A "valuable secret" cure for hydrophobia called for a mixture of
camphor, opium, digitalis, and molasses, followed by lobelia in frequent doses.
Portsmouth Journal copied in Edwardsville *Illinois Advocate*, August 19, 1831.

[84] Dr. John Monroe, *The American Botanist and Family Physician* . . . (Whee-
lock, Vt., 1824), 10.

[85] One of the first important medical botanical works in the United States was
Dr. Jacob Bigelow's three-volume *American Medical Botany, being a Collection
of the Native Medicinal Plants of the United States, Containing their Botanical
History and Chemical Analysis, and Properties and Uses in Medicine, Diet and*

Root and herb collecting was a routine activity for all and a part-time vocation for some.

One of the earliest and most interesting of the Indian medicine books in the West was Peter Smith's *The Indian Doctor's Dispensatory,* published at Cincinnati in 1813.[86] It was designed especially for the citizens of the West. "The natives of our own country are in possession of cures, simples, etc., that surpass what is used by our best practitioners." With that idea in mind Smith reduced all diseases to two kinds: those of (1) plethora and irritation; (2) debility, weakness, and languor. After a brief introduction he listed ninety prescriptions which ranged from the Home Ipecacuanha or Indian Physic to the famous *Leotrill* which he got from Flanders. There were the usual purges, tonics, and poultices, an interesting concoction for cure of derangement or mania, and the late discovery of snail cure for cancer.

Two prescriptions were fairly unique.[87] "Preserving the teeth, and curing an odious taste in the mouth, may always, I presume, be effected by this little simple process: Only wash and rinse your mouth every morning in your own urine. . . . Relief from the ill taste I have proved, and I do not think the remedy worse than the disease. Those who know this in their youth, and will not try it, who can pity them when they groan with the tooth-ache!" The other was "for a diarrhoea, or looseness of the belly," and was particularly efficacious and given with success to both man and beast. "Take the yard or pizzle of a buck (get it saved and dried by a deer hunter), reduce it to powder, put a spoonful of the powder in a bottle with a pint of spirits; take this solution in small quantities, every hour, till relief is obtained."

Better known than Smith's book were Dr. Richard Carter's

---

the Arts (Boston, 1817–20). Practically simultaneously appeared Dr. William Paul Barton's two-volume *Vegetable Materia Medica of the United States or Medical Botany* (Philadelphia, 1818, 1825), a compendious treatise of botanical descriptions and medicinal properties of plants indigenous to the United States. Another such was the two volume *Medical Flora; or Manual of the United States,* of Constantine Samuel Rafinesque (Philadelphia, 1828, 1833).

[86] *The Indian Doctor's Dispensatory, being Father Smith's Advice Respecting Diseases and Their Cure: Consisting of Prescriptions for Many Complaints: and a Description of Medicines, Simple and Compound, Showing Their Virtues and How to Apply Them,* by Peter Smith of the Miami country (Cincinnati, 1813).

[87] But not original. See, for example, Catullus, *Carmina,* XXXIX, and Strabo, III, 164. Modern science has finally caught up with Dr. Smith as witness the boom in dentrifices including carbamide (urea) and dibasic ammonium phosphate in the late 1940's.

A Valuable, Vegetable, Medical Prescription[88] and the book of his son-in-law, Dr. S. H. Selman, published at Columbus, Indiana, in 1836.[89] Dr. Carter, after a youth practically devoid of education but full of afflictions, became interested in medicine. He settled and practiced in Garrard County, Kentucky. His system was a combination of Indian medicine, mysticism, Carter, and poetry. Carter mixed his "receipts," of which there were sixty-three, by the barrel (some of them were two pages in length) and spiced them with quantities of poetry, homilies, and crude woodcuts of certain nefarious characters of the animal world. Some of his tales are hard to beat. Besides consumption and poetry Dr. Carter was particularly authoritative on the "hypo." This dread disease, otherwise known as "ennui," manifested itself by dullness, fear, indefinite pains, and lack of desire to attend to any business. It was confined to the male of the species; females had "hysterics." It could be caused by hard drink, fevers, gout, night air, scolding companions, or intense thought. When established, it was very hard to exterminate for it became "engratiated and in a measure second nature." The best treatment indicated was cheerful company and light diet.[90] As for hysterics, gold filings given in honey night and morning had been known to cure a person who had been too weak to work for three years. "Or take bear's gall and put it in rum and drink as a bitter is excellent for this disorder; and when the choaking is bad, a teaspoonful of wheat flour mixed in water and drank, will stop it."[91]

Dr. Selman also held the faculty (the regular doctors) in contempt. He ran the gamut from "ager" to snake bite, but was

---

[88] The rare two-part edition bears the title: *A Short Sketch of the Author's Life, and Adventures from his Youth until 1818, in the First Part. In Part the Second, A Valuable, Vegetable, Medical Prescription, with a Table of Detergent and Corroborant Medicines to Suit the Treatment of the Different Certificates* (Versailles, Ky., 1825). An earlier single-part work, bearing the title *Valuable Vegetable Medical Prescriptions for the Cure of All Nervous and Putrid Disorders*, had been published ten years earlier at Frankfort.

[89] See note 71.

[90] "I heard of a man once who became so desperately in love with a young woman, that on her denying him, (although he had ever been considered a prudent man, and managed his estate well,) yet he became so extravagant, as to patiently sit for three months on a goose egg. If this was not the hypo, it was very much like it, if not worse." Carter, *A Valuable, Vegetable, Medical Prescription*, 44–45. For more detailed discussion of Dr. Carter, see Pickard and Buley, *The Midwest Pioneer: His Ills, Cures, and Doctors*. 47–71.

[91] Carter, *A Valuable, Vegetable, Medical Prescription*, 135.

particularly good on the "Incubus or Night-Mare." This misery could be caused by anxiety, despondency, or intense thought, possibly also by diet. The remedy was a blood purification effected by the following recipe: Into a copper kettle and five quarts of water put a handful each of bark of the yellow poplar, dogwood (from the north side), wild cheery, yellow sarsaparilla root, and the roots of the running briar. Boil slowly to two quarts, add a pint of whiskey, and take a tablespoonful two or three times a day.[92] Let the diet be confined to chicken, squirrels, beef, mutton, and broths not too highly seasoned.

In addition to Indian medicine men, Botanics, and whatnot, the pioneer doctor had to fight superstitions and the arts of the amateur healer. "Among the most disagreeable things attending the practice of medicine, are the prejudices the physician must constantly meet with, either in the mind of the patient, or in those of his friends. It is easier to cure the bodily complaints of an hundred persons, than to eradicate the prejudice from the mind of one."[93] Sickness and death, surrounded as they were with an air of the supernatural, easily called forth the folklore of primitive medicine. Powwowing, charm cures, and magnetic healers all had their devotees.[94] Those who possessed "the

---

[92] This recipe has been characterized by a recent writer as sounding "like something invented by a bartender with the female trade in mind." R. E. Banta, "The Indian Doctors," in *The Wabash Bulletin*, XL, 24 (Jan., 1942).

Other "Indian doctor" books published in the area included Robert L. Foster's *The North American Indian Doctor, or Nature's Method of Curing and Preventing Disease According to the Indians* (Canton, Ohio, 1838); Daily's *The Indian Doctor's Practice of Medicine, or Daily's Family Physician;* and James Cooper's *The Indian Doctor's Receipt Book* (Uniontown, Ohio, 1855). The latter was one of the few to include the horse in the family; "certain cures" were provided for founder, heaves, farsey, windgall, bots, and sweeny. One can imagine Dobbin's delight, especially in summer, after he got his treatment for the bots—"Drench the horse with sweet milk and molasses."

[93] A country physician in Madison *Indiana Republican*, August 1, 1833.

[94] There have been hundreds of books on magic, necromancy, "Egyptian Secrets," witchcraft, *hexadukt'r*, powwowing, etc. One of the standard works published in America was John George Hohman's *Long Lost Friend*, which went through many editions and was still being published and sold a hundred years later. For a reprint see A. Monroe Aurand, Jr., *John George Hohman's Long Lost Friend; or, Book of Powwows* (Harrisburg, Pa., 1930), a curious hodgepodge of bibliography, argument, testimonials, and accounts of twentieth-century "witch" murder trials. Many additional remedies are copied here. See also William J. Hoffman, "Folk-Lore of the Pennsylvania Germans," in *Journal of American Folk-Lore*, I (1888), 125-35, and II (1889), 23-35, 191-202; Thomas R. Brendle and Claude W. Unger, *Folk Medicine of the Pennsylvania Germans* . . . (Norristown, Pa., 1935). There is no adequate study of Midwest folklore and medical superstitions. Considerable material may be found in newspapers and reminiscences, but much such lore passed with the older generations. A comparison with the folk medicine and superstitions of the Pennsylvania Germans (Fogel, *Beliefs and Superstitions of the Pennsylvania*

power" guarded it carefully and passed it along with discretion, always to one of the opposite sex. A man might tell a woman a charm, or a woman tell a man, but if man told man or woman told woman, the charm was lost. Some formulas were community property, but others were jealously guarded, perhaps recorded on sheets in the family Bible along with births, deaths, and the proper time to plant beans. A fortunate few individuals—a seven-months' baby or the seventh son of a seventh son—were born with special curative abilities. Some were gifted with the knack of "blowing out the fire" and were called upon to treat burns. Others by magic words and a red thread could cure erysipelas.

Many persons had implicit faith in the charm cures; they charged failures to some deficiency or dereliction on the part of the patient rather than believe them a fault of the cure. Besides, there was frequently an "out" in the formula itself, such as "Corn beef and cabbage is good for a blacksmith with cramps, but ain't worth a d—n for cramps in a minister."[95] All honor was granted the cure last used before the body mechanism, in spite of the remedies, was restored to its natural condition. Madstones, loadstones, various woods and minerals were widely used, and the astrological signs heeded. July and August were the "dog days" when Sirius cast a baneful effect on the blood and air. Wounds would then become infected, disease was readily caught, and even the old swimming hole was viewed askance for its paludal influence.

From prenatal days to the grave and even after, the life of an individual was hedged round by these practices. Woe betide the pioneer baby who, in his anxiety to get into the rapidly developing Northwest, decided to enter society a month early. Only seven-months'-premature babies were supposed to live. (And should the powers that be defy the laws of nature by deciding that he shouldn't enter the world at all, 'twas said the use of the water in which nine eggs were boiled would do the trick.) Delayed entry could be expedited by quilling, but this was

---

Germans, 267–335) and of those of the southern mountain people in our own day is interesting, since these groups furnished two of the important ingredients in the Midwest mixture.

[95] Joseph D. Bryant, "Sunshine and Shadow in Medical Endeavor," in *Transactions of the Indiana State Medical Association*, 1905, p. 39.

hardly a superstition.[96] The rattle of a rattlesnake sewed in a black silk cloth and put in the hands of the parturient woman, provided she neither knew what the bundle contained nor opened it, was said to hasten delivery. Once the baby's arrival was satisfactorily explained to the other children—that he had been discovered in the spring, creek, the cabbage patch, or the midwife's apron—he began to run the gamut of superstition and home cure.

Any birthmarks could be obliterated by rubbing with the hand of a corpse or the head of a live eel for three successive mornings. If baby's face was washed in his baptismal water, he would be beautiful. If Mama cut his hair before he was a year old, she thereby cut short his life; if she pared his nails before nine weeks, he was doomed to the life of a thief. Crawling through an open window or between the legs of tables and chairs (unless he crawled back the same way) would immediately stop his growth. If a child were "afflicted with short growth," the string which measured his length and showed it less than seven times the length of his foot was looped, the child was passed through the loop three times while words were repeated, and then the string was twined around the grindstone. When the string wore out, the child would be of proper length.

Should he look into a mirror before he was nine months old his life would be full of trouble. Were the empty cradle carelessly rocked, measures must be taken immediately, else colic would result. Scrapings from the table cover or a spoonful of baptismal water would be administered. If croup threatened, the right front foot of a mole tied around baby's neck with a black thread would prove effective. Relief could also be afforded by the sufferer's standing on the warm spleen of a freshly slaughtered beef until the spleen grew cold. Better still, a hair of the child's head hidden in a hole bored in an ash or oak tree would prevent the ailment. This preventive ceased to operate when the child grew to the height of the hole. If convulsions occurred, pouring baptismal water over the peony bush or covering the infant with his father's wedding coat would effect a cure. Since most of baby's fits were caused by worms, treatment with either specifics or charms might be used. For the violent type (of fits) a little

[96] See below, note 178.

bag containing the leg of a toad worn around the neck was known to be good. Almost as effective as this or pumpkin-seed tea was conjuring in the name of God. Were bedwetting baby's weakness, fried-mouse pie, burned-hog's bladder powder, or spanking with a bake-oven mop was reputed to help.

Whooping cough could be conquered by a bag of little live ground bugs hung around the neck, white ant tea, or passing the sufferer through a horse collar three times. If this was not convenient, he could eat the cast-off skin of a snake, or eggs obtained from a person whose name had not been changed by marriage, drink mare's milk or tea made of blue clover blossoms, or wear a piece of stolen blue ribbon. His parents might place him in the hopper of a mill until the grist was ground; or they might seek to transfer the affliction to nine worms placed in a bottle and hidden, or to a live fish, which, after being returned to the water, gave the ailment to his fishy friends, as was evident from the fact that thereafter they came to the surface of the water to cough. Kissing a Negro before the age of one year would prevent whooping cough entirely. The ravages of diphtheria could be warded off by a poultice of cow dung held in place by means of a stocking turned wrong side out. Baby should never be left alone with the house cat, for the latter was likely to steal his breath. If, however, baby suffered from marasmus and was puny and short of energy, he could eat out of the cat's dish; the cat would die, but the baby's vigor would be restored. About the only thing the baby did not have to worry about was snake bite, for that could not happen to him until he was seven years old. Then, when bitten, if he did not approve of good liquor or gunpowder, he could tie on a toad to draw out the poison. If the toad died, another was tied on. When the toad lived, all the poison was out. Carrying an onion in the pocket provided against snake bite but, if a person were bitten, it was necessary for him to eat the heart of the offending reptile if he would gain further immunity. Spitting into the mouth of the snake would kill it and prevent further harm, or the curse of Adam might be put upon it, and then it would sneak away and die of shame.

Once the child was past infancy the repertory of possibilities in both diseases and remedies widened. The best charm for earache was the insertion of the kinkiest hair to be had from a

Negro's head, or oil from the ears of a weasel of the same sex as the sufferer. If immunity from toothache had not been acquired by rubbing the child's gums during the first six months with the brain of a rabbit or the rattles of a rattlesnake, or if Dr. Smith's recipe had not been followed, the pain could be eased by picking the offending tooth with a splinter from a tree struck by lightning, a coffin nail, the needle used in making a shroud, the nail of the middle toe of an owl, or a woodcock's tongue. Further recurrence could be prevented by paring the nails only on Friday or Sunday and burying the parings on the north side of the house, or by putting on the left stocking and right coat sleeve first when dressing. Biting into an apple immediately after coming home from first communion guaranteed exemption from toothache pains, too, as did wearing around the neck a string which had been used to hang three mice, or one on which was suspended a rabbit's tooth.

Ague could be handled by wearing a spider around the neck or having the sufferer take some of his own urine. Horse chestnuts or sweet potatoes carried in the pocket would cure piles, fried rattlesnake, tuberculosis, soup made of chicken—feathers and all —would cure constipation. For epilepsy one might eat the heart of a rattlesnake, sleep over the cow stable, or be passed three times through the crotch of a forked hickory tree which had been wedged open. If the tree healed and grew, the patient would recover. A wool stocking around the neck would fend off colds, while mumps could be eradicated by rubbing the swellings against the pig trough, or even chips from it. Wounds and injuries might be prevented by the right eye of a wolf inside the right sleeve; they could be cured by treatment with wound wood—ash severed before sunrise on Good Friday with three strokes of the ax and gathered by the "doctor" after the sun had shone on it. In addition to such specifics as cobwebs and horse manure, excessive bleeding could be stopped by shifting the pocket knife from one pocket to another or repeating the charm, "Christ's wounds were never bound," etc. For foot injury a piece of turf the shape of the foot was cut out and replaced upside down. A dried eelskin would relieve sprain, while the blood from the amputated tail of a black cat would take care of shingles. Eating from a blue dish, thrusting a live fish down the throat then returning it to the water, or wearing a spider sewed in a thimble around the neck might relieve a cough. A bag of camphor or asafetida worn around the neck would fend off all ills. Contagious diseases, sties, warts, boils, carbuncles, coughs, and colds all yielded to folk and charm cures of weird and wonderful mien.[97]

In addition to Indian medicine, powwowing, folk cures, and mechanical aids, many people resorted to household remedy or domestic medicine books for aid in times of illness. These books contained both the cures of the regular doctors and those of the vegetable kind; often they were hard to distinguish from the numerous offerings of Botanics or Eclectics, about the only criterion being whether or not they recommended bleeding and calomel. The number published in the West is not definitely known. Many were of limited circulation, confined largely to the locality in which they were published; others of foreign origin, such as that of Dr. William Buchan, *Domestic Medicine; or the Family Physician: Being an Attempt to Render the Medical Art More Generally Useful with Respect to the Prevention and Cure of Diseases* (Edinburgh, 1769), went through many editions in the United States. It has been said that the influence of this book was "greater than any other similar work ever published."[98] Often these books were so similar that it is apparent that they were copied from their predecessors, yet occasionally one would have distinguishing features, such as specializing in strong alcoholic remedies. They varied in size from the six-page *A Physician at Hand or a Collection of Receipts and Cures to Heal Diseases and Wounds of Various Kinds,* by Dr. W. Smith (Wooster, Ohio, 1829), with its even dozen recipes, to the thousand-page *Domestic Medicine or Poor Man's Friend, in the House of Affliction, Pain, and Sickness* . . . (Knoxville, 1830), by Dr. John C. Gunn, which is known to have had 213 "editions."[99]

---

[97] For a more detailed list of cures, see Pickard and Buley, *The Midwest Pioneer: His Ills, Cures, and Doctors,* 75–85 and 316–18.

[98] Hugh P. Greeley, "Early Wisconsin Medical History," in *The Wisconsin Medical Journal,* XX (1922), 564.

[99] Other domestic medicine books include: Dr. Anthony A. Benezet, *The Family Physician; Comprising Rules for the Prevention and Cure of Diseases; Calculated Particularly for the Inhabitants of the Western Country, and for Those Who Navigate Its Waters* (Cincinnati, 1826); A. Weyer, *The Family Physician or Poor Man's Friend, and Married Lady's Companion: Containing a great variety of Valuable Medical Recipes, designed to assist heads of Families, Travellers, and*

Some people thought that diseases were part of the penalty man paid for his sins, hence only God could effect a cure; others blamed the devil and were willing to stick by remedies which he understood. But in cases of fatality it was the doctor who was held responsible, since he had had the last chance. As one old doctor said, "The principal position of the doctor was dealing in second hand goods, and a bad quality at that."[100]

To the notion of many people who made a living at manual labor, lawyers, bankers, teachers, and to a certain extent doctors, were a parasitic class—useless and extravagant luxuries at the best. As frontier society became more complex, each of the vocations established its usefulness. First to do so were the doctors.

§ §

Much has been written of the country doctor. He was an important figure in pioneer life. An individualist in an age of individualism, he conformed to no set type, but in general has fared well at the hands of history. Like the preacher he was often a jack of several trades—might farm, hunt, or do some smithing in odd hours. In the early days wolves and wildcats kept him company on the solitary night journeys through almost trackless woods, but his nerves were steady and weird cries were not so dangerous as overhanging branches, hidden holes, and swollen streams. As did the judge and minister, he sometimes rode circuit over his territory. Tireless, fearless, often gruff, yet sympathetic, the doctor maintained a personal relationship with his people more intimate and vital than did minister or lawyer. Though frequently short of learning, intolerant of rivals and given to petty quarrels, he was abundantly possessed of those qualities which made his humanity triumph over both nature and human

---

Sea-faring People in Curing Disease (St. Clairsville, Ohio, 1831); anonymous, Travellers Pocket Medical Guide (printed by Wilcox, Louisville, 1833); Buell Eastman, Practical Treatise on Diseases Peculiar to Women and Girls . . . (Connersville, Ind., 1845); H. D. Mason, Symptoms and Treatment of All Diseases (Cedarville, Ohio, 1843); William Matthews, A Treatise on Domestic Medicine and Kindred Subjects; Embracing Anatomical and Physiological Sketches of the Human Body (Indianapolis, 1848).

[100] Dr. William H. Wishard, in Transactions of the Indiana State Medical Society, 1889, p. 12.

selfishness, and himself usually a figure at the same time feared, loved, and venerated.

His equipment was simple: perhaps mortar and pestle, pair of balances, some homemade splints and bandages, a few drugs, possibly a small set of instruments, and, of course, horse and saddlebags. By the late 1830's most of the better equipped doctors also carried stethoscopes,[101] tooth forceps, and a few obstetrical instruments. In the absence of complicated equipment the doctor relied upon his fingers, his eyes, ears, and nose. Temperature and pulse he could feel; color of skin, lips, eyes, and nails meant much, as did the sound of voice, cough, and breathing of the patient. He could smell out a case of typhoid or measles.

A contemporary description by a member of the profession covers the essentials:

The doctor had to be his own pharmacist. He made his own pills and tinctures, compounded all his medicines, and generally carried all he required, as, with saddle-bags across his horse, he wended his way from house to house, administering to the sick and ailing, always welcome and often regarded as an angel of mercy, although his homely garb and rough appearance looked anything but angelic. His life was one of peril, toil and privation. The country was new and thinly settled, and his rides were long and solitary; his patients were scattered over a wide expanse of territory; his travel was mostly performed on horseback, and its extent and duration was measured by the endurance of himself and his horse. He struggled through almost unfathomable mud and swamps and swollen streams. He was often compelled to make long detours to cross or avoid the treacherous slough. His rest was often taken in the saddle, sometimes in the cabin of the lonely settler. From necessity he was self-reliant and courageous. Every emergency, however grave, he was generally compelled to meet alone and unaided, as it was seldom assistance could be procured without too great an expenditure of time and money. His fees were small and his services were often paid for in promises, seldom in money, of which there was but little. The products of the country, called by the people "truck," was the general and most reliable circulating medium, and with this the doctor was usually paid. But there is a bright side to this picture. The kindly life of a new country, and the dependence of its inhabitants upon each other,

---

[101] This instrument was in use in southern Ohio in the early 1830's but not in other parts of the state until after 1835. Dr. Howard Dittrick, "The Equipment, Instruments and Drugs of Pioneer Physicians of Ohio," in *Ohio Archaeological and Historical Society Publications*, XLVIII (1939), 201–3. Dr. Drake in Cincinnati in 1830 was urging his readers to give the stethoscope a trial. He devoted several pages of his journal to a summary of Rene T. H. Laennec's *Treatise on the Diseases of the Chest*. See *Western Journal of the Medical and Physical Sciences*, III (1830), 68–99.

gave the doctor a strong hold upon the affection and gratitude of those among whom he lived and labored. They loved him when living and mourned for him when dead.[102]

As indicated above, the pay of the country doctor was uncertain, and when received, was often in the form of produce. At the end of a year's service, including care in two smallpox epidemics, an early Wisconsin doctor had received $68 in cash.[103] Even Chicago's city physician as late as 1861, when the population was more than 135,000, received an annual salary of only $600, and was required to furnish all medicines.[104] Another, at the forks of the Kalamazoo, apparently for somewhat less than a year's work, reaped much gratitude and "for service, advice and medicine—12½ cents,"[105] and an old German physician in Illinois in 1842 received a stove for sixteen office visits (at 37½ cents), solutions, and powders.[106]

The frontiersman, self-reliant and proud, and generally poor, was usually reluctant to call for the doctor, considering it a waste of both time and money. When the doctor was called, he often had to compete with all present and thereabouts to justify his system. Hence, perhaps, the bold treatments in these, the heroic days of medicine.

To the pioneer patient the lancet was a familiar implement. One of the commonest types was much like a pocket knife with a small cleaver on the end of the blade; others were merely long, tapering blades. Improvements brought the spring lancet which could be set to penetrate to a definite depth. "Bleed to

---

[102] Dr. Robert Boal of Cincinnati, quoted in Otto Juettner, *Daniel Drake and His Followers* (Cincinnati, 1909), 87–88.

[103] Dr. John C. Reeve, "A Physician in Pioneer Wisconsin," in *Wisconsin Magazine of History*, III (1919–20), 308.

[104] Dr. Morris Fishbein, "Some Physicians' Fees," in *Bulletin of the Society of Medical History of Chicago*, II (1919), 181.

[105] Etolie T. Davis, "Memoir of Ebenezer Grosvenor," in *Michigan Pioneer and Historical Collections*, XXXVIII (1912), 703.

[106] Fishbein, "Some Physicians' Fees," 181. In a day of scarcity of specie and small change and prevalence of makeshifts, a Doctor Murdock, of Brookville, Indiana, in 1825 issued scrip bills "good for one dose of medicine." These were known as "Puke Bills." Patients rarely came back for the second dose. *Atlas of Franklin Co. Indiana . . .* (J. H. Beers & Company, Chicago, 1882), 95. Medical charges varied. Village and country doctors were not organized and fees were not standardized. The Indiana law of 1816 fixed fees at 12½ cents per mile of travel by day, 25 cents at night, but these were not adhered to. In the towns, informal agreements were sometimes made. For instance, Springfield, Illinois, physicians in 1840 agreed on the following scale: daytime visit in town, $1.00, up to four miles $2.00; and 50 cents additional for each mile. Prices double for night visits. Verbal advice, $1.00; each dose of medicine, 50 cents; vaccination, $1.00; natural parturition, $5.00 to $10; fractures, $5.00 to $10; amputation of leg or arm, $25 to $100; lithotomy, $100 to $200. *Sangamo Journal*, April 10, 1840.

syncope" was the almost inevitable advice to practitioners. Arms of the patient were often so scarred from repeated bleeding that locating a vein for another bleeding became a difficult task. Many believed that bleeding from the right arm when the pain was on the left side would be fatal, for death would result from drawing the pain across the heart.

Although some physicians were more liberal than others in their blood taking, most books of the period recommended the withdrawing of 10 to 12 ounces at a time. Dr. Samuel Gross fixed the amount at 16 to 24 ounces and said that the patient felt cheated if less were removed. The *Cyclopoedia of Practical Medicine* (Philadelphia, 1845) recommended adjusting the amount to the action of the heart and pulse; for apoplexy it suggested 40 to 50 ounces. In 1811 the *Medical Repository* reported the case of Captain Niblett, from whom was taken in fifty bleedings 600 ounces of blood in a period of two months. This was in addition to blood taken by cups and leeches. It is hard to believe that the victim lasted for two months, much less recovered, as accounted.

Besides the lancet, leeches and cups were used to bleed. Cups were of various types—some bell-shaped and made of glass, others of glass and brass with stopcocks or valves. The air might be sucked out by mouth or hot sealing wax applied within the cup to expel the air. In use, too, was the lancet cup, a brass box about two inches square with one end slotted to contain the concealed knives. These were expelled by means of a spring which, when released by a trigger, swept them upward and forward at the same time. Ordinarily twelve knives were used, six moving counter to the other six. As described by a patient, the doctor put the ". . . brass box to my left side, pressed hard down on it, pulled a trigger, and twelve sharp knives slashed into my flesh. Then he burned a piece of alcohol-saturated cotton in a small glass, or cup. This drove the air out. While still aflame but expiring, this was applied over the twelve little incisions which had been made in my side. As the air was exhausted in the cup and no more could get in, the cup 'sucked' blood."

Leeches, after being dried, were encouraged to take hold by covering the skin of the patient with cream, sugar, or blood. If still indifferent to the job, they might be activated by throwing them into a saucer of beer, "until they become quite lively. It will be seen with astonishment how quickly they bite."[107]

The blister, the seton, and moxa were also called into play. The seton was a thread or horsehair introduced through a fold of the skin and kept there to "maintain an issue," or irritate and inflame. Or a pea or small lump of lint would be kept in an incision in the thigh or leg. The moxa was a coil of carded cotton treated to burn slowly, so that when placed on the skin it would irritate steadily. By judicious use of bellows the physician would blow so that the moxa might burn as slowly as possible without being extinguished.

In cauterizing infection and wounds it was the iron heated to gray heat which was most irritating and torturous, hence the most effective. For fevers and delirium the patient was bled until faint and relaxed, an emetic of ipecac administered, then a cathartic (calomel), then opium to allay irritability of internal organs. Meanwhile the sufferer was probably confined in a closed room, sandwiched between feather beds, and forbidden cooling drinks.

To cure the dumb ague some thought it was necessary to bring on the shakes. "Carry then your patient into the passage between the two cabins—strip off all his clothes that he may lie naked in the cold air and upon a bare sacking—and then and there pour over and upon him successive buckets of cold spring water, and continue until he has a decided and pretty powerful smart chance of a shake."[108] Wet sheets wrapped around the sufferer were also used to drive out the fever. If pneumonia resulted, the cure was bleeding, tartar emetic, and calomel.[109]

[107] *Western Lancet* (Cincinnati), V (1843–44), in *Ohio State Medical Journal*, XXXV (1939), 1329.

[108] Hall, *The New Purchase*, 254.

[109] Alfred Patton, "Medical History of Vincennes," in *Transactions of the Indiana State Medical Society*, 1874, pp. 35–45. Bleeding was considered proper at the beginning of all inflammatory fevers, inflammation of the lungs, intestines, bladder, stomach, kidney, throat, and eyes, and good for coughs, headaches, rheumatism, apoplexy, and epilepsy. Benezet, *Family Physician*, 464. Bleeding and calomel treatments were probably most ably presented in the United States by the philosophical Benjamin Rush (1745–1813) of the College of Philadelphia and Pennsylvania University.

Dr. John Esten Cooke of Transylvania and Louisville carried the Rush calomel-and-purge treatment to the extreme. He believed that all diseases, particularly fevers, arose from cold or malaria, which weakened the heart and thus produced an accumulation of blood in the *vena cava* and in the adjoining large veins of the liver. Consequently, calomel and other cathartics which acted on that organ were the cure. "If calomel did not salivate and opium did not constipate, there is no telling what we could do in the practice of physic," represented the main idea of Cooke, who has been called "the most elaborate of all American Systematizers."

No indirect attacks, these, but frontal assaults. As one of the stalwart doctors of the days of vigorous medication said: "We went into it with our sleeves rolled up, and generally came out satisfied with the result of our work."[110] And another:

We used no manner of temporizing treatment, but aimed our agents directly at the extermination of diseases. Opium, ipecac, tartarized antimony, nitrate of potassa, spirits mindereri and spirits of nitre, with other means too tedious to mention, were all frequently brought into requisition. Under the above manner of treating a case of remittent fever it was no uncommon thing on our second visit to find our patient sitting up feeling "pretty well, except a *little weak*," and within a few days able to return to his ordinary avocations.[111]

In case of death there probably was no second visit. It was said that the rigorous system of the pioneer doctor "killed quick but cured slow." The doctor himself was sometimes referred to as "Death on the Pale Horse." "When we hear of a man's getting well, after being given over by the doctors, we can't help thinking how lucky he was to be given over by the doctors." That the doctors were sincere in practice of such treatment is evidenced by the fact that many tried their own medicine, with fatal results. That any patients survived both disease and cure speaks wonders for their constitutions and powers of resistance.

Though the practices of the pioneer doctors seem indeed crude, the western doctor did not noticeably lag behind the general advance of medical science. As Dr. William H. Welch, first dean of the Johns Hopkins Medical School, later said: "The best of these men were, withal, abreast in knowledge, training and skill

[110] Dr. Wilson Hobbs, in *Transactions of the Indiana State Medical Society*, 1889, p. 24.

[111] Dr. Joel Pennington, "President's Address," in *Transactions of the Indiana State Medical Society*, 1873, pp. 11–12. The following, written in the light of later knowledge, shows a different view of the early doctor: "Then he would say, 'yes, I see, all run down, very weak, bilious, debilitated. We must draw off all the bad blood and give you a chance to make new and get strong again, give me a bowl and a bandage.' They were brought and the poor victims gave up poor thin blood that was merely keeping the heart beating. . . . The doctor forgot his lance one day and so took his jack knife and sharpened it on his boot leg and bled all of the family of Mr. Reagan. When he came to little Susan the hurt and fright were so great that she died in his arms. He came to our house but mother would not let him touch one of her children. Father was growing worse and tried the doctor's remedy, in fifteen minutes he was dead. Another doctor came who said that was no way to do, he never bled his patients, he wound them in a wet sheet. A promising young man . . . was wrapped in a cold wet sheet and died. Yet another doctor came and he sent a man and team down to Grand Ledge to get a load of hemlock bark which he would steep strong and give them hemlock sweats when they were so weak that they died from the heat and exhaustion." Margaret Lafever, "Story of Early Day Life in Michigan," in *Michigan Pioneer and Historical Collections*, XXXVIII (1912), 675.

with their contemporaries of the Atlantic coast; they were men of striking originality, substantial contributors to the sum of medical knowledge and art, powerful influences in the material, as well as the medical development of what was then the far west."[112] Many of the discoveries and inventions of the period were adopted at quite an early date by frontier physicians— vaccination, stethoscope, microscope, anesthesia.

Surgery had made some progress since the time of the American Revolution, when operations were often mere butcheries, fractures were clumsily and painfully treated, and antiseptic surgery and anesthesia unknown. No small part of that progress might be traced to frontier regions where conditions incident to life made quick and bold decisions on the part of attending physicians a necessity. Important contributions were made by western doctors who possessed little in the way of instruments or facilities, but much of daring and courage.

In 1809 Ephraim McDowell, of Danville, Kentucky, who had more than a local reputation as a surgeon, was called to attend a pioneer wife who seemed pregnant, but had passed her time with no sign of delivery. McDowell decided it was a tumor which must be removed immediately, but so dangerous and unprecedented was the proposed operation that he would not attempt it except in his own office. The woman rode sixty miles to Danville on horseback in midwinter, resting the protuberance on the pommel of the saddle. It was said that a committee of local doctors and prominent citizens endeavored to prevent the operation. Doctor and patient, however, had made their decision. "The day having arrived, and the patient being on the table, I marked with a pen the course of the incision to be made, desiring him [Joseph Nash McDowell, his nephew] to make the external opening, which, in part, he did; I then took the knife, and completed the operation . . . ," while the patient gritted her teeth and recited Psalms. Five days later the patient made her own bed, and on the twenty-fifth day drove home, to live thirty-one years longer.[113] Again in 1813 and 1816 Dr. McDowell performed

[112] Address at Centennial Celebration of the College of Physicians and Surgeons, Columbia University, June 11, 1907, in *Papers and Addresses* (3 volumes. Baltimore, 1920), III, 292–93.

[113] August Schachner, *Ephraim McDowell, "Father of Ovariotomy" and Founder of Abdominal Surgery* . . . (Philadelphia, 1921), 67. Mrs. Jane Todd Crawford, the patient, is buried near Graysville, Sullivan County, Indiana.

similar operations, but when he published his article in the Philadelphia *Eclectic Repertory and Analytical Review* in 1817 he was
not believed until he demonstrated two other operations.[114]

At Newtown, Ohio, in 1827, Dr. John Lambert Richmond,
with a few simple instruments, performed what is reputed to be
the first Caesarian operation west of the Allegheny Mountains.
Lithotomies, or operations for stones, had been performed a number of times at Transylvania in the early 1820's, and were soon
executed by a few of the more skillful doctors. Dr. Benjamin W.
Dudley of Transylvania, probably the West's most distinguished
surgeon, was credited with more than two hundred, with only
4 per cent mortality.

In physiology, as well as surgery, the Midwest made a contribution. At Mackinac in 1822 Alexis St. Martin, half-breed
employee of the American Fur Company, had the misfortune to
have a shotgun loaded with buckshot discharged at close range
into his abdomen. The result was a large hole out of which came
portions of ribs and lung. The wound was treated and the man's
life saved by Dr. William Beaumont, surgeon at the military
post. The wound, however, failed to close, except for an inside
covering of a fold of the stomach wall. This accidental provision
of a window to a human stomach was taken advantage of by
Dr. Beaumont, who observed the digestive processes under different conditions over a period of months in 1825. The subject,
somewhat sensitive over being known as "the man with a window
in his stomach," ran away, went back to work, married, reared
a family, and lived many years. He was persuaded to submit to
further observations from 1829 to 1831. As a result of this
experimentation, Dr. Beaumont was able later to publish his conclusions, the first important study in this field in the world.[115]

---

[114] Dr. Henry E. Sigerist, *American Medicine* (New York, 1934), 89.

[115] Dr. William Beaumont, *Experiments and Observations on the Gastric Juice
and the Physiology of Digestion* (Plattsburg, N. Y., 1833; reprinted in England,
1847). A brief account of this case may be found in George H. White, "Alexis
St. Martin, of Mackinaw, the Subject of an Important Discovery in Physiology,"
in *Michigan Pioneer and Historical Collections*, XXVI (1894–95), 646–50. The best
account of this subject at the present time is Dr. Jesse S. Myer, *Life and Letters
of Dr. William Beaumont* . . . (St. Louis, 1912). Two early Beaumont notebooks
edited by Genevieve Miller were published under the title *William Beaumont's
Formative Years* (New York, 1946). The influence of Dr. Beaumont's work on his
contemporaries and successors has been well presented by Dr. George Rosen, *The
Reception of William Beaumont's Discovery in Europe* (New York, 1942).

§ § §

Opportunities for education of doctors were limited. Transylvania University at Lexington established a medical department in 1799, but it did not really begin to function until 1819, at which time there were six instructors and seven graduates.[116] Dr. Daniel Drake, after one year's service on the faculty, established his own school at Cincinnati in 1818, which in 1819 was chartered by the legislature as the Medical College of Ohio.[117] Drake was soon out of his own school and by 1826 four other men were lecturing, with subjects grouped as follows: anatomy,

[116] Dr. Robert Peter, *The History of The Medical Department of Transylvania University* (*Filson Club Publications*, No. XX, Louisville, 1905), Appendix, 166. See also his *Transylvania University, Its Origin, Rise, Decline, and Fall* (*Filson Club Publications*, No. XI, Louisville, 1896). So unimportant was the work of the Transylvania medical department prior to 1819 that the following statement by Dr. G. W. H. Kemper is substantially correct: "Prior to 1816 there was not a medical college west of the Allegheny Mountains." "Medical History of Indiana's First Century," in Jacob P. Dunn, *Indiana and Indianans* (5 volumes. Chicago, 1919), II, 788. By 1834 the school had had 2,810 students and given 699 medical degrees. In 1820 and 1834 "considerable sums" (about $25,000) were spent for a medical library, which was purchased largely in Paris, the successor of Edinburgh as Europe's medical center. For the influence of Transylvania in Indiana, see Leon Zerfas, "Medical Education in Indiana as Influenced by Early Indiana Graduates in Medicine from Transylvania University," in *Indiana Magazine of History*, XXX (1934), 139–48.

The College of Philadelphia in 1769 had the first medical faculty in the United States—John Morgan, Benjamin Rush, Thomas Bond, etc. It was suppressed in 1779, and the University of Pennsylvania established, but it returned to life in 1783 and the two schools merged in 1791. Philadelphia remained the medical center of the United States throughout this period.

[117] *Liberty Hall and Cincinnati Gazette*, October 19, 1819. Dr. Drake continued to attempt to organize various schools in competition with his first. Some failed; others were absorbed. Edward D. Mansfield, *Memoirs of the Life and Services of Daniel Drake, M. D.* . . . (Cincinnati, 1855), gives the main facts in the life of this versatile but somewhat cantankerous pioneer physician, and of the Medical College. See also Charles D. Meigs, *A Biographical Notice of Daniel Drake, M. D.* (Philadelphia, 1853), and Dr. Otto Juettner, "Rise of Medical Colleges in the Ohio Valley," in *Ohio Archaeological and Historical Society Publications*, XXII (1913), 481–91. Dr. Juettner in his *Daniel Drake and His Followers* gives the most comprehensive account of early midwestern doctors. J. Christian Bay, "Dr. Daniel Drake, 1785–1852," in *Filson Club History Quarterly*, VII (1933), 1–17, gives additional material on Dr. Drake's role in midwestern medical education.

The Medical College of Ohio was organized and opened in the autumn of 1820; it held its first commencement in April, 1821, when, after a public examination, degrees were conferred upon seven. In 1821 the college had thirty students, but Dr. Drake was ousted and returned to Transylvania. The next year the Cincinnati school had no students. In 1825 it had 30, as contrasted with Transylvania's 281; 1830, 124 to 210; and in 1834, 83 to 247, in spite of the advantage of city location, hospitals, etc. After legislative investigation the college was reorganized in 1835 and taken over as part of Cincinnati College, which Drake had helped organize in 1818–20. Its advertisements at that time mentioned new hospital and clinical facilities. Fees were $15 for each lecture or $90 for all per term. Candidates for graduation were to be twenty-one years of age, must have had three years of medical work under some reputable practitioner and two courses of lectures, or have been a practitioner for four years plus one course of lectures.

physiology, and surgery; chemistry and pharmacy; materia medica and obstetrics; theory and practice of medicine.[118]

The Louisville Medical Institute was opened in 1837 and Vincennes University offered a series of medical lectures the same year, but the medical department of neither the St. Louis University nor Missouri University was actively functioning until after 1840.[119]

Comparatively few of the practitioners in the West were medical school graduates, or had even "attended lectures."[120] Entry into the medical profession was almost as easy as into the law. A young man "read medicine" with some local doctor, rolled his pills, mixed his powders, and took care of the horses. After a time he was ready to doctor on his own.[121]

Medical books and professional periodicals were scarce. If the doctor possessed one book on each of four or five fields of medicine, he was considered fairly well equipped.[122] Newspapers sometimes published articles on medicine as they did on agriculture, travel, and phrenology. For instance, in 1821 the Cin-

[118] *Western Sun and General Advertiser*, September 23, 1826.

[119] Joseph Nash McDowell, nephew of Ephraim McDowell, organized the Kemper Medical School at St. Louis in 1839. In 1845 when Kemper College was finding it difficult to keep going, the medical school became the Medical Department of the University of Missouri. Later it became the Medical Department of the Missouri Institute of Science. The Medical Department of St. Louis University was established in 1836, but did not begin to function until 1842 when Charles Alexander Pope took over. The warfare between "Pope's College" and "McDowell's College" existed for years.

[120] Dr. W. H. Wishard thought that in 1825 in Indiana not over 10 per cent of the physicians were graduates of medical colleges and not over 25 per cent had ever attended any lectures. *Transactions of the Indiana State Medical Society,* 1889, p. 7. In Ohio it is estimated that the percentage rose from around 10 to approximately 20 by 1835. Frederick C. Waite, "The Professional Education of Pioneer Ohio Physicians," in *Ohio Archaeological and Historical Society Publications,* XLVIII (1939), 190.

[121] This living-in type of apprenticeship was gradually supplanted by the regular daytime instruction type. Since under the latter system board and room were not furnished and the doctor could not expect much in the way of labor from his apprentice, a regular fee was charged. This was frequently $100 per year. A rough standard of apprenticeship was three years. Upon completion the preceptor would issue a certificate. Unless some form of examination was required by the local medical society, this certificate, when registered, entitled the holder to practice medicine. If the young physician became a member of a medical society, he was likely to rate a little higher. Men who held the college medical degree were always careful to display the M. D. on their prescriptions and signs.

[122] Many still used books published in the eighteenth century, such as Benjamin Bell's *Surgery,* Alexander Hamilton's *Obstetrics,* and William Cullen's *Practice of Medicine,* the latter reprinted in the United States in 1806, 1816, and 1822. Later the works of Drs. Rush, Thomas, and others came into use. There is no way of knowing how many of the early doctors had access to John Hunter on *Blood, Inflammation and Gun Shot Wounds.*

cinnati *Liberty Hall* published a long series by "Hippocrates." Number 17 was on "Emetics," number 18 on "Blood Letting." The first American medical journal, *The Medical Repository* (New York, 1797–1824), had slight circulation in the West. In 1820 was founded *The Philadelphia Journal of the Medical and Physical Sciences*, which in 1827 became *The American Journal of the Medical Sciences*. Also at Philadelphia was published the *Eclectic Repertory and Analytical Review*. It was not until 1827, however, when Dr. Drake began publication at Cincinnati, of his *Western Journal of the Medical and Physical Sciences*, that a professional periodical was generally available in the West.[123] The next year at Lexington was begun *The Transylvania Journal of Medicine and the Associate Sciences*.

There was no important treatise on medicine by a western doctor until Dr. John Eberle's *A Treatise on the Practice of Medicine* (2 volumes. Philadelphia, 1830) and Dr. Samuel Gross's *Elements of Pathological Anatomy*, which appeared at Philadelphia in 1839. Another outstanding work was Dr. Drake's two-volume *Diseases of the Interior Valley of North America . . .* which was published in the early 1850's.[124] Alexander von Humboldt pronounced this "a treasure among scientific works" and Benjamin Silliman of Yale classified it as "an enduring monument of American genius." Later critics, evaluating American medical books, stated that, though it was not possible to make a

---

[123] In 1822 the *Western Quarterly Reporter* (Cincinnati) ran for six issues and in 1826 the semimonthly *Ohio Medical Repository* was started. Dr. Drake joined the editors, Drs. Guy W. Wright and James M. Mason, and in 1827 the publication was changed to the monthly *Western Medical and Physical Journal* which in Volume II became the *Western Journal of Medical and Physical Sciences*. In 1839 when the medical department of Cincinnati College was dissolved, the *Journal* was transferred to Louisville and united with the *Louisville Journal of Medicine and Surgery*. The *Journal of Health*, started at Philadelphia in 1829, also circulated in the West.

[124] This monumental and original work was the product of nearly a quarter of a century of travel and observation from Hudson Bay to the Gulf, from the mouth of the St. Lawrence to the Rockies. The contributions in the fields of geography and physiography are as important as in medicine. Topographical and Hydrographical Etiology, Climatic Etiology, and Physiological and Sociological Etiology comprise Volume I. The first volume got a laudatory thirty-page review in the *British and Foreign Medico-Chirurgical Review* of London. *Daily Cincinnati Gazette*, July 9, 1851. Nothing was too insignificant to arouse Drake's curiosity in relation to disease. Though he arrived at some rather fantastic conclusions, on the whole his attitude was scientific. He almost discovered germs without a microscope. Besides Mansfield, Juettner, etc., cited above, Drake's scientific work is discussed in Arthur Deen, "Frontier Science in Kentucky and the Old Northwest, 1790–1860" (MS. thesis, Indiana University, 1938), 269–88, and Pickard and Buley, *The Midwest Pioneer: His Ills, Cures, and Doctors*, 132–33, 152–54.

great list, one could make a strong one, and on that list Drake's work was among the strongest.

Dentistry as a profession was only beginning. Ordinary tooth-aches were treated with home remedies such as peppermint oil. When too far gone the tooth was looped with a string and pulled by a friend, or the string was hitched to a springy bent sapling which when released would yank out the offender. Difficult cases were taken to the country doctor, who, with a tortuous crank-like lever known as a "pullikin," sometimes achieved the same result. When teeth decayed without excessive pain, the dead stumps and roots were, as a rule, not interfered with. Plugs of tinfoil were sometimes used to advantage by fastidious persons, as this substance showed less conspicuously than gold leaf. Once the teeth were extracted it was impossible for the average pioneer to replace them, and toothless gums were common among older folk. Some thought that diseases of the teeth were more common in this country than in England or Germany.[125]

Aside from natural wear and tear, the salivating effects of the overdoses of calomel, and possibly the fevers and constitutional afflictions were no doubt aggravating factors. By the 1820's dentists were available in the larger towns of the West, and itinerant dentists, many of them mere tooth pullers, were traveling over the country. One such traveling practitioner, in the seven years between 1830 and 1837 which he devoted entirely to dental surgery, reported that he had "travelled between 25 and 30 thousand miles in different parts of the United States."[126]

These itinerant dentists were not always accorded the greatest regard; for example, one writer used more than a column of the front page of the Cincinnati *National Republican and Ohio Political Register*[127] to discuss "The Tooth-Drawer" who "is a most savage little animal" and "desires that the world had but one tooth that he might wrench it out by a single twist!"

[125] Leonard Koecker, surgeon, dentist, M. D., and member of the Academy of Natural Sciences of Philadelphia, *Principles of Dental Surgery* . . . (London, 1826), reviewed in *Western Medical and Physical Journal,* I (1827–28), 333. It was recognized at this time that diseases of the mouth were more prevalent in civilized than in savage life. Among the causes assigned was, "It is the law of the animal economy, that the organ oftenest thrown into high excitement, is most liable to disease. Now the civilized state is one of wealth and luxury; it is emphatically an eating state."

[126] Columbus (Ohio) *Daily Journal and Register,* December 6, 1837.

[127] August 10, 1824.

A dental college opened in Baltimore in 1840 was said to be the first and only one of its kind in the United States. In 1828, however, Dr. John Harris, of Bainbridge, Ohio, who in the preceding year had opened a "School of Medical Instruction," announced: "From his knowledge of the Medical Profession Surgery and Dental Surgery in particular, he flatters himself that he shall be able to render general satisfaction to all, who may have occasion to employ him."[128] From 1835 to 1836 Dr. Harris gave dental instruction at Transylvania, and in 1836 tried to obtain a charter for a regular university dental institution in Ohio, but failed. In 1845 a dental college was founded by Dr. James Taylor at Cincinnati.[129]

Advertisements appeared for "Dental Surgery—natural teeth inserted," and by 1840 there was in use in Cincinnati a "new substance, like clay, [which] pushed firmly in the teeth, hardens in a day or two like the tooth itself."[130] Numerous remedies for toothache were advertised in the newspapers in the 1830's. Among others were Dr. Brown's extract of gall and creosote, and Dr. Hitchcock's "Magnetic Odontica, the dream of the alchemists realized."

Eye trouble received little attention. But few people used their eyes consistently for close work. When vision got bad, various spectacles from the stock of the peddler or general store were tried on until one was found to fit. Although astigmatism was discovered at the very beginning of the century, and cylindrical lenses were being ground at Philadelphia in 1828, the rudiments of optometry were known by only a few, so spectacles only magnified and took care of "long-sightedness" and "short-sightedness." A few eye specialists began to appear by the late 1830's. Dr. Waldo, of Columbus, for instance, announced in his "card": "Special attention to Diseases of the Eye. Artificial Eyes inserted." It was probably easier to get a satisfactory glass eye than a fitted pair of glasses. Dr. Drake's Cincinnati Eye Infirmary, founded in 1827, pioneered in institutionalized care.

[128] Chillicothe *Supporter and Gazette,* February 21 to December 3, 1828.

[129] For information relating to early dental education in Ohio, see articles by Edward C. Mills, in *Ohio Archaeological and Historical Society Publications,* XLVIII (1939), 243–56, XLIX (1940), 386–97, LI (1942), 294–312, and LII (1943), 356–72.

[130] *Ohio State Journal,* September 21, 1833; *Cincinnati Daily Gazette,* February 14, 1840. Such a feat in an era of hard times and bank failures called forth the comment that it was now possible to mend almost everything except dishonesty.

The warfare between the "regulars" and the "quacks" of the medical profession was long and bitter, but who was which was often hard to determine.[131] Generally speaking it was the calomel-mercury-bleeding doctors, or allopathists,[132] who were regarded as the orthodox members of the profession; at times the botanic or nonmineral medicine men seemed not only to have greater number and popularity on their side, but more of sense and science as well.

As late as 1883 in Indiana seventeen different kinds of practicing "doctors" were reported: eclectic, botanic, homeopathic, uroscopian, old Thomsonian, hydropathic, electric, faith, spiritual, herbalist, electropathic, vitapathic, botanico-medical, physio-medical, physio-electric, hygeo-therapeutic, and "travelling."[133] More than three quacks to every regular were reported in Wisconsin, and early Michigan's high death rate was said to result from their presence. Indiana was adjudged "a sinkhole in medical practice"; Ohio was condemned as a "paradise of the incompetent."[134]

It was Samuel Thomson,[135] however, who with his *New Guide to Health; or Botanic Family Physician* established the system with the largest popular following. This system was predicated on the idea that all diseases are the effect of one general cause and can be removed by one general remedy. Heat is the substance of life; absence of heat is the cause of disease; heat is the remedy. No one ever died of a fever, said Thomson; he always

---

[131] Even the best of the regulars indulged in some theories or practices which had as little scientific basis as those of the irregulars. Dr. Drake, for instance, in his spontaneous combustion theory, maintained that, under certain conditions, the human body could explode and actually burn up. *Western Journal of the Medical and Physical Sciences,* II (1828), 69. His cure for drunkenness was also interesting: sulphuric acid in bitters.

[132] The "allopaths" or regulars used remedies designed to produce effects different from those of the disease treated, as contrasted with "homeopaths," whose remedies produced effects similar to those of the disease under treatment. "Allopath" was a term of derision applied to the regulars by members of the homeopathic belief.

[133] Dr. George Rowland, "Medical Legislation," in *Transactions of the Indiana State Medical Society,* 1883, p. 172.

[134] George H. Weaver, "Beginnings of Medical Education in and near Chicago," in *Bulletin of the Society of Medical History of Chicago,* III (1925), 346; Burr, *Medical History of Michigan,* I, 16; William H. Lopp, "Quacks and Quackery in Indiana," in *Transactions of the Indiana State Medical Society,* 1883, p. 118; Eugene H. Roseboom and Francis P. Weisenburger, *A History of Ohio* (New York, 1934), 413.

[135] Thomson was born in 1769 at Alstead, New Hampshire. As a result of his early favorable experiences with Indian doctors and other irregulars, and unfavorable contacts with regulars, he evolved his own system of irregularity.

got cold first. His treatment called for emesis by the use of *Lobelia inflata,* steam baths, and a group of vegetable medicines numbered from one to six, designed to stimulate and heat internally.

The "hot stone steam system" was pointedly attacked. In 1809–10 Thomson was charged with murder following the death of a patient, but was acquitted, perhaps much better off for the resultant publicity.[136] A few years later, March, 1813, he received a patent giving him exclusive right to administer six concoctions in the healing of specific diseases.[137] Even before the granting of the patent (1806), however, Thomson sold "family rights" to practice his system. Persons buying these rights automatically became members of "Friendly Botanic Societies." With the appearance, in 1822, of his *A Narrative of the Life and Medical Discoveries of Samuel Thomson . . . To Which is added an introduction to his New Guide to health or Botanic Family Physician,* the purchaser received for $20 both the book and a diploma which conferred upon him the right to practice the patented system.[138]

From 1822 to 1837 Thomsonianism enjoyed a popularity more extensive than that of any other of the unorthodox systems. It spread throughout New England, down the coast as far as Georgia, and westward from New York and Pennsylvania into the Old Northwest, where Ohio became its focal point. Agents were dispatched "By different directions, Eastward and Southward, et cetera, and in their several routes, to have an opportunity to give all their principal Agents, and many others a

---

[136] For accounts presenting the trial from both sides, see Thomson, *Narrative,* 93–104, and Barton, *Vegetable Materia Medica,* II, 188–95, quoting 6 *Tyng,* 134. In Boston in 1824 (?) Thomson published a pamphlet, *Learned Quackery Exposed; or, Theory According to Art. As exemplified in the practice of the Fashionable Doctors of the present day,* which contained a poem which he claimed to have been written in Newburyport jail in 1809. This poem had been circulated as a handbill "as a looking-glass in which the doctors might see their own conduct and the effects of their medicine on patients in cases of pleurisy and fevers, when treated according to art. . . ."

[137] Ten years later this patent was replaced by a fourteen-year right, which before its expiration was renewed for another fourteen-year period.

[138] For a copy of this diploma, see Lucius P. H. Zeuch, *History of Medical Practice in Illinois* (Chicago, 1927), 326. Under one title or another the book ran through thirteen editions—the later ones mostly published in Ohio—and according to its author, sold more than a hundred thousand copies. One edition was even translated into German for would-be practitioners of Pennsylvania and eastern Ohio.

personal call."[139] These agents were authorized to sell the system to any and all who could be persuaded to buy. Some of the Thomsonian advocates gave lectures.[140] Numerous botanic medical books were published, by converts as well as agents.[141] As another means of furthering their cause, the Botanics started in 1832 at Columbus *The Thomsonian Recorder, or Impartial Advocate of Botanic Medicine*. With the growth of the movement other periodicals were established.

Botanic medicines, which were widely advertised in general newspapers as well as the special botanic publications, were dispensed both wholesale and retail in Cincinnati, Louisville, Indianapolis, St. Louis, and elsewhere.[142] The need for these medicines may be readily observed by a glance at some of the intricate Thomsonian cures.[143]

So successful was the propagation of Thomsonianism that by 1835 the Botanics maintained that half of the people of Ohio relied upon their system; the regular doctors conceded one third.

[139] *Thomsonian Recorder*, II, 74 (Dec. 7, 1833).

[140] For example, Dr. Samuel Robinson, a Cincinnati clergyman, *A Course of Fifteen Lectures, on Medical Botany, denominated Thomson's New Theory of Medical Practice; in which the Various Theories that have Preceded it, are reviewed and compared; delivered in Cincinnati, Ohio* (Columbus, 1829).

[141] Among others in the Middle West: Charles Miles (in 1825 general agent for Thomsonian promotional sales at Columbus), *New and Improved System of Medical Botanical Practice* (Cleaveland, 1829); Horton Howard (controller of western headquarters at Columbus, 1827–31), *An Improved System of Botanic Medicine* (3 volumes. Columbus, 1832), also published by J. Kost of Cincinnati in 1852 in a one-volume edition; J. E. Carter, *The Botanic Physician; or Family Medical Adviser* . . . (Madisonville, Tenn., 1837); anonymous, *The Medical Instructor, or the Cause and Cure of Disorders, expressed in Plain, Easy Language, and Intended for the Great Benefit of Mankind* (printed by S. and C. A. Preston, Norwalk, Ohio, 1835).

[142] Directions for the medical preparations recommended by Thomson in his book were quite general and indefinite; he warned his followers that the most efficacious remedies were manufactured by establishments which he either owned or controlled. The largest of these, located in Cincinnati, supplied much of the western territory.

[143] "I gave him the warming medicine very freely, such as Nos. 2 and 6, *Composition,* &c. I rubbed the surface of the body freely with cold water, vinegar and salt, mixed—repeating these applications several times, while over the steam. After about an hour I applied cold water and vinegar by means of a towel— then dressed and put him to bed, gave him an emetic, repeating the dose till I had given him twelve large teaspoonsful of the Third Preparation. It operated slowly after several hours. I then resumed the use of the medicine first prescribed. I gave freely of Nos. 2, 3, 4, 5, and 6; Nerve Powders, Stomachic Bitters, Conserve of Hollyhock and Golden Seal. I prepared bitters of equal parts of Golden Seal, Columbo Root, Nerve Powders, Unicorn Root, Balmony, Poplar Bark, with enough Bitter Root to obviate or remove costiveness, and Cayenne sufficient to make the medicine quite warm. This course I pursued, using alkalies, such as Pearlash, Sal Aeratus, &c, . . . I proceeded afterwards to take him through another full course of medicine, then resumed the treatment with tonics and stimulants as before." *Thomsonian Recorder*, II, 174 (Mar. 1, 1834).

By 1839 they claimed three million followers in the United States. The reasons for the popularity of Thomsonianism are fairly obvious. Its relative simplicity made a wide appeal. It linked up closely with Indian herb practice, belief in which was deep-seated in the minds of many people. The Thomsonians offered a solution to the problem of shortage of doctors, particularly in those regions where the population was growing rapidly. The ease with which a person might become a "doctor"—the purchase of a *New Guide* for $20—made practicing medicine possible for many who could not afford medical school or the cost of preceptorial training. The Botanics also cashed in upon the prejudice of the popular mind against the regular doctors. Certainly not the least among the appeals of Thomsonianism was its democracy. Many people had an innate distrust of "book larnin'," whether in their "public sarvints," their preachers, or their doctors. Medicine, following government and religion, was now placed in the hands of the people.

Naturally such a good thing as Thomsonianism—financially, at least—found it difficult to maintain its integrity. Heresy breeds heresy; there threatened to be as many prophets as followers, as many "schools" of botanic medicine as individual Botanics. Thomson's despotism was resented by many of his followers, even his own sons. Another cause of dissension was the question of schools. Active internal conflict began as early as 1827 when Dr. Wooster Beach, of New York, organized the "Eclectic" or "Reformed" system of botanic medicine. Another faction headed by Horton Howard, of Ohio, in 1832 established themselves as the "Improved Botanics," but with the death of their leader in the cholera epidemic the following year this offshoot began to disappear. Not until 1838, however, did a formal schism occur. In that year was formed the "Independent Thomsonian Botanic Society," headed by Dr. Alva Curtis;[144] the old guard became known as the "United States Thomsonian Society."

For a while three main groups of Botanics were apparent: the True Thomsonians, the Physiomedicals (Independents), and the Reformed Botanics or Eclectics. The True Thomsonians soon dropped the name of their founder and called themselves

[144] See Jonathan Forman, "Dr. Alva Curtis . . . ," in *Ohio Archaeological and Historical Society Publications*, LI (1942), 332–40.

simply Botanics. Many of their better members deserted to one of the other factions; by the time of the Civil War the Botanics, as an organization, had practically disappeared.

Curtis, meanwhile, was organizing his Independents into a new school of thought which he called Physiomedicalism, a system different in little more than name from the old Thomsonians. In practice, however, the Physiomedicals did believe in the necessity of establishing schools of training. Newspapers in the autumn of 1837 carried announcements for their school which was to be opened in Columbus. Prospects were considered good for a large class: "We are even informed that we shall be *honored with the presence of several M. D.'s. This is right and proper.*" Not until March, 1839, was the "Literary and Botanical-Medical Institute of Ohio" incorporated, with the powers of a university. The following autumn its medical department was opened as The College of Physicians and Surgeons, and in 1841 it moved to Cincinnati where it continued to exist under different names until 1885.

The third faction of Botanics, the "Eclectics" or "Reformists," was headed by Dr. Wooster Beach of New York who in 1827 set up a Reformed Medical Academy of New York, a school without a legislative charter. By 1829 arrangements were made with the Worthington [Ohio] College trustees, which permitted Beach to use their charter and set up his school in the West. In December of the following year the Worthington Reformed Medical College was opened. Under Dr. Thomas Vaughan Morrow the school prospered, until the townsfolk, enraged by the practice of students obtaining cadavers from the local burying grounds, wrecked Dr. Morrow's home and practically demolished the college. It then (1840) moved to Cincinnati where from 1845 to 1848 its enrollment was greater than that of any of the schools of the regulars.

Like the schools of the regulars, the Eclectic Institute was characterized by internal disagreement which at times threatened its existence. Particularly was this so after the death of Morrow. So antagonistic were the factions at one time that one group seized the building of the school, implanted a "six-pound" cannon in the hall, barricaded the doors and windows, and held out for two days and two nights against an opposition whose attack was finally broken up by the arrival of the police and mayor. After a court ruling had favored the defensive group, the offense set up its own school in other quarters, and not until some three years later was there effected a reconciliation between the two groups.[145]

A minor division of the Botanics were the Botanico-Medicals, whose origin and life history are not clear. In 1830 their strength was confined largely to three central Atlantic states and Ohio. A few years later they were prominent also in Indiana. The Bloomington *Medical Investigator*, apparently intended as their organ, ran for a few numbers in 1847. It reported the organization of various county societies, one with more than sixty members. Their system differed but slightly from that of the other Botanics; it embodied the usual impossible remedies garnished with a few sprigs of common sense.

Besides the various more or less classified Botanics there were some who simply called themselves "eclectics" (with a small "e"), and offered to use any system, regular or irregular. The patient—or if he were too ill to vote, his friends or relatives—was permitted to name his own poison; the eclectic would administer it. Considering the variety of choices—since hydropathy, vitapathy, homeopathy, and other practices soon had their followings—one is forced to admit the versatility of these accommodating doctors.[146]

However much the various groups of reformers of the Botanic tribe might differ among themselves, they usually stuck together in

[145] The period of uncertainty ended in 1862 with the coming of Dr. John M. Scudder, under whose firm hand the school became the leading medical college of Cincinnati in the 1880's.

Attempts had been made by both Morrow and Beach to organize the various factions of Botanics against their common enemy, the regulars, but they had not been entirely successful. A National Eclectic Medical Association existed from 1848 to 1857; it was revived in the 1870's, in which period Eclectic practice was at its height. That the Eclectic or Reformed practice lasted longer than any of the groups formed after the demise of pure Thomsonianism may be directly traced to the quality and training of its leaders.

[146] The period following 1840 was one of flux, confusion, and transition. It is impossible to keep track of the schisms, mergings, and crossings-over. Thomsonians not only became Eclectics, Physio-Medicals, and Botanics; some joined the regulars. In the records of the regular medical schools of the period are occasional references to applicants who had previously been Thomsonians. Others went over to the water-cure system, and a number took up homeopathy. On the other hand, at times the competition of "the People's Doctors" was so severe that the regular doctors were forced to adopt their methods or lose their own practice. Far more regulars became irregulars than one would realize from reading the formal medical histories of the period.

their struggles for equal legal rights and in criticism of the regulars. They accused the latter not only of bleeding arms but pocketbooks as well, and of endangering life by their poisonous mineral medicines. Ordinarily none too certain of their chemistry, anatomy, or materia medica, they were proud of their botanic orthodoxy, as was the old doctor who assured the newcomer from a medical college that he never administered any mineral medicine whatsoever except the iron in the "cast steel" soap from which he made his pills.

More than a few of the faint in heart adopted homeopathy, the "science of littles." The homeopaths sought to cure with remedies which would produce on a healthy person effects similar to the symptoms of the disease to be cured.[147] Infinitely small or diluted doses of medicine were held to be most potent physiologically. One critic of this idea said it was about as sensible as to expect even a German to be able to detect beer at the mouth of the River Spree after a glass had been spilled several miles upstream. Another critic compared the homeopaths to their doses: one figure of little value followed by a perfect battalion of ciphers. Still the system was said to have cured a hypochondriac who, believing himself a goose, had procured an egg and begun to set. " 'Like cures like' . . . it takes a goose to cure a goose! He [the doctor] ordered a pair of feather breeches to be worn by the patient and a dozen eggs. The spell and the eggs were broken together, and the patient was himself again. Very eggstraordinary, was it not?"[148] A Wisconsin practitioner said of homeopathy, "He who actually believes it, is an ignoramus. He who does not believe it and practices it is dishonest." They "amuse their patients with inert doses of medicines; they depend wholly upon rest or exercise as the case may be, dietary restrictions, and upon the natural resources of the system." Another regular critic charged, "Well, whosoever employeth a homeopathic doctor and is holpen thereby hath confessed hysterics already unto condemnation."

Some of the homeopathic medicines were quite thin as, for in-

[147] Homeopathy, formulated in Germany in the late eighteenth century by Samuel Christian Friedrich Hahnemann, was introduced into New York in 1825 by Hans Burch Gram. In 1836 the Allentown Academy, first of the American homeopathic schools, was chartered in Pennsylvania.

[148] *Cincinnati Lancet and Observer*, I (1858), 59–60.

stance, the pigeon soup made by hanging two pigeons in the kitchen window so that their shadow fell in a ten-gallon pot on the stove. After the shadow was boiled ten hours over a slow fire, one drop of the mixture was to be given in a glass of water every ten days. Since according to the theory of homeopathy every medicine, if sufficiently diluted and attenuated (Hahnemann thought the thirtieth dilution most efficacious, though he had carried the process of dilution on to a point where the resultant compound contained one-superbillionth of the original medicine), would become a deadly poison, some persons were pernickety enough to inquire what would be the effect of taking none at all.

In 1836 the first of many homeopathic practitioners in the Middle West, a Dr. Cope, was reported near Plymouth in Richland County, Ohio. Dr. Cope, whose treatment consisted of a single dose, repeated in two weeks in "radical" cases, was reputed to have had remarkable cures and a large practice. Soon a German doctor began practicing in Delaware County, Ohio, giving to his patients "very little pills," and in typhoid cases administering one dose, then returning at the end of a week "to see how it was working." Cincinnati's first homeopathic doctor was Dr. Wilhelm Sturm, a personal student of Hahnemann who set up shop there in 1839. He is said to have acquired a large practice and much fame throughout the Ohio Valley. The next year one of the founders of the Allentown Academy, Dr. Joseph H. Pulte,[149] came to Cincinnati.

A number of homeopaths were practicing in Kentucky in the late 1830's. When in 1840 Dr. I. G. Rosenstein published his *Theory and Practice of Homeopathy* at Louisville, he received letters of approbation from several local doctors, but he stated that "the whole *west* and *south* is still a barren field." In Wisconsin and Indiana homeopaths offered little real competition to the regulars until later in the century. In 1837 Dr. Samuel G. Mitchell, of Indianapolis, became a convert. "He tried to practice it here, but it was not popular at that time. People did not think they were getting enough for their money." Homeopathy did not appear in Michigan until 1843, when Dr. S. S. Hall was

---

[149] Among the books on homeopathy by Ohio doctors those by Dr. Pulte were outstanding. His *Homœopathic Domestic Physician*, published in 1850, and *Woman's Medical Guide*, 1853, were well known.

listed as the first doctor of this belief. By 1840 relatively few homeopaths were to be found in Illinois.[150]

In the period in which medicine was making the transition from a very uncertain art to a more or less exact science the internecine warfare in the profession was not only prolonged, but open and, like politics and religion, a matter of important public knowledge and concern. Although the main battle line was drawn between regulars and irregulars, with many participants and followers on both sides refusing to wear uniforms for fear of identifying themselves too certainly with what might be the losing army, there were innumerable battles and skirmishes within the ranks of each host.

However uncertain the regulars were regarding the tenets of their own faith, they did agree on two things: first, that medicine constituted a body of knowledge which required some little time and effort to assimilate; and second, that the integrity of the profession should be defended against any and all who sought to break it down.

Most irritating and obnoxious to them, because they were most numerous and aggressive, were the Botanics. The Botanics' contention that the mineral medicines of the regulars were poisons and that the patient was overcharged was bad enough, but the idea that humanity was being bettered by the administrations of every blacksmith or peddler who got a copy of Thomson, threw away the tools of his trade, and set up doctoring, was demoralizing. And in medicine, as in other fields, the task of combating ignorance with knowledge was a difficult one.

The regulars pointed out that it was certainly a stretching of the intent of the patent law of 1793 to take advantage of the words "or composition of matter" to include drugs and methods of curing disease. The hands of the more conservative and modest of the regulars were tied somewhat by the "ethics of the profession."[151]

Examples of the price paid for "quackery" were constantly printed and circulated. A contemporary letter pointed out the

[150] Homeopathy later reached the peak of its development in the Old Northwest in the region around Chicago where in the late 1850's 40 per cent of all the homeopaths in the world were said to have been located.

[151] Well presented, for example, in an article on the honor of the profession, danger of quacks, weakness of the law, etc., in *Sangamo Journal,* May 10, 1834.

danger of these "Unlicensed Doctors, alias Quacks." "It is one of the severest curses to a new settlement that quacks of every description find refuge there, but none do more mischief to society than the self-dubbed doctors, who in numerous herds deal death and destruction in the shape of pills, powders, tinctures, etc."[152] The "hot-stone steam system" received its share of blame for needless sacrifice of life. "When a few of them shall be convicted of murder or manslaughter and find their way to the halter or state's prison, the practice being found unprofitable, may be laid aside."[153]

A sense of humor, itself a critical sense, was an effective weapon, but most doctors were too worked up over the irregulars and "quacks" to use it; they could not see anything funny about the situation. Homeopathy, of course, with its doctrine of infinitesimals, affected the risibilities of pioneer wits, to say nothing of hydropathy, phrenology, vitapathy, and the like.

Ironically enough, even "quacks" attacked quacks. Anthony Hunn of Kentucky was furious in his attack against both mercury users and irregulars. He said he had seen calomel "cause the teeth, those valuable instruments of our most substantial enjoyments, to rot, perhaps fall out; and the upper and lower jaw bones to come out in the form of horse shoes!" Hunn said he used "analeptic equalizers," let his patients alone, and claimed eminent success. He appealed to the medical profession to supply information to the great mass of the people who were the prey of quackery. "Quacks, conjurers, Faith-doctors, Indians, Negroes, Cancer-women, etc., will be preferred only by a people bedizzened by ignorance and prejudice and at war with their own dearest interests."[154]

Perhaps the ballad on "Calomel" was written by some of Hunn's followers as propaganda against the regulars. One version had eleven stanzas and ended:

> The man in Death begins to groane
> The fatal job for him is done
> His soule is wing'd for heaven or hell
> A sacrifice to Calomel.

[152] "Observer," in *Edwardsville Spectator,* July 17, 1821.
[153] Ravenna (Ohio) *Western Courier,* August 20, 1825.
[154] Anthony Hunn, "An Essay on Bilious Fever and Calomel, etc.," reviewed in *Western Monthly Review,* II (1829), 465–67.

Physicians of my former choice
Receive my counsel and advice
Be not offended though I tell
The dire effects of Calomel.

And when I must Resign my breath
Pray let me die a natural death
And bid you all a long farewell
Without one dose of Calomel.[155]

More difficult to handle was the providential-humanitarian-uplift approach of the irregulars. Not only did Samuel Thomson have a "Call from Providence, and a degree from the God of Nature," but hydropathy, phrenology, mesmerism, Grahamism, and, to a certain extent, homeopathy got inevitably intertwined with the aura of Democracy, associationalism, eclectic love, and free-soulism. Though the followers of many of the more strenuous of these urges allowed themselves plenty of right of way on either side of the straight and narrow path of orthodox religion, they were never loath to call attention to the fact that their enemies were heathen and atheist. So with the irregular medicos.

Contributing to the common belief that the regular faculty were frequently unbelievers was the practice of dissection, considered by many as a desecration of God's highest work, the human body—the temple of man's soul. The charges regarding the morals and religion of the regulars were harder to meet than the criticisms of their medicines. Sometimes lecturers urged regulars to "embrace and revere the purity of Primitive Christianity; let it secure you against Infidel Sentiments." When in 1824 Dr. Charles Caldwell of Transylvania defended the medical profession on the basis of natural religion, as important and as God-given as revealed religion, his address was considered heretical, that of a freethinker.[156]

[155] Brewster (ed.), *Ballads and Songs of Indiana,* 309–10. That calomel was not without its defenders is illustrated by lines "Written During a Bilious Attack," which ended:

"Then Calomel, thou great deliverer! come;
Purge from my eye this ochre hue,
And clear my head again;
Make me benevolent and true
And just to other men;
And the first worthy deed I do,
I'll own, O Calomel! my virtue is from you."
Western Monthly Magazine, I (1833), 304.

[156] *Western Monthly Review,* I (1827), 155–57. Caldwell's *Introductory Address on Independence of Intellect* was published at Lexington in 1825. He also defended

As frontier communities settled—often promoted by a land boomer—lawyers and doctors of doubtful qualifications hurried in; sometimes the doctor and preacher were brought by the promoter as an additional talking point. Though these unlicensed doctors might be "the pest of regular practitioners, the tools of knaves, and the bane of society," as the more intelligent people were aware, the majority of the people often defended them on the same grounds that they opposed legislation which required stock owners to fence in their animals: such legislation was class legislation in favor of those who owned improved bulls, and the services of free scrub bulls were better than no bulls at all. So with medical regulation; it would protect a vested interest.

The problem of regulation of doctors was an old one. The Code of Hammurabi, as well as others of ancient times, contained provisions regarding fees and malpractice, and the Salic law of the Franks had medical provisions, such as "If any one have given herbs to another so that he die, he shall be sentenced to 200 shillings (or shall surely be given over to fire)." The whole subject of legal regulation of licensing of doctors was intimately involved with the organization of, and qualifications for membership in, the medical societies.

In Ohio, largely through the efforts of Dr. Samuel P. Hildreth, of Marietta, a law was enacted in 1811 which divided the state into five medical districts, in each of which a board of three censors or examiners was to be appointed by the General Assembly. The boards were to satisfy themselves as to the moral character and medical knowledge of the applicant for license. Unlicensed physicians were not forbidden to practice, but could not use legal processes to collect fees. A year later licensing privileges were put into the hands of the President and Fellows of the Medical Society of the State of Ohio and the state was divided into seven medical districts for administration. The names of one hundred twenty physicians were written into the law. (At the first "convention," at Chillicothe, November, 1812, only five delegates appeared, whereas the law required ten; it

the teaching of Natural Religion at Transylvania in a written debate with Dr. James Fishback, pastor of the First Baptist Church of Lexington. *The Correspondence Between Dr. Charles Caldwell—and Dr. James Fishback . . . ,* was printed at Lexington in 1826, as was Caldwell's *Medical and Physical Memoirs.* His *Autobiography* was published in Philadelphia in 1855, the second year after his death.

adjourned sine die.) By this law those who practiced without licenses not only could not use the law to collect fees, but were subject to fines of from $5.00 to $100 for each offense. Fines levied were to be shared by the informant and the medical societies. The fines were changed by subsequent laws.

The next General Assembly repealed this law and returned to the law of 1811. Between 1813 and 1821 the law was amended, repealed, and re-enacted at least three times. In 1818 graduates of recognized medical institutions were made eligible to licenses without examination. By law in 1821 each of the nine circuits of the courts of common pleas was constituted into a medical district, and in each district a board of five censors was appointed to examine medical candidates annually. The board also was to elect a delegate to the Medical Convention of Ohio, a corporate body, which was to meet annually at Columbus, and be given exclusive power to license candidates and prescribe "periods and methods of study and the qualifications of candidates." After five medical conventions were held, the legislature gave up; in 1833, largely as a result of the botanic lobby, it repealed all laws for the regulation of physicians and surgeons.[157] Some carping criticism questioned the right of the legislature to regulate medical practice, but the attitude of the regulars of the profession was that it had the same right as to regulate marriage.[158] Such right, however, seemed to mean little, since irregular practice thrived. Not until 1896 was anything like effective regulation undertaken.[159]

The law having failed to effect medical organizations, it was left to the doctors to take action. Frequently they disagreed when they tried to do so. For instance in the summer of 1821 when proposals were made for a Cincinnati Medical Association which might standardize fees and establish professional standards, a member of the faculty of the Ohio Medical College argued against it. "Justice" in a letter to the *Liberty Hall and*

[157] *Laws of Ohio*, 1810–11, pp. 19–23; 1811–12, pp. 58–65; 1812–13, pp. 28–33; 1817–18, pp. 105–6; 1820–21, pp. 28–35; 1832–33 (general), p. 27.

[158] Letter in reply to criticism, in *Ohio State Journal*, December 28, 1826. The first medical convention adopted a set of stiff requirements among which were good moral character, knowledge of Greek, Latin, and "Mechanical Philosophy, two years practice with some reputable physician and at least one course of lectures from some 'respectable Medical Institution.'" Worthington *Franklin Chronicle*, July 2, 1821.

[159] Donald D. Shira, "The Legal Requirements for Medical Practice" [in Ohio], in *Ohio Archaeological and Historical Society Publications*, XLVIII (1939), 188.

Cincinnati Gazette particularly attacked the proposal that members of the Association not consult with doctors who were non-members. Other criticisms followed. Similar arguments and differences were encountered by most of the early attempts at forming medical societies.

The "Medical Conventions of Ohio" were open to all regular physicians from 1835 to 1851; membership was "individual" and voluntary. Notice of the first triennial meeting "To be holden . . . January 1, 1838" appeared in the Columbus *Daily Journal and Register*. The object was "organization, advancement and elevation of the Medical Profession as well as the promotion of objects of general benevolence." All "Scientific Practitioners of Medicine and Surgery" of Ohio were invited, also "Brethren from the sister States who can make it convenient." In 1846 the Ohio State Medical Society was organized. In the early years a large part of its work had to do with encouraging the formation of, and passing upon the requirements of, the local or auxiliary societies. About a dozen of these were functioning by 1850. Despite urgent requests on the part of the state society, these societies were still largely indifferent and dilatory in furnishing reports on membership, papers read, and actions taken.

In Indiana the First General Assembly made each of the three judicial districts into a medical district and provided for boards of censors to regulate the practice of physic and surgery, examine candidates, grant licenses, and fix fees. The members of each board of censors were named in the statute. Persons who showed qualifications and "reasonable evidence of their moral character" were to be admitted to the "board" of their district, a body "corporate and politic." No person not a member of these "boards" (local societies) could have the benefit of the law for collecting any charges. An act of 1819 excepted from this provision any person who was already practicing in the state in 1816. The same act provided for a state medical society with powers to license physicians. Any person who practiced without a license from the state society (or a district society in the interim) was subject to a fine of from $10 to $20 for the first offense, and double thereafter. The money so collected was to go to the state society for the promotion of medical science. (By amendment in 1823 it was switched to the county seminaries.)

Following the law of 1816 the censors of the first district met at Vincennes in June, 1817, examined five candidates, and organized the board for the district. At the meeting in May, 1819, two delegates were selected by ballot to meet with those from the two other districts to form a state medical society. At the same meeting it was resolved that no person be admitted to examination before the censors if he could not produce satisfactory evidence of having "studied physic and surgery for the full term of three years"; also a committee was appointed to choose a delegate to meet in convention to formulate a district pharmacopoeia.[160]

Although delegates had been appointed in 1819 to form a state medical society, it was not until the following year that an organization was effected. Just why the setup under the 1819 law was unsatisfactory is not clear, but at any rate in 1825 another law provided all over again for the organization of the Medical Society of the State of Indiana; a quorum of five representatives of the county societies was empowered to create this body. From the wording of the law ("the society when thus formed") it would appear that no society was formed under the law in 1819. This time the society was given the additional power to establish "a uniform system of the course and time of medical study" to qualify for license.

How effective this was may be judged from the law of 1830 which said that "owing to defects in the law regulating the practice of physic in this state, the medical societies which now exist, have never been legally organized, and the provisions of the act are such as do not induce a large portion of qualified physicians to become members of any medical society, or sufficiently to guard against licensing unqualified men to practise medicine. . . ."

To remedy these evils the law legalized the existing societies when they should file their names and officers with the proper county recorders; all powers granted by the law of 1825 were extended to them; and all licenses granted by them in the interim were recognized. It was provided that after one year no person not regularly licensed in Indiana, or in an adjoining state of

[160] *Laws of Indiana*, 1816–17, pp. 161–65; 1818–19, pp. 77–78; 1822–23, p. 118; Leon Zerfas, *Indiana Medicine in Retrospect* (reprinted from *Journal of the Indiana State Medical Society*, XXIX [1936]), 10–12.

which he was a resident, or not "at the passage of this act a resident practitioner of medicine in this State" could recover anything by law for medical services. But there was a big "Provided": nothing in the act was "to affect the right of females to practice midwifery, or apothecaries or others not professing to prescribe or practise medicine, from selling medicine and recovering payment therefor."[161]

This last section had the effect of leaving the state wide open to whosoever wished to engage in medical practice; farmers, blacksmiths, and others frequently tried their hands at it.

Local medical societies continued to exist, but though notices of their meetings appeared in the newspapers, one surmises from the frequent "reorganizations" that attendance was small and interest languishing. The Indiana State Medical Society was revived in 1849 and its continuous existence dates from that year.

Illinois, too, started off with an impressive paper effort. In 1817, since "well regulated medical societies have been found to contribute to the diffusion of true science and particularly to the knowledge of the healing art," the Territory was divided into two medical districts by a meridian running north from the mouth of the Ohio. The medical society of each was empowered to examine students and grant diplomas. After organization of the societies no one was to practice physic or surgery without a diploma; the penalty was disqualification "forever after" from use of the law for collecting any debts incurred by such unauthorized practice. Practicing rights of those who came into Illinois Territory with licenses from their former states were recognized. Assessments of $10 each upon members of the societies were authorized "for the purpose of procuring a medical library and apparatus, and for the encouragement of useful discoveries in chemistry, botany, and such other improvements as the majority of the society shall think proper."

In 1819 the first General Assembly divided the state into four medical districts in each of which was to be "held a board of physicians." These boards or societies when organized were to examine students and present diplomas. Persons who did not have diplomas from medical schools or who had not previously

---

[161] *Laws of Indiana*, 1818–19, pp. 77–78; 1825, pp. 36, 40; 1829–30, pp. 91–93.

practiced in the state had either to pass an examination before a society or be disqualified from collecting any fees by use of the courts. All physicians were required by this law to render to the president of the medical society of his district "a true and accurate record of all the births, deaths and diseases which may take place within the vicinity of his practice." Any physician who refused to attend the state meetings of the said societies was to be fined $5.00.

That this law was not enforced may be concluded from the fact that, under the law of 1825, which divided the state into five districts, the "practicing physicians" of each district were authorized to elect a censor. The five censors so selected were to meet at Vandalia in November and form a board to examine candidates and grant licenses. Those with medical school diplomas or licenses from any "respectable medical society" were not required to submit to examination. Once the board of censors was organized it could certify the censor and physicians of each district, or their appointees, to conduct the examinations. Any person who practiced physic contrary to the provisions of this law was subject to a fine of $20, which was to go to the county poor fund.

Only about twenty persons attended the first meeting of the "Illinois Medical Society" (the board of censors) which was held at Vandalia in November. Most of these were applicants for licenses.

The law of 1825, in its last section, provided that the board of censors lay before the next General Assembly a plan for a permanent system of licensing. If they did so, nothing came of it, for on January 25, 1826, the legislature repealed the law of 1825 and no further legislation for this purpose was passed until 1877.[162]

In 1819 the Governor and Judges of Michigan Territory incorporated the Medical Society of Michigan. When a quorum, not less than four in number, of physicians then practicing in the Territory, should meet and organize, the society would constitute a corporate entity. The society was given the right to elect by ballot two new members each year from physicians residing

---

[162] *Laws of Illinois Territory*, 1817–18, pp. 21–25; *Laws of Illinois*, 1819, pp. 233–35; 1824–25, pp. 111–13; Vandalia *Illinois Intelligencer*, November 18, 1825.

in the Territory. County societies were authorized to be formed in the same manner. Physicians who became members were to be excused from jury service and militia duties in time of peace. No person, unless duly certified in another state, was to commence the practice of physic or surgery until he be examined and certified by one of the societies established by this law. No society was to examine any candidate until he furnished testimony that he had studied with a respectable practitioner for the full term of three years. If any candidate felt he did not get just consideration from one of the county societies, he might present himself to the society of the Territory of Michigan. Any one who practiced contrary to the provisions of this law was to be liable to a fine of $25 for each offense and forbidden to use the courts to collect fees for services.

In 1825 an amendment prescribed four years of study, after the age of sixteen, "with a regular physician and surgeon," but one year of classical studies or one course of lectures at a medical college might be counted as one year of this preparation. Physicians from outside the Territory were required to file a copy of their diplomas or certificates with the society of the county where they practiced. Another amendment in 1829 declared that any person who practiced medicine outside the provisions of the law should be deemed guilty of a misdemeanor, punishable by a fine not to exceed $100, imprisonment up to six months, or both.

In 1838 an elaborate law re-enacted many of the provisions of the law of 1819. County societies already created were recognized. The penalty for unlicensed practice was merely to be denial of court procedure for collecting fees.[163] After due notice, and filing of evidence in writing, licenses of physicians might be annulled for "infamous crimes, habitual drunkenness, or gross ignorance or incompetency," by a two-thirds vote of the members present of a county society.

In 1843 the penalties of the law of 1838 for unlicensed practice were repealed, but if "any person who proposes to be a physician or surgeon, or shall hold himself out to the public or

[163] *Revised Statutes of Michigan*, 1838, pp. 172–78. Dr. Laertus Conner in an address before the Michigan Medical Society in June, 1902, said that fines for unlicensed practice were eliminated by this law. Burr, *Medical History of Michigan*, II, 398.

any person employing him to be such," should be guilty of neglect or malpractice, action might be had at common law.

Three years later (1846) a law of thirty-seven sections went through the whole business once more of erecting a state medical society, county societies, and fixing their powers to examine and license. Section 36 declared unlicensed practice a misdemeanor punishable with one year's jail sentence and a fine of $1,000, or both.[164] This section was repealed by law in 1851. In 1849 the supreme court of the state had, in the case of *Sulton* v. *Facey*, refused to decide who was a doctor.[165]

Wisconsin in 1841 incorporated the Medical Society of the Territory of Wisconsin and provided for the organization of county societies along the general model of those set up by law in Michigan, from which it had recently been separated. Yet in 1883 the secretary of the Wisconsin State Board of Health wrote: "I do not know how the impression has gone abroad, as it has, that we have a law regulating the practice of medicine, for we have none."

Such a statement would have been substantially correct, as far as results were concerned, for any state in the Middle West prior to the Civil War. The laws cited above serve as samples for the region; they are evidences of intent rather than records of accomplishment in determining who was a doctor. The story was about the same in the states bordering the Old Northwest. The organization of the American Medical Association in 1846 was supposed to stimulate and strengthen the movement for state societies and regulation. In 1850 a meeting was held at Cincinnati and the 1859 meeting was at Louisville. Although influential in encouraging organization of state societies, the national association had no important immediate effect in tightening state regulation in the West.

The penalties of fines were seldom, if ever, enforced. The usual penalty on irregulars of not being able to use the courts to collect fees meant little; the regulars could not collect their fees even with the aid of the courts. For all practical purposes, anybody was a "doctor" who called himself a doctor.

[164] *Laws of Michigan*, 1843, pp. 41–42; *Revised Statutes of Michigan*, 1846, pp. 168–73.
[165] *Sulton* v. *Facey*, 1 *Manning*, 243.

§ § § §

Prevalence of superstition and practice of charm cures were, after all, largely negative evils. But with the growth of the traffic in patent medicines there came a positive menace, and one which a hundred years of education in the era of science have not been able to eradicate. Strange as it may seem, times the rise of the patent-medicine business was synchronous with, and dependent upon, the development of education and the newspaper. The schools made it possible to read, the newspaper furnished something to read. The newspaper made the patent-medicine business, and the medicine advertisements sustained the newspaper.[166]

Most "patent" medicines never did have patents; rather they were proprietary medicines, possibly invented or concocted by the person whose name was attached, but more often only sold under that name. Since a patent served to convey the idea of government sanction, perhaps recommendation even, peddlers of proprietaries, either by direct statement or implication, sought to create the notion that their particular product was a patented medicine. Though by and large possessed of a fair sense of appreciation of the ludicrous—himself a lover and creator of tall tales—the pioneer could get taken in by his own badger fight. Change the name of the game, take it out of his immediate experience—after all, the word in print was hard to get around. The bigger the lie the harder to disprove. Allowing a discount of 90 per cent, there still remained enough potency in the cure-all to warrant a try. Besides, the pitchmen had put on a good show; the artist was worthy of his hire. If his product did not cure rheumatism or sweeny, it might clean a copper kettle or soften a pair of stiff boots.

The ailing pioneer, uncured by home remedies or local quacks,

[166] The only other considerable source of income of the country newspaper was the public printing—laws, notices, etc. In the *Hamilton* (Ohio) *Intelligencer* in 1840, a seven-column, four-page sheet, two columns of page one and seven columns of page four were patent-medicine advertisements. The editor later announced that the big Evans Fever and Ague Pills advertisement would be reduced so as to give more room for reading matter; he frankly admitted such ads were necessary to maintain the paper. Otherwise country newspapers would need a circulation of two thousand instead of a few hundred. "The bones are sold with the beef." June 18, November 6, 1840. A Fort Wayne editor *pro tem.* in 1847 noted that "Every village newspaper from the North to the South, and from the East to the West, is filled with their trash." When the regular editor returned, he repudiated not only the political blunders made by his understudy, but the *faux pas* in connection with advertising policy as well. *Fort Wayne Times and People's Press,* August 21, September 11, 1847.

was ever willing to place his trust in the promises of the wonderful elixirs and cure-alls which came in bottles. The word in print carried more authority than word of mouth. Advertisements picked at random from any newspaper will serve as samples of the hundreds that appeared weekly in the period between 1815 and 1840. A three-column advertisement in the *Western Sun* of July 15, 1815, proclaimed the virtues of the thirteen patent medicines of Dr. T. W. Dyott, M. D., of Philadelphia, guaranteed to cure anything from gout to female disorders.[167] Dr. J. Shinn advertised Dr. Swaim's Panacea, good for scrofula or King's Evil, ulcered or putrid sore throat, skin and bone diseases of ulcerous character, syphilis, etc. Testimonials were appended from two members of the faculty of the University of Pennsylvania.[168] LaMott's cough drops, "peculiarly adapted to the present prevailing disorders of the lungs leading to consumptions," Vegetable Rheumatic Drops, Dr. Felix's celebrated Liver Pills, Hay's liniment for dropsy, swelling, sores, and rheumatism, Morrison's Pills—a sure remedy for diseases running from consumption to epilepsy—Dr. Peter's pills for fevers and the blood,[169] Hepatica Triloba for coughs, consumption, and liver complaints, and Dr. Fahnestock's Vermifuge, which could be

[167] See also *Illinois Intelligencer,* September 23, 1825, etc.

[168] Vincennes *Western Sun and General Advertiser,* June to December, 1824; *Hamilton Intelligencer and Advertiser,* May, 1824 ff. According to Dr. Drake, "Dr." Swaim was a saddler and harnessmaker of New York who from contacts with ostlers and farriers got the urge to become a doctor. Having obtained some sort of recipe proposed by a French physician, he moved to Philadelphia and began to advertise his panacea at $3.00 per bottle. He sent an agent to England and soon laudatory notices of the medicine appeared in Liverpool and elsewhere. One of the emphasized virtues of this medicine was its efficacy in curing diseases incurred by taking too much mercury (calomel). When it was revealed that Swaim's cure-all, besides borage, senna, and sassafras, contained corrosive sublimate, the strongest of the mercurial preparations, the popularity of his medicine waned somewhat, but it continued to be sold for many years. Daniel Drake, "The People's Doctors," in *Western Journal of Medical and Physical Sciences,* III (1830), 416.

[169] Dr. Peter claimed to be graduated from Yale College and the Medical College of Berkshire, Massachusetts, and combined literature with his science:
"The King of terrors looked a while,
As though his soul was turned to bile,
At that unsparing scourge of ills
By all men known as Peter's Pills.
The Pills of Peter's stop the slaughter
And leave the blood as pure as water.
Now Peter makes, I've heard him say,
Five hundred thousand Pills a day,
So that the chance is very small
Of People dying there at all,
For soon the cheeks so marked for doom
Begin like any rose to bloom."

safely administered to the tenderest infant, were a few of the widely advertised remedies. The patent of Dr. Galleckes of Germany, "The Greatest of Human Benefactors," possessed triple powers derived from the vegetable, animal, and mineral kingdoms, and by filling the vacuum in the materia medica, proved the conqueror of physicians. Dr. Rafinesque contributed his Pulmel for "Curing and Preventing the Consumption or Chronic Phthisis."[170] This was available in syrup, balsam, balsamic syrup, lotion, or milk, wine, sweet chocolate in cakes or liquid, sugar, honey, lozenges, powders, and pulmelin or concentrated salt.

Two very important new medicinal discoveries of the 1830's were "Kreosot" and the tomato. The former, it was found, would resist putrefaction and preserve meat. Soon it was being recommended for both external and internal use; for sores and wounds it was the best remedy known. "People afflicted with the dreadful disease cancer, after having been despaired of by the most skilful physicians, have been completely cured by Kreosot."[171]

The lowly tomato rapidly rose from its position as a doubtful comestible to that of a sort of dietary and medicinal panacea. Doctors began to promote it vigorously. Dr. Bennet, Professor of Midwifery, Hygiene, and Acclimatement at the Medical College of Lake Erie, was no more enthusiastic than many others when he stated that the tomato was one of the most powerful deobstruents of the materia medica, and in certain liver affections probably the most effective and least harmful agent known. It would prevent bilious attacks, serve as a remedy for dyspepsia, was successful in treating diarrhea, and would render one less liable to cholera. It should be eaten daily, raw or cooked.[172] The medicine men were right up with, if not ahead of, the doctors. Phelps' Compound Tomato Pills, Dr. Miles' Compound Extract of Tomato, and other brands were advertised as substitutes for calomel and "peculiarly adapted to the treatment of *bilious fevers*

[170] *The Pulmist; or, Introduction to the Art of Curing and Preventing the Consumption or Chronic Phthisis* (Philadelphia, 1829). For details of the life of this eccentric character, see Richard Ellsworth Call, *The Life and Writings of Rafinesque* (*Filson Club Publications*, No. X, Louisville, 1895). Some of Rafinesque's ideas on medicine are also contained in his *Medical Flora*.

[171] *Vandalia Whig*, October 23, 1834.

[172] *Ohio Farmer and Western Horticulturist* (Columbus), August 1, October 1, 1835; *Cincinnati Daily Gazette*, August 29, 1837, September 16, 1839.

and other diseases in which a *torpidity* or congestion of the *liver* and *portal circle* prevail," at prices somewhat higher than a modern bottle of catsup. In fact, Extract of Tomato was "undoubtedly one of the most valuable articles ever offered for public trial and inspection." From poison to panacea in five years—yet this rapid inflation did not spoil the tomato, a previtamin vitamin which ultimately made good on its merits.

Dr. Robertson's "Stomachic Elixir of Health," Dr. Godbold's "Vegetable Balsam of Life," Carter's fluid extract of Sarsaparilla, Evans' Camomile Pills, Resurrection or Persian Pills for fever, ague, pregnancy, etc., and the famous Extract of Wa-ahoo, an Indian medicine for consumption, all had their devotees.

The medicine ads seldom made a direct appeal to the babies. Their mothers were reminded, however, that Irish Moss was "valuable as a diet for infants afflicted with Debility, Derangement of the Stomach, and for those brought up by hand or after weaning." If babies were restless and their mothers aware of the dangers of too frequent use of soothing syrups which contained opium—which they probably were not—a harmless substitute was recommended: smear baby's fingers with thick molasses, then put half a dozen feathers into its hands. The youngster would pluck feathers from hand to hand until it dropped asleep. When it awakened, supply more molasses and feathers.

A medicine had to be good to compete with Merchants' Celebrated Gargling Oil for Man and Beast, which was deservedly popular in the cure of "Spavins, Sweeney, Chapped Hands, Cake Breasts, Sore Nipples, Piles, &c." (No testimonials from the horses were attached.) Hemmbold's Genuine Preparation of Highly Concentrated Compound Fluid Extract of Buchnu was a "joy to the afflicted. . . . Beware of Quack Nostrums and Quack Doctors." Dr. Sappington's Vegetable Febrifuge Pills—a simple treatment for a simple disease; Farr's Ague Tonic; Beckwith's Anti-Dyspepsic; Dr. Taylor's Balsam of Liverwort; French Jejube Paste, "a valuable article"; Stout's Highly Improved . . . or Great Western Fever Panacea; Dr. Chipman's Vegetable Blood Purifier; McLean's Strengthening Cordial Blood Purifier—illustrated by before-and-after-taking pictures; Dr. Guysott's Extract of Yellow Dock; Wistar's Balsam of Wild Cherry; Dr. Phillips' Diarrhoea Syrup; Moffat's Vegetable Life Pills and

Phoenix Bitters; Dr. Duponco's Golden Periodical Pills for Females; Dr. R. Thompson's Pelvic Corset; Jayne's Hair Tonic and Expectorant; Carthusian Cough Drops; Bartholomew's Pink Expectorant Syrup; Circassian Lymph for pimples, scurvy, and rash; Dr. Baker's Specific—for seminal weakness and venereal diseases, "may be used by either sex with entire secrecy"—all were offered by the newspapers.

Dr. M. S. Watson's Great Invincible Birgharmi Stiff Joint Panacea, discovered on the Nile, "has astonished every beholder, and no discovery in Medicine since the day of the illustrious Hippocrates, is probably equal in amount of usefulness to the one under consideration." In one six-month period it had cured 8,300 cases of stiff joints, chronic rheumatism, white swelling, contracted spinal cords, and gout, a record which paled before that of Dr. Townsend's Sarsaparilla, "The Wonder and Blessing of the Age, the most extraordinary Medicine in the World," which in a five-year period cured 100,000 persons, including 15,000 incurables, or Dr. Easterly's Iodine and Sarsaparilla which within three years cured more than 25,000 severe cases of disease: 3,000 of scrofula, 2,000 dyspepsia and indigestion, 1,000 gout and chronic inflammatory rheumatism, 2,000 general debility, 2,500 liver complaint, dropsy, and gravel, 1,500 different forms of female complaint, and 6,000 of syphilitic or venereal coughs, pimples, salt rheum, and headaches.

Attempts to supplant the old family bottle of bitters were made by Dr. Lin's Temperance Life-Bitters and Chinese Blood Pills. (The Chinese lived to "such immense ages" because they purified their blood.) Time and space forbade the listing of all the brilliant effects of this medicine, even by the proprietor. But beware! "FRAUDULENT COUNTERFEITS will be attempted." Then there was Dr. John Bull's Great American King, truly a sovereign remedy, which ruled its subjects from the principal office in Louisville. In comparison "the power of the crowned heads of Europe sink into insignificance . . . European Kings employ the power vested in them to increase the riches of the rich and lordly, and to reduce to greatest misery and degradation, the poor and dependent. Our American King goes forth with equal willingness to the lordly mansion and humble cabin, ready alike to administer relief and to offer health and happiness to the lofty and lowly the rich and poor." This medicine, "The Tenth Wonder of the World," was at the people's command. "All those who still suffer, and will not accept the proffered Balm, deserve not the pity of their families."

The famous Hygeian Vegetable widely advertised in the 1830's was recommended as a cure for consumptions, cholera morbus, inflammation, dyspepsia, fevers, ague, indigestion, diseases of the liver, gout, rheumatism, lumbago, dropsy, St. Vitus dance, epilepsy, apoplexy, paralysis, green sickness, smallpox, measles, whooping cough, and syphilis—in fact for all complaints and disorders to which the flesh was heir.[173] In use, also, was crude oil (petroleum), which marketed as "American Oil" was widely used for rheumatism, consumption, dyspepsia, colic, and wounds. Jew David's or Hebrew Plaster had no equal in the world for removing all seated pains, whether in the joints, back, or breast, "also corns, wens and humours." These products, with scores of other "Balsams," "Expectorants," "Vegetable Compounds," pills, liniments, syrups, elixirs, compounds, and tonics adorned the pages of the papers or were peddled by pitchmen and "professors." Many were nationally advertised, whereas others were local discoveries.

Doctors and medical societies might protest and cry out against such fraud and quackery, but the rantings and ravings of the "medicine men" were not to be stifled or their products eliminated, as the long life of many of these remedies and the ample fortunes of their promoters bear witness. Even the newspapers, possibly not yet sufficiently commercialized to be muzzled, reprinted articles from eastern papers and added their own warnings against the dangers of the great gullibility on the part of the people:

However lenient we are at present with respect to the notorious, illiterate empirics, that infest this country, more care was taken formerly, of the

---

[173] A Dr. Gallopore who advertised in the *Pittsburgh Statesman* that he could cure "all disorders incident to the human body, without exception, no matter what may be the age, circumstances, or place of residence of the afflicted patients," did not even need to see the patients, but merely know the precise time of their birth. By his pills he could cure all accidents, including those persons supposedly scalded to death by the bursting of boilers, struck by lightning, injured by fallen trees, etc., and could keep anyone in perfect health so he could drink two gallons of alcohol per day (which, said the editor of the *Cleaveland Herald,* was almost as bad as so much new whiskey). *Cleaveland Herald,* June 11, 1829. "Absolutely certain" cures for cancer were widely advertised.

Peoples constitutions, and their health was not suffered to be infected by these poisoners of whole countries.

· ·

Any idle mechanic, not caring longer to drudge at day labor, by chance gets a dispensatory, or some old receipt book, and poring over it, or having i: read to him (for many of these present doctors cannot read), he finds that mercury is good for the itch, and old ulcers; that opium will give ease; and that a glass of antimony will vomit.

Down goes the hammer, or the saw, razor, awl, or shuttle—and away to work to make electuaries, tinctures, elixirs, pills, plasters, and poultices . . .

. . . hundreds of little infants are yearly destroyed by the very remedies the unhappy parents were prevailed on to administer in order to destroy these supposed worms, which never existed but in their brains.

Cobblers now set up for regular-bred physicians; hacney coachmen and barbers for anatomist & natural philosophers; washer women for chymists; tumblers . . . and scavengers, for bone-setters, and occulists, c&. Nothing can equal the ignorance of such empirics but the stupidity of those people who buy their unwholesome preparations.[174]

§ § § § §

In spite of the diseases and heavy mortality, births exceeded deaths, and population increased. Early marriages and large families were the rule, for a young man could support a family as soon as he could do a man's work on the farm. Said a western congressman in 1824:

Why sir, you may visit the humblest cottage in our country, and you will find everything to admire. So soon as the faithful dog, by his saluting bark, announces that a stranger is coming, your astonishment would commence; you would have the singular felicity of beholding a most delightful spectacle —about twelve or thirteen fine, ruddy, well-formed, hearty-looking young *Democrats,* would run out to see the stranger; and upon entering the house, you would be met by a very plain, unaffected woman, to all appearances about thirty years old, whose countenance would at once tell you to make yourself easy; you would meet with kindness, and, in casting your eyes around, you would see two more little fellows, who were too small to run out at the first alarm.[175]

This case was probably no more typical than the description was accurate, yet it indicates an ideal or culture trait of the time. Politicians and statesmen thought of votes, man power, increas-

---

[174] *Western Sun and General Advertiser,* July 6, 1826.
[175] Robert P. Letcher, in *Annals of Congress,* 18 Congress, 1 session, 2325.

ing wealth. Some parents thought of children as economic assets, others took seriously the injunction to be fruitful and multiply, or took pride in their large broods as evidences of virility and social standing; many gave the matter little or no thought. At any rate children came in almost annual crops. In the journals and reminiscences of the period, records for the most part from the more advanced and articulate classes, the prayers for large families are usually followed by a depressing record of early deaths.[176]

As for the poorer and less responsible folk, they were troubled neither by "imperative duties," nor post-mortem introspection.

Births, weddings, funerals—episodes in the simple annals of the lesser folk, events in the lives of their betters. For many of the pioneer women, rugged and accustomed to hard physical labor, childbirth was not an event to interfere seriously with the routine of life.[177] Often far from the services of a doctor when her time came, the wife was dependent upon the help of neighbors, among whom there probably would be one who made profession to midwifery.[178] Nevertheless, when added to the other hardships of life, the burden of too frequent childbearing and inexpert attention usually exacted its penalty. All too many women lost their bloom with their teens, were tired out and run down by thirty, and old at forty. Tombstones in the churchyards bear testimony that many a wife died young, to be followed by a second who contributed her quota and labors, and perhaps a third who stood a good chance to outlive the husband.[179]

[176] See, for example, "Autobiography of Abel Mills," in *Journal of the Illinois State Historical Society,* XIX (1926–27), 94–239 *passim.*

[177] Instances are told of outdoor births in the winter, after which the mother carried the child several miles to shelter, neither the worse off for the experience.

[178] Some of these midwives or neighbors as well as pioneer doctors were very skillful at child delivery. Puerperal infections and other dangers which have to be so carefully guarded against in modern hospitals were rare. One practice which was used to expedite matters in hard cases was "quilling." A little dry snuff blown through a goose quill into the nostrils of the mother would bring on a sneezing paroxysm. This in turn sometimes effected the desired results. Babies so introduced into the world might be spoken of years later as "Quilled Babies."

[179] By way of idealization of the "good old days": "Mothers rejoiced rather than mourned, as they are apt to do nowadays. Then a mother's joys were her children, now they are in the way of these gay women, who want cards and society; in the way of these poorer ones who think they can't provide for them. Have devoted mothers, like many other things, gone out of style? Lord, send a reform to the women of today! Bring them back to the life of the good-sized family circle of boys and girls. . . . Oh, Lord, bring my beloved land back to home life and motherhood again." "Autobiography of Clarissa Gear Hobbs," in *Journal of the Illinois State Historical Society,* XVII (1924–25), 620–21. Mrs. Hobbs was born

Babies being no rarity, they received no special attention: they were raised, not reared. The same rule of thumb or trial and error methods that applied to crops or cattle were good enough. The science of infant care was not yet, and instead of a vitamin, baby got a bacon rind, sometimes attached to a string so that when accidentally swallowed it might be recovered. When weaned, usually by the almanac, youngsters began to eat corn bread, biscuits, and "pot likker" like grown-ups. The fittest survived, and the rest "the Lord seen fitten to take away."[180]

Even among people of means there was a certain carelessness regarding health. Quite modern was the description—not to be taken too seriously—of practice of some of the young ladies:

Again, young ladies at school, and sometimes with their parents, will resolve to become extremely pale, from a notion that it looks interesting. For this purpose, they will substitute for their natural food, pickles of all kinds, powdered chalk, vinegar, burnt coffee, pepper and other spices, especially cinnamon and cloves; others will add to these paper, of which many sheets are sometimes eaten in a day; and this is persisted in till the natural appetite for wholesome food is superceded by a depraved and morbid desire for everything but that which is nutritious; cordials and bitters are then sometimes resorted to, in a vain attempt to restore the healthy tone of the stomach, till at least, the cheeks, originally pale—for fresh and blooming colour is very rare in the complexions even of the healthiest and youngest in America— become death-like in their hue, the whole frame withers, and a premature grave receives the unhappy victim. So indifferent, however, are parents to the welfare of their children, or so unable or unwilling are they to exercise parental authority to check this evil in the bud, that they look on, if not without disapprobation, at least without any vigorous effort to avert the evil; . . . Such practices as these, added to the other causes, . . . sufficiently account for the decayed and decaying state of health among the female population of the United States.[181]

---

in 1829. The "good-sized" families still exist among the remnant of some of the pioneer stock of feeble-minded strain in some of the counties of southern Indiana and Illinois. Social workers and attendance officers can supply some appalling information of families of a dozen or more children, with the usual conditions of disease, idiocy, illegitimacy, juvenile delinquency, incest, and all the rest. The maintenance charges on the public treasury are likewise sizeable, but the true pioneer spirit of individualism and *laissez-faire* still prevails.

[180] "The western women felt that water was a deadly application for babies. They kept their babies' heads covered with a thick calico cap until they were several months old, in which time a black surface would form and cover the scalp. They would then commence a season of cleaning by saturating the head with either hog or 'bar's' (bear) grease, and then as it would come loose, pick off the black coating. As it would usually come off in large blotches, it gave a sad, leopard-like appearance to the little 'honey.' " [Christiana H. Tillson], *Reminiscences of Early Life in Illinois by our Mother* (Amherst, Mass., 1873), 94.

[181] Buckingham, *The Eastern and Western States of America*, III, 71.

Were conditions such as these to continue another fifty years, this observer of 1840 predicted that it would require a new race of settlers in the West to supply the worn-out constitutions of the old ones, just as new lands were required to replace the worn-out fields of the seaboard states.

Yet indifference and ignorance were slowly giving way before more enlightened views. *The Journal of Health,* begun at Philadelphia in 1829, gave practically its entire attention to temperance in the use of liquor and tobacco, to fresh air, exercise, and cleanliness. It attacked feather beds (except for the aged), corsets, and quackery. It advocated the same bodily exercises for boys and girls and recommended walking, gardening, tennis, and open-air games for all. Dancing under proper limitations was a "highly salutary species of exercise," and pursuit of a game called golf, formerly played in Scotland, was said by some to prolong life ten years.[182] The following paragraph on health, reprinted in some of the newspapers from Sears' *New Family Recipe Book* may have expressed ideas far ahead of the times, but such advice was becoming the rule rather than the exception:

Rise early. Eat simple food. Take plenty of exercise. Eat what best agrees with your system and resolutely abstain from what hurts you, however well you may like it. Have nothing at all to do with quacks and do not tamper with quack medicines. Let those who love to be invalids drink strong green tea, eat pickles, preserves and hot biscuits. Have your bed chamber well aired and have fresh linen every week. It is not healthy to sleep in heated rooms.[183]

Not all the advice of this nature, however, was so sensible, though on the whole the science of the editors was certainly equal to that of the average medical practitioner. Gunn's *Domestic Medicine or Poor Man's Friend,* first published in Tennessee in 1830 (later at Springfield, Ohio), was in its twelfth edition in 1838, and claimed sales of 100,000 by 1839. About one eighth of the work treated "Of the Passions"—fear, anger, hope, joy, jealousy, grief, religion, intemperance, and love—a combination of mental hygiene, morality, and advice to the lovelorn.

[182] *The Journal of Health,* I, 133. Sarah Josepha Hale was shortly to make sensible living, exercise, and fresh air one of her major crusades. Ruth Finley, *The Lady of Godey's* (Philadelphia, 1931), 131–33, 154; and files of *Godey's Lady's Book,* 1830–77.
[183] See, for instance, *Indiana Journal,* August 20, 1825, for health rules copied from Porter's *Health Almanac,* and the Madison *Republican and Banner,* July, August, September, 1834, for hints and articles on health.

"When the passions run counter to reason and religion, *nationally* and *individually*, they produce the most frightful catastrophes." Joy and hope were beneficent passions, though the
latter might have dangerous consequences. Fear was a base passion, and aggravated disease, while cowardice "disorders and
impedes the circulation of the blood; hinders breathing with freedom; puts the stomach out of order, as well as the bowels; affects
the kidneys and skin, and produces bad effects on the whole
body. . . ." Jealousy usually had to do with love but might be
merely a disease of talking. Love was one of the master passions
and embraced all the complicated and powerful faculties of man.
Its effects were determined largely by training and education.
"No woman possessed of a judicious education . . . ever became
the victim of a *broken heart.*" Religion concerned not only the
moral condition of mankind, but health and diseases of the physical system. Medical drugs were inadequate to restrain those joys
or remove those sorrows which spring from the mind itself. Resort must be had to the restraining powers and the consolations
of religion and morality, for the pleasures and pains of the imagination commence where those of the memory and the understanding terminate. Within twenty years advances in the publishing
arts made possible in this popular book beautiful colored plates
on Love, Jealousy, Intemperance, Infidelity, and the like, which
ranged from the beatific to the ridiculous.

The rise of the drug trade paralleled the development of medicine. In a few cities such as Cincinnati, Columbus, Indianapolis,
Springfield, St. Louis, Detroit, and later Chicago, stores which
engaged in both wholesale and retail activities found enough business to warrant such specialization.[184] Such stores carried drugs,
patent medicines, paints, perfumes, dyes, optical supplies, surgical instruments, glassware, and store furnishings. In the average
towns the drug stores were the department stores of the day, and
sometimes competed with the general store with a stock of hard-

---

[184] Drug distributors such as J. J. Smith Jr. & Co., "Apothecaries Hall" (Johnson
and Lott), both of St. Louis, Mitchell's in Cincinnati, and others, advertised in
papers throughout their territory. Paints, oils, varnishes, dye stuffs, patent and
botanic medicines, and "fancy articles," were carried in stock, as well as English,
French, American, and other drugs. Advertisements may be found in widely scattered newspapers of the 1820's and '30's.

ware, notions, and even groceries and dry goods.[185] Liquor was often sold, and soda water with syrup flavors was dispensed in the 1830's.[186] Proprietary or patent medicines did not constitute such an important part of the stock as one might think, for the bookstores or stationers often enjoyed exclusive privileges on many of these brands. Some stores advertised botanic medicines, Thomsonian remedies, and vapor baths.

Although much of the stock for the physicians or "saddlebag trade" was imported from the East,[187] it was manufactured or prepared by the druggist or his apprentice. Sugar of milk, gum arabic, opium, bloodroot—in fact most powders except jalap, rhubarb, and ipecac—were produced by tedious work with pestle or mortar.[188] Tinctures and ointments were also made. Tincture of iron was made from iron rust, the result of the action of nitric or muriatic acid fumes on thin plates of iron. "Mercurial ointment was a tedious job. What it would require forty years ago, fifteen days to make, will not take fifteen minutes now."

Indigo, logwood, fustic, nicwood, madder, and cochineal were worked up into dyestuffs, ink was prepared, plasters were made, and burning fluid of alcohol and turpentine mixed. It would be

[185] Albert E. Ebert, "Early History of the Drug Trade of Chicago," in *Transactions of the Illinois State Historical Society,* 1903, p. 245. George W. Sloan, *Fifty Years in Pharmacy (Indiana Historical Society Publications,* III, No. 5, Indianapolis, 1903), 334. From the 1840's drug stores confined their business more strictly to drugs, only to become general stores again in the twentieth century.

[186] Dr. Daniel Drake fitted up in his drug store at Cincinnati in 1816 what was supposed to have been the first soda fountain in the West.
Brandy, port, and sherry were for medicinal purposes. Later, when the temperance movement came, "Kentucky Wine" was sold, but not as whiskey. Editors often noted the coming of the soda fountain to town, and gave the drinks a free boost in their papers. A popular drink of the period was Sarsaparilla Mead, which was advertised not only as a thirst quencher, but as an aid to digestion and a preventive of fevers, headaches, indigestion, and diarrhea. Portsmouth *Western Times,* June 27, 1829; Piqua *Courier and Enquirer,* July 29, 1837.

[187] Philadelphia was the center of the English chemical trade, while New York supplied French, Spanish, German, and Italian articles, and Boston the East India importations such as spices, indigoes, nutmegs, cinnamon, cloves, gums, etc. A typical advertisement was that of Dr. G. Dawson of Pittsburgh, who carried fresh drugs and medicines—family, patent, and horse—surgeons' instruments, trusses, mortars, pestles, syringes, nipple glasses, oils, varnishes, paints, dyes, perfumery, all sorts of chemicals, gums, etc. Ravenna (Ohio) *Western Courier,* May 21, 1825.

[188] "Sugar of milk came in what we called 'cobs' because it looked somewhat like an ear of corn. A stick 12 or 14 inches long was put in the saturated sugar solution which crystallized about the stick. This was extremely hard to powder. A man might work it in a mortar all day and not get more than a pound. A day's work might not furnish more than two pounds of powdered gum arabic." Sloan, *Fifty Years in Pharmacy,* 335, writing of the 1840's. "The ponderous iron mortar, a tincture press and a Swift's drug mill were the ever present dread of the apprentice." Ebert, "Early History of the Drug Trade of Chicago," in *Transactions of the Illinois State Historical Society,* 1903, p. 244.

difficult to estimate the amount of drugs manufactured in any region. The census of 1840 listed the value of drugs, paints, and dyes in Ohio at $101,000, Indiana $47,000, Illinois $19,000, and Michigan $1,500.[189] The larger stores supplied the drug stores and merchants of the smaller towns and peddlers who worked the country districts in covered wagons. Castor oil, sweet oil, essence of lemon, peppermint, cinnamon, and wintergreen, cordials, soda, seidlitz powders, quinine, calomel, horehound, salts, borax, copperas, saleratus, alum, herbs, and patent medicines figured prominently in such trade. Paints, perfumes, dyes, surgical instruments, glassware, and shop equipment were usually carried in stock. The bottle and balances, or pestle and mortar, were signs of the drug store. The doctors seldom wrote prescriptions but usually mixed their own medicines, rolling the pills and folding the powders into neat little packets. During the scarce money days the druggists as well as the peddlers would accept beeswax, ginseng, flax and hemp seed, and other articles in trade.

[189] U. S. Census, *Compendium of the Enumeration of the Inhabitants and Statistics . . . of the Sixth Census* (Washington, D. C., 1841). This seems very low; it would appear that Samuel Thomson's western manufactory at Cincinnati or the eclectic tincture concentrate producers, to say nothing of the patent-medicine makers, alone would exceed this amount.

VI

Pioneer Life—Social and Cultural Backgrounds

We live under republican institutions, where the whole power of the government is in the hands of the people, and where every act of sovereignty is but an emanation of the public will. No mighty monarch graciously assumes the burthen of conducting our affairs; no hereditary parliament kindly relieves us from the difficult task of enacting our laws; no established church in charitable consideration of our weakness, deigns to accept the tithe of the produce of our labors, in return for the amiable office of directing our consciences in the world, and selling us the right of admission to a better existence. In government, in religion, in social life, we think our own thoughts, and act at our own pleasure.

James Hall, *Western Monthly Magazine*

THE homespun fabric of pioneer life was held together by the hard, coarse warp thread of the material struggle, but the color, the design, the quality, were supplied largely by the filling of activities, practices, and processes which, if not peculiar to, were at least characteristic of, society in the new West in the period of founding. Times were when the fight for mere existence left no surplus of time or energy for education or culture as commonly understood, and life degenerated into a vicious circle of days and years of grinding toil for the necessities to sustain the body, in order that other days would come in which to repeat the process. Yet at its worst the pioneer's world offered to even the most barren of lives something of amusement, of social relationships, of joys and sorrows over and beyond the material—and at its best a richness of background which afforded setting for lives more complete and rich in many respects than is possible to most under the unstable conditions of a highly specialized modern industrial society, often geared to a tempo beyond the capacity and power of humans.

The pioneer's world was essentially a man's world, and life possessed that robustness of flavor, that element of gusto and spontaneity which characterized the activities of people engaged in the harsher pursuits and in more direct contact with nature. The seclusiveness or propensity for solitude of the ultraindividualistic type of the early half-hunter, half-farmer class, was exceptional rather than common. From the first cabin raisings and logrollings in the wilderness to the time when muster days, political barbecues, country fairs, and Saturday trips to town became regular affairs, men found occasion to get together. There was leisure time for all at certain seasons, and for some at all seasons; even after strenuous physical labors in harvest field or timber clearing, there seemed always to be a surplus of energy to manifest itself in rough practical joking, raucous laughter, tall tales, feats of strength and skill, in whiskey drinking, and fighting. Even the labor was spiced with the spirit of competition, as when the logrolling, house-raising, or corn-husking crowd was divided into two gangs, under leaders, to race to a finish.

Among the fairly strenuous sports were throwing the maul,[1] pitching quoits, lifting weights, or "pulling a man down." In quoit throwing a flat stone of twenty to sixty pounds was pushed from the shoulder while the pitcher toed the mark. Pulling a man down could be played with hand spikes, each man at one end, and on opposite sides of a log, or with a round stick grasped by both and started overhead. Running, jumping—high, broad, and half-hammon (hop, step, and jump)—pole jumping (for distance mostly), tug of war, crack the whip, and "rastlin' " were popular. Somewhat less arduous were horseshoe pitching, leap frog, town ball, "stink base," "chicken," "slap jack," and "I spy." Even grown men played industriously at marbles, to the neglect of more serious labors. A cruel game which called for no mean order of skill and furnished no end of merriment was gander pulling. A tough old gander whose neck had been stripped of feathers and then well greased, was tied feet up to a strong springy limb. Bareback riders, whose horses were given a good urge with a switch in the hands of men stationed some yards back, sought to pull off the gander's head. Fluttering and squawking, the old bird was an elusive object, and sometimes caught and held too long, merely unhorsed the contestant, who was thereby disqualified. Sometimes small rings were substituted for the gander, to be speared on a stick as the rider went by.

[1] A sort of cross between the Highland "tossing of the caber" and the modern hammer throw.

Horses being animals of common interest, the question as to which of two horses could travel faster frequently came up. Tests of speed were arranged spontaneously on any level stretch, and money or its equivalent in skins or whiskey changed hands. There were no "race horses" or any considerable organized racing north of the Ohio until the rise of the county fair. One of the early newspaper notices of racing was that in the Cincinnati *Liberty Hall*, November 18, 1806; it announced races at Lawrenceburg, Indiana. Notices of the "Whitewater" races appeared in the same paper two years later. In December, 1825, "Polly of Portage," a Warren, Ohio, horse of some local fame, was duly challenged by the Trumbull Jockey Club, and $300 posted on a hundred-rod race. The race was run in the snow, which was pushed aside to form a path. Bets totaled three or four times the purse. Because it was the first race run in the county, and many interested persons were unable to attend on account of the weather, the editor of the Ravenna *Western Courier* gave a one-column, rod-by-rod account of it. Other races followed, and in May, 1,500 people saw "Polly" beaten by "Billy" in Cleveland.[2] Ten years later the editor of the *Cleveland Herald* apologized for not having noticed the extensive racing with Kentucky and Virginia horses which had been taking place, and reported that "Orazabo" won the mile and $75 in 1:53.[3] Correction was made next day, and three heats of two miles each were reported in 3:53, 3:48 and 4:03.

In the autumn of 1835 a public meeting was held in Cleveland to do something about gambling at the race course, but someone, fearing violence, put out the lights, and apparently nothing was done.[4] Most races were run on the roads. Now and then an irate "citizen" or "father" would protest these "unlawful assemblages of idle and dissolute persons who had congregated for the purpose of *running horses*." They were bound to lead to drunkenness, gambling, and every species of profligacy and crime.[5] By 1840 county fairs and other associations were holding regular races. The Springfield Illinois Association charged an entry fee of $25 for its two-year-old, one-mile sweepstakes. Other races

---

[2] Ravenna *Western Courier*, December 10, 1825; January 7, 1826; *Cleaveland Herald*, May 12, June 2, 1826.
[3] *Daily Cleveland Herald*, June 23, 1835.
[4] *Ibid.*, October 6, 1835.
[5] Letter in *Hamilton* (Ohio) *Intelligencer*, June 27, 1839.

were for older entries and the sponsors "hoped that farmers would take a deep interest in testing the qualities of their stock."[6]

A question of even more vital and widespread interest wherever men were gathered, was, "Who is the best man?" Modesty was not particularly an obsession among certain types of men, and interesting proceedings were often inaugurated by the agitation of friends or by the unadorned announcement: "I'm a better man than you are." If the contest was friendly and for sport's sake, a rough set of rules was followed. The casualties suffered in "rastlin'" were the usual thumped skulls, friction burns, and occasionally a broken bone.[7] Not all matches were friendly, however, for frequently the contestants got mad. Besides there was always a tough or rowdy element, to whom wrestling appeared too inconclusive, and who under the stimulus of whiskey or motivated by "bad blood," began with fisticuffs and ended up in the old-fashioned fight or gouging contest. Even here there were rules which sought to restrict the fracas to "far holts," see that it was "fit fair," and that it ceased when one party cried "nuff." But since the rules permitted striking, biting, hair pulling, scratching, kicking, gouging, and stamping upon a downed man, they did not unduly cramp the participants' style. Whereas wrestling ended when one contestant was downed, this point was but the beginning of a serious fight. Shins were cracked, ears bitten—sometimes off—windpipes garroted, and teeth knocked out, but the *coup de grace* of the expert fighter was not executed until he had his opponent on his back, knees in the pit of his stomach, and thumbs on his eyeballs. Then the pressure was applied, and if stubbornness or pride held back the word of surrender, eyeballs were popped out of their sockets. Some bullies wore long horny thumb nails, sharpened to a keen edge, further to facilitate this operation.[8]

[6] Springfield *Illinois State Register,* August 21, 28, 1840.
[7] Among the pioneers were men of great strength, endurance, and phenomenal roughness, but their physical endowments were not usually backed with any specialized training or skill. For example, in wrestling, there was little use of the powerful leg muscles for squeezing the opponent into submission; in high jumping the jumper went over "sitting up"; in putting the weights the contestant stood flat-footed. It is the writer's guess that only in weight lifting, chopping, throwing, standing jumps, walking, and ability to "take it" in fisticuffs, could the strong men of the period equal the modern athlete. And, of course, in shooting.
[8] "Women of that day attended none of these rough and exciting sports of men. Foot-ball had not yet come to pollute the taste of that day to its brutal grade of barbarity and cruelty." Haines, "Social Life and Scenes in the Early Settlement of Central Illinois," in *Transactions of the Illinois State Historical Society,* 1905, p. 38.

The militia musters, elections, public sales, shooting-matches, and Saturday afternoons in the towns or at the cross-roads "grocery," or "coffeehouse," as the drinking places were called, were the principal scenes of these passages at arms. On such occasions many a fellow who was ambitious of pugilistic renown was sent home to family in a sadly undone condition, to be nursed back to a semblance of his former self by his sympathetic wife. With the bellicose disposition as a basis, there was no lack of entrances into a quarrel and the wished-for fight. Differences of opinion were not even necessary. Neat clothing, correct speech and a gentlemanly bearing were often a sufficient provocation to the bully who had a distaste for these effeminacies, and lacking these he could, without departing too widely from recognized custom, "renown it" by drawing a circle about himself with a stick and defying anyone to enter the space thus appropriated; or sometimes, after loading up with whisky, he essayed to terrorize a town, profanely swearing he could "whup" the best man or all the men in it, till some one accommodated him.[9]

Dearest of all sports to the heart of the pioneer was the shooting match, for it was here that he could exhibit a proficiency in his special skill, one acquired through years of practice with the long rifle, defender of his home, support of his life, his tried companion in war and peace.[10]

The small bore rifle with its five-foot barrel, slender grip, and narrow stock was, in comparison with modern rifles, an awkward-looking and unbalanced weapon, but in matter of accuracy up to a hundred yards, was equal to the best. Bullets were molded at home, dumped into the ashes to cool, and the lead rims and tiny necks trimmed off with a pocket knife. For accurate charges powder was poured from the translucently polished cow horn into a measure made of the tip of a deer antler; but for rough estimate, powder in the palm of the hand sufficient to cover the bullet was the rule. Powder tamped in, a patch of linen greased with tallow was laid over the muzzle, and the bullet rammed home with the hickory ramrod.[11] Flint inspected and firepan filled—on later guns, cap adjusted—the triggers were set and the marksman was ready for action. He planted his feet with left side toward the mark, cocked the piece, and as he raised it, down came his head, back went his shoulders, and outward bent his knees, as man and rifle became one. The muzzle was lowered past the mark and

[9] Parker, "Pioneer Life," in *Indiana Magazine of History*, III, 2.

[10] For guns and their manufacture in the West, see Chapter IV.

[11] For emergency loading the bullet might be merely wet in the mouth and the moisture depended upon to hold it against the powder. The rule regarding the amount of powder in relation to size of bullet has proved generally correct by modern measurements; the larger the bullet (and the greater its shock power) the less powder (and velocity) needed in proportion.

slowly raised until, with both eyes open, the bead was drawn and the trigger lightly squeezed.[12]

Shooting practices varied. Distances usually ran from 75 to 100 yards, and the shooting was either offhand or from a rest, with a yardage advantage for those who shot offhand.[13] A favorite target was an inch square of white paper with a diamond hole cut in the center, and mounted in a six- or eight-inch blackened circle on a shingle or board. The number of shots was agreed upon and each man fired his string without interruption or haste. The winning score was determined by adding the distances of all shots from the center of the diamond. A shot outside the circle usually disqualified the contestant. Other times the contestants would drive the nail. At forty paces one out of three shots of a good marksman would hit the nail.[14]

Shooting matches had their conventions or ethics, but in a sport in which even extra heartbeats might seriously affect the results, there were subtler ways of getting the marksman's nerves on edge. "I remember one old man who threw down his rifle in a rage, shouting, 'He throwed me off, Gawd damn it. Ol' Jeff Whatley throwed me off, a-clickin' of his Gawd damn' tongue agin.' "[15] Sometimes for practical joking or betting purposes the uninitiated were introduced to the art of bewitching a rifle. The conditions were that after the gun was rested for the shot, the bewitcher be permitted to pass his hand up and down the barrel. This done, he was willing to bet that the marksman could not even hit the tree, and if the bewitcher had craftily slipped into the muzzle a small extra bullet, his bet was safe. Prizes might be a half barrel of whiskey, a beef, a turkey, or a goose. If shooting for beef, the best two shots got the hindquarters, the next two the forequarters, while the fifth had to be content with hide and

---

[12] Experts disagreed on whether it was best to keep both eyes open, or squint. Practice probably was guided by whether the rifleman was right-eyed or left-eyed, since only one eye controls sighting. The double trigger locks made it impossible to cock the piece until one trigger was "set." The remaining trigger was then ready to go with the slightest pressure.

[13] Those who used rests either shot prone ("fired on his belly"), sat down and used a stool or box, or stood and used a crotched stick or rested the muzzle against a tree. The target was set at the desired height for each contestant.

[14] John James Audubon, *Delineations of American Scenery and Character* (New York, 1926), 60.

[15] Randolph, *The Ozarks*, 250.

tallow. When shooting for turkeys, the head of the prize itself was the mark, "bill shots not counting."[16]

Since powder varied greatly in quality, it was necessary for the rifleman to try out each new batch to determine the proper charge for best work. Somewhere near the hunter's cabin was likely to be a shooting tree. When the bullet carried up at 20 rods, the charge was considered to be about right. Periodically the test bullets were dug out of the hacked and scarred tree with an ax or other implement and remelted.

As innately characteristic of the Upland South pioneer as love of the long rifle was his attachment to hound dogs. These prominent-ribbed, velvety-eared, sad-eyed representatives of the dog world, never sufficiently fed for fear of dulling the keenness of scent, were bred, raised, swapped and bet on—more valuable than a horse, but probably no more pampered than children. Not much to look at, regarded by the worthy wife as a nuisance around the house, the hound came into his own when the blasts of the hunting horn rallied the pack. As the melodious but weird voices reverberated over hill and hollow, their owners thrilled with the music. These voices revealed to them every step of the hunt, every triumph and mistake of their favorites, which hounds were leading the pack, and which were giving out, even though they caught "nairy" sight of fox or hound the whole night through.[17]

Women folk did not participate in or even witness these sports, but if the meeting were at someone's house, perhaps used the

---

[16] See Hall, *The New Purchase*, Chapter XVII, for an excellent account of a shooting match.

A national Muzzle Loading Rifle Association was organized in 1933 and Indiana had the largest number of members. *Outdoor Indiana*, July, 1936, p. 5. Local and sectional meets are frequently held. Although the marksmen use black powder, homemade bullets, and the old rifles, the technique of loading, charges, etc., has become quite complicated. In addition to the scores of books on old rifles and shooting, the files of *Muzzle Blasts* (Portsmouth, Ohio, 1940–) are most useful for study of the subject.

[17] The foxes seemed to enjoy these runs as much as the hounds and hunters, and although the fox was legitimate prey for gun or trap, to catch a veteran runner with the hounds was more or less of a community tragedy. Gray foxes soon took to earth, but a good red fox was good for from ten to twenty hours. Fox-hunting organizations, meets, and periodicals are still maintained in southern Indiana and Illinois, although the woods and foxes have become scarce. The folklore, rules, and finesses of this sport, so far as the author knows, have never been collected, and may pass with the memories of the old timers who knew them. The reception given MacKinlay Kantor's *The Voice of Bugle Anne* (New York, 1935) would seem to indicate that many still cherish sentiments for hounds who haven't seen a fox in years. Hound breeding has long since become as specialized as horse breeding, with resulting distinct American strains based in part on the pioneer mongrels.

occasion to get together on their own account. Their absence from the men's doings gave the men ample freedom for the exercise of their natural propensities in the way of drink, language, and pranks which ran the gamut from snipe hunting to the old badger fight. Meanwhile, the women were probably visiting, gossiping, and engaging in cooking bouts. More to their liking were the various sociables which began in any community just as soon as several families had settled within a radius of a few miles of each other. Some of these combined work and pleasure, others were for fun only.

Corn huskings appealed to all, old and young, male and female.[18] On the day or evening appointed, neighbors assembled in the barn, where the corn was heaped in a long pile. Leaders were selected, sides chosen, the corn pile divided into two equal parts by a rail, and the contest was on.

The yells of defiance, mingled with whoops and yells in Indian style, arose in one continued medley, and reverberated far through the woods, whilst an unceasing shower of corn streamed through the air . . . many of the ears flying wide of the mark, and one now and then making a dubiously tangential movement, which brought it into contact with the body of some unlucky wight. Shortly after the commencement, there were some new arrivals, toward whom the tide of vociferation was directed. "Come along, Andy—go ahead—whoop, here's the major—halloo, major, graze it—well done, *Kurnel*,—look at him—see how he cuts gravel—whoop, halloo," etc.[19]

Hands flew fast, ears thumped on the floor, and the chatter and merriment were heightened when now and then some young swain found a red ear and sought to exercise his right to kiss the girl of his choice; or a maid found one, took it to her favorite, and got a red cheek in return. All seemed confusion yet:

> It was for all that, order of its kind,
> 'Twas fun and useful industry combined.
> Nobody thought to do such things by rule,
> And run a husking like a village school.
> The hour passed on, and forward went the work,
> Off went the husks, with grip, rip, and a jerk,
> The ears were tossed into the crib, and lower

---

[18] By 1840 in the towns such simple amusements appeared countrified and rude. Masquerades and fashionable balls were the thing. Even so, all liked "to recur to the pastimes of our ancestors." Piqua *Courier and Enquirer*, November 18, 1837.
[19] Oliver, *Eight Months in Illinois*, 75.

> Each moment grew the unhusked pile before,
> While larger grew the husk pile in the rear,
> When lo! at nine the barn floor was all clear![20]

When the corn was all shucked, the floor was cleared and a barn dance, with food and refreshment, served to end the evening with the proper fillip.

> A better feast no king was ever at
> Than that 'round which the hungry huskers sat.
> Blithe maidens served with dignity and grace,
> But the chief attention at the place
> Where sat the young men. Quick were they to spy
> Whose cup was empty and who wanted pie,
> And each desired dish was soon supplied,
> Till all were served, and all were satisfied.
> Supper was ended, evening duties done,
> The girls must go but must not go alone!
> They went in pairs as things into the Ark,
> No matter then had it been twice as dark.
> What then was said beneath the midnight moon,
> Was brought to light by weddings the next June.[21]

A game sometimes played by men and boys at corn huskings was a variety of "Who's got the thimble?" Seated close together in a circle with knees drawn up, the players passed a small object around through the tunnel thus formed, with cries of "Brogue it about!" When the person in the ring pounced upon someone suspected of having the object, he was likely to be pommeled with it from the opposite side of the circle.

Fulling parties were held in the earlier days. The raw cloth from the loom was laid out on the floor, lathered with warm water and suds, and the young men sitting in two rows, worked it with their bare feet until it was properly shrunk. Quilting parties were of interest to the women and no doubt tongues wagged in rhythm with the needles.[22] Spinning parties, apple parings, rag cuttings,

---

[20] Luke Woodard, *Pioneer Days* (Richmond, Ind., n.d.), 11.
[21] *Ibid.*
[22] It was customary among certain classes of people for the women to remain in the background before strangers. This fact was noted by travelers, but was an individual rather than a class characteristic. At any rate, when the women got together among their friends, there was seldom any dearth of conversation.

"During the short time we sat, before and after supper, there were scarcely half a dozen words of conversation, an occurrence quite characteristic of the people, when the sexes are met. The silence of the woods is not half so oppressive, a pin can't fall without being heard and the jaws of those who yawn through sheer

carpet tackings, wool pickings, even chicken and goose pickings, were often as not made excuses for sociable and festive occasions.

For young unmarried folks such excuses of necessary toil were not required; the frolic was sufficient justification in itself. Where general prejudices against dancing existed, in communities dominated by certain religious sects, the gathering was known as a play party, otherwise as a frolic, hoedown, or "bussing bee."[23]

News of a frolic was passed around and everyone was welcome. About candle lighting on the appointed day the young people began to drift in, on foot, horseback, ox cart, bobsled, or however; the girls dressed up, the young men like as not in their everyday clothes. In good weather the party was conducted outside in the moonlight. Preliminary reserve was soon broken down —perhaps a jug in the offing helping with the men—and the activities got under way. A young man might offer a young lady his arm and begin marching around, to be followed by other couples. The voices took up the tune:

> We're all a marching to Quebec;
> The drums are loudly beating,
> The Americans have gained the day,
> And the British are retreating;
> The wars are o'er, and we'll turn back
> To the place from whence we started;
> So open the ring and choose a couple in
> To relieve the broken-hearted.

At "open the ring," all held hands and formed the circle, one was inside, and as he chose a partner the song became:

> Green grow the rushes, O!
> Kiss her quick and let her go!
> But don't you muss her ruffle, O!

A somewhat snappier start began with the "snap and catch-'em," whereby a snapping of the fingers in the face of one of the

---

weariness, are heard cracking right and left. The men generally are not very talkative, but I believe the women are much like women all the world over, and I have in some instances overheard them unfasten the sluices of their eloquence, and fairly maintain the character of their sex." Oliver, *Eight Months in Illinois,* 185.

[23] Quakers, Disciples (Campbellites), Methodists, Baptists, and Presbyterians generally forbade dancing. The distinction in the mind of proper folk between the play party and "hoedown" was similar to that which later existed between card playing with conventional cards and playing the same games with a different kind of cards.

opposite sex was a challenge to chase and catch, in which contest the girl, whether capturer or captured, always lost and paid the penalty with a kiss.[24] Then to the tune:

> Come Philander, let's be a marching
> Every one his true love serching.

or the familiar one of "Skip to my Lou, my darling," the many variations of marching and choosing, skipping, double shuffling, and kissing began. "There was a rhythm to the whole thing, a certain keeping time to the music, but this rhythm was almost as much of the arms, head and body as of the feet. The players bowed, they knelt, they kissed, they promenaded, they swung, each keeping time to the singing in whatever way his innate sense of dance directed." Other marching plays were "I suppose you've heard of late of George Washington the Great," "Sailing on the boat when the tide runs high," "King William was King James' son," "We are marching in to the Ivory O!" "Charley Cole," "Old Dusty Miller," "Jersies Blue, to you I call," "Oh! Sister Phoebe, how merry we were the night we sat under the juniper tree," "Roxie Ann," "We'll All go Down to Rowser's," and scores of others. The songs used in some instances were descended from ballads of bygone days, others were of American patriotic significance. The Weevily Wheat song, long a popular favorite, was probably of Scottish Jacobite ancestry.[25] There were various versions, one of which follows:

[24] "Sometimes an old settler 'snapped up' his wife, or was 'snapped up' by her, when we would have a race of an unusually amusing character." A.D.P. Van Buren, "The Frolics of Forty-Five Years Ago," in *Michigan Pioneer and Historical Collections,* V (1882), 305.

[25] Systematic study of the play party and dance tunes of the Midwest frontier has just begun in recent years. Brief treatments and reproductions of words and music may be found in the *Journal of American Folk-Lore,* XX (1907), 275–77; XXIV (1911), 295–318; XXV (1912), 268–73; XXVII (1914), 289–303; XXVIII (1915), 262–89; XXXII (1919), 486–504; XXXIII (1920), 91–132; XXXIV (1921), 111–20; in Van Buren, "Frolics of Forty-Five Years Ago," in *Michigan Pioneer and Historical Collections,* V, 304–9; and in Randolph, *The Ozarks,* Chapter VI. Leah Jackson Wolford, *The Play Party in Indiana* (*Indiana Historical Collections,* IV, Indianapolis, 1916) gives a glossary of terms, diagrams and description of play, together with words and scores of several dozens of the songs. Recent studies include: Charles J. Finger (comp.), *Frontier Ballads* (New York, 1927); Harvey H. Fuson, *Ballads of the Kentucky Highlands* (London, 1931); John A. and Alan Lomax (comps.), *American Ballads and Folk Songs* (New York, 1934), and *Folk Song U.S.A.* (New York, 1947); John Jacob Niles (ed.), *Songs of the Hill-Folk* (New York, 1934); Richard Chase (comp. and ed.), *Old Songs and Singing Games* (University of North Carolina Press, 1938); Emelyn E. Gardner and Geraldine J. Chickering (comps.), *Ballads and Songs of Southern Michigan* (University of Michigan Press, 1939); Mary O. Eddy (comp.), *Ballads and Songs from Ohio*

Oh I don't want none o' your weev'ly wheat,
    An' I don't want none o' your barley,
But I want some flour in half an hour,
    To bake a cake for Charley.

Th' higher up th' cherry tree
    Th' sweeter grows th' cherry,
Th' more you hug and kiss a gal
    Th' more she wants t' marry!

Yes, Charlie he's a fine young man,
    Oh Charlie he's a dandy,
An' Charlie is the very lad
    Thet stole th' striped candy.

Grab her by th' lily-white hand
    An' lead her like a pigeon,
Make her dance th' Weevily Wheat
    An' lose all her religion!

Over th' river t' feed them sheep
    On buckwheat cakes an' barley,
We don't kear whut th' ol' folks says—
    Over th' river t' Charlie.

"Old Dan Tucker," a stand-by in the period after 1840, was a minstrel show hit of the early 1840's. "Dixie" came somewhat later. Dan D. Emmett of Mount Vernon, Ohio, was the author of both songs. Forfeit plays were interspersed among the marching games and it was from "building the bridge," "picking cherries," and "keeping post office" that the parties got their title of "bussing bees." "Hurly burly" and other such fun-creating games were also enjoyed.

From marching and swinging games to dancing was but a step;

(New York, 1939); Brewster (comp. and ed.), *Ballads and Songs of Indiana*; Henry M. Belden, *Ballads and Songs Collected by the Missouri Folk-Lore Society* (*University of Missouri Studies*, XV, No. 1, Columbia, 1940); Ira W. Ford, *Traditional Music of America* (New York, 1940); Frank Luther, *Americans and Their Songs* (New York, 1942). See also Marshall Bartholomew, *Mountain Songs of North Carolina* (New York, 1926); Henry E. Mellinger, *Folk-Songs from the Southern Highlands* (New York, 1938); and Eloise H. Linscott, *Folk Songs of Old New England* (New York, 1939).

Harry R. Stevens has made a careful listing of the ballads and songs of the period from contemporary newspapers in "Folk Music on the Midwestern Frontier 1788–1825," in *Ohio Archaeological and Historical Society Publications*, LVII (1948), 126–46.

The Library of Congress and the School of Music of the University of Wisconsin are engaged in recording old songs and folk music of the area. The work of Alan Lomax in this field is outstanding.

in fact those games were dancing.[26] Musical instruments were scarce, the commonest being the fiddle, and "the devil was in the fiddle." As the dulcimers, organs, and pianofortes came in, they, too, were under moral suspicion. Besides, they were discredited because "a music box would make no man a good hep-mate." Nevertheless, it sometimes happened that after the more strict among the old folks had gathered up the children and started for home, a smuggled fiddle would be produced. A few magic passes of the bow across the strings of the devil's own, nerves began to tingle and feet to respond, and soon some brazen hussy would step out onto the floor with her partner. The appeal of the ele-mental rhythm of the "mountaineer music" was not to be denied, and as "Monnie Musk," "Zip Coon," "The Devils Dream," "Old Soomer Licked the Ladle," and all the rest were punctuated with the cries of the fiddler, even some of the more sedate among the grown-ups warmed to the occasion, fell into the figures of the Virginia reel, jig, "hoedown," or French Four, "cut the pigeon wing," and executed many a "double-and-twisted-lord-massey" for the edification of the young folks.[27]

Of course, there were some in each community possessed of such moral turpitude as to attend regular "hoedowns" or dances. The fiddler, holding his instrument on his chest and grasping his bow in the middle, let go, went off and kept on, all in rhythm. The gayer dancers "cut the double shuffle," jumped high in the air, clicked their heels together three times, and never lost a step to the music, while "Whoopees!" escaped as naturally from the performers as did the "Amens!" in another setting. They

> Danced all night, 'til broad daylight,
> And went home with the girls in the morning.

For such derelictions, people sometimes got "fiddled out of church" or "churched," unless, of course, they could prove that they had not crossed their feet while walking to and fro with the music.

[26] The heavy shoes and boots and rough uneven floors ordinarily restricted the country dances to those used to such facilities.

[27] The mountaineer music or "barn dance" music is as typically "American" as the Negro music or cowboy music. As with the ballads, its ancestry was Scottish, perhaps with a Spanish strain; it was developed by the "Scotch-Irish" pioneers. The full flavor of the pathos is given only by the lazy flat nasal drawl of the Upland South voices.

These parties were not only sources of amusement in themselves, but were important agencies for promotion of the age-old pursuits of wooing and wedding. About the only other opportunities for group contacts were offered by church, spelling bees, and singing school. In spite of the numerous testimonials to the effect that flirting was an unknown art in pioneer life, other than documentary evidence seems to indicate that, by whatever name described, the art or process by which a maid gets a man has changed least of all the old-time customs. There were bashful and awkward swains in those days; also bold bad men. Not only was John frequently overawed with Sally's presence, but there was the raw humor of the boys to be faced. If he "beaued her home" and asked her not to tell, she might give her promise, saying that she was as ashamed of it as he was.

Much of courtship took place in the home, which had few accommodations, but youth found a way. In the cabins and more modest houses, parlor, living room, kitchen, and bedroom for the old folks, were likely one and the same. Sunday evenings in winter the family hearth was the favorite location for lovers.

A tallow candle or greasy lamp would cast a faint sickly ray on the nervous swain as he shifted first one leg, then the other, over his knee and tried to keep up a conversation with the family group. If the girl happened to be the oldest of the family, there was the additional annoyance of several urchins, winking, blinking, and tittering until they grew tired and were ordered to bed. Then there was a short respite for the young man, who proceeded to turn a "searchlight" on the old folks. Although there was no one authorized to send them into retirement, it was well understood that if they were friendly to the beau they would avail themselves of the earliest opportunity to vacate the harthstone and leave the way clear for the "commencement exercises" of the evening. But if they wished to show their disapproval of the young man's attentions they would stay up and sulk until a late hour. Sometimes when the girl did not wish any further annoyance, or was after another beau, she would get "pap" and mother to "sit him out" until midnight. This was a polite way of informing him that "his room was better than his company."[28]

A few weeks of steady company ordinarily established the right of way for the young man, and the courtship once accepted, the community expected an early marriage. Sometimes the young woman got too many beaux on her string and complications

[28] Major, *Pioneers of Morgan County*, 288–89.

resulted, but since the economic obstacles to early marriage were normally not insurmountable, there was considerable less freedom of companionship between the sexes and less prolonged playing at love for amusement or experience, than practiced by young folks of a later period. Although the girls frequently sang at the play parties:

> I am too young, I am not fit,
> I cannot leave my mamma yet,

they hesitated not even at fourteen or fifteen, when the right young man popped the question.

Weddings were gleefully anticipated not only by the parties immediately concerned, but by the whole community, for the event meant several days of feasting and frolicking for young and old. For more formal ceremonies, an "invite," probably composed by the local schoolmaster, was carried from house to house by the groomsman.[29] Ordinarily no invitation except word of mouth was necessary, and the nuptial hospitalities were extended to all the neighborhood.

Certain customs were more or less common to the weddings of ordinary folk. On the day of the wedding the groom and his friends might assemble at his father's home and start their journey on horseback, so as to arrive at the bride's home about noon. When the party got within a mile or less of the house, two members were selected to "run for the bottle." The winner brought back the trophy, usually corn whiskey, distributed its contents, and the party continued to its destination in good spirits.

The simple marriage ceremony was solemnized by someone with ministerial license. The bride might be dressed in the wedding

---

[29] Hall, *The New Purchase*, 132, gives a copy of the special invite to the minister, issued in the 1820's in a backwoodsy community of southern Indiana:

"Rev. Mr. Hilsbury asqr.,—you are pertikurly invited to atend the house of mr. Abrim Ashford asq. to injine upon i the yoke of konjegal mattrimunny with his dater miss Susan Ashford as was—thersday mornin next 10 aklok before dinner a. m.

> mr. Joseph Redden
> your humbell sarv't
> mr. William Welden, groomsman."

"p.s. don't say nuthin about this 'ere weddin that's to be—as its to be sekrit—and to morrer Billy Welden's goin to ride round and give the invites—and all your settlemint's to be axed."

Later, among the socially correct in the towns, it was considered proper for the bride to stay hidden from idly curious eyes for several weeks after the bids were out. *Journal of the Illinois State Historical Society*, III, No. 2 (July, 1910), 41.

dress of mother or aunt, perhaps previously used in more genteel
surroundings and preserved all these years for the occasion; or
in gaily colored calico, fine book muslin or cambric, tight-laced
jacket, bobinet cap, cotton stockings, and kid slippers. The
groom, too, took matters seriously, and if possible would procure English broadcloth at $6.00 a yard, silk lining, buckram,
velvet for collar, silk twist and a half-dozen shiny brass buttons,
and turn the job over to a tailor. But like as not, the bride was
gowned in linsey-woolsey and the groom in honest homespun and
shiny new cowhide boots, and when it was all over, they were
just as much married as anyone else.[30]

Preparations for the wedding dinner took days. The neighborhood was scoured for china, pewter, and silver, for linen and
cooking utensils. Neighbors and relatives aided in the cooking.
Improvised tables of boards on wooden horses, often outdoors,
were laden with the best the land could offer. "The table fairly
reeled under the weight of roast beef, pork, and turkey, stacks of
cakes, pies, and crullers, with corn and wheat bread, butter and
home-made molasses—all plentifully interspersed with cabbage,
beans, potatoes, baked custard, pickles, catsup and pepper-
sauce."[31] Or better still, the description of one not accustomed to
the abundance and appetites of the frontier:

First, then, and middle most, an enormous pot-pie, and piping hot, graced
our center, overpowering, with its fragrance and steam, the odours and
vapours of all other meats: and the pot-pie was the wedding dish of our
Purchase, par excellence! The pie to-day was the doughy sepulchre of at
least six hens, two chanticleers, and four pullets. . . . What pot could have
contained the pie is inconceivable, unless the one used for "tarrifying the
barr." Why, among other unknown contributors, it must have received
one half peck of onions! And yet it is to be feared that they who came after
us were potpieless. . . .

Around the pie were wild turkeys. . . . The poor birds, however, were
so done, over and under too, that all native juices were evaporated, and
the flesh was dry as cork: but by way of amends quarts of gravy were

---

[30] At Springfield, Illinois, a bride in short skirt and groom in foxskin cap rode
into town on the same horse. Another person rode ahead, carrying a pole with the
bride's handkerchief held aloft. The groom took a long swig from his "tickler" and
the party repaired to the squire's place. *Sangamo Journal,* February 16, 1833. In
outlying communities, during a hard winter or if "the roads were bad," "weddings"
as well as funerals, were sometimes solemnized, or celebrated, en masse, months
later or whenever the minister could get around.

[31] Major, *Pioneers of Morgan County,* 291.

judiciously emptied on our plates from the wash-basin-bowls. That also moistened the "stuff'nin," composed of Indian meal and sausages. . . .

But who can tell of the "sasses?" for we had "biled petaturs!"—and "smashed petaturs!"—and "petatursis!" i. e. potatoes rolled into balls as big as marbles, and baked brown. And there were "bil'd ingins!"—"fried ingins!"—and "ingins out of this here pie!" Yes, and beets of all known colours and unknown tastes!—all pickled in salt and vinegar and something else! And there were pickled cucumbers, as far as salt and water could go; and "punkun-butter!"—and "punkun-jelle!"—and corn bread in all its glory!

Scientifically inserted and insinuated among the first course, was the second; every crevice and space being wedged up. . . . This second course was chiefly custard; and that stood in bowls and teacups of cadaverous white, encircled by unknown flowers. . . . But we had also custard pies! And made with both upper and under crusts! And also maple molasses, (usually called "them 'ere molassissis,") and preserved apples, preserved water melon-rinds, and preserved red peppers and tomatoes—all termed, for brevity's sake, . . . "sarves."

A few under crusts, or shells, were filled with stewed peaches and apples. . . .

Among the curiosities were the pound cakes, as numerous as apple dumplings, and about as large. These were compounded of some things found in pound cakes every where, and of some not found, maple sugar being, evidently from the taste, the master ingredient; but their shape—that was the beauty! All were baked in coffee-cups! And after being disencupped, each was iced all over, till it looked for all the world, exactly like an ill-made snow ball! The icing, or snowing, was a composition of egg, starch, and a species of double rectified maple sugar, as fine and white as table salt.

In addition to all these matters tea and coffee were severally handed, while the girls in attendance asked each guest—"Do you take sweet'nin?"[32]

Such was the abundance for culinary and gastronomic exhibitionism in a region which had been Indian country but a brief dozen years before.

Formalities counted for little. If the table could not accommodate all, men and boys were seated first, and with much boisterous conversation well seasoned with witty shafts, sometimes more or less crude, aimed at the bride and groom, the feasting continued until all were more than satisfied. By late afternoon the women had cleared away the remains and the old folks went home. The young people, unless dancing was barred, remained to dance; four-handed reels and square sets continued into the small hours. In some communities it was customary for the newly married

[32] Hall, *The New Purchase*, 154–56.

couple to be excused about midnight; with many bits of advice, the girls put the bride to bed, and with jokes practical and otherwise, the men did the same for the groom. The merrymakers continued to visit the couple at intervals and take them lunch, until the party broke up.

The following day, at the groom's home, was held the infare. The same people attended, another race for the bottle took place, another feast, and another dance. If the groom had built a cabin or house, or when one was ready and the couple moved in, a charivari—called shiveree—was in order. All the noisemaking implements were assembled, and the burlesque serenade might result in anything from turning loose a greased pig in the party, to kidnaping the bridegroom.[33]

Townsfolk varied the customs somewhat, and there were some who sought more formality and dignity.[34] Others, either for purposes of ostentation or possessed of genuine hospitality, opened the doors and fed the neighborhood. "There were people crowded into the house, to overflowing, nearly 600 it was said, and it was talked about for years, 'the big wedding the Captain gave his daughter.' "[35]

The importance of matrimony was impressed upon the minds of girls; there was no niche for the unmarried woman in a society in which a woman was comparatively useless except as wife and housekeeper. Failure to get married was more than a personal disappointment; it was more or less an economic calamity. The

[33] See Hall, *The New Purchase*, 445–51, for description of a "shiver-ree." An excellent description of a simple pioneer Ohio wedding may be found in Merle Estes Colby, *All Ye People* (New York, 1931), Chapter VIII.

[34] "My dress of White Satin very rich and thick dead white. The bosom made with folds across, with one row of shell trimming around the neck, two rows on the sleeves. The skirt *long without* any *trimming* deep blonde on the sleeves. My gloves white kid satin on the tops and edged with blonde. My hair was plaited behind and my Grecian curls were curled very beautifully and worn behind curls in front. Mock orange blossoms were sent to me to wear in my hair. I wore them in front buried in my curls and beautiful white rose in behind. My shoes were of *light kid* they were *entirely white* at candle light. My pocket-kerchief was trimmed with deep lace."

And the groom: "It was a rich suit of Broad cloth black satin vest, stock, *frock* coat, boots very handsome made for the express purpose, a pocket handkerchief that I gave him. his appearance was very fine looked extremely handsome very animated. his attendants were dressed in the same style."

From an Indianapolis wedding performed in 1840 by Henry Ward Beecher. Letter of Catherine Noble Davidson, June 6, 1840, Indiana State Library, published in *Indiana Magazine of History*, XVI (1920), 303–7.

[35] "Autobiography of Clarissa Emely Gear Hobbs," in *Journal of the Illinois State Historical Society*, XVII, 655.

girl who reached her early twenties without matrimony was likely to be regarded with a combination of pity and blame, and doomed to spinsterhood. And the lot of spinsters was not particularly happy. To remain at home with the old folks, or live around with married brothers and sisters, seeking by hard and often unappreciated work to compensate for their keep, uncertain of anything which they might call their own—this was the common fate of maiden aunts, hard enough certainly to lead many women to marry men of coarser nature and lesser talents than themselves. Those same facts gave to marriage a certain amount of permanence. The day when the economic independence of women would give them a new status was a generation or two in the future. Consequently much could be forgiven a man, if only he was a good provider.

Besides funerals and weddings there were church camp meetings, muster days, court days, political meetings, and trips to town or village for trading, or even "down river" with produce, which served to break the hard routine of rural life and gave opportunity for social contacts.[36] Yet withal there remained much of drabness and loneliness, particularly in the outlying regions, or

[36] For church and camp meetings, see Chapter XIV. As for muster days, they were usually anything except serious military training. Between the War of 1812 and the Civil War the efficiency of the militia of the midwestern states reached the vanishing point. Only now and then did an officer drill troops with weapons. As social and political meetings musters were important. As late as 1845 the adjutant general's office of the state of Indiana was unable to report the strength of the Indiana militia for the simple reason that the commanders of divisions and brigades had not reported to him. At that time the adjutant received $100 per annum and provided his own fuel and stationery.

A description of a Sangamon County, Illinois, militia muster in 1840 is typical: "Certainly there are few more ridiculous scenes than a military muster under the present (dis) order of things. Several hundred men formed in what is called a *line* (although it can hardly be called a straight, and as little a curved, or any other known mathematical line) in every variety of posture and position—some sitting, some lying, some standing on one foot, some on both, and well-spread at that; equipped, too, or non-equipped, with every variety of coat and shirt sleeves, and every variety of weapon, among the latter, however, the corn-stalk, the umbrella and riding whip predominating almost to uniformity; every man grumbling and thinking the time wholly thrown away; some impatient for the grog-shop, and some for the horse race, and some to attend to their business—certainly, there is very little of the military in this display!" Quoted in Isabel Jamison, "Independent Military Companies of Sangamon County in the 30's," in *Journal of the Illinois State Historical Society*, III, No. 4 (Jan., 1911), 23.

Sandford Cox relates the story of a captain who, disgusted with the ragged line of men with guns and sticks, threw his cocked hat on the ground, then his shirt, then his sword on top of that. "He then rolled up his sleeves and shouted with the voice of a stentor: 'Gentlemen! form a line, and keep it, or I will thrash the whole company!'" The line was formed. *Recollections of the Early Settlement of the Wabash Valley* (Lafayette, Ind., 1860), 35–36.

in those isolated sections where even today roads are impassable for months at a time to all except horseback travelers. For men and children it was not so bad; for women it was worse, and many of them accepted the drawbacks more or less from necessity rather than choice. Dr. Daniel Drake, who traveled thousands of miles through the region, was aware of the problems of the wife of the emigrant, who, "surrounded by difficulties or vexed with hardships at home, provided with no compensation for what she has left behind, pines away, and wonders that her husband can be so happy when she is so miserable."[37] To the half-hunter, half-farmer individualist there was a deep-seated appeal in the comparative solitude; he had a distaste for too frequent or too close contact with his fellows.[38] (Women more rarely possessed this nature.) For others the frontier struggle was an ordeal to be lived through for the rewards at stake. George Flower, among others, made it clear that on the frontier, labor fell more constantly upon the women than the men.

In the toils incident to a large family, there are times and seasons under the best management, when all the nerve and sinew that a woman can muster, must be put in actual requisition. . . . If their good sense prevails, and they resolutely undertake what is necessary to be done, with cheerfulness and good will, they will find kind neighbours to teach and assist them, and what is yet better, they will be their own best friends.

The outlying settlements were not so good for the educated female.[39] No doubt many women besides the one Birkbeck met were suffering "from the lone."

[37] Harriet Martineau, *Retrospect of Western Travel* (3 volumes. New York and London, 1838), III, 224.

[38] "All his feelings, all his reasonings, are influenced by the loneness in which they were conceived. His associations are not tinctured with the busy crowds and homes of cities, but with the still solitudes of the primeval forest. He has not learned to philosophize on the ebbs and flows in the destinies of congregated millions, but he has wandered and mused on the banks of some leviathan river, rolling its waters along, whither he knows not, whence he cannot tell,—a dream, a mystery." Oliver, *Eight Months in Illinois*, 155.

"In wandering through the woods where solitude seems to hold undivided reign . . . it is not uncommon to find originals odd enough to make the fortune of a human menagerie, such as will doubtless form, at no distant day, a new resource for the curious. If any of the experimental philosophers of the day should undertake a collection of this nature, I recommend the woods of the West as a hopeful field for the search. Odd people are odder in the country than in town, because there is nothing like collision to smooth down their salient points, and because solitude is the nurse of reverie, which is well known to be the originator of many an erratic freak." Kirkland, *Western Clearings*, 207.

[39] *The Errors of Emigrants*, 26–27.

Those were indeed unjoyous days,
When plodding o'er the lengthen'd ways,
The partner of his lot—his bride,
With broken spirits by his side,
Whose tendered heart, more us'd to melt,
A keener, longer anguish felt,
At thought of friends and home she lov'd,
To such a distance now remov'd;
When brightest hopes of future gain
Could ill assuage their mutual pain;
When enterprise, almost subdued,
Had lost its nerve and hardihood,
And fain would yield to love and tears
The boasted plans of future years.
But pride still pointed out the goal,
And goaded on the lagging soul,
While happier hopes and visions rise,
To gild anew the western skies,
And turn'd the retrospective view
To forward scenes of brighter hue.[40]

As the home was the center of the domestic economy of the pioneer's world, so was it the center of his social life. Here work and play were combined. The domestic crafts for both men and women gave other than mere utilitarian satisfactions. Spinning, weaving, dyeing, cooking for the women; making things with tools, possibly breeding animals, or experimenting in horticulture for the men, were as much avocational as vocational. Hunting and fishing were within reach of most, as were the pleasures of roaming the woods in search of herbs and roots, activities which remained as recreations long after they had ceased to be necessities.

Almost as characteristic of the settlers from the South as proficiency with the long rifle and love of hound dogs, was the "sang" hunting habit. To the untrained eye the ginseng plant looks suspiciously like any one of a dozen weeds which may surround it; but the woods habitué could spot it fifty yards away, and if he did not want it at the time, would file the location away in his memory with dozens of others scattered over miles of woods, and return to it later. Dried ginseng roots were generally accepted in trade, but the hunting habit was as much a game with

---

[40] Henry Whiting, *The Emigrant*.

nature and an expression of the collector's instinct as a commercial pursuit.[41]

Long winter evenings usually found the family around the fireplace—the women and older girls busy at spinning or knitting, the men resting, the children roasting apples, chestnuts, scraping out turnips with a round-ended knife, or popping corn. Grandmother—and no pioneer home seemed complete without one—might be prevailed upon to tell stories of the wars with Britain, or mighty hunting tales. Reading was not a popular pastime, and it was the exceptional family which possessed aught besides a well-thumbed almanac, a Bible, a spelling book, and possibly a copy of Foxe's *Martyrs*. Not before the 1830's did newspapers circulate generally, and then not regularly.[42]

Now and then about dusk came the traveler or land looker, seeking guidance or shelter. Did he know his manners, he would "Hello the House!" from a distance, and not dismount and approach until he had received recognition; for although, traditionally, the latchstring hung out, the stranger did not come too close unannounced, especially after dark, or when the men folk were not in evidence. Once accepted, the best at hand was placed at his disposal; but he was likely to pay well in conversation, for, though tight lipped and inexpressive in many respects, the settlers were also curious and inquisitive. Many youngsters got their first lasting impressions of the world outside from the tales of the travelers, listened to with wide-eyed, childlike interest. Also from time to time came peddlers, tinkers, colporteurs, and the hawkers, and walkers who vended their wares and furnished entertainment.[43]

Visiting, when neighbors were not so numerous or close, was much indulged in—not brief, conventional calls, but real family

[41] Up to 1840 ginseng roots were quoted in prices current at about the same price as whiskey, i.e., 15 to 30 cents. Even though the plants were fairly numerous in the early period, it would take a lot of travel and digging to gather four or five pounds, since they shrank about half in weight when dried. The Chinese market was apparently insatiable. It seems that the Chinese had a method of clarifying or rendering the roots transparent. Michaux states that ginseng so processed sold at $6.00 or $7.00 per pound in Philadelphia, and that the "secret" was sold in Ohio and Kentucky for $400. Whether the secret worked or not is not clear. Michaux, *Travels to the Westward of the Allegany Mountains*, 202. In modern times ginseng has sold as high as $8.00 to $12 per pound. Like furs, the chief output now comes from "farms." Many of the pioneers developed the "sang" chewing habit. The root had a pleasant, sharp sweetish taste and no effects so far as the writer knows.

[42] For books, newspapers, and periodicals, see Chapter XV.

[43] Peddlers are described in Chapter VII, 558–61.

visits, planned ahead and with a day or days set aside for the purpose. On foot, horseback, in the ox cart, wagon, or bobsled, depending on circumstances and season, went the family to the home of friends or relatives. Men boomed their greetings, while the women, feigning surprise, exclaimed, "Well, I swan!" or, "My land to goodness!" amid much fluttering and making over one another and the children. The big boys exchanged rough challenges, the girls giggled, and the younger children were awkwardly silent. While the men looked after the horses and around the place, the women repaired to the kitchen; soon all got together over the big meal which was the most obvious manifestation of hospitality. Etiquette required the women to volunteer in the preparation and dishwashing, and the hostess to protest. For ordinary "run in" visits between women it was proper for the hostess to continue with her work, and for the visitor to bring some work along.

Although there were numerous chores to do at home, possibly even some schoolwork, boys and girls found ample time for fun and amusement. They seldom lacked companionship in the numerous company of brothers, sisters, and neighbors. Younger children did not have access to "5 and 10" stores, and were without the gaudy and diverting toys of the modern age; but homemade balls of yarn, dolls, dishes, and animals were just as interesting, and far more lasting. Now and then some little girls were fortunate enough to get some cabinetmaker's miniature sample furniture models for her doll's establishment, or some tiny "real china" from back East. Needless to say most girls knew the uses of the various household utensils and could dress their own dolls.

For the boys, homemade sleds, wagons, bows and arrows, slings, and noisemakers such as whistles of paw paw or other slippery wood, bull fiddles, drums, and the like were always to be had; they were all the more enjoyable in that the idea and its manufacture were personal affairs. Add a pair of skates from the forge of the blacksmith, perhaps a gun—and the whole outdoors to use it in—and life was quite tolerable for the boys.

Christmas was celebrated with homemade candies—taffy or "lasses candy" predominating—popcorn strings and balls, fancy cookies, and perhaps some dates and figs from the store. Although presents were common at this season, Christmas was not yet the highly commercialized institution which it has since become. One looks in vain in the newspapers for any indication in advertisements or news that the Christmas season was different from any other. People of Yankee origin hardly honored the festival, but emphasized Thanksgiving instead.[44]

Boys and girls received most of their education not at school, but firsthand, from their environment of woods, animals, and growing things. Pets were plentiful—dogs, cats, goats, lambs, sometimes ponies, 'coons, and other wild animals. And the outdoors, not stripped of trees and neatly divided by barbed-wire fences, but marked only by streams, gullies, woods, caves, briars, and thickets, possessed mystery and romance. Beyond the next turn of the woodland cowpath would at least lurk a groundhog or a 'possum, if not a bear or an Indian.

Winter was fine enough, although it had its drawbacks, but sugar-making time was a harbinger of spring. While the unmarried couples kept the fires burning all night and sparked on the side, the children hoped that the maple-sugar cakes would soon materialize.

> And sugar-making time to me
> Was like an annual jubilee.
> In iron kettles rudely swung;
> On dogwood poles and forks, and hung,
> 'Twixt burning logs, day after day,
> We boiled the liquid sweet away.
> I watched the golden syrup boil,
> And ever and anon the while,
> With wooden paddle filled my cup
> And dipped the waxy nectar up.
>
> My boy's enjoyment was complete,
> And once a year my face was sweet!
> But woe to him who takes no care,

---

[44] The *Detroit Gazette,* November 29, 1825, remarked that Thanksgiving had just been observed in the eastern states, and wished that such a national institution, "one of those good old customs," were observed in Michigan Territory. One of the earliest of the infrequent references to Christmas was in the Green Bay *Wisconsin Democrat,* December 22, 1836: "Christmas with all its happy associations, is close at hand." The *Cleveland Weekly Advertiser,* December 28, 1837, said: "The anniversary of this ancient festival occured on Monday last. . . ." The editor thought that such festivals should be observed. Americans were too serious and bent on money-making, and certainly there was no danger of overdoing such celebrations. The *Quincy Whig,* December 28, 1839, had an article on Christmas and carried the now familiar, "Merry Christmas—Happy New Year."

> And lets his taste become his snare!
> 'Twere well if Eve had tasted less,
> And so with me I must confess.
> Eve, I suppose, grew sick at heart,
> And I in an adjacent part.[45]

Sassafras tea cleared the "humors" from the system, and mixed with sugar molasses was no mean drink. Bare feet were in order by the time the redbud and dogwood were in blossom, and the swimming hole had been tried before the walnut leaves had unfolded.

The woods ably supplemented the household larder in the difficult task of filling the stomachs of growing youngsters. Earliest spring fruits were the service[46] (pronounced "sarvis" by the pioneer) berries, to be found on the bushes in June, and eaten before the squirrels and birds attended to that job. Too large a helping set the teeth "on edge," but these little berries were not to be passed up on that account. Next came the luscious mulberry, on trees which literally invited climbing. The berries were usually full of bugs, but the bugs were also full of berries, so it made little difference to crows, squirrels, and children. About the only difference was that the squirrels probably showed better judgment as to the quantity consumed and suffered less from the inevitable stomach-ache which followed. Delicately flavored wild strawberries, often transplanted to gardens, helped tide over until green apples were in season. The blackberry grew in cut-over land, in pastures, fence corners, on poor hillsides, or most anywhere, but reached its best in the woods openings where the juicy berries were an inch long. Tasty raspberries were not so plentiful, nor was the delicious dewberry. Autumn brought the paw paw, persimmon, and crab apple, the red and black haws, grapes, and nuts.

> When nuts were ripe, I understood
> Just where to find them in the wood.
> I ne'er forgot the rich paw-paws,
> Nor where to find the ripe black haws.[47]

Walnuts and butternuts kept hands stained for weeks; but the

---

[45] Woodard, *Pioneer Days*, 13–14. Micah P. Flint's description of the sugar camp in his poem "The Hunter" is better poetry but no more inspiring.
[46] The Juneberry, shadbush, or *amelanchier*.
[47] Woodard, *Pioneer Days*, 6.

hickory nut, some large and thick shelled, others small and thin, was more prized. In some of the valleys were the tall pecans, and scattered here and there the hazelnut.

These fruits of the woods were known to young folks, whether they lived on farms or in town. Only in the prairie regions might they miss some of them. Some way or other things wild always tasted better than products of the garden or orchard, perhaps because they called for no labor.

Nor was knowledge confined to edibles. Boys and girls learned the names of the trees and wild flowers—not their botanical names, but their common names—where they grew, what they were good for. And so with animals, domestic and wild.

> I was no thief, but laid a claim
> To every calf and colt that came,
> And at first sight gave each a name.
> I had a share in every flock,
> And I was rich in fowl and stock.
> The eggs were mine, and night and morn,
> I ransacked shed, and stack, and barn;
> In vain did gander, standing guard,
> Dispute my rights in poultry yard!
> With cornstalk, keeping him at bay,
> I bore the round white prize away!
> In vain did turkey hide her nest
> In brush, or wood, where I made quest.[48]

Chickens and other fowl fell within the province of the women folk, and gathering the eggs or spotting the nest of the old hen who persisted in hiding out was the girls' job. They learned the vagaries of the foolish fowls, the silliness of the chickens, the errantry of the turkey, and the flightiness and raucousness of the guinea fowl. When the girls insisted that these creatures were the dumbest of all creation, the boys could remind them of the cows, or, better still, the sheep, which, for want of something better to do, would get on their backs and swell up and die in the absence of someone to turn them over. Since most boys were hunters, fishermen, and trappers, they knew the habits and uses, if any, of foxes, 'coons, 'possums, muskrats, weasels, skunks, and other local varmints; of owls, hawks, buzzards, pheasants, part-

---

[48] Woodard, *Pioneer Days*, 5.

ridge, and waterfowl; of fish from the savage muskie and proud bass to the lowly catfish and the crawdad.

Boy Scout classes were not necessary to teach boys woodcraft, handicrafts, or cooking. The average boy knew how to shoot or trap any of the animals of his region, to skin, clean, and eat them in the most efficient manner. Even though school at times interrupted this larger education, it was not permitted seriously to interfere. In going to and from school the straight path was not always taken; side forays and scouting expeditions were always in order, important discoveries were mentally catalogued for further attention.

When more formal amusement was desired, there were games in abundance. "Forfeits," "grunt," "ships come to town," "going to market," "pussy wants a corner," "drop the handkerchief," "bobbing the apple," "hiding the thimble," and many others, had their basis of appeal either in nimbleness of mind or body required, in the forfeit, or in the mirth-provoking fun produced. At home and at school "blackman," "three cat bat," "fox and geese," "run sheep run," "andy over," "bull pen," and various forms of shinny, some of them played with fire-hardened sticks and quite rough, served as outlets for excess energy. Skating, sleighing, sledding, and bobsledding were popular winter sports for young people. These sports were not confined to a few weeks or days, for the forests protected the snow, and sleighs, cutters, spiders, jumpers, and bobsleds served as romantic settings for many parties and romances.

Spelling bees and singing schools were social rather than intellectual pursuits. The exceptional interest in orthography was owing as much to the competitive feature and chance for distinction which this branch of "book larnin'" offered as to the fact that ability to spell was the chief criterion by which an educated person was judged. Rivalries carried beyond the schoolhouse walls; girls spelled boys; young folks competed against the old; community against community. Families and individuals vied for prizes and honors; the distinguished spellers were known far and wide. Even the reputable spelling masters were marked men, and as much sought after as successful basketball referees of a later day. These were the days of loud or blab schools, before the idea of "silent reading" had received any emphasis. Hence the generally prevalent method of spelling by syllable and repeating.[49] "Merely rattling off the letters in a word, as is often done in schools, is not spelling. Spelling is properly arranging the letters in their syllables and these in the word. Letters are to the word what words are to the sentence." So the diminishing lines held bravely, partisans and spectators held their breaths, until one side had spelled down the other. Food was then in order, and a good time was had by all.

Singing schools were usually conducted by a master on the sub-scription basis; to make a living he tried to keep several going at the same time. Or he may have been the local schoolmaster, possessed of a pitch pipe, a pair of waving arms, and some kind of a voice. Sometimes rival schools existed in the same community and joint meetings and contests were held. Of the New England singing master it was said that "the doctor, the minister, even the 'variety store keeper' were neither of them scarcely noticed, when *he* was present. In the 'meetin' hus' and at all jollification he was *the* lion." Unless young, handsome, single, and well comported, the singing master in the West, outside the schoolroom, was hardly such an important personage.

Music books were written in the famous "buck wheat" notes, four in number and recognizable without reference to their posi-tions on the staff. The four notes mi, fa, sol, la were repeated to form the octave: fa, sol, la, mi, fa, sol, la, fa. Later came the round note system and the figure note system. Among the early music books were the *Missouri Harmony,* the *Christian Psalmist, Sacred Melodeon* and books by Dr. Lowell Mason and A. D. Filmore. The *Eolian Songster,* which contained "sentimental, patriotic, naval, and comic songs," was published by U. P. James, of Cincinnati, in the early 1830's. The same publisher put out *The American Minstrel* and *The United States Songster.*

The singing parts were treble or air (modern soprano) sung by men and women, tenor or double air, for both men and women, and bass for men. Alto and baritone were not used. Well-trained singing masters had great difficulty in getting their scholars to restrain their voices; the latter judged the quality of the music by its volume. "For pure and wholesome social enjoyment, few

[49] For example: "incomprehensibility," "i-n, in; c-o-m, com; incom; p-r-e, pre; incompre," etc.

recreations surpassed the old country singing-school, and there at the same time were trained many sweet singers for the local churches, as well as for the homes." But it can hardly have been the interest in music alone which led the young folks to the popular refrain, "I am so fond of singing schools I can't stay away, oh, I can't stay away."

Debating clubs, moot courts, and literary societies, organized alike in villages and rural communities as soon as the most pressing of material problems were solved, were also as much social as intellectual in nature. The wide interest in politics and debating was manifested in general attendance of young and old at court sessions to hear the lawyers argue, and gain the stimulation of declamation. Many a pioneer youth hoped to reach the pinnacle of Henry Clay by way of the *Kentucky Preceptor*, which he studied and practiced on the domestic animals, patient victims of his "elocution."

Although December 25 might be completely ignored in the newspapers, not so January 8 (Jackson day) in the Democratic Republican press, and July 4 in the papers of both parties. These dates were celebrated by illuminations, dinners, and much speech-making. On these occasions as well as at dedication exercises, local meetings, and honorary dinners, numerous toasts both arranged and voluntary were offered. Among the subjects certain to be listed were "the day we celebrate," "the Constitution," "the Union," "the state," "the army," "the navy," "the heroes of '76," "the elective franchise," "the rights of man," "education," "agriculture," "manufactures," and "to the fair." The events which led to a free republic were fresh and important in the minds of the people; although the toasts may often have been stereotyped, they were more than mere formalities.

"The Constitution of the United States,—the best in the world, may it ever remain inviolate"; "The United States, my adopted country, may her independence be as permanent as the rock of Herculaneum"; "Washington,—his memory will be adored while liberty shall have votaries"; "Jefferson,—to the political world he said, 'let there be light, and there was light' "; "Our free institutions,—may they never be sapped by the intrigues of faction, nor demolished by arbitrary force, but ever stand as impregnable citadels of the rights of man"; "The elective franchise,—in proportion to the purity with which it is exercised, will be the purity of our government"; "The ballot box and the cartridge box—the former powerful in expressing, the latter in defending the will of Republicans"; "Education,—the fountain of virtue, the friend of liberty, the bane of despotism"; "The Western Hemisphere,—may it become as famous for peace and freedom, as the eastern is for bloodshed and tyranny"; "The will of the people,—let the Servant who disobeys it tremble!" Toasts such as these were as frequent on the tongues of the pioneers as the latest tune or joke came to be with the advent of the radio.

More variety was usual in honoring the women, a toast seldom overlooked. "The Fair,—on man nature tried her 'prentice hand, and then she made the Lasses"; "The Fair,—our most valuable *productive* class. 'Paul may plant and Apollos water, yet *woman* alone can give the increase.' While we look upon a union of the States as necessary for the perpetuation of our republican government, let us not forget that the union of the sexes and the raising of young republicans, is a necessary part of our duty as patriots"; "The American Fair,—may they ever be adorned with the beauty of Venus and the virtue of Diana; be endued with the wisdom of Minerva, and possess the excellencies of Ceres"; "The Fair, —may the virtuous be fair and the fair be virtuous."

Not all were as dignified and classical as these samples. At a July 4 meeting in Madison, while the discussion was still warm over the location of Wisconsin's capital, was given the following: "May the enemies to Madison have everlasting itching and be deprived of the pleasure of scratching," and "Long corns and short shoes to the enemies of James D. Doty."[50]

The young cities of the West offered a wide range of amusements, with Cincinnati at first far in the lead. "Theatricus," whose attempt to interest "the good people of Cincinnati" in a theater in 1815 had run into considerable opposition from those who thought his enterprise would cultivate dissolute practices and prove deleterious to all principles of morality and decorum, was back on the job four years later, raising money for a $5,000

---

[50] Madison *Wisconsin Enquirer,* July 6, 1839. Representative lists of July 4 toasts may be found in the *Cleaveland Herald,* July 17, 1821, the *Hamilton* (Ohio) *Intelligencer and Advertiser,* July 15, 1822, the Vandalia *Illinois Intelligencer,* July 28, 1825, and the *Sangamo Journal,* July 7, 1838.

building; by 1828 plays were presented throughout the season.[51] Within five years Cincinnati had two theaters. Traveling theatrical corps visited the leading towns, and by 1835 even in the New England settled Western Reserve Mrs. McClure and company were playing "Honeymoon," "Othello," "Hunchback," and other plays to overflowing houses.[52]

The circus came "with the greatest variety of performances ever produced in the United States," including singing, dancing, riding feats, wire dancing, vaulting, tumbling, sleight of hand, and Mme. Robert who balanced a musket with fixed bayonet, point down, on her tooth. Prices were 50 cents for a box seat and 25 cents in the pit. "Grand menageries" of living animals were ever advertised. At Columbus the "Great Lion" was exhibited for four days in 1819 for 25 cents, but by 1838 it took the "Gigantic Giraffe or Cameleopard" to rate the same price.[53] The elephant or "great natural curiosity" might have been seen at Mr. Whipple's Hotel in Detroit in 1819 for 50 cents,[54] while at Hamilton in 1834 the "giant Rhinoceros or *Unicorn*," together with the other animals—all to be seen for 25 cents—got a four-by five-inch woodcut and two columns of publicity in the *Intelligencer*.[55] There was nothing like the animals for arousing interest. In Detroit in competition with a theatrical corps and a great magician "who ate fire and did a number of other odd things," it was the two traveling menageries which drew the crowds. Some people would even forego their whiskey to see them.[56]

Not even hard times and pecuniary difficulties deprived the people of their taste for rational amusements. By the middle 1830's towns of two or three thousand population were offering

[51] *Liberty Hall and Cincinnati Gazette*, January 11, 23, March 3, 1815; *Cincinnati Daily Gazette*, November-December, 1828. The Chillicothe *Weekly Recorder*, January 15, 1815, was quite worried about the inordinate pursuit of carnal pleasure and sought to have the legislature act. "It appears to be a sad evidence of depravation, and ominous of much evil to society, if to the vain pleasure of balls and assemblies now eagerly and systematically pursued, must be added the fascinating and corrupting entertainments of the stage."

[52] *Cleveland Herald*, July 2, 7, 1835. For a discussion of the theater, see Chapter XV.

[53] *Columbus Gazette*, April 1, 1819; *Ohio State Journal*, October 12, 1838. Cuts were used in the papers in the 1820's for the circus and animal advertisements. By the middle 1830's ads were of the display type.

[54] *Detroit Gazette*, November 26, 1819.

[55] *Cleaveland Herald*, August 24, 1827; *Detroit Gazette*, September 4, 1827; *Hamilton Intelligencer*, August 21, 1834.

[56] *Detroit Gazette*, June 28, 1825.

fair opportunities. In 1833 Cleveland had in the course of a few weeks a theatrical corps, two equestrian companies, the Siamese twins, General Black Hawk and his retinue (the ladies did not kiss him as in New York), then a female "orang-outang," as well as the great Fourth of July celebration—certainly "sufficient to satisfy the votaries of pleasure."[57] Soon the balloon ascension, "a sublime affair," was to be seen. At Cincinnati in 1835 the band played "Hail Columbia," and the big bag actually ascended. When a small black dog was let down in a parachute, the delight of the 2,000 spectators was complete.[58]

"Museums" exhibited wax figures of great heroes and scoundrels of history and "grand panoramic views" of Greece, Rome, or battle scenes from the late wars. The "National Panorama and American Museum of Wax Figures" was touring the West in 1815. It showed General Washington, the Goddess of Liberty, Stephen Decatur, Napoleon Bonaparte, Marie Louisa, Thomas Parr, Benjamin Franklin, and "Othello murdering Desdemonia, a sleeping beauty with her infant by her side," for 25 cents. Smoking was prohibited.[59] A "Grand Exhibition of Natural Curiosities" which included an enormous living anaconda or great Mountain Serpent, the chameleon of America, the *Real Asp* of Egypt, and the head of a cannibal New Zealand chief handsomely tattooed, was available at the same price. In 1816 lovers of the arts had an excellent opportunity to gratify both their tastes and their patriotism by visiting Mr. Gray's panorama of the gallant achievements of Macdonough and Macomb and the bombardment of Fort McHenry.[60]

Letton's Museum in Cincinnati in 1828 exhibited several thousand natural curiosities, a number of wax figures, an equestrian statue of Gen. Andrew Jackson, together with a splendid cosmoramic painting of the Battle of New Orleans. "Christ Rejected" did not draw the crowds, which seemed to prefer the wax works. The editor of the *Gazette* trusted that there was no less moral feeling and religious taste in Cincinnati than in the smaller towns.[61]

[57] *Cleveland Herald*, July 13, 1833; Ravenna *Western Courier*, August 1, 1833.
[58] *Hamilton Intelligencer*, April 9, 1835.
[59] Hamilton (Ohio) *Miami Intelligencer*, January 26, 1815.
[60] *Liberty Hall and Cincinnati Gazette*, December 9, 1816.
[61] *Ibid.*, January 16, 1827.

The same complaint regarding attendance was not registered in 1834 against the nightly exhibit in the upper story of one of the museum buildings of "the final place of torment in the other world, with all the agreeable accompaniments that the imaginations of the vulgar delight in conceiving as belonging to it." Even persons who frowned upon the theater defended this spectacle for the "good moral effect it would produce."[62]

Persons interested in developing the terpsichorean arts in Cincinnati did not have to confine themselves to the simple dancing games so enjoyed by their country brethren. Monsieur Ratel's dancing academy was offering lessons in the allemande, hornpipe, waltz, and the minuet in 1817; even in the depression year of 1819 the Cincinnati Cotillion Club held as many as eight dances in a season.

Musical instruments were being advertised by the 1820's. Next in popularity to the violin were the flutes and other wood winds. Pianos were manufactured on a small scale in Cincinnati prior to 1820. Instruction in music was offered by the Ratels at the same time they opened their dancing academy. Amateur musicians organized a Haydn society which in 1819 gave concerts and even performed a symphony.

First notices of phrenology lectures appeared with Dr. Cranium in 1822; within a few years the western towns were full of "professors" who "amused and instructed presentable gatherings." The chief promoter of the "popular pastime" (originated in Europe by Drs. Gall and Spurzheim) was Dr. Charles Caldwell, of Transylvania, whose book, *The Elements of Phrenology*, was widely circulated. He delivered a course of lectures at the Western Museum in Cincinnati in 1827–28. Naturally the new "science" attracted many quacks, but the more serious phrenologists were groping after a fashion for the science of psychology.[63] Articles and reviews, as well as advertisements of "professors,"

[62] The exhibit is more fully described in Chapter XV, 577–78.

[63] See, for instance, Dr. Charles Caldwell's defense of phrenology in his review in the *Western Monthly Review*, I (1827–28), 357–65. Also review of the pamphlet, "New Views of Penitentiary Discipline and Moral Education and Reform," in *ibid.*, III (1829–30), 50. A Dr. Sewall advertised his lectures at Springfield, Illinois, with a column of testimonials from such well-known men as Daniel Webster, John McLean, John Sergeant, and John Quincy Adams. Adams' testimonial was something of a boomerang. He classified phrenology with alchemy, judicial astrology, augury, etc. Like Cicero he did not understand how two augurs could meet and look each other in the face without laughing. Springfield *Sangamo Journal*, August 2, 1839.

appeared often in the newspapers after 1830. Best known of the phrenologists after Spurzheim's death was the Scotsman, George Combe, who spent two years, 1838 to 1840, lecturing in the eastern cities. He came West only to see Dr. Caldwell and William Henry Harrison, but his lectures were closely followed by many western papers. His two-volume report on his travels, *Notes on the United States of North America During a Phrenological Visit*, is better known for its description of the country than for its phrenological data.

For twenty years phrenology flourished. Serious followers expanded its possibilities to the control of personality—even crime might be eliminated when the science was mastered—but the general populace was not entirely convinced. In 1849 "A Skeptic" was advising, "Go everyone and get your heads examined."[64] Many did.

More stimulating even than phrenology were the "laughing gas" exhibitions. The notice of such a performance in a northern Ohio town in 1821 read:

> Dr. Brooks proposes to administer 10 to 15 doses of the protoxide of azote, or the exhilarating gas, in the Warren Hotel on Tuesday next at 3:00 o'clock p. m. The sensations, produced by this gas are highly pleasurable and resemble those in some degree attendant on the pleasant period of intoxication. Great exhilaration, an irresistible propensity to laugh, dance and sing, a rapid flow of vivid ideas, an unusual fitness for muscular exertion, are the ordinary feelings it produces. These pleasant sensations are not succeeded by any debilitating effects upon the system. A more full account of this gas will be given on the evening of the exhibition. Tickets of admission may be had at the printing office.[65]

These exhibitions unknowingly served a more valuable use than mere amusement, for they were furnishing experience in the use of anesthetics.

Billiard tables, ninepin alleys, gaming tables, and coffee houses were common enough to give the lawmakers and puritanical citizens something to worry about, not to mention the Public Garden and the Ball Room.[66] Competing with these in drawing

---

[64] *Cincinnati Daily Gazette*, January 3, 1849.
[65] Quoted in Pickard and Buley, *The Midwest Pioneer: His Ills, Cures, and Doctors*, 114.
[66] Columbus *Ohio State Journal*, August 17, 1827; *Cincinnati Daily Gazette*, July 31, 1837.

power, at least periodically, were protracted meetings conducted by a popular preacher of one of the evangelical sects.

> His Congregations are famed for the number of young and handsome girls that attend them; and these draw a corresponding number of gay young men. His addresses are described as being more to the imagination than to the reason; his voice is spoken of as melting and tender, his imagination fervid; and his language eloquent and amatory; and as he indulges in the privilege, when his female converts are young and handsome, of "greeting them with a holy kiss," his popularity is by many thus accounted for.[67]

With more amusements and places to go,[68] certain classes in the young cities naturally paid more attention to dress. More women came to rely upon dressmakers and milliners for their dresses, capes, and mantles of linens, worsteds, and silks, many of them cut from imported fabrics. Merchants carried stocks of shawls of many colors, and various accessories. Leghorn bonnets "with a flaring front-piece and a curiously placed crown, the whole resembling an inverted coal-scuttle, decked out with brightly-colored ribbons and artificial flowers," and other such creations were popular. One English traveler found the more fashionable of Cincinnati as well clothed as Londoners. "But the females of the middle and lower orders, though gaily dressed, often go without shoes and stockings; indeed most of the females in the western country go without them, at least in summer."[69] He must have mistaken children for "females." This was hardly a fair observation. Other travelers noticed as many well-dressed women and pretty faces on the streets of Cincinnati as in New York. Although, in the absence of manufacturers' and stylists' organizations, fashions did not change seasonally or even annually, nevertheless, the desire to be in style existed.

Nor did the women have a monopoly on color and fancy design. Cuts of frock and dress coats, cassimere and fancy pantaloons, vests, shirts, and collars were appearing in Cincinnati papers in the late 1820's, and within a few years these articles were available in the smaller towns. Silk, velvet, marseilles, and

---

[67] Buckingham, *Eastern and Western States of America,* II, 395–96.
[68] To Michael Chevalier, however, Cincinnati seemed a wearisome abode to anyone interested in gaiety and amusement. See below, 389.
[69] Woods, *Two Years' Residence on the English Prairie,* 99–100.

valencia vestings; Italian silk cravats; silk and linen handkerchiefs; silk, linen, horseskin, and beaver gloves; silk half-hose;
silk and satin vests; and silk hats for gentlemen were carried in
stock by Vincennes merchants in the 1830's.[70] The local dandy
of the period was likely to be decked out in a long-tailed double-
breasted blue broadcloth coat trimmed in a double row of gold-
plated buttons, a buff or fancy vest, buff or fawn tight-fitting
trousers, and neat tailored boots. A silk stock or "choker" over
a stiff buckram frame held high a head topped off with a bell-
crowned beaver or silk hat.[71]

Cincinnati, the pride of the West, by the 1830's had its
"society," poised and gracious enough to win "the high respect"
of Miss Martineau, who was familiar with Europe as well as
America. There were garden parties and teas, literary clubs
and concerts, art exhibits and charity bazaars. True, Easterners
and Westerners sometimes sought to accentuate and perpetuate
their differences in background and distinctive observances, but
this only contributed to the interest.[72] At the other extreme,
Chicago, a raw but booming village, took "some allowable pride
in . . . its society. It is a remarkable thing to meet such an assem-
blage of educated, refined, and wealthy persons as may be found
there, living in small, inconvenient houses on the edge of a wild
prairie."[73] "The society of Detroit is very choice; and . . . has
continued so since the old colonial days," reported the same
visitor.[74]

§

In speech, as in blood, the Middle Westerner of the pioneer
period was essentially "American"—that is, his language was a
blend, with the Southern Appalachian element generally predominating. The speech of the southern highlands was a survival
of Anglo-Saxon of the Elizabethan Age, with some "Scotch-

---

[70] *Western Sun.*

[71] A one-and-a-half-column article in the Cincinnati *National Republican,* May
14, 1824, described the dandy mathematically, anatomically, chemically, metaphys-
ically, botanically, and topographically.

[72] Martineau, *Retrospect of Western Travel,* III, 241.

[73] Harriet Martineau, *Society in America* (2 volumes. 4th ed. New York, 1837),
I, 261.

[74] *Ibid.,* I, 233.

Irish," "Pennsylvania Dutch," and Indian influences.[75] Description is difficult because of the local variations in pronunciation and vocabulary, and the peculiarities and vagaries of syntax and inflection. Strong verbs were made weak and weak verbs strong. The mountaineer "blowed," "ketched," "drawed," "knowed," "seed," and was "borned"; but he also "clum," "div," "retch," "drug," "et," "snuck," and "skun." Old forms were common. He "taken" things to town, and he "heered" or "hearn say." "Afeared" for "afraid," and "et" for "ate" were of good English ancestry.[76] Cases, moods, auxiliaries, relatives, agreement of subject and verb, as well as tense, were treated with true Elizabethan indifference: "Me and her was a-sparkin'," "Hit shore is me," "She seed he and I a-comin' down the road."

"Yourn," "hisn," "hern," "ourn," and "theirn" were commonly used possessives. Adjectives served as adverbs: "I could ketch him easy"; as verbs: "I shore didn't aim t'contrary that ol heifer fr'm Hell Holler," "Hit darknin' out doors," "He'll sly outen the law"; and as nouns: "Them Pea Ridge folks is all hatefuls, an' if they'r a-lookin' fer trouble they'll shore get a lavish of it"; verbs as adjectives: "He warn't thoughted [intelligent] enough"; and as nouns: "Did you all get the invite (or give-out)?" Nouns were used as adjectives: "Them dang fool houn' dogs," and as verbs: "Don't fault th' young-un jes' fer bein' puny," "That 'ar shoat'll meat th' hull fambly a month,

[75] Among helpful articles for brief study of this subject: Maristan Chapman [Mary and Stanley Chapman], "American Speech as Practised in the Southern Highlands," in *The Century Magazine,* CXVII, No. 5 (Mar. 1929), 617–23; J. H. Combs, "Old, Early and Elizabethan English in the Southern Mountains," in *Dialect Notes,* IV, Part IV (1916), 283–97; Vance Randolph, various articles and word lists on the Ozark folk speech in *American Speech,* III, 1–13, 401–7; IV, 205–6; V, 16–21, 198–208, 264–67, 424–30; and in *Dialect Notes,* V, Part IX (1926), 397–405, Part X (1927), 472–79. The many-volumed *Linguistic Atlas of the United States,* sponsored by the Council of Learned Societies, is to contain a volume on Kentucky and the Old Northwest states. This work is still in the process of preparation and will deal far more comprehensively with this subject than anything in existence.

Pennsylvanische-Deutsche in its various forms was a blend of the Palatinate, Württemberg, Rhine country and Swiss dialects of two centuries ago, with a mixture of English up to 12 or 15 per cent. See introduction to "A Dictionary of the Non-English Words of the Pennsylvania-German Dialect," Marcus Bachman Lambert, editor, in *The Pennsylvania-German Society Proceedings,* XXX (1924), viii, ix.

Many of the first Americanisms were borrowed from the Indian. Examples: moose, skunk, hickory, pecan, paw paw, raccoon, chinquapin, chipmunk, persimmon, squash, hominy, pone, canoe, moccasin. Henry L. Mencken, *The American Language* . . . (1st ed. New York, 1919), 40–44; *Journal of American Folk-Lore,* XX (1907), 240.

[76] "Afeared" is the regular participle of "affear," whereas "afraid" comes from "affray." For "et" see *Oxford Dictionary.*

easy," "Waitin' so purty and patientable to bride her man."[77]

Beyond the knowledge of Elizabethan forms, or grammar and idiom, is required an understanding of the spirit of the folk who created this speech. The frontiersman refused to be restricted in style by law of grammar no less than law of Parliament or Congress.[78] Clearness in expression was preferred to grammatical correctness, and brevity to clearness. In tone nasal, and in delivery usually deliberate, yet easily distinguished from the Yankee nasal drawl, this speech ordinarily kept the flat *a* of colonial times, preferred *i* to *e* in such words as "get," dropped final *g*'s, elided, contracted ("ary," "nary," "howdy," etc.), and changed pronunciation from time to time and place to place.[79] Pronunciation and emphasis played an important part, but grammatical shift of parts of speech, word compounding, word coining, use of obsolete comparatives and superlatives, together with imaginative and picturesque speech figures, added appreciably to the expressiveness. Double identifying nouns such as "kitchen-room," "shootin'-iron," "rifle-gun," "ham-meat," "ridin'-critter," "man-person," and "cow-brute" were common, as well as such obvious compounds as "carrytale," "lackbrain," "wantwit," "breakvow," and "clutchfist."

There were verb compounds, such as "tale-bearing" and "lie-swearing." Adjective compounds came easily: "sweet-meaty," "hind-leggy," "dumb-brutely," "sheepsy," "stuff and non-setty"; and compounded superlatives were effective: "mud-piedest," "dry-uppedest," "shut-pocket'dest," "sought-afterest," "up-and-comin'-dest," "nothin'-doin'dest," and "flea-huntin'dest." Hybrids

---

[77] Several of the expressions are cited from contemporary mountain speech.

[78] "But the nervous expressions, and almost startling boldness, of western phraseology would lose half its vividness and power when transferred to paper." Hoffman, *A Winter in the West*, I, 51.

"Language, ideas, manners, customs—are all new; yes, even language; for to the instructed person from one of our great Eastern cities, the talk of the true backwoodsman is scarce intelligible. His indescribable *twang* is, to be sure, no further from good English than the *patois* of many of the English counties. But at the West this curious talker is your neighbor and equal, while in the elder country he would never come in your way unless you sought him purposely to hear his jargon." Mrs. Kirkland, *Western Clearings*, preface, vi.

[79] Some specimens of pronunciation: "agin," "bar" (bear), "keer" (care), "kiver" (cover), "crap" (crop), "aig" (egg), "fotch," "holp," or "hep" (help), "jiste" (joist), "laig" (leg), "obleeged," "rensh" (rinse), "sich," "yander." The broad *a* vogue originated in England about 1780 and later came to Boston. C. H. Grandgent. "Fashion and the Broad A," in *The Nation*, January 7, 1915, pp. 13–14. Noah Webster made *bath* and *path* rhyme with *hath*.

with borrowed prefixes and suffixes were created: "disremember," "ingrateful," "onsartin'," "unproper," "unthoughtedly," "disturbment," "revilement," "sadful," "argyfy," "teachified," and so on, as well as words with diminutives or redundant suffixes such as: "tittery," "tumbly," "withery," "frecklsy," "quicksy," "slickery," "tickle-sweety," "stillsome," "patientable," and "virginous."

Vocabularies were rich, flexible, and sometimes strong. Such words as "brash" (hasty, brittle), "bound" (determined), "beatenest" (hard to beat), "bresket" (energy), "bee-gum" (beehive), "clever" (kind, accommodating), "cazan" (cause), "crick" (creek), "dunk" (dip), "dauncy" (half-sick), "enjoy" (entertain), "fitten," (decent), "lavish" (a large quantity), "guess" (think), "heap" (a great deal), "middlin' " (fair, tolerable), "passel" (parcel, of people, etc.), "poke" (bag), "powerful" (exceedingly, extraordinary), "racket" (fight), "ruction" (quarrel), "reckon" (guess, wonder), "red up" (tidy up), "whang" (thong), "swan" (swear—"I swan," etc.), might necessitate a glossary for one unfamiliar with the speech. But "contrarious," "cumfluttered" (confused), "caterwampus," "flopdoodle," "fractious," "mozy," "ornery," "peart," "piddlin' " (trifling or puttering around), "sashay," "triflin'," and "tetchous" (touchy) are practically self-explanatory. More expressive still are descriptive words and phrases such as "fritter-minded," "gone franzy," "plumb moonshined," "buck-eyed," and "hippoed"[80] (applied to mental states), "lickety splittin'," "lickety brindle," "gimlet-eyed," "chisted out" (swelled up), "sow-belly" (pork), "granny woman" (midwife), "woodscolt" (illegitimate child), and "lollygagin' " and "tomcattin' " (applied respectively to slushy and promiscuous sexual behavior).[81]

This was the foundation speech of the majority of the folk who populated southern Illinois and Indiana, predominated in parts of Ohio, and figured prominently in the settlement of the northern parts of these states as well as in Wisconsin and to a certain

---

[80] Hippo usually meant some old crone versed in medical lore of the charm or Indian remedy type. Hippoed meant sick, overcome by symptoms, overdoctored, etc.

[81] Samples here are of words widely used. For glossaries with many words of more local usage, see the novels of Maristan Chapman [Mary and Stanley Chapman]: *Homeplace* (New York, 1929), *The Happy Mountain* (1928), *The Weather Tree* (1932), etc.

extent in Michigan.[82] As one went farther north from the Ohio more often was heard the speech of Middle States men—Germans, York staters, some Quakers—and the various Yankee accents which prevailed in the Reserve, in Michigan, eastern Wisconsin, and northern Illinois. Some words the Yankee had in common with the Southerner: cover was still "kiver" and chair was "cheer"; "ary," "fit," "rid," and "his'n" sounded much the same. But pronunciation as well as accent contrasted noticeably when he said "deestrick" for district, "sile" for soil, "kag" for keg, "quishion" for cushion, "sneck" for snake, "idear" for idea, and pronounced stone, coat, and boat with short o's. Names of many things were different ("beetle" for maul, "shack" for mast, "rifle" for whetstone, "shakes" for clapboards), but it was in enunciation and peculiarities of expression that differences were most noticeable. When the New Englander swore he was inclined to say "I vum," "I swan," "goll darn," "golly crimus," "by cripes," and otherwise evade the issue.

The western man ripped out remorseless oaths, swearing a blue streak with a remarkable breadth of expression. Whereas a Hoosier described himself as "catawampously chawed up," the Yankee was merely a "gone sucker." Inquire about his health, and he tells you he is "so as to be crawlin'!" As one contemporary observed: He talks of "spunkin' up to an all-fired, tarnation,

[82] As a result of the writings of Eggleston (*The Hoosier Schoolmaster,* etc.) and others, the idea of a Hoosier dialect and "hoosierisms," grew up. There are no "hoosierisms" any more than "suckerisms" or "buckeyeisms." In spite of the modifications brought on by time and schools a native of a rural county in southern Illinois or Indiana will need no special training to speak the language of the mountaineer of Kentucky, ridge runner of the Ozarks, or cotton tenant in Arkansas. This is apparent from a comparison of word lists in *Dialect Notes,* more obvious when the speech is heard firsthand.

"The so-called Hoosier dialect, where it survives at all, is the speech of the first American settlers in Indiana, greatly modified by time and schooling, but retaining, both in employment of colloquial terms and in pronunciation, the peculiarities that were carried westward from tide water early in the nineteenth century. The distinctive Indiana countryman, . . . speaks a good deal as his Pennsylvania, or North Carolina or Kentucky grandfather or great-grandfather did before him, and has created nothing new. His speech contains comparatively few words that are peculiar to the State or to communities within it; but in the main it shares such deviations from normal or literary English with the whole Southwest." Meredith Nicholson, *The Hoosiers* (New York, 1915), 46–47.

J. Richard Beste, *The Wabash: or Adventures of an English Gentleman's Family in the Interior of America* . . . (2 volumes. London, 1855), I, 280, writing of Indianapolis: "For notwithstanding the disagreeable nasal tone and drawling whine in which most of them speak, and not withstanding a few national phrases and the peculiar use and pronunciation of certain words, it must be admitted that the American people, in general, speak English without provincial dialect or vulgarisms."

slick gall, clean grit, I tell yeou neow"; and, naturally he has a "kinder sneakin' notion arter her." If she were to tell him to "hold his yawp" he would admit that he felt "kinder streaked, by golly!" He describes a man as being "handsome as a picter, but so darnation ugly"; or as "a thunderin' fool, but a clever critter as ever lived"—ugly being Yankee for wicked, and clever for good-natured.

A plain girl is as homely as a hedge-fence. A Yankee brags that he is a hull team and a hoss to let. You can't tucker him eout. It beats all natur heow he can go it when he gets his dander up. He has got his eye-teeth cut, true as preachin'. He gets hoppin' mad, and makes all gee agin. He is dreadful glad to see you, and is powerful sorry you enjoy such poor health.

I am inclined to think the Western vocabulary more copious than that of the Yankee proper. The language, like the country, has a certain breadth and magnitude about it. A Western man sleeps so sound, it would take an earthquake to wake him. He is in danger pretty considerable much, because somebody was down on him, like the whole Missouri on a sandbar. He is a gone 'coon. He is down on all cussed varmints, gets into an everlasting fix, and holds that the longest pole knocks down the persimmons. A story smells rather tall. Stranger, he says, in bar hunts I am numerous. He says a pathetic story sunk into his feelings like a snagged boat into the Mississippi. He tells of a person as cross as a bar with two cubs and a sore tail. He laughs like a hyena over a dead nigger. He walks through a fence like a falling tree through a cobweb. He goes the whole hog. He raises right smart of corn and lives where there is a smart chance of bars. Bust me wide open, he says, if I didn't bulge into the creek in the twinkling of a bedpost, I was so thunderin' savagerous.[83]

Besides the quaint but descriptive expressions of this type, probably characteristic of the uneducated in any time or place, there was an abundance of slang, and ephemeral and crude localisms. Unfortunately travelers often failed to record them. "I have not mentioned the fact of the existence of a multitude of singular and uncouth phrases and words, as characteristic of the West, for I have deemed them utterly unworthy of notice. I have heard some scores of them in my tours, but such of them as are not the coinage of rude boatmen, or of still more ignorant hunters, are of eastern origin, and claim no pretensions to regard in this

[83] Thomas L. Nichols, *Forty Years of American Life* (2 volumes. London, 1864), I, 385–86.

work."[84] Another Easterner characterized western speech even more briefly. "Indeed the whole conversation at the west is *racy* —it smacks of the soil."[85]

Naturally current events affected speech. For example, anyone knew in the 1830's that "to swarthout" (after Samuel Swarthout of New York) meant to default and flee. To "go the whole hog" meant to have refreshment or to vote a straight ticket; "to have steam up," ready to go. When political ferment or reform movements got to humming, people were warned "not to mistake the whizzing of the safety valves for the bursting of the boilers." "Have you seen the elephant?" must have originated as a result of the tour of the great pachyderm. The question (and answer) usually had connotations but remotely related to menageries. When a man had "seen the elephant" he had been everywhere, seen everything, perhaps was, in the language of a later period, "fed up." Profanity, of course, abounded. "It is a lamentable fact that this vice is extremely common in the valley of the Mississippi. . . . So much so, that many gentlemen, and clever men in other respects, are in the habit of using profane language, when they are scarcely aware of it. . . ."[86]

Of folklore, proverbs, and superstitions, the West had no distinctive variety, and made few original contributions. The most-used gems of wisdom were those which had stood the test of time—those used in colonial times, in England, Germany, even in ancient lands. "Buying a pig in a poke," "A chip off the old block," "He cut a real swath," "A hard row to hoe," "He's been through the mill," "He'll never amount to a hill of beans," "He's come to the end of his rope," "Short horse soon curried," "It comes and goes like the old woman's soap," and hundreds of others, saws and sayings as well as proverbs, which comprised a considerable part of ordinary speech, antedate the new West.

Nor can the habit of the smart answer or "wisecrack" be said to be indigenous to the West, although it certainly was characteristic. To his tall tales, practical jokes, and witty replies the Westerner gave his peculiar twist—and how he loved them. To

---

[84] R. B., *View of the Valley of the Mississippi: Or the Emigrant's and Traveller's Guide to the West* . . . (Philadelphia, 1832), 93. The author is said to be either Robert Baird or Richard Bache.

[85] A. D. Jones, *Illinois and the West*, 165.

[86] R. B., *View of the Valley of the Mississippi*, 343.

the greeting "How do you do?" a keen citizen would reply, "About as I please, stranger, how do you do?" If he were asked, "Where does this road go?" he might aptly observe, "Don't go nowheres, mister, stays right there." If asked how his potatoes turned out, he would say, "Didn't turn out at all, had to dig 'em out." And so on. Such pat answers were used over and over on friends as well as strangers, and never seemed to die out as do slang and current expressions. The river boatmen, professional teamsters, later the lumberjacks and other workers with a vocational pride or *esprit de corps,* had their special collections; the reputations of such heroes as Mike Fink and Paul Bunyan rested as much upon their ready wit as upon prodigious feats of valor and skill. The embarrassing question, the successful baiting of a rival, above all the *riposte verbale* were often more decisive than a fight, and longer remembered.

Though the common speech was less used by the educated and those of wider contacts, still there was always a tendency for even these classes to speak with somewhat less grammatical correctness and propriety of diction than they had knowledge of. Correct pronunciation and too much attention to diction was put in the same category as fastidiousness in dress, and was regarded as "stuck up."[87] Lawyers who aspired to office, newspaper editors, even preachers, had to be careful about such matters. To many, however, such precaution was unnecessary. Not too exceptional was the legislator from Columbiana County, Ohio, who spoke of the "hebias kawpus law" and referred to "Jefferson's immanuel" address. "Zelious," "magnanimious," "scurlious," "philanthripic," "embazzle," "inoquivocably," "reitriate," and "oughter" were favorites with him. He was reported as using "rise up enmassey" and saying "his garden are cut, his house are kept by the state."[88]

Lack of acquaintance with books and a knowledge of the classics, history, and philosophy was ordinarily no handicap to the active-minded Westerner. He relied heavily upon personal contacts, conversations, and firsthand knowledge. "Fluencey of language, with an ease and power of expression which sometimes

[87] James Whitcomb Riley, "Dialect in Literature," in *Forum,* XIV (1892–93), 467; Sulgrove, *History of Indianapolis,* 89.
[88] The Columbus correspondent in the *Cleveland Herald and Gazette* (weekly). March 25, 1840.

swells to the dignity of eloquence, and often displays itself in terms of originality, at once humorous and forcible, constitute the conversational resources of the western man."[89]

§ §

"I do not think that American peculiarities of language are so remarkable as those of character and manners—or, in other words that Americanism is so much in speech, as in thought, feeling, and action," said an American who lived in England.[90] So it was with Westerners in comparison to Easterners in America. Some of the causes of the distinctiveness in western character and attitudes are obvious.

By heritage the western peoples came by certain characteristics honestly, for the West drew unto itself copiously of the bold, the aggressive, the capable, as well as of the discontented, the unsuccessful, even the lawless. The older folks, the successful, the conservative, when they came, were a small minority.

The West offered special advantages for the poor man, particularly if industrious and patient.[91] Yet wealth did not come quickly, nor ultimately to everyone. Nor were the opportunities of the West to be counted upon to take the place of lack of ability on the part of emigrating merchants, doctors, and lawyers. A fifth-rate lawyer from Boston, expecting to find himself shortly a judge or a member of Congress from a western town, would likely find that he was still a fifth-rate lawyer.

Indeed, a man of respectable talents coming from the east or south finds here many and powerful competitors, and will have to work his way to favor or wealth in his profession, much as he would elsewhere. It is true there is less competition because there is a wider field, the facilities are multiplied and multiplying, instead of being nearly exhausted, as is the case in the east. A young man of enterprise and a small capital, whether in law, medicine, engineering, surveying, or in the mercantile business, stands a much fairer chance to succeed in either here, than any where east or south, because not only is his field larger and competition less, but new sources of wealth and power are developed every day, and more and more. But the

---

[89] Hoffman, *A Winter in the West*, I, 266–67.
[90] Nichols, *Forty Years of American Life*, I, 389.
[91] The arguments are well presented in W. Kirkland, "The West, the Paradise of the Poor," in *The United States Magazine, and Democratic Review*, N. S., XV (July–Dec., 1844), 182–90.

same talent, tact and industry are requisite here as elsewhere. The difference is, he *must* succeed here, elsewhere he *may*.[92]

Western society was society on the make. The American's desire "to better his condition" at times developed into an encroaching spirit, yet the pioneer was jealous of his possessions and willing to take the law in his own hands to defend them. If at times he seemed selfish, morose, and suspicious, at others he was openhanded, hospitable, and credulous. Courage he had, dis-passionate and stoical, and patience—especially for vengeance. Generations of Indian fighting saw to that. Restless he was, but also calm and deliberate. Pride and personal dignity backed a self-reliance which had something of egotism but little of arro-gance. "It was a calm, just estimate of his own capabilities—a well-grounded confidence in his own talents—a clear, manly un-derstanding of his own individual rights, dignity and relations." A certain graveness of mien seemed in keeping with the sterner realities of his environment—"a melancholy looking face, with its mild blue eyes and sharpened features." Yet on the other hand Miss Martineau thought Americans "the most good tem-pered people in the world" who offered a "general example of cheerful helpfulness" (excepting for the apparent coldness of persons in hotels and shops).

It has been said that there was little of romance in the make-up of the pioneer, although much in his environment. Yet Timothy Flint was right when he said: "There is more of the material of poetry than we imagine, diffused through all classes of the community." Not the poetry of verse but the poetry of life. Lack-ing were artistic costumes, folk music, and art comparable to that which European or Mexican peasants might produce.

Luxury and taste are, in general, the offspring of refinement and of ripened age. . . . The great body of the people of the west are employed, not in trailing vines, but in acquiring their support. A wheat field is more pleasing to their taste than a flower garden. A well-ploughed lot is more satisfactory to their eye than the most exquisite painting of a Raphael or a Claude. They would prefer seeing a gristmill working on their own stream, to the sight of the sculptured marble of the Venus or the Apollo![93]

[92] A. D. Jones, *Illinois and the West*, 103-4.
[93] James H. Lanman, "The Progress of the Northwest," in *Hunt's Merchants' Magazine* (New York, 1839-70), III (July-Dec., 1840), 39.

But this process of making a living was art; basic art. Truly, for those who had the capacity, coming West, making a farm, a home, creating good things and enjoying them, was as much a way of satisfying the innate craving for romance and art as it was a process dictated by economic necessity. There was on the part of the individual a sensing of the magnificent, a feeling of the fulfillment of destiny. In this the influence of a more grandiose nature played its part. Measureless forests, big waters "whose sweep is over uncounted leagues," and the onward reaching prairies—these tended to release the inward impulses and restless energies, to create freedom of thought and expression and a feeling of the newness of life.

This quality was displayed in marked degree by the Kentuckians, who more than any other single people influenced the Ohio Valley states of the Old Northwest. Charles Fenno Hoffman thought them "individually the most characteristic and interesting people in the Union" (though by no means as useful members of society as New Englanders). Descended as they were largely from military men and hunters, inheriting not only the experience of Indian warfare but life in broad and fertile meadows and forests, they were distinguished by the traits natural from such an origin. "There is an off-handedness—if I may use the term—a fearless ardour, a frankness and self-possession about them that engages your good-will at once; while you are both interested and amused at the exaggerated tone of sentiment, half-romantic, half-vain-glorious, which their ideas and expressions betray." The Kentuckian's well-known loyalty to his state was never better expressed than by the boatman who ferried the traveler across the Ohio: " 'No, stranger, there's no place on the universal 'arth like old Kaintuck: she whips all "Out-west" in prettiness; and you might bile down cr'ation and not get such another State out of it.' "[94]

Kentuckians were fortunate in having good "press agents," even from an early date; yet they had no monopoly of these traits. The "Buckeyes," "Hoosiers," "Suckers," "Wolverines," and later the "Badgers" were generally quite as proud of their states, their nicknames, and equally satisfied with themselves.[95]

[94] Hoffman, *A Winter in the West,* II, 139–41.
[95] "Hooshier," "Sucker," "Badger," and "Wolverine" were used by Hoffman (*A Winter in the West*) in 1833. "Buckeye" was already well known. The application

In spite of an aggressive self-reliance, a certain "boadaciousness" of spirit, there was just the suspicion of an inferiority complex in the attitude of the Westerner. In a region where dress was rough and serviceable, clay mud or dust covered the boots, and haircuts or shaves were infrequent, the average man looked askance or worse upon anyone who appeared dressed up or otherwise seemed to be "puttin' on airs."[96] At least one traveler warned others to lay aside their good clothes west of Pittsburgh in order to avoid staring, adverse comment, and sometimes expectoration with a purpose.

When an Indiana politician electioneered for office in 1826 in a new-fangled borrowed buggy, he was advised by friends to hide it and proceed on horseback or foot. As late as the 1840's, when Congressman George H. Proffit attended a basket meeting

---

of four of these names is obvious, though the origins in point of time are not clear. Early miners in the Mineral Point region really did burrow; some stayed all winter, whereas others came back in spring with the suckers. Reuben Gold Thwaites, "Wisconsin's Emblems and Sobriquet," in *Wisconsin State Historical Society Proceedings*, LV (1907), 303–4.

The word "Hoosier" (hoohier, hoosher) gives more trouble. The earliest reference known is that in a letter in the Indiana State Library from James Curtis at Oregon, Holt County, Missouri, February 24, 1826, to his uncle, Joseph Beeler, of Indianapolis. Curtis wrote: "The indana hoesiers that came out last fall is settled from 2 to 4 milds from us." See *Indiana History Bulletin*, XXVI (1949), 75–76.

One explanation of the origin of the term came by way of Mordecai M. Noah, of New York, and was based on a doubtful story of a recruiting officer of the War of 1812 who called hussars "hoosiers." Another explanation traced the word to days of early settlement and survey when the cabin greeting was "Who's here." More likely the sobriquet was one of many used by the Ohio River boatmen to designate a real man, a word equivalent to "ripstaver," "scrouger," "snorter," "bulger," "hoover," "screamer," "roarer," etc., words which never attained later respectable standing. By some caprice the term came to be confined solely to those boatmen who lived on the Indian shore and then to those on the Indiana stretch and finally to Indianans. Piqua (Ohio) *Courier and Enquirer*, February 17, 1838. See also Jacob P. Dunn, "Origin of the Word Hoosier," in *Indiana Magazine of History*, I (1905), 85–96. Charles Collins of the *Chicago Tribune* (Book Section, August 29, 1943) advanced the theory that *houssieres* (French for "the bushy places") is the simple and proper explanation.

Although the general connotation of the term was a boorish or crude person, by 1833 ex-Governor James B. Ray of Indiana was defending the name as synonymous with gentleman. Springfield *Sangamo Journal*, October 12, 1833. The nickname was no doubt helped in its transition to respectability by the famous poem "The Hoosier's Nest," by John Finley, which was published in the Indianapolis *Indiana Journal* in 1833. Commenting upon the poem, the *Quincy* (Ill.) *Whig* said, "The citizens of our sister State of Indiana are pretty generally known throughout the West, by the singular appellation Hoosher. . . . The picture will answer also for the wilder parts of Illinois." September 28, 1839.

[96] Toilet facilities at taverns, on boats, etc., were simple. Enough water to wash one's face and hands at mealtime was considered adequate. "In fact I have found it more difficult in travelling in the United States, to procure a liberal supply of water at all times of the day and night in my bedchamber, than to obtain any other necessity." James Stuart, *Three Years in North America* (2 volumes. New York, 1833), II, 273.

in his district with a silk hat and fine carriage, he broke up the meeting but lost votes. Old taxpayers shook their heads and refused to see their "servant" so bedecked. The fastidious traveler who hung up a blanket to protect his bed from public gaze at the tavern saw the horny fist of a son of toil pull it down with the exclamation, "There's too damned much privacy here." And James Whitcomb, later governor of Indiana, almost "got off on the wrong foot" when it was discovered that he wore a night-shirt. Too much of nicety or style in speech, dress, or manners was openly resented, either as a mark of softness of the "effete East," or as an assumption of superiority because of station or wealth. When the "professor's" wife improvised a screen behind which to retire in a crowded house it was regarded as "powerful proud doings of stuck up folks." "And sorry am I to say that in the Purchase, as in some other places, such opinion is formed and similarly expressed about *extra* cleanliness, decency, modesty, learning and the like: if these things exceed your neighbour's they subject you to suspicion, often to dislike, and not infrequently to rancorous persecution."[97]

So also in Michigan Territory, where the New England rather than the Upland South heritage prevailed.

There seems to be in the forming stages of society, at least in this Western country, a burning, restless desire to subject all habits and manners to one Procrustean rule. Whoever ventures to differ essentially from the mass, is sure to become the object of unkind feeling, even without supposing any bitter personal animosity. . . . As was the accusation of witchcraft in olden times—a charge on which neither evidence, judge nor jury, was necessary to condemn the unfortunate suspected,—so with us of the West is the suspicion of pride—an undefined and undefinable crime, described alike by no two accusers, yet held unpardonable by all. Once establish the impression that a man is guilty of this high offence against society, and you have succeeded in ruining his reputation as a good neighbour. Nobody will ask you for

[97] Hall, *The New Purchase,* 81.
"Society here at present seems almost entirely free from the taint of aristocracy— the only premonitory symptoms of that disease, most prevalent generally in old settled communities, were manifested last week, when John I. Foster bought a new pair of silver plated spurs, and T. N. Catterlin was seen walking up street with a pair of curiously embroidered gloves on his hands." Cox, *Recollections of the Early Settlement of the Wabash Valley,* 19.
". . . of all places in the world to live on the shady side of public opinion, an American backwoods settlement is the very worst." Kirkland, *A New Home— Who'll Follow,* 219–20.

proof; accusation is proof. This is one of the cases where one has no right to be suspected. The cry "Mad Dog!" is not more surely destructive.[98]

Westerners, being a social and gossipy people, probably regarded desire for privacy as a species of pride. "There is a sort of community of feeling . . . of all men and womens affairs and motives. . . . You are in a house of glass." No one, especially a stranger, dared to want to be left alone. Seclusion was regarded as "a species of neglect, if not offense, which is decidedly felt, though it may not be expressed. You may sin and be wicked in many ways, and in the tolerant circle of American Society receive a full and generous pardon. But this one sin can never be pardoned, and if you want to be elected constable, squire or president, be sure you never commit it."[99]

When one comes to a discussion of the manners and habits of the people of the Midwest frontier, he enters upon dangerous ground. A heated argument may nearly always be started at any pioneer-society meeting by opening the subject as to whether the manners of the earlier period were crude or uncouth. Someone is sure to rise and deny with vehemence that his ancestors were boorish, apparently with the feeling that their character has been impugned. Yet the truth remains that the majority of them probably were.

Not only in the West, but generally throughout the United States, public relations between the sexes were characterized by extreme diffidence and stiffness. European travelers noted that at church, lecture, picnic, or rally, the women sat, congregated, or marched separately, and there was lacking the freedom of relationship which would be expected in a country so proud of its

[98] Mrs. Kirkland, *Western Clearings,* 217, 221–22. Nor is the following statement necessarily contradictory: ". . . for every one on the frontiers dresses just as he pleases, and whether he has his blankets and skins made up into coats and boots, or wears them loose about his person, no one comments upon it. The utmost freedom of dress prevails; and you may see the same person three days in succession with a leather hunting-shirt, a surtout of scarlet woollen, or a coat of superfine broadcloth just from St. Louis, all worn in any company with the same air of independence; and while several colours and textures frequently combine in the same dress, the result is of course an outrageous violation of taste in individual instances, but great picturesqueness of costume upon the whole: the very figure whose apparel is most obnoxious to the laws of good taste as last enacted by fashion, being often that which, of all others, a painter would introduce into a landscape to relieve its colours, or copy for some romantic charm of its own." Hoffman, *A Winter in the West,* I, 306–7.
[99] Flower, *Errors of Emigrants,* 35.

freedom.[100] It appeared at times as though the menfolk deprecated the very existence of the women as somehow a manifestation of weakness in themselves.

In matters of etiquette, attention to the lesser niceties and conventions in relation to women, there were individuals, to be sure, who were governed by the best rules of gallantry of Old Virginia or by the polite standards of Boston, but such was not the general practice among the majority of the people. In a society in which the woman usually got up first in the morning and built the fire, milked the cows, took care of the garden, fetched wood and water, and sometimes worked in the fields, she was seldom regarded as "the weaker sex."[101] Most women had no time to cultivate an interesting pallor, or the art of attractive fainting.[102] Tobacco was frequently used by women. A few smoked "segars," more used the pipe, but probably snuff was more common than either. This substance was either collected on the chewed end of a stick or placed behind the gum; in strength it was more than the equivalent of the tobacco the men chewed. Men generally prided themselves on possessing the sturdy virtues of manliness, honesty, bravery, and respect for women, yet saw no inconsistency in referring to their spouses as "old woman," occupying the best (or only) chair, eating first, and keeping their hats on, regardless. When a man and woman walked a narrow path, the man

[100] Basil Hall seemed actually to worry about this strange state of affairs (*Travels in North America*). William Oliver, *Eight Months in Illinois* (pp. 122–23), speaking of a Fourth of July celebration in a small town: "After the ladies had all passed, the gentlemen followed, in similar style. . . . It would have been considered the very height of indecorum had one of the beaus offered his arm to any of the ladies. . . . the demeanor I have alluded to prevails at all the public meetings of the sexes, and is a national trait." At the speaking the audience sat or reclined on the ground, "the ladies on one side of the waggon, and the gentlemen on the other."

[101] There were hardy, strong women aplenty. A sample description of a pioneer athlete: "Miss Jinsey Collins was the strongest woman in the county. She was about medium height, weighing 130 pounds. It was said that she could shoulder three bushels of wheat, standing in a half-bushel [about 180 pounds without moving the feet]. She could swing an ax like a logger, and was a good hand in a clearing. She could ride as wild a horse as the average man. In winter time she was usually attired in linsey-woolsey, with a red bandana tied about her head. She had dark brown eyes and hair, with complexion to match, and was more useful than showy." Major, *Pioneers of Morgan County*, 255.

[102] Yet a Michigan pioneer had a wife who was subject to fits of hypo. After stopping work several times, riding miles for a doctor and returning to find her about her affairs as usual, he remonstrated, and told her he didn't believe the spells necessary. Whereupon she proclaimed: "Elmer Bacon, 'tain't no use talkin', I *can* have fits, and I *will* have em." James H. Lawrence, "Pioneer Recollections," in *Michigan Pioneer and Historical Collections*, XVIII (1891), 371–72.

walked ahead;[103] when they got in a wagon, the man likely climbed in first. The woman usually lugged the infants and packed the bundles. On the other hand, Charles Dickens in his travels saw no woman "exposed to the slightest act of rudeness, incivility, or even inattention," and Miss Martineau thought that the manners of Americans ("the best I ever saw") showed to their greatest advantage "as to the gentlemen, in travelling." The women, however, when traveling, were "like spoiled children when the gentlemen are not present to be sacrificed to them;— in the inn parlour, while waiting for meals or the stage; and in the cabin of a steam-boat. I never saw any manner so repulsive as that of many American ladies on board steam-boats."[104]

Although the ordinary manners of the backwoodsman may have been crude ("They are barbarous enough," said Mrs. Kirkland), on one thing it was agreed: in time of sickness and death among friends and neighbors he was a gentle creature, "his whole soul is melted, and his manners could not be amended by false Chesterfield himself. A delicacy not always found among the elegant, will then temper his every look and movement to the very tone of the time."[105] George Flower, generally impressed with the affability, kindness, and good temper of Americans, thought that the backwoodsmen—rough hard hands, beard and all—possessed the qualities of civilized people no less than the wealthy farmer of the East. "Consideration of kindness for the helplessness of infancy and the bereavement of widowhood is one of the most pleasing traits in the American character, individually and nationally."[106]

To public manners, as well as dress and external appearance, the people of the West were somewhat indifferent. As society became more democratic, a freer and easier intercourse developed. Clerks and farmers were accustomed to "swap" drinks and play cards with congressmen, army officers, or judges. Deference or servility based on social inferiority was nonexistent, and, on

---

[103] Possibly a survival of the day when the man went ahead with his rifle, or maybe, just indifference or reluctance to give any outward show of deference. As Lincoln said to Mary Todd when she chided him on his lack of some of the finer points of manners, "How can you attach such great importance to matters so trivial?" Katherine Helm, *The True Story of Mary, Wife of Lincoln* (New York, 1928), 80–81.
[104] *Society in America*, II, 187, 214.
[105] Kirkland, *Western Clearings*, vii.
[106] *Errors of Emigrants*, 27.

the part of many, rudeness was common; the son of the judge became the apprentice of the shoemaker, the son of the congressman the apprentice of the carpenter. Some persons were chilly and self-centered, others impertinently curious as to personal affairs of strangers. Tobacco chewing, promiscuous and copious spitting—"a perfect storm and tempest of spitting"—dram drinking, and prolific profanity abounded on steamboats, in taverns, and other public places. There is no denying that the tobacco situation was serious; the majority of the men reserved the sovereign right to let the tobacco juice fall where gravity commanded, particularly in public places.[107] Not only the bare floors of public buildings, taverns, and steamboats, but the carpets of boarding houses and hotels were subjected to prolific and odoriferous dosages of the brown juice. Wise, though aesthetic, observers mentioned, only to dismiss, "the nauseous subject." There was nothing they could do about it.

Emphatic and heated arguments over politics, bragging accounts of slick transactions in business, or rough and coarse horseplay were common; yet a crude wit and originality, tinged with gross exaggeration and some drollness flavored it all. Nevertheless, the fierce reply or flat contradiction was seldom heard; one remembered that he was confronting the "sovereign people." At the table, especially if no ladies were present, each person took care of himself, reached liberally, and bolted his food, in the silence required by the etiquette of the West.

Timothy Flint believed the better-class people in the West not inferior to the same kind of people back East:

Although we have so often been described to . . . [the] traveller, as backwoodsmen, gougers, ruffians, demi-savages, a repulsive mixture, in the slang phrase, of the "horse and the alligator," we confidently hazard the opinion, that when a little accustomed to the manners of the better class of people among us, he will institute a comparison between our people and his own, not unfavorable to us. There is evidently more ease and frankness, more readiness to meet a wish to form an acquaintance, sufficient tact, when to advance, and how far, and where to pause in this effort, less holding back, less distrust, less feeling as if the address of a stranger were an insult, or a degradation.[108]

[107] The *Chicago Democrat*, October 26, 1836, had a good description of the various arts and practices of the tobacco chewer. It told of the delicate young female who, talking to a "lip-cud-holder," was fascinated and horrified by the manipulation of the cud "like a toad in a monkey's mouth."
[108] Timothy Flint, "National Character of the Western People," in *Western Monthly Review*, I (1827–28), 135.

It was not necessary to be a Mrs. Trollope to find much to be improved in the behavior of the average Westerner.[109] Well-bred and cultured persons might well resent, and hold themselves aloof from, such commonness of behavior, or else accept it all as part of the life in a new world, to be made the best of. For those who aspired to be politicians, preachers, merchants, and editors, there was no other alternative; some liked it, others pretended to.[110]

As regarded morals, so inadequately defined and difficult to evaluate in any period or place, the West offered about whatever the observer wished to find. Early settlers of the "better class" were possessed of much theoretical piety, frequently more manifested in their laws than in private conduct. The conflict in American life between the puritanical heritage—the penchant for self-improvement and the regulation of the other fellow's conduct—on the one hand, and the frontier heritage—individualism, resentment against regulations—on the other, has never been better demonstrated than on the Midwest frontier.[111] As Rudyard Kipling later said, the American had a "cynic devil in his blood,

> That bids him flout the Law he makes,
> That bids him make the Law he flouts."

In keeping with the great American urge, many laws regulating rigid Sabbath observance and gaming were passed. Ohio in 1816

---

[109] Frances Trollope, in *Domestic Manners of the Americans* (London, 1832), gives one of the most prejudiced and most widely resented descriptions written by any foreign traveler. Speaking of Cincinnati she said, "The total and universal want of manners, both in males and females, is so remarkable, that I was constantly endeavoring to account for it."

[110] The British travelers of the "period of Tory Condescension" found it hard to accommodate themselves, but even some of them were quite rational on the subject, especially if they came in early life. Said Stuart: "No people consider it so great a hardship to be obliged to eat or associate with those whom they consider to be their inferiors, in point of station, as the British." *Three Years in North America,* II, 266. Not all were so tolerant. Hamilton wrote: "One circumstance may be mentioned, which is tolerably illustrative of the general habits of the people. In every steamboat there is a *public* comb and hair-brush suspended by a string from the ceiling of the cabin. These utensils are used by the whole body of the passengers, and their condition the pen of Swift could alone adequately describe. There is no tooth-brush, simply, I believe, because the article is entirely unknown to the American toilet." [Thomas Hamilton] *Men and Manners in America,* by the author of *Cyril Thornton* (Philadelphia, 1833), 296. For distinction between the early travelers interested in practical affairs in America and the later experience-seeking upper-class type, see Nevins (comp. and ed.), *American Social History as Recorded by British Travellers,* introductions to the various parts.

[111] Ohio, for instance, to 1836 had passed fifty-three volumes of laws of which only two volumes of general laws were in force at the time. James Hall in his review of Salmon P. Chase's *Statutes of Ohio,* in *Western Monthly Magazine,* V (1836), 633.

made persons over fourteen years of age who engaged in "sporting, rioting, quarrelling, hunting, fishing, shooting, or . . . common labor" (works of charity and necessity, such as ferrying, etc., and Seventh-day observance excepted) subject to fines of from $1.00 to $5.00. Disturbing religious meetings, swearing by God, Jesus Christ, or the Holy Ghost, playing bullets across the street, or running horses in town were punishable by fines of 50 cents to $5.00; for puppet shows, wire dancing, or tumbling, there was a $10 fine.[112]

The third session of the Illinois legislature provided that "If any person shall hereafter bring into the State . . . or shall sell or offer for sale any pack of playing cards, or any dice, billiard balls, or any other device or thing intended, or made for the purpose of being used at any game; shall, on conviction, be fined in the sum of not exceeding $25." Practically the same law was passed again in 1836. Yet the pack of cards came with the packs of the earliest traders, and the billiard table so surely that it roughly marked a milestone in the development of a new region. A Columbus, Ohio, ordinance of 1826 provided a $5.00 to $20 fine for each twenty-four hours at a ninepin alley, ball alley, or gaming of any kind, and a $10 fine for serenading or making a noise with "drums, bells, fifes, horns, pans, kettles or with any thing whatsoever."[113] The Ohio law of 1831 which voided all agreements made on any sport or pastime was so stringent that numerous indictments were blamed upon the folly of the law rather than the baseness of the people.[114]

Governor James B. Ray, of Indiana, advocated more searching and efficient laws against gambling. "There is no offense in our penal code, which is more frequently committed; and no violation of law which escapes with such general license and impunity."[115] Young folks gambled, as did their elders and the Indians before them. A Cincinnati schoolteacher protested in print against these widespread vices. When a boy was called by his mother, he grabbed a handful of marbles and amidst much cuffing and

[112] Hamilton (Ohio) *Philanthropist*, May 31, 1816.
[113] *Ohio State Journal*, August 17, 1827. The penalty against ninepins was evaded in the West by using an extra pin. Oliver, *Eight Months in Illinois*, 120–21.
[114] A two-column criticism of the law was printed in the Piqua *Western Courier and Enquirer*, September 3, 1836.
[115] Message, December 8, 1829.

cussing yelled, "Damn the old ——, she might let me play another game." She was certain such habits led to idleness, tardiness, profanity, fighting, and stealing.[116] When the United States postal regulations directed that mail be carried on the Sabbath, hot protests were made on the grounds that the postmasters were being deprived of religious freedom and the authority of God violated.[117] When the *Walk-in-the-Water,* the first steamboat to reach Detroit, made its departure on Sunday, there was much ado about it on the part of respectable citizens. The action was defended by some on the grounds of probable necessity, but even they decided it might have been better to wait until Monday.[118]

Lotteries, however, seemed not to have been included among the immoralities by the strict-minded. Public buildings, bridges, charities, even churches were financed by lotteries. The managers of the Indiana canal lottery of 1817, for a canal at the Falls of the Ohio, were put under state bond. By act of the Ohio legislature a lottery was held to relieve one Elisha Barrett and to rebuild his woolen factory. There were to be 4,829 prizes ranging from $8,000, first prize, to 4,401 $3.00 prizes, a total of $32,004. Tickets were $3.00.[119] The St. Louis Hospital lottery advertised that at one third the cost one had fourteen times greater chance of the same prize than in the Mammoth New York Lottery.[120] Prizes totaled $10,000. The Virginia Dismal Swamp Lottery, with prizes from $30,000 on down to fifty of $1,000, tickets $12 each, advertised out of the St. Louis manager's office in 1831.[121] The New York Consolidated Lottery advertised "Christmas Presents worth $40,000" in the same year. In 1839 advertisements for the Richmond lottery, Petersburg lottery, Alexandria lottery, and the Great Mammoth all appeared in the same issue of the *Sangamo Journal.*[122] Similar notices appeared in the papers of Cincinnati, Cleveland, Detroit, and other places. They were running the patent medicines a close second as space buyers.

[116] *Cincinnati Daily Gazette,* March 17, 1836.
[117] Indianapolis *Indiana Journal,* January 14, 1830.
[118] *Detroit Gazette,* August 28, 1818.
[119] *Cleaveland Herald,* November 6, 1828.
[120] Springfield *Sangamo Journal,* April 20, 1833.
[121] Edwardsville *Illinois Advocate,* October 28, 1831.
[122] February 28, 1839.

The use of whiskey was general. As a commodity it was produced on innumerable farms, and available at "groceries" at from 15 to 25 cents a gallon.[123] From cabin raising and logrolling to muster assembly and political barbecue, no important work could be accomplished without its use. Von Schweinitz, the missionary, viewed a militia muster at Madison, Indiana, at which candidates for Congress, governor, and legislature made speeches. Although he said drinks were not served at respectable inns, yet "I have rarely seen so many people drunk and nowhere so many brawls and rows, for the populace of Indiana develops a fearful rudeness on such occasions."[124] Canal contractors supplied whiskey to their workmen,[125] stores frequently kept a barrel and tin cup on hand free for customers; candidates for office placed bottles in groceries and other strategic points with their names on them, and the row of empties by election day served as a rough index of public opinion. Or on election day barrels bearing the party labels would be set near the public well or polling place, with tin cup attached, and by the time the votes were in, the barrels would be empty and the men full. All classes of people were given more or less to dram taking—farmers, traders, printers, lawyers, and even many ministers,[126] women as well as men. "When I commenced the practice of law in the spring of 1818," wrote Judge Isaac Naylor, "I found the besetting sin of early members of the bar to be intemperance and gambling.

[123] The John Hancock grocery in Springfield, Illinois, advertised with a difference:
> All you that does good liquors choose,
> Come taste my Gin, if not my muse;
> I've Brandy, Rum, and Whiskey too,
> And one or t'other, sure, will do.
> Old Ned I keeps, but rather deer,
> Besides a butte of Pittsburg beer,
> And when I gets 'em I shall sell,
> The best of figs and Mackerell;
> With other things I need not mention,
> That's quite sufficient here to hint on;
> Come, Suckers, Come, nor deem me rash
> If I say come too, with the cash!
> The times are hard on all, we know it—
> But hardest still upon the poet.

Sangamo Journal, June 28, 1832.

[124] The Journey of Lewis David von Schweinitz to Goshen, Bartholomew County in 1831 (Indiana Historical Society Publications, VIII, No. 5, Indianapolis, 1927), 230.

[125] Ohio Archaeological and Historical Society Publications, XXIV (1915), 336.

[126] J. Edward Murr, "Lincoln in Indiana," in Indiana Magazine of History, XIV (1918), 63–64.

About nine-tenths of the members of the bar were slaves and victims of these vices."[127]

Some writers have maintained that the oldtime whiskey was not strong and would not readily intoxicate, but this does not seem to have been the fact. There was "cheap" whiskey, then, as now, variously called "40 rod" whiskey, "red eye," "rot gut," and other pet names; ability to stand up under it would have been evidence of superhuman prowess. Intoxication was all too prevalent, both private and public, although some witnesses found actual conditions better than they had expected. "Though whiskey is drunk like water, considering the large population of Ohio and Indiana, I have seen fewer drunkards than I expected. Men drink it by the quart & even the wealthy prefer it to any of the foreign liquors."[128]

Quite a little flurry of temperance reform came in the 1830's. Long articles on the subject appeared in the newspapers, and editorial comment called attention to the movement. "Intemperance has been called the national vice of Americans, and one is almost ready to acknowledge the correctness of the charge, from observing on election, muster and other public days, so many persons in a state of beastly intoxication," said the Richmond (Indiana) *Public Leger*. It advocated that Congress levy a heavy tax on distilleries, and the legislature secure the property of habitual drunkards to their children. Intemperance was said to be "the most brutalizing vice of which a man can be guilty."[129] The address and attendant write-up of the Bond County (Illinois) Society for the Suppression of Intemperance in 1826 filled ten columns in the *Illinois Intelligencer*.[130] It included sermons, moralizing, and pathos; it listed Dr. Benjamin Rush's nine consequences of alcohol, including madness. (Only spontaneous combustion was overlooked.) The secretary of the Indianapolis Temperance Society defended the points stoutly, but the editor of

[127] Judge Isaac Naylor, "An Autobiography," in *ibid.*, IV (1908), 139. *The Medical Repository*, XIX (1818), preface, iii, after indicting Americans for over-eating, continued: "and it ought likewise to be observed, that the quantity of ardent spirits drank by our people, exceeds everything of the kind, that the world can produce; the appetite for inebriating drink seems to be increasing and insatiable."

[128] Samuel B. Judah, "A Journal of Travel from New York to Indiana in 1827," in *Indiana Magazine of History*, XVII (1921), 348.

[129] *Public Leger*, January 29, August 5, 1825.

[130] September 9, 16, 1825. In 1826 this society became the Illinois Society for Suppression of Intemperance.

the *Indiana Journal* would not commit himself too definitely.[131]
A few years later "wives and mothers" were petitioning the
General Assembly to discontinue the licensing of the grog shops
or "sinks of pollution."[132] By 1830 five societies had been organized in Michigan Territory.[133] Soon many long addresses made
to temperance societies and lyceums were being published.
"Almost every weekly paper brings us fresh intelligence of the
most horrid crimes, committed through grog shop influence, and
yet some grog sellers are raising the cry of persecution. . . ."[134]
A committee of the Detroit Common Council reported in 1834
that the number of licensed groggeries was excessive. Each year
$90,000 was spent for liquor, in which there was neither wealth
nor nourishment—enough to buy 500 sheep, 500 cattle, 500
horses, and to build 4 brick seminaries.[135]

Touching descriptions of the drunkard's home—cold, hungry
children, beaten wife, poverty, and squalor—sought to call
attention to the liquor evil.[136] In Cincinnati the coffee houses were
submitted to a barrage of attacks; as "nurseries of disorder,
debauch and crime" worse than anywhere on the face of the
globe, they were held a disgrace to the "Queen of the West."[137]
A city ordinance was passed which required the consent of two
thirds of the residents of the district for licensing and location.
Even tobacco suffered an attack now and then, as when "Escula-
peus, Jr.," climaxed a two-column article with "smoking mothers
have crying children."[138]

It was not only among the rivermen of the Ohio and canal
diggers that fighting and violence were to be found. A rowdy
element in most communities could be relied upon to furnish a
certain amount. Thieving, banditry, horse stealing, and murder
occurred in varying proportions. Contradiction in evidence is
common. For instance, writing of the people around Pontiac,
Michigan, in the late twenties, Dr. D. L. Porter said: "The
people are rough as Tartars, the majority intemperate, all or

---

[131] *Indiana Journal*, December 3, 1829.
[132] *Ibid.*, December 26, 1837.
[133] Detroit *North-Western Journal*, February 24, 1830.
[134] *Cincinnati Journal*, quoted in *Piqua Gazette*, November 16, 1833.
[135] *Detroit Journal and Michigan Advertiser* (semiweekly), April 22, 1834.
[136] *Cincinnati Daily Gazette*, April 3, 5, 1830; *Indiana Journal*, October 17, 1834.
[137] *Cincinnati Daily Gazette*, July 31, 1837. Columns of discussion of temperance
and crime continued to appear for months.
[138] *Hamilton* (Ohio) *Intelligencer*, January 5, 1827.

nearly all drink some. They have been, and the mass of people here now are, the most wicked set that ever lived in the U. S. A."[139] Yet of the region around Yankee Springs a few years later an early resident wrote: "Thefts and robberies were unknown, although large quantities of money were carried by travelers and it would have been an easy matter for it to change hands had there been the desire for it by designing persons." Fifteen thousand dollars in specie was regularly transported from Detroit to Grand Rapids for Indian payments "without a care or thought of being robbed."[140] On the other hand a Muskingum bank cashier absconded with several thousand dollars in 1819,[141] the Cincinnati branch of the Bank of the United States was robbed of $8,000 in specie in 1822, and the Illinois State Bank was entered and $4,200 in specie removed in 1823.[142]

Bank robberies, however, were comparatively rare, but business ethics were probably neither better nor worse than elsewhere, though much was heard of questionable practices and deals resulting from the speculative fever prevalent in the West, and the flimsy banking systems. Mail robberies were more numerous. Between 1815, when the first commitment was made to the Ohio penitentiary, and 1822, horse stealing, larceny, and counterfeiting led the list of crimes in that order. Up to 1826, 548 commitments had been made, including 5 women.[143]

That crime was a problem is obvious. Newspapers of the 1820's were full of notices of murders, suicides, robberies, and defalcations. "Barbarous Murder," "Horrible Crime," "Atrocious Outrage," "Terrible if True," "Horrid Murders," "Distressing Narrative," and similar headlines dot the pages. "Another Outrage Upon Our Borders," cried an Edwardsville, Illinois, paper,[144] when another duel was fought by outsiders. "It is high time that Illinois should cause her territory to be respected; it has too long been the *slaughter house* of the high and hot bloods of other States." "Never at any time since the formation

---

[139] Letter quoted in Burr, *Medical History of Michigan*, I, 262.
[140] Mrs. Mary D. Hoyt, "Founding of Yankee Springs," in *Michigan Pioneer and Historical Collections*, XXX (1905), 294–95.
[141] Hamilton (Ohio) *Miami Herald*, January 19, 26, 1819.
[142] Vandalia *Illinois Intelligencer*, March 29, September 27, 1823.
[143] Hamilton (Ohio) *Intelligencer and Advertiser*, December 9, 1822; Columbus *Ohio State Journal*, November 28, 1826.
[144] *Illinois Advocate*, September 2, 1831.

of the constitution of the United States, has so many murders and robberies been perpetrated, as within the last, and present year, and all the robberies and murders were committed for money. Such is the fact, that we scarcely receive a paper but contains a mail robbery, a murder, or the execution of a murderer. And in proportion as money becomes scarce, we may suppose that crimes will become more common," was the report from Cleveland.[145] "Villainy" was the title of a Detroit editorial in 1818. While imports were being made, literature pursued, and advances taking place, "crimes are multiplying and the vigilance of the officers of justice almost constantly defeated. . . . It is evident that there is either a want of energy in our criminal laws or an impardonable laxity in their administration; otherwise we cannot account for the circumstance, that old offenders, having repeatedly committed the same crime, and having been as often prosecuted, still remain at liberty within the country, growing hoary and hardened in their iniquity."[146]

A society for prevention of theft was organized in 1830,[147] yet in 1834 the Detroit jail suspended operations for want of tenants—some thought the public had lost confidence in this supposedly safe institution because it had recently been made a government repository for defaulting postmasters[148]—and at the same time drunken brawls, and depredations of wandering gangs were reported as almost nightly occurrences.[149] *"Citizens Look Out,"* warned the *Advertiser* a little later. "Our city is infested with a gang of desperate rogues, whose depredations are attempted on a bold scale. We would caution householders and shopkeepers to be on the look-out."[150] When in one term of court in Cincinnati in 1835, twenty persons were sentenced to prison, and one to be hanged, on convictions of robbery with intent to kill, arson, counterfeiting, and the like, it was certainly but further "proof of the degeneracy of the times."[151] "It has been a subject of frequent remark, for some time past, that suicides, murders and other atrocities, have recently mutliplied in a highly alarm-

---

[145] *Cleaveland Register,* March 9, 1819.
[146] *Detroit Gazette,* May 29, 1818.
[147] Detroit *North-Western Journal,* April 14, 1830.
[148] *Detroit Journal and Michigan Advertiser* (semiweekly), June 17, 1834.
[149] *Ibid.,* March 4, 1834.
[150] *Detroit Daily Advertiser,* July 14, August 8, 1836.
[151] *Hamilton* (Ohio) *Intelligencer,* November 5, 1835.

ing degree . . . ," said the *Ohio State Journal*,[152] and since the increase seemed to be in direct ratio to the efforts to improve the moral condition of the human race, it surmised that one cause might be the great notoriety given such crimes by the periodical press.

Concerning public villainy and public opinion the St. Louis *Daily Pennant* wrote in similar tone :[153]

Every day brings us, close packed upon each other, accounts of crime and villany, committed by men hitherto considered respectable. Why is this? Are the laws more lax than formerly? No; but the fact is this—and a lamentable one it is—that public opinion has become depraved, and the standard of private and official honesty is gradually falling. The complaisance with which a bank or government "defalcation," as it is politely termed, is now regarded, will soon extend to all species of fraud, swindling and robbery—so that, a man who is arraigned for an unsuccessful attempt to defraud his neighbor, will become an object of public sympathy and pity, rather than disgust and execration. The onward march of crime must be checked—and speedily; otherwise the world will revert back to its primitive state of barbarism, and spurn all law but one—that might is right. . . . We are sorry to see editors joking at the frequent instances of rascality which leak out from the corrupt sink of wealth and power. It is no joke—it is but a specimen of the entire rottenness within; . . . and we learn to look lightly upon that which is sapping the foundations of moral and political freedom.

Judge James Hall, an assiduous and reliable observer of the West, noticed a discrepancy between its domestic morals and its popular sentiment. He thought that there was as much industry and private virtue in the country as ever, yet the discussions in the better periodicals and newspapers "displayed a dissoluteness altogether incompatible with the genius of a sober-minded people." The same derelictions were discernible in literature. Bad brandy and bad books produced the same effect in Judge Hall's mind. As for the politicians: "There never was a period in the history of our country, in which its public men have sought popularity, power, and office, with so much avidity, or have shown so little scruple, as to the means by which their purposes might be effected."[154]

Sexual morality is even more difficult to estimate. This subject

152 July 1, 1833.
153 June 17, 1840.
154 *Western Monthly Magazine*, III (1835), 248.

was rarely mentioned in pioneer recollections, private journals, or referred to in the newspapers. (Scandal sheets and blackmail columns were not yet known.) Yet now and then an item got recorded. In 1827 the *Bloomington* (Indiana) *Gazette* said: [155] "At the March term of the Monroe Circuit Court at Bloomington, a gentleman was fined fifteen dollars; and a lady sentenced to twenty-five days imprisoment for *bundling* three times. It is hoped this decision will put a stop to this indecent manner of sparking, so common among the youngsters of Ohio, Pennsylvania, and Carolina." Seeing this item the editor of an Ohio paper queried: "Why should the male be fined fifteen dollars only, and the female (the weaker vessel), thrust within the four walls of a loathsome jail, there to be imprisoned for twenty-five days?" Furthermore, "The insinuation that such a practice prevails among the 'youngsters of Ohio' is a base falsehood; and it is a fact beyond contradiction, that but seldom any other mode of *sparking*, than that of *bundling*, prevails in the State of Indiana; and it is hoped the example set the people of other States by this *important decision*, will have a salutary effect on the morals of the Indianans."[156] Stories of this sort no doubt gave birth to the long articles on kissing, which appeared now and then, and on "The practice of Courting after Bed Time." It was unnecessary. One should court openly and seek a wife in daylight. The "innocent kiss" was like dram drinking; one was not enough. Ruin was the inevitable consequence. It was a relic of superstition and opposed to the cultivation of virtue and piety. "Is it polite? Is it genteel? Is it Christian? Yes, we ask, is it decent?"[157]

Some of the youth of Ohio were having their troubles, too. In 1833 the "Society for Inquiry" in Western Reserve College appointed a standing committee on lewdness. (Whereupon "Sylvester" wrote in to inquire whether the purpose was to encourage lewdness.) Charges were made that lewd practices were engaged in by preachers, physicians, and the wealthier and more respected people of society. By actual count three fourths of the young men were found guilty, yet they moved in the best of society. The statements of the committee were challenged as the fanatical

[155] Copied in *Piqua Gazette,* May 2, 1827.
[156] *Ibid.*
[157] *Hamilton Intelligencer,* March 30, 1837.

pryings of a self-appointed band of virtuous sisters, and some thought that the committee painted such an attractive picture of vice as to encourage it.[158] Antivice societies of this sort were not to be taken too seriously. The Chillicothe society, which was meeting as early as 1814, gives an idea of their nature. Although in a non-Puritan settlement, its object was to "discountenance, discourage and suppress every species of vice," especially profanity, violation of the Sabbath, ardent spirits, gambling in every form, theatrical amusements, shows, balls, and other activities.[159]

The "ancient evil" was a problem in the western cities, as elsewhere, from their beginning. Laws and resolutions seemed to have had little effect. Said the *Detroit Daily Advertiser:* "We rejoice to know that the city authorities are alive to the necessity of checking, by the strong arm of the law, the progress of open licentiousness among us. The vice has fearfully increased within the corporation limits during the past year, and has at length reached such a crisis and assumed so bold and unblushing a character as to cause the moralist to shudder at the possible consequences." The peace had been broken by nightly outbreaks of the most outrageous nature; pistols and guns had been used. Perhaps a law similar to that of Wisconsin Territory, which provided a $500 fine and banishment for keepers of disorderly houses, would help. "If the keepers of every house of ill fame in this city were to be punished with equal severity, we should probably hear less of the beastly outrages that are rapidly degrading certain purlieus to the loathsome condition of the Five Points."[160]

It is easy to say that sexual irregularity was rarer in rural regions in earlier days than today. Generally speaking it was more harshly condemned. Taboos on sex applied to conversation; the subject was not usually mentioned in mixed company, and largely "in ribald jest among the men." Male animals were euphemistically named in the presence of women, but ewes, cows, mares, sows, and the like were respectable enough. There were

---

[158] *Observer and Telegraph,* June, July, 1833, as reported in Ravenna *Western Courier,* June 20, July 18, 1833; *ibid.,* July 3, 1834.

[159] *Weekly Recorder,* July 19, 1814.

[160] *Detroit Daily Advertiser,* June 16, 1838. A mob in Louisville attacked and burned two houses "occupied by persons of ill fame" in 1832. Two were killed. *Daily Herald and Gazette* item quoted in *Sangamo Journal,* August 11, 1832.

other words with possible sexual connotations that were more or less prudishly frowned upon. Pregnancy was not mentionable in mixed company, and of course "bastard" was much too harsh. In spite of these restrictions it seems that young people had a general notion of what it was all about, and that a fair amount of "tomcattin' " took place the "woodscolts" or illegitimate children in any community bore witness. Barnyard biology did not explain a lot of things, however, and ignorance and superstition regarding sex was amazing, even among adults. Early marriages and scattered population no doubt served to restrict irregular relationships, as did jealousy and lack of freedom of companionship between the sexes; but even incest was all too common among the lower classes in the more isolated regions. Laws against bigamy were strict but hard to enforce. The Illinois law still in force in 1824 subjected both male and female offenders to one to three hundred lashes on the bare back, fine, imprisonment, and loss of right to testify in court.[161]

Criticism of western morals emanated from New England, where morality and religion were considered one and the same. Speaking of Ohio immediately after the war, a New England preacher wrote: "South of New Connecticut, few Bibles or religious tracts have been received for distribution among the inhabitants. The Sabbath is greatly profaned, and but few good people can be found in any one place."[162] A missionary from the Massachusetts Missionary Society reporting in 1815 on the "Territories," had said: "We have travelled through them—have seen the nakedness of the land, and our eyes have affected our hearts. We have heard the cry, *Come over into Macedonia and help us*. . . . The character of the settlers is such as to render it peculiarily important that missionaries should early be sent among them. Indeed, they can hardly be said to have a character. . . ."[163] Of the Illinois country around Edwardsville in 1831 another preacher wrote: "This part of Illinois has been peopled chiefly with emigrants from Virginia, Kentucky, and Tennessee.

[161] Vandalia *Illinois Intelligencer*, December 31, 1824.
[162] Quoted in Carrie P. Kofoid, "Puritan Influences in the Formative Years of Illinois History," in *Transactions of the Illinois State Historical Society*, 1905, p. 272.
[163] Samuel J. Mills and Daniel Smith, in *The Panoplist and Missionary Magazine* (Boston), XI (1815), 179, 183.

The state of morals is generally very low, yet there are many pleasant families in this region. . . ."[164] The *Sunday School Journal* in an article by a preacher from the West had said that "A manifest tendency to atheism or heathenism, was evidently produced in *one or two stages of family descent,*" upon persons emigrating to the West. "Their manners, intellectual character, and morals, *if in the meantime friendly intercourse with their neighbors was continued,* sunk progressively lower and lower, till they had lost all the superiority they possessed at the first migration of the parent stock."[165] At a Boston meeting a clergyman asserted that "the majority of the people, of the adult males, of the western states, *doubt the divine origin of religion,*" and the *New-England Magazine* published an article in which it was stated that "the population of the valley of the Mississippi may be set down as half infidel."[166]

However accustomed the Westerner was to having his devils exorcised by his preachers, he was the last to submit gracefully to such charges from New England. By 1830 a sense of sectional pride had been developed, a western-mindedness, sensitive, aggressive, thoroughly patriotic to the locale. None had been more instrumental in developing this consciousness than Judge James Hall,[167] who came to the defense of the character of the West. He believed that any difference in attitude towards religion was in favor of the West. There were no seaports or large towns, few "ignorant and debased foreigners," and "there is no question that the farming population, as a class, is that in which there is most sobriety, sedateness, and sound morals."[168]

As for introducing "the social and religious principles of New England into our country," he was at a loss to know what they were and poked fun at the idea. "On the whole, we see no great fault to find with our *social* principles—nor do we know of a single *social principle of New England,* which we do not practise,

---

[164] Extracts from the "Memoir of Alvan Stone," in *Journal of the Illinois State Historical Society,* III, No. 4 (Jan., 1911), 89.

[165] Quoted in *Western Monthly Magazine,* III (1835), 107.

[166] *Ibid.,* and "Atheism in New-England," in *New-England Magazine,* VII (Dec., 1834), 502.

[167] Founder of the *Illinois Monthly Magazine* (Vandalia, 1830–32) and editor of the *Western Monthly Magazine* (Cincinnati, 1833–36). See Chapter XV. Other western editors were as outspoken as Hall; see, for instance, Richmond *Indiana Palladium,* June 10, 1825, September 9, 1826.

[168] *Western Monthly Magazine,* III (1835), 109.

nor an unsocial principle, which is condemned there, that would
not be repudiated here. If there be a difference, it is that we have
a little more of the social principle than they."[169]

When the Reverend Lyman Beecher, of Lane Seminary in Cincinnati, published *A Plea for the West*,[170] Hall attacked him as a
recent and insincere convert to the merits of the West, and quoted
from Beecher's previous appeals to the East in which he had
begged New England's sons to come into the West and act as a
leaven to produce a saving influence, on the assumption that "uncultivated virtue was cultivated vice."[171]

Regarding education and general ability, Hall said,

> The people of those States [six Western states] have subdued the wilder-
> ness, have framed constitutions, enacted laws, organized civil institutions,
> introduced the useful arts, and cultivated the social principles, in great
> harmony and with signal success by the aid of their own *uncultivated
> virtues*. They have now in complete organization the whole complex
> machinery of law and government; and they number among their citizens,
> gentlemen who make and who expound laws, clergymen, physicians, mer-
> chants, artists, and farmers, who are as capable as those of other states,
> and possess as much general intelligence.[172]

Gershom Flagg, writing from Illinois, inquired "whether that
Old sarpent called the Devil is drove out of Vermont or whether
he is still roving up and down the country seeking whose Chickens
he can catch and devour. I see or read and hear that there [is]
great uneasiness by our religious friends [in] the East about the
cause of Religion in the valley of the Missipi &. &. I do not see
but the cause flourishes as well here as in other places the people
here contribute freely for the support of Preachers both in money
and good living which you know is the main thing."[173] When a
Philadelphia church petitioned the Pennsylvania legislature for
a lottery to raise funds, a Western editor wrote: "Would it not
be advisable for those missionary societies in the East, who pro-
fess to be so anxious about the 'heathens' in the West, to spend
a portion of their funds in converting the members of this church

[169] *Western Monthly Magazine*, II (1834), 656.
[170] Cincinnati, 1835.
[171] *Western Monthly Magazine*, III (1835), 320. Beecher's sermon from the
Lowell (Mass.) *Journal* is quoted in *ibid.*, II, 656.
[172] *Western Monthly Magazine*, II (1834), 658.
[173] Buck (ed.), "Pioneer Letters," in *Transactions of the Illinois State Historical
Society*, 1910, p. 182.

to Christianity?"[174] Peter Cartwright also spoke out against those who criticized western morals and ignorance.[175]

Not all New Englanders were adversely critical of the West. Abner D. Jones, generally a reliable observer, writing in 1838, said:

Well do I know that a very vague and utterly false estimate of the morality as well as the literature of the west is held by the majority of the people at the east, and I feel it my duty for one to do my part towards disabusing them thereof. No eastern man of reflective mind can spend a few weeks even, in *society* here, and not undergo a thorough change in the estimate brought by him from his home. . . .

I do not say that there is not a favorable comparison to be made between New England and the west, in point of morals, in behalf of the former, yet, I can but think there is a more unfavorable impression existing among us respecting western morality than an examination into the subject will warrant.

Of the country along the Ohio he made the following fair estimate:

Many of the towns I found beautiful; and in all of them I witnessed the supremacy of the utilitarian spirit, which, while it is rearing towns and villages all over the wilderness west, is but too careless of the moral growth. The amount of grog-shops which curse every western town and city, would astonish every man from New England. As far as my knowledge extends, I do not think the average high, when I say, that in towns in every eighth, and in cities in every twelfth tenement, ardent spirit is an article of traffic. What can be expected of the morals of the west? And yet, in justice I must acknowledge, that I have not seen half a dozen men drunk since I left Boston. Nor do I think that the tone of morality is at such low ebb as we have been accustomed to suppose. Indeed, in society, embracing not only the upper, but middling classes, there is a high standard of morality; and gross violations thereof are by no means winked at. True, it is more chivalrous than christian, but it embraces the fundamental principles of honor, patriotism, integrity and charity. We find here *the best materials to work upon*; rude and unrefined, they may be, but containing the elements of the best social organization.

Nor do the tidings of violence and wrong which are daily wafted to our ears from this far land, check my confidence in the redeeming virtue of the west. We abuse ourselves when we take these rough samples as specimens of the western character. We ought to reflect that the strange, and the cruel, and the bloody, are far more likely to reach us than the

[174] Richmond (Ind.) *Public Leger*, January 29, 1825.
[175] "The Valley of the Mississippi, or the Moral Waste," in Springfield *Sangamo Journal*, August 30, 1834.

good, which is less notorious because it is less strange. And the reign of
Lynch law here, is, by no means, to be taken as evidence of the *lawlessness*
of the land, but otherwise. The country is large, wild, young, and sparsely
settled, and it is, in many cases, exceedingly difficult to obtain justice at all;
and it is, nine cases in ten, only a sense of justice that erects this extra-
judicial tribunal, whose decisions, however opposed to Coke and Blackstone,
are generally such as these eminent jurists would have legally sanctioned.[176]

The frontier churches held both ministers and members to
strict moral accountability, as the number of church trials indicates. Although the number of church members in the average
community was relatively small, their influence was no doubt
greater in proportion than their numbers.[177]

An estimate of the character of the West and of its people is
meaningless without due consideration of those mental attitudes
and complexes, so infrequently recorded by its inhabitants, but
lived and felt by them. Inarticulate though the people were, western consciousness was a reality, expressed in no uncertain terms
by the leaders, and recognized by outside observers.

In Congress when John Randolph, of Virginia, accused the
Westerners of suffering from "a greediness for gain . . . from
habits of indolence, of profusion, of extravagance,"[178] and made
fun of their dress, appearance, manners, and habits, a Kentucky
congressman came to their defense and declared statements of
this nature could only be the result of inexcusable ignorance of
the character, the feelings, the intelligence, and the habits of the
Western people.

Their external appearance is not the most fashionable and elegant kind;
they are not decorated in all the style, the gaiety, and the taste of a dandy
of the first water. Their means are too limited and their discretion is too
great, I trust, for the indulgence of such foppery and extravagance. . . .
But . . . it is not to the exterior of men we should look. Fortune affords
advantages which may enable one to appear well, when, in truth, there is
nothing worthy of admiration. It is the conduct, the deportment, the principles of men, we should examine. Will the people of the West . . . fear
an examination of this sort? . . . Who can boast of a preference over
them? . . . Let the firmness, the valor, the suffering of the people of the
West . . . be forgotten. . . . Withhold if you choose, the gratitude of the
nation; but I beg of you to do justice to their private virtues, to allow them,

[176] *Illinois and the West,* 24–26, 27, 79–80.
[177] William W. Sweet, "The Churches as Moral Courts on the Frontier," in *Church
History,* II (1933), 21.
[178] *Annals of Congress,* 18 Congress, 1 session, part I, 1298.

at least a character for integrity of motive, for benevolence of heart, for hospitality of conduct. . . . Their hospitality is without ostentation, without parade, without hypocrasy; it is not contaminated, and I trust never will be, by the fashionable vices which might be enumerated, as the tip of the *ton* in some other places . . . he [the Westerner] utters not the commonplace, unmeaning compliments; he speaks the language of his heart . . . dressed, sir, not in fine ruffles and broadcloth, with powdered hair, but in good, substantial, plain clothes, manufactured by the industry of his wife; and, upon entering into conversation with him, an ample theme for reflection would be afforded; you would wonder how one in his humble station could have known so much, upon so many subjects, with such limited opportunities. . . . Sir, these are the very citizens of whom the nation ought to be proud. They constitute the bone, and sinew, and strength, of your Government.[179]

John Ludlum McConnel recognized four outstanding traits in the Westerner. First, his desire to better his condition. "His spirit is eminently encroaching." He was inclined to take the straightest path, even over the property of others, but was quick to warn off trespassers. Second, he was seldom conscious of having done wrong. Not usually impetuous, he rarely acted until he was sure of himself, hence his aversion to apologies. He "thinks a safe retreat worse than a defeat with slaughter." Third, he was restless and fond of change—a little selfish. He had no deep affection for the soil. His character seemed hard-featured but was neither unsocial nor morose. He was hospitable and accommodating. Some of these traits he had before emigrating, but the wilderness brought out self-reliance, courage and a realistic attitude. The border type despised organization, even military. "This self-reliance was not an arrogant and vulgar egotism. . . . It was a calm, just estimate of his own capabilities—a well-grounded confidence in his own talents—a clear, manly understanding of his own individual rights, dignity, and relations." He was "stout of heart, strong of hand—calm, sagacious, unterrified," neither easily disconcerted nor excitable. This was not just fortitude or passive courage; it was active. Thirst for blood was not a force. His hatred of the Indian was inherited. God made the earth; to him the continent was vacant. As for romance, life was too serious for poetry and the wilderness did not cultivate it. The pioneer was not a dreamer, but matter-of-fact, in many respects

[179] Robert P. Letcher, in *ibid.*, 18 Congress, 1 session, part II, 2523–25.

simple as a child, credulous. He "had nothing of the faculty which enables us to detect falsehood, even in matters of which we know nothing by comparison and analogy." (This is McConnel's poorest generalization.) Finally, another characteristic, traceable to the same source, the stern reality of his life, was the pioneer's gravity:

> The agricultural population of this country are, at the best, not a cheerful race. Though they sometimes join in festivities, it is but seldom; and the wildness of their dissipation is too often in proportion to its infrequency. There is none of the serene contentment—none of that smiling enjoyment— which, according to travellers like Howitt, distinguishes the tillers of the ground in other lands. *Sedateness* is a national characteristic, but the gravity of the pioneer is quite another thing; it includes pride and personal dignity, and indicates a stern, unyielding temper. There is, however, nothing morose in it: it is its aspect alone, which forbids approach; and that only makes more conspicuous the heartiness of your reception, when once the shell is broken. Acquainted with the character, you do not expect him to *smile* much; but now and then he *laughs*: and that laugh is round, free, and hearty. You know at once that he enjoys it, you are convinced that he is a firm friend and "a good hater."[180]

Perhaps what this observer missed was the spontaneous gaiety of European peasants, however poor, in their festivals, folk dancing, and musicals. For some reason the American environment was not conducive to this sort of thing. The Westerners, however, did have the spirit of hospitality, of sincere simplicity which characterizes peoples who live close to the soil, qualities which compensated in part for lack of some of the graces of more cultured parts.

> The wild new country, with all its coarseness and all its disadvantages of various kinds, has yet a fascination for the settler, in consequence of a certain free, hearty tone, which has long since disappeared, if indeed it ever existed, in parts of the country where civilization has made greater progress. The really fastidious, and those who only pretend to be such, may hold this as poor compensation for the many things lacking of another kind; but those to whose apprehension sympathy and sincerity have a pre-eminent and independent charm, prefer the kindly warmth of the untaught, to the icy chill of the half-taught; and would rather be welcomed by the woodsman to his log-cabin, with its rough hearth, than make one of a crowd who feed the ostentation of a *millionaire*, or gaze with sated eyes upon costly feasts which it would be a mockery to dignify with the name

[180] John Ludlum McConnel, *Western Characters or Types of Border Life in the Western States* (New York, 1853), 110–16.

of hospitality. The infrequency of inns in a newly settled country leads naturally to the practice of keeping "open house" for strangers; and it is rare indeed that the settler, however poor his accommodations, hesitates to offer the best he has to the tired wayfarer. Where payment is accepted, it is usually very inconsiderable; and it is seldom accepted at all, unless the guest is manifestly better off than his entertainer. But whether a compensation be taken or refused, the heartiness of manner with which every thing that the house affords is offered, cannot but be acceptable to the visitor. Even the ever rampant pride, which comes up so disagreeably at the West, where the outward appearance of the stranger betokens any advantage of condition, slumbers when that stranger claims hospitality. His horse is cared for with more solicitude than the host ever bestows on his own; the table is covered with the best provisions the house affords, set forth in the holiday dishes; the bed is endued with the brightest patchwork quilt—the pride of the housewife's heart; and if there be any fat fowls— any white honey—any good tea—about the premises, the guest will be sure to have it, even though it may have been reserved for "Independence" or "Thanksgiving."[181]

Perhaps no better contemporary estimate of the Westerner is to be found than that of the Reverend Edward Thomson, who in the 1850's hoped that his sketches might be "valued by the antiquarian." Thomson in his essay on "Western Character" emphasized the following: first, the Westerner was possessed of "much philosophy, but little metaphysics"; his philosophy, however, was practical rather than speculative. Though he would not deprecate the value of speculation, he had little opportunity to indulge in it for there was everything to be done—"the forest to be felled, the city to be built, the railroad surveyed, the swamp cleared, political, social, and religious systems to be organized; a study under such circumstances would be like a study in a vessel short-manned and swept by the tempest."

Another characteristic of the western man was that, though he had more of the real than the imaginary in his thoughts, he was by no means lacking in the latter. He was in the "midst of broad plains, lofty mountains, majestic streams"; he could allow his mind free scope in depicting the creations of nature, familiarity with which created a tendency to excite the imagination and stimulate figurative language.

[181] Kirkland, *Western Clearings*, 1–2. See also John James Audubon, *Delineations of American Scenery and Character*, 79.

This love of nature bore a close relationship to the Westerner's love of freedom:

For the most part he is not brought up, but brings himself up. He is
free in his manners; he has neither the skulking of a menial nor the strut
of a lord; he meets you with a look of conscious integrity, an air of confidence and fearlessness, a mien that bespeaks a contented condition, and a
manner rustic as a patriarch's. He has no rules of politeness but his behavior
makes you feel at ease in his company. . . . He is free in speech as well as
manners; he gives you your title if he thinks of it, if not, no matter; he
accords to you your claims after you have demonstrated them; he tells you
that he prefers his own taste to yours, and, after hearing your opinion, he
gives his own, which he thinks much better; he frankly puts you on guard
against your infirmities, and tells you of your faults; and he is willing that
you should communicate with him as freely as he does with you; if you
engage him in debate, you will find him a fearless, outspoken, and trenchant
antagonist—scorning all artifice, concealing no truth, acknowledging what
is against himself, and candidly conceding what he cannot maintain; he
goes heart uppermost. Whether he be friend or foe you know it—you will
find him sincere. . . .

He eats when he is hungry, and drinks when he is thirsty; he sows and
reaps when he gets ready, whether the moon's horns are up or down; he
goes in and comes out as he pleases, without consulting the almanac. . . .

You silence a western man because he pronounces hy-per-bo-*le* *hy*perbole,
or cue bono *cui* bono, or pronounces belle in two syllables. . . . As well
attempt to stop the Mississippi with a paddle.

The western man had an abhorrence of unnecessary forms in
business and law and particularly in religion.

Necessity is a great simplifier and organizer. . . . If the devil is in a
barrel and there is no law to get him out, he will knock him on the head
and spill his liquid brains, or, if he do not, his wife will. Though he sometimes uses the club of the unwritten law, he rarely squeezes out the venom
of the written one; and when he resorts to force it is from *good* impulses,
not *bad* ones—it is with a view not to *subvert,* but to *supplement* the
statute.

Westerners loved liberty—liberty was public, freedom personal. They had rational views of civil liberty which respected
the state, and religious liberty which respected the church. They
were honest. Honest in the

extensive sense, as descriptive alike of principles, conduct, and temper of
mind. . . . They are not honest merely in the negative sense—they consider
each other's welfare. View them in all situations in which the rights and

interests of others are concerned, and you will find them possessed of a character which, in this fallen world, is remarkable for integrity. Are they competitors, they are fair; are they judges, they are equitable; are they umpires, they are reasonable.[182]

Timothy Flint, missionary, editor, geographer, and student of the West, said in characterizing this region:

Its most obvious features are a buoyancy, a confidence, self-complacency, and daring, a perfect command, at all times and places, and under all circumstances, of at least all that the person knows—a hardihood—a spirit, finely denominated in the phrase of the country, a "pushing" spirit, which every competitor with a Kentucky lawyer, merchant, doctor, or candidate for election, or office, well knows, fears, tries to imitate, and attempts to ridicule.[183]

It was this volatile self-confidence, willingness to support all claims with a fight, which led the young physician to find no difficulty in the most unknown case, and the young attorney to start on a scale of utmost grandeur and terminate in a sublime tempest of eloquence. This spirit, when accompanied with learning, talent, mind, and application, carried everything before it.

Caleb Atwater, pioneer Ohio historian, in discoursing on the character traits and vital contributions of the pioneer, wrote:

In this State we have no rule of court etiquette which requires the introduction of a citizen, by a head of a department, to our Chief Magistrate, before any business can be transacted with him. . . . If grandeur has found in our national capital and in Europe, a splendid palace and a lofty dome for its abode, its dwelling place in Ohio is in the heart of its possessor. Our grandeur is a moral one, and the humblest citizen can approach it without impediment whenever he wishes to do so.[184]

The fact that Ohio, with a population of 3,000 in 1790, had, in thirty-seven years grown to 800,000 appeared fabulous in retrospect. In 1790 "the Indian boy was exercising his skill with the bow where now the tyro is embuing his mind with the wisdom of past ages. . . ." The hum of business prevailed where had been but the sighing of the forests; luxuries were common which took

[182] Edward Thomson, D.D., LL.D., *Sketches Biographical and Incidental,* edited by the Reverend D. W. Clark, D.D. (Cincinnati, published by L. Swormstedt & A. Poe for the Methodist Episcopal Church at the Western Book Concern, 1856), 220, 221, 230–33, 237.
[183] In his review of Marshall's *History of Kentucky,* in *Western Monthly Review,* I (1827–28), 275.
[184] Address at Columbus, in *Ohio State Journal,* July 5, 1827.

Europe centuries to win. Great was to be the future. "Who can foresee the event?"

We of this generation are but pioneers; we have done much, but nothing in comparison with what the next generation will do. We are their "hewers of wood and drawers of water"; we came and saw and conquered, but the spoil is theirs; ours is emphatically the age of *bile*—theirs will be the golden. The State of Ohio has progressed with a rapidity that has far outstripped the most sanguine anticipations. We feel no disposition, however, in looking forward to her maturity, to indulge in castle building. Everything around us—improvement in building—the bustle of business in villages— the emigration of intelligent and enterprising men—the successful prosecu- tion on the canals—the improvement in roads—the increased travel and facilities afforded to travellers—the increased attention to education—public opinion chastened and operating more powerfully on society—a higher tone of moral feeling pervading the community—these and a variety of other facts show distinctly, that Ohio is rapidly progressing in all that renders a people happy and respectable.[185]

Atwater thought Ohio distinguished from other communities by its morality. A general abhorrence of slavery, absence of sui- cides and intoxication, and the judging of each man on his merits, characterized the people. He attributed the general diffusion of order and the moral and peaceable habits to the larger proportion of ministers of the gospel than in any other state.[186]

Homilies of this nature came no nearer the truth than the much-resented writings of the more snobbish of the British trav- elers, "depraved men, whom a long career of subserviency had rendered callous to every principle of honor."[187] When Thomas Hamilton, in his *Men and Manners in America,* described the gulping and swallowing with which Americans pitchforked their food down their gullets, their bluntness and inquisitiveness, their entire lack of learning, and said of the Ohio boat passengers that he had never seen anything so disgusting in human shape, with morals and manners alike detestable,[188] James Hall's ire was

---

[185] Atwater, "Prospects of Ohio," in *Ohio State Journal,* July 12, 1827.

[186] *The General Character, Present and Future Prospects of the People of Ohio* . . . (Cincinnati, 1827), *passim.* See review in *Western Monthly Review,* I (1827– 1828), 183.

[187] James Hall in *Western Monthly Magazine,* I (1833), 517.

[188] *Men and Manners in America,* 30, 71, 196, 296. Hamilton found the catalogue of sins of these people so complete that he was disappointed that it did not include one more—hypocrisy. "Of hypocrisy, however, they were not guilty."

Patrick Shirreff, one of the most judicious of reporters, distinguished between the cabin passengers, whom he found generally civil, temperate, well dressed and decent, and the deck passengers, many of whom were coarse and profane but still civil. He, better than any other, probably had the explanation for Hamilton's acer-

aroused. Statements of this sort were "wilful and deliberate false-hoods . . . intentional and wicked fabrications, and corrupt per-versions of the truth, written in an abusive spirit of calumny . . . the result of an arranged plan of national detraction."[189]

Yet Michael Chevalier,[190] who amply confirmed Mrs. Trol-lope's account of the sociable manners of the people, received the approbation of the doughty editor. "His views are in general sagacious, and his opinions decidedly favorable to us."[191] Che-valier saw in bustling Cincinnati evidences of the "industrious feudalism," which he thought characterized the nineteenth cen-tury.

The moral aspect of Cincinnati is delightful to him, who loves labor before every thing,—to whom labor holds the first rank. But whoever has a taste for pleasure and expense, whoever would wish to plunge often into amusements and gaity, would find that this beautiful city, with its pure sky and picturesque scenery, is a wearisome abode. It would be even much worse for a man of leisure, desirous of consecrating a good part of his life to the culture of the fine arts and the rest to enjoyment. For him, life would not be there supportable, it would not be even passable. He would be blasted by politics—for there is a feeling in the United States, that men of leisure are so many foundations for an aristocracy; anathematized by religion—for the sects, though so different, all agree in condemning all kinds of pleasures, such as feast, luxuries, gallantry, even the fine arts; . . . Surrounded, completely enclosed by habit of labor, and by political axioms, and religious prejudices, it would be necessary to resign himself to an existence analogous to the crowd, or fly and seek an abode less opposed to his tastes in the great cities. . . .

Chevalier's insight was keen and his judgments fair. He noted the lack of respect toward sovereign authority in the West, where

---

bity. In the first place, the latter came into the West with a servant and then was ashamed to use him. "This circumstance of itself was sufficient to sour him with all the country contained, as well as to create in others an unfavourable impression towards himself. It was surely an odd proceeding to send 'for a bottle of champagne from the inn', when he was on board a steam-boat. The reason assigned for having done so—'tolerably tired of the poison called brandy'—perhaps accounts for much he has written regarding America—a potation of this liquid, followed by 'cham-pagne', being one of the most deceptious mediums which things can be viewed through, and I shall leave future visitants of the United States to determine whether much he has described has reality, or the fantasies of his imagination." *A Tour Through North America; together with a Comprehensive View of the Canadas and United States. As Adapted for Agricultural Emigration* (Edinburgh, 1835), 279–80.

[189] In his review of *Men and Manners,* and of *Transatlantic Sketches,* by Capt. J. E. Alexander (Philadelphia, 1833), in *Western Monthly Magazine,* I (1833), 515, 517.

[190] "Letters on America," in *Western Monthly Magazine,* IV (1835), 404–14.

[191] *Ibid.*

the authority of the "rulers" and their salaries were on a par. There were governors who did not govern, and judges likely to be indicted. To call the chief magistrates of the states commanders in chief of the military and naval forces was a farce, when they had no more authority than a corporal. Yet the spirit of obedience was there. The authority of public officials might be questioned, but not that of innkeeper, coach driver, or steamboat captain. Travelers came at the call of the innkeeper's bell, ate whatever was put before them, stopped at the pleasure of the driver or captain, and stood for inconvenience, upsets and worse, without complaints. "It has often been remarked of the founders of empires, from the days of the Romans until those of Buccaniers, that their lives were a strange mixture of absolute independence and passive obedience. The immense empire of the West is another apt illustration of this remark."[192] Looking through the externals, Chevalier saw the character of the West:

In the west, all are equal; but not with a nominal equality, not equal on paper merely. There every man with a coat on his back is a gentleman; quite as good as his neighbor, and who has no idea of putting himself out for any body. He thinks only of himself, without bestowing a thought upon his neighbor, from whom, in return, however, he expects not the least civility. This is rude, to be sure, but no unkindness is mixed with it; on the contrary, it is done so naturally that you cannot take offense at it. A western man is rough, but not quarrelsome; he is touchy to be sure, and proud of himself, and above all of his country, but yet not disagreeably or impertinently so. Once but penetrate beyond his coating of vanity and egotism, and you will find him a man of sense and even of generous feelings. You will find him a close calculator, and yet susceptible of enthusiasm—passionately fond of money, and yet far from being avaricious—nay often very prodigal; harsh and awkward, because he has neither time nor opportunity to modulate his voice, and soften his manners. Rough he may be, but not disobliging; on the contrary, he aspires to be a man of the world, and for such would like to pass, but unfortunately has cultivated his farm to rather more advantage than his manners. It is quite natural that the first generation of the west should bear the impress of the hard labor amid which it has been reared.[193]

Alongside this homespunness of western life existed symptoms of aspirations to a less solid life. A traveler on the Springfield, Illinois, stage in the early 1830's noted with what reluctance a

[192] Michael Chevalier, "The Western Steamboats," in *Western Monthly Magazine*, IV, 414.
[193] *Ibid.*, IV, 412–13.

woman of "delicate appearance, a sylph-like form, regular features, and a lively manner" finally consented to compromise with the cold weather by putting on a pair of wool stockings, which her husband bought for her, over the silk ones which she was wearing. "Like many of her countrywomen, she had feet and ankles of exquisite formation, and perhaps in the display of this gift of nature, she made a sacrifice of her health."[194]

Perhaps Thomas Hamilton was right when he doubted:[195]

No woman, conscious of attraction, was ever a republican in her heart. Beauty is essentially despotic—it uniformly asserts its power, and never yet consented to a surrender of privilege. I have certainly heard it maintained in the United States, that all men are equal, but never did I hear that assertion from the lips of a lady. On the contrary, the latter is always conscious of the full extent of her claims of preference to admiration, and is never satisfied till she feels them to be acknowledged. And what zephyr is too light to fill the gossamer sails of woman's vanity! The form of a feature, the whiteness of a hand, the shade of a ringlet, a cap, a feather, a trinket, a smile, a motion—all, or any of them, or distinctions yet finer and more shadowy, if such there be—are enough, here as elsewhere, to constitute the sign and shibboleth of her fantastic supremacy. It is in vain, therefore, to talk of female republicans; there exists, and can exist, no such being on either side of the Atlantic, for human nature is the same on both.

Commenting on the "Fashionable Follies of Ornamental Young Ladies" of about 1830, the *Western Monthly Review* said:

It is a sad and lamentable truth, after all the incessant din we have heard, of the march of mind, the talks about Lyceums and the interminable theories, inculcations and eulogies of education, that the present is an age of unbounded desire of display and notoriety, of exhaustless and unquenchable burning ambition; and not an age of calm, contented, ripe and useful knowledge for the sacred privacy of the parlor. Display, notoriety, surface, and splendor, these are the first aims of the mothers; and can we expect, that the daughters will drink into a better spirit? To play, sing, dress, glide down the dance, and get a husband, is the lesson; not be qualified to render his home quiet, well ordered and happy.[196]

Others, too, were worrying about the degeneration of the "gentler sex" and pondering over the good old days when women were useful as well as ornamental. Mrs. Sarah Josepha Hale, the

---

[194] Shirreff, *A Tour Through North America*, 285.
[195] Quoted in *ibid.*, 298–99; see also Hamilton, *Men and Manners*, 65.
[196] III (1829–30), 403.

influential editor of *Godey's Lady's Book,* was beginning her life-
long crusade in favor of exercise and health for women. Although
doctors recommended sweeping, polishing furniture, rope jumping, battledore, and modified calisthenics for sedentary females,
Mrs. Hale recommended the spinning wheel. "From the universal, yet gentle exercise it affords the limbs, the chest, and the
whole frame, it is altogether the best mode of domestic calisthenics that has hitherto been devised."[197]

Milking as an exercise was advocated by some. They pointed
out that thirty years earlier it was as hard to find a man milking
as it was a woman mowing. But times had changed. Girls now
hardly knew—or at least pretended not to know—whether milk
came from the udder or the horns. This was bad from many
angles. Women were cleaner, more patient, and gentler. Men
had to milk too early and too late. "The morning air would be
bracing to their muscles, (if the modern girl has any muscles, for
there begins to be a reasonable doubt in this matter); and the
odor of the cow has been long known to be, and is often recommended by physicians as medicinal."[198]

Derelictions of this sort were not confined to the women. There
were such things as "dandies" in the West. It had been said that
there were three sexes: men, women, and dandies. A dandy was
a person who had people pick up things for him. Western editors
usually pretended that such animals were confined to the eastern
seaboard, and one hoped that the wisdom of the western state
legislatures would prevent their spreading to the interior.[199]
Either the legislatures failed to act or else the laws were not enforced. Thomas Peirce of Cincinnati thus described him or it:

> Behold a pale, thin-visaged wight,
> Some five feet, more or less, in height;
>   Which, as it frisks and dances,
> Presents a body that, at most,
> Is less substantial than a ghost,
>   As pictured in romances!

. . . .

[197] *Farmer's Reporter and United States Agriculturist* (Cincinnati), 1833.
[198] Springfield *Illinois State Register,* November 9, 1839, quoting the *New England Farmer.*
[199] *Detroit Gazette,* January 8, 1819.

Around its neck a stiff cravat;
Another tightly drawn o'er that,
  And over these, a dozen
Enormous ruffles on his breast;
And close below a tiny vest,
    For gaudy colors chosen.

. . . .

With trowsers welted down each side,
And spreading out almost as wide
  As petticoats at bottom;
A small dumb watch some cent'ries old,
With twenty keys and seals of gold—
  No matter how he got 'em.

To dangle at a lady's side,
Whene'er she takes a walk or ride,
  A thing extremely handy:—
These constitute—as fashions run
In eighteen Hundred twenty-one—
  A *Cincinnati Dandy*.[200]

Even though the words were proscribed by colleges, one editor decided that it was an "eventful," "wonderful," "pro-di-gi-ous" age. "In all soberness, change has become a passion; and the time is coming when men will laugh at our awkwardness and simplicity, and count us little better than Hottentots."[201]

These then, were some of the characteristics of the people of the West. Their history was homely but it was original, like nothing else in the wide world "and so various that successive travellers [and historians] may continue to give their views of it for years to come, without fear of exhausting its peculiarities."[202] As the nonliterary practical-minded English traveler so soundly concluded: "It may be easily supposed that the character of such a mixed population exhibits no near approach to individuality [uniformity]."[203] The emigrants carried the mixed heritage of

[200] *The Odes of Horace in Cincinnati* . . . (Cincinnati, 1822), Ode VII.
[201] Detroit *North-Western Journal*, January 30, 1830.
[202] Kirkland, *Western Clearings*, preface, vi.
[203] Oliver, *Eight Months in Illinois*, 73. When Daniel Drake, who knew the West as did few others of his day, started a chapter on the "State of Society" in Cincinnati in 1815, he found it a formidable undertaking and excused himself by stating: "This cannot, of course, be pourtrayed with the same facility and exactness as in older communities." *Natural and Statistical View; or, Picture of Cincinnati*, 166.

the older communities, conditioned by the struggle with the wilderness, the Indian, and their comparative isolation. Among them were the best elements of the hardy population of earlier colonial frontiers, and some of the worst; also men of intellectual attainments, some with classic educations, destined for leadership in any community. The desire for better homes, broader opportunities, greater wealth, was the dominating motive. A certain stamina of independence, of aggressiveness, and of faith lay deep in the breasts of these people.

They have been called coarse, ignorant, lawless, and violent, which at all times some were, and at some time most were. This, of course, was the result largely of the failure of law made for the older societies to function under the peculiar conditions of the frontier. Until communities were stabilized and law was generally applicable, the individual code ruled, sanctioned by the strong arm or ready gun of the pioneer. The cultural life of the settlers and their institutions were as fresh and simple as the log houses which they built, inelegant and crude, but with lasting qualities. In estimating these people and their work, the contempt of superiority is no less to be guarded against than the idealization which ascribes superabundance of vision, courage, industry, and virtue to them. After all, they were just folks, doing their day's work, and caring little for the verdict of history.

VII

Trade, Travel, and Transportation

Under the influence of that fell spirit of demagoguism which has swept over our land, it has become fashionable to flatter the agricultural and laboring classes, because they are the most numerous, and wield the greatest power at the ballot boxes; while a systematic effort has been made, to decry the merchant and the banker, and to stigmatise their business as inimical to the liberty and prosperity of the country. We might pass over these incendiary doctrines with the contempt they deserve, if it were not for the wide spread mischief which they work, by deluding, to their own injury, the numerous classes whom they are intended to cajole and flatter. The laborer and mechanic are taught to dislike the banker, whose means furnish them with daily employment, and the farmer's mind is diligently imbued with a settled hatred for the merchant, without whose assistance his crops would rot upon the field. The prosperity of the country, its peace, its character, and its credit, are deeply affected by the too successful influence of these wretched intrigues. The masses are imbued with the opinion that wealth and poverty, commerce and labor, education and the want of education, constitute hostile interests; and the legislative halls are disgraced by an abject subserviency to those prejudices, which has banished justice, and patriotism, and manly freedom of thought, from that high sanctuary of sovereign power.

James Hall, *The West: Its Commerce and Navigation*

WHILE the pioneers of the Ohio Valley were pushing back the Indian, clearing the woods, and founding towns, far to the north in a wilderness hardly disturbed, still prevailed the fur trade. The early French explorers in the region of the St. Lawrence failed to discover either precious metals or the long-sought passage to the Orient, but they did find the Indian and the beaver (*castor*) and began the fur trade which, in the eighteenth century, came to play a part in international affairs comparable to that played in our own times by oil, rubber, and nitrates. At first the furs, which were all the Indian had to offer for the white man's goods, were incidental to the traffic in fish, but they became in time the chief interest of Frenchmen in the New World, and it was the fur trade, rather than royal monarchs, feudalism, or religion, which determined the nature and fate of the colonial establishment of France in North America.

In the early period the tribes came annually with their canoes and pelts to Three Rivers, or Montreal, but as the beaver retreated westward and tribes near at hand began to play the part of middlemen, it became necessary for the traders to penetrate deeper and deeper into the Indian country towards the Great Lakes and beyond. The contact of European and Indian cultures seriously conditioned both. The Indian was soon dependent upon the trader for metal pots and knives, blankets, guns, and traps, but these valuable articles as well as ornaments and liquor could be had for old used fur robes and garments, as well as prime pelts.[1] Agriculture came more and more to be neglected for the chase, and the Indian to be transformed from a natural conservationist into a destroyer of the beaver people.

Under the paternalistic French system, favored individuals or groups were usually given monopoly privileges in the fur trade, prices were fixed by law, and the number of licensed traders was carefully limited. But while favored companies came and went, fishermen and peasants, army officers, ex-soldiers, and merchants traded on regardless; these *coureurs du bois,* or unlicensed traders, thronged into the wilderness, attracted by the freedom, the thrills of adventure, and the chance for profits. Many adopted the Indian way of life and became progenitors of a race destined to play an important part in the fur trade of later periods, as well as in the Indian wars and western settlements. Since French official policies were so largely influenced by the vested interests of the fur trade—and these were often in conflict with the aims of the missionaries—intrigue and corruption were all too common. When Radisson and Groseilliers, who had successfully ventured into the Sioux country of the Far West, had thousands of furs confiscated by the governor of Three Rivers, they turned willing ears to the plans of a group of English adventurers and helped persuade Charles II of England to charter the Hudson's Bay Company in 1670.[2]

In 1664 the English took over New Netherlands by right of

[1] Indian robes, worn next to the body with fur turned in, were more valuable than new furs, for the long hairs were worn down and the short fur became oily and soft, and felted into a finer product.

[2] The charter was granted to the "Governor and Company of Adventurers of England Trading into Hudson's Bay."

conquest, and from 1670 onward the French faced the keen competition of her powerful rival from two directions. The posts of the "Great Company" tapped the regions adjacent to Hudson Bay and from New York the English, aided by the Iroquois, strove to divert the trade of the Great Lakes region to the Hudson. The French countered by establishing posts at Kingston, Michilimackinac, and other points on the Lakes and the Upper Mississippi. The long beaver war had begun.

La Salle's vision of an Indian fur empire in the Mississippi Valley passed with his failure to establish a colony at the mouth of that river, but others followed and carried on. Eventually French military posts and trading stations dotted the West from Biloxi and New Orleans up through the Illinois country to connect with La Baye, Michilimackinac, Detroit, and the St. Lawrence. Although France yielded Acadia, Newfoundland, and the Hudson Bay country to England by treaty at the end of Queen Anne's War in 1713, there were those who claimed that she rightfully possessed title to all of North America.

The English established Fort Oswego on Lake Ontario, and aggressively supported their allies, the Iroquois, in increasing trade activities at the expense of the French in the Great Lakes region, while the French expanded their control from New Orleans up the Mississippi and into the Lower Ohio region. A half century of conflict was necessary to settle the issue. When the French began to occupy the Upper Ohio Valley, not only were Virginia, Pennsylvania, and other colonies vitally interested but even England was aroused to the importance of the stakes in America. The struggle for the Ohio precipitated the last of the colonial wars. By the Treaty of Paris, 1763, France surrendered all territory east of the Mississippi and south of the Hudson Bay country (excepting Florida) to England; Louisiana, stretching west from the Mississippi to the Rockies, went to Spain; Spain ceded Florida to England.[3]

England was not immediately to reap the profits of the con-

---

[3] A general review of the French fur trade may be had in George M. Wrong, *The Rise and Fall of New France* (2 volumes. New York, 1928). Harold A. Innis in *The Fur Trade of Canada* (Toronto, 1927) and *The Fur Trade in Canada* (New Haven, Conn., 1930) gives a scholarly analysis of the subject from the beginning to 1729. Excellent chapters may be found in Kellogg, *The French Régime in Wisconsin and the Northwest*. Constance Lindsay Skinner in *Beaver, Kings and Cabins* (New York, 1933), gives a readable popular story.

quest of New France, however, for the Indian uprising known as Pontiac's Conspiracy disrupted the fur trade in the Northwest. The King's Proclamation of 1763 sought to hold back the settlers until a plan for administering Indian affairs and the fur trade could be formulated. Meanwhile, French traders continued to predominate in the Illinois country. When Sir William Johnson, superintendent of Indian affairs for the "Northern Department," attempted to concentrate the Indian trade at Niagara, Detroit, Oswego, Michilimackinac, and Fort Chartres, he ran into opposition from Canadian merchants and Governor Guy Carleton, of Quebec. Though he planned to open additional posts at Green Bay, St. Marys, Sandusky, St. Joseph, and on the Wabash and Miami (Maumee), his plans for imperial regulation failed, and the problem was turned back to the colonies. Since the colonies in turn failed to control the trade, England tried once more, with the Quebec Act, to bring order out of chaos in the West. Canadians as well as Yankees protested, but the American Revolution prevented the working out of any effective plans of regulation. Measures were enacted by the Quebec legislative council, and the friendship of the Indians was cultivated, but little more was accomplished. Traders moved from Albany to Montreal during the war, the St. Lawrence trade to the interior was strengthened, and penetration into the far Northwest followed.

Many English and Canadian merchants thought their government had gone too far in yielding to the Americans valuable fur territory by the treaty of 1783, but despite the lack of a definite policy in the period following, England continued to hold on to the western posts on United States soil and to allay the fears of the Indians who felt they had been betrayed by their late allies.

Since the British feared that American traders would divert the trade down the Mohawk-Hudson route, they banned them from the upper country and prohibited the export of furs to the United States. The main centers of British trade in the Northwest during this period were Detroit and Michilimackinac.

Detroit was the chief depot for the country around Lake Erie, the Maumee-Wabash valleys, and part of the Illinois country, while Michilimackinac drained the area west of Lake Michigan. Farther to the northwest beyond Superior lay the vast area with outlet by way of the Grand Portage route. Influential Montreal merchants in 1783 organized the North West Company to exploit this region and operate on a continental scale.[4] Estimates of 1784 placed the annual value of the fur trade for these three regions at about £150,000; of 1794 at about £200,000.

The United States fully appreciated the importance of the fur trade in the Northwest, and in 1786 the Confederation Congress created a Northern and a Southern Indian department with separate superintendents. Trading among the Indians was restricted to licensed American citizens. President Washington more than once emphasized the importance of a controlled trade as a factor in Indian diplomacy and favored government development of the trade. A law in 1795 set aside $50,000 for the establishing of government trading posts; the next year $150,000 was added, and within the next dozen years posts were in operation at Detroit, Fort Wayne, Chicago, Sandusky, Michilimackinac, and elsewhere.[5]

Although the British surrendered the western military posts under Jay's Treaty in 1796, rivalry for trade and influence with the Indians on American soil did not cease. It became one of the causes of the second war with England, and not until the Treaty of Ghent in 1814 was the British supremacy broken.

American trade suffered from a lack of cheap manufactured goods, consequently Montreal still held the advantage over Albany in the trade in American territory. Leadership in the recovery of the fur trade and re-establishment of the Albany–New York route was taken by John Jacob Astor and his American Fur Company. The United States factory system of 1795–96 paved the way, and the North West Company served as example and stimulus. Astor, a New York merchant and fur trader, had incorporated the American Fur Company in 1808 to compete with the North West and Michilimackinac companies, a greater part of whose furs came from United States territory;[6] in 1811 he concluded a five-year agreement with representatives of these

[4] Really a partnership or common-law company. Gordon Charles Davidson, *The North West Company* (*University of California Publications in History*, VII, Berkeley, 1918), 13; Wayne E. Stevens, *The Northwest Fur Trade 1763–1800* (*University of Illinois Studies in the Social Sciences*, XIV, No. 3, Urbana, 1928), 106, and documents cited.
[5] *American State Papers, Indian Affairs*, II, 181–82.
[6] Incorporated in New York for twenty-five years, capital stock might be $2,000,000 after two years. The act may be found in Kenneth Porter, *John Jacob Astor* (2 volumes. Cambridge, Mass., 1931), I, 413 ff.

companies for the formation of what came to be known as the South West Company. The fur trade of the New York and Montreal companies was to be conducted by joint account so as to avoid double losses from competition, the North West Company agreed to keep off United States soil, and the South West Company out of Canada except in part of the Lake Huron area.[7] During the war the Canadian traders established themselves on United States soil, and in 1815 Astor signed a renewal of the agreement for five years, hoping meanwhile for a United States law which would enable him to get control of the whole business.[8] In April, 1816, Congress enacted a law which restricted Indian trade within United States territorial limits to citizens of the United States.[9] Astor's influence was sufficient to secure enough licenses for Canadians for his own immediate needs, and in 1817 he purchased his partners' interest in the South West Company.[10]

Unencumbered by alliances, Astor was now ready to go after furs in the Great Lakes region in earnest. He owned and directed the American Fur Company, and his political connections were strong. Robert Stuart and his fellow Astorian, Ramsay Crooks, were appointed agents to handle the company's business from Montreal, New York and Michilimackinac, clerks and *voyageurs* were sent west, and in the spring of 1817 the various outfits were dispatched into the Indian country from Michilimackinac. The Hudson's Bay Company still offered competition, as did representatives of lesser companies and strongly entrenched private traders. In addition was the opposition afforded by the military officers, Indian agents, and government factors.

The United States factory system among the Indians, as begun in 1795–96, was designed to secure the friendship of the Indians, protect them from unscrupulous traders, weaken the British influence, and provide a means of trade control.[11] Between 1802

[7] Porter, *John Jacob Astor*, I, 254–55.

[8] Astor to Secretary of State James Monroe, December, 1816, cited in *ibid.*, II, 691. Astor knew from the Superintendent of Indian Trade that the government intended to keep the British traders out of the United States. *Ibid.*, 695.

[9] U. S. *Statutes at Large*, III, 331–33. There seems to be no proof that Astor secured the passage of this law, as often stated, but it seems probable.

[10] George Graham to Governor Lewis Cass, in Reuben Gold Thwaites, "The Fur Trade in Wisconsin, 1815–1817," in *Wisconsin Historical Collections*, XIX (1910), 458.

[11] For its purposes, see *Wisconsin Historical Collections*, XX (1911), 26–28. For a brief study of the factory system, see Edgar B. Wesley, "The Government Factory System Among the Indians, 1795–1822," in *Journal of Economic and Business*

and 1821 the system was renewed or extended by a dozen laws. In 1811 the capital was increased to $300,000 plus appropriations for salaries of factors and clerks. The Detroit factory was discontinued after 1805, the Fort Wayne factory was burned by Indians in 1812, and the Sandusky, Mackinac, and Chicago factories were also lost at the outset of the war. The last named was reopened in 1816 and new factories were established at Green Bay and Prairie du Chien. The factors ordered their goods from the Superintendent of the Indian Trade, who was limited to the purchase of domestic goods. Shipment to the stations was often difficult and always expensive. Factors were discouraged from selling goods to whites and forbidden to trade on their own account or to sell liquor.

Army officers and government factors distrusted Astor's company and its intentions, for many of his agents had been on the British side during the war, and his desire to have the government trading houses abolished was well known. But Astor's influence was too strong. In 1816 Secretary of War William H. Crawford requested both the commanding officer and the Indian agent at Mackinac to give Astor's agents "every possible facility and aid in the prosecution of their business, that [might] be compatible with your public duties,"[12] and the next year he requested Governor Cass, of Michigan Territory, to do the same. Cass apparently so favored the company that even Crooks was surprised.[13] He aided in the ousting of the Mackinac agent, Maj. William H. Puthuff, whom the company could not win over, and shortly Crooks and Stuart were threatening the agents at Green Bay and Prairie du Chien. Even so, the year 1817 was not particularly profitable to the company, and Crooks and Stuart wrote Astor that if his representation did "not produce the abolition of the factories, now no longer necessary: or at least create a thorough change in their present organization, it will in our opinion

---

History, IV (1931–32), 487–511; Katherine Coman, "Government Factories: An Attempt to Control Competition in the Fur Trade," in American Economic Association, *Papers and Discussions,* 1911, pp. 368–88; Royal B. Way, "The United States Factory System for Trading with the Indians, 1796–1822," in *Mississippi Valley Historical Review,* VI (1919–20), 220–35.

[12] Quoted in Thwaites, "The Fur Trade in Wisconsin, 1815–1817," in *Wisconsin Historical Collections,* XIX, 414.

[13] For an analysis of the impression that Cass accepted money for his favors, see Porter, *John Jacob Astor,* II, 723–25, note 54.

be imprudent in you to continue interested in the trade."[14] Private capital and political influence, combined with superior goods, underselling, use of liquor, and the power of traders frequently intermarried with the Indians, proved too much for the government system. The factories at Green Bay and Chicago were practically out of business by 1821. Cass advocated the ending of the system, and when Senator Thomas Hart Benton, of Missouri, joined in the fight, a bill for discontinuing it was passed in the spring of 1822.[15]

The government factory system, though well intended in purpose, had not worked well in practice. Goods at cost and a fair price for furs did not compensate in the Indian's mind for lack of credit, presents, and liquor. Private traders gave all three, and by following the Indian into his hunting country, usually intercepted the best of his furs, and frequently were better diplomats as well.[16] Although not profit-making in intent, the failure of the factory system to pay its way no doubt weakened support. The War of 1812 caused losses equal to about one sixth of the capital; bad debts and unsalable goods further depleted it. At the end of twenty-seven years only about half the capital was recoverable. The fact was, government-managed fur traders could not successfully compete with private traders. Secretary of War Calhoun, however, believed that the experiment was not all loss:

It was commenced, and has been continued, from motives both of prudence and humanity; and though it may not have fully realized the expectations of its friends, it has no doubt produced beneficial effects. If wars

[14] Quoted in Reuben Gold Thwaites, "The Fur Trade in Wisconsin, 1812–25," in *Wisconsin Historical Collections,* XX (1911), 31.

[15] Benton was retained as attorney by the American Fur Company during the period in which he worked for this bill. Porter, *John Jacob Astor,* II, 714, based on Ramsay Crooks' and Robert Stuart's letter books and other data. Maj. John Biddle, Indian agent at Green Bay, had written to Benton criticizing the report of the superintendent of the establishment. He defended the traders and thought that with slight modifications of the law, the whole trade would best be left to individual enterprise. The chief evil, he stated, was the liquor traffic. *Detroit Gazette,* April 26, 1822. The American Fur Company was defended by the *Gazette* (May 24, 1822) when the Washington (D. C.) *National Intelligencer* published a letter charging that the United States factories could not compete with their domestic blankets against the duty-free ones which the company brought in from Canada. The *Gazette* letter stated that Astor's company, as well as others, bought their blankets in Boston and New York and paid thousands in revenues into the United States treasury annually.

[16] Private traders misrepresented the system, telling the Indian it was intended to get him in debt in order that the United States could take his lands, and that the factor sold goods intended as presents to the Indians. *American State Papers, Indian Affairs,* II, 82.

have not been entirely prevented by it, they probably, without it, would have been more frequent; and if the Indians have made but little advances in civilization, they probably, without it, would have made less.[17]

The methods, and to a large extent the working personnel of the fur trade in the Northwest, remained French throughout the English and into the American period. The *bourgeois* or proprietor gave way to the agent or factor, but the *voyageurs* or boatmen remained indispensable. Originally descriptive of travelers or explorers in general, the term *voyageur* eventually came to be applied to the boatmen and subtraders. The two classes, *mangeurs de lard* (pork eaters) and *hivernants* (winterers), were separated by sharply drawn lines. The "pork eaters" were novices, supposedly incapable of living on the customary ration of a quart of lyed corn (or dried peas) and two ounces of tallow or grease per day, and were used only as boatmen. The *hivernants,* on the other hand, were seasoned veterans who were often entrusted with subtrading posts in the interior where they remained over winter, and who were never reluctant to lord it over the apprentices.

The *voyageurs* were recruited largely from around Quebec and Montreal—later from Detroit and Mackinac—and signed on for a term of years. Usually unlettered, simple and childlike in their ways, superstitious, often lazy and unambitious outside their season's work, these men were prodigies of skill and endurance in the canoe or behind the sled. Proud, jealous, boastful, yet courteous, distinguished by their costumes, songs, and traditions, the *voyageurs* constituted a unique and picturesque class. Working costumes consisted of a red wool peaked cap—from under which their long hair hung—shirt, breechcloth or breeches, leggings, and moccasins. A gaudy sash from which hung a beaded bag or pouch, sometimes a blue capote, and the small-bowled clay pipe completed the outfit.

The taste for color and decoration was not limited to the person, but applied to the *voyageur's* pride, his canoe. The trade canoes were of different sizes and styles, but all modeled on the Indian bark canoe. They varied in size from the light 10- or 15-foot canoe, weighing about 50 pounds, to the giant 35- or 40-foot

[17] *Ibid.,* II, 182.

Montreal canoes capable of carrying several tons of cargo.[18] For use on the smaller streams and lakes the standard was the *canot du nord,* about twenty-five feet in length and with capacity of a ton and a half besides crew. The canoes were often covered with color designs as brilliant as the Indian used on his body, and in bow and stern were placed red feathers or plumes as testimonials of the craft's worthiness.

Most important of the crew of eight for the "North canoe" were the bowsmen and the steersmen, one of whom was likely to be the song leader. The middle men occupied closely spaced seats suspended from the gunwales and with short light cedar blades paddled Indian fashion, with choppy strokes at forty or more to the minute. Twelve to fifteen hours per day, broken by brief but regular rest intervals, when pipes were lighted, was a normal day's work. In fair water four to six miles per hour were covered; distances were usually measured in "pipes." On lakes if *"la vieille,"* or the old woman of the wind, was favorable, a light mast was set up and better progress made. If not, sacrifice of some garment in the water was made to court her favor. *Voyageur* songs, ballads, jingles, sometimes ribald and obscene doggerel, set the rhythm of the stroke and whiled away monotonous hours.[19] Ordinary headwinds were met and conquered with grim pulling, but on the lakes many days were wasted "wind bound."

[18] "The northwest canoe . . . is constructed wholly of bark, cedar splints, the roots of the spruce, and the pitch of the yellow pine, . . . and these articles are fabricated in a manner uniting such an astonishing degree of lightness, strength, and elegance, and with such a perfect adaptation to the country, and the difficulties of northern voyages, as to create a sentiment of mixed surprise and admiration. Those of the largest size, such as are commonly employed in the fur trade of the north, are thirty-five feet in length, and six feet in width. . . . They are constructed of the bark of the white birch tree . . . which is peeled from the tree in large sheets, and bent over a slender frame of cedar ribs, confined by gunwales, which are kept apart by slender bars of the same wood. Around these the bark is sewed, by the slender and flexible roots of the young spruce tree, called *wattap,* and also where the pieces of bark join, so that the gunwales resemble the rim of an Indian basket. The joinings are afterwards luted, and rendered water tight, by a coat of pine pitch, which, after it has been thickened by boiling, is used under the name of *gum.* . . . A canoe of this size, when employed in the fur trade, is calculated to carry sixty packages of skins, weighing ninety pounds each, and provisions to the amount of one thousand pounds. This is exclusive of the weight of eight men, each of whom are allowed to put on board a bag or knapsack of the weight of forty pounds. In addition to this, every canoe has a quantity of bark, wattap, gum, a pan for heating the gum, an axe, and some smaller articles necessary for repairs. The aggregate weight of all this may be estimated at about four tons." Schoolcraft, *Narrative Journal,* 68–69.

[19] A number of these songs "of their canoes, of their country, of their life, of their loves, of their church" are reproduced in Grace Lee Nute's interesting book, *The Voyageur* (New York, 1931).

White water or rapids were the delight of the seasoned *voyageur*; they furnished excitement and opportunity to exhibit particular skill. Shooting the rapids, under power so as to furnish steering leverage, grazing boulders and sliding over others by the narrowest of margins, guided by a sixth sense and a teamwork between crew and steersmen apparently derived from the subconscious, was great fun if all went well. If not, came damaged cargoes, wrecked boats, and lost lives. Going upstream, shallower currents were breasted by the crew going overboard and pushing and lifting, sometimes by towing or cordelling. Getting in and out of water often ice-cold, with no time to dry clothes until evening, was part of the day's work. Always there was the spirit of rivalry, whether in canoe or behind the sled, which gave vent not only to tall talk, bragging, and contempt for the weak, but in racing and feats of endurance hard to imagine.

Portages, unlike shooting rapids, were tedious and backbreaking monotonies; on many a trip more time was spent in carrying than in paddling. The impassable rapids and shallows did not always permit easy portage paths, nor did the carrying places between lakes and streams. Uneven and difficult paths over logs, boulders, and through brush were the rule. Packs of merchandise or skins were done into packages or "pieces" of approximately ninety pounds. The extraordinary carrying accomplishments were all the more remarkable, as the *voyageurs,* though well developed in shoulders and arms, were light and spindly in the legs. "The muscular carriers vied with each other in their powers of endurance, and their capacity to carry heavy weights. Two pieces, or one hundred and eighty pounds, were the ordinary charge that the men were expected to carry, but instances were not rare when individual voyageurs of exceptional strength and activity bore three, and even four pieces on their backs for considerable distances without stopping, rivaling in these feats the famed porters of Constantinople."[20] Even chafed backs or boils were not allowed to interfere with the work.[21] Hernia, naturally, was a common disability, though colds seem to have been rare.[22]

In camp the peas or corn, bits of pork, and perhaps some bis-

---

[20] *The Unfinished Autobiography of Henry Hastings Sibley . . .* , edited by Theodore C. Blegen (Minneapolis, 1932), 13.
[21] Extract from Sherman Hall's diary cited in Nute, *The Voyageur,* 47.
[22] *Ibid.*

cuits, were boiled into a thick mess in the big kettle. These standard rations were always supplemented when possible with berries, game, bird eggs, fish, or wild honey. Pemmican[23] or pressed buffalo or other meat was indispensable on winter trips. In camp the overturned canoe or the blanket and the sky furnished shelter in summer, and a windbreak, bank of snow, and a fire, protection in winter.

After 1815 the less frequent use of the St. Lawrence outlet for furs from the Northwest released many of these Canadian boatmen, and Astor soon got around the law restricting the employment of only American citizens in the trade. Ramsay Crooks wrote:

It will still be good policy to admit & freely and without the least restraint the Canadian Boatmen. these people are indespensable to the successful prosecution of the trade, their places cannot be supplied by Americans, who are for the most part are [sic] too independent to submit quietly to a proper controul, and who can gain any where a subsistence much superior to a man of the interior and although the body of the Yankee can resist as much hardship as any man, tis only in the Canadian we find that temper of mind, to render him patient docile and perserving. in short they are a people harmless in themselves whose habits of submission fit them peculiarly for our business and if guided as it is my wish they should be, will never give just cause of alarm to the Government of the Union   it is of course your object to exclude every foreigner except those for whom you obtain licenses.[24]

Henry Hastings Sibley, who, as head of a district, had charge of hundreds of traders, clerks, and boatmen, testified to the fidelity and honesty of the Canadian French *voyageurs*.[25] The same qualities seem in general to have been possessed by the traders as well, though the latter were often regarded as a tough and hard lot. As a class the trader has suffered somewhat from the description and charges which emanated from the army men and

[23] Meat pounded fine over which hot grease was poured and allowed to solidify.
[24] Crooks to Astor, spring 1817, in American Fur Company letter book at Mackinac, cited in Nute, *The Voyageur*, 203–4. The abandonment of the long canoe route via the St. Lawrence, development of steamboat traffic on the lakes, canals, railroads, and the advance of the agricultural frontier into the Wisconsin country, brought about the decline of the *voyageur* class. They went into lumbering and elsewhere and by 1850 had practically disappeared.
[25] Sibley, *Unfinished Autobiography*, 13. Sibley was a fur trader with Astor's company at Mackinac, later frontier politician, congressman, first governor of Minnesota, and a regent of the state university.

missionaries, who could hardly be expected to see eye to eye with him.

Perhaps no body of men have ever been so misunderstood and misrepresented. . . . To them have been ascribed not only all the evils and outrages that are the accompaniments of extreme frontier life, where law is unfelt and unknown, but they have been charged with fraud and villainy of every conceivable description. . . . With too much self respect to contradict charges so absurd and improbable, and with an undue contempt for public opinion, it is not surprising that scarcely a voice has been raised, or a pen wielded in his behalf. There is an unwritten chapter yet to be contributed to the records of the Northwest, which will place the Indian trader in a proper light before the country, while it will not seek to extenuate either his defects or vices.[26]

As a rule uneducated, often married to Indian women, the traders were possessed of energy and a capacity to meet and handle varied problems incidental to their business. Yet there were among them men of education and culture who chose to endure the hardships and perils of an occupation, which, once entered, was seldom forsaken. The peculiar fascination of this hazardous life, so rarely financially remunerative to the average trader, lay in part, no doubt, in the charm of the surroundings, the romance of wild regions inhabited by savage beasts and men, and the adventures and dangers which gave zest to existence. There is ever the tendency for many civilized men to revert to the primitive as the normal condition of life, and to the freedom from restraint of artificial trammels which the wilderness offers. Among the Indians the trader was a man of importance—their counselor and friend—and esteemed in proportion to the degree in which he identified himself with their interests. Even the bitter warfare among rival traders was flavored with something of romance and chivalry. Although trade wars were serious business and hostilities often progressed through the recognized stages of unfair competition—seduction of the best hunters from former alliances by gifts, bribery, intimidation, and the like, to actual violence—nevertheless, when traders met, the amenities were observed, hospitality generously offered, and no reference made to the unfortunate incidents. In need of provisions, medical aid,

[26] Henry H. Sibley, "Reminiscences; Historical and Personal," in *Minnesota Historical Collections*, I (1872), 463.

or assistance in emergencies, the trader could usually count on the best, even from a hostile camp.[27]

In the technique of competition the American Fur Company was a past master. Green Bay traders were forced to organize and buy their outfits from the company, were restricted to a definite area, and yet opposed on all fronts by Astor's company, and finally broken. In 1824 Congress required the Indian agents to designate certain places for the carrying on of the Indian trade and forbade trading elsewhere. This law was supposed to have been promoted by the company, as it would force independent traders to meet it on its own chosen ground. Soon there were protests from the company regarding the operation of the law, but it was retained as necessary for the regulation of the liquor traffic.[28] The company continued to squeeze out or absorb its competitors, and to expand on all fronts except in the Detroit area. This city had long been a center for individual traders, and being the easternmost post, was most affected by the influx of settlers. It was well aware of the importance of the Indian trade and was anxious concerning St. Louis' ambition to establish itself as the chief center in the West.[29] At Detroit the company was forced to retrench for a while, but by 1831 the city seems to have become a department headquarters as had Mackinac and St. Louis. By 1828 in the Northern Department—Great Lakes and Upper Mississippi — the company bought 95 per cent of the $250,000 to $300,000 worth of furs handled at Mackinac. The company continued to play politics, sought tariff concessions, sought to oust recalcitrant Indian agents such as Maj. Laurence Taliaferro at St. Peters, and even won over Col. Thomas L. McKenney, former superintendent of the government factory system, to support it in reclaiming goods condemned by John Tipton, agent on the Wabash, for violation of the liquor law.[30]

The problem of liquor and the Indian was not only one of trade but vital in the whole matter of the Indian policy of the government, the relation of the Indian to the settlers, and the welfare, even survival, of the Indian himself. The effects of in-

---

[27] Sibley, *Unfinished Autobiography*, 15.
[28] It was reaffirmed in 1834.
[29] A number of articles on the subject appeared in the *Detroit Gazette*, January—March, 1821.
[30] Porter, *John Jacob Astor*, II, 758–59, 803–4.

Scene in Hotel. *Lefevre J. Cranstone*

"I've Seen the Elephant." Ross County, Ohio, 1829

The Landing Place at Natches on the Mississippi

Wooding Station on the Mississippi

2nd May 1828

From original sketches by Basil Hall, 1828

toxicating liquor on the Indian were out of all proportion to the amount consumed, more like those of a drug such as heroin. Even a moderate amount would as a rule turn a fairly peaceable and respectable Indian into a raving madman, as likely to attack friend or family as an enemy.

Prior to 1822 government policy with reference to the use of liquor among the Indians was uncertain, but some of the territorial governors, such as William Henry Harrison, of Indiana Territory, and Ninian Edwards, of Illinois Territory, had tried hard to prevent its use. Generally speaking, Astor's company, firmly entrenched, capitalized, and administered, stood in a position to profit more, in the long run, without the use of liquor, for the sober Indian was a good judge of goods and more likely to be a permanent customer. But once liquor was resorted to by any in the keen competition for Indian trade, its use was practiced by all. The Hudson's Bay Company used liquor, and sometimes it got across the American border; individual traders smuggled it to aid their trade against superior goods and often better prices of the company, and soon the agents of Astor's company were equally involved.

As a result of the ensuing lawlessness, Congress by law in 1822 forbade traders to take liquor into the Indian country, under penalty of forfeiture of all goods.[31] Even then large quantities went in, for it was not always clear what was "Indian country." Citizens other than traders were not affected, and liquor was permitted for use of the "engages" or employees. As a result the law was frequently of no consequence, and the Indian country was flooded with liquor, the American Fur Company's representatives being among the most frequent offenders. When army officers or Indian agents went after the company and when its posts were threatened with search, Astor wrote to the Secretary of War reminding of past suits and threatening others, with the desired effect. A stricter law was enacted in 1832 which provided that "no ardent spirits shall be hereafter introduced, under any pretence, into the Indian country."[32] Even this did not abolish the traffic, for the American Fur Company which distributed 8,776 gallons to ten outfits at Mackinac in 1832, put out 5,573

[31] U. S. *Statutes at Large*, III, 682–83.
[32] *Ibid.*, IV, 564.

gallons to the same number in 1833.[33] By this time Astor's company could beat its rivals not only at price cutting but at liquor selling as well.

It is difficult to arrive at any accurate estimate of the value of the fur trade. In the Northern Department of the American Fur Company probably $125,000 was put into goods and wages (including 4,500 engages) annually, during this period, and $250,-000 to $300,000 worth of furs taken out.[34] With all of its advantages of capital, organization, political influence, and competitive technique, Astor's company never did become a monopoly. The fur trade by nature was difficult to monopolize; competition, stamped out in one spot, broke out in another, and a very considerable volume of traffic was handled by independents. Astor himself complained steadily of the unprofitable state of the business; in 1834 at the age of seventy and in ill health, he sold his interest. The Northern Department went to Ramsay Crooks and associates and kept the company name. Although the constant encroachment of the settlements upon the Indian lands year by year diminished the importance of the Indian trade in this department, and constantly modified the nature of the fur trade, nevertheless, the trade remained, even in the most settled parts of the region, and throughout our period, a far more important business than one might estimate.[35]

§

The fur trade depended not upon man-made highways or improvement in transportation facilities as did the commerce which developed from agriculture and manufacturing. The Ohio River, the only important navigable river flowing towards the west in eastern North America, served as the great natural highway, not

[33] Porter, *John Jacob Astor*, II, 812.

[34] It was estimated in 1819 that importations for the fur trade at Detroit were about $150,000, and exports much greater. *Detroit Gazette*, August 13, 1819. Fur prices held firm in 1821, a very acceptable condition for the hard times, but the *Gazette* (July 1, 1821) could not but wish that some of the dollars could go into permanent improvements, rather than in payment of debts for imports. In 1830, fur peltry and hide exports were listed as $335,000 of a total of $400,000. Detroit *North-Western Journal*, January 13, 1830. Most of the records of the New York office of the American Fur Company were destroyed in the fire of 1835.

[35] For the fur trade after 1834, see Chapter XII.

only for the immigrants who came into the Northwest, but for their commerce as well. "The means of internal navigation without the expense of cutting canals, are truly extraordinary; add to which, the facilities of export afforded by those fathers of waters, the Ohio, Mississippi, and Missouri, present a picture of future greatness dazzling to conceive—impossible to estimate," said Fearon.[36] "The rude and uncultivated state of the western country—the extensive field opened for industry and enterprise; and the opportunity afforded by the number and extent of our navigable streams for increasing in commerce, and in wealth, furnish at all times a most pleasing reflection,"[37] wrote one who looked daily at the Ohio. And Henry Clay said that in all his travels he had never seen a "section for which God had done so much and man so little."[38]

The canoe, which served the fur trade so well, even long after the coming of the steamboat, proved inadequate for the needs of a people moving west and had begun to go out of general use even before the Revolution. Pirogues and batteaux were on the decline thereafter.[39] Galley batteaux were built at Pittsburgh by the Philadelphia trading firm of Baynton, Wharton, and Morgan in 1765, and along the Monongahela during the Revolution. While the pack-horse freight service developed to connect the East with the forks of the Ohio from 1760 to 1790, western boat builders were developing the peculiar craft which bore the burden of traffic until replaced by the steamboat and railroad. These boats did not originate on western waters, but it was there that they made their fame. Pole boats, flatboats, and arks had been used in colonial days as early as 1685, and probably originated on the Connecticut and Delaware rivers.[40]

A description of these boats must of necessity be general and composite, for in common with the fish of the streams and lakes, they were not only numerous in variety but were given names

[36] Fearon, *Sketches of America*, 255. A strong and optimistic statement from this cautious traveler who was usually skeptical and "anti."

[37] *Portsmouth* (Ohio) *Gazette*, March 10, 1819.

[38] Charles H. Ambler, *A History of Transportation in the Ohio Valley* (Glendale, Calif., 1932), 22.

[39] *Ibid.*, 29; Archer B. Hulbert, *Waterways of Westward Expansion* (*Historic Highways*, IX, Cleveland, 1903), 103.

[40] Seymour, Dunbar, *A History of Travel in America* ... (4 volumes. Indianapolis, 1915), I, 39, 277.

which varied with the locale and person using them.[41] Certain general types stand out, however.

The pirogue or dugout was of simple construction, often ran to forty or fifty feet in length, and could carry several tons' burden. It was propelled by oars or poles. Sometimes a big poplar pirogue would be split lengthwise, the halves ribbed together and planked over, and a keelboat be the result.[42] Skiffs were made of planks; the batteaux were essentially big skiffs, able to accommodate a family. They were propelled downstream by oars or sweeps, and poled upstream.

The keelboat, developed from the batteaux, took its name from the longitudinal timber which gave it rigidity and bore the brunt of collisions. The hull of stout planks over ribs was from 5 to 10 feet wide, up to 80 feet in length, and housed over except for the narrow deck which ran all the way around. A mast and sail were part of the usual equipment. Going downstream, if the wind was not favorable, sweeps were used to assist the propulsion of the current, but it was in upstream navigation that the light-draft keelboat played its most important part. In normal currents and over firm bottom upstream propulsion was effected by poling. The technique of poling varied, but in all cases it was backbreaking labor. In the smaller boats in medium current the crew of eight polemen lined up at the prow, four on either side, facing downstream. At the command of the steersman, the long iron-shod ash poles were "set" sloping upstream, the upper end was placed against the shoulder socket, feet gripped the cleated deck or extension runways, and with bodies stooped or braced at an acute angle, the crew walked the boat upstream under their feet. This method worked when enough momentum could be gained so that at the command of "shift" or "lift" the men could run back to the front without the boat backsliding.

In strong water, or with the larger boats, poles were set by two's or four's, and a continuous chain or treadmill system applied. The main drawback to this method was that unless extra-

[41] "You can scarcely imagine an abstract form in which a boat can be built, that in some part of the Ohio or Mississippi you will not see, actually in motion." Timothy Flint, *Recollections of the Last Ten Years* . . . (Boston, 1826), 16.
[42] Samuel T. Covington, "Pioneer Transportation on the Ohio River," reprinted in *Indiana Magazine of History*, IV (1908), 129–33, from the *Rising Sun Local*, April 27, 1877; Otto M. Knoblock, *Early Navigation on the St. Joseph River* (*Indiana Historical Society Publications*, VIII, No. 4, Indianapolis, 1925), 187.

wide runways were provided, the men had to lift their poles clear of the water, jump to the roof of the cargo box, and carry them awkwardly to the bow again. Boatmen were proud of their prowess, and anyone lost caste among his fellows who could not hold up his end, or who let the boat turn cross-channel in the fast water. Head polemen were selected from among those whose records were clear. But after all, the main idea was to get upstream, and if better progress could be made, the tow rope or cordelle was used. Shore line and water permitting, the men might pull the boat, otherwise the rope would be fastened to a tree or anchor and the boat pulled up to it by hand-over-hand operation, then a new anchor found and the process repeated. This was known as cordelling. Cordelles were often a thousand feet long and fastened to the top of the mast so as to clear intervening brush. Pulling the boat along by overhanging shore branches or "bushwhacking" was sometimes possible. A boat and cargo of 10 to 40 tons, and crew of 8 to 20 men did well to average 6 miles per day upstream.

Keelboats bore the burden of upstream freight traffic, and as packets, took care of most of the passenger traffic on the Ohio until displaced by the steamboat. Their light draft made keelboats practicable on water never accessible to the steamboat, and like the pack train on land, they served to connect the settlements with the main thoroughfares and the outside until the Civil War period and later.[43]

Among the cumbersome rectangular craft of light draft used for downstream transportation there is considerable confusion of terminology.[44] There were flatboats, Kentucky boats, Orleans

[43] Types of keelboats, poling methods, etc., are described in Knoblock, *Early Navigation on the St. Joseph*. Bruno Vinette, "Early Lumbering on the Chippewa," in *Wisconsin Magazine of History*, IX (1925–26), 442–47, describes the use of keelboats in connection with lumber rafting in the 1850's. Keelboats are well covered in Leland Dewitt Baldwin, *The Keelboat Age on Western Waters* (Pittsburgh, 1941).

[44] Compare Dunbar, Hulbert, and Ambler, for instance, for differences among the three and contradictions within. It is useless to try to classify these boats rigidly, as a brief glance at the contemporary travels or newspapers would indicate. James Flint, *Letters from America*, 73, 86, 131, speaks of "Arks or family boats" 9 or 10 feet wide and of varying lengths, roofed over; of a "family boat sailing" (rowing) up river; and of a "flat ark." Fortescue Cuming in his *Sketches of a Tour to the Western Country* . . . (Pittsburgh, 1810), 79, 98, mentions a "covered flat," and a "large square flat, roofed. . . ." Estwick Evans, *Pedestrious Tour*, in Thwaites (ed.), *Early Western Travels*, VIII, 257, wrote, "The flat boat or ark is of a clumsy construction." John Woods, *Two Years' Residence on the English Prairie*, 75, 129, saw an ark covered with boards and later met "three large flat

boats, arks, broadhorns, Kentucky broadhorns, barges, rafts, and so on. Generally speaking, a flatboat was any boat which was flat, and in common parlance in the West the term was more often used in connection with the scowlike craft, undecked and not cabined over, which took the produce of the West down river.

In a narrower sense, the flatboat was a heavy framed rectangular craft 8 or 10 feet wide and 30 or 40 feet long, whose hull rose 3 or 4 feet above water, and above which, usually covering the whole, was built a heavy, flat-topped cabin or houselike structure 4 or 5 feet high. Doors were at the ends, or in the roof; windows or loopholes were in the sides. A stern sweep, side sweeps or poles, often a short bow oar known as the "gouger," kept the boat in the current; it was ill adapted to upstream navigation.[45] "Kentucky boats" or "New Orleans boats" were flatboats, named for their destinations, the former probably smaller, not so well built, and perhaps only partially cabined or roofed over. The term broadhorn was apparently applied to either flatboat or ark, if it had the big sweeps, sometimes of curved design, projecting from the sides like horns.[46] The housed-in flatboat was the product of the Ohio[47] and the chief reliance of westward movers as long as protection was needed from the Indians.

When this protection was no longer necessary, the ark, earlier used on the Delaware and the Susquehanna, came into more general use. It was a shallow hull of vertical sides and slightly V-shaped or square ends, was not ordinarily decked or housed, but might have one or more shacks or shelter cabins on it. Lengths might run to more than one hundred feet. The ark was built for its one trip downstream and no doubt got its name from its ample

boats loaded with flour, bacon, whiskey, tobacco, horses, and pine and cherry planks," apparently open boats. John Bradbury in his *Travels in the Interior of America in the Years 1809, 1810, and 1811 . . .* (2d ed. London, 1819), reprinted in Thwaites (ed.), *Early Western Travels*, V, 203, 301, "passed no fewer than thirteen arks or Kentucky boats," which were square ended and covered. A. D. Jones, *Illinois and the West*, 35, spoke of "immense rafts of timber and flat boats, peopled with immigrants."

[45] Hulbert, *Waterways of Westward Expansion*, 113. "It was the boat that never came back, a downstream craft solely," p. 119. Yet on pages 113–18 is quoted Audubon's description of an upstream trip in a barge, which the author calls an *Orleans* boat, but on the next page (119) both *Kentucky* and *New Orleans* boats are flatboats. "Vessels of the flatboat type rarely proceeded upstream." Dunbar, *History of Travel*, I, 286.

[46] William H. Venable, in *Footprints of the Pioneers in the Ohio Valley* (Cincinnati, 1888), speaks of "Kentucky boats" or "broadhorns," 15 by 50 or 80 feet and covered with an arched roof.

[47] Dunbar, *History of Travel*, I, 284.

capacity and variety of cargo. The flatboat has been described as "a mixture of log cabin, fort, floating barnyard and country grocery."[48] Eliminate the fort, enlarge the barnyard and put it out in the open, add cabins, implements, kegs, boxes, wagons, more men, women, children, horses, pigs, fowls, dogs, dishes, furniture—the noise and confusion of domestic processes from milking to washing clothes for several families—and we have the ark. "Perhaps no other craft that ever moved on land or sea provided such episodes and contrasts, such diverse pictures of tragedy and revel, as did the flatboats in which the vast host of floating pilgrims travelled the interior rivers of America from about 1788 until as late a date as 1840,"[49] unless it was the ark. Boats of this type were broken up at the end of the trip and the lumber used for various purposes. Some were knocked apart at the mouth of the Ohio where their cargoes (and timbers even) were loaded on steamboats and shipped up to St. Louis.

For heavy freight service, especially during the earlier period before superseded largely by the keelboat, were the barges. Early barges were "huge boxes, covered and uncovered, square at each end, and flat bottomed."[50] From the batteau they took better shape and became "great, pointed, covered hulks carrying forty or fifty tons of freight and manned by almost as many men."[51] They have been described as resembling the keelboat, schooner, and ship's long boat,[52] and carried a mast, sails, and rudder. Covering or protection was provided by a center house or an allover roof. Oars aided the current in downstream navigation, and sails, poles, and rope were used against the current.

From the barge and keelboat developed the Ohio River packet boat, for fast freight and passenger service. Fifteen or more feet wide, up to one hundred in length, and equipped with mast, sails, poles, and rudder, some of these boats offered the best in river travel prior to the steamboat. As early as 1794 a Cincinnati-Pittsburgh line was advertising separate cabins for men and women and "conveniences . . . on board each boat, so as to

[48] Dunbar, *History of Travel*, I, 272.
[49] *Ibid.* Perhaps Dunbar is now speaking of the ark, for this description does not fit his definition of a flatboat.
[50] Hulbert, *Waterways of Westward Expansion*, 106.
[51] *Ibid.*, 113.
[52] Dunbar, *History of Travel*, I, 286; Ambler, *Transportation in the Ohio Valley*, 43; Venable, *Footprints of the Pioneers*, 92–93.

render landing unnecessary."[53] But by the middle 1820's the discriminating traveler thought there was not much pleasure to be derived from a passage on board a keelboat.

> It forms a species of wooden prison, containing commonly four rooms; the first for the steward, the second a dining room, the third a cabin for gentlemen, and the fourth a ladies' cabin. Each of these cabins was provided with an iron stove . . . on the sides were our births, in double rows, six feet in length and two broad. In former times this manner of travelling was generally resorted to on the Ohio and Mississippi; the application of steam, however, has superseded these primitive conveyances, and I hope to the regret of no one.[54]

By 1815 those interested in the development and prosperity of the West were well aware of the relation between transportation routes and the balance of trade. The importance of the Ohio as an emigrant route was recognized. Many had come and brought in money, but "emigration must continue equal benefits, or *new* channels and modes of transportation must be resorted to, to pay for all the British merchandise which will be imported this fall." People should ask themselves whether they had done everything possible to encourage exportation. There were too many importing houses. Seasonal downstream traffic glutted New Orleans' markets and prices fell. "We must learn to ascend our natural current as well."[55] A partial solution to this problem was seen with the coming of the steamboat to western waters.

Robert Fulton and his associates[56] sent Nicholas J. Roosevelt west in 1809 to survey the Ohio and Mississippi and look over political conditions. Roosevelt reported favorably on both rivers and the chances for privileges; in December, 1810, the Ohio Steam Boat Navigation Company was incorporated by the Indiana territorial legislature. Through political connections the Livingston associates got from the legislature of Louisiana Territory a grant of exclusive rights to steam navigation in the Territory for fourteen years.[57] Meanwhile they had built at

---

[53] *Centinel of the North-Western Territory*, January 11, 1794.

[54] [Karl Postel], *The Americans as They Are* . . . (London, 1828), 53–54.

[55] Cincinnati *Liberty Hall*, August 21, 1815; *Zanesville Express*, August 31, 1815.

[56] Robert Livingston, De Witt Clinton, Robert R. Livingston, and Daniel D. Tompkins, etc.

[57] April, 1811. The company's plans for an eastern monopoly, granted a second time in 1803 for twenty years, were not working out so well.

Pittsburgh the *New Orleans*.[58] Late in October, 1811, this boat steamed down to Cincinnati, to Louisville, back to Cincinnati, then, when the waters rose, with Roosevelt, his young wife, new baby, and a Newfoundland dog for passengers, it ran the Falls at Louisville, got by the snags and the new dangers created by the great earthquake, and reached New Orleans. For two years the boat was used in the New Orleans-Natchez traffic.

The following year the small stern-wheel *Comet* was built by Samuel Smith under the Daniel French patent; in 1814 the Fulton company built the 340-ton *Vesuvius*. Both boats were the deep-draft, seagoing type, with engines in the hold; once down the river they could not repass the Falls. The 75-ton *Enterprise* was the next boat of the independents; under Capt. Henry M. Shreve it reached New Orleans in time to be of service to General Jackson against the British. In May, 1815, taking advantage of high waters and cutoffs, Shreve made the trip back to Louisville in twenty-five days.[59] During the summer the *Enterprise* arrived at Cincinnati from Pittsburgh in four days, then went from Cincinnati to Louisville, reloaded, and got back to Cincinnati in six more days.[60] "The celerity and safety with which this boat descends and ascends the current of these waters—must be equally interesting to the farmer and the merchant."[61] Such performances were astonishing to those accustomed to the slow progress of keels and barges—three or four months up from New Orleans. "The navigation of the Mississippi is from new circumstances every day becoming more important," noted the businessman.[62] Soon the steamboat of 200 tons would be seen towing a

---

[58] There is dispute as to whether this boat was a side- or stern-wheeler. Woodcuts in early directories portray it differently. (See Ambler, *History of Transportation in the Ohio Valley*, plate 117.) Dunbar calls it a stern-wheeler. It was probably a side-wheeler, with the 1808 improvement permitting independent motion of the two paddle wheels, for the first three Fulton boats had vertical engines, impossible with stern wheels. George B. Merrick and William R. Tibbals, "Genesis of Steam Navigation on Western Rivers," in *Wisconsin State Historical Society Proceedings, 1911*, p. 102; Archer B. Hulbert, *The Ohio River* (New York, 1906), 332. The *New Orleans* was 138 feet in length, 26½ beam, deep draft, and cost about $40,000.

[59] *Niles' Weekly Register*, VIII, 320 (July 1, 1815); Portsmouth (Ohio) *Western Times*, January 14, 1830.

[60] *Zanesville Express*, August 17, 1815.

[61] *Pittsburgh Gazette*, June 15, 1815, cited in Ambler, *History of Transportation in the Ohio Valley*, 126.

[62] William C. Anderson to Thomas Sloo, Jr., November 27, 1815, in *Quarterly Publication of the Historical and Philosophical Society of Ohio*, VI, No. 2 (April—June, 1911), 17.

barge of equal size upstream and the West could cease its ever-lasting tribute to Pennsylvania and the East.[63] Not only were the commercial possibilities recognized, but those for pleasure as well.

After trying out a smaller boat, Captain Shreve and his associates in 1816 built the pretentious *G. Washington*, which inaugurated several improvements on the Fulton and French patents. By substituting fixed horizontal cylinders for oscillating vertical, it was possible to put the machinery on deck instead of in the hold, and thus make a boat which would run on the water instead of in it. Flues in the boilers saved fuel, double high-pressure engines gave increased power, and two-wheel cranks at right angles gave a steadier application of power.[64] Double decks and passengers' rooms named after the states were added features. When the *Washington* reached New Orleans she was seized by the Fulton-Livingston company.[65] Already their case against the *Enterprise* had been appealed to the United States Supreme Court. The company offered Shreve an equal share in patent rights if he would arrange to lose his case and admit its claims, but he refused, spent a fortune, and ultimately was vindicated by the Supreme Court.[66]

This controversy between monopoly rights and free navigation caused considerable discussion in the West, a section never favorable towards special privileges. Newspapers flared up and

[63] Cincinnati *Liberty Hall*, September 11, 1815.

[64] James T. Lloyd, *Steamboat Directory and Disasters on Western Waters* (Cincinnati, 1856), 44.

[65] But the suit was withdrawn when the court put the company under bail for damages in case they lost the suit.

[66] Suits against the owners of the *Washington* and two other boats came up in the United States District Court at New Orleans in April, 1817, but the Court decided it had no jurisdiction. Another case pended for some time, but the Louisiana statute apparently remained a dead letter and independent boat operations increased. In 1824 in *Gibbons* v. *Ogden* the Supreme Court ruled against the monopoly and opened the navigable waters of the nation to all. John Fitch, who operated the first steamboat in American waters, in his petition to the Congress of the Confederation in 1787 had said, "I do not desire at this time to receive emoluments for my own private use, but to lay it out for the benefit of my country. . . ." Fitch, who had some bad luck in family affairs as well as in steamboat promotion, left a record to the Philadelphia Library, to be opened thirty years later. "I know of nothing so perplexing and vexatious to a man of feelings as a turbulent Wife and steamboat building. I experienced the former and quit in season and had I been in my right senses I should undoubtedly have treated the latter in the same manner." Fitch died destitute and heartbroken in Kentucky, with the request that he be buried on the banks of the Ohio, "where the song of the boatman would enliven the stillness of his resting place, and the music of the steam engine soothe his spirit." Emerson W. Gould, *Fifty Years on the Mississippi* (St. Louis, 1889), 18.

called for action. They pointed out to Congress and state legislatures the effects of the patent-rights tie-up on navigation and the West. Freight rates from Philadelphia to Pittsburgh had again advanced to $8.50 per hundred and might go to $15 in spring and fall when merchants needed goods. It was high time for the western country to arouse from its lethargy. In February, 1816, the Ohio legislature requested their congressmen to use their influence to settle the squabble.[67] Kentucky did likewise and stated her intention to maintain inviolate the right of her citizens to navigate the Mississippi. In 1822 Ohio retaliated against the New York law which gave exclusive rights by forbidding any person to land any passenger on the shore of Lake Erie from any steamboat which received passengers from any steamboat whose owners operated under the New York law.[68] It would have been difficult to enforce court decisions upholding the monopoly, for the West had never quite got over the idea that if necessary they could always take New Orleans by force.

In March, 1817, Captain Shreve started the *Washington* on her second round trip from Louisville to New Orleans, which was made in forty-one days. The upstream trip in twenty-five days under normal river conditions, served to dissipate the doubts concerning the possibility of upstream navigation. Westerners were thrilled with this achievement. Shreve was feted at Louisville and in the excitement predicted that in time boats would come from New Orleans to Louisville in ten days. The audience was not entirely convinced, but enthusiastic nevertheless. The same season a boat with cargo made the 1,500-mile down trip in seven working days (not counting two days on a bar).[69] In 1818 the *Vesuvius* made the down trip more than once in seven days, and the *James Ross* came up in fourteen days.[70] In 1829 the *Huntress* and the *Tecumseh* made the up trip in a little over eight days,[71] and the

---

[67] The Ohio legislature had been petitioned to pass a law to defend any citizens, and pay any damages, against use of steamboat patent rights. Feeling became very bitter against "any quack" who sought to monopolize what it regarded as "a public necessity to the people of a large section of the country." William F. Gephart, *Transportation and Industrial Development in the Middle West* (*Columbia University Studies in History, Economics and Public Law*, XXXIV, No. 1, New York, 1909), 80.

[68] *Detroit Gazette*, March 8, 1822.

[69] *Niles' Weekly Register*, XII, 143 (Apr. 26, 1817).

[70] *Ibid.*, XV, 267 (Dec. 12, 1818); XVI, 319 (July 3, 1819).

[71] *Ohio State Journal*, May 25, 1827; Portsmouth (Ohio) *Western Times*, January 14, 1830.

Wm. Tell came from Pittsburgh to Cincinnati at the rate of
thirteen miles per hour.[72] Such was "the wonderful evidence of
the power of steam." "What a progress is this against the currents of the rivers of the West—what a field does it present to
the speculative mind, disposed to anticipate the future condition
of things."[73]

Meanwhile, the steamboat had made its appearance on the
Great Lakes and begun a traffic on the world's greatest inland
waterway system, a traffic destined ultimately far to surpass that
of the western rivers. The *Walk-in-the-Water* was built at Black
Rock near Buffalo, under Livingston-Fulton rights, and made her
first trip to Detroit in late August, 1818, in about four days.[74]
This boat of 330 tons and passenger capacity of 200 or more, was
equipped with two masts, schooner rigged, two 16-foot paddle
wheels, low pressure engine, and could average around 8 miles
per hour. "The Elegant Steamboat" was the headline greeting in
the *Cleaveland Gazette*.[75]

The Detroit Lyceum had appointed a committee to meet and
examine this interesting visitor whose arrival had been well
heralded. The Indians along the Detroit River were also interested. "Nothing could exceed the surprise of the sons of the
forest, on seeing the *Walk-in-the-Water* moving majestically and
rapidly against a strong current, without the assistance of sails or
oars—they lined the banks above Malden and expressed their
astonishment by repeated shouts of Ta-i-yah-niche (Surprise)."[76]
The report was that a big canoe would come drawn by a sturgeon.
Some did not believe this, but seeing what they could not understand, grunted and turned away in disgust. Shortly the *Walk-*

---

[72] Indianapolis *Indiana Journal*, April 24, 1827.

[73] *Niles' Weekly Register*, XVI, 319 (July 3, 1819).

[74] The *Ontario*, built at Sackets Harbor, New York, and the Canadian *Frontenac*,
built near Kingston, had been used on Lake Ontario early in 1817. Letters of Daniel
Dod and John Dod Ward of September, 1816, and April, 1817, quoted in Argosy
Book Stores *Catalogue No. 177*, items 277, 278, seem to settle beyond doubt the
priority of the *Ontario* over the *Walk-in-the-Water*. See also H. A. Musham,
"Early Great-Lakes Steamboats—The *Ontario* and the *Frontenac*," and "*The Walk-
in-the-Water*," in *American Neptune*, III (1943), 333–44; V (1945), 27–42. The
Frontenac was 170 feet long, had a beam of 32 feet, and displaced 700 tons; she
also had three masts. The *Ontario* was much smaller: 120 feet in length, with a
24-foot beam, and about one third the tonnage of its rival. For early trips and
additional references, see Arthur Pound, *Lake Ontario* (*The American Lake Series*,
Indianapolis, 1945), 318–20.

[75] September 1, 1818.

[76] *Detroit Gazette*, August 28, 1818.

in-the-Water was running on regular nine-day schedules between Buffalo and Detroit.[77] In 1820 the 200 miles from Buffalo to Cleveland were made in 29 hours, and the Buffalo to Detroit run in 62 hours, an average of 5 miles per hour.[78] The boat was wrecked in a gale in 1821. The next year, equipped with the salvaged engine of the *Walk-in-the-Water*, the *Superior* of 400 tons was launched at Buffalo; smaller boats followed.[79] The *Walk-in-the-Water* was also the first steamboat to enter Lake Michigan; in 1821 it carried 200 passengers from Detroit to Green Bay and made the round trip in 13 days. The first to reach Chicago were the vessels which bore General Scott's army westward to suppress the Black Hawk uprising in 1832.[80]

Apropos the possibilities opened by the coming of the steamboat to the Great Lakes, the *Detroit Gazette* said: "The most gigantic speculations upon the subject of the western part of the United States soon become sober and serious truths, and calculations apparently the most visionary are rendered erroneous only because they are exceeded by the reality."[81] At a Fourth of July celebration at Detroit in 1830 Henry Whiting, army officer and poet, said:

> And where was e'er the modern wight,
> Who, though possess'd of second sight,
> Twice eight years since, could see a boat
> Within the shadowy future float?
> Or see one lying at Black Rock,
> (For Buffalo then had no dock,)
> Compell'd to lay the straits below,
> Till "horn-breeze" or a storm should blow.—[82]

The first steamboat—a keelboat with an engine—to reach St. Louis was the *Zebulon M. Pike* in 1817.[83] It was greeted with cheers and the firing of cannon. Two years later the *Independence*

---

[77] *Cleaveland Register*, August 24, 1819.
[78] *Cleaveland Herald*, May 9, 1820; Schoolcraft, *Narrative Journal*, 47.
[79] For list of early Lake boats, captains, etc., see Francis A. Dewey, "A Sketch of the Marine of Lake Erie Previous to the Year 1829," in *Michigan Pioneer and Historical Collections*, IV (1881), 79–81.
[80] Milo M. Quaife, *Chicago's Highways* (Chicago, 1923), 36, and *Lake Michigan* (*The American Lakes Series*, Indianapolis, 1944), 138, 144.
[81] November 20, 1818.
[82] *The Age of Steam* (Detroit, 1830). "Horn-breeze" referred to oxen, sometimes used to help against the wind.
[83] *St. Louis Republican*, article on Western Steamboat Navigation cited in Springfield *Sangamo Journal*, February 2, 1832.

went some distance up the Missouri, and in 1822 regular traffic was begun between St. Louis and the Fever River in Illinois.[84] The next spring the *Virginia,* "The Clermont of the Upper Mississippi," reached Fort Snelling.[85] Also in 1823 the *Florence* navigated the Wabash as far as Terre Haute;[86] in 1826 the *American* went to Lafayette.[87] The next year the *Lawrence* with 125 tons of cargo reached Covington,[88] and in 1828 the 52-ton *Triton* from Louisville got up the West Fork of White River almost as far as Spencer on its way to Indianapolis.[89] In 1828 steamboats went up the Illinois to Naples, the next year to Pekin, and in 1830 to Peoria. In 1831 there were 186 arrivals at Naples and 17 at Peoria.[90] In 1829 the *Winnebago Chief,* launched at Green Bay with a Cleveland-built engine, began to ply the Fox River between Green Bay and the Wisconsin portage.[91] In 1832 when, after much publicity, the 150-ton *Talisman* ascended the Sangamon River as far as Springfield, the people felt that that young settlement was no longer an inland town.[92]

The introductory period was over. Building of steamboats had developed rapidly. Statistics vary, of course, but a general idea can be had from the widely cited contemporary estimates. The Chillicothe *Supporter* in 1819 listed by name 35 western boats varying in tonnage from 40 to 443, and 29 building.[93] A year later the *Louisville Public Advertiser* listed by name 72 boats as belonging to the "Western Navigation Traffic."[94] By 1823 the list had grown to 79[95] and the next year to 130, of which 22 had

[84] Gould, *Fifty Years on the Mississippi,* 114, 116.

[85] *Minnesota Historical Collections,* II (reprint, 1889), 107; VIII (1898), 376 ff.; George B. Merrick, *Old Times on the Upper Mississippi* (Cleveland, 1909), 187; *Minnesota History,* IX (1928), 347; *Wisconsin Historical Collections,* II (1856), 152.

[86] Vincennes *Western Sun and General Advertiser,* May 10, 1823.

[87] *Ibid.,* April 22, 1826.

[88] *Indianapolis Gazette,* April 3, 1827.

[89] Indianapolis *Indiana Journal,* May 15; Lawrenceburg *Indiana Palladium,* May 24, 1828.

[90] Pease, *The Frontier State,* 191.

[91] *Detroit Gazette,* June 11, 1829; *Cleaveland Herald,* June 18, 1829. Considering the rapids of the Fox this statement sounds questionable. For importance and advantages of Fox-Wisconsin navigation, see *Green-Bay Intelligencer,* October 24, 1835.

[92] *Sangamo Journal,* January 26, February 16, March 29, 1832.

[93] April 7, 1819. *Niles' Weekly Register,* XVI, 144 (Apr. 17, 1819), listed 40 built since 1812, 7 wrecked, burned or abandoned, 33 plying, and 28 building.

[94] Copied in *Edwardsville Spectator,* November 7, 1820.

[95] *Hamilton* (Ohio) *Intelligencer and Advertiser,* November 24, 1823. The Vandalia *Illinois Intelligencer,* November 8, 1823, quoting the *National Gazette,* listed 77.

sunk and 4 burned.[96] One hundred twenty-five boats totaling 23,834 tons had been licensed by the collector of the port of New Orleans for the Mississippi trade, of which 60 of 10,800 tons were active;[97] in 1826 tonnage on western waters was listed at 20,500.[98] At Louisville 51 different boats were listed (9,338 tons) which made 182 arrivals during the year.[99] The list of one-inch steamboat advertisements in 1832, with a small cut at the head of each, occupied one whole column in the *Cincinnati Daily Gazette.* It was estimated that $14,000,000 had been spent on 323 boats of 56,000 tons on western waters through the year 1829.[100] The *Portsmouth Times* listed 911 arrivals in 1829.[101] The 1834 official list of boats in operation was 230 of 39,000 tons;[102] in 1842 it was 450 of 126,278 tons. Concerning such lists a Wisconsin editor said: "The exact number of steamboats on Western waters,—the exact number of fiddlesticks!" No one knew. By the time they could be counted a half dozen new ones would have been built and an equal number sunk or destroyed.[103] By 1834 the tonnage of the Ohio and Mississippi steamboats exceeded that of the Atlantic seaboard or of the British Empire.[104]

Increase in steam tonnage on the Great Lakes was not so rapid—from approximately 330 tons (the *Walk-in-the-Water*) above Niagara Falls in 1820 to about 15,000 tons in 1838.[105] In 1827 the *Henry Clay* made the round trip between Buffalo and Detroit in 3 days and 19 hours,[106] and daily service was begun in 1830.[107] Six years later the *General Porter* made the trip from Buffalo to Detroit in 30 hours, or about 25 hours running

---

[96] *Liberty Hall and Cincinnati Gazette,* April 30, 1824.
[97] *Hamilton Advertiser,* March 18, 1825.
[98] Cincinnati *Saturday Evening Chronicle,* cited in *ibid.,* March 9, 1827.
[99] *Louisville Advertiser* in *Indiana Journal,* April 24, 1827.
[100] *Western Monthly Magazine,* II (1834), 316.
[101] In *Cleaveland Herald,* January 29, 1830.
[102] *Western Monthly Magazine,* II (1834), 316.
[103] Burlington *Wisconsin Territorial Gazette,* March 17, 1838.
[104] Hulbert, *The Ohio River,* 337. Of course it must be remembered that ocean steam navigation got off to a later start.
[105] William L. Bancroft, "Early Commerce of the Upper Lakes," in *Michigan Pioneer and Historical Collections,* XXI (1892), 354–55; *Cleveland Herald and Gazette* (weekly), August 7, 1839. Buffalo customs house figures for 1827 listed 53 American vessels in the upper lake traffic, with tonnage of 3,611, not counting the two steamboats *Pioneer* and *Chippewa.* This apparently was nonsteam tonnage. *Buffalo Journal* cited in *Cleaveland Herald,* December 21, 1827.
[106] *Liberty Hall and Cincinnati Gazette,* June 25, 1827.
[107] *Cleaveland Herald,* March 25, 1830.

time.[108] Six steamboats were advertised for the navigation of
Lake Erie in 1826[109] and only 2 or 3 were added in the next few
years.[110] In 1833 Great Lakes steamboat owners formed their
first association: 11 boats, which represented an investment of
$360,000, carried 61,485 passengers—42,956 of them west out
of Buffalo. Three trips were made to the upper lakes, two to
Chicago, and one to Green Bay. The next year there were 18
boats in the association. It was dissolved in 1836 and accurate
statistics for numbers and business were no longer kept.[111] By
1837 there were between 40 and 50 steamboats engaged in the
lake trade.[112]

Steamboats ceased to be a novelty at Green Bay in 1835, when
39 schooners and 9 steamboats entered the port.[113] Chicago in
1833 had 4 boat arrivals from the lower lakes—about 700 tons—
but two years later there were 250 arrivals or 22,500 tons. A
dozen boats might frequently be seen in the harbor at one time.
In 1836 there were 456 arrivals (57,500 tons) between April
and December, of which 49 were steamboats. Among the competing lines which advertised were the United States Line, the only
steam freight line, the Telegraphic, Washington-Eagle, New
York and Oswego, and Troy and Oswego lines.[114]

Total lake tonnage in 1838 as listed in the report of the United
States Treasury was 36,388, of which 15,426 was steam tonnage.
Another association was formed in 1839, when all steamers
except the *Illinois* and the *North America* agreed to eliminate
fare and rate cutting.[115] By this time a regular line of 8 boats of

[108] *Detroit Daily Advertiser*, August 16, 1836.
[109] Columbus *Ohio State Journal*, April 27, 1826.
[110] Dewey, "A Sketch of the Marine of Lake Erie," in *Michigan Pioneer and Historical Collections*, IV, 80; *Cleaveland Herald*, December 21, 1827. There were about one hundred vessels of all types navigating the lakes in 1831, with tonnage of about 7,000. *Detroit Journal and Michigan Advertiser*, November 9, 1831.
[111] James L. Barton (secretary of the association), "Commerce of the Great Lakes," in *Merchants' Magazine and Commercial Review* (Freeman Hunt, editor, New York, 1839–1870), XV (1846), 349.
[112] *Daily Cleveland Herald*, December 6, 1836, stated there were 50, but the complete list in the weekly *Cleveland Herald and Gazette* of May 27, 1837, gave 42 plus 10 building. Also *Detroit Daily Advertiser*, May 2, 1838. United States Treasury statistics on annual tonnage built on the Great Lakes may be found in *Report on Steam Navigation in the United States*, by T. C. Purdy, 6, 11, in *Report of Tenth Census* (1880), Volume IV. The *Buffalo Commercial Advertiser* cited in *Milwaukee Advertiser*, June 10, 1837, listed 42 active steamboats on Lake Erie and 6 building.
[113] *Green-Bay Intelligencer*, December 9, 1835.
[114] *Chicago American*, 1835–36, *passim*.
[115] *Detroit Daily Advertiser*, May 25, 1834.

from 350 to 650 tons each was formed to run from Buffalo to Chicago. Sixteen days were required for the round trip. In 1840 there were 225 sailing vessels and 61 steamboats on the Great Lakes—total value of which was more than two million. Earnings alone in 1841 were listed at a million and a half.[116] An idea of rates from Buffalo to Chicago in the 1830's may be had from the following: "Cabin passage, found" $20; steerage passage $10; light freight 75 cents per 100 pounds, heavy freight 50 cents per 100 pounds, excepting near the close of the season when the freight rates were higher. Rates had fallen about one third since steam service commenced west from Detroit. Although the amount of money invested in sail was only slightly more than half as much as in steamboats, total earnings were more than twice as much.

One of the important and picturesque operators on the Lakes was Oliver Newberry, who came from Buffalo to Detroit in the early 1820's. From the retail business he branched out into many activities. To facilitate his own transportation he built a small sloop in 1825. Within a few years he owned a fleet of schooners and brigs distinguished particularly for their Napoleonic names. With his own shipyard as well as fleet Newberry rightly deserved the title "Admiral of the Lakes."

Improvements in engineering and construction of steamboats kept pace with the increase in numbers. The wide shallow-draft hull first emphasized by Shreve and the adoption of independent engines for each side wheel aided measurably in river navigation. As the low-pressure single engines gave way to high-pressure double engines, which often cost from $10,000 to $20,000,[117] the open cabins and pilot houses were superseded by staterooms, saloons, and promenade decks. Pilot houses were glassed and engine odors closed off. The first cabin steamer on the Lakes was the *Michigan*, built by Oliver Newberry, in 1833. This boat, with a deck 156 feet long, 3 masts, 2 smokestacks, and 2 low-pressure engines, provided 48 berths for gentlemen and 60 for ladies. The *James Madison*, put on the Lakes in 1837, was 181

---

[116] *Hunt's Merchants' Magazine*, II (1840), 525; *Chicago Democrat*, March 14, 1843.

[117] Harkness and Vorhees of Cincinnati gave the cost of seven engines in 1835 as $11,000 to $13,000 each. *Cincinnati Daily Gazette*, December 11, 1835. The engine of the *Madison* (1837) cost $20,000. *Buffalo Commercial Advertiser* in *Cleveland Herald and Gazette* (weekly), May 27, 1837.

feet in length, had a 30-foot beam, and was of 700 tons burden. There were 30 berths in the ladies' cabins with stairs leading to the dining cabins, which had 23 berths for gentlemen. Around the dining cabin were 15 staterooms with 2 berths each, and on the hurricane deck was the saloon with 12 berths. The high-pressure engines with 28-inch cylinders and 8-foot piston stroke developed 180 horsepower. The boat cost $75,000.[118]

Before the year was over, the new *Cleveland* was ready, with 120 cabin berths for gentlemen, 12 below for ladies, besides 10 staterooms with 3 berths each. Total length was 186 feet, beam 29 feet, and tonnage 575. Cylinder bore was 56 inches, piston stroke 10 feet; the paddle wheel was 24 feet in diameter and turned 24 times per minute. Cost was $85,000.[119] The *Illinois*, built by Newberry at Detroit in 1838, was 205 feet long, had tonnage of 775, and was second in size only to the *Natchez* on the Mississippi. More seaworthy than the *Michigan* with its separately operated paddle wheels, the *Illinois* could make the Buffalo-Chicago run in five days. Soon to surpass the *Illinois* in size, but not in elegance, was the *Great Western*, 781 tons, 34-foot beam, 186 feet long, with 27-foot wheel and 300 horsepower engine. The upper-deck cabin arrangement gave more space on the main deck for cargo. The first ship on the Lakes was the *Julia Palmer*, built at Buffalo in 1836; the first propeller steamer was put in operation in 1841.

In the 1830's artificial ornamentation and superficial elegance on steamboats touched the ridiculous, to give way to more practical and substantial development in the golden era of the steamboat which followed. The earlier boats had neither whistles nor bells, but by 1830 the whistle was probably second in importance only to the engine. The *Illinois*, however, used a cannon. Boats came to be known by their whistles. A really superb whistle, like a perfect bell, seemed to be impossible of exact duplication, and sometimes was passed on from boat to boat, a soul which refused to conform to the limitations of the body.

Relatively few people, of course, traveled on the luxury boats. Deck passage, whether on the river boats or lake boats, though more comfortable than most stagecoach travel, offered few con-

[118] *Cleveland Herald and Gazette* (weekly), May 27, 1837; *Milwaukee Advertiser*, January 28, 1837.
[119] *Cleveland Herald and Gazette* (weekly), October 13, 1837.

veniences and no luxuries. As late as 1838 a traveler on a lake steamer wrote that the scene presented in the deck cabin among the deck passengers was worthy the pencil of a Hogarth. The scene impressed him:

Shades of night & my great grandmother. Here lie stretched in wild disorder & promiscuous confusion upon the floor like the slain on the field of battle in all shapes & positions both sexes & all ages, the man of gray hairs & the tender infant, the rosy cheeked damsel & the sturdy wood chopper. Here is crying & scolding & snoring & groaning. Some in births & some on chairs & trunks & settees & the rest on the floor. Some sitting & some lying, some dressed & some undressed, some covered & some uncovered & naked; some are stretched on beds, others on matrasses & cushions & cloaks & not a few are trying to find the soft side of the hard floor. Such is a steamboat life on Lake Erie, a scene which I do not soon wish to experience again.[120]

The effects of the steamboat on transportation were not so sudden and revolutionary, as gradual and momentous. Early boats were slow, unreliable, and the captains frequently unaccommodating. Then, too, traffic was dependent upon the stage of the river. Several months of low water in summer and ice in winter left normally only spring and autumn months for navigation. Some seasons, such as 1819, when navigation was practically closed to steamboats from April to the following February, were bad for steamboats. Heavy freight of comparatively low value, such as coal, lumber, and crude iron, could not ordinarily bear the cost of steamboat shipment. Keelboats continued for years to supplement the steamboat in seasons of low water, and the flatboat and barge to carry the bulk of the heavy produce. In 1817 there were 20 or 30 barges, averaging 100 tons' burden, available on the Ohio–Mississippi.[121] Making one round trip per year, total tonnage would be 2,000 to 3,000 for upstream cargo. There were probably 150 keelboats averaging 30 tons each on the Upper Ohio. In 1834 upstream freight traffic was estimated at nearly 1,200,000 tons.[122] Most of this was handled by steamboats, but the total steamboat capacity, allowing five up trips per year, would not account for all of it. Pirogues and keelboats were still used extensively and were not supplanted even on the Ohio–

[120] "Charles Minton Baker's Journal from Vermont to Wisconsin" (1838), in *Wisconsin Magazine of History*, V (1921–22), 398.

[121] Morgan Neville in the *Western Monthly Magazine*, II (1834), 318, gives the figure as 20; Portsmouth (Ohio) *Western Times*, January 14, 1830, gives 29.

[122] *Western Monthly Magazine*, II (1834), 318.

Mississippi until the middle 1830's, by which time steamboats capable of "running on a heavy dew" were in use.[123]

So also with downstream traffic. New Orleans receipts in 1816 were under $10,000,000,[124] but in 1818–19, the year the success of the steamboat was assured, they rose to almost $17,000,000.[125] The steamboats did not carry all of this increase; they did, however, furnish an easy return for the flatboatmen, and thus made possible three or four trips a year by the flats and rafts instead of one.[126] In 1823 it was estimated that 69,000 tons valued at $3,590,000 went downstream past the Falls, and this did not include iron castings, salt, gunpowder, and white lead.[127] In 1832 some 4,000 flatboats descended the Mississippi with 160,000 tons. Passenger fares from Pittsburgh to New Orleans had been about $60 and freight rates $6.75 per hundred prior to the steamboat.[128] Freight per hundred from the Atlantic seaboard to Pittsburgh had been $5.00 to $8.00. By 1823 the average cabin passenger fare from Pittsburgh to New Orleans was near $35,[129] but ten years later it was possible to get deck passage (covered and with berths) which included meals, for $8.00.[130] Upstream fares had been about $100; on steamboats they were about one third higher than down-river fares. Downstream freight rates declined proportionately, but the greatest change was in upstream rates. Whereas it had formerly cost $7.00 to $10 per hundred to get goods from the coast to Cincinnati via Pittsburgh, goods from New Orleans could now be laid down at Cincinnati at $2.00 to $3.00, and sometimes as low as $1.00 per hundred

---

[123] Covington, "Pioneer Transportation on the Ohio River," in *Indiana Magazine of History*, IV, 129; "Journal of a Tourist," in *Western Monthly Magazine*, III (1835), 338.

[124] *History of Domestic and Foreign Commerce of the United States*, by E. R. Johnson, *et al.* (2 volumes. Carnegie Institution of Washington, 1915), I, 213.

[125] *Ibid.*

[126] Chevalier, "Letters on America," in *Western Monthly Magazine*, IV, 411–12.

[127] *National Gazette* in *Illinois Intelligencer*, November 8, 1823.

[128] *Liberty Hall and Cincinnati Gazette*, June 24, 1816.

[129] *Hamilton* (Ohio) *Intelligencer and Advertiser*, November 24, 1823. Ohio River passenger rates, 1823:

Cincinnati to New Orleans	1,480 miles,	8 days	$25
New Orleans to Cincinnati	" "	16 "	$50
Cincinnati to Louisville	130 "	15 hours	$ 4
Louisville to Cincinnati	" "	30 "	$ 6
Pittsburgh to Cincinnati	449 "	60 "	$12
Cincinnati to Pittsburgh	" "	5 days	$15

National Gazette in *Illinois Intelligencer*, November 8, 1823.

[130] *Wheeling Advocate*, cited in *Western Monthly Magazine*, III (1835), 398.

pounds.[131] Because of the more or less unrestrained competition as well as seasonal factors, rates were not constant. Low waters might increase the rates several fold.

Low waters and obstructions were not confronted by the lake boats, but storms were more of a problem than on the rivers. Sailing-vessel service improved steadily. In 1829 the schooner *Mariner* made the round trip from Cleveland to Green Bay in fourteen days,[132] but six years later freight was reaching Chicago from New York in twenty days.[133] A sail vessel left Buffalo daily for Chicago in 1836, but a steamboat only every 10 days.[134] Yet of the approximate 100,000 passengers who left Buffalo for the West in 1833, the 11 steamboats carried nearly 43,000.[135] New boats and services in the later 1830's, elimination of storage of freight at canal transfer points such as Buffalo, and lowering of steamboat rates, all helped facilitate traffic. Steamboat fares, Buffalo to Detroit, in 1839 were $8.00 cabin, $3.00 steerage, while freight to Chicago was 62 cents per hundred.[136] A boat such as the *James Madison* could "make [probably gross] $20,000 on a single trip."[137]

As population and traffic increased, the individualistic nature of the earlier steamboat operation proved less satisfactory to all concerned. For the boat operator there were frequently short cargoes and loss of profits, while for the shipper there were uncertain schedules and rates. In 1825 about thirty of the Louisville boat operators arrived at an agreement on rates for barrel goods and some of the owners operating above Cincinnati effected some sort of organization in 1828.[138] Of more importance was the organization in 1832 of sixteen of the boats in the Louis-

---

[131] *Western Monthly Magazine*, II (1834), 318. In 1820 the steamboat *Manhattan* delivered merchandise from New York to Shawneetown, Illinois, at three cents per pound. *Western Herald and Steubenville Gazette*, May 6, 1820. In 1829 boat owners above the Falls agreed on the following freight rates: Pittsburgh to Cincinnati, 45 cents per hundred; to Louisville, 50 cents; Wheeling to Cincinnati, 40 cents; Wheeling to Louisville, 45 cents; Cincinnati to Louisville, 12½ cents. Upstream fares the same. Pork and whiskey from Cincinnati to Louisville, 20 cents per barrel. *Scioto Gazette* in *Hamilton Intelligencer*, May 5, 1829.
[132] Including six days at anchor. *Cleaveland Herald*, May 14, 1829.
[133] *Chicago American*, September 25, 1835.
[134] *Ibid.*, August 6, 1836.
[135] Governor William L. Marcy's message, in *Chicago Democrat*, February 4, 1834.
[136] *Cleveland Herald and Gazette* (weekly), June 5, 1839.
[137] *Milwaukee Advertiser*, June 10, 1837.
[138] *Cincinnati Daily Gazette*, September 30, October 8, 1828.

ville–New Orleans trade into the Ohio and Mississippi Mail Line.[139] Among the advantages supposed to result were reduction of costs, stabilization of rates, avoidance of overloading, elimination of racing and unsafe practices, and the establishment of reliable schedules. The later history of the Line is obscure, but it was probably the first notable example of the organizations which began in the late 1830's and became so prominent in a later period. Some of these were the loosest of "lines" which required merely waiting turn for cargo and staggering departures, while others were real combines or pools, which required deposits up to 45 per cent of all receipts on the part of members. This pool, when divided, helped compensate for cutthroat rates and losses suffered by single boats.

In addition to its effect on traffic, the steamboat created employment, business, and a demand for materials. Boat building became a leading business along the Ohio from Pittsburgh to New Albany; also in Cleveland and Detroit.[140] Morgan Neville estimated that from 1817 to 1829, $5,600,000 had been spent in building and $2,800,000 in repair; including operations the total was $14,000,000. In 1834 annual operating expenses were estimated at $4,600,000, of which wages constituted 36 per cent, wood 30 per cent, and provisions 18 per cent.[141] Wood handling for the boats was a boon to the river farmers. Prices ran from $1.50 to $5.00 per cord. Coal was available at four to five cents per bushel at points above the Scioto and again below Shawneetown.

Despite its importance, steamboating was not a profitable investment. Only those particularly fortunate were able to net 6 per cent on their capital. Snags and other hazards of navigation took their toll; explosions and fires were likewise regarded as unavoidable hazards. Since the average life of a boat was thought to be but four or five years, boats were often cheaply and flimsily constructed; managers were frequently incompetent persons,

---

[139] Plans and arguments were set forth in an advertisement in the *Cincinnati Daily Gazette*, November 20, 1832. Other references to the Line may be found in *ibid.,* December, 1832, to June, 1833.

[140] A list of western steamboats, 1811–35 (not including those on the Great Lakes) by name, tonnage, place built, and "how destroyed" is included in James Hall, *The West: Its Commerce and Navigation* (Cincinnati, 1848), 149–64. These figures vary somewhat from other tabulations published at the time.

[141] From Morgan Neville's article in *Western Monthly Magazine*, II (1834), 316–18. Reprinted in Hall. *The West: Its Commerce and Navigation*, 129–30.

which fact further assured accidents. Competition, rate cutting, and questionable practices for getting business were other factors.

The number of steamboats which met unfortunate ends exceeded the number of those which wore out.[142] Of the boats built prior to 1826, 41 per cent had been lost or destroyed by that date; almost three fourths of this loss was due to fire.[143] Morgan Neville, a student of river traffic, listed 66 boats as put out of service in the two years, 1832 and 1833, of which 24 were snagged, 15 burned, and 15 abandoned. He estimated the annual loss at 12 per cent in number or 10 per cent in tonnage. The losses on western waters in 1838 were listed at 80, of which 37 were snagged, 17 sunk, 8 blown up, and 6 "collapsed."[144] Indifference, carelessness, and poor construction, high-pressure boilers, and racing, with its supposed advertising value, were the chief causes. Steam engineering was in its infancy and little attention was paid to tensile strength, pressure per square inch, and safety valves. The use of river water necessitated frequent boiler cleaning (on the Missouri almost daily). If this was neglected, anything might happen. A "hot engineer" was one who ignored the steam and water gauges, if any, and measured pressure by the weight hung on the safety valve. Hot engineers and "close pilots" were much in demand. Sometimes boats were locked together and ran in this way for miles, while part of the steam was shut off and the boilers pushed with dry ash and pine, to raise a good head of steam preparatory to the breakaway. When the signal came, excitement would prevail among the women as well as the men. "I have very often stood by the side of the 'Randolph's' boilers when shoving her and imagined I could see them breathe like an old horse with heaves and still I don't believe it was imagination. . . ."[145]

The results were reported in constantly recurring headlines: "Terrible Steamboat Disaster," "Another Explosion," etc.[146] By

[142] See list in *ibid.*, 149–64.
[143] Gephart, *Transportation and Industrial Development*, 80.
[144] Hall, *The West: Its Commerce and Navigation*, 134; *Alton Telegraph* in *Hunt's Merchants' Magazine*, I (1839), 356.
[145] Wilson Daniels, "Steamboating on the Ohio and Mississippi," in *Indiana Magazine of History*, XI (1915), 124.
[146] Accounts of some of these may be found in Hall, *The West: Its Commerce and Navigation*, Chapter X. Some of these explosions threw fragments of machinery and bodies onto both shores of the river. Although forty or fifty lives might be lost, the newspapers seldom got beyond the modest headlines of the period, that is, letters about one-eighth inch high.

the late 1830's these were becoming so common that public opinion was being aroused. "The steamers on the Ohio and Mississippi appear to be going into a wholesale destruction of human life. We scarcely have time to notice one horrible catastrophe before another of an equally, if not more heart rending description, is announced," said the *Piqua Courier*.[147] It advised travelers not to risk themselves or their families in such floating castles but to patronize those boats built on the low-pressure principle and whose captains were reliable and not addicted to racing and *brag* voyages. The *Detroit Advertiser* announced that it would have no mercy on racing boats, and severely criticized two of its favorite boats, one of which landed Cleveland passengers, including one invalid, at the outer end of a 1,200-foot pier at 2 A.M. in order to save time.[148] In 1837 Indiana passed "An Act to prevent disasters on Steam Boats," to go into effect when similar laws should be passed by Illinois and Kentucky. It provided for an engineer to examine and certify steamboat owners. The same year Illinois passed a comprehensive steamboat law which specified full and competent crews, established traffic rules, and forbade racing and carrying of explosives.[149] Wisconsin Territory also enacted a law to regulate machinery and crew, river passing, and night navigation. Violators were made liable to damages. Races were outlawed and if lives were lost while racing, the master was to be charged with high crime and misdemeanor.[150]

Navigation of the Ohio–Mississippi presented its problems. First to learn of the riffles and wooden islands, changing bars and currents, were the explorers and *voyageurs* of an earlier day. By the time westward emigration began to use the river, knowledge respecting its navigation was generally available. In 1801 Zadok Cramer, a Pittsburgh printer, began publication of *The Navigator*,[151] a useful and popular work which ran through twelve editions. In 1825 Samuel Cumings, of Cincinnati, began

[147] *Piqua Courier and Enquirer*, May 5, 1838.
[148] *Detroit Daily Advertiser*, August 3, 1838.
[149] *Laws of Indiana*, 1836–37 (general), pp. 76–78; Vandalia *Illinois State Register and People's Advocate*, September 8, 1837.
[150] *Detroit Daily Advertiser*, June 16, 1838.
[151] *The Navigator; or, The Traders' Useful Guide to Navigating the Monongahela, Allegheny, Ohio and Mississippi Rivers.* . . . See Buck, *Travel and Description*, 43, for sketch of various editions.

his *Western Pilot*.[152] He used Cramer's *Navigator* as a foundation, without mentioning the fact, but added new charts, checked up on surveys, and otherwise kept up to date. These guides mapped the rivers by sections, listed all obstacles and dangers, showed the channel, and paralleled the charts with textual instructions such as: "*Dead Man's Island*. Channel to the right. As you approach the island, keep well towards the right shore, round the large bar at the head of the island, then keep to the left. . . ." The *Navigator* also discoursed upon types of boats and the importance of sound workmanship, equipment, handling the boats, dangers, and how to avoid them.

The common dangers were snags, ice, bars, falling banks, wooden islands, and sunken wrecks. As banks were undermined, thousands of trees found their way into the streams. Roots weighted with dirt might anchor the trunk and leave it set firmly as a planter, or fix it at one end only, and at an angle, leaving one end free to weave up and down as a sawyer. Sawyers were particularly dangerous as they might point either up- or downstream, ready to impinge on their jagged points any object which hit them with force. The period of vibration of sawyers was sometimes twenty minutes or more, in which case a boat might arrive just in time to meet the unknown danger. "Sleeping" sawyers never appeared above the surface, the only warning being the slight riffle or change in color of water apparent only to the experienced eye. Ice became most dangerous when a boat or ark got caught on a bar or landed in an exposed position, in which case ice might pile up and sink it. Bars were constantly shifting, and might cause a lot of heavy work if encountered.

Islands were not so bad, for they were usually protected by bars at the upper end. But this was not true of the wooden islands, or masses of driftwood which became anchored. In a stream which might vary from three or four feet in depth with a lazy current, to eighty or ninety feet with rushing volume, as did the Ohio, problems of navigation were presented which

---

[152] *The Western Pilot; Containing Charts of the Ohio River and of the Mississippi, from the Mouth of the Missouri to the Gulf of Mexico; Accompanied with Directions for Navigating the Same; and a Gazetteer* . . . (Cincinnati, 1834 edition). See Buck *Travel and Description*, 92–93, for history of this work.

did not exist in lake navigation or on most of the eastern rivers.[153] When floods were at their height, most boats were tied up, but ordinary high waters were taken advantage of by even the largest steamboats to ascend the Falls at Louisville.[154] Low waters in summer and early autumn frequently tied up steamboats and brought the keelboats to the front. In November, 1818, it was estimated that three million dollars worth of goods was piled up at Pittsburgh awaiting a rise in the Ohio,[155] and in October, 1819, more than a dozen steamboats were aground near Louisville waiting for water.[156] In the dry summer of 1830 keelboats were at a premium; freight rates from Pittsburgh to Cincinnati and Louisville were $1.00 to $2.00 per hundred, but when steamboats ran again, they fell to 20 or 30 cents. The summer of 1838 was also dry. The *Illinois State Register* explained its reduced sheet by the fact that its paper had "been waiting on the banks of what was once the Ohio River since September last."[157] After

[153] Outstanding flood or "fresh" years on the Ohio were 1772, 1784, 1813, 1815, 1832, and 1847. The early floods, of course, did not cause much destruction to navigation or farms, although they covered the bottom lands from 6 to 8 feet deep. Three feet of rain fell in the late summer and autumn of 1831, or about 54 inches for the year, as compared with a normal 40 inches. Heavy snows were followed by a quick thaw which broke up the ice. More snow and heavy rain followed in January and February, 1832, and the Ohio reached its highest mark prior to 1937. On February 10 the river was 32 feet above low water mark at Pittsburgh, at Wheeling it was 48 feet above on the 12th, and the next day 50 feet above at Marietta. February 18 and 19 the river reached 62 feet above low water mark at Cincinnati and 60 feet at Louisville. Water Street, Cincinnati, was navigable by steamboats. The *Robert Fulton* used the street to clear the *Uncle Sam. Cincinnati American*, February 14. All previous records were broken, said the papers. It has been reasoned, however, that the flood of 1772 was about 5 feet higher, since the flood of 1832 lacked that much of backing up Wheeling Creek to its falls, which did occur in 1772. Samuel P. Hildreth, "Brief History of the Floods of the Ohio from 1772 to 1832," in *Journal of the Historical and Philosophical Society of Ohio*, I (1872), 51. Houses, barns, mills, boats, even "a church passed the city [Cincinnati] with the steeple standing, bound for New Orleans we presume—a poor market." For the flood of 1832, see *Steubenville Herald*, February 15; *Cincinnati American* (extra), February 17; *Commercial Daily Advertiser*, February 27; Louisville *Prices Current*, February 18. In December, 1847, the Ohio rose 14 feet in 24 hours and again reached 62 feet above low water mark. In the great flood of 1937 which broke all records, the river reached about 80 feet above low water mark at Cincinnati and 87 at Louisville. The 1937 mark was 28 feet above "flood stage"; it has been estimated that the flood of 1772 was 24 feet above. It would seem that the clearing of the forests has not been the important factor in causing floods that we have been led to believe.

[154] *Liberty Hall and Cincinnati Gazette*, March 2, 1822; Madison *Indiana Republican*, April 28, 1828, March 18, 1830; Lawrenceburg *Indiana Palladium*, February 25, July 8, 1826; Indianapolis *Indiana Journal*, October 25, 1829.

[155] *Niles' Weekly Register*, XV, 267 (Dec. 12, 1818); Portsmouth (Ohio) *Gazette*, December 10, 1818.

[156] Faux, *Memorable Days*, 201.

[157] November 23, 1838.

the low waters the following winter brought ice. By the time navigation was opened some of the merchants' shelves in western towns badly needed replenishing. The next summer was no better. It was "a very good river while it lasts but it makes a very poor summer wear." Again in the autumn of 1840 there was "a whole raft of boats aground in the Ohio River."[158]

The Falls at Louisville, a drop of about twenty-five feet in two miles, constituted a permanent obstacle.[159] Smaller steamboats could make the down passage with fairly high waters, but only rarely came back. This established a division point; most of the steamboats navigated either from Pittsburgh to Louisville or from Louisville down river. Shippingport developed as a result of transfer activities across the two-mile portage, hence the teamsters were natural opponents of a canal.

In 1805 an Indiana Canal Company was organized in the hope of obtaining a land grant to build a canal at the Falls. That same year the first Indiana territorial assembly issued a charter for the company whose stock was to be tax-exempt. A time limit of nine months was set for beginning, and six years for completing the canal.[160] Whether or not influenced by a U. S. Senate report which favored the Kentucky side, the company failed to act, and nothing came of the project.

The United States Government in 1810 promoted a canal project at the Falls, as did Kentucky five years later, but the latter was scared out in part by talk of a canal on the Indiana side. The war held up further plans, but in 1817 the Indiana Assembly chartered the Ohio Canal Company. Authorized capital stock was $1,000,000, the company was given the right of eminent domain for both right of way and materials, and was to finish a canal by 1822. Cincinnati was strongly in favor of this "Jeffersonville–Ohio" canal.[161] Although it was stated that ample funds would be forthcoming from capitalists along the Ohio and

---

[158] *Quincy* (Ill.) *Whig*, November 23, December 1, 1838, August 24, 1839, October 10, 1840.

[159] See George Croghan, "A Selection of Letters and Journals, Relating to Tours into the Western Country," in Thwaites (ed.), *Early Western Travels*, I, 136; John Melish, *Travels in the United States*; Jervis Cutler, *Topographical Description*; and others for descriptions of the Falls.

[160] Philbrick (ed.), *Laws of Indiana Territory, 1801–9*, 154–63; *American State Papers, Miscellaneous*, I, 419, 479.

[161] *Laws of Indiana*, 1816–17, pp. 219–28; *Liberty Hall and Cincinnati Gazette* and Cincinnati *Western Spy*, autumn and winter of 1817–18.

east to the mountains, nothing happened. When the Indiana Assembly met again the following year, a second company was chartered to be known as the Jeffersonville Ohio Company. The old charter was canceled but its main provisions were retained in the new one. Additional privileges were granted, including the right to raise $100,000 by lottery. The time for completion was extended to 1824. A ditch was dug the length of the two-and-a-half-mile stretch around the Falls, but funds ran out, and the venture languished.[162]

Louisville promoters incorporated the Louisville and Portland Canal Company in 1825, capital $1,000,000. The United States Government bought 2,350 of the 10,000 shares. The canal was built on the Kentucky side and was opened in December, 1830; during the first year it handled 406 steamboats, 421 keel- and flatboats, and took in $12,750 in tolls. Its financial success was phenomenal as the income in twelve years more than paid the cost, but its facilities were soon inadequate. Locks were too small for the larger boats, boats could not pass each other in the canal, and delays resulted with serious financial losses to the boat owners. Tolls were high (60 cents per ton) and constituted a heavy tax on river traffic, sometimes equal annually to one fifth or even one half the cost of the boat.[163]

On the Mississippi between St. Louis and the Falls of St. Anthony were two sets of rapids. The lower or Des Moines Rapids, some 200 miles above St. Louis, were about 11 miles long with a 24-foot fall. The upper or Rock River Rapids were approximately 15 miles long and had a fall of about 26 feet. Since narrow channels and sharp turns made these difficult, early steamboats without sufficient power to breast the current were compelled to warp over by anchoring a cable and winding it around the main paddle wheel shaft.[164] Keelboats did the same with man power.[165] Cargoes had to be lightened and the delays and

---

[162] *Laws of Indiana*, 1817–18 (special), pp. 57–67; Logan Esarey, *Internal Improvements in Early Indiana (Indiana Historical Society Publications*, V, No. 2, Indianapolis, 1912), 65–69; Corydon *Indiana Gazette*, quoted in Madison *Indiana Republican*, January 16, 1817. The lottery advertisements were widely printed in the papers in 1819.

[163] Hall, *The West: Its Commerce and Navigation*, 78–83.

[164] Dr. Moses Meeker, "Early History of the Lead Region of Wisconsin," in *Wisconsin Historical Collections*, VI (1872), 278.

[165] See Timothy Flint, *Recollections of the Last Ten Years*, letter 12, for excellent description of this difficult task.

lighterage fees proved costly. When water was too low for steamboat navigation, freight charges increased about 100 to 150 per cent.

Agitation for aid from the Federal Government for river improvement began early. There was talk of spending millions in the East for canals, said the Cincinnati *Liberty Hall* in 1816, why not some on the canals already dug, the western rivers?[166] A beginning was made in 1824 when Congress appropriated $75,000 for removal of snags; small appropriations continued, despite Jackson's attitude on internal improvements, for about twenty years. Captain Shreve harnessed two powerful small steamboats together and "Uncle Sam's Tooth-puller" straddled the obstructions and removed thousands of them from the Lower Ohio and the Upper Mississippi. Whereas from 1822 to 1827 losses of $1,360,000 of cargo were credited to snags in the Ohio and Mississippi, the next five years saw these reduced almost three fourths.[167] Various plans for removal of sandbars were debated: wing dams to narrow the current and force it to maintain its own channel, cutting channels through the bars, and converting the stream into slack water by dams and locks. The first two were tried with indifferent success. The river continued to place and remove its bars. Shallow-draft boats lessened the danger and delay, but even so, knowledge of how to "spar off"[168] was among the presumed qualifications of any captain worthy of the name. Boats on the Great Lakes were not concerned with snags and low waters, but faced equal dangers from ice and storms.

The lesser rivers presented similar problems and the states did the best they could to keep them open to navigation. Indiana, for instance, in 1820 declared most of the navigable rivers to be public highways, open to the free use of all. Fines levied against obstructors were assigned to the school fund.

Professional boatmen and rivermen constituted a noteworthy and distinctive class in the new West, well known to travelers and emigrants in their day and preserved to us in tradition and literature. "There is not on earth a class of men of a more peculiar

[166] February 5, March 18, 1816.
[167] Hall, *The West: Its Commerce and Navigation*, 60.
[168] Heavy timber spars were set on the bottom, and by means of steam power and tackle fastened to the boat's hull, the boat could be lifted and shoved over at either end; or it was scooted forward or "walked over" by spars on either side. For description see Merrick, *Old Times on the Upper Mississippi*, 74.

and marked character, than the western boatmen."[169] The earliest professional boatmen on the Ohio and Mississippi developed from the fur trade of colonial days, but as the westward migration set in, their numbers were augmented by discharged soldiers from the western armies, lawless and unscrupulous men from the older regions, and venturesome pioneers from the western settlements.

The life was attractive because of its color and danger, its freedom, its periods of ease, and the opportunities offered to see the world. From the Allegheny to the farthest reaches of the Arkansas, from New Orleans to the Yellowstone, the boatmen roamed in labor and adventure, subject only to the law of their kind. Before the steamboat, river work was rough and hard, and it produced a class of rough and hard men. Whether they were the toughest class in the West cannot be proved, but in their own opinion there was no doubt about it, and this view is often supported by others.[170] The redoubtable but semimythical Mike Fink, joker, fighter, and king of the boatmen, voiced the sentiments of his class when he bellowed his boast:

I'm a Salt River Roarer! I'm a ring-tailed squealer! I'm a reg'lar screamer from the ol' Massassip'! WHOOP! I'm the very infant that refused his milk before its eyes were open, and called out for a bottle of old Rye! I love the women an' I'm chockful o' fight! I'm half wild horse and half cockeyed-alligator and the rest o' me is crooked snags an' red hot snappin' turtle. I can hit like fourth-proof lightnin' an' every lick I make in the woods lets in an acre o' sunshine. I can out-run, out-jump, out-shoot, out-brag, out-drink, an' out fight, rough-an'-tumble, no holts barred, ary man on both sides the river from Pittsburg to New Orleans an' back ag'in to St. Louiee. Come on, you flatters, you bargers, you milk-white mechanics, an' see how tough I am to chaw! I ain't had a fight for two days an' I'm spilein' for exercise. Cock-a-doodle-doo![171]

Fink and his kind lorded it over the flatboatmen, "black-guarded" or out-reparteed the landsmen with whimsical vulgarity, fed snuff to the farmers' sheep and got paid for taking away these victims of the "bloody murrain," shot, drank, gouged and

---

[169] R. B., *View of the Valley of the Mississippi*, 128.

[170] Estwick Evans admitted their conspicuousness for intemperance and swearing, but found them less quarrelsome and pugnacious than he had been led to expect. *Pedestrious Tour*, in Thwaites (ed.), *Early Western Travels*, VIII, 260.

[171] Walter Blair and Franklin J. Meine, *Mike Fink, King of Mississippi Keelboatmen* (New York, 1933). A similar challenge may be found in Mark Twain *Life on the Mississippi*.

boasted, sang and spent their wages. Lanky, bronzed, lacka-
daisical, or indifferent appearing, the boatmen, like the Canadian
voyageur, had to meet the high standards set by his pride in his
work and the opinion of his fellows.

In his normal state he was silently waiting for something to happen,
knowing quite well it certainly would. When the bomb of circumstance
exploded the human creature was on that dot of time transformed into a
combination of rubber ball, wildcat, and shrieking maniac, all controlled by
instantaneous perception and exact calculation. After the tumult he subsided again into his listless lethargy of waiting, the monotony being endured
by chewing tobacco and illustrating the marvelous accuracy with which he
could propel a stream of its juice for any distance up to fifteen feet.[172]

The distinguishing dress of the boatman consisted of a red
flannel shirt, a blue jerkin or coat which reached to the hips,
brown trousers of linsey-woolsey, and a cap of skin or fur, or a
hat. The boatman, like the trapper, the teamster, the drover,
later the lumberman, had his peculiar vocabulary and used a picturesque language of simile and metaphor, more than usually
interspersed with profanity. He spoke of going "fernenst" the
current, and of "reverend" sets (when his pole got a solid set
against a firm log). When he demanded haste, he yelled "start
yer trotters" or "shake yer skids." Things happened "quicker
nor an alligator can chaw a puppy." A silent person was "dumb
as a dead nigger in a mud-hole," and a drowned man was "choked
to death like a catfish on a sand-bank." A difficult task was
"harder nor climbin' a peeled saplin' heels uppard." After hours
or days of quiet drifting downstream, when the emergency came,
"Hell's a snortin' " said the boatman, as he went into action.

A Frenchman was considered best at paddle or oar, but a
"Kentuck" the best man at a pole. When working laboriously up
rapids or through chutes, straining at the poles, swimming out
with the cordelle in mouth, pushing, and pulling, the boatman
showed his stuff. "It would be incredible to any one who had not
seen such men, and had full opportunities to become acquainted
with their character, the hardihood and endurance of which they
are capable."[173] These men of course regarded the first steamboats with contempt, but were compelled grudgingly to give way

[172] Dunbar, *History of Travel*, I, 293.
[173] Timothy Flint, *Recollections of the Last Ten Years*, 94.

before their advance. Long after their labors ceased to be of importance on the Ohio and Mississippi, they were necessary on the lesser streams. Something of the more lawless and outrageous spirit of earlier days disappeared; they became less intemperate and more civil in address, but their essential character remained the same—"boldness, readiness to encounter almost any danger, recklessness of consequences, and indifference to the wants of the future, amid the enjoyments, the noise, whiskey and fun, of the present. It is a mournful fact, that their own inclination, as well as their mode of life, almost constantly exclude them from the means of moral and religious instruction. Their condition is beginning, however, to excite Christian sympathy, and to elicit suitable efforts for the promotion of their reformation."[174] Regardless of the lack of moral qualifications, never very significant when it comes to doing the rough work of the world, the western boatmen did their part as nation builders, and deserve a place in its history as well as trappers and teamsters, farmers and missionaries, prospectors and railroaders. A romance surrounded their lives which made them more than mere laborers in the minds of travelers and settlers.

The boats float by their dwellings on beautiful spring mornings, when the verdant forest, the mild and delicious temperature of the air, the delightful azure of the sky of this country, the fine bottom on the one hand, and the romantic bluff on the other, the broad and smooth stream rolling calmly down the forest, and floating the boat gently forward,—all these circumstances harmonize in the excited youthful imagination. The boatmen are dancing to the violin on the deck of their boat. They scatter their wit among the girls on the shore who come down to the water's edge to see the pageant pass. The boat glides on until it disappears behind a point of wood. At this moment perhaps, the bugle, with which all the boats are provided, strikes up its note in the distance over the water. These scenes, and these notes, echoing from the bluffs of the beautiful Ohio, have a charm for the imagination, which, although I have heard a thousand times repeated, and at all hours, and in all positions, is even to me always new, and always delightful. No wonder that the young, who are reared in these remote regions, with that restless curiosity which is fostered by solitude and silence, who witness scenes like this so frequently, no wonder that the severe and unremitting labours of agriculture, performed directly in the view of such scenes, should become tasteless and irksome. No wonder that the young along the banks of the great streams, should detest the labours of the field, and embrace every opportunity, either openly, or if minors, covertly, to escape and devote themselves to the pernicious employment of boating. And

[174] R. B., *View of the Valley of the Mississippi*, 128.

Boatmen and passengers. From original sketches by Basil Hall

Vehicles (Indiana Yearly Meeting of Friends, 1844)

Stone Bridge in Ohio. *Lefevre J. Cranstone*

in this view we may account for the detestation of the inhabitants along
these great streams towards steam-boats, which are every day diminishing
the number of small boats and boatmen, and which have already withdrawn
from the western waters, probably ten thousand from that employment.
And yet with all these seductions for the eye and the imagination, no life
is so slavish, none so precarious and dangerous. In no employment do the
hands so wear out. After the lapse of so very short a period since these
waters have been navigated in this way, at every bend, and every high
point of the river, you are almost sure to see, as you stop for a moment,
indications of the "narrow house"; the rude monument, the coarse memorial, carved on an adjoining tree by a brother boatman, which marks that
an exhausted boatman there yielded his breath, and was buried.[175]

The poet as well caught the sentiment:

> O, boatman! wind that horn again,
> For never did the listening air,
> Upon its lambent bosom bear
> So wild, so soft, so sweet a strain!
> What, though thy notes are sad and few,
> By every simple boatman blown,
> Yet is each pulse to nature true,
> And melody in every tone.
> How oft in boyhood's joyous days,
> Unmindful of the lapsing hours,
> I've loitered on my homeward way
> By wild Ohio's banks of flowers;
> While some lone boatman from the deck
> Poured his soft numbers to the tide,
> As if to charm from storm and wreck
> The boat where all his fortunes ride!
> Delighted Nature drank the sound,
> Enchanted echo bore it round
> In whispers soft and softer still
> From hill to plain and plain to hill
> Till e'en the thoughtless, frolic boy,
> Elate with hope and wild with joy,
> Who gamboled by the river side,
> And sported with the fretting tide,
> Feels something new pervade his breast,
> Change his light step, repress his jest,
> Bends over the flood his eager ear
> To catch the sounds far off, yet dear—
> Drinks the sweet draft, but knows not why
> The tear of rapture fills his eye.[176]

---

[175] Flint, *Recollections of the Last Ten Years*, 15–17.
[176] William O. Butler, "The Boatman's Horn," as printed in Frankfort (Ky.)
Commonwealth, Springfield *Sangamo Journal*, and other papers, 1836.

Some of the keelboatmen finished their days in the old life, but many went over to the new way. The post of pilot, the most difficult and important on the steamboat, was usually filled by one who had gained his minute knowledge of the river from scores of trips in the flat- and keelboats. No light by night or "diamond boards" by day marked the path in the early days of steamboating. There were no searchlights to cut the darkness ahead. The pilot reckoned by natural landmarks, sounds, echoes, and a sort of sixth sense. He carried a minute knowledge of almost every rod of hundreds of miles of river, and could see in the dark far better than most men. The pilot was also the captain on many of the early boats. When bigger boats came, the pilot ranked next to the captain, but by the unwritten law of the service, the "old man," even though he might be the owner of the boat and himself a licensed pilot, did not interfere with running the boat. The pilot and the captain were the aristocracy of steamboatmen; by the 1840's their pay and position made them the figures most admired by the youth not only of the river towns, but of the interior as well.[177]

Early captains were frequently arrogant and independent, but it was soon realized that qualifications other than mere ability to manage a boat were necessary. The years brought professional traditions as well as increased responsibilities. Sometimes captains came from the mate's position, more often from the pilot house. They were expected to know the river, be able to handle men, understand something of business and shipping, and stand as the owner's chief representative before the public. This the better captain did in high degree. A few were uncivil, profane, and disagreeable, but they were the exceptions. "I have travelled in many of the steam-boats in the Valley of the Mississippi, and I have almost uniformly found their commanders urbane, attentive, patient, vigilant, and disposed to do every thing that could be done to render the voyage—often long and tedious, and demanding uncommon patience in the master of the vessel,—pleasant to the passengers."[178]

As the luxury boats opened the golden age of the steamboat in the late 1830's, the organization on the boat became more complex. Chief mate and second mate, chief clerk and second

[177] Larger boats sometimes carried two pilots. Salaries ran from $125 to $200 a month.

[178] R. B., *View of the Valley of the Mississippi,* 339.

clerk, engineer, and steward all became keymen. The clerk handled the business, and the steward ran the galley or kitchen. Here he was czar of his domain. A good steward might get a mate's pay, or even a captain's pay. The amenities and conventions as well as rules and regulations fixed the duties and relationships among the officers. Cabin crews and firemen might be composed largely of free Negroes, but deck crews and stevedores were as a rule white common labor, and worked under the driving power of the clerk.[179] Proudly breasting the current of the Ohio and Mississippi or sweeping downstream between the wooded shores and penetrating the quiet with its bugle call or jarring it with the rumble of its whistle, a top-class boat was a beautiful sight; within its cabins and on its decks might be found a cross section of the people of the West.

> Thence, might be heard, back on the breezes floating,
> The mingled murmur of an hundred tongues;
> Deep politicians, arguing and voting,
> With heads prophetic, and untiring lungs,
> Profoundly settling, as the steam-boat went,
> That knotty problem, our next president.
>
> And from within, came joyous, though remote,
> Songs from the gay, and laughter from the young,
> While ever and anon, with clarion note,
> High o'er the rest, the stirring bugle sung,
> 'Till the rous'd echos started at the sound,
> And answer'd from their solitudes around.
>
> Along the guards, like lovers arm in arm,
> Some exercising coxcombs wheel'd, and march'd,
> Their snow-white ruffles, done up to a charm,
> And their broad collars admirably starch'd;
> While on the stern, a group of ladies fair,
> Were sitting out to take the morning air.
>
> .   .   .   .
>
> The Mississippi, with its full spring tide,
> Swept in its torrent majesty along,
> And down its breast, in all her painted pride,
> Rush'd a gay steam-boat, with her crowded throng
> Cleaving the rapid flood, and spurning back,
> Its swiftest wave, for lingering in her track.[180]

[179] The Irish seemed to pre-empt this work in the later period, as they did canal and railroad building.

[180] From Micah P. Flint's "Meander, A Western Epic," in *Western Monthly Review,* I (1827–28), 594.

Besides the professional boatmen, there were many more whose lives were intimately bound with the western rivers. Not all boat business concerned itself with transportation. Traveling shops on boats worked the river towns and the river itself. Cabinetmaking, groceries, notion peddling, tin making, blacksmithing, groggeries, horse-trading establishments, puppet shows—in fact, almost every business activity found on land—could be found on the Ohio–Mississippi. Fishermen, ferrymen, and the numerous class of shiftless hangers-on, the "river rats" or squatters on the right of way, who eked out an existence by one means or another, must not be overlooked.

More important still was the part the river played in the lives of thousands of Westerners, emigrants who arrived by the river, businessmen who bought goods in Pittsburgh or Philadelphia, but especially farmers, who made one or more trips to New Orleans with produce. However important the canal, railroad, or highway later became, it is doubtful whether they ever possessed the appeal of the river and the trip to New Orleans. Many were the young men who got their first view of the outside world from a flatboat and their introduction to the big wicked city at the end of the ride. New Orleans was a story unto itself. In pre-steamboat days the trip back was usually made on foot. Assuming that the proceeds from the produce or wages were not all left in New Orleans, there was still Natchez under the Bluff, the rendezvous of gamblers, prostitutes, and boatmen. Also "footpads" on the way. By the 1830's deck passage upstream could be had for $6.00 to $8.00, passengers finding themselves and perhaps helping wood the boat. Cards, drinks, and songs helped these "fellows of infinite jest" amuse not only themselves but the cabin passengers as well.

§ §

The waterways and the Indian trails were the white man's first pathways into the interior,[181] and from earliest times to the

[181] Many of the Indian trails followed the paths laid out by the buffalo in his migrations. For maps of Indian trails, see Archer B. Hulbert, "The Indian Thoroughfares of Ohio," in *Ohio Archaeological and Historical Society Publications*, VIII (1900), 264–95; George R. Wilson, *Early Indiana Trails and Surveys* (*Indiana Historical Society Publications*, VI, No. 3, Indianapolis, 1919), 349–457.

present, interest and dominating importance has shifted back and
forth from water to land routes. The French came into the West
by the waterways, but the first important American migration
was by Boone's road and the Cumberland Gap. The Ohio was
all-important for a while, then was overshadowed in part by the
National Road and the turnpikes. The steamboat and the canal
brought water navigation again to the front, only in turn to be
supplanted by the railroad, which after its period of supremacy,
had to yield to in part, if not be supplanted by, the highway and
waterway and the airways.

The use of wheeled vehicles—chairs, chaises, and carriages or
coaches—which became common in the colonies in the latter part
of the eighteenth century, as well as the need for freight transportation and postal service, led to the development of roads.[182]
Bridle paths or pack-horse traces were widened, sometimes
straightened, and the higher climbs detoured. By 1740 the more
important cities in the middle and northern colonies were connected by some sort of roads.[183]

Two of the important roads which led to the West were
the result of military expeditions: Braddock's Trace from Fort
Cumberland on the Potomac to near the forks of the Ohio
(1755), and Forbes's Road, or the Old Glade Road, westward
from Philadelphia to Carlisle, Ligonier, and Pittsburgh (1758).
These former trader's traces were opened at just the time that
the wagon began to supersede the pack horse. Boone laid out the
trail through Cumberland Gap to Boonesborough in 1775, but
the branch west through Crab Orchard to the Falls of the Ohio
and on to Vincennes soon became a more important road.[184] The
Genesee Road from Albany west past the Finger Lakes was open
through to Buffalo near the end of the century, and a trail con-

[182] In Boston owners of horse coaches were regarded as of questionable sobriety
and morality as late as 1687, but almost a century later (1772) there were eighty-
four vehicles in the town. In 1697 Philadelphia had about thirty wheeled contrivances (including carts), but Connecticut had no carriages until about 1750
and few until after the Revolution. Dunbar, *History of Travel*, I, 48, 205.

[183] The first regular transportation service on roads dates from about 1732 when
weekly stage-wagon service began between Burlington and Amboy, New Jersey.
Competition had reduced the time from Philadelphia to New York, about ninety
miles, to three days by 1756. *Ibid.*, I, 180, 183.

[184] Followed by Benjamin Logan when he left the Henderson party in 1775 and
established Logan's Station. The distance from Philadelphia by way of the Great
Valley—Wilderness Road to Louisville was about seven hundred miles. Despite its
being the longest of the land routes to the interior, it was the path by which
thousands of Virginia and Middle States' emigrants came to the Northwest.

tinued through Erie, Cleveland, Sandusky, across the Black Swamp, to the Maumee and on to Detroit before the War of 1812. The first turnpike in the country, the Philadelphia and Lancaster, sixty-two miles long, was built by chartered company as a result of an act of 1792, and opened in 1794. The Lancaster and Susquehanna was opened by 1803.

To connect Pennsylvania and the East with the Kentucky settlements by a land route usable the year round, and to supplement the Ohio as an emigrant route, Ebenezer Zane was authorized by Congress in 1796 to open a road through the Northwest Territory between Wheeling and Limestone (Maysville, Kentucky). This first road in Ohio determined the important settlements of the following years. Where it crossed the Muskingum, Zanesville developed, at the Hockhocking, Lancaster, and at the Scioto, Chillicothe.

By 1812 an east and west road ran from Marietta to Cincinnati by way of Chillicothe. Roads ran from Cincinnati to Dayton, Chillicothe to Franklinton (Columbus); in the northeast corner of the state roads connected Cleveland, Warren, Canton, and New Lisbon with Beaver, Pennsylvania, on the Ohio. Trails ran from Cincinnati to Greenville and Fort Wayne, and from Zanesville and Columbus to Sandusky.[185] The more important settlements in the southern parts of Indiana and Illinois territories were likewise connected by roads or traces.

The Cumberland Road, or Old National Road, was of particular importance to the Northwest. In answer to persistent demands from the West, Congress in 1806 took the first step toward uniting the Atlantic Coast and the Mississippi by a government highway.[186] The law provided for laying out a road four rods wide from the Potomac to the State of Ohio, and that the consent of the states concerned be given. The commissioners appointed to select the route were to seek the shortest, most feasible route

[185] Maps of Ohio from 1813 to 1825 such as the Melish-Tanner map of "The Seat of the War in North America (1813)," F. Lucas (1815), J[ohn] Kilbourn (1820), H. S. Tanner (1823), A. Finley (1824?), and others, give the impression of a fairly well-established road net. Most of these "roads" were mere unimproved trails.

[186] In the Ohio enabling act of 1802, 5 per cent of the net proceeds from the sale of government lands lying in the state were to be used to build "public roads, leading from the navigable waters emptying into the Atlantic, to the Ohio, to the said State, and through the same." Next year it was changed so that 2 per cent should be used for roads to the state, and 3 per cent in the state. The same provision was later made for Indiana and Illinois.

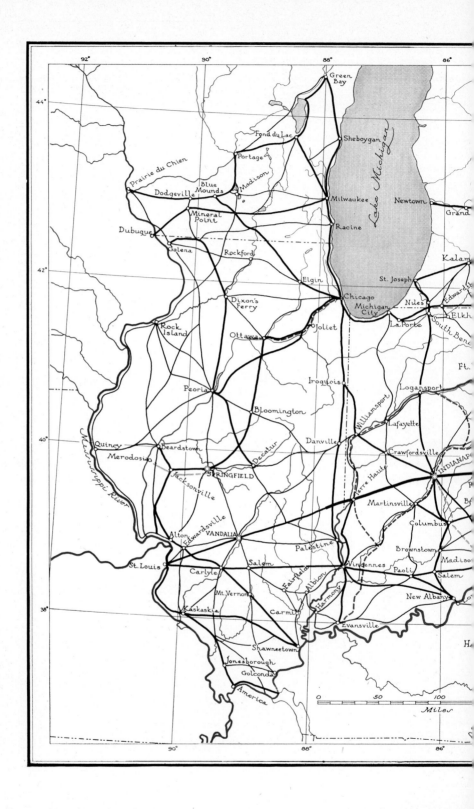

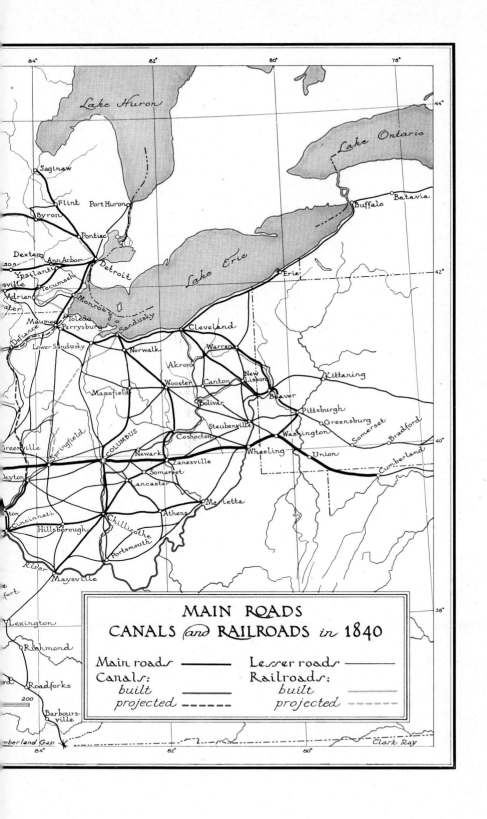

MAIN ROADS
CANALS *and* RAILROADS *in* 1840

Main roads ——— Lesser roads ———
Canals:
built ———
projected ------
Railroads:
built ———
projected ------

which would most diffuse the benefits, and reach a point low enough on the Ohio to ensure certainty of navigation. Sectionalism and politics caused delay in selection of a route, but in 1811 contracts were awarded and construction began. In general, from Cumberland to Laurel Hill, the last range of the Alleghenies, the line of Braddock's Road was followed, then a line west to Brownsville on the Monongahela, to Washington and Alexandria, Pennsylvania, and to the Ohio at Wheeling.[187] The road was incomplete but open to traffic in 1817 and the next year United States mail coaches were running from Washington to Wheeling.

In 1820 Congress appropriated $141,000 to complete the section between Washington, Pennsylvania, and Wheeling, and $10,000 for laying out the road from Wheeling to a point on the Mississippi between St. Louis and the mouth of the Illinois River. The earliest built sections were already wearing out, so in 1822 Congress passed a bill "for the preservation and repair of the Cumberland Road." This brought forth President Monroe's veto on constitutional grounds and precipitated a violent political and constitutional controversy which lasted for years. In 1823 Monroe signed a bill similar to the one of the preceding year; in 1825 he approved the act appropriating $150,000 for continuation of the road from Wheeling to Zanesville, Ohio, and completion of surveys through the seats of government of Ohio, Indiana, and Illinois to that of Missouri. This act was in part the counter of the other Middle States against New York and her bid for the commerce of the West by the Erie Canal. It was hailed with enthusiasm by the people of the Northwest.

The old portions of the road were now macadamized (crushed stone) and in some parts repairs practically amounted to a rebuilding. Drains, retaining walls, culverts, bridges, and stone masonry were repaired and improved. Construction west from

[187] The selection of Wheeling as the Ohio River terminus was a source of high glee to Zanesville citizens, who were keen rivals of those of Steubenville. Editors of the leading papers of the two towns had been calling names, but when Wheeling was selected, the editor of the *Zanesville Express* said Steubenville could take it out in laughing. The editor of the Steubenville *Western Herald* thought the demonstration premature and asked, since it took 10 years to build 30, how long would it take to build 220 miles of the road. The answer came promptly: "73 years, 3 months and 30 days." *Zanesville Express*, April 11, May 9 ff., 1816. Shortly Steubenville was promoting a Pittsburgh to Steubenville Turnpike. *Western Herald and Steubenville Gazette*, May 22, 1818.

Zanesville began in 1825–26 and soon the line was a busy scene. Farmers round about hired to contractors during off seasons, and laborers trooped in. Commissioner Jonathan Knight, who had laid out the line to Columbus, left that place in the summer of 1826 to survey on to Indianapolis;[188] he finished the survey to the western boundary of Indiana in September, 1827.[189] Other appropriations followed [190] and the road was completed to Columbus in 1833. The Indiana line was reached a few years later. The $60,000 appropriation of 1830 was used for building the sections sixteen miles east and twelve miles west out of Indianapolis. Contract bids were advertised for in Illinois in 1831;[191] these included sixteen bridges. Citizens' meetings were held in Edwardsville, Alton, and elsewhere,[192] and after Commissioner Joseph Shriver's report regarding extension of the road to Missouri, enthusiasm ran high.[193] But building lagged. In 1833 Secretary of War Lewis Cass suspended the superintendent, some thought because of intemperance, and the year following the chief engineer refused further estimates of cost for 1835. "Will the people of Illinois submit to this?" asked the *Illinois Advocate*.[194] Work on all but a thirty-mile stretch west of the Wabash was suspended in 1836, much to the disgust of Vandalia.[195] Contracts on the section between Terre Haute and Vandalia were let in 1837. Four years later the traveler noted that "most part of this road is nothing more than a track . . . the timber cut down and re-

---

[188] Columbus *Ohio State Journal*, August 17, 1826.

[189] Indianapolis *Indiana Journal*, September 4, 1827; see also *Indianapolis Gazette,* September 26, November 30, 1826, January 19 ff., 1827, and Richmond (Ind.) *Public Leger*, November 11, 1826. Under an earlier survey of 1820 the road would have passed about fourteen miles south of Indiana's newly located capital. The Indiana General Assembly petitioned Congress (*Laws of Indiana*, 1820–21, pp. 142–44) and that body specified that the line be moved north to accommodate Indianapolis. See Lee Burns, *The National Road in Indiana* (*Indiana Historical Society Publications*, VII, No. 4, Indianapolis, 1919), for a general account of the road in Indiana.

[190] For summary of appropriations, see Archer B. Hulbert, *The Cumberland Road* (*Historic Highways*, X, Cleveland, 1904), appendix. From 1806 to 1844, when $1,359 was appropriated for arrearages on the survey to Jefferson, Missouri, thirty-four appropriation acts were passed. Despite Jackson's stand against Federal aid for internal improvements as shown by his Maysville Road veto in 1832, he supported the National Road and signed ten appropriation bills for it.

[191] Edwardsville *Illinois Advocate*, June 3, 1831.

[192] *Ibid.*, December 9, 1831.

[193] Made in January, 1830, published in full in *ibid.*, December 23, 1831.

[194] December 20, 1834.

[195] Vandalia *Illinois State Register and People's Advocate*, August 26, 1836.

moved, the stumps being left." The road was eventually opened to Vandalia in 1852.

After Monroe's decision that the United States could not maintain the road, it was turned over to the states by sections as soon as built. In 1828 Pennsylvania and Ohio passed laws to provide for maintenance and accepted completed portions between 1831 and 1834.[196] Congress gave up the road in Indiana in 1848, and the state leased it to the "Plank Road Company." The road was never macadamized beyond Indiana.

The Old National Road was (and again is) one of the great vehicle roads of the world. In its eastern sections, eighty feet wide with a thirty-foot center of broken stone one foot deep, with culverts and bridges of cut stone and waterproof mortar, this road furnished a bond between East and West. It carried mail, emigrants, and freight. The road was never so important to Indiana and Illinois as to Pennsylvania and Ohio, for much of the through traffic was diverted by the Ohio River,[197] and other means of transportation were competing strongly by the time the western stretches were completed. Yet there were times when tolls were greater on the section west of the Monongahela than on the eastern.

It is impossible here to trace the development of a road system in the Northwest in the quarter of a century following the War of 1812.[198] The necessity for roads was so pressing and obvious that the subject was, with politics, the most discussed. From the message of Governor Worthington, of Ohio, in December, 1815, to the end of the period, it is safe to say that not a message was delivered by any governor in any of the states, which did not emphasize roads. Legislatures debated, politicians promised, newspapers alternately complained and promoted, but progress was necessarily slow in a region where dollars seemed even

[196] Ohio, by law in 1831, authorized tollgates every twenty miles and fixed rates. Tolls in that year were $2,777 but increased in 1839 to $62,496, the high mark. In 1836 the Ohio part of the road was placed under the Board of Public Works.

[197] Thomas B. Searight, *The Old Pike* . . . (Uniontown, Pa., 1894), 298, estimates two fifths of the travel was diverted at Brownsville.

[198] There are numerous articles and monographs on canals and railroads, but no systematic study of the development of roads has been made. The material for such a study will be found not so much in the statute books, but in the correspondence of military men, county histories, newspapers, and mail-contract awards. For a bibliography on roads, see Dunbar, *History of Travel*, and *History of Transportation in the United States Before 1860*, compiled by Caroline E. MacGill, *et. al.* (Carnegie Institution of Washington, 1917).

scarcer than settlers, and the work to be done proved too great for the capacity and resources of the "light and simple" governments elected by the people.

A few of the more important road projects prior to the period of systematic state internal improvements deserve mention. Two or three turnpike companies were incorporated by the Ohio legislature between 1809 and 1812, and in 1818–19 several works were originated by chartered companies, but it was not until 1821 that commissioners appointed by the Ohio legislature, with the aid of the Indians, blazed the trees and marked a road over the 109 miles from Piqua to Fort Meigs.[199] Petitions were presented to the legislature the next year for the much-needed road from Cleveland to the Ohio in Columbiana County,[200] but the road was not provided for until 1823 and not built until the years following. The same year Congress granted lands to Ohio for completion of the road from Cleveland to the Maumee within four years.[201] In 1827 "Junius" was "highly gratified in finding a pathway through a forest, which four years ago, was dismal and impassable."[202] This path did not become a road for a number of years. In 1839, following a legislative appropriation, surveys were made and contracts let on portions of it.[203]

The turnpike era was at hand and canals just in the offing. Both stimulated road building, the first because of the improved methods, the second by creating the necessity of connecting the canals with the interior. Columbus could not wait for the canal; in 1826 John Kilbourn was promoting the Columbus and Sandusky Turnpike Company recently chartered by the legislature. Congress granted land, and sales and building went on simultaneously.[204] Rates on freight to Lake Erie were supposed to fall from $1.25 per hundred to 50 cents on its completion. Within a few years turnpike companies were being chartered by the

---

[199] *Piqua Gazette*, October 18, 1821.
[200] *Cleaveland Herald*, February 26, 1822.
[201] Right of way had been granted from the Firelands to the Maumee by treaty at Brownstown in 1808 with the Chippewa, Ottawa, Potawatomi, and other tribes.
[202] Columbus *Ohio State Journal*, February 15, 1827.
[203] *Cleveland Herald* in *Daily Chicago American*, May 13, 1839.
[204] *Ohio State Journal*, August 31, 1826, March 15, 1827, May 8, 1828. Congress granted an alternate section on each side of the road, for the half of its 105 miles which ran through United States lands, or about 32,000 acres. About $868 per mile was the estimated cost. Governor Trumbull's message, December, 1827. *Cincinnati Daily Gazette*, December 20, 1827.

dozen and stock was being sold on all sides.[205] Special state laws permitted counties to subscribe to stock in private turnpike companies; a law in 1836 authorized the governor to subscribe state funds to private turnpike company stock in an amount equal to private subscriptions. Improved roads were regarded by some citizens as even more important than politics. The *Cincinnati Gazette* thought that six miles of improved roads were more important than all the political conventions of the preceding six months.[206] If Cincinnati expected to share in the trade of eastern and northern parts of Indiana, all interested parties would have to get together behind promotion of turnpikes; of particular importance was the completion of a road to intersect the Michigan Road to Indianapolis. No longer could Cincinnati expect continued growth without effort.[207]

Indiana, too, was building roads. A network of Indian traces had covered the region, with focal points at the Wabash-Maumee portage (Fort Wayne) and White River at Fall Creek (Indianapolis).[208] The earliest road of importance was the Louisville-Vincennes road along the old "Buffalo Trace," which was in use in early Northwest Territory days and surveyed in 1805.[209] The survey for a road or trace from Cincinnati to Vincennes was begun in 1799 and probably finished in 1801–2. It was later described as running through Rising Sun, Madison, Salem, and French Lick, across both forks of White River, and on to Vincennes, a distance of 201 miles, and known as "Kibbey's Road."

Other roads or trails connected the leading settlements along

[205] Especially in the southwest part of the state. Among turnpike companies were the Hamilton, West Chester, and Sharonville; the Colerain, Oxford, and Brookville (1832); the Dayton, Centreville, and Lebanon; the Dayton and Springfield; the Dayton and Greenville; and the Dayton and Bellefontaine (1838). *Hamilton Intelligencer*, May, 1832, *passim; Liberty Hall and Cincinnati Gazette*, April 18, 1832; *Dayton Journal*, April 24, 1838; *Ohio State Journal and Register*, April 27, 1838. By 1838 the Ohio legislature had incorporated eighty such companies. W. D. Gallagher, "Ohio in 1838," in *The Hesperian*, I (1838), 8.
[206] *Liberty Hall and Cincinnati Gazette*, January 16, 1832.
[207] *Cincinnati Daily Gazette*, February 18, 1835.
[208] George S. Cottman, "The First Thoroughfares," in *Indiana Magazine of History*, III (1907), 13. Wilson, *Early Indiana Trails and Surveys*, is the best account of the Indian trails and first surveys.
[209] Also called the Kentucky Road, Vincennes Trace, Clarksville Trace, Harrison Road. The Buffalo Trace ran somewhat to the south of the modern Louisville–Vincennes road (U. S. 150). By 1816 there were two routes from the Falls to Vincennes, both of which used parts of the Buffalo Trace. For detailed description and maps of the trace, see George R. Wilson and Gayle Thornbrough, *The Buffalo Trace* (Indiana Historical Society Publications, XV, No. 2, Indianapolis, 1946).

the Whitewater, Ohio, and Wabash rivers. A road ran south
from Vincennes to the Ohio over the Red Banks Indian trail, and
north to Terre Haute; Governor Harrison blazed this trail on
to the Wabash in 1811. Military roads were built east and west
across the north and south Indian trails before and during the
War of 1812. In 1818 Jacob Whetzel blazed a trace westward
from the Whitewater (Franklin County) to the West Fork of
White River (Morgan County). The Three Notch Road followed the Indian trail from the Falls of the Ohio to the new
state capital in the wilderness; Berry's Trace, coming from the
settlements in southeastern Indiana, joined it on the East Fork
of White River.

The legislature in December, 1821, projected more than two
dozen roads, several of which were to lead to the new capital.[210]
One of these, from Vincennes to Indianapolis, was laid out two
years later by dragging a log with an ox team, through the
woods, prairies, and marshes.[211] One of the earliest wagon roads
out of Indianapolis was the road east to the Whitewater Valley,
which connected in Wayne County with the Cincinnati-Greenville
road. It was later superseded by the National Road. The road
from Indianapolis to Fort Wayne was also laid out; it followed
the Indian trail closely.[212] Another important road led from the
Falls (New Albany) by way of Salem, Bedford, and Bloomington, one branch going on north to the Wabash, and one northeast
to Indianapolis.

After Indianapolis was assured of a position on the National
Road, a north and south road was desired. The military importance of such a road was emphasized, besides it was thought

[210] An appropriation of $100,000 was made from the United States Three Per
Cent Fund, a state fund agent was appointed, and likewise a commission of three
to supervise the laying out and building of the roads. The undertakers (contractors) were allotted five-mile sections and allowed to take stone, timber, and
other materials from adjacent lands. The roads were to be cleared 48 feet wide,
timber under 18 inches in diameter to be cleared even with the ground, more than
18 inches to be cut off at the usual height of 12 inches. Appropriate milestones and
guide posts were to be erected. This act may be regarded as the foundation for the
first state highway system of Indiana. *Laws of Indiana*, 1821–22, Chapter 81. The
first report of the state agent and a map of the roads projected may be found in
Messages and Papers of Jennings, Boon, Hendricks, edited by Logan Esarey
(*Indiana Historical Collections*, XII, Indianapolis, 1924), 457–70.

[211] This road (Indiana 67) remained full of inexplicable turns for a number of
years after Indiana was covered with a network of paved automobile highways,
and was not thoroughly resurveyed and paved until 1939–40.

[212] Richmond *Public Leger*, October 22, 1825; Indianapolis *Indiana Journal*,
October 11, 1825.

that the project would expedite the removal of the Indians from the fertile lands north of the Wabash. During the treaty negotiations with the Miami and Potawatomi in 1826, the commissioners (Governor James B. Ray and John Tipton of Indiana, and Lewis Cass of Michigan) succeeded in obtaining land from the Potawatomi for such a road.[213]

The only mention of a road recorded in the treaty Journal was made by Governor Ray, who told the Indians: "We wish to make a road from Indianapolis, our great village, to Lake Michigan."[214] But article two of the treaty, in addition to other land cessions, provided that "as evidence of the attachment which the Potawatomi tribe feel toward the American people" they were giving up a strip one hundred feet wide from Lake Michigan to the Wabash, plus one section of good land for each mile of the proposed road.

Thus began Governor Ray's "Grand Project." "This grant severs the remaining Indian possessions; and when the land granted for this purpose is settled, it will weaken the attachment of the Potawattamie to his country."[215] (By 1838 the attachment of the Potawatomi was sufficiently weakened, and along this road John Tipton started them on the "Trail of Death" which led to the Indian country west of the Mississippi.)

Congress in 1827 gave Indiana the sole right to dispose of the land grant. Followed several years of legislative debate and surveys. Madison was finally agreed upon in 1830 as "the point" on the Ohio for the southern terminus. Two years later contracts were let for a road to be cleared 100 feet wide, 30 feet to be grubbed and graded. The interesting story of the construction and financing of this road, the biggest state project up to this time, cannot be related here. By the end of 1835 more than $200,000 had been spent, but land sales were more than adequate to cover this expenditure. The 265 miles from Madison by way of Greensburg, Indianapolis, and Logansport to South Bend were open by 1836 and usable eight months out of the year. After 1836 this road was merged into Indiana's general internal im-

[213] See map of Indian cessions, 111.

[214] The original of the treaty Journal is in the National Archives. It is printed in the *John Tipton Papers* (3 volumes. *Indiana Historical Collections*, XXIV, XXV, XXVI, Indianapolis, 1942), 576–92.

[215] Governor Ray's message, in *House Journal*, 1826–27, p. 52.

provements system; the road was never "finished" any more than any road is ever finished.[216]

In 1829 the road from Indianapolis to Crawfordsville, Williamsport, and "thence to the State line, in a direction to Chicago," was provided for by the legislature. A westward extension joined the Vincennes-Chicago road at Old Bunkum (Iroquois) and contributed heavily to Chicago traffic. As the northern part of the state settled in the late 1820's and early 1830's, roads were extended along the Wabash from Terre Haute to Fort Wayne; from Fort Wayne several roads fanned out toward southern Michigan, and a road from Lafayette crossed the Kankakee swamps to intercept the Chicago-Detroit road at La Porte. The first really improved roads did not come until the state started its internal improvements program, 1835–36.[217]

Illinois in territorial days had but few main road lines. An old road ran from Fort Massac on the Ohio westward to Kaskaskia and on up the Mississippi to St. Louis; another, the Goshen Road, from Shawneetown northwest to Carlyle, Edwardsville, and Alton. The Vincennes-St. Louis road ran east and west and coincided with the Goshen road for a few miles west of Carlyle. About midway across the state a branch led from it southwest to Kaskaskia. Other roads led from Kaskaskia by way of Belleville to Edwardsville, and from Shawneetown north to Carmi and Albion. In 1816 Congress authorized the construction of a road from Shawneetown to Kaskaskia; two years later contracts were let for building, "the road to be cut thirty-three feet wide and all timber taken off, the stumps to be very low." The Vincennes-St. Louis road lay beyond the settled regions in 1815 and was merely a prairie trace, without houses to accommodate the traveler. It was used more by 1818, however, and stopping places began to appear.

In addition to these main roads, by 1818 "most of the settlements [were] connected by practicable roads, at least for packers and travellers on horse back."[218] From Vincennes an old Indian trail led northwest through the Vermilion Salt Springs (Danville) and on toward Lake Michigan. Other trails from the

---

[216] The only adequate history of the Michigan Road is by Geneal Prather, MS. thesis, Indiana University, 1941.
[217] See Chapter XII.
[218] Samuel R. Brown, *Western Gazetteer* (1817), 28.

Upper Wabash Wea towns joined this trace. In 1825 Gurdon S. Hubbard, American Fur Company superintendent of the Illinois River trade, ceased to depend upon uncertain water travel and began to use pack ponies. Trading posts were established along the trail from Chicago to the mouth of the Wabash, and this route became known as Hubbard's Trace; it was also known as the Vincennes Trace or State Road. State Street, Chicago, preserves its memory. Indiana traffic from the Indianapolis-Crawfordsville-Williamsport road joined the State Road at Bunkum (Iroquois), Illinois, or else came in by way of the Lebanon-Lafayette road. In the 1830's this road was filled with emigrant wagons, produce, and cattle on the way to Chicago. The road was notoriously bad.[219]

The legislature of 1823 "laid out" a dozen roads, among them roads radiating from Vandalia to Shawneetown, Kaskaskia, Alton, Palestine, and other points. Nineteen hundred dollars was appropriated, and when the roads, which were to be four rods wide, were marked out, the county commissioners were to cut, work, and maintain them.[220] Two years later three more roads were "laid out" and a turnpike company incorporated. County districting and supervisors were provided for, and road work of two days or its equivalent was required of men between twenty-one and fifty years of age. In 1833 the roads from Alton to Beardstown, and Alton to Springfield were approved, the Springfield-Beardstown road was surveyed, and a survey begun of a road from Grafton on the Mississippi to Springfield, Bloomington, Ottawa, and Chicago.[221]

In 1831 Cook County began development of the upper end of the Potawatomi Trace which ran along the high prairie path from Chicago southwest towards Ottawa on the Illinois; three

[219] Elmore Barce, "The Old Chicago Trail, and the Old Chicago Road," in *Indiana Magazine of History,* XV (1919), 9–10; *Chicago Democrat,* June 18, 1834.

[220] Vandalia *Illinois Intelligencer,* March 1, 1823. The roads were: Vandalia to Shawneetown; Vandalia to Kaskaskia; Vandalia to Covington, Brownsville, Jonesborough and America; Vandalia to Golconda via Mt. Vernon and Frankfort; Vandalia to Palestine; Vandalia to Alton; Vandalia to Illinois on the Mississippi; a road to intercept the St. Louis-Vincennes road at the Little Wabash; a road from Fairfield to intercept this road at any point on its way to Vandalia; a road from Fairfield via Albion to the west bank of the Wabash opposite Harmony; a road from Fairfield to Carmi; and a road from John M'Callas' dwelling to the Wabash opposite Vincennes.

[221] Springfield *Sangamo Journal,* January 26, May 18, 1833.

years later stagecoach service was projected to St. Louis. Other roads to Ottawa ran by way of Naperville and the Fox River Valley, and by the Des Plaines and Illinois River valleys through Joliet. Steamboats were supposed to be able to make Ottawa, but river navigation was not to be relied upon, and a road soon paralleled the river from Peoria to Joliet, to connect at Peoria with roads from Springfield and Decatur. In 1825 Oliver W. Kellogg blazed a trail from Peoria to Galena and an alternate path was opened by John Boles the next year. From Peoria another road was opened along the west side of the Illinois River to Quincy. A wagonload of lead was driven from Galena to Chicago in 1829, but not until after 1832 when General Scott went from Chicago to Naperville, Dixon's Ferry on the Rock River, and thence by Kellogg's Trail to Galena, was a road developed. (His army followed a more northern route by way of Beloit and Rock River.) In 1836 the state provided for a northern road by way of Elgin on Fox River, Midway (Rockford), and on to Galena. In the absence of ferry or bridge across the Fox at Elgin, travelers scrambled across as best they could until 1837; a ferry was maintained across the Rock River, however. Mail went through as far as Rockford by stage on January 1, 1838.

The only road (trail) into Michigan Territory at the end of the War of 1812 was that used by General Hull in 1812. In 1818 Congress, for military reasons largely, began to improve this trail around the end of Lake Erie to the falls of the Miami (Maumee) where it would connect with the trace across the Black Swamp and to Sandusky and Cleveland. The same year a wagon and team got through to Detroit from Pontiac in three days. The survey of this road into the interior was completed on to Saginaw in 1823 and stages ran on it for a while three years later.[222] Governor Lewis Cass inspected the Indian trail toward Chicago in 1820, and in his report did his best to advertise the country. The Saginaw treaty of 1819 opened new lands into which a road was necessary before they would sell.

By the Chicago treaty of 1821 with the Chippewa, Ottawa, and Potawatomi the United States acquired the right to build a road through the Indian country from both Detroit and Fort

---

[222] *Detroit Gazette,* January 17, 1823; August 15, 1826.

Wayne to Chicago. Father Gabriel Richard, territorial delegate to Congress, got $3,000 appropriated for the Detroit to Chicago survey. Much more was used, however, before the 263 miles were completed in 1832. Since a straight-line route necessitated cutting of much timber, the surveyors took the path of least resistance and followed the sinuous path of the Great Sauk Trail south and west through (or by) the later settled towns of Ypsilanti, Jonesville, Coldwater, Bertrand (just south of Niles), and thence into Indiana and around the southern end of Lake Michigan. Little was done toward construction until 1830 and then the Black Hawk trouble and the cholera caused delay.[223] By 1831 dirt and logs made a fairly solid road to Ypsilanti, and stages could get through as far as Tecumseh. Beyond lay merely a wagon track or trail, but coaches got through to Niles in 1832, and from Niles to Chicago in the next year.[224] This road was, in a way, an extension of the Erie Canal route, and together with the St. Joseph's Road (Territorial Road), which ran west to the Kalamazoo Valley and south to the St. Joseph (authorized by the territorial government in 1829, and opened about five years later), played a very important part in the settlement of southern Michigan.[225]

In 1830 no overland road connected the western side of Lake Michigan with the Mississippi. In 1829 James Duane Doty, a companion, and a guide left Green Bay, plunged into unsettled expanses, and emerged at Prairie du Chien. This journey marked a route which later became the Military Road. The same year petitions were sent from Green Bay to Congress for a road from Green Bay to Chicago. Congress recognized the need for these roads and in 1830 appropriated money for surveys. The surveys were made during the next two years. The road to connect Forts Howard (Green Bay), Winnebago (Portage), and Crawford (Prairie du Chien), was regarded as of particular importance for military purposes. From Green Bay it ran along the east side of the Fox River and Lake Winnebago, headed southwest to the portage, followed along the south side of the Wisconsin for about

---

[223] In discussing the need for the improvement in 1827, Senator Smith, of Maryland, thought there was some danger of trees growing up in it, if built, as it would not be used. *Detroit Gazette,* February 13, 1827.

[224] Carl E. Pray, "An Historic Michigan Road," in *Michigan History Magazine,* XI (1927), 335.

[225] See Chapter X for development of settlement and roads in Michigan and Wisconsin territories.

half the remaining distance (to the later Helena), turned south to Dodgeville, then ran due west and crossed the Wisconsin about a half-dozen miles from its mouth at Prairie du Chien.[226] By 1837 a road forked off some 15 miles above Fort Winnebago, ran up the west side of Lake Winnebago and the Fox River, and recrossed the Fox a few miles from Green Bay.

Lewis Cass, now secretary of war, ordered construction started on the Military Road by the troops in 1835.[227] The road was soon open from the Mississippi to Lake Winnebago,[228] but the dense forests delayed the completion of the eastern half until 1838. On the prairies mile stakes were set; in the woods a path two rods wide was cleared. Rough corduroy construction made the swampy places passable, and crude bridges spanned the streams.[229] The road was usable in winter and summer months.

Congress in 1832 provided for establishment of the post road from Chicago to Green Bay, but in 1835 the road was still little more than an Indian trail.[230] North from Milwaukee it followed the lake shore to the mouth of the Sheboygan, then bore north-west to the Manitowoc Rapids (about a dozen miles inland), then due north to Green Bay. An alternative trail forked off northwest of the mouth of the Sheboygan and crossed the Mani-towoc about two miles from its mouth. Stage service (a lumber wagon drawn by horses) to Milwaukee began in 1836; in 1839 the stage required forty hours to make the one hundred miles. Further appropriations were made by Congress in 1838, but be-yond Milwaukee, through unsettled country, it was necessary to carry the mail on foot. Five days were required to get the mail over the 160 miles between Green Bay and the Illinois line. The other route to Green Bay, from Milwaukee to Fond du Lac and on the Military Road the rest of the way, remained a primitive trail until 1831. Unlike the Detroit-Chicago road or the Vin-cennes road, the Green Bay road was not an avenue of heavy emigrant or freight traffic. It was too close to the lake, which

---

[226] Map in H. E. Cole, "The Old Military Road," in *Wisconsin Magazine of History,* IX (1925–26), 49. Hinman and Dutton, *Map of Wisconsin Territory* (Philadelphia, 1838).

[227] *Green-Bay Intelligencer,* July 13, 1835.

[228] *Ibid.,* July 23, 1835.

[229] Cole, "The Old Military Road," 50.

[230] The *Green-Bay Intelligencer,* April 9, 1835, thought this road, along with the $17,000 appropriation, was apparently "smothered in the safe of some public functionary."

offered easier communication, and was used largely by local traffic and necessary through travel from Chicago to Green Bay.

The Michigan territorial government provided for a road from Milwaukee to the Mississippi by way of Platte Mounds in 1834, and the next year for roads from Blue Mounds to the Illinois boundary in the direction of Chicago, and from Milwaukee to Lake Winnebago.[231] Local roads connected Prairie du Chien, Dodgeville, Mineral Point, and other settlements with Madison City, Galena, and Chicago in the 1830's. Maps of this period show no roads in the southeast corner of later Wisconsin, that is, between Madison, Milwaukee, and Chicago, since this region was not open to land entry until 1836. A party of thirty workmen in ten days cut through a trail from Milwaukee to Madison, the new Wisconsin territorial capital, in 1837. The early military roads were of minor importance in the development of what was to become Wisconsin, and not until 1838–40, with Congressional aid, were roads developed out of Southport (Kenosha), Racine, and Milwaukee.[232] Local road work was practically nonexistent. The *Miners' Free Press* in 1837 stated that not a county on the west side of the Territory had assessed and received a day's work on the roads.[233]

To speak of roads as being "provided for" or "laid out" conveys no idea of the means for travel and transportation available to the people in the early days. A road in a statute book or on a map was one thing; the actual road might be anything from a morass to a passable affair. The best of the roads, with one or two exceptions, were about equal to the outlying unsurfaced country roads of southern Indiana or Illinois of today. From 1815 to 1840, and later, the story was the same, even on the oldest and most traveled roads. In 1841 an English traveler was somewhat surprised when on one of the state roads in Illinois over which the mail stage was routed he found that a settler had obtained clay for his house chimney by digging a big hole in the middle of the road. This he admitted to be unusual on a state road, but almost anything could be expected on the lesser roads, up to and including building fences across them. "In some places,

---

[231] *Ibid.*
[232] J. H. A. Lacher, "The Taverns and Stages of Early Wisconsin," in *Wisconsin State Historical Society Proceedings,* 1914, p. 132.
[233] Mineral Point (Wis.) *Miners' Free Press,* July 21, 1837.

where the country is getting peopled up, the roads are flung about from one farm to another, in a manner perfectly vexatious and perplexing."[234]

In eastern Ohio in 1814 the roads were described as intolerable, shocking, wretched, and devilish. Horses expired on them, axles and wheels snapped, and coaches of Kentucky nabobs upset.[235] Fearon said Zane's road had ruts worn deep enough to bury a horse in; people could not settle in the rich region around Columbus because they could not get in.[236] Produce could not get into Cincinnati in the early part of 1823 because the roads had been almost impassable for months.[237] The same situation existed at Columbus in 1828, and mails came through on horseback until April, when stages again ran.[238] Ordinary delay in mails was to be expected, said the editor of the *Cleaveland Herald,* but he did think six to eight days sufficient to cover the 150 miles from Columbus.[239] Five years later, a family moving from Dayton into southern Michigan, started with two wagons—two yoke of oxen hitched to one, a team and a yoke to the other. It took twenty-one days to make the 234 miles; some days only three miles were made. The horses wore out, and more oxen were purchased. At the bad places all eight oxen were hitched to one wagon at a time.[240]

Probably no road in the country received more Irish blessings than the Black Swamp road between Sandusky and the Maumee. The mild winter of 1837–38 saw tons of mail accumulate at each end. It took one to two weeks for Detroit papers to reach Cleveland, and Michigan was practically cut off from the East.[241] It was said that a team of horses drowned in a mudhole, the bottom of which had fallen out. Of this road, as well as others, the story was told that one of a party found a beaver hat in the road, but when at risk of his life he waded out to it, he found a man under it and called for help. Whereupon the man under the hat pro-

[234] Oliver, *Eight Months in Illinois,* 195.

[235] *Zanesville Express and Republican Standard,* November 28, 1816.

[236] Fearon, *Sketches of America,* 234; Columbus *Ohio Monitor,* November 28, 1816. The *Monitor* was constantly discussing the lack of roads.

[237] *Liberty Hall and Cincinnati Gazette,* January 24, March 14, 1823.

[238] *Cincinnati Daily Gazette,* January 8, 1828; *Ohio State Journal,* April 10, 1828.

[239] *Cleaveland Herald,* February 1, 1828.

[240] A. B. Copley, "Sturdy Pioneers of Van Buren and Cass," in *Michigan Pioneer and Historical Collections,* XXXVIII (1912), 639.

[241] *Cleveland Herald and Gazette,* February 2, 1838.

tested, "Just leave me alone, stranger, I have a good horse under me, and have just found bottom."[242] Inhabitants along this road were accused of having a proprietary interest in the various mudholes; the right to pull out travelers at a price was mutually recognized as belonging to the nearest proprietor. It was said that in dry seasons some fostered their mudholes carefully; one tavern keeper, on selling out, offered his interest in a particularly profitable mudhole and actually found a buyer.

Speaking of the Detroit-Chicago road the *Advertiser* said, "The road from this place to Ypsilanti looks at certain times as if it had been the route of a retreating army, so great is the number of wrecks of different kinds which it exhibits."[243] In 1837 the stages left Detroit at 8 A. M. and arrived at Ypsilanti, thirty miles, at 2 A. M. The passengers had walked nearly one third of the way and helped the coach. Miss Martineau decided that Juggernaut's car would not have survived on such a road. Farther west "It was pleasant to stand on some dry perch, and watch my companions through the holes and pools that I had passed. Such hopping and jumping; such slipping and sliding; such looks of despair from the middle of a pond; such shifting of logs, and carrying of planks, and handing along the fallen trunks of trees."[244]

On the road from Toledo to Jackson County, Michigan, by way of Dundee and Tecumseh, travelers had to pay tribute to the proprietors of mudholes, whose ox yokes stood ready, for a consideration, to help the unfortunates out.[245] In 1829, John Biddle, newly elected Michigan territorial delegate to Congress, in order to reach Washington in early winter, was said to have taken a Canadian pony, cut across by way of the Chicago Trail to the southern end of Lake Michigan, followed the Indian trails to the Wabash, and reached the capital in thirty days.[246]

In Indiana the road north from the Ohio toward Bloomington was described as follows: "Travelling by land becomes of course, travelling by water, or by both; viz., mud and water. Nor is it

[242] Also told of the swamp on the Detroit-Pontiac Road (*Michigan Pioneer and Historical Collections*, VI [1884], 16), and of streets in various western cities.
[243] *Detroit Daily Advertiser*, December 24, 1836.
[244] *Society in America*, I, 239.
[245] Joseph M. Griswold, "Some Reminiscences of Early Times in Brooklyn, Jackson County, Michigan," in *Michigan Pioneer and Historical Collections*, XXVI (1894-95), 256.
[246] Col. Henry Raymond, "Fifty Years Ago," in *ibid.*, IV (1881), 100.

possible if one would avoid drowning or suffocation to keep the law and follow the blazed road; but he tacks first to the right and then to the left, often making both losing tacks; and all this, not to find a road but a place where there is no road . . . so we did enter souse into the most ill-looking, dark coloured morasses, enlivened by streams of purer mud crossing at right angles, and usually much deeper than we cared to discover."[247] The Indianapolis *Indiana Journal* suspended publication for two weeks in early winter, 1825, because of delay in getting paper through from Cincinnati.[248] Even such a well traveled road as the Louisville-Vincennes road was impassable for loaded vehicles in spring when the surface broke through,[249] while the National Road as late as 1838 was in a state of dilapidation in eastern Ohio. Between Columbus and Zanesville it was so cut up that it was doubted whether it would be usable after another winter.[250] In 1835 a traveler passing through Indiana "got on to the National Road, then building, but the late rains & immence travell made the road intolerable. Some times we were obliged to take the woods to escape the mud, & even there travellers often got stuck fast."[251] It was considered by some about as passable (by boats) as the Wabash Canal. City streets were no better. Chicago mudholes were such as to require extra teams to pull out coaches or wagons.

Most of these roads were at best only cleared and partially graded paths, and at worst mere traces made "by one man on horseback following in the track of another, every rider making the way a little easier to find, until you came to some slush, or swampy place, where all trace was lost, and you got through as others had done, by guessing at the direction, after riding at hazard for miles until you stumbled on the track again."[252]

Although the improvements in road engineering which resulted from the work of McAdam and others were known by 1825, and

[247] Hall, *The New Purchase*, 50.

[248] Such notices were very common among papers throughout this period.

[249] In 1828 a traveler coming from St. Louis to Vincennes said that the stretch of road between the Embarrass and the Wabash bore the name of Purgatory. "The road from Vincennes to Louisville is even worse than what preceded it." Mrs. Basil Hall, *The Aristocratic Journey* (New York, 1931), 283. Coaches as late as the 1850's sometimes used the front axle only in order to get through with the mail.

[250] *Cincinnati Daily Gazette*, July 16, 1838.

[251] Alfred Brunson, "A Methodist Circuit Rider's Horseback Tour from Pennsylvania to Wisconsin, 1835," in *Wisconsin Historical Collections*, XV (1900), 271.

[252] Flower, *English Settlement in Edwards County, Illinois*, 120.

road-building materials were commonly available, the task of constructing good roads was too great for the financial resources and politicians of the new states. In Indiana, for instance, there was apparently no important road improved with either stone or gravel prior to 1832.[253] The original contract specifications for the National Road in Indiana called for maximum grades of 4 per cent and grubbing and removal of all stumps in the thirty-foot center, but these proved far too expensive to carry out. Modifications were soon made; in Indiana and Ohio only trees of less than 1 foot in diameter were to be cut level with the surface, those up to 18 inches might be left with 9-inch stumps, and those over 18 inches with 15-inch stumps. "All stumps within the said centre of thirty feet must be rounded and trimmed in such a manner as to present no serious obstructions to carriages."[254] In the remaining 50 feet all stumps were to be no higher than 18 inches. Later instructions called for grubbing out the stumps in the center path, but the holes left were practically impassable. It was said that there were stage drivers expert enough to tell, even on a dark night, whether or not they had strayed from the center path. Ninety per cent of the 150 miles of the road through Indiana was through timber.[255] Since the grubbing and grading was carried on intermittently whenever appropriations were available, despite the abundance of dirt, gravel, stone, and timber along the way, the work had to be done over and over, and at no time was the road in good condition. The engineers' reports of 1838 and 1839 indicated that the construction was poor, the bridges weak, the road badly washed and in need of regrading before stone surfacing would do any good.

Common practice on roads in the timber sections was to lay logs crosswise in the low or swampy stretches, but corduroy roads were never satisfactory. In the thin-soiled areas, such as southern Indiana, roads frequently followed the stream bottoms, where vehicles took the ledges, loose rock, and occasional water holes much as they did the stumps on other roads. Streams were always problems when not fordable. Ferries, and sometimes bridges, were private enterprises, usually subject to local regulation. Prim-

---

[253] Indiana *Geological Report*, 1905, p. 24.
[254] Vincennes *Western Sun and General Advertiser*, September 12, 1829.
[255] Commissioner Jonathan Knight to Senator William Hendricks, February 4, 1830, in Indianapolis *Indiana Journal*, April 14, 1830.

itive bridges of various types were thrown together. Some were
"shaking bridges," others were bridges of planks laid loose on
stringers which floated on the water. Unless the planks were replaced after each passage, there was no bridge for the next comer.
On the more important roads bridges were, of course, more substantial. Since fine craftsmanship in stone masonry and woodworking was available, the art of bridge building was on the
whole far in advance of that of road building.[256] Some of the all-
wood bridges, trussed and braced in keeping with modern engineering principles, were not only pleasing in design, but remained
serviceable into the day of the automobile and paved highway.[257]

Roads made possible vehicular travel, mail, and wagon transportation, but horseback travel and pack-horse transportation
were only gradually supplanted. Cleveland had stage service to
Painesville in 1818;[258] six years later semiweekly stages ran to
Pittsburgh and every other day to Buffalo.[259] Steubenville was
connected with Pittsburgh in 1820. The same year a stage line
was established between Vincennes and Louisville, the first in
Indiana.[260] Three years later the *Louisville Morning Post* was
agitating for through mail-stage service to St. Louis by way of
Vincennes.[261] This was begun the following spring. Passenger
fare for the three hundred miles was $21.[262] This was not the
first stage in Illinois, however, for in 1819 a stage with accommodations for four passengers, fare $4.00, was operating be-
tween Kaskaskia and St. Louis.[263]

Michigan's first public stage was run from Detroit to Mt.
Clemens—weekly, just after the boat arrived—in 1822.[264] In
1825–26 the stage to Upper Sandusky ran all winter, disregard-
ing the thaws and bad roads; in the spring a new four-horse

---

[256] Of the $1,136,600 allotted by Congress to building the National Road in In-
diana, $513,099 was spent for bridges and masonry. Indiana *Geological Report,*
1905, p. 35.
[257] The National Road bridge over the Whitewater at Richmond erected in 1835
was of sawed oak timber on stone abutments. Bolts were forged in the blacksmith
shop at the bridge. It stood the weather, floods, and traffic for eighty years.
[258] *Cleaveland Gazette,* August 11, 1818.
[259] *Cleaveland Herald,* December 10, 1824.
[260] Vincennes *Indiana Centinel,* April 15, 1820. The stage left Vincennes at
6 A. M. Wednesdays and made the 126 miles to Louisville by 1 P. M. Fridays.
[261] *Western Sun and General Advertiser,* November 8, 1823.
[262] *Ibid.,* May 1, 22, 1824.
[263] Kaskaskia *Illinois Intelligencer,* January 20, 1819.
[264] *Detroit Gazette,* May 31, 1822.

stage began trips to Pontiac, and another line operated to Ann Arbor.[265] Six years later coaches were getting through on the Chicago Road (and the Niles–St. Joseph extension) to St. Joseph. By 1828 those who dreaded the trip across Lake Erie could go by "safe, cheap and comfortable conveyance," all the way to Buffalo for $11.[266]

Columbus in 1825 claimed that no other town in the western country had the advantage of so many stage routes. Weekly stages ran to Portland; semiweekly to Zanesville, to Delaware, and to Cincinnati by way of Springfield, Dayton, and Hamilton. Stages to Chillicothe ran three times a week.[267] Two years later there were thirty-two arrivals and departures weekly of the eight stages, plus six horse mails. The Cincinnati-Columbus-Portland stage became a daily and the fare was reduced to $12.[268] When daily stages between Cincinnati and Cleveland, which were started in 1830, made the trip in four days, people began to look back upon the hard old days when one got a good horse, a carbine, a brace of pistols, and hoped to get through in a week or two.[269] The "northern mail" from Buffalo began to arrive daily in Cleveland in 1832,[270] and in Detroit in 1834.[271]

Mail stages ran regularly, at least summer and autumn, between Indianapolis, Lawrenceburg, and Madison in 1830;[272] four years later the fast mail coach enabled the traveler to go from Indianapolis to Madison in one day, sleep on the Ohio packet, and breakfast in Cincinnati the following morning.[273] In 1835 a new four-horse stage line was in use from Leavenworth on the Ohio by way of Milltown, Paoli, Bedford, Bloomington, and Martinsville, to Indianapolis.[274] Springfield, Illinois, in 1834 began to be served by a new four-horse stage line which connected it with St. Louis, Terre Haute, Vandalia, and Peoria. Stages ran once or twice a week. The 130 miles to St. Louis were covered in two days, the fare being $6.50; the 156 miles to Terre

[265] Ibid., March 28, April 4, 1826.
[266] Ibid., August 28, 1828.
[267] Columbus (Ohio) Gazette, June 30, 1825.
[268] Ohio State Journal, May 31, June 26, 1827.
[269] Cleaveland Herald, June 24, 1830.
[270] Ibid., January 5, 1832.
[271] Detroit Journal and Michigan Advertiser (semiweekly), June 17, 1834.
[272] Indianapolis Indiana Journal, November 3, 1830.
[273] Ibid. (semiweekly), May 31, 1834.
[274] Ibid., May 15, 1835.

Haute required three days, fare $8.00. About the same time more or less regular stages were running from Peoria to Galena (three days; fare $10), Peoria to Ottawa, Ottawa to Chicago; also in the lead-mining region between Galena and Mineral Point, and from Galena to Chicago.[275] Stages ran daily from Peoria to Springfield in 1838 and triweekly to Galena, Ottawa, and Rushville. Green Bay and Chicago were getting occasional stage service in 1836, this being one instance at least in which the stage was ahead of the road.[276]

By the late 1830's all of the Northwest, excepting Wisconsin Territory and northern Michigan, was covered with a network of stage lines, while over established routes in the more thickly settled parts there were frequently competing lines. From Cincinnati, for example, in 1838, one might take a choice of two daily lines for Columbus, Wheeling, Cleveland, or Sandusky; take a stage daily for Dayton, Springfield, Piqua, Lawrenceburg, Indianapolis, Terre Haute, Lafayette, and Springfield, Illinois; to Hamilton and Oxford; and to Georgetown and Lexington, Kentucky. Thrice a week he could have service to Chillicothe, Lancaster, and Zanesville, to Burlington and Lawrenceburg, to Batavia and West Union, and to Lebanon. To Franklin and Monroe the stage ran weekly.[277] Fares were being reduced. Cincinnati to Columbus was $5.00, Columbus to Wheeling the same, while intermediate hauls were made at the rate of five cents per mile.[278]

Although stages took over the mails on the main roads, much of the mail was handled on horseback, some even on foot.[279] Quite an expansion in the number of post roads (mail routes) took place after the law of 1814[280] which provided that mail service be arranged from the nearest post office on any post road, to any courthouse established or to be established. Many of these new mail lines were in outlying regions. The advertisements

---

[275] Lacher, "Taverns and Stages of Early Wisconsin," in *Wisconsin State Historical Society Proceedings*, 1914, p. 133; *Chicago Democrat*, February 25, 1834.

[276] Harry E. Cole, *Stagecoach and Tavern Tales of the Old Northwest* (Cleveland, 1930), 53.

[277] *Cincinnati Daily Gazette*, August 25, 1838.

[278] *Ohio State Journal* (daily), July 17, 1837.

[279] The establishment of post roads (mail lines) can be followed in the *Annals of Congress*. A chronological map of post roads from earliest territorial days would furnish a very accurate picture of the progress of settlement in the Northwest.

[280] U. S. *Statutes at Large*, III, 130–33.

for mail contracts in Ohio in 1823 consisted of hundreds of items and filled an entire five-column page.[281] A majority of the routes were traveled on horseback. As late as 1834, the postmaster general's report stated that "half of the intelligence of the country is still carried in saddle bags," and the proportion in the Northwest was probably higher.

Detroit got mail from the East once a week in 1823, by way of the Black Swamp road. Eastern papers were frequently six weeks on the road, as they were held up when the mails were heavy to equalize the pony load.[282] The mail which was supposed to arrive at 10 A. M. was usually late, and was closed to outgoing mail the same evening. Unless handled promptly, replies had to wait a week. The following year semiweekly service was begun, and in 1826 Sandusky was boasting of thrice-a-week service.[283] By 1834 Detroit had not only daily eastern mail, but also to and from Chicago, while mail came from the South three times per week.

Towns such as Shawneetown and Vandalia did well to get mail from the cardinal points once per week by 1825–26.[284] Semiweekly coach mail service between Chicago and St. Louis was announced for 1834.[285] By this time Springfield had semiweekly mails to and from St. Louis, Vandalia, Peoria, and Edwardsville, and weekly mail to and from Terre Haute, Monmouth, and Quincy.[286] Three years later the 112 mail contracts in Illinois required seven columns of newspaper space to list.[287]

Mail routes, however, were like the roads: they existed but did not always function; complaints of failure of the mails are almost as common in the newspapers as patent-medicine advertisements. Since so many of the newspapers depended upon their "exchanges," failure of the mails frequently resulted in issue of a small-sized sheet or a mere skeleton paper. "Our exchanges failed to arrive," was sufficient excuse for the editor. Hamilton, Ohio, in 1825 claimed it took eastern papers 11 to 12 days to

[281] *Western Herald and Steubenville Gazette,* July 26, 1823.
[282] *Detroit Gazette,* February 14, 1823.
[283] *Ibid.,* December 17, 1824, February 7, 1826.
[284] *Illinois Intelligencer,* March 1, 1823, January 9, 1824, September 9, 1825; Shawneetown *Illinois Gazette,* February 18, 1826.
[285] *Sangamo Journal,* December 14, 1833.
[286] *Ibid.,* January 11, 1834.
[287] Vandalia *Illinois State Register and People's Advocate,* July 22, 1837.

arrive, whereas formerly they got through in 8 or 9.[288] Corydon, Indiana, subscribers protested it took more than a week to get their Indianapolis papers, when they should have got through in 5 or 6 days.[289] Vandalia papers were 11 days reaching Edwardsville in 1832, and letters were 30 days traveling 150 miles. Eastern papers were held up for weeks at Vincennes. The *Illinois Advocate* was reprimanded by the mail contractor for stating that foot travelers actually passed the mail.[290] New York papers got through to Chicago in 1835 in "the amazing time of 62 days."[291] Chicago letters and papers reached Springfield in 7 to 10 days, whereas passengers made it in 3 days.[292] Detroit papers reached Green Bay by way of Chicago in 11 days in 1835, but frequently they were routed by way of Galena and then came through in 26 days.[293] After listing mails which arrived weeks late, the *Wisconsin Territorial Gazette* (Burlington) found that the mail rider threw overboard the mail when it was too hot, too cold, or used his judgment about what to carry. "There is a point beyond which endurance is contemptible and cowardly."[294] Especially when Congress was in session did people protest when

---

[288] *Hamilton Advertiser,* December 27, 1825.

[289] *Indiana Journal,* May 31, 1825.

[290] Edwardsville *Illinois Advocate,* April 6, 1832. A few months earlier the *Advocate* wrote: "People living at a distance will be astonished to learn with what rapidity travelers are whirled over our prairies. For instance—a gentleman in St. Louis wishes to go to Vandalia to pay his taxes (distance sixty-four miles), he steps into the Mail Stage, and is set down in Vandalia, in little less than two days. . . . Thus we go on improving, and there are many persons *now* living, who are sanguine enough to think, that the time will yet arrive, when Mail Stages will travel from St. Louis to Vandalia in one day . . . but we confess we are not of that number, unless greater improvements are made than any yet seen in this state." November 4, 1831.

This description of the "rapidity of the lesser mails" was supplemented, July 20, 1833, by the account of the speedy coach: "It appears . . . that the celebrated Snail still continues to transport the mail from Belleville to St. Charles by way of Edwardsville and Alton at the rate of between three and four miles an hour, over one of the best roads in the State. This is quite an improvement. Last year you might get *twelve* hours ride (24 miles) between Edwardsville and Belleville, for a dollar—you now get but little more than half of that time for the same money. This is the same stage, about which so much noise was made last year, in consequence of its taking fire from the rapidity of its motion and burning out a part of one of the wheels by which she was so disabled as to occasion its being laid up awhile for repairs—since which it is understood they have reduced its speed. We hope our friend of the Ridge Prairie will give us an account of her motions from time to time."

[291] *Chicago American,* November 21, 1835.

[292] *Sangamo Journal,* July 29, 1837.

[293] *Green-Bay Intelligencer,* June 13, 1835.

[294] September 14, 1837.

papers failed to arrive, as one miss put them two weeks behind.[295] "It has been asserted that nothing is so uncertain as the female —except the mail. . . ."[296]

Part of the difficulty was no doubt the result of the practice of carrying newspapers outside the mail. This practice was apparently permissible by postal regulations if stipulated in the carrier's contract, in which case it was regarded as part of the pay.[297] When in 1827 the postmaster general ruled that a quarter of a year's postage should be paid to the postmaster in advance, some postmasters held up the papers and confusion resulted. Others winked at the "outside carrying" and let the papers through, even though not in the carrier's contract. In the late 1830's the *Cleveland Herald* often ran a column headed "In Advance of the Mail." It got the eastern papers directly from boat passengers—smart journalism for the time.[298]

During the Jackson period opposition newspapers complained constantly of the mails, and said that the Democratic papers usually got their exchanges on time.[299] That all such complaints were not political is indicated by the number of Democratic papers which also stated their grievances. The *Chicago Democrat* said that Amos Kendall's penuriousness might make a good showing to Congress, "but it is a mighty incubus to the administration in the West."[300] Protests against carrying mails on the Sabbath abounded in the period about 1830, but most of it emanated from the religious press and had little effect.

Mail between Green Bay and Chicago—240 miles—was still carried on foot during the 1830's. The carrier, accompanied by an Indian guide, set out with sixty pounds of mail, two sacks of parched corn, and blankets, depending upon the Indians for food. One night's rest in Chicago and he began the return trip. The round trip took a month; the pay was $60 to $65.[301] This service

---

[295] Indianapolis *Indiana Journal*, January 3, 1828. Most of the papers subscribed to by distant residents were weeklies.

[296] *Western Monthly Magazine*, V (1836), 219.

[297] *Scioto Gazette* in Portsmouth *Western Times*, March 8, 1827.

[298] *Cleveland Herald and Gazette* (weekly), July 19, 1838.

[299] Such protests were regular items in the *Ohio State Journal, Liberty Hall and Cincinnati Gazette, Indiana Journal*, and other important Whig papers, 1829–33.

[300] September 26, 1838. The *Democrat, Alton Spectator*, and *Wisconsin Territorial Gazette* were outspoken Democratic papers.

[301] "Narrative of Alexis Clermont," in *Wisconsin Historical Collections*, XV (1900), 452–57.

was discontinued in 1834 but was soon restored.[302] November and December, 1838, issues of the *Green Bay Democrat* reached Cleveland by the middle of February. The editor of that paper had received some news of the Wisconsin territorial legislature meeting at Burlington, by way of the Washington *Globe,* in sixty days.[303] While such service existed in the outlying regions, stages had brought through President Jackson's message in 1829 with "unparalleled expedition." The message, delivered Tuesday noon, reached Columbus Wednesday at 11 P. M.—420 miles over bad roads.[304] Of course this was showmanship, not regular schedule, but in 1833 the regular mail which left Washington at 7 P. M. arrived at Wheeling in the early morning of the second day following (fifty-five hours), at Columbus the next morning, and at Cincinnati the morning following.[305] From Portsmouth to Sandusky the schedule was three days. Other regular stage routes averaged about the same time in good weather, and this speed was not materially bettered until the railroad took over the mails.

In 1837 express mail service was begun on horseback on the National Road. It was to handle newspaper slips, public dispatches, stock quotations, and private letters, at triple postage rates. Riders were expected to average ten to twelve miles per hour, day and night, and thus cut the stage mail schedule in half. Some Whig papers were not favorable to this latest improvement of Amos Kendall, postmaster general under Jackson and Van Buren. The *Richmond Palladium* said that as a producing rather than a speculative community, people would be satisfied to receive the eastern papers and letters in five or six days, and that the extra expense should be borne by those who benefited.[306] From 1825 to 1838 regular postal rates for letters of a single piece of paper were: up to 30 miles, 6 cents; 30 to 80 miles, 10 cents; 80 to 150 miles, 12½ cents; 150 to 400 miles, 18¾ cents; over 400 miles, 25 cents. Letters of two pieces of paper called for double postage, and single sheets weighing over one

[302] *Chicago Democrat,* December 17, 1833; *Green-Bay Intelligencer,* August 2, 1834.
[303] *Cleveland Herald and Gazette,* February, 1838.
[304] *Ohio State Journal,* December 11, 1829.
[305] *Ibid.,* May 4, 1833.
[306] *Richmond* (Ind.) *Palladium,* March 10, 1837.

ounce, quadruple postage. These rates were approximately half the rates of 1815, but still high enough to account for the practice of vertical lines of script written crosswise upon the horizontal lines, and sometimes even diagonal lines superimposed upon these.[307] The thin paper was self-enveloped, sealed, and, if important, sent in duplicate or triplicate, in separate mails, as a precaution. The sender did not always pay the postage, often counting on the recipient's eagerness for a letter to break down his resistance. Although the postal regulations did not require payment in United States coin, any kind of coin was frequently scarce. Not infrequently letters were wrapped in brown paper and sent with a waybill, as would be a parcel of freight.[308]

By the time roads in the West permitted stage lines, the stagecoach had reached that point in its evolution where it had become streamlined. Originally a boxlike structure similar to the stage wagon, only lighter, or modeled after private carriages with flat top but curved bottom, the coach took on curves until it became elliptical in shape. Just why this form is not apparent, as streamlining for lessened wind resistance was certainly not a factor, and the shape noticeably lessened head room and besides left no space for baggage on top. It was probably merely a matter of fashion. The body contained two or three transverse seats for three passengers each, had side doors and was mounted or suspended high above the axles on plaited or riveted leather thongs or thorough braces, in lieu of springs. The result was a somewhat wobbly, top-heavy vehicle. Small luggage might be taken inside, stored with the driver, or put under the seats, but the infinite variety of odd-shaped carpetbags, leather trunks, hatboxes and such, necessary to carry the furbelows of male and female fashion, presented a problem. The baggage boot at the rear could not hold all, but soon the coach top was utilized as well. By the middle 1830's the flat-topped Concord coach began to replace the "football" bodies, and no other material changes took place until the stage went out of use.[309] Not only

---

[307] Which, with the fine script, faded ink and browned paper, give the historian something to worry about.

[308] *Transactions of the Illinois State Historical Society,* 1906, p. 75.

[309] The development of shape in relation to function in water and land vehicles offers some interesting comparisons and contrasts. Naturally the clipper ship and light-draft steamboat were developed to slip through or over the water long before any thought was given to body design of land vehicles. Not until speed became

were stagecoaches the last word in the wagonmaker's art, but in color, finish, and fine-line painting, were not surpassed until a generation of automobile use brought new processes and perfections. Coaches, like steamboats, and later Pullman cars, usually had names.

Stage drivers, as well as steamboat captains, and later railroad conductors, were persons of importance. "Mail carriers, baggage masters, engineer, conductor, collector and sometimes quite active artillery men," were these masters of the high seat. Because of exceptional size, affability, skill in driving, ability to hold liquor, or a record run, reputations of famous drivers extended far beyond their working territory.

When the coach horn blew, the tired horses perked up to bring the stage rolling smartly up to the tavern, and the driver tossed the lines to the boy, walked into the bar, banged his whip butt on the floor, and called for three fingers of whiskey, or when after a change of horses, the driver cracked his whip and started off with a flourish, the tempo of life in the immediate vicinity livened up.[310] Loafers drifted in and petty affairs ceased for the while, for with the stage came news and gossip; drivers were men of the world, and authorities on many subjects besides horses and roads. "He was the man of authority with whom even the schoolmaster would esteem it a most distinguishing

---

much greater was it necessary to consider air resistance. More remarkable has been the failure of improvements in body design to carry over from one type of land conveyance to another. The railroad coach started where the stagecoach began, not where it left off. So with the automobile and the airplane. Each began again with a box- or cratelike structure, apparently uninfluenced by changes in either stage- or railroad coach design.

[310] The stage driver's whip was an article of great importance, seldom ever let out of his hands. Bought from one of a few famous whip makers or made by the driver, it was to the stage man what the bow and arrow was to Robin Hood, custom-made rifle or fishing rod to the modern sportsman, or the highly specialized tool to the artisan. The stock of hickory or water-seasoned oak was from six to eight feet long, with heavy butt, usually weighted with lead, and tapering shaft. The lash was braided of soft strands of leather with interwoven linen threads perhaps, and tapered from about a half inch to a quarter or less, in the last half of its length. The lash was about twice the length of the stock. On the end was the cracker of several feet, braided of silk and shoemaker's thread waxed with beeswax. The proud driver rebraided or replaced the cracker every trip or two. The whip in the hands of the crack coachman was used to speak a language of its own to the horses. It could warn, persuade, steady, even caress. It could pick off a horse fly without ruffling the hair, or it could split open the toughest hide. Ordinarily the horses were never struck with the whip. It was a rule with some companies that they never be. The necessary noise in a race, or the flourish of impressive start or grand arrival, was made by "giving them the silk."

honor to have been found in company or in confidential conversation."

The seat by the driver was regarded as one of honor. Many were the feats of skill and nerve executed by these men, undertaken perhaps to save time, because of rivalry with competitors, or simply to show off and give passengers a ride to remember. Comfort-loving or nervous passengers wisely avoided the fast mail coaches; least of all would they ride with the President's message. On such special occasions brakes were rarely touched, steep descents and hairpin turns were taken on the dead run, and the driver trusted to Providence or the party in power to get him over or around the ruts, rocks, or stumps with nothing more disastrous than a well-jolted load of passengers.[311]

Ohio in 1827 passed a law for the safety of passengers, which made it illegal to run horses to pass another coach, or to keep from being passed, or to leave horses attached to the coach and unhitched, with passengers in the coach. Violators were subject to fine as well as damages.[312] Wages of drivers were $12 to $20 per month. In northern states in winter, coaches were often placed on runners, the horses harnessed with bells, and the passengers, covered with buffalo robes and provided with foot warmers, enjoyed a clean ride free from dust or mud.

Many were the adventures and travel stories of stagecoach passengers. Tickets were not sold but passengers were waybilled like livestock; preachers and children commonly traveled half fare or "second class." It was said that Windy Bob McPheters on his Indianapolis-Louisville run, would pause at the bottom of steep hills and call out, "All first class passengers get out and walk, all second class passengers get out and push." At times, when stuck in mudholes, all passengers got rails and logs and lent a hand, if they wished to continue their journey. On the National Road and elsewhere, competing stage lines maintained keen rivalry. At one time or another there were the Pioneer Line, the National Line, the June Bug Line (predicted not to survive until the June bugs came), and the Shake Gut Line. At

[311] Such record runs as were made over the National Road in the East were not ordinarily possible on any of the western roads in our period. On one trip the run from Uniontown to Brownsville, Pennsylvania, twenty miles, was made in forty-five minutes. One of Van Buren's messages was brought from Frederick, Maryland, to Wheeling, 222 miles in 23½ hours.

[312] *Hamilton Advertiser*, April 6, 1827.

central points where coaches waited for exchange of passengers, the drivers often raced each other to the first relay. Sometimes horses were changed in a minute and the race continued. Much prestige and consequent financial advantage was supposed to attach to victory. Likewise considerable prestige was assumed on the part of folks in the country and villages as the result of having ridden on the stage. Probably Mrs. Jones, at the quilting party, would casually remark, "when we rode the stage to Indianapolis," with the same smug implications as indulged in by her descendant of a later day when she said, "Now when we flew down to Havana." And of the two, no doubt the stage ride was by far the more strenuous adventure.[313]

Not quite as interesting, but just as important as the stagecoach was the freight wagon, the best known type of which appeared in Pennsylvania in the 1750's, and probably took its name from a breed of heavy horses developed in the Conestoga Valley. The body was sturdy, built with flaring sides and a floor which curved upward at either end to prevent the load from sliding on the steep hills. The high, heavy-spoked, wide-tired wheels were well dished and toed in for additional strength. The pole, or wagon tongue, was rigid and only the wheel team—the largest— could do any holding back. They were aided by the long-levered "patent lock" or brake, which could be manipulated either from the ground or the rider's seat. Hoops supported a sail-cloth cover, while on the sides beneath the body hung water and tar buckets, feedbox, extra chains, and toolbox. Bodies were almost invariably painted blue, with red trim and running gear.

Most teamsters owned their horses, hence took pride in their outfits. They kept harness greased and by way of ornamentation put on brass or "ivory" studs and rings, hames' bows with cone-shaped bells, or heavy shoulder housings or protectors of bear-skin dressed with the hair on. The bells of particular teamsters were graded in size and produced a harmonious rhythm as they jingled along. By law of the road, if a wagon got stuck and was pulled out by the same number of horses of another teamster,

---

[313] Besides the work of Dunbar and Cole, much general material on stagecoach days may be found in Alice Morse Earle, *Stage Coach and Tavern Days* (New York, 1908); Marion Nicholl Rawson, *From Here to Yender* . . . (New York, 1932); George Estes, *The Stagecoach* (Cedarwood, Ore., 1925); and John Winston Coleman, *Stage Coach Days in the Bluegrass* . . . (Louisville, 1935).

the bells and housings went to the better outfit. Drivers usually walked and managed their six-horse teams with a single line to the lead horse, and the long whip. A series of quick jerks on the line, fastened for convenience to the hame of the nigh wheel horse, indicated "gee," and a steady pull meant "haw." The driver walked on the left or, if he rode, it was on the nigh (left) wheel horse. Harness was heavy—back bands more than a foot wide—and the traces were heavy chains.[314] There were freelance wagoners, but the majority worked for established companies or freight lines. Some of these lines ran one or more wagons daily, changed horses every eleven miles day and night, and averaged about thirty miles per day.[315] A ton and a half for four horses was a good load on fair roads, but some of the great wagons with eight-inch tires and eight horses could haul three times as much. Six horses was the standard team for the Conestoga wagon. These big-topped, brightly painted land freighters lumbered ponderously along, and whether singly or in caravans, they presented an imposing sight. They served their purpose well until the railroad ended their day. Their modern counterpart is the motor truck.

Teamsters had the general reputation of being a hard lot. But so did the boatmen, the canal builders, and later the railroader, the lumberjack, the miner, the cowboy, and the truck driver.

These people, who drive teams . . . were to me, in their manners and way of living, a new species, perfectly unique in their appearance, language and habits. They devote themselves to this mode of subsistence for years, and spend their time continually on the road. They seemed to me to be more rude, profane, and selfish, than either sailors, boatmen, or hunters, to whose modes of living theirs is the most assimilated. We found them addicted to drunkenness, and very little disposed to assist each other. Such was the aspect they presented us. We were told, there were honorable exceptions,

[314] For cut and description of a Conestoga wagon, see Thomas Wilson, "The Arkansas Traveller," in *Ohio Archaeological and Historical Society Publications*, VIII (1900), 296–300. The teams and wagons are portrayed in John Omwake, *The Conestoga Six-Horse Bell Teams of Eastern Pennsylvania* (Cincinnati, 1930).

In many regions of the Midwest common usage later reversed the position of the "nigh" and "off" horses. After a thorough investigation of the subject the author gives up; the only conclusion he can venture is that the "off" horse is the one farthest away from the observer.

[315] Two wagons a day were started by the Philadelphia and Pittsburgh Transportation Company in the spring of 1818, and such lines were extended on west as the National Road was built. *Western Herald and Steubenville Gazette*, April 18, 1818.

and even associations, who, like the sacred band of Thebes, took a kind of
oath to stand by, and befriend each other. I often dropped among them,
as by accident, that impressive tract, the "Swearer's Prayer"! I was pleased
to remark the result of their reflections, as they read the tract, apart on
their window seats. In some it seemed to produce a momentary thought-
fulness; in others a smile; and again in others, a deep growl of acquiescence,
very like that which every one has heard, who has attended a council of
Indians, and heard them express a kind of reluctant assent to terms proposed to them.[316]

Descriptions of this type, of course, emanate largely from the
more protected or civilized classes, the preachers, travelers or
literary folk. To these observers, then or now, common man,
closely scrutinized, is likely to prove crude and tough. To a
sensitive preacher, writer, or college professor of today not only
might sailors, stevedores, and miners, but factory workers or
even college undergraduates, viewed in their native haunts, be
regarded as "a new species, perfectly unique in their appearance,
language, and habits." Nevertheless the professional teamsters
or freighters were not ordinarily welcomed at some of the regular taverns, but either camped out or put up at those which
specialized in the patronage of teamsters and drovers.

> There custom always called a halt,
> To water, rest and take a drink;
> And, not unlikely, while they stopped
> A jig was danced, or horses swapped;
> And so, perchance, a broken link
> The smith was hurried to renew,
> Or tighten up a loosened shoe,
>
> Meantime, the jolly wagoners stood
> And swaggered 'round the old-time bar—
> The latticed nook, the landlord's throne,
> Where he presided, all alone,
> And smoked his cheap cigar,
> And reckoned up the tippler's bill
> For whiskey, at a "fip" a gill;
>
>   .   .   .   .   .   .
>
> They sat in all the different ways
> That men could sit, or ever sat;
> They told of all their jolly days,

---

[316] Timothy Flint, *Recollections of the Last Ten Years*, 8–9.

And spat in all the different ways
That men could spit, or ever spat;
They talked of horses and their strength,
And spun their yarns at endless length.[317]

Stagecoaches and Conestoga wagons were not the only vehicles
which traveled the roads. On the National Road regular traffic
was augmented by the stream of movers which continued to the
West. A company of Middle States families, well equipped with
Conestoga wagons and family possessions, leading and driving
extra horses, neat cattle and hogs, might be followed by a single
couple in an old-fashioned, high-wheeled carriage which could
straddle the stumps and ford the streams. Virginia and Carolina
travelers of the better-to-do class favored lighter wagons of the
Conestoga type, with single teams. Poorer folk from the Upland
South used the little carts and wagons made of tough young oak
without nail or iron tires, pulled by unshod, scraggly little southern ponies. There were two-wheeled Philadelphia carts, four-
wheeled New Jersey carts, and push carts. And some people
walked.[318] Local farm wagons, traveling farm machinery, hay-
racks, barouches, phaetons, chariotees, gigs, buggies, and occasionally a handsome private carriage suspended from high goose-
neck springs, as well as droves of hogs and cattle cluttered the
road. Past these now and then would dash the special messenger
on horseback, the country doctor, or the express coach. To one

[317] H. L. Fisher, of York, Pennsylvania, 1888, in Omwake, *Six-Horse Bell Teams*,
130–34.

[318] The Velocipede, accellator or "hobby horse," which was introduced from
England and manufactured by Boston coachmakers as early as 1819, was mentioned in western papers, but apparently not seen on western roads. Chillicothe
Supporter, June 9, 1819. Nor was the twenty-ton "automotive vehicle," invented
by a Mr. Parker, of Illinois, which could be driven twenty miles a day on any
turnpike, with twenty-five bushels of coal. *Hamilton Advertiser*, May 20, 1825.
The evening campsite of a group of families crossing the prairies in Illinois
was described as follows: "But you should see all this motley multitude, just as
they have encamped for the night. Horses, cattle, dogs, hogs and sheep spread
over the prairie far and wide; the wagons at convenient distance and grouped in
a most neighborly method, each with its cheerful camp fire blazing, and its camp-
kettle sending forth its grateful steam and appetite-quickening odor, round which
you behold the female inmates of each family busily engaged in supper preparations. Meanwhile the men liberate their dusty teams, and after rubbing them down,
turn them loose upon the rich and unfenced pastures, or grease their axles, and
repair any injuries sustained by the rough usage of the wilderness roads over
which they have made, it may be, a hazardous and dangerous way. To fill up the
picture, scores of happy children, glad to escape the dull monotony of their slow
and toilsome march, mingle in clans, capering and shouting on the beautiful level,
plucking the thousand wild flowers which bedeck their playground, or rolling in
very plenary of joy on the luxuriant carpet which covers the whole space for many
a mile around." Jones, *Illinois and the West*, 32–33.

who cherished memories of the road in its heyday, this last left the most powerful impression.

With the tinkling of the bells, the rumbling of wheels, the noise of the animals and the chatter of the people as they went forever forward, the little boy who had gone to the road from his lonesome home in the woods was captivated and carried away into the great active world. But the greatest wonder and delight of all was the stage coach, radiant in new paint and drawn by its four matched horses in their showy harness, and filled inside and on top with well dressed people. I think yet that there has never been a more graceful or handsome turnout than one of these fine old stage coaches drawn by a splendid team of matched horses, and driven by such drivers as used to handle the ribbons between Richmond and Indianapolis. We could hear the driver playing his bugle as he approached the little town, and it all seemed too grand and fine to be other than a dream.[319]

On lesser roads there were fewer of the fine coaches, freighters, and carriages, more of nondescript wagons, carts, and sleds. Around Detroit, excepting for a few carriages among the old families, the primitive French carts prevailed until about 1840.

In the 1830's on the roads into Chicago from the South and East might be seen the "Yankee Wagon," a long-coupled, low-box-bed, narrow-tread, two-horse affair. Also the Hoosier wagon, or the western version of the Conestoga, not quite so well kept, certainly not drawn by such splendid Pennsylvania horses as possessed by the teamsters along eastern sections of the National Road, but massive and capacious, perhaps drawn by oxen. In vehicles as in manners, customs, language, and politics, the Yankee and southern civilizations competed. To haul 40 bushels of wheat 100 to 200 miles to Chicago, receive 40 cents per bushel, pay expenses for a week on the road, and still have a profit, called for efficiency in transport as well as economy in food of man and beast. Although taverns sprang up along the roads, many teamsters or farmers carried their own food and camped out. A professional teamster class such as existed on the National Road was not in evidence elsewhere in the West, so the farmer-teamsters patronized the regular taverns.

Over the roads also traveled thousands of neat cattle, hogs, horses, and sometimes turkeys. Droving from the Northwest to eastern markets developed in the early 1820's and continued to

[319] Benjamin S. Parker, in "The Hesperian Tree" (1903), quoted in *Indiana Magazine of History*, III (1907), 77–78.

be quite a business until the railroads were built. Stock was driven from Pickaway County, Ohio, to Baltimore in 1822.[320] Two years later, a traveler on the National Road between Fredericktown and Washington, Pennsylvania, "met continually droves of hogs, often 600 together, being driven, usually from Ohio and even Indiana, to Baltimore."[321] Twelve hundred cattle passed through St. Clairsville in a few weeks, to "sell at $35 a head and help pay for a few gewgaws from the East."[322] Soon large droves of cattle were coming all the way from Missouri, and going East.[323] When the prospectus of the village of Danville, Illinois, was being set forth in 1833, one of its chief advantages was thought to be its situation on the road from Vandalia to Indianapolis, a "great thoroughfare for drovers." Almost 6,000 animals had passed on their way East the preceding summer, as well as others to Michigan, Chicago, and markets to the south.[324]

Droving cattle were mainly of two types. The three-year steers or "stock cattle" were destined mainly for the farmers of eastern Pennsylvania, who "fed them out" for a year longer. The four-year fatted bullocks went on through to markets in eastern cities. A northern droving route led through Pennsylvania to Dunkirk, New York; another across the Ohio River ferry at Wellsville and to Pittsburgh and Philadelphia; while the southern route ran by way of Wheeling to Bedford and Philadelphia, or to Cumberland, Maryland, and to Baltimore. These three routes corresponded roughly to the later routes of the New York Central, Pennsylvania, and Baltimore and Ohio railroads. As the railroads worked westward to Dunkirk and Pittsburgh, these points usually became the end of the drive. Other droving routes led to Cincinnati, Chicago, and lesser towns which became butchering and shipping centers. The stalwart semi-razorbacks of the Wabash country of Indiana went in droves to Chicago in the 1830's and from southern Indiana and Ohio they went to Cincinnati in such quantities as to give that city the title of Porkopolis.

[320] I. F. King, "The Coming and Going of Ohio Droving," in *Ohio Archaeological and Historical Society Publications*, XVII (1908), 247.
[321] *Diary of William Owen*, 49.
[322] *St. Clairsville Gazette* in *Columbus* (Ohio) *Gazette*, May 26, 1825.
[323] Indianapolis *Indiana Journal*, June 16, 1830.
[324] *Danville Enquirer*, first number, August 5, 1833, reprinted in *Journal of the Illinois State Historical Society*, IV (1911–12), 351.

Stock buyers sometimes worked in a district until their purchases were completed, then arranged an assemblying point for the animals. The start of an organized drove was almost as exacting an event as the roundup later became on the great plains. Farmers would drive in their whole flocks, then the animals to be driven away were separated at this time. By the terms of sale, the farmer was required to furnish help on this occasion. Other buyers would start out with a few dozen animals and count on picking up other increments along the way.[325]

Ordinarily droves contained from one to two hundred animals, although larger droves were not rare. Horses could average better than twenty miles per day, "stock cattle" about nine, fat cattle seven, and if accompanied by hogs, not so much. Even the leaner types of hogs of the period sometimes had to be trained for their road work; they were driven around in the fields by boys for a number of days before starting. The loss of time resulting from a mixed drove of cattle and hogs was more than compensated for by the saving in feed, as the hogs could subsist on the undigested grain which fat cattle left.

For larger droves, a crew of several men was required. The boss drover, on horseback, carried in hand a "black snake" whip, and in saddlebags some extra clothing for the other men. Another mounted man was necessary as a flanker at crossroads or when passing through forests. At the head of a cattle drove a man on foot usually led an ox, while one or more footmen urged on stragglers from the rear. At the noonday pause the boss rode ahead and made arrangement for the night. Drovers, like freighters, seldom stayed at the regular taverns, but at "drove stands," which were farmhouses with adequate pens and supplies to accommodate the droves and drovers. To save money at toll bridges and ferries, the lead ox and a few cows were ferried across and the rest swam. Blacksmiths were located along the line to shoe whatever animals (cows or horses) became lame from tender feet. Pay of drovers was about $15 per month, and the return home on foot was allowed for at the rate of 50 cents and 33 miles per day. Fast walkers could do 40 miles and save a dollar or so. Corn in the shock was usually available along

[325] See Oliver, *Eight Months in Illinois*, 105–8, for a good description of the task.

established droving routes at 37½ cents per shock or 25 cents per bushel.

Droving was not only a nuisance to traffic but hard on the roads. The tendency for the cattle to follow in line created great ruts or "cattle billows" in the soft mud, which remained hard and rough when summer suns baked the roads. In winter, clay roads became impassable for vehicles after the droves had churned up the roadbed, and in summer clouds of dust marked the progress of a drove.

§ § §

Wherever the traveled road, there also was to be found the tavern. Along the earlier or less used roads and in the more remote regions the tavern was like as not a log house, indistinguishable from the pioneer's dwelling. In fact, the settler was often, in self-defense, forced to hang out a sign—"keep public"— for his house was so located that more travelers applied for lodging than his slender resources could handle without charging. In these taverns the accommodations were of the crudest. Homemade furnishings such as were common in the pioneer cabin prevailed: puncheon floors, fireplace, a ladder to the loft, crude table and benches, beds or bunks without rope springs and mattresses, but with clapboards covered with straw or grass, sometimes known as "prairie feathers," and cooking equipment to match. These wilderness taverns, located at cross trails, at ford or ferry, often formed the nucleus around which developed the village or town. Then the log house was replaced and a more pretentious public house came into being.

Although the taverns of the West had not the generations of history behind them, nor the quaintness and flavor possessed by the old inns of New England or Old England, nevertheless the better type, such as were to be found along the National Road and other important highways, and in the towns, maintained the best traditions of the older inns. Usually built rectangular in shape, of poplar and walnut timbers, or of brick, with large outside fireplace chimneys of stone, large living room, dining room, and lean-to or separate-wing kitchen, they were placed close to the roadside. A prominent feature of the big room, furnished with ladder-back and splint bottom chairs, heavy settees, drop-leaf, gate-leg, or trestle tables of cherry or maple, walnut or oak, and a woven rag carpet, was the bar. Not necessarily a long counter, just as often a narrow shelf over a swinging door, it was equipped with sufficient mugs, pitchers, pewter cups, and demijohns to serve the drinks of the day. In taproom or cellar were the kegs and hogsheads, equipped with spigots and bungs, perhaps rows of dusty bottles reposing in the dark. The first-class tavern keeper prided himself on being able to supply the favorite drinks of Yankee, Southerner, or Westerner. Madeira, port, sherry, cognac, gin, and Jamaica spirits, as well as domestic favorites such as apple jack, cherry bounce, peach brandy, cider, and the ever present corn whiskey, would be in demand. Flip, "rhum," syllabub, sling, metheglin, toddy, and many other drinks could be had.

In the kitchen of such a hostelry would be heavy tables or waist-high shelves, fireplace or stove and oven, copper and brass kettles, pans, pots, firkins, platters, and other necessary accouterments. Permeating all was what one might call the "tavern odor," a combined smell of man, horse, food, liquor, salt pork, and wood smoke, so penetrating that it became deeply embedded in the furnishings, even in the wood of the tables.[326] Sleeping rooms upstairs, ample barns, and lots for the horses and a good springhouse or other source of water supply, completed the material equipment of such a hostelry. The hanging sign in front, with its bear, bull, wolf, plow, eagle, picture of George Washington, or other symbol or inscription was common but not necessary.[327] Under the assumption that "good wine needs no bush" (bough, foxtail, or other symbol to attract attention), many of the best known places had no signs. Their reputations were secure in the personality and hospitality of their landlords and the excellence of their meals. Of them it might well be said:

> Who e'er has travelled life's dull round
> Where'er his stages may have been
> Will sigh to think he still has found
> His warmest welcome at an inn.

[326] So permanent was this "smoke house" scent that it is distinctly perceptible in the kitchens of taverns which have not been used for generations.

[327] "The sign board, however large it may be, never in any instance contained in one line the name of the owner, one or two letters at the end of the name being put over the others in a reduced size, and this was evidently the fashion," or just the result of poor planning. Oliver, *Eight Months in Illinois*, 202.

The landlord in genial affability carried the front for the establishment, but its success depended also on the less conspicuous but hard drudgery of wife, daughters, or "hired help." The cooking and serving for patrons of uncertain numbers, the scrubbing and washing of linens and dishes, carrying of water, providing of candles, cleaning of lamps, and innumerable other duties kept them busy. A capable stableman or handy man was also a necessary asset.

The average tavern in the West was something between the primitive log shelter and the better-type places. Accommodations and equipment were crude rather than elegant, but hospitality and food were abundant. To the stand-bys of pork, potatoes, and corn meal were added game and vegetables in season. Hot breads, usually served at all meals, butter, milk, pickles, conserves, and pies varied in quality with the skill and industry of the tavern keeper's wife. Good coffee was not so common as good whiskey. Ablutions performed at the water trough, the pump, or even the near-by branch—tin wash basins for the ladies—the tired and dirty traveler might expect to sit down to first-class board.

Good sleeping accommodations were not so certain, for the rule was to lodge all who came. Since beds were all too frequently at a premium, doubling up with strangers was the custom. Some landlords were accused of filling beds to capacity and then later removing sound sleepers to the floor to accommodate late-comers. Privacy was often either not regarded as necessary or was impossible under the conditions. An improvised curtain, or temporary withdrawal of the men to permit women to retire, was the best that could be expected under ordinary conditions. Change of bed linen for different guests was not customary, and, of course, cleanliness depended upon the individual tavern keeper.[328] Bed vermin were all too frequently met with and often, like houseflies, tolerated "with wondrous equanimity," although in justice to the average tavern mistress it should be said that the former were regarded as somewhat less acceptable. As to the flies, they were a minor nuisance. Switches of leaves, strip-paper brushes, or a sort of punkah suspended over the table and operated by a child during meals, was considered the ultimate in

[328] When Mrs. Kirkland, novelist of early Michigan life, tried to get fresh sheets, after having seen a liberal supply of newly laundered ones in the kitchen, the girl protested, "You know damp sheets is dreadful unwholesome—and there ha'nt nobody slept in these beds but some very *nice* gentlemen."

refinement. In the absence of screens the near-by stable yard and its ever present manure pile made sure the supply of flies was abundant. "Flies everywhere! Flies in everything! Flies on everything!" Germs and such had not yet caused any worry about flies or lack of ventilation.

Western manners were always in view at the taverns, and wayfaring Englishmen or Easterners were never loath to criticize the ever present profanity, seegar, chewing, and spitting as well as gulping of food and loud talk. If civilizations be rated by the number of tines on the forks used, this was a one-tine (the knife) civilization.

The fundamental idea of the diner was to convey the food from the table to his teeth; the precise method of its conveyance thither being a matter of subsidiary concern. In his main purpose he was successful, and if the methods by which bread and meat are transported to their final destination have also improved with the lapse of years, it is well to remember that those earlier generations were sturdy men who fearlessly met whatever emergency confronted them, whether the problem was the conquest of the wilderness or the impalement of a distant potato.[329]

The knife conveyed peas as well as potatoes, hot drinks gurgled in by way of the saucer (both proper enough), and a goodly hunk of bread and "gedunking" took care of the rest. Were hand linen provided, habit—or scorn—probably prevailed, and the back of the hand or coat sleeve served instead. Minor refinements, when provided, were likely to be ignored or abused in use.[330] In other words, the practices were those of the average citizen, in any time or place. Though they may differ in the superficialities, they remain the same fundamentally, whether in a log tavern or "the world's finest hotel."

Taverns were social and news centers as well as stopping places for travelers. Here the town loafers congregated, whittled, expectorated, and watched the world go by. News items, as well as their names, were often jotted on the register by travelers; the stage drivers were traveling news services in themselves.

[329] Dunbar, *History of Travel,* I, 216.

[330] Count Francesco Arese of Milan noted a sign in one of the leading hotels of Louisville in 1837: "'Gentlemen are particularly requested not to deface or remove the files of newspapers from the reading room: waste paper can be had on applying at the bar!!' In spite of such a positive and solemn sign, not a paper had been respected. It is to be remembered, too, that the season of fevers or other illnesses had not yet begun!!" "Translations from the Notes of an Italian Count," in *Mississippi Valley Historical Review,* XX (1933–34), 385.

Town or township meetings, local party conventions, court sessions, as well as dances and parties, often utilized the big room; preachers or strolling bands of actors performed there, and Jackson Day or Fourth of July celebrants gathered round the tavern table. Sometimes an impromptu performance of "The Arkansas Traveller" or other simple plays would be put on, and when word was passed around, the neighboring residents packed the barroom along with the tavern guests.[331]

In the larger towns the taverns aspired to the title of "hotels," and were known under imposing names such as the "American House," the "Columbian Hotel," or more simply as "the Gumey House" or "the Smith House." They often displayed the "sign."[332] Charles Fenno Hoffman spoke of the Pearl Street House in Cincinnati as rivaling the best hotels in New York and said that one of the Louisville hotels was "much superior in external appearance and interior arrangement to any establishment of the kind we have in New York." And the Englishman, William Oliver, apropos of hotels in Dayton, said, "Indeed few objects in the country are more surprising to the stranger, than these establishments, which, at first sight, often appear so disproportioned to the other accessories." Hotels such as these differed from the country and village houses only in size. Only the finest provided for heat in the sleeping rooms; indoor toilet facilities of course were unknown. The bar was more elaborate, possibly there was a reading room, but the landlord was still a very important personage, who knew and was known by his guests. In good establishments the landlord or waiters carved the principal joints at table or side table. Ice water was

[331] For an excellent account of one version of "The Arkansas Traveller," see Wilson's "The Arkansas Traveller," in *Ohio Archaeological and Historical Society Publications*, VIII, 303–6. The main outline of the performance was as follows: An Arkansas squatter is trying in vain to play on his fiddle a tune he had heard in New Orleans, but can remember only the first part. A traveler comes along, begins conversation, and seeks lodging. The squatter, interested in his tune, parries the stranger's polite conversation with crude repartee and frontier "wisecracks," meanwhile playing over and over the first part of the tune. Eventually when he learns the stranger knows the last part of it, his attitude changes at once and nothing is too good for him. Whereupon the stranger takes over the fiddle and plays the last part of the tune, but can't be persuaded to play the first part. The auditors enjoyed particularly the simple jokes and smart replies between the squatter and traveler, and the many possibilities offered the performing wits to show off appealed to their type of humor.

[332] For example, the Bell Tavern in Vandalia in the 1820's, "the sign of the Bell"; Union Hall (Louisville), "the sign of the Indian Queen"; the Columbian Hotel, Vandalia, "the sign of General Washington."

served during summer, and the quantity of meat was less than in the outlying places. Since servants were expensive, meals were served at fixed hours. Fixtures were plain and meager, but serviceable. Patrick Shirreff, one of the most observing and judicious of the British travelers, stated that in his whole experience with American hotels, largely in the West, he "did not receive an uncivil answer, or experience neglect from any one connected with the establishment." Landlords were not so fawning in manner as those in Britain, but equally civil and eager to oblige. Although the soft tone was perhaps not so prevalent among guests in the West, still it was a civil tone.[333]

Hotel advertisements appeared regularly in the newspapers; they usually emphasized bed, board, bar, and stable facilities, though rates were rarely listed. By the late 1830's it was possible for a town of a few thousand population, such as Quincy, Illinois, to boast of a hotel four stories high and with eighty or more rooms.[334] Though Chicago had no hotel of importance in 1835, the new Lake House was enlarged and improved and by 1839, with a row of small furnaces in the kitchen, was ready "for simultaneous preparation of a variety of nick-nacks a la mode the French." "Suites of parlors" and a reading room were also available.[335] Detroit lacked good hotel facilities until about 1835. Hotels improved in size and conveniences as one traveled east from St. Louis to Cincinnati and Pittsburgh.

Tavern rates were ordinarily regulated by the county boards which granted licenses, but prices did not vary as much from place to place as did the type of tavern and service. In Crawford County, Indiana, in the 1820's a night's lodging was fixed at 25 cents, as were meals and horse feed for 24 hours. Whiskey was listed at 12 cents the pint, peach brandy at 18 cents, and wines and French brandy at 43 cents.[336] In Martin County lodging was 12½ cents, meals 37½ cents, one horse feed 12½ cents, and horse's lodging 62½ cents. Whiskey was 12½ cents the half pint,

---

[333] *A Tour through North America,* 288. Shirreff, speaking of eastern hotels, said that waiters were usually addressed in whispers and that the habits of some persons from Britain who sought to command attention by oaths and noise were not suitable to this region of America "where the mild and unassuming are never neglected." Compare with Miss Martineau, who only complained of hotel servants.

[334] *Quincy Whig,* November 17, 1838.

[335] *Daily Chicago American,* April 29, 1839.

[336] Commissioners' records, January, 1825, cited in H. H. Pleasant, "Crawford County," in *Indiana Magazine of History,* XVIII (1922), 148.

and French brandy or foreign spirits 62½ cents.[337] The B. Brown and S. Henderson Inn in Indianapolis charged $2.50 for a week's board and lodging and $2.00 for the horse. By the day meals and lodging for one person and horse were $1.25.[338] In southern Michigan it was possible to get lodging and two meals for as little as 18 cents.[339] Cook County, Illinois, in 1831 fixed prices in its two taverns at 12½ cents for lodging, 25 cents for breakfast and supper, 50 cents for dinner, and 18¾ cents for a pint of whiskey.[340] A fairly standard price in many regions was 25 cents for lodging, for each meal, and for hay and lodging for the horse. City prices were $1.00 to $2.00 the day.

Generally speaking, people traveled the highways in the earlier period not for pleasure but from necessity. The hardships and delays, the dirt and the dangers made travel unattractive to all but a few hardy souls. Impositions were practiced by proprietors of public conveyances. Overloading was common, and running off schedule or stopping short of the destination at night to benefit some tavern in league with the line was another custom. Once off the few good roads, the mudholes, impassable fords, or makeshift bridges were constantly to be faced, to say nothing of uncertain lodgings, possible runaways, "road agents," and cutthroats. Some taverns were run by people of criminal status, and served as headquarters for horse stealing and robbing gangs. The unsuspecting traveler was choice prey because of absence of friends and connections to aid him or trace his disappearance. One did not always have to obtain a list of names of the cutthroats and villains, and look them up for adventure as did Dr. R. L. Mason in Illinois in 1819.[341] Nor was it always possible for the traveler to pass through in daytime districts known to be dangerous. Conditions of road and weather might leave no choice as to the night's lodging.

Not only was travel hard work; it was expensive. Measured in dollars it was two or three times modern day costs, and in

[337] Carlos T. McCarty, "Hindostan—A Pioneer Town of Martin County," in *Indiana Magazine of History*, X, No. 2 (June 1914), 58. For the county rates in Jackson, Floyd, and Switzerland counties, see *ibid.*, X, No. 4 (Dec. 1914), 275; XVII (1921), 220; XX (1924), 195.

[338] *Indiana Journal*, December 3, 1829.

[339] Quaife, *Chicago's Highways*, 173.

[340] *Ibid.*, 174.

[341] Richard Lee Mason, *Narrative*, 40.

purchasing power still more. Tavern rates were reasonable, but they comprised the minor part of the expense. Stages at 5 or 6 cents per mile did not reach all points by any means. Beyond, it was necessary to hire whatever sort of rig or conveyance was available, at whatever price. Sometimes none was to be had, but the determined traveler might secure one horse from one person, another from another, a set of harness from a third, a cart or wagon from a fourth, and then find a driver to take him on to his destination.

Tolls at ferries, bridges, and on highways mounted up for those who traveled in private conveyances or hauled stuff to markets. Ferries often charged 50 to 75 cents for wagon and horses, 12½ cents for man and horse, 6¼ cents for a footman or a horse, 4 cents the head for neat cattle, and 2 cents for a hog. These rates varied greatly from place to place and tended to become less as improvements and traffic developed.[342] Ohio in 1832 provided for tollgates every 10 miles along the National Road with rates at 5 cents for each 20 sheep, hogs, or neat cattle, 1½ cents for horse or ox, 4 cents for horse and rider, 12½ cents for a two-horse pleasure vehicle, and a sliding scale for wagons, based on width of tires and number of horses. A four-horse wagon would average about 12½ cents, but if the tires were over six inches wide, there was no toll. School children, persons going to church, funerals, and militia musters traveled free; those living on the road could arrange a yearly toll payment.[343]

Yet travel was constantly on the increase. When hot weather, dust, and sickness came to the city, "then it is that the sound of driver's horn, the cracking of his whip, and the rattling of wheels, are music to the ear—the best kind of music, for they have not been set to notes, that tease the sense of hearing by the monotony of recurring sounds."[344] Judge James Hall, traveling in 1835, noted a change in the type of traveler met in the West.

[342] The ferry across the Mississippi at St. Louis was probably the most expensive: horse and rider 50 cents, foot passenger 12½ cents, each head of neat cattle 50, other cattle 37½, merchandise per hundred 8 cents, gig and horse $1.25, two horses and wagon $1.75, etc. Wagons loaded with "cole," brick, corn, and firewood $1.00, with produce $1.50. Empty wagons returning in ten days, no charge. Vandalia *Illinois Intelligencer,* December 3, 1824.

[343] Columbus *Ohio State Journal,* June 23, 1832.

[344] James Hall, "Travels in Hot Weather," in *Western Monthly Magazine,* II (1834), 487.

In addition to the "young, bold, active, adventurous and indigent," who formerly furnished the mass, the older folks, the wealthy and timid were beginning to venture their money and bodies in the West.

"But in addition to those who compose the stream of emigration, there is a concourse made up of gayer spirits, mingled with not a few of the more substantial individuals, who are the great lights, as well as the great fixtures, of the land, and who a few years ago, would as soon have thought of going to China, as of coming to the west." Parties of pleasure, the gentry of Boston, New York, and Philadelphia were finding the way and realizing that travel to the interior might possess educational advantages next in importance only to dancing, singing, and phrenology. At hotels in Cincinnati, Louisville, and elsewhere might be seen gay bridal parties from down East, venerable citizens of New York, or spruce Quakers from Chestnut Street—"all on hobbies, gee up and gee ho, jaunting it merrily through the wide west, with as little fatigue, and as little sense of danger, as formerly attended a trip to Saratoga." Men of the church, of affairs, politicians, came out to look over the western people. "Fashionable parties have made the adventure, and returned without being gouged, scalped, knocked into a cocked hat, or used up to a mere grease-spot, and a visit to the west is ascertained to be not only safe but in good taste. . . . What with railroads, macadamized turnpikes, and canals, one may whisk off from the seaboard to Cincinnati in six or seven days, at an expense not worth naming, and with ninety-nine chances to one, against the mishap of a broken neck, or even a dislocated limb."[345]

The people of the West, too, were becoming more mobile. Sight-seeing and pleasure, as well as business, were taking more travelers into the cities, down river to New Orleans, up the Mississippi to the Falls of St. Anthony, east to Niagara, Saratoga, and other watering places.[346] Travel was becoming so prevalent that western papers copied a long article of warning from New England, which stated that the rage for travel was one kind of extravagance rapidly on the increase in our country,

[345] *Ibid.*, IV (1835), 87–88.
[346] Notice of pleasure boat trips were becoming more frequent by 1840.

and if the old-time habits of our ancestors continued to break up, it would be well if our virtue and freedom did not follow them. Nations do not plunge to ruin, they start slowly at first.[347]

The increasing travel was the result largely of improved facilities. The need of a road or canal in a given place might not be so obvious, nor the amount of traffic and travel apparent to warrant its expense, yet once constructed, it to a certain extent created its own traffic and encouraged social as well as commercial intercourse. By the end of the 1830's distances were being measured in hours rather than miles.[348]

§ § § §

Important as were the rivers and roads, they were thought inadequate for the needs of the rapidly growing West. Canals were discussed in America as early as 1700. Franklin wrote in 1772 in favor of a Susquehanna-Schuylkill canal; within a year Washington was discussing the feasibility of connecting the Potomac and the Ohio rivers. Manasseh Cutler, when promoting emigration to the Ohio Company lands in 1787, called attention to the possibilities of connecting the Ohio and Lake Erie and Hudson routes. Twenty years later Senator Thomas Worthington, of Ohio, proposed that the Secretary of the Treasury report a plan for opening roads and making canals. Gallatin's report of 1808 on internal improvements brought results in the Cumberland Road, but it was New York's project of the Erie Canal which set off the sudden and somewhat forced canal-building boom of the period 1820 to 1840.

When, in 1811, the Erie Canal Commission called upon the states to support New York's appeal for United States aid, Ohio was the only one to join in warm support. Congress failed to help, but so great was New York's desire to be linked up with the interior, and so energetic were Governor Clinton's efforts, that the state undertook the project alone. When "Clinton's Big Ditch"—363 miles long and costing almost $13,000,000—was completed in 1825, Pennsylvania, New York's chief rival for the western commerce, could stand it no longer. After warm

[347] *Massachusetts Journal* in *Hamilton* (Ohio) *Intelligencer,* September 29, 1829.
[348] *Cleveland Herald and Gazette* in *Daily Chicago Democrat,* June 8, 1839. For instance Cleveland was 84 hours from New York, 72 hours from Green Bay, 10 hours from Detroit, 96 hours from Chicago.

debates regarding the merits of canals versus the new means of transportation called "railroads," the legislature acted in 1826; soon work was begun on the great Pennsylvania Canal to connect the Susquehanna River with the Ohio. This was the beginning of a gigantic system of state improvements which in the early 1830's made possible four-day passage from Philadelphia to Pittsburgh. From Philadelphia to Columbia on the Susquehanna the traveler journeyed on the horse-car railroad, with stationary steam engines to pull the cars by cable up the hill near Philadelphia and let them down again near Columbia. Followed 172 miles of canal travel to Hollidaysburg, then 36 miles of inclined planes and cable assistance to Johnstown. Later canal boats built in sections were transferred bodily to the rail trucks so that the passenger or freight need not transfer. One hundred four miles of canal completed the distance to Pittsburgh.

Interest in canals was not confined to New York and Pennsylvania, but developed simultaneously in the West. In 1815 Niles wrote: "The exigencies of the nation, during the late war, has raised up an astonishing zeal in all parts of the United States, to secure all those advantages of roads, bridges and canals, &c which our country so happily presents to us."[349] The Cincinnati *Liberty Hall* was gratified to see the spirit of internal improvements manifesting itself throughout the state of Ohio as well as sister states of the West.[350]

In his message of 1817 Governor Thomas Worthington, of Ohio, gave much attention to the subject and a resolution was introduced in the legislature. The next year Governor Ethan Allen Brown recommended a survey for a canal to connect the Ohio and Lake Erie. Hard times of 1818–19 delayed action. William Henry Harrison's resolution in the legislature of 1819 instructed the senators and requested the representatives to obtain Federal laws to encourage roads, canals, and commerce, and recommended the state to do the same.[351] Three canal commissioners were provided by law in the next year but Congress did not co-operate.[352] Governor Brown came back to the subject

[349] *Niles' Weekly Register*, IX, 202 (Nov. 18, 1815).
[350] November 20, 1815.
[351] Chillicothe *Supporter*, December 22, 1819.
[352] The *Liberty Hall and Cincinnati Gazette* encouraged the legislature to act and pointed to New York's action in the face of ridicule. Nevertheless, it thought that "in the present state of affairs" not much could be done without aid from the General Government. February 18, 1820.

in 1821 and a legislative committee made an elaborate report.[353] The advantages of a shorter route to the East, convenience, and profits were considered. Cost was estimated at $2,500,000 and it was thought that revenue from the canal would pay for construction in six years.

By the law of 1822 the Governor was authorized to appoint an engineer and a board of seven commissioners to examine the different routes and make a report. Canal meetings had been held at various places. The dangers and risks of the voyage to New Orleans, the overstocked and glutted markets there as a result of seasonal shipping down river, the unhealthful climate, the saving in time, were all emphasized. Also the water power and resultant revenue, which would be made available at the locks. Cincinnati, Cleveland, Columbus, and other newspapers took up the idea. The *Liberty Hall* said to go ahead with the exploration and if present resources and credit were not sufficient, that problem could be taken up in time.[354] The Columbus *Ohio Monitor* did not wish to disparage New Orleans and her lowland markets, "but to our people they have proved a grave." It asked the people to co-operate by furnishing details regarding topography, streams, and other features to the canal commissioners.[355] Cleveland thought the project feasible and was for it.[356] Steubenville was interested in the Ohio and Erie project but also in the Chesapeake and Ohio Canal.[357] The Ravenna *Western Courier* was so stimulated that it indulged in prophesy. In "the Year 2150 anticipated," it reported news items on the arrival in Washington of a congressman from California by way of a canal at Darien, and that the population of New York was two million people.[358] "If internal improvements have changed the aspect of countries naturally barren and unfruitful; if agriculture and commerce have been promoted by the opening of roads and canals, through rocky and mountainous districts,

[353] Governor Brown came to be known as the "Father of Ohio Canals." The report may be found in Ohio *House Journal*, 1821–22, pp. 177 ff., or *Liberty Hall and Cincinnati Gazette*, January 19, 1822.

[354] January 19, 1822.

[355] April 13, August 10, 1822.

[356] *Cleaveland Herald*, May 21, 1822, and different articles during spring of 1822.

[357] *Western Herald and Steubenville Gazette*, October, 1823.

[358] Cited in *Hamilton Intelligencer and Advertiser*, December 2, 1822.

what an incentive to industry and enterprise is presented to the people west of the mountains."[359]

Under the direction of James Geddes, one of the Erie Canal engineers, nine hundred miles of surveys were made, and various feasible routes found.[360] The canal commission reported in 1823, and was authorized to make more detailed surveys. The original plan was to run the canal from the Miami to the Scioto River and to Lake Erie, and thus traverse the state from the southwest to the northeast corners. This was found impracticable because of high ground between the two rivers, so in the second report of 1824 the commission recommended the Scioto-Licking-Upper Muskingum route.[361] The report of the next year gave more details of this route as well as the Miami-Maumee route from Cincinnati to Toledo.

Meanwhile, ex-Governor Worthington pointed out in a widely published essay that Ohio's estimated population of 800,000 cultivated only two and a half million acres out of the sixteen million subject to taxation. As long as it cost more to haul a load of produce twenty-five miles over poor roads than the load was worth, little increase in acreage cultivated or taxes collectible could be expected. A canal would cut such costs many fold, and quick progress could be expected.[362]

Schools, canals, and a taxation system had all come to the front in state politics in 1824 and the legislature elected in that year was ready to act. On February 4, 1825, the law was passed "to provide for the internal improvement of the State of Ohio, by navigable canals." It created a board of seven canal commissioners, which was to select three of its members as an active board; a canal fund; another board of three to handle the canal

---

[359] *Portsmouth Gazette*, March 10, 1819.

[360] Five were considered practicable: Mahoning and Grand River route, Cuyahoga and Muskingum (Tuscarawas branch), Black and Muskingum (Killbuck branch), Scioto and Sandusky, Maumee and Great Miami. *Report of the Canal Commissioners to the General Assembly of Ohio*, 1823.

[361] Important acts, reports, and other documents relating to Ohio canals, were compiled and published by John Kilbourn in the *Civil Engineer, and Herald of Internal Improvement*, which he published weekly at Columbus from June to November, 1828. These issues and some additional documents were included in a volume issued by Kilbourn in 1832 under the title *Public Documents Concerning the Ohio Canals.* . . . For the 1823 and 1824 reports, see pages 31-40, 54-79.

[362] *Liberty Hall and Cincinnati Gazette*, September 24, 1824.

fund; and empowered this board to borrow $400,000 for 1825 and up to $600,000 in any succeeding year.[363]

"The laws that were enacted by the last General Assembly will produce a new era in our history," said the editor of the *Columbus Gazette*.[364] "The time seems to have arrived for the commencement of a liberal system of Western internal improvement," said the *Liberty Hall* as it congratulated the people of Ohio on the prospects before them. "Retrenchment and economy are not creative,"[365] and all but a few of the papers of the state agreed.[366] Chillicothe celebrated the bill's passage with salutes by the militia and a general illumination.[367] The town expressed its "gratification at an event so auspicious to the future prosperity of the State."[368] There was some little opposition to the measure, but it quickly subsided.[369] The *Steubenville Herald*, edited by the able James Wilson, opposed the borrowing system and the certain high taxes; and the *Sandusky Clarion* doubted that funds could be obtained at reasonable terms. Such doubters were overwhelmed with editorials and articles in the important Cincinnati, Columbus, Cleveland, and other papers.[370]

The law authorized two canals—the Ohio and Erie from Portsmouth on the Ohio to Cleveland by way of the Scioto–Muskingum route, and the Miami Canal from Cincinnati to Dayton along the Miami River. This was a compromise, for there were those who insisted on three canals, one in the east

[363] For the financial end of the Ohio canals, see Chapter XII. The act may be found in *Public Documents Concerning the Ohio Canals,* 158–65; *Columbus Gazette,* February 8, 1825; *Liberty Hall and Cincinnati Gazette,* January 28, 1825.

[364] February 24, 1825. The school law and tax law were also enacted (see Chapters VIII and XIII). Timothy Flint, in his *Western Monthly Review,* I (1827–28), 73, said that primary schools were the levers which moved the intellectual world, and that canals, railways, and steam-navigable waters were becoming the same to the empire of science and thought.

[365] February 1, 1825.

[366] The *Columbus Gazette* noted only four of the forty-eight state papers on its exchange list opposed to the Ohio and Erie Canal, with one or two on the fence. March 24, 1825.

[367] A common practice in way of a celebration in this period was to place candles or lamps in the windows of all residences and thus light up the town.

[368] *Cleaveland Herald,* February 18, 1825, quoting the "Chillicothe Gazette" [*Supporter and Scioto Gazette*] of February 3.

[369] Chillicothe *Supporter and Scioto Gazette,* May 5, 1825.

[370] *Liberty Hall and Cincinnati Gazette,* March 1, July 18, August 2, September 20, 1825; *Columbus Gazette,* January 1, 8, 18, 27, etc., 1825; *Ohio State Journal, passim.* The editor of the *Cincinnati Literary Gazette* thought Wilson was probably honest in his opposition, but felt he would create a false impression in the East. Cited in *Portsmouth Gazette,* April 29, 1825. The *Cleaveland Herald* during the early months of 1825 contained little besides canal articles.

by way of the Muskingum–Cuyahoga route, one in the center by way of the Scioto–Sandusky route, and the one in the west up the Miami to the Maumee. By the route selected for the Ohio Canal, the more thickly populated areas were served. Engineers were appointed and despite some discussion regarding the route,[371] an opening celebration was planned for July 4, Ohio's twenty-first birthday.

On the appointed date Governor De Witt Clinton and party were met at Cleveland by Governor Morrow and escorted by stage to Newark. At the Licking Summit, three miles out, "before a concourse of 10,000 people," Governor Clinton lifted the first shovelful of dirt, Governor Morrow the second, and other dignitaries contended for the honor of the third. The great Ohio Canal was under way. Thomas Ewing, the orator of the day, said: "The grand work, which is this day begun, is the effort of our infant state, yet in the cradle of her prosperity." Governor Clinton thought that every citizen would say:

See what my country has done in her juvenile state! And if she has achieved this gigantic enterprize in infancy, what will she not effect in the maturity of her strength, when her population becomes exuberant and her whole territory in full cultivation. And your sister states, and the civilized world, will be astonished. It will exhibit a spectacle, unprecedented and amazing. An infant wielding the club of Hercules, and managing the lever of Archimedes with irresistible power. When the eagle, in its first flight from the aerie soars to the heavens, looks at the sun with an unfailing eye, and bears in its talons the thunderbolts of Jove, who will not admire this sublime sight.[372]

The Clinton party then participated in celebrations at Dayton, Hamilton, and Cincinnati, then on July 21 at Middletown lifted

[371] James Kilbourne was one of its chief advocates and printed an eleven-column article in the *Delaware Patron*, March 24, 1825.

[372] Accounts of the celebration may be found in Ravenna *Western Courier*, July 23, Zanesville *Republican*, July 9, 1825, and most of the important Ohio papers. The account of the commencement was published in pamphlet form at Lancaster, Ohio; a reprint may be found in the *Ohio Archaeological and Historical Society Publications*, XXXIV (1925), 63–99. The most complete history of the Ohio canals is C. P. McClelland and C. C. Huntington, *History of the Ohio Canals, Their Construction, Cost, Use, and Partial Abandonment* (Columbus, 1905). Ernest Ludlow Bogart, *Internal Improvements and State Debt in Ohio* (New York, 1924), emphasizes the financial aspects. Articles which cover the subject in general are George White Dial, "Construction of the Ohio Canals" (with map), in *Ohio Archaeological and Historical Society Publications*, XIII (1904), 460–81, and Charles N. Morris, "Internal Improvements in Ohio 1825–1850," in *Papers of the American Historical Association*, III, No. 2 (1889), 107–36. Henry S. Tanner, *A Description of the Canals and Rail Roads of the United States . . .* (New York, 1840) contains useful maps, diagrams, and data.

the first dirt from the Miami Canal. Following this the "Father of Internal Improvements" continued in triumphal tour amidst the ringing of bells and firing of cannon to Chillicothe, Circleville, Lancaster, Zanesville, Cambridge and other towns.

First contracts were let for work on the Miami Canal in July, and work began. From Middletown to Hamilton the ditch followed the Miami Valley, then was carried across a plain to the southeast at a level of six to ten feet above the surrounding country. Locks brought it down to the level of Mill Creek and other locks to the "Nine Mile" level which led to Cincinnati. Spring floods which undermined the aqueduct piers and other obstacles brought delay, but work was completed to the head of Main Street, Cincinnati, and in July, 1827, crowds assembled to see the water turned in. Great disappointment resulted when the water did not flood the canal. It merely soaked into the dry bed. By November, however, enough had collected to carry three boats from six miles north of Cincinnati to Middletown. Shouts and the roar of cannon marked their progress. Then the water was turned out to let the banks settle. Work continued in 1828, and in January, 1829, Dayton celebrated the arrival of four canalboats from Cincinnati. A few weeks later the steam canalboat, *Enterprise*, made the trip. Locks to let the canal down the 112-foot drop to the Ohio were finished in 1830. This completed the 66-mile[373] stretch between the Mad River and the Ohio, which came to be known as the Miami Canal.

Work on the Ohio Canal got off to a slower start. By the end of November, however, 1,500 to 2,000 men were at work north of Portage Summit. Awarding of contracts caused some delay, for in 1826 there were nearly 6,000 bids for the 110 sections south of Portage Summit.[374] The digging and hauling continued in snow and mud during the winter of 1826–27,[375] only to be slowed considerably by the bad malarial summer of 1827. By spring work was under way on the deep cut at Licking Summit.[376] Work on the Portage Summit and forty locks along the Cuyahoga progressed so rapidly that on July 3, 1827, Governor Trimble and party left Portage Summit in the brightly painted *State of*

[373] The length as stated in the *Report of the Canal Commissioners, 1833.*
[374] *Ibid.*, 1826.
[375] *Liberty Hall and Cincinnati Gazette*, January 12, 1827.
[376] *Lancaster Gazette* cited in *Piqua Gazette*, May 2, 1827.

Ohio for Cleveland, thirty-eight miles away.[377] They were met outside Cleveland by the *Pioneer*, and a procession, prayers, orations, and feasting followed.[378]

The 109 miles from the Summit to Dresden, with a drop of 238 feet in 29 locks, were finished in the next two years. The ditch crossed the Tuscarawas by a dam, and recrossed it by an aqueduct, as it did the Walhonding. At Dresden the side cut of two miles let out the water from the two summits into the Muskingum. From Dresden the canal entered the Licking Valley and by 19 locks ascended the 160 feet to Newark, 174 miles from Cleveland. On July 10, 1830, a little more than five years after Governor Clinton started the canal, the first boat arrived at Newark from Cleveland. The immediate improvement in Cleveland business was noticeable; flour-mill workers, butchers, mechanics, and businessmen were kept on the run.

The stretch from Newark by way of the south fork of Licking across to the Scioto and down the west side to where the canal entered the river two hundred yards from its mouth at Portsmouth, completed the main canal. Navigation was open from Lake Erie to the Ohio in 1832. Total length, including feeders, was 333 miles.[379] There were 152 lift locks, 9 guard locks, 16 aqueducts, and 155 culverts.[380] The most important feeder was the 11½-mile stretch at Columbus opened in 1831. When in the early autumn the *Governor Brown* arrived at Columbus from Circleville, the *Liberty Hall and Cincinnati Gazette* boasted that within twelve months communication would be opened from New York to New Orleans through the heart of one of the finest countries in the world. "It will be understood and will flourish, as it was commenced and completed, without the aid of free trade, or any other species of nullification."[381] The main ditch of both the Ohio and the Miami canals was 40 feet wide at the water

---

[377] *Hamilton Advertiser,* July 14, 1827.

[378] Among the toasts offered: "George Washington," "The Present Administration," "Domestic Manufacturers," "Bunker Hill," "Canals and Roads," "Heroes of the Revolution," "The Governor of Ohio." *Cincinnati Daily Gazette,* July 14, 1827.
Statistics on shipment of goods on this section to the end of the year are published in the *Cleaveland Herald,* December 28, 1827. Wheat and whiskey led as exports, salt and merchandise as imports.

[379] The Ohio Canal proper was 308 miles long with 1,206 feet of lockage.

[380] *Report of the Canal Commissioners,* 1833.

[381] October 4, 1831.

line, 26 at the bottom, and 4 feet deep. The cost of the former
was about $4,245,000, and the latter $900,000.

Canal building was not a new venture in the history of mankind, but even so the engineering problems presented taxed the
best abilities of the generation, as did railroads, automobiles, and
aviation at a later date. Building a ditch which would hold
water, carrying it across rivers, providing for locks to overcome
several hundred feet of change in level, securing an adequate
water supply at the higher levels by means of reservoirs and
feeders was no simple task, and all the more difficult in that dirt,
wood, and stone had to do the work done later by reinforced
concrete and structural steel.[382] But at such practical tasks Americans have ever been more ingenious than in solving the attendant
financial problems.

Contracts were let for the following essential operations:[383]
grubbing, clearing, mucking and ditching, excavation and bank
building, locks and culverts, puddling, and protection. Clearing
of all stumps extended twenty feet on each side. Some excavation
was in rock, some under water. Locks and culverts were constructed of stone or wood; culverts and back walls of locks were
covered with puddle, a combination of gravel and wet clay,
packed by the feet of animals or manual tampers. Protection
against erosion of banks was provided with stone pavement or
loose stone. Seepage, dams, and aqueducts probably presented the
most difficult construction problems. Where the Ohio Canal
crossed Summit Lake a tow bridge of dikes and floating bridges
was built.

Labor for the work was supplied largely by Ohio farmers and
their sons, although a large number of Irish and German laborers
were employed. Gangs camped in shanties near the job during
working seasons and lived the rough life customary to men
engaged in construction labor.[384] Work in water and new land
rendered the men fit subjects for the prevalent malarial fevers.

[382] The best presentation of engineering practice in canal building is William
Strickland, *Report on Canals, Railways, Roads, and other Subjects, made to "The
Pennsylvania Society for the Promotion of Internal Improvement."* Strickland was
an architect and engineer who was sent to England and told to get the actual con-
struction details on canals, locomotives, and railroads. His report, published at
Philadelphia, 1826, contains 72 folio copper-plate engravings.

[383] *Report of the Canal Commissioners,* 1833.

[384] The original settlement at Akron was a canal shanty town.

Often work almost ceased in the July-August period. During the early years pay was 30 cents per day plus board and one to three jiggers of whiskey. As a result of Pennsylvania's vast improvement program and the competition offered by the building of the National Road and other works, wages were later increased.[385] The resident engineer had general supervision of the work, made the estimates, and certified to the acting canal commissioner as to work done by the contractor. The assistant engineer and his staff laid out the work, made measurements, and reported on quantity and kinds of materials. The contractor drew his money from deposits made by the Canal Fund Commissioners on requisition of the Board of Canal Commissioners, and paid his men. The bank-note pay was often accepted in trade at a discount. In the mad scramble for contracts some honest bidders underestimated obstacles and costs. Provisions and materials advanced even faster than wages. Others were dishonest bidders who figured on squeezing out a profit somehow, and these sometimes forgot to pay their laborers.

Governor Allen Trimble, of Ohio, in his message of 1826 had stated that the spirit of internal improvements, like the spirit of freedom, was contagious; he hoped that its influence would spread far and wide to each section, and thus unite the discordant passions of men into one great zeal for the general good. And James Kilbourne in his Congressional campaign said that the way to prosperity was easy: Extend the Miami Canal to Lake Erie, build one from near Pittsburgh to Lake Erie, another from Muscle Shoals to the "Tumbeckby," connect the Illinois River and Lake Michigan, extend the Cumberland Road, build other roads into the West and South and thus "get away from foreign dependence, encourage domestic industry and build up American markets."[386] The demand for internal improvements which sprang up after the War of 1812 was being fostered by the National Republicans, who by the "American System" sought by national aid to co-ordinate roads and canals with the protective tariff and the Bank of the United States into one great national system of

---

[385] Laborers were in demand in 1828 on the Pennsylvania Canal at $12 to $15 per month. *Civil Engineer, and Herald of Internal Improvement*, August 16, 1828.

[386] In his address to the voters of the eighth district. *Ohio State Journal*. September 28, 1826.

economy.[387] The western states, impatient of results, could not wait, so embarked upon their own plans. Henry Whiting, of Detroit, celebrated the new developments in verse:

> At mention of the word *canawl*,
> (Lord Byron makes it rhyme with call,)
> What hydrostatic wonders rise,
> And spread before the mental eyes!
> Where now does Erie sally forth?
> Her *flood-gate* still is near the north:
> But has she now no shorter sluice,
> By which she lets her waters loose?
> That leads them, as by magic wand,
> Adown the intervening land,
> Where Mitchell, with his bottled tide,
> Made Erie old Van Hudson's bride?
> Yes, "Clinton's ditch!" as 'twas y'clept,
> By those who nature's footsteps kept,
> And thought that streams, against their will,
> Should ne'er be made to climb a hill;
> That Hudson had no right to take
> A drop of water from the lake;
> That still it should descend the Fall,
> For old St. Lawrence own'd it all.[388]

Indiana was not far behind Ohio. Governor Jonathan Jennings in 1817 referred to Governor Clinton's letter regarding the practicability of a canal to connect the Ohio–Mississippi system with the Great Lakes.[389] The Vincennes *Western Sun* promoted a system of internal improvements,[390] and throughout the next dozen years the "system" was one of the leading issues in state affairs.[391] Interest in canals was quiescent for a period, although memorials were sent to Congress for aid. When James B. Ray was elected governor in 1825 on an internal improvements platform, serious agitation began. Seth M. Levenworth pointed out to the legislature that since Indiana sold her goods through one port and imported through another, she had to pay a double profit. Since it took a year for money to come from New Orleans and be sent East, interest was also an item. Ability to sell in the

[387] For internal improvements as a political issue, see Chapters IX and XI.
[388] *The Age of Steam.*
[389] Message, December 2, 1817. Indiana *House Journal*, 1817–18, p. 8.
[390] Esarey, *Internal Improvements in Early Indiana*, 79–80. This is the standard monograph on the Indiana canals.
[391] *Ibid.*, 80.

East would save the people money.[392] And John Ewing of the Senate reported regarding canals:

The statesmen and philosophers of the age, have exerted their best faculties to establish the theory and the practicability of this system, combating in their progress, ignorance and prejudice, timidity and heedlessness, in all variety of forms. . . . The scintillations of these mighty geniuses, like "the day spring from on high," have visited every hemisphere, and the benign influence will continue to unfold and expand the beauties of a God of nature, and the mysteries of political economy, until the *Danube,* like the *Nile,* the *Mississippi* like the *Thames,* and the *Wabash* like the *Hudson,* shall exhibit one great theatre of splendid and successful exertion.[393]

Even the citizens on the Lower Wabash, whose outlook was down river, passed resolutions for the Wabash and Erie Canal.[394]

The General Assembly in 1826 incorporated the Whitewater Canal Company, capital $1,000,000, work to be begun in two years, charter to run to 1860. The state reserved the right to buy one fourth of the stock and provided that, if profits exceeded 25 per cent per annum, tolls might be applied to reduce the same to 18 per cent.[395] The Richmond *Public Leger* called this "wind work," and apparently was right, as no canal came of it.[396]

Meanwhile interest in a Wabash–Lake Erie canal was developing. When Jonathan Jennings in Congress in 1822 backed a bill for such a canal the Vincennes *Farmers and Mechanics Journal* became enthusiastic.[397] Congress in 1824 donated a 320-foot right of way through the public domain for a Wabash–Maumee canal, but Governor Ray and the Assembly maintained the state should receive a section of land for each mile. Under pressure from Indiana's representatives Congress in 1827 donated to the state a strip of land one half of five sections wide, on each side of the canal from the mouth of the Tippecanoe to Lake Erie, reserving alternate sections to the United States. The canal was to be begun in five years and finished in twenty.[398]

[392] Indianapolis *Indiana Journal,* March 20, 1827.
[393] Indiana *Senate Journal,* 1825, pp. 168–69.
[394] *Indiana Journal,* September 5, 1826. The Richmond *Public Leger,* however, thought it was much too soon to think of embarking upon canal building. December 17, 1825, October 21, 1826.
[395] *Laws of Indiana,* 1825–26, pp. 29–36.
[396] February 3, 1827.
[397] February 20, June 26, 1823.
[398] U. S. *Statutes at Large,* IV, 236. This amounted to about 3,200 acres for each of the 213 miles of the proposed work. Indiana claimed 557 sections of land or 356,480 acres. A part of this had already been sold and the Indian title had not been extinguished to a large portion of it. Richardson, "History of the Wabash and Erie Canal," MS. thesis, Indiana University, 1925.

Indiana accepted this grant in 1828, and created a canal commission of three members,[399] but nothing was done because of the sectional warfare between the "Ohio-Whitewater" faction and the "Wabash" men. Besides, railroads were being considered favorably by many, among whom were the speaker of the house and the governor.[400] Cost, too, was an item. In its report the commission pointed to the proved utility and practicability of canals as well as to their democratic nature. They could be used by any person at any time. A new commission, appointed in 1830, employed an engineer and began surveys. Canal land sales were advertised,[401] but an added difficulty was the fact that part of the canal would have to pass through Ohio.

Congress in 1828 had given a similar grant to aid Ohio to extend the Miami Canal to the Maumee River. One section of this law authorized Indiana to transfer to Ohio, on agreeable terms, the part of the Wabash and Erie Canal lands which lay in the latter state. Agents of the two states conferred at Cincinnati the following year and an agreement was made whereby Ohio would take over the lands and build within fifteen years that part of the canal which would lie within her boundaries.[402] Ohio, however, feared that the Wabash and Erie Canal would be a competitor with her own canals which she was building at state cost, and her Assembly refused to ratify the agreement for a number of years. The canal opponents caused trouble in the Indiana legislature, but it finally ratified the joint agreement. An additional law of 1832 provided for a Canal Fund Commission,[403] land sales were reopened, and work ordered to begin.

At Fort Wayne on Washington's birthday, the Hon. Charles

[399] *Laws of Indiana*, 1827–28, pp. 10–12, 138–39.

[400] Governor Ray said that the Congress grant gave no choice, but believed a good argument could be put up for a railroad. Message of December 4, 1827. Indiana *House Journal*, 1827–28, p. 20; *Indiana Journal*, December 11, 1827. The *Journal* refused to take sides on the canal-railroad issue, but thought it would be just and wise for the General Government to yield its sovereignty over the public lands to the states in which they lay.

[401] *Cleaveland Herald*, July 1, 1830.

[402] *Indiana Journal*, January 7, 9, 1830. The *Journal* copied accounts from the *Hamilton Intelligencer* and the *Ohio State Journal*.

[403] *Laws of Indiana*, 1829–30, pp. 172–73; 1831–32, pp. 3–8. O. H. Smith, *Early Indiana Trials and Sketches*, 70, tells of the debate on passage through the House. Able arguments for and against the canal had been made, when Col. John McNary, the chosen orator of the Wabash, got the floor. Raising himself on tiptoe and facing the chair he said: "Mr. Speaker, our population on the Wabash am great, but our resources for salt am slim. SALT! they can not emigrate up the Wabash." This ended the debate. There was no reply.

W. Ewing and Commissioner Jordan Vigus officiated at the beginning celebration. Contracts were let and the labor shacktowns began to appear in the Maumee-Wabash valleys. About a thousand men were at work in the summer of 1834. "Corkers" and "Way Downers" (or Corkinians and Far Downers) paused long enough now and then to crack each other's skulls in settlement of long standing difficulties—no one seemed to know just what—but the work went on.[404] On July 3, 1835, three canal boats went from Fort Wayne to the forks of the Wabash, and the next day the opening of this thirty-two-mile summit section was celebrated by proper proceedings.[405] The wooden aqueducts were rotten by the time this section was opened, but the legislature had already voted to extend the canal on to Lafayette, said to be a great commercial center and steamboat landing. The canal was to cross the Wabash behind a dam, but at Birmingham Bluff it was to be built out in the river and protected with riprap.[406]

The land-sale receipts paid for only a small part of Indiana's expenditures on the Wabash and Erie Canal. By November 1, 1839, total expenditures were more than $2,000,000 of which $274,000 came from canal lands. Most of the remainder was borrowed.

Indiana's transfer of 292,000 acres of canal lands was authorized by Congress in 1834 and ratified by the Ohio legislature, which in March provided for the building of the eastern part of the Wabash and Erie Canal.[407] Construction began in 1837 and was completed in 1842 to the junction with the Miami Extension. The Wabash and Erie Canal was opened from Lafayette to Toledo, 187 miles, July 4, 1843; the event was celebrated at Fort Wayne with an oration by Lewis Cass.

By the law of Congress of 1828 Ohio was to begin work on the Miami Extension within five years and complete the project within twenty. Ohio accepted the terms the same year, authorized construction from Dayton to the Maumee in 1831, and began

---

[404] For sample riots with statistics, see *Indiana Journal*, March 25, September 9, 1837.

[405] Letter from Fort Wayne in Piqua (Ohio) *Western Courier*, August 8, 1835; *Indiana Journal*, July 31, 1835. Hugh McCulloch's seven-column address may be found in the *Journal*, September 18, 1835.

[406] *Laws of Indiana* (general), 1834–35, Chapter 16. The Report of the Canal Commissioners and of the Engineer was published in the *Indiana Journal*, January 9, 13, 1835.

[407] *First Report of the* (Ohio) *Board of Public Works,* 35.

work in 1833. This 114-mile canal, 50 feet wide at the surface and 36 at the bottom, and 5 feet deep, was not completed until 1845.

The brisk canal activity on the part of Ohio, Indiana, and Congress stimulated private enterprise. The Sandy and Beaver Canal of 73 miles to connect the Ohio River near Little Beaver Creek with the Ohio and Erie Canal at Bolivar, was started by an incorporated company, as was the Warren Canal from Lebanon to the Miami Canal. The latter was abandoned by the company in 1836, taken over by the state, and completed in 1840. The Pennsylvania and Ohio Canal of 93 miles, from Akron on the Ohio Canal across to join the Pennsylvania and Erie, was built by a private company in 1836–40. The Cincinnati and Whitewater was begun in 1839 by a private company which received aid from Ohio and Indiana. The Hocking Canal, 56 miles, from the Ohio Canal southeast to Athens, was begun by a private company but finished by the State of Ohio. In 1836 Ohio created a Board of Public Works to supersede the canal commissioners; the legislature also authorized the Walhonding Canal of 25 miles, and the Muskingum Improvement, as well as the taking over of the above-mentioned works.

A canal between the Great Lakes and Mississippi by way of the Illinois River—possibility of which was noted by Jolliet more than a century and a half earlier—was among the earliest western projects considered. The War Department in its survey in 1819 reported the headwaters of the Chicago and Des Plaines rivers so close together that during wet seasons Mackinaw boats of six or eight tons could pass from one to the other without portage, and that in time of strong east winds the waters of Lake Michigan undoubtedly flowed down the Illinois River.[408] In 1822 the economic arguments for a connection with eastern markets were presented by the *Illinois Intelligencer*.[409] Despite some opposition from areas not situated to benefit by such a canal, the Illinois legislature of 1822–23 passed a canal bill and set up a commission of five members to survey the route and estimate the

[408] *American State Papers, Miscellaneous*, II, 555. Summary in *Niles' Weekly Register*, XVII, 309 (Jan. 8, 1820). The best history of the Illinois and Michigan Canal is James W. Putnam, *The Illinois and Michigan Canal, A Study in Economic History* (*Chicago Historical Society's Collection*, X, 1918).

[409] November 30, 1822.

Steubenville, Ohio. *"Drawn from Nature by Whitefield"*

A Road Accident near Thornville, Ohio. *George Harvey*, 1841

cost. In 1825 a private corporation was authorized to accept any land grants, build the canal, and charge tolls. The state reserved the right to purchase the work in fifty years at cost plus interest. Daniel Pope Cook, Illinois' very energetic congressman, pointed out the dangers of this action; it was repealed in 1826.[410]

In 1827 Congress gave Illinois a land grant similar to that given to Indiana, and two years later the legislature set up a canal commission of three members. Ex-Governor Edward Coles, although in general favoring railroads, thought the region between the Illinois River and Lake Michigan well adapted to a canal.[411] But the new commission in its report of 1832 recommended a railroad rather than a canal. In March, 1833, the canal commission was abolished and a state examining board reported its books correct. The Senate, calculating that goods came from the East cheapest by way of the lakes, instructed the committee on internal improvements to examine into the expediency of a railroad or turnpike from Chicago to the head of navigation on the Illinois River.

Joseph Duncan, who had worked for the Illinois and Michigan Canal while in Congress, was elected governor in 1834. He believed canals more useful than railroads which "are kept in repair at very heavy expense and will last but about fifteen years."[412] "Peorian," in a long article in the *Sangamo Journal*, pointed out the monopolistic and undemocratic nature of railroads,[413] and the *State Register* said the reputation of the state was at stake; if the Assembly did nothing Illinois would become a mere "bye word." "This is an age of internal improvement, and it cannot be, that Illinois will stand with folded arms, and see

[410] A four-column article in the *Illinois Intelligencer*, November 18, 1825, set forth Cook's view. He argued that if the proposition was good enough to attract private capital, it was good enough for the state to undertake. The editor disagreed, for Illinois was already pledged to the limit of its resources.

[411] "Communication to the Antiquarian and Historical Society of Illinois," in *Illinois Monthly Magazine*, I (1830–31), 25. The map and profile survey of the proposed route as surveyed in 1830 may be found in U. S. *House Reports*, 23 Congress, 1 session, No. 546. The Edwardsville *Illinois Advocate*, October 21, 1831, said that the need for the Illinois and Michigan Canal was becoming more apparent daily; it cited the case of a St. Louis merchant who by importing goods by way of the lakes to Chicago, by wagon to the Illinois River, thence by boat to St. Louis had saved more than a week in time and almost enough insurance to pay the costs of transportation.

[412] Elizabeth Duncan Putnam, "The Life and Services of Joseph Duncan," in *Transactions of the Illinois State Historical Society*, 1919, pp. 129–30. See also Duncan's message to the legislature, 1834.

[413] February 15, 1834.

Ohio and Indiana rushing forward in the cause of internal improvements, and herself make no efforts."[414] Many railroad and canal meetings were held during the autumn.[415] In the ensuing legislature there was a sharp division between members from the northern and southern parts of the state, but a canal bill was finally passed. At first the credit of the state was not to be pledged for loans, but this provision was soon changed. The canal act was passed, but by this time the sectional or local interests and the railroad advocates had thrown open the whole question of a state internal improvements system. This was the big issue which faced the legislature in 1836–37.[416]

In the discussions but little attention was paid to the possibilities of canals as passenger carriers, but as soon as canals were opened people sought to travel on them in such numbers that plans had to be made for their accommodation. Passenger traffic on the western canals was never so heavy as in the East, for by the time the canals were finished the railroad was offering better facilities.

The first canalboats were modeled after the keelboats or barges of river fame, and built with pointed bow and stern, rounded bottoms, and narrow beam; they were about 50 to 60 feet long. Soon it was found that these features were not necessary in quiet waters, so a blunt-ended, wider and flatter boat became standard. The cabin walls rose five or six feet above the hull, and the flat roof served as promenade deck for passengers during fair weather. When it was found that passenger traffic was to be a considerable item, passenger boats were designed which became fairly well standardized. In the bow was a small cabin for the crew of a half-dozen men, then came the ladies' dressing room, followed by the ladies' cabin. In the middle and rear, excepting for the cramped cook's quarters, was the large room for men, which served as cabin, dining room, and sleeping parlor. At meal

---

[414] *Illinois Advocate and State Register*, January 7, 1835. See also series of articles in *Chicago Democrat*, September, 1835. The *Democrat* almost two years earlier had called attention to the indifference of Illinois as compared with the activity of Michigan and Indiana; it suggested that Illinois get busy. *Sangamo Journal*, January 11, 1834.

[415] *Sangamo Journal*, autumn 1835.

[416] For the Illinois state internal improvements system, see Chapter XII. The lengthy report of the committee on internal improvements in the legislature was published in full in the *Illinois Advocate and State Register* January 14, and in the *Sangamo Journal*, January 24, 1835.

time the crew set up the trestle tables and at evening they attached or let down the narrow shelves or bunks, three in a tier, to provide sleeping facilities. Not infrequently a cabin equipped with forty-two berths would accommodate more than twice as many sleepers. Under such conditions the floors and even the tables were used. Were a passenger unable to sleep because of heat, mosquitoes, or lack of ventilation, his chances for a soothing stroll on the deck were slim, for if, in the darkness, he succeeded in getting to the floor without stepping on a fellow passenger, he was most certain to get lost in a maze of baggage and clotheslines strung to take care of clothing.

Established lines on the most traveled canals usually maintained two types of passenger service. The regular or line boats, as a rule, supplied neither food nor bedding, and traveled about two or two and a half miles per hour. The luxury or packet boats, for those in a hurry, were extra-fare service, and averaged a mile or so greater speed per hour. Five cents per mile was a common fare on the packets, two or three cents on the line boats.[417]

Bright colors were not confined to Conestoga wagons and stagecoaches, for packet lines vied with one another in the variety and elegance of the hues with which they decorated their boats. Line boats were often crowded with emigrants coming West, who with their plunder and children, more or less stoically endured the crowded conditions and slow progress. Some fitted out family boats and with their own horses came all the way from New York into the Ohio and Indiana canals. Travel, even on the packets which made forty or fifty miles per day, was tedious and monotonous. It lacked the variety and attractiveness of steamboat travel. Scenery along canal routes was not likely to be as interesting as on the rivers. Going through locks provided some excitement, or for the young bloods, jumping on and off the boat at bridge crossings or locks to follow the tow path for a piece, but ordinarily there was little besides the changing of horses to break the even tenor of the slow progress. The passing of the canalboat as a means of travel was not regretted by many. Horace

[417] Since the five cent fare included meals, there were some, in the East at least, who boarded just before meals, ate, then got off and walked back a mile or so, all for five or ten cents.

An Ohio inventor, not satisfied with the canalboats then in use, constructed a vehicle with runners to run on ice and yet able to float should it break through. *Columbus Sentinel* in *Indiana Democrat*, January 13, 1832.

Greeley, who remembered the line boats of "a cent and a half a mile, mile and a half an hour" fame, expressed a general sentiment when in later life he said: "I say nothing about 'the good old times'; but if anyone would recall the good old line boats, I object."[418]

§ § § § §

The early railroads in America were, in general, conceived of as improved turnpikes, which would offer improved facilities for vehicular transport by horsepower. Various "railways" of wood, with horsecars, had been used around quarries, kilns, or mills from 1795 to 1826. Only a few pioneering minds associated this improvement with steampower. One of these, Oliver Evans, of Pennsylvania, petitioned his state in 1786 for the monopoly of propelling vehicles by steam on the roads of the state. The Pennsylvania legislators questioned his sanity, but Maryland was more patient and gave him a grant. In 1804 he put wheels under his five-horsepower steamboat and ran it through the streets of Philadelphia under its own power; in 1812 he offered to wager $3,000 that he could make a steam carriage which would run 15 miles per hour on good level railways.

John Stevens, of New Jersey, in 1811 applied to his state for the right to build a railroad, and the next year wrote *Documents Tending to Prove the Superior Advantages of Rail-Ways and Steam Carriages over Canal Navigation.*[419] Stevens believed railroad construction should be undertaken by the General Government, but the War of 1812 intervened, to be followed by a period in which strict-construction ideas prevailed. So American railroads evolved under private auspices.

When Stevens submitted his argument for a railway to the New York Canal Commission, Evans realized the obstacles to be overcome. He wrote:

When we reflect upon the obstinate opposition that has been made by a great majority to every step towards improvement; from bad roads to turnpikes, from turnpikes to canals, from canals to rail-Ways for horse carriages, it is too much to expect the monstrous leap from bad roads to rail-Ways for

[418] *Recollections of a Busy Life* (New York, 1869), 64.
[419] Dunbar thinks this probably the first published work on the subject. *History of Travel*, III, 881.

steam carriages, at once. One step in a generation is all we can hope for. If the present shall adopt canals, the next may try the rail-Ways with horses, and the third generation use the steam carriages. . . . I do verily believe that the time will come when carriages propelled by steam will be in *general use,* as well for the transportation of passengers as goods, travelling at the rate of fifteen miles an hour, or 300 miles per day.[420]

Stevens, as well as others, having tried unsuccessfully to get financial backing for various railroad projects, in 1820 built an experimental steam railroad on his estate in New Jersey, and a locomotive to pull the cars around the track. This was probably the first American-built locomotive. Three years later Pennsylvania granted Stevens a charter to build a railroad from Philadelphia to Columbia. Much doubt existed as to the possibility of steam being able to operate over such a distance—73 miles— but Stevens argued that each mile was just a repetition of the first mile. People with money admitted that railroads might serve a purpose across portages or to supplement canals, but were unwilling to invest their funds in them as basic means of transportation. Interest was aroused, however. In 1824 the Pennsylvania Society for the Promotion of Internal Improvements was organized, and a civil engineer, William Strickland, was sent to England with secret instructions to get a practical and specific knowledge of the best and most economic methods of constructing canals and railroads, together with information on locomotives. The committee wrote their agent: "Much excitement prevails in this state upon the question whether railroads are superior to canals, and the inquiries that are in progress in relation to them are in the hands of men of ingenuity and well disposed to the cause of internal improvements. . . . The importance of correct information in relation to them is thus greatly increased."

Important treatises on railways were appearing in England at this time,[421] and they found their way into American newspapers or were reprinted in this country. Although England had been making iron rails for almost a century, and locomotives for twenty years, most of these works deprecated the "ridiculous expecta-

---

[420] *Niles' Weekly Register,* III (1812–13), Addenda, 5.
[421] Thomas Tredgold, *A Practical Treatise on Rail-Roads and Carriages, Showing the Principles of Estimating their Strength, Proportions, Expense, and Annual Produce, and the Conditions which Render them Effective* . . . (London and New York, 1825); Nicholas Wood, *A Practical Treatise on Railroads* . . . (London, 1825, Philadelphia, 1832).

tions" of any general system of steam carriage, or speeds of twelve or eighteen miles per hour. George Stephenson, to get the ear of Parliament, was warned not to "damn the whole thing" by mentioning such speeds as twenty miles per hour. Not until Stephenson's *Rocket* made its demonstration in 1829 was there a significant change in the attitude of the English.

Meanwhile, the work of the pioneer railroad advocates in America was bearing fruit. Railroads struck the popular imagination; by 1825 china and glassware, wallpaper, and sheet music were being ornamented with designs of railroads and trains. Cuts appeared in a few newspapers between 1825 and 1830, as well as many columns of discussion regarding construction and mechanics, the use of railways as highways, and their economic possibilities.[422] Strickland's Report of 1826 was followed by public meetings and immediate activity. Baltimore had seen New York and Philadelphia reach into the West with canals; it staked its future on the railroad. The Baltimore and Ohio was chartered by Maryland in 1827. On July 4, 1828, Charles Carroll, last surviving signer of the Declaration of Independence, laid the cornerstone amid befitting ceremonies.

The West followed this project with keen interest. Long articles were copied from eastern newspapers.[423] Meetings were held at Marietta, Zanesville, Indianapolis, and elsewhere. The *Scioto Gazette* demonstrated that the new railroad should be continued from the Ohio River on to Chillicothe, Hamilton, and Terre Haute.[424] The *Hamilton Advertiser* published a full-column editorial on the subject[425] and the *Cleaveland Herald* pointed out that a Chesapeake and Ohio canal would cost twelve millions while the railroad would cost only five; also that canal rates, Pittsburgh to Baltimore, would be $5.85 per ton as compared with $2.50 for the railroad.[426] An Indianapolis mass meeting sought to get the railroad to extend its line through Ohio,

---

[422] The *Ohio State Journal*, November 11, 1825, had two articles, one on the history of railroads, the other on arguments for and against. The Lawrenceburg *Indiana Palladium*, May 13, 1825, devoted most of the front page to railroad material copied from the *Baltimore American*. Readers were told what railroads were, how locomotives operated, etc.

[423] Particularly *Ohio State Journal*, March—April, 1827, December, 1829.

[424] Copied in *Liberty Hall and Cincinnati Gazette*, May 18, 1827.

[425] June 1, 1827.

[426] April 20, 1827.

Indiana, Illinois, and on to the Mississippi.[427] A Cincinnati businessman wrote: "Who knows but that in a few years you will be coming from the West in Steam Carriages on Railways at 10–14 miles per Hour, you no doubt hear what is going on in Baltimore, the projected railroad from thence to the Ohio."[428]

The first section of the Baltimore and Ohio, thirteen miles out of Baltimore, was built for horse-drawn vehicles, but by the time it was completed in the spring of 1830, the success of the locomotive was being demonstrated. The tests of Stephenson's *Rocket* in England in 1829 impressed the public; the same year Peter Cooper demonstrated his miniature *Tom Thumb* over several rods of the Baltimore and Ohio track, and the year following, having improved his machine, pushed a car and twenty-four passengers over the thirteen miles in one hour and fifteen minutes. The prowess of the *Tom Thumb* was successfully disputed by the stagecoach interests, when a horse, on a parallel track, drew its car in ahead of the locomotive. This triumph was short-lived, however.

Other railroad plans were under way and further prepared the public mind. The little sixteen-mile coal line in Pennsylvania, the Carbondale and Honesdale, imported the nine-horsepower English *Stourbridge Lion*, which made a trial trip in the summer of 1829. The Charleston and Hamburg in South Carolina tried horsepower locomotives, sailing cars, and then in 1830 tried out an American-made locomotive,[429] which pulled a car with several passengers 21 miles per hour and ran alone at 30 miles per hour. The *West Point*, which replaced the *Best Friend* in 1831, protected its passenger car against boiler explosion by a car of cotton bales. The Mohawk and Hudson completed seventeen miles of track between Albany and Schenectady in 1831; after a brief use of horsecars, it decided to follow the Carolina plan. On August 9 the *De Witt Clinton*, built in New York, made a memorable trip. Carrying three passenger coaches and a half-dozen flat cars loosely connected by chains, the new locomotive created havoc

[427] *Indiana Journal*, July 31, 1827.
[428] James Brown to Thomas Sloo, Jr., April 3, 1827, in *Quarterly Publication of the Historical and Philosophical Society of Ohio*, VI, No. 2, pp. 43–44.
[429] The New York-built *Best Friend of Charleston*. This was the first locomotive made in America for regular use on a railroad. It probably was the first to run off the track and furnished the first explosion, when a Negro fireman, annoyed at the hissing escape valve, sat on the lever to keep it closed.

among the horses of the spectators along the way, set fire to the umbrellas and clothing of the passengers, jolted them out of their seats starting and stopping, but completed its run in less than an hour, including stops. The next month it made the trip in thirty-eight minutes and far outdistanced the horsecars.

Even before this success, the western mind was already building railroads all the way to the Mississippi. It had been well prepared by newspaper publicity, crossroads discussion, and legislative debate. In 1826 James Kilbourne, prominent Ohio politician, wrote that the best judges in the East thought that railroads with their lower costs and greater speed, would supersede canals. He advised the legislature, regarding a Columbus-to-Sandusky canal, to issue a charter for either a canal or railroad, and leave it up to the company.[430] The next year arguments were presented to the Indiana legislature that railroads were not only cheaper but possessed greater possibilities. To increase the speed of a canalboat from two to four miles per hour, one would have to increase the number of horses four times, but horsepower could not continue to follow the law of the square of the velocity because horsepower decreased with the speed. This was not true of steam, because once initial "axletree" friction had been overcome, doubling of power doubled the speed.[431] Three- to six-column articles, mostly extracted from C. Maclaren's essay on railroads, were published in the *Indiana Journal* in 1827,[432] as were also pages of Thomas Tredgold's treatise copied from eastern papers. This important Indiana paper believed that railroads were not only daily becoming more important, but were decidedly preferable to canals in the minds of both experimenters and public.[433] Thomas J. Larsh, editor of the *Richmond Palladium*, preferred railroads to canals, despite the great interest of his county in canals:[434]

A few years ago, even one year ago, Railways were only thought practicable, where canals could not be constructed. Now it is contemplated to

[430] *Ohio State Journal*, January 12, 1826. Kilbourne added one and one-half columns of extracts from the report of the *Liverpool and Birmingham*, February 23, 1826.

[431] Seth M. Levenworth, in committee of the whole on the internal improvements bill in the House. *Indiana Journal*, March 20, 1827. Apparently no one questioned Mr. Levenworth's physics.

[432] May 8, July 3, 1827.

[433] *Ibid.*, March 17, 1830, August 14, 1835.

[434] *Richmond* (Ind.) *Palladium*, August 27, 1831.

construct one, between two important places connected by a navigable river!

And we venture the prediction that the man is now living, who will see Pittsburg and Cincinnati connected by a Railway. . . . The beneficial effects of the canals of the United States have been great—they have exceeded the expectations of their most sanguine friends; and we boldly affirm, that there is no comparison between a Railway and a Canal. . . .

Larsh could not understand the apathy of his section towards a "Rail Road" from Richmond to connect with the Miami Canal at Hamilton.

> Rouse! fellow citizens, Rouse! Let your energies lie no longer dormant —let us not be the last to engage in the good cause. The resources of Wayne County, already rich, populous and flourishing are not yet half developed. There is an immense quantity of unimproved water power in this county, calculated to drive any species, and almost any amount, of machinery. So soon as this cheap and rapid means of transportation is in operation the water power will be occupied—large capitalists will be induced to settle amongst us—the price of property will be doubled—the farmer will find a market at home for his surplus products—the very timber, which is now in his way, will be converted into money, the mechanic, the manufacturer, the merchants, the publican, and even the printer will be benefitted. . . . Of course, in a pecuniary point of view the benefits would be immense; but when we come to take into consideration, the moral influence it would have on society, particularly the rising generation, the widest stretch of the imagination is incompetent to comprehend the results.

In the *Palladium* in 1832 began a series of elaborate discussions of railroads by John Test, prominent lawyer and politician. Governor James B. Ray, who had argued for railroads as early as 1827, in his message of 1830 suggested that the Great Lakes be united with the Ohio by a railroad from Detroit across Michigan and by way of Indianapolis to the Ohio. He visioned in time a "grand scheme of railroad concentration at Indianapolis."

The Mohawk and Hudson had not yet laid its track before the ambitious project of a great railway was being promoted "to connect the Canals and navigable waters of the states of New York, Pennsylvania, Ohio, Indiana, Illinois, Missouri; and the Michigan, North-West, and Missouri Territories; opening thereby a free communication, at all seasons of the year, between the Atlantic States and the great valley of the Mississippi."[435]

[435] Pamphlet, New York, 1829. Extracts in *Western Monthly Review*, III (1829-30), 19–24.

This was variously referred to as the Atlantic and Michigan, Atlantic and Mississippi, Great Western, and Atlantic and Great Western. The distance from New York to the Rock Island Rapids was calculated at 993 miles; the cost was estimated at $8,000,000 to $11,000,000. Timothy Flint, editor of the *Western Monthly Review*, contemplated its effects: The West needed only transportation facilities to cover its noble forests and fertile prairies with population; in half a century this would probably be one of the most salubrious climates in the world.

We suspect this to be the most magnificent project that was ever proposed, in the sober conviction of practicability, in any age or country. It actually made our head ache, to stretch our thoughts from one extremity of this proposed chain to the other. We stood still, shut our eyes, and attempted fixedly, to imagine the thousands of loaded teams continually gliding along the iron track, bound in opposite directions, and as continually speeding their everlasting course up the hills and down the vallies, as the roll of the rivers beneath them, or the lapse of time.[436]

Flint thought it not improbable that within a hundred years, canals and railways would be as common as ordinary roads then were.

The *Detroit Gazette* in its first important notice of railroads,[437] predicted that in twenty years the great canal of New York would be filled up and that the broad and beautiful lakes would be of no use. In time it would be possible to get in a carriage over a steam engine and at 30 to 40 miles an hour travel east to breakfast the next day in New York. "Wild and visionary as these predictions now seem to the reader, we are mistaken if we do not consider them as sober calculations. . . ."

The dream of a Pennsylvania businessman who had just used the railroad seemed fantastic at the time. He saw railroads shooting off in every direction; men kept individual sulkies for business use; some found it cheaper to live in their carriages than in houses. "In every direction we saw huge shanties in motion with artisans at work—women on top cooking—children squalling—all the operations of domestic arrangements going on. . . . the fashion had come up of having no permanent location—

---

[436] *Western Monthly Review*, III (1829–30), 20.
[437] December 17, 1829.

the whole country was over run with wanderers—cities were deserted...."[438]

So rampant was the enthusiasm for railroads, and so far-reaching their possibilities, that some facetious protests were heard. A canal stockholder advanced the following argument:

He saw what would be the effect of it; that it would set the whole world a-gadding. Twenty miles an hour, sir.—why, you will not be able to keep an apprentice boy at his work! Every Saturday evening he must have a trip to Ohio to spend a Sunday with his sweetheart. Grave plodding citizens will be flying about like comets. All local attachments will be at an end. It will encourage flightiness of intellect. Veracious people will turn into the most immeasurable liars. All conceptions will be exaggerated by the magnificent notions of distance. Only a hundred miles off—tut, nonsense, I'll step across, madam, and bring your fan! . . . And then, sir, there will be barrels of pork, cargoes of flour, chaldrons of coal, and even lead and whiskey, and such like sober things that have always been used to slow travelling—whisking away like a sky rocket. It will upset all the gravity of the nation. . . . Upon the whole, sir, it is a pestilential, topsy-turvy, harum-scarum whirligig. Give me the old, solemn, straight forward, regular Dutch Canal—three miles an hour for expresses, and two rod jog-trot journeys—with a yoke of oxen for heavy loads! I go for beasts of burden; it is more formative and scriptural, and suits a moral and religious people better—none of your hop skip and jump whimsies for me.[439]

Others thought that railroads would have pernicious moral effects. Physiological arguments were also advanced: the human body was not constituted to function at speeds as great as 25 miles per hour. The heart would be unable to pump the blood against such a speed. These predictions had little effect, for in 1832 a flurry of railroad chartering began in Indiana which resulted in 31 charters in five years, all in advance of any construction.[440] Although capital was somewhat reluctantly forth-

[438] *Sangamo Journal* (quoting *Philadelphia Bulletin*), October 6, 1832.

[439] *Western Sun and General Advertiser*, July 24, 1830. A passenger on the way from Washington to Philadelphia in 1841 mentioned the rush and bustle to get choice seats on the cars. "The way we fly across the country is like the wind. . . . so much speed at times we cannot count the panels of fence on the way." *Diary of William Sewall, 1797–1846*, edited by John Goodell (Lincoln, Ill., 1930).

[440] 1832: The Lawrenceburg and Indianapolis; the Madison, Indianapolis, and Lafayette; the Ohio and Lafayette; the Wabash and Michigan (Lafayette to Lake Michigan); the Harrison and Indianapolis; the New Albany, Salem, Indianapolis, and Wabash; the Richmond, Eaton, and Miami; and the Ohio and Indianapolis.

1834: The Evansville and Lafayette; the Indianapolis and Lafayette; the Leavenworth and Bloomington; the Indiana Northwest Railroad Company (Michigan City to Terre Haute); and the New Albany and Jeffersonville.

coming, these were not mere wildcat projects, for on the charters appeared the names of many of the more responsible business- and public men in the state. The Lawrenceburg and Indianapolis was most prominently promoted. Notices of stock subscriptions abounded and two thousand shares were said to have been taken by the spring of 1834.[441] In May estimates of cost were $2,500 per mile or $250,000 for the eighty-eight miles; by December the estimate was placed at $6,033 per mile.[442] Aside from the one and one-quarter mile experimental track laid down by this road near Shelbyville, no railroad track was opened in the state until 1838.[443]

The whole question of railroads versus canals was open, and the legislature, considering a general system of internal improve- ments, prepared in 1835 to make railroad as well as canal surveys. It was hoped to complete six or seven hundred miles before the next meeting of the Assembly.[444]

In Ohio the first railroad charter was granted in 1830 to the Ohio and Steubenville, a road which never got beyond the charter stage. Soon public meetings were held and the legislature became

---

1835: The Buffalo and Mississippi (across Northern Indiana); the Indianap- olis and Montezuma; the Frankfort, Delphi, and Michigan; the Michigan City and Kankakee; and a short line from Charlestown to the Ohio River.

1836: The Evansville and Vincennes; the Crawfordsville, Covington, and Illinois; the Princeton and Wabash; the Perrysville and Danville (Illi- nois); the Lafayette and Danville; the Bethlehem and Rockford; the Jeffersonville and Vernon; and the Madison and Brownstown.

1837: The Michigan City and St. Joseph (Michigan); the Indianapolis and Michigan City; the Hudson and New Buffalo (Michigan); the Fort Wayne and Piqua (Ohio); and the Mount Carmel (Ill.) and New Albany.

[441] Lawrenceburg *Indiana Palladium, Shelbyville Republican, Indiana Journal,* February—May, 1834.

[442] *Indiana Journal,* May 10, December 2, 1834. This estimate was for a single track of wrought-iron rails ⅝ by 2¼ inches laid on 6-by-8-inch oak stringers; stringers to be laid on 9-by-5-inch sleepers 8 feet long. Sleepers were to be 4 feet apart, each end to rest on 1 cubic foot of crushed stone. It included grading, superstructure, and a horse path of broken stone 4 inches deep.

[443] The first railroad report in the state was rendered to the legislature by the Lawrenceburg and Indianapolis in December, 1834. This road had opened its 1¼ mile of railroad with "one cut of five feet, one embankment of five feet, and one of ten, two curves and two bridges" on July 4, 1834. Cost of construction was $1,975, the car cost $222.12½, horses and drivers $12.62. Sixty dollars were taken in as fares from "between six and eight hundred persons" on that date, and immediately returned to the stockholders as dividends. The 12-page report strongly advocated railroads and pointed out the prospective increase in values of timber, stone, and firewood, as well as transportation and market facilities; it anticipated a 15 per cent dividend from the beginning. Indiana *Senate Journal,* 1834–35, pp. 63–75. For construction of the Indiana railroads, see Chapter XII.

[444] *Indiana Journal,* May 15, 1835.

interested. "The Railroad fever is permitted to rage unmolested in both houses," reported the *Cleveland Advertiser*. Ten charters were granted in 1832, the most important of which was for the Mad River and Lake Erie road (Springfield to Sandusky) which gave the state the right to purchase after forty years. Contracts for grading the first division of this road between Sandusky and Tiffin were let, and at Sandusky on August 17, 1835, an inaugural celebration was held. A twenty-four-gun salute was fired and speeches made. Governor Joseph Vance and General William Henry Harrison were guests.[445] The first thirty miles were not completed until five years later.

Illinois, too, was hearing railroad rumblings. As early as 1825 the *Illinois Advocate* noted the incorporation and promotion of a company, capital stock $3,000,000, to begin within three years a railroad from Vincennes to Danville, Paris, and Chicago.[446] Accounts of the Great Western project received some notice in 1829, and a few railroad meetings were held in 1831 to consider a railroad from Lake Erie to the Mississippi.[447] A Quincy meeting recommended that the Great Western proceed from Buffalo to that town, while a Jacksonville meeting considered the practicability of a railroad from Springfield to the Illinois River by way of Jacksonville.[448] Jacksonville in 1832 advanced the idea of a road from that town to the Illinois River, while two years later George Forquer, James Adams, and other important politicians thought a railroad to connect the Mississippi with the Wabash by way of Beardstown, Quincy, Springfield, Decatur, and Danville more practicable than a canal. The editor of the *Sangamo Journal* advocated substituting a railroad for the Illinois and Michigan canal; Vandalia and Pekin meetings approved the idea.[449] Rushville resolved for estimates on a road from that town to the Illinois River. Early in 1833 a bill to charter the Chicago and Illinois railroad failed by one vote in the Senate,[450]

---

[445] *Cleveland Herald*, September 5, 1835.
[446] *Illinois Advocate and State Register*, January 24, 1825.
[447] Pease, *The Frontier State*, 205.
[448] *Sangamo Journal*, December 29, 1831; January 5, 1832.
[449] *Ibid.*, March 1, 8, 22, 1832. Many articles on railroads from British and eastern papers appeared in the *Journal* during the summer and autumn of this year.
[450] *Ibid.*, March 9, 1833.

but later in the year Springfield was agitating for a special session to charter the road from Chicago to the Illinois River.[451] Representatives from Adams and Schuyler counties met in 1835 to promote a similar road to link up the Wabash and Erie Canal with Quincy by way of Springfield and Jacksonville; they recommended another to the Ohio by way of Vandalia.[452] Governor Joseph Duncan, advocate of canals, gave these plans no support, however.[453] Many railroad meetings were held during 1835–36 for by that time the question of building a central railroad from Cairo to Peru was becoming an issue in state politics. Another year and Illinois railroads had found important enough friends to make a beginning.[454]

The Legislative Council of Michigan Territory in 1832 incorporated the Detroit and St. Joseph Railroad Company. The road from Detroit to the mouth of the St. Joseph River, which was permitted to utilize steam, animals, or other power, was to be completed within thirty years; the state was given the privilege to purchase at cost, plus 14 per cent interest. Forty-four miles of this road (Detroit to Ann Arbor), which eventually became the Michigan Central, were in operation by 1840. But though this was the first Michigan charter it was not to be the first railroad, for the Erie and Kalamazoo began operations prior to that date.

In Wisconsin Territory—set off in 1836—the settlements were not sufficiently advanced to be ready for railroads. The territorial Assembly during its first year petitioned Congress for a railroad from Lake Michigan to the Mississippi, to take care of the 14,000,000-pound-per-year lead production.[455] Tanner said in 1840: "With the exception of some surveys authorized by Congress, nothing has been done in this section of the United States in the way of canals or railroads."[456]

---

[451] *Sangamo Journal*, September 28, October 5, 1833.

[452] *Ibid.*, December 19, 1835.

[453] See Illinois *Senate Journal*, December 1, 1834, for his arguments against railroads.

[454] *Sangamo Journal* and *Illinois Advocate and State Register*, 1835-36.

[455] *Belmont* (Wis.) *Gazette*, November 23, 1836.

[456] Tanner, *Canals and Rail Roads of the United States,* 220. Railroads were proposed from Milwaukee to the Mississippi, from Lafontaine to Lake Winnebago, from Belmont to Dubuque, and from Belmont to Dodgeville via Mineral Point. Also a canal from Milwaukee to Black River. For the building of the railroads of the Northwest, 1836 to 1840, see Chapter XII.

§ § § § § §

Long before the American settler displaced the Indian in the Northwest, the possibilities of the region for commerce and industry were foreseen. Gen. Thomas Gage, commander of the King's troops in the colonies, in 1770 saw no advantage in increasing the settlements in the "remote country," for though they might produce naval stores, wines, silks, and other commodities,

their very long Transportation must probably make them too dear for any Market. I do not apprehend the Inhabitants could have any Commodities to barter for Manufactures, except Skins and Furrs, which will naturally decrease, in proportion as the Country increases in People, and the Desarts are cultivated so that in the Course of a few years, Necessity would force them to provide Manufactures of some kind for themselves: And when all Connection upheld by Commerce, with the Mother-Country shall cease, it may be suspected that an Independency on her Government will Soon follow.[457]

This view in part determined a colonial policy which lost an empire to England, but the United States did not repeat this error with its colonies. The Ordinance of 1787 and a liberal land policy indicated a different attitude. Nevertheless, as the West settled, it found itself in somewhat the same economic relationship to the East that the colonies had been to England. After all, sectionalism is but nationalism divided up. As the settlers advanced in great numbers into the Northwest following the War of 1812, they soon found themselves owing the government (or speculators) for their land, and eastern merchants for their necessary purchases. Despite the hardships of the first few years in the wilderness and prairie, a surplus for export soon became available in heavy staples such as grain, meat, whiskey, lumber, and livestock. The problem then, was one of markets, transportation, money, and credit. Then as now, a degree of stable prosperity depended upon a rough balance not only between the geographic sections, but between agriculture, industry, and commerce. Achievement of such a balance necessitated the solution of a difficult problem in conflicting interests.

Following the war came the usual period of good prices and

[457] Gage to Lord Hillsborough, November 10, 1770, in Clarence E. Carter (ed.). *The Correspondence of General Thomas Gage . . . , 1763–1775* (2 volumes. New Haven, Conn., 1931–33), I, 277.

speculation. Europe needed raw materials and our foreign commerce increased several hundred per cent in the next few years. The western land boom was on, state bank notes flooded the country, and the price of land and agricultural products was high.[458] At Chillicothe in 1816 corn was selling at 37½ cents, wheat at 75 cents, beef at 6¼ cents, bacon at 10 to 12½, potatoes at 50 cents, and hay at $8.00 per ton.[459] "Attention! Farmers and Others Seriously!" was the heading of a notice by a farmer who had news of crop failures in Europe and a $12-per-barrel price for flour in Baltimore. He wished all farmers to be informed so as not to sell at half price; the times were right for getting even with both Europe and eastern merchants who had been making farmers sell bank notes at 10 to 20 per cent loss.[460] Corn at Vincennes went from 25 cents in 1816 to 50 cents in February, 1818, when wheat was $1.00, pork $4.50 per hundred, and beef $3.00 to $4.00.[461]

Similar prices prevailed in Illinois,[462] with pork at $4.00 to $7.00 per hundred and butter at 12 to 50 cents. Wood ashes brought 8 cents a bushel at Hamilton, Ohio, in 1817, and pearlashes $150 per ton at Cleveland the next year.[463] Flour at Detroit was $11 to $12 the barrel in 1817, pork $26 to $30, lard $20 the hundred, potatoes 75 cents, cordwood $4.00, whiskey $1.00 to $1.25 the gallon, while corn and wheat were $2.00 per bushel.[464] Prices fell somewhat the following spring, but were still high.[465] At Cleveland corn sold at 50 to 62 cents, wheat at $1.00, ham at 19 cents, lard at 12½, and whiskey at 50 to 62½ cents.[466] The *Zanesville Express* in the early summer advised farmers to get their wheat to New Orleans before mid-December, for the previous winter flour had been $15 and ships had had to leave that port in ballast for lack of cargo.[467] The flatboat traffic down river

---

[458] For land sales and speculation, see Chapters III and X; for currency and banking, Chapter VIII.
[459] Chillicothe *Supporter*, September 2, 1816.
[460] *Ibid.*, November 26, 1816.
[461] David Thomas in his "Additional Notices of the Western Country," in *Travels*, 191.
[462] Buck (ed.), "Pioneer Letters," in *Transactions of the Illinois State Historical Society*, 1910, p. 162.
[463] Hamilton (Ohio) *Miami Herald*, September 26, 1817; *Cleaveland Register*, October 6, 1818.
[464] *Detroit Gazette*, September 26, 1817.
[465] *Ibid.*, February 20, May 29, 1818.
[466] *Cleaveland Register*, October 6, 1818.
[467] Cited in *Liberty Hall and Cincinnati Gazette*, June 16, 1818.

was heavy. One person counted 643 flatboats headed for New Orleans on his trip upstream.[468] Merchants were speculating in commodities, farmers in land, everyone directly or indirectly in the flimsy money of the state banks.

The false delusions of artificial wealth increased the demand of the farmer for foreign productions, and led him to consume in anticipation of his crops. The country trader, seduced by a demand for more than his ordinary supply of merchandise, was tempted to the extension of his credit, and filled his stores, at the most extravagant prices, with goods vastly beyond what the actual resources of his customers could pay for, whilst the importing merchant, having no guide to ascertain the real wants of the community but the eagerness of retailers to purchase his commodities, sent orders abroad for a supply of manufactures wholly disproportioned to the effective demand of the country. Individuals of every profession were tempted to embark in speculation, and the whole community was literally plunged in debt. *The plenty of money,* as it was called, was so profuse, that the managers of the Banks were fearful they could not find a demand for all they could fabricate, and it was no unfrequent occurrence to hear solicitations urged to individuals to become borrowers, under promises as to indulgences the most tempting.[469]

As usual, such conditions tempted many to live by speculation rather than labor; fictitious values were given to all kinds of property. "Specie was driven from circulation as if by common consent, and all effort to restrict society to its natural conditions was treated with undisguised contempt."

Deflation came rapidly in the late summer of 1818. The contraction in money and credit was accompanied by an abrupt drop in prices of commodities and property values. Wheat was locally quoted at 25 to 75 cents, and flour sold at $2.50 to $3.00 per barrel. Corn and whiskey were about 12½ cents, eggs 1 to 3 cents per dozen, pork $1.25 to $1.75 per hundred, chickens 37½ to 75 cents per dozen, and so on. The break in prices and the uncertain state of the currency disrupted business. Honest traders as well as speculators were severely penalized. Sixty- and ninety-day bills drawn on New Orleans preceded the merchant and his produce to that city, and when he sold, he had to do so at half price.[470] By 1820 corn at Cincinnati was down to 10 cents, wheat to 25 cents, and whiskey would not sell at 15 cents per gallon. Two bushels of wheat would scarcely pay for one pound of coffee;

[468] *Niles' Weekly Register,* XIV, 344 (July 11, 1818).
[469] Gouge, *A Short History of Paper Money and Banking,* part II, 65.
[470] See Chapter VIII for more extended discussion of the conditions in the West.

flour, after being hauled sixty miles by wagon, brought $1.50 a barrel; chickens sold at 1 to 6 cents each.[471] "Distress is beyond all conception. Sherriff sales occur almost daily." A handsome gig and a valuable horse brought $4.00, an elegant sideboard $3.00, three beds with bedding, $3.00.[472] Men, businesses, banks, were all broke. But little specie was to be had; merchants issued small notes—25 cents and lower—payable in dry goods, groceries, or drink. Spanish pistareens (about 17 cents in value) were cut into 6 pieces whose total value was about double that of the original coin. Tavern meals were 25 cents in cut money, $1.00 in paper.[473] Conditions as portrayed at Vincennes in the winter of 1822 were typical:

A few years past Vincennes was the very emblem of prosperity: every wind wafted her some good. Our houses were filled with inhabitants, our streets were crowded with citizens, the noisy hum of business resounded in our ears, all was life and activity. How sadly is the picture reversed. More than one third of our dwelling houses are destitute of inhabitants, our population has decreased nearly or quite one half, our ready property has suffered a greater diminution. Buildings that a few years ago rented for $200 to $300 per annum now rent for $50 to $100. . . . An universal despondency prevails.[474]

There were the usual discrepancies, lack of uniformity and maladjustments in prices. The *Pittsburg Statesman,* July, 1819, complained that despite the hard times, scarcity of money, difficulty of getting *passable rags* (bank notes), flour was $10 a barrel and produce of every kind high. "Nothing of a chattel kind is depreciating, except bank stock."[475] But by 1821 flour was $1.00 per barrel, whiskey 15 cents per gallon, and sheep and calves $1.00 per head. The complaint now was that foreign goods were at the same old prices: it took a bushel and a half of wheat to buy one pound of coffee, one barrel of flour to buy one pound of tea, and twelve barrels to buy one yard of broadcloth.[476] Detroit was complaining in 1819 that while wages had fallen in the East, one had still to pay $1.00 per day for common

[471] "Historical Sketches—No. 1," in *Genius of the West* (Cincinnati, 1853–56), IV, 34 (Feb., 1855).
[472] Letter in *Cleaveland Herald,* August 29, 1820.
[473] *Cincinnati Pioneer* (Cincinnati, 1873–85), III (1874), No. 3, p. 14.
[474] *Western Sun and General Advertiser,* February 16, 1822.
[475] July 17, 1819.
[476] *Pittsburg Mercury,* in *Niles' Weekly Register,* XX, 180 (May 19, 1821).

labor, $2.00 to $2.25 for masons and carpenters, $6.00 to $8.00 per month for housework, a shilling a pound for poor mutton, 10 cents a pound for poor beef, and $20 to $25 per barrel for ordinary pork. Certainly prices should be no higher than in 1817 when $5.00 came to pocket oftener than $1.00 does now.[477]

The *Cleaveland Register* felt the times to be badly out of joint.

Hard times are cried by everyone, and yet we pay the war prices for everything. We must have tea at two dollars per pound, coffee at 50 cents and everything else in the same proportion. We must pay the laborers upwards of a dollar per day—the mechanic two or three—we must pay for boarding four or five dollars per week.—What! And still cry hard times! Shame on such inconsistency—the times are not hard here, or we could not pay so extravagantly for everything.

Debt was piling up, everyone was pushing everyone else one step down. "Such a scene as has never been exhibited in Ohio is about to take place," as the poorer classes were reduced to a state of indigence and want.[478] Some thought the most disastrous results were other than material. Despondency prevailed, society and good fellowship were torn up by the roots. "Envy, hatred, malice, and their train of evil passions, are taking deep hold of our minds. We see, every day, monsters in human shape distressing their neighbors, and wringing the widow's heart." Sheriffs' and constables' sales abounded on all sides. "Honesty has fled from the world, and Sincerity has fallen asleep; Piety has hidden herself, and Justice cannot find the way; the Helper is not at home, and Charity lies sick; Benevolence is under arrest, and Faith is nearly extinguished; the Virtues go a-begging, and Truth has long since been buried; Credit is turned crazy, and Conscience is nailed to the wall."[479]

Although the second Bank of the United States drew the brunt of the blame in the West,[480] some critics were sure the people had been offending Providence with luxurious living and lax morals, while others thought they saw some connection with the past wars. America had fattened at the expense of Europe and expected the emoluments of prosperity to continue indefinitely.

[477] *Detroit Gazette,* September 17, 1819.
[478] *Cleaveland Register,* September 28, 1819.
[479] *Ibid.,* August 10, October 5, 1819.
[480] See Chapter VIII.

Mathew Carey thought that to blame the banks was to mistake the symptom for the cause. The real cause lay in a state of unbalanced foreign trade and unbalanced national economy within. Too many people were farming and raising foodstuffs in the face of diminishing foreign demand, while we did not manufacture enough to meet our own needs.[481]

Some in the West blamed, in addition to the Bank—"The Great Mammoth of the East"—the ungenerous policy of the General Government towards the western country. Either as a result of unpardonable ignorance or willful neglect, it taxed the West higher than the East (counting payments for government land), yet the revenues were spent in the East. Not 1 million of 26 millions spent by the United States in 1818 were spent in the West, complained Ohio papers.[482]

The depression merely intensified the arguments of sectional interest. Editors, letter writers, and politicians as well as businessmen argued that the West would have to establish its own manufactures, its own markets, that the Ohio River would have to be used both ways, that exports would have to exceed imports.[483] "As long as we import more than we export we will always be in a bad way," said "A Friend to Domestic Manufactures."[484] It did no good to rant about banks when the real cause of pecuniary distress was that the West bought more than it sold.[485] Societies were organized along the Ohio for Domestic Industry and Economy. Cleveland businessmen recommended the idea to their brethren along the Lake shore.[486] Edwardsville citizens met to recommend a system of domestic economy compatible with the conditions of the people of the western states.[487] Farmers were warned that they must give up their hopes of a general European

[481] Carey, in his preface to *The Crisis* . . . (Philadelphia, 1832). Mathew Carey wrote some sixty pamphlets on the subject of manufactures, tariff, and agriculture about this time.

[482] Letters by Dion on "The Interest of the West," in *Liberty Hall and Cincinnati Gazette*, May, 1819; Chillicothe *Supporter*, May—June, 1819.

[483] Articles, editorials, and exchanges in *Liberty Hall and Cincinnati Gazette*, August, 1815. The *Western Herald and Steubenville Gazette*, February 17 and 24, 1818, gave seven columns to John Melish's letter to President Monroe in which he emphasized the 75-million-dollar deficit in the United States from foreign trade for the preceding three years, and noted the unemployment which resulted.

[484] *Western Herald and Steubenville Gazette*, November 2, 1822.

[485] *Ibid.*, April 17, 1819.

[486] *Cleaveland Register*, February 15, 1820.

[487] *Edwardsville Spectator*, October 9, 30, 1821.

war to ameliorate distressing conditions.[488] Relief was to be had otherwise:

Farmers of the West, you have too long deceived yourselves—you have depended on foreign work-shops, for your wearing apparel—you have depended on foreign countries for your tea and coffee—retrench your expenses —manufacture your wearing apparel, and substitute milk for tea and coffee —use economy, industry and prudence—then will your pockets be lined with money, your bodies and minds invigorated with wholesome food, and clothed with substantial raiment of your own manufacturing.—Then will poverty cease to stare you in the face. You will no longer witness your goods exposed to sale under the hammer of the sheriff nor be dunned by the merchant for the last pound of tea or coffee—the by word "Hard Times," will cease to be heard, and you will once more enjoy peace and prosperity.[489]

With Detroit the problem was still more local, for the lack of agricultural development in Michigan Territory necessitated that most of the meat and other foodstuffs be imported from Ohio. After seven years in which to get started, and with enough acres cleared to feed six times the population of the Territory, it was time to cut down on imports, said the *Gazette*. Not three families manufactured their wearing apparel, there were not five looms in the Territory, and not a single carding machine or fulling mill within one hundred miles of Detroit.[490] Prices remained high. Despite importations, flour was $7.50, corn 50 cents, pork $12, beef $10, whiskey 50 cents, and butter 18 cents.[491] The first flour manufactured outside Detroit arrived from Pontiac in 1825.[492] Most of the 3,000 hogs butchered in Detroit in 1826 came from Ohio and Kentucky.[493]

Transportation costs, too, were regarded as vital contributing factors. Freight from New York to Detroit by land was $4.50 to $5.00 per hundred pounds. In 1821 when flour at Baltimore, New York, and Philadelphia was $7.50 to $8.50 and $10 at New Orleans, at Cincinnati it was $3.75.[494] In 1823 wheat sold at $1.44 and flour at $7.25 in New York; at Cleveland the prices

[488] *Detroit Gazette,* June 1, 1821.
[489] *Cleaveland Register*, December 8, 1818.
[490] *Detroit Gazette,* May 11, 1821.
[491] *Ibid.,* December 26, 1823.
[492] *Ibid.,* December 13, 1825.
[493] *Ibid.,* January 17, 1826.
[494] *Western Sun and General Advertiser,* November 24, 1821.

were 62½ and $3.50.[495] In Indiana and Illinois, where there were roads, hauling charges were 50 cents to $1.00 per hundred for twenty miles. Corn would not pay carrying charges for that distance. Northern Ohio looked forward to completion of the Erie Canal. "When this temporary depression and langor shall have passed by, and works of internal improvement now in agitation are consumated, business will resume its former aspect, the value of property will be enhanced, and Ohio, instead of being *out of the world* . . . will be deemed a position sufficiently central, and a mart of no inconsiderable traffic."[496]

The impression prevailed in the minds of many people, however, that transportation improvements, banking reforms, relief and stay laws, and the like were not all that was required. The causes of hard times were largely individual extravagance, love of "showing out in our families, dressing off our daughters," and like display. When individuals quit calling for relief, acted with sense and judgment, got back to some of the simplicity of former times, abandoned hackneys for gigs which they could pay for, then more prosperous days would return.[497]

Hard times furnish ample evidence of the state of affairs in the news of the day. News of recovery is not so noticeable. Recovery is slower and less spectacular than panics and deflation. Gradually losses, bad debts, forfeitures, and inflated values were written off and forgotten. Emigration picked up again, land prices advanced, commodity prices stabilized, and conditions improved. In 1822 land near Fort Defiance brought $2.50 to $12.50 per acre and some as high as $30.[498] Cincinnati real estate recovered more slowly; not until ten years after the deflation, when the opening of the Miami Canal and other factors furnished stimulus, did values again approach those of 1817–18.[499] New Orleans prices remained low and trade dull, for some time.[500] As a result

---

[495] *Cleaveland Herald*, May 15, 1823.

[496] *Ibid.*, November 6, 1821.

[497] Portsmouth (Ohio) *Scioto Telegraph*, August 3, 1820; *Niles' Weekly Register*, XVIII, 231 (July 1, 1820).

[498] *Piqua Gazette*, in *Hamilton Intelligencer and Advertiser*, August 26, 1822.

[499] In 1827, for instance, a 740- by 100-foot lot which in 1817 sold at public sale for $4,000, sold at private sale for $2,100. *Cincinnati Pioneer*, III (1874), No. 3, p. 16.

[500] In 1823: Ohio flour $3.50 to $4.00, lard 9 to 10 cents, prime pork $9.00 to $11, cargo pork, $7.00 to $8.00, whiskey 28 to 30 cents, ham and bacon 7 to 9 cents. In 1828: Flour $3.75 to $4.00, lard 5½ to 6½ cents, mess pork $11.50 to $12, whiskey 21 cents, ham 7½ cents, ginseng 12½ cents and no demand, mess beef $8.00 to $10 the barrel. *Liberty Hall and Cincinnati Gazette*, January 24, 1823; *Cincinnati Daily Gazette*, June 18, 1828.

of eastern demand, flour at Cleveland advanced from \$2.50 to
\$5.00 the barrel in 1823,[501] but this was an exceptional price.
Cincinnati exported about 15,000 hogs (2,700,000 pounds) in
the autumn and winter of 1822, and 26,000 barrels of whiskey
were brought in, mostly for export.[502] Exports gradually increased
from 1823,[503] but price changes were slight.[504]

Since agriculture was the basic source of production and wealth
in the Northwest throughout the period, a brief survey of the
regions and their products may aid in the understanding of the
economic history.[505] Ohio, which the settler had found inhabited
by the Indian a short half century before, was roughly two hundred miles broad and long—a land of rolling to level country,
bounded on the south by a great river, on the north by an inland
sea, and traversed in all directions by navigable streams. Agriculturally, the state was by 1825 showing five more or less distinct areas, each of which had a principal staple product which
was not the main product of any of the others.[506]

Stretching from the Pennsylvania line along the Ohio to the
mouth of the Little Scioto, and reaching back from twenty to

[501] *Cleaveland Herald*, February 5, 1822, June 5, 1823.

[502] *Liberty Hall and Cincinnati Gazette*, January 1, 1823. The 1820 census listed
552 distilleries in Ohio—three fifths in the Scioto and Miami valleys—which used
600,000 bushels of grain. In 1825 there were more than one hundred distilleries
which produced two hundred gallons or more per year on the Miami River above
Franklin.

[503]

Year	Flour, bbls.	Whiskey, bbls.	Flaxseed oil
1823	27,206	—	—
1824	29,560	—	—
1825	45,000	9,000	264
1826	—	13,000	700
1827	58,000	18,000	9,000

From the *Cincinnati Daily Gazette*, January 4, 1828.

[504] Cincinnati market prices, 1828: flour \$3.00 to \$3.75 per bbl., wheat 50 cents,
corn 25 cents, whiskey 18 cents, apple brandy 18 to 20 cents, peach brandy 75 cents,
beeswax 22 cents, honey 62 to 75 cents gal., feathers 23 cents lb., ginseng 14 cents
lb., linen cloth 18 to 20 cents yard, candles 11 cents lb. Some of the articles bought
by farmers: coffee 16 cents, salt 62 cents bu., tea \$1.35 lb., powder \$5.00 to \$7.50
keg, glass (8 by 10) \$4.50 the box, calico 18 to 20 cents, tickings 19 to 28 cents,
almonds 18 cents lb., figs 15 cents lb., sperm candles 33 cents lb. Other articles:
French brandy \$1.50 gal., rum \$1.50, Holland gin \$1.40, Madeira \$3.00 to \$4.00,
port \$1.75 to \$2.50, bar iron \$90 to \$100 ton. *Cincinnati Daily Gazette*, October 31,
1828.

[505] For agriculture, see Chapter IV.

[506] The southeastern counties of Ohio were the nonglaciated portion of the state;
they were hilly, rough, but with small bottom lands. The remaining three fourths of
the state was largely level to rolling glaciated plains; bottom lands were more
prevalent in this area. The western half of the state was largely limestone soil;
the eastern half largely acid sandstone-shale, but with local limestone areas within.
Corn and clover dominated in the western half; grazing, dairying, and sheep raising
in the eastern half.

sixty miles at different points to the counties of Fairfield, Licking, Tuscarawas, and vicinity, was the mineral belt—coal in the northeastern part, salt and iron in the southwestern. To the north of this region from Columbiana and Jefferson counties on the east, west to the Scioto Valley, and north of the National Road on to the Upper Miami Valley, lay the small grain belt. Columbiana, Stark, Wayne, and Richland were known as the "backbone counties." There were many "Pennsylvania Dutch"; livestock and wheat were their specialties. Running north and south from Sandusky on Lake Erie, through Union, Madison, Fayette almost to the Ohio, and crossing the grain belt, was the beef belt. The nine counties in and around the Western Reserve in the northeast corner of the state, constituted the grazing or dairy-products area. In the southwest corner, south of the National Road, west of the Scioto, was the corn and hog belt. All of these regions to a certain extent produced the same products—excepting the minerals—and overlapped, but by reason of soil, custom, or transportation and market facilities, each came to be known mainly for the products named.[507]

The most outstanding of the Ohio agricultural regions was the Scioto Valley, rich first- and second-bottom land, which stretched for sixty or seventy miles along the river, with an area of about four million acres. Although in the early 1820's cultivated largely for corn, it was estimated the valley could produce a million bushels of wheat annually.[508] Hog and cattle production was heavy, but by 1830 there were exportable surpluses of flour, whiskey, hides, oil, beeswax, beans, hemp, poultry, and even rags.[509] Although corn and wheat remained the staple crops, rye, oats, barley, and buckwheat were produced extensively, but like potatoes, were consumed largely at home. It was possible to raise

---

[507] *Cleveland Herald and Gazette,* May 17, 1838; Gallagher, "Ohio in 1838," in *The Hesperian,* I, 9; see also Lloyd, Falconer, and Thorne, *Agriculture of Ohio,* 10–11.

[508] *Cleaveland Herald,* August 13, 1824.

[509] In the absence of reliable figures, some estimates are interesting. The *Scioto Gazette* (in *Cleaveland Herald,* March 19, 1829) estimated annual exports of the valley at 36,000 fat cattle, 70,000 stock cattle, and 5,000 fat hogs. At the Chillicothe canal celebration in 1831, it was stated that 10,000 cattle for eastern markets were being fed that winter in the valley, as well as 2,000 for domestic consumption. Export values of these (at $30 per head) as well as 35,000 head of stock cattle (at $15 per head), 25,000 head of stock hogs (at $3.50), and 60,000 barrels of pork, were placed at $1,500,000. *Scioto Gazette* extract in *Ohio State Journal,* December 1, 1831.

100 bushels of corn per acre on some of the Scioto and Miami bottoms, but 60 bushels was more nearly average for the corn lands. Wheat averaged about 25 bushels on the better wheat land. Wool, poultry, and dairy products played an increasingly important part in export trade. Hemp and tobacco were also raised. The yellow leaf tobacco was cultivated for a while on the Western Reserve, but its culture declined, as did that of the highly promoted mulberry which was to make silk one of the important products of the West.[510] Of fruit, the apple was Ohio's best crop.

Indiana was not so distinctly sectionalized agriculturally as Ohio. The difference in products between the richer valleys such as the Whitewater and Lower Wabash, and the interior uplands of southern Indiana, seems to have been in quantity rather than in kind. Even after settlement of the prairie lands of the north-central region and the Upper Wabash valleys there appeared no marked differentiation in the period prior to 1840. Corn, hogs, livestock, and their derived products remained the staples.

Southern Illinois even more than southern Indiana remained essentially a hog and hominy region.[511] "Our husbandry is yet in a rude state," wrote Judge Hall in 1830;[512] the deep sandy loam of the Illinois prairie was not yet utilized to its best advantage. Wheat, often sowed in new land indifferently prepared, was only fair, while facilities for threshing were most primitive. Cotton, tobacco, and the castor bean were cultivated to some extent, mostly in the southern counties, but fruits and vegetables were neglected. Farmers either lacked the leisure or else the desire and skill necessary to develop the art of horticulture, in the absence of cash markets. There was little for export besides pork, beef, venison hams, and some hides. Ordinarily farmers took to local markets their cordwood (at 75 cents to $1.00), potatoes, chickens, butter and eggs, and some fruit.

As noted earlier agriculture in Michigan Territory was not sufficiently advanced to play any important part in the commerce of the period to 1836. Six years after the war of 1812–14, despite

---

[510] See Chapter IV for silk culture.
[511] George Flower to Senator Asher Robbins, in *Cincinnati Daily Gazette,* July 12, 1838.
[512] James Hall, "Notes on Illinois," in *Illinois Monthly Magazine,* I (1830–31), 126, gives a very good brief review of Illinois agriculture and its prospects.

the fact that enough acres were cleared to support several times the population, foodstuffs were still being imported, largely from Ohio. Naturally prices were high, with flour at $7.50, corn at 50 cents compared to 10 to 12 cents in the interior of Ohio, pork $12, and beef $10.[513] No flour was milled for export, except at Detroit, prior to 1825. Farmers had not had any surplus beyond the needs of the settlers and emigrants, and were advised to get busy.[514]

Agriculture, in its relation to commerce and industry, was seriously affected by factors which necessitate but minor consideration today. Besides the influence of the weather and seasons upon crops,[515] there was its effect upon roads, river shipping, packing, and other activities. Roads were at their best in winter when frozen or in summer when dry—the very seasons when river navigation was at its worst. River navigation was at its best in the spring and late autumn when roads were at their worst. At no time did the maximum combined facilities of land and water transportation coincide with the crop and hog peak; also the absence of storage and preservation facilities further complicated matters for the shipper of agricultural products. The fact that the railroad offered a solution to this seasonal problem is probably the most important explanation of its spontaneous and enthusiastic reception.

Until 1840 and after, the flatboat on the Ohio and Mississippi was the means by which the great bulk of the produce of the Northwest was conveyed to market.[516] In the earlier days local buyers, merchants, even farmers, made their boats, often capable of 350,000 pounds burden, but later boats were made by regular builders and available at the chief ports. When the spring freshets came, even creeks which would later be almost dry, floated the flats to the rivers. The cargoes of corn, pork, beef, bacon, whiskey, lumber, livestock, flax, beeswax, lime, and poultry, reached New Orleans and glutted the market in April and May. In 1820 the estimated 2,400 boats which passed the Falls of the Ohio carried 1,804,000 pounds of bacon, 200,000 barrels of flour, 20,000 of pork, 62,000 bushels of oats, 100,000 of corn, 10,000

[513] *Detroit Gazette,* May 11, 1821, December 26, 1823.
[514] *Ibid.,* December 23, 1825, January 17, 1826.
[515] For the weather and agriculture, see Chapter IV.
[516] For flatboat construction and operation, see *ante,* 414-15.

barrels of cheese, 160,000 pounds of butter, 466,000 pounds of lard and 11,207,000 fowls.[517] In the spring of 1826, 152 flatboats passed Vincennes, headed south with 250,000 bushels of corn, 100,000 barrels of pork, 10,000 hams, 2,500 cattle, 10,000 pounds of beeswax, 3,600 venison hams, besides many hundred tons of miscellaneous produce.[518] In November, 1834, at Shawnee-town, before the pork shipping season had yet begun, one observer noted that an average of 25 flats per day during daylight went down river loaded with flour, whiskey, corn, mules, sheep, cattle, and lumber. Later, the same observer, coming up past Memphis, met 60 in 9 hours, saw 20 tied at one place and 12 at another, and met 77 the next day. In the 12 days from New Orleans to Louisville about 900 flats with some 450,000 barrels of cargo were observed.[519] Best estimates placed the number of flatboats which annually descended the Mississippi during this period at 4,000, and their tonnage at 160,000.[520]

Packing these cargoes for best results required knowledge and care no less than that required to run them down river. Even boats built from sap-free lumber, and well calked, let through enough bilge water to spoil flour or grain. Wise shippers put in the bottom a layer of dunnage—locust bundles, hoop poles, oak pipe staves, etc.—to guard against this danger.[521] Flour packed too tight, or in barrels of green staves often spoiled. Many

[517] *Niles' Weekly Register*, XX, 239 (June 9, 1821).

[518] *Western Sun and General Advertiser*, June 17, 1826.

[519] *Cincinnati Evening Post* in *Indiana Journal*, May 29, 1835. Reliable data on the volume of down-river traffic does not exist. Judge James Hall compiled tables of New Orleans receipts from New Orleans newspapers which were based on wharfmasters' reports, from 1825 to 1834 in his *Statistics of the West* (1836), *Notes on the Western States* (1838), and *The West: Its Commerce and Navigation* (1848). Although the bulk of these imports came from the region north of the Ohio, what percentage is not known. Some interesting changes in this period can be noted. Bacon hams increased from 367 hhds. to 7,318, bulk bacon from 211,000 lbs. to 615,000 lbs., pork from 15,000 to 92,000 bbls., bulk pork from 146,000 lbs. to 2,603,000 lbs., lard from 486 bbls. and 34,000 kegs to 2,300 bbls. and 199,000 kegs, beef from 1,200 bbls. to 5,400 bbls., hides from 11,000 to 41,000, flaxseed from 180 to 3,700 bbls., flour from 140,000 to 320,000 bbls., staves from 615,000 to 2,000,000, and ginseng from 150 to 13,600 lbs. Tallow, whiskey, brandy, cider, beeswax, deer- and bearskins, held fairly steady. Corn meal, furs, hemp, and bear oil diminished noticeably. New items were pig iron, western coal, and western lime.

[520] James Hall, *Statistics of the West*, 247.

[521] Newspapers often copied letters of instruction regarding shipping—types of containers, packing, protection against weather, and spoiling. For example, Chillicothe *Supporter*, December 24, 1816. The Governor and Judges of Michigan Territory in 1819 provided for the inspection of provisions and lumber. Beef and pork were classified and an inspector appointed. Fish barrels of white or red oak, white ash or pine were to hold 29 to 30 gallons; half barrels, 15 gallons. Construction was regulated in detail. *Detroit Gazette*, June 18, 1819.

barrels spoiled because not dried and cooled before packing, or the flour was not acceptable because not ground fine enough.[522] Louisiana by law in 1820 appointed an inspector and three re-packers for beef and pork and the careless shipper might have to pay up to $1.12 per barrel for inspection and repacking.[523] Pork and beef were classified into mess, prime, and cargo.[524] Barrels were supposed to be of seasoned white oak or white ash, 18 inches between chimes and 28 inches long.[525] Two pecks of coarse salt, 6 per cent saltpeter, besides pickle (saturated salt solution) were required per barrel. Beef required more salt than pork and some maintained that a half bushel was not enough for the warm damp climate of New Orleans. Packing in the towns, like butchering on the farms, was largely a seasonal industry. Since a freezing temperature was required to chill the carcasses, ordinarily operations could not be carried on until November, nor continued later than February or March. Within this period abnormally warm weather might necessitate suspension of activity or result in spoiling of meat, or extremely cold weather, even in the Cincinnati region, frequently closed the establishments. Impassable roads also had to be reckoned with. The seasonable nature of employment in the packing industry was not such a problem, for labor was not so specialized and could be found among farmers, artisans, and general laborers who at other seasons worked at other jobs.

Some of the Cincinnati packing houses were built of brick three stories high and covered several acres. The division-of-labor system was in use and represented one of America's first disassembly lines. From the death blow through the finished product the hog moved down the line; the workers stood still. "The mallet,—the knife,—the axe,—the boiling caldron,—the

[522] *Liberty Hall and Cincinnati Gazette,* July 1, 1816.

[523] Portsmouth (Ohio) *Scioto Telegraph,* June 29, 1820; *Hamilton Advertiser,* November 29, 1825.

[524] Mess pork was to consist wholly of the sides of well-fattened hogs. A barrel of prime pork might include two hams, a head and a half (but no ears, snouts, or brains), the rest to consist of three shoulders with shanks off at the knees, sides, neck, and tail pieces. Cargo pork was any part of the hog which was merchantable, but not to contain more than four shoulders and two heads per barrel. Mess beef was brisket and choice side pieces. Prime beef: not over one half a neck, two flanks, two legs, some side pieces, etc. Cargo beef: good pieces of four to twelve pounds weight, not more than half necks, three flanks, two legs, etc., as in prime.

[525] Quarter-bound barrels of twelve hoops were legal, but a full bound barrel required eighteen hoops. Barrels contained about two hundred pounds.

remorseless scraping-iron,—have each done their work; and the fated porker, that was but one minute before grunting in the full enjoyment of bristling hoghood, now cadaverous and 'chapfallen,' hangs a stark and naked effigy among his immolated brethren."[526]

Cincinnati as yet had no rivals to her position as premier port of the Northwest. From about 5,000 in 1815 to more than 30,000 population in 1836, the Queen City was often referred to as Porkopolis. Exports in 1826 were estimated at a million dollars; in 1832 at four million; in 1835 at six million.[527] During the winter of 1832–33, 85,000 hogs were slaughtered, a year later 123,000, while by 1835, including those brought in by wagon and the Miami Canal, the number was 162,000.[528] In 1834, 90,000 barrels of flour came in and 55,000 barrels of whiskey. Fifty stages and sixty mails arrived weekly.

Although the volume of stuff bought up at 40 to 50 per cent of New Orleans prices and shipped to New Orleans was large, it seems that comparatively little cash was brought back into the Northwest.[529] Prior to 1840 farmers rarely received more than 2 cents a pound for hogs on the hoof, and 1½ to 3 cents for cattle. Buyers would pay about $25 for a yoke of oxen, $1.00 a head for sheep, 50 cents for a bushel of flaxseed, 10 to 15 cents for corn, and $10 to $50 for horses. Allowance had to be made for slaughter, packing, spoilage, loss in shipping, accidents, and delays, as well as a fluctuating market. The merchants either bought goods in the New Orleans market or applied their proceeds on debts back East. The smaller shipper nearly always sold in a glutted market, spent some money seeing the sights in New Orleans, made some purchases, and used the balance for steamboat fare home. If he made the return trip on foot, he ran the hazards of robbery and the gambling centers at Natchez and elsewhere.

[526] Hoffman, *Winter in the West,* II, 138. Miss Martineau also described the process in *Retrospect of Western Travel,* II, 45.

[527] [Benjamin Drake], "Cincinnati at the Close of 1835," in *Western Monthly Magazine,* V (1836), 28.

[528] In November, 1834, upwards of 30,000 hogs went through Brookville, Indiana, on their way to Cincinnati. Brookville *Indiana American,* November 29, 1834.

[529] An Illinois congressman in 1824 viewed with distrust the West's connection with New Orleans. He said that beef and pork not put up with imported salt spoiled in the southern climate and that one sixth of the flour shipped in the past five years had spoiled.

New Orleans prices fluctuated widely, aside from the general cyclical changes from depression to good times. For instance, in the autumn of 1821 flour was quoted at $10 the barrel ($3.75 in Cincinnati), while a year later it was $5.00 to $6.00, and by December, "$3.50 to $4 and dull."[530] Beef and pork prices were somewhat more stable. The New Orleans market was offering less in the way of prospects after about 1827; this fact accounts in large part for the enthusiasm for canals and railroads. In 1835, after the completion of the Pennsylvania Canal to Pittsburgh, it was possible to ship cotton to Philadelphia from as far down as Nashville in twenty-one days for a trifle over $1.00 the hundred.[531] This choice of markets gave the western producer and merchant the advantages of selling in eastern markets where he did his buying.

The effects of the canals on shipping prices and land values were obvious, and call for but passing notice. Ohio, of course, benefited first. In 1826 goods reached Columbus from Philadelphia in thirty days at a cost of $5.00 per hundred, whereas, as a result of the Erie Canal, New York goods could be had in twenty days at $2.50. Three years later goods made the 1,100-mile all-water trip from New York to Dayton at $17.25 per ton or at one third the former rate. Johnson and Wilkinson advertised at Vincennes in 1827 to forward goods from New York to Pittsburgh in seventeen days at $2.25 per hundred, but would lay them down at Sandusky in twelve days for $1.25.[532] Regions back from the Ohio and Lake Erie were given access to markets. Agricultural produce from the interior, with no local markets and no transport facilities often would bring no price whatever.[533] In 1817 flour was $15 in Sandusky but $6.00 to $6.50 in Columbus, Chillicothe, and vicinity; corn was $1.50 compared to 40 to 50 cents. In 1825 interior Ohio wheat was 20 to 30 cents and corn 10 to 12 cents.[534] These prices more than doubled between 1825 and 1832.[535] Wheat at Massillon, Ohio, one hundred

---

[530] Cincinnati *Western Spy* in Vincennes *Western Sun and General Advertiser*, November 24, 1821, and October 26, 1822; *Liberty Hall and Cincinnati Gazette*, January 1, 1823.

[531] *Philadelphia Gazette* in *Western Monthly Magazine*, III (1835), 398.

[532] *Western Sun and General Advertiser*, April 7, 1827.

[533] *Report of the Canal Commissioners*, 1833; Ohio *House Journal*, 1834, p. 329.

[534] *Niles' Weekly Register*, XII, 144 (Apr. 26, 1817).

[535] *Report of the Canal Commissioners*, 1833.

miles west of Pittsburgh, sold higher than at points sixty miles farther east.[536] Higher prices raised land values and increased production. Newark land prices increased 50 per cent as soon as digging of the Ohio Canal began.[537] The influence of the canals extended back at least one hundred miles on either side and, of course, reached beyond their termini. The canal commissioners reckoned the saving on transportation in the first year, 1832, at $312,156.[538]

Among the products shipped from the interior by way of Cleveland in 1832 were 288,700 bushels of wheat, 54,000 barrels of flour, 13,800 barrels of pork, 353,000 pounds of lard, 85,700 pounds of cheese, 2,150 barrels of whiskey, 657,000 feet of lumber, 271,000 pounds of pot- and pearlashes, and 13,000 pounds of mineral coal. Into the state by the same port came 29,939 barrels of salt (145,697 bushels at 56 pounds per bushel), 7,600 barrels of fish, 190,000 pounds of gypsum, and more than 5 million pounds of merchandise.[539] At Cincinnati 97,500 barrels of flour had arrived by the Miami Canal, 40,400 of whiskey, 19,700 of pork, 31,500 kegs of lard, 1,877,000 pounds of bulk pork, and 12,000 cords of firewood; merchandise cleared (entered) amounted to 6,000,000 pounds.

The Portsmouth end of the Ohio Canal began to contribute its part by 1836. Although by 1835 exports from points in central Ohio near the canal had a choice of four routes to the coast,[540] this was not the case with the produce from most regions. Chillicothe was apparently the dividing point for pork and whiskey.

---

[536] Dial, "Construction of the Ohio Canals," in *Ohio Archaeological and Historical Society Publications*, XIII, 479.

[537] *Indiana Journal*, August 30, 1825.

[538] *Report of the Canal Commissioners*, 1833. Table reprinted in Bogart, *Internal Improvements in Ohio*, Appendix A.

An idea of canal rates may be had from the order of the Ohio Board of Canal Commissioners in 1829: general merchandise 4 cents per ton per mile for the first 100 miles, 3 cents per mile for each additional 100 miles; paper, glass, nails, wool, and cotton manufactured in Ohio, 2 cents and 1 cent; flour, wheat, whiskey, black salts, seeds, provisions, furniture, wagons, etc., 1½ cents and 1 cent; corn, oats, rye, barley, 1 cent.

[539] *Report of the Canal Commissioners*, 1833.

[540] (1) South by the Ohio Canal to Portsmouth, thence either to New Orleans by flat- or steamboat; (2) up the Ohio to Pittsburgh by steamboat, thence by Pennsylvania's system of canals and roads, to Philadelphia; (3) north on the canal to Cleveland, by lake ship to Buffalo, thence by the Erie Canal to Albany and New York; (4) from Cleveland through the Welland Canal (opened in 1833) and to Montreal. Some traffic went east through the Welland Canal to Oswego and thence to Albany. Some went by Erie Canal to Rochester and thence to Montreal.

From north of that place goods cleared through Cleveland; from south by way of Portsmouth. But most producers were not so well situated. Many miles lay between the farm and the canal or river. Then each of these routes had its advantages and drawbacks. As a consequence products for certain areas and of certain kinds tended to follow certain routes. Northern Ohio used the canal and the lakes, but the remainder of the Northwest which had a surplus for export, still used the river. The bulk of the wheat (83 per cent) went northeast, but the flour went largely to New Orleans (70 per cent). Practically all of the corn and pork went south (98 and 96 per cent), as well as most of the tobacco (87 per cent) and the whiskey (95 per cent). Wool went east as did most of the hemp.[541]

But a few statistics will not tell the whole story. As expressed at the time:

The effects of these improvements upon the prosperity of the state cannot be developed in a few sentences. They have afforded to the farmer of the interior, an easy access to market, and have enhanced the value of his farm and his productions. They have facilitated intercourse between different sections of the state, and have thus tended to make the people more united as well as more prosperous. They have furnished to the people a common object of generous interest and satisfaction. They have attracted a large accession of population and capital. And they have made the name and character of Ohio well known throughout the civilized world, as a name and character of which her sons may be justly proud.[542]

Indiana and Illinois commerce had to wait until after 1836 for canals, but shared indirectly in the benefits of the Ohio canals. Much local shipping still followed the rivers. Shipping notices in the newspapers of any river town give an idea of the amount: "Louisville to La Fayette," "Terre-Haute to Cincinnati," "La Fayette to Shawneetown," "Madison to St. Louis," and scores of others appear in the papers. The Indiana Canal Commissioners in 1829 estimated the annual trade of the Wabash at 7,000 barrels of salt and 10,000 barrels of pork. Three thousand barrels of whiskey and a like quantity of pork came from Terre

[541] Albert L. Kohlmeier, *The Old Northwest, as the Keystone of the Arch of the American Federal Union* (Bloomington, Ind., 1938), 20. This data is based on a study of the canal documents and commercial reports of Ohio, Pennsylvania, New York, Canada, and the United States.

[542] Salmon P. Chase, *Statutes of Ohio* . . . (3 volumes. Cincinnati, 1833–35), I, 46. A good contemporary summary of the canals and their relation to Ohio economic life may be had in Gallagher, "Ohio in 1838," in *The Hesperian,* I (1838), 1–17.

Vincennes Race Track. *Charles A. Lesueur*

Indiana Knobs (near New Albany, Indiana)
G. N. Frankenstein

Sugar Camp. *Charles A. Lesueur*

Aboard the Philanthropist. *Charles A. Lesueur*

Haute alone.[543] In the winter and spring of 1830–31 no fewer than fifty-five steamboats ascended the Wabash while several hundred keel- and flatboats descended.[544] Shawneetown, the gateway to eastern Illinois, was established by the United States government as a port of entry. St. Louis dominated the western side of the state and developed into a steamboat port second only in importance to Pittsburgh and Cincinnati. Alton and Cairo were never able successfully to contest its dominance. River boats went up the Illinois to Naples in 1828, to Pekin the next year, and to Peoria in 1830. Illinois towns grew up and steamboat connections were established with St. Louis even before the towns along the Ohio were aware of their existence. In 1830 a bill of goods destined for Beardstown and unloaded by mistake at Shawneetown was held for some time because the location of Beardstown was not known.[545] Yet steamboats were regularly plying between that town and St. Louis. In 1831 there were 186 arrivals at Naples, 32 at Beardstown, and 17 at Peoria.

Both the steamboat and the canal gave impetus to the rapid development of Great Lakes commerce and shipping. The rise of Cleveland dates from the opening of the Ohio Canal. The village which in 1826 believed that the good gravel soil of its streets "will forever render it unnecessary to pave them"[546] was ten years later indulging in the luxury of paved sidewalks on Superior Street.[547] The city became boom conscious; articles on its growth and prospects appeared regularly. Two slaughtering establishments in January, 1829, were killing 1,400 hogs weekly and it was estimated that 50,000 hams would be put up that season.[548] Buffalo received during the navigating season of 1830–31 heavy shipments of goods from the West, mostly from Ohio.[549]

[543] In *Western Sun and General Advertiser*, February 7, 1829.
[544] *Illinois Monthly Magazine*, II (1831–32), 100.
[545] James Hall, *Notes on the Western States* (Philadelphia, 1838), 265.
[546] *Cleaveland Herald*, April 21, 1826.
[547] *Daily Cleveland Herald*, November 17, 1836.
[548] *Cleaveland Herald*, January 8, 1829.

[549]
267,900 bu. wheat	359,000 pipe staves
86,900 bbls. flour	3,500 packs furs and pelts
11,800 bbls. ashes	29,000 lbs. wool
4,800 bbls. whiskey	149 tons hemp
6,900 bbls. pork	242 bales of feathers
1,600 bbls. beef	4,206 boxes of glass
4,319 kegs butter	5,760 lbs. western bar iron,
1,273 bbls. lake fish	lumber, stone, rags, etc.

Buffalo Journal in *Cleaveland Herald*, February 2, 1831.

At Massillon wheat sold at 73 to 76 cents, but on the Ohio at 54 cents. Much canal wheat went by way of Rochester, New York, to Montreal, for wheat went from Canada to the West Indies duty free, whereas wheat shipped directly from the United States bore a duty of $1.33 per bushel.[550] Advertisements called attention to the fact that freight rates on flour were 25 cents per barrel cheaper by way of the Welland Canal to Rochester and Montreal, than by way of Buffalo. Foreign exports from Cleveland grew from less than $5,000 in 1831 to approximately $250,000 in 1833, mostly to Montreal. As a result the commissioners of both the Erie and Ohio canals reduced tolls 25 per cent in the summer of 1833. Lake business was said to have increased 100 per cent at Cleveland between 1830 and 1833. New buildings were going up and new business houses were being opened.[551] To July, 1833, 230 vessels, excluding steamboats, arrived, compared to 142 of the preceding year;[552] in the first eleven months of 1836, there were 1,822 arrivals and departures of ships other than steamboats.[553] Canal traffic was up 50 per cent, and almost 10,000 barrels of pork had been exported. Lowering of the rates on both the Erie and Ohio canals brought much traffic from Illinois, Indiana, Kentucky, and Tennessee. Goods could come from New York to Cincinnati at slightly above $2.00 per hundred weight.[554] Rapid growth continued; in 1836 wheat and flour ex-

---

[550] *Cleaveland Herald,* February 17, March 24, 1831. Wheat entered Canada from the United States duty free by act of 1831.

[551] *Ibid.,* January 5, 1833.

[552] *Ibid.,* July 13, 1833.

Figures on boat arrivals and estimated exports and imports as given in *ibid.,* September 21, 1833:

	Boats Arriving	Exports	Imports
1825	75 (21 steamboats)	$50,000	$132,000
1829	314 (90 steamboats)	222,000	568,000
1832	1,070 (470 steamboats)	1,500,000 (est.)	2,000,000

The collector of the port showed goods arriving (via canal) in 1832 at 43,694,000 lbs.; cleared (going in) 18,700,000 lbs. In 1833, 70,000,000 lbs. and 23,580,000 lbs. Important commodities listed as arriving and clearing were:

1832—arrived (going out)—1833		1832—cleared (coming in)—1833	
288,700 bu. wheat	386,000	29,900 bbls. salt	28,400
54,000 bbls. flour	98,000	7,600 bbls. fish	4,000
13,800 bbls. pork	22,700	5,260,000 lbs. merchandise	9,896,000
363,000 lbs. lard	498,000		
12,900 bu. coal	49,100		
261,000 lbs. ashes	175,800		

Ibid., January 4, 1834.

[553] *Daily Cleveland Herald,* December 6, 1836.

[554] *Hamilton Intelligencer,* September 28, 1834.

ports alone were valued at more than $1,700,000.[555] Cleveland eagerly awaited the opening of the Wabash and Erie Canal, which would tap the heart of Indiana, and add volume to this traffic.

Cincinnati was not unaware of these developments, and cast anxious eyes toward the day when much traffic would be diverted from the Dayton-Cincinnati route into Lake Erie. It was up to Cincinnati to back the Mad River and Lake Erie Railroad.[556] In 1835 it was estimated that Cincinnati's exports were $6,000,-000. There had been 2,237 steamboat arrivals. Receipts included 90,000 barrels of flour and 55,000 barrels of whiskey; 162,000 hogs had been slaughtered—all of this with only the river, the Miami Canal, and two improved turnpikes of 12 and 16 miles respectively towards Lebanon and Columbus. The city was looking forward to the extension of the Miami Canal from Dayton to the Maumee Bay, and of the pikes to Chillicothe, Columbus and Wooster, Springfield, and to the Indiana line toward Brookville. Also to the extension of the National Road through Indiana and the building of the Cincinnati and Charleston, Lawrenceburg and Indianapolis, and Miami to Lake Erie railroads. Incidentally it was predicting a population of 100,000 by 1850.[557]

Soon the commercial rivalry between the Ohio cities and the lake cities was as keen as among the eastern cities for the trade of the West.

Meanwhile the larger strategy of the New York, Philadelphia, Baltimore trade war was taking form. These three cities lay more or less in a line which roughly paralleled the southern shore

[555] *Exports*

		Value	*Imports*	
Bu. wheat	464,000	$ 534,000	22,214	bbls. salt
Bu. corn	392,000	215,000	4,082	bbls. lake fish
Lbs. flaxseed	11,500	12,800	133,384,900	lbs. mdse.
Bu. coal	84,900	8,492	1,314,000	lbs. furniture
Bbls. flour	167,500	1,234,000	1,500,000	lbs. gypsum
Bbls. pork	13,495	203,000	294,000	ft. lumber
Whiskey	7,257	72,570	1,351	thou. shingles
Butter lbs.	900,000	99,000	37	pair millstones
Lard lbs.	636,000	63,600		
Pig iron	1,031,500	15,000		
Hhds. tobacco	3,851	192,000		

Daily Cleveland Herald, January 3, 1837.
[556] *Liberty Hall and Cincinnati Gazette,* September 5, 1833.
[557] [Drake], "Cincinnati at the Close of 1835," in *Western Monthly Magazine,* V (1836), 27-31.

of Lake Erie,[558] and no shortest line of communication to the West had yet been effected. When New York lost business to Montreal, rates were lowered on the Erie Canal and construction of a railroad from the Hudson to Dunkirk was begun. Philadelphia was linked with Pittsburgh by the completion of the western section of the Pennsylvania Canal in 1835 and was reaching west by the Sunbury and Erie Railroad, chartered in 1837. The Pennsylvania and Ohio Canal from Beaver, on the Ohio River, by way of Warren to Akron, where it connected with the northern end of the Ohio Canal, was another important link in this chain by which Philadelphia hoped to reverse considerable of the western traffic which went to New Orleans. Baltimore, with an eye on both Philadelphia and New York, had run the Baltimore and Ohio Railroad to Pittsburgh, and the Chesapeake and Ohio Canal was making its way to the Ohio.[559]

Whoever stood to win in this rivalry, Cleveland was in a strong position. It was not anticipated that a great volume of business would be reversed and sent south on the Ohio Canal, for rates per hundred from Portsmouth to Philadelphia would be $2.00 as against 75 cents by way of the Welland Canal.[560] Besides the volume gained from the opening of the Wabash and Erie Canal would more than offset any such loss for, because of seasonal advantages, much of that business would enter the Ohio Canal at Cleveland, take the Pennsylvania and Ohio Canal across to Beaver, be towed up the Ohio to Pittsburgh, and thence go to either Philadelphia or Baltimore.[561]

Toledo and Detroit were other lake cities which shared in the gains of the early 1830's. Toledo, but recently called Port Lawrence or Vistula, was destined to wait several years for the opening of the Wabash and Erie Canal. It was in 1836 a town of about 2,000 inhabitants with several busy hotels; 12 to 20 steamboats arrived daily.[562] Detroit reported arrivals and departures

---

[558] More noticeable on a globe map.

[559] A two-column discussion of the situation at the end of 1836, with a map, may be found in *Cleveland Herald and Gazette* (weekly), June 3, 1837, and another survey of the situation in an article, copied from the *Cincinnati Chronicle* in *Cincinnati Daily Gazette*, February 22, 1837.

[560] *Cleveland Herald*, January 4, 1834.

[561] Cleveland to Philadelphia by this route was 582 miles, by railroad it would be 432. To New York by water was 706 miles as against a possible 600 by rail.

[562] *Toledo Gazette* in *Detroit Daily Advertiser*, July 13, 1836.

daily, of 3 steamboats with some 200 passengers and 50 tons cargo. Thirty steamboats of the largest class worked between Detroit and Buffalo. Besides, there were 150 vessels in navigation with an average daily arrival of 3, with 100 tons cargo. During the seven months navigating season it was estimated that 1,000 persons arrived and departed daily, and that 400 tons of freight arrived.[563] Detroit thought that the importance of the lake traffic was not generally appreciated along the Atlantic seaboard. Forests surrounding the vast inland seas had given way to thriving villages, and harbors but recently occupied only by the Indian canoe were "crowded with shipping and resounding with the hammer of the artisan and the song of the sailor. . . . There is room for empires to spring up around the borders of the seas which cluster on our Northern boundary. The tide of emigration has turned thither with a fullness and force that nothing can check; and it is easy to foresee that the time cannot be far distant when the lakes will be whitened with the sails of an extensive commerce."[564]

Milwaukee and Chicago were growing young towns whose names began to appear in the commercial news. In 1831 goods reached St. Louis by way of Chicago at a saving of one third over the New Orleans route. Two years later several hundred barrels of beef were shipped by Oliver Newberry from Chicago to New York by way of Albany at $13 the ton. Weekly boat arrivals from Buffalo were listed in 1834. Next year 255 sailing ships arrived at Chicago, and in 1836, 383 ships and 49 steamboats.[565] Many of these boats stopped at Milwaukee, which was becoming a distributing point for this part of Michigan Territory, as was Chicago for northern Illinois.

The Great Lakes, in addition to serving as highways for commerce, themselves produced one of the important articles of com-

[563] *Detroit Daily Advertiser,* December 20, 1836. In 1818 the entries at the port of Detroit were: 3,501 barrels of flour, 2,843 of salt, 1,948 of whiskey, 888 of pork, 295 of fish, 693 firkins of butter, 5,062 bushels of corn, 1,042 head of beef cattle, and 1,435 hogs. Cleared from Detroit, mostly to the military posts on the upper lakes: 2,024 barrels of flour, 1,282 of salt, 753 of cider, 1,478 of fish, 105 of pork, 394 of beef, 453 of whiskey, 153 firkins of butter, and 1,280 bushels of corn. *Detroit Gazette,* August 13, 1819. In 1830 there were more than 1,000 entrances and clearances of boats at Detroit with an estimated cargo value of $5,000,000. *Detroit Journal and Michigan Advertiser,* November 9, 1831.
[564] *Detroit Free Press* quoted in *Cincinnati Daily Gazette,* February 14, 1835.
[565] Pease, *The Frontier State,* 190, 191.

merce. The Indian had long recognized the importance of the fish, largely sturgeon, lake trout, and whitefish, which were so plentiful and at times easily speared in the Sault and elsewhere, or else caught through the ice, or in nets.[566] Early trappers and traders showed some interest, but it was not until the American Fur Company began the development of commercial fishing that fish became an important article of commerce. In 1817 the Lakes catch was estimated at 3,000 barrels, but Detroit citizens seemed not to be interested.[567] The next year only 295 barrels of fish were entered at the port of Detroit and 1,478 barrels cleared. One hundred barrels sent to Cincinnati were all lost because they would not sell.[568] Articles in the *Detroit Gazette*[569] called attention to the want of enterprise on the part of Michigan citizens, emphasized the importance of the fisheries, and suggested means for improvement and development. Although by 1824, 1,600 barrels were taken at Grosse Isle alone, fish seldom appeared in the Detroit market.[570] Whitefish, which had been held in low esteem in Ohio and New York markets and would hardly sell at 50 cents per hundred pounds, were by 1825 much in demand at $3.00 to $4.00 the hundred, with orders for thousands of barrels piling up.[571] By 1830 an estimated 8,000 barrels, valued at $40,000, were marketed.[572] A few years later one of the American Fur Company agents was expecting the fisheries of Lake Superior to be more profitable than the fur trade.[573] By 1837 Samuel Abbott, Mackinac agent of the company, reported that 4,000 barrels would be taken by the company that season in Lake Superior. Total takings for 1837 were estimated at 13,500 bar-

[566] Also herring, and in the streams pike, perch, bass, pickerel, etc. John T. Blois, *Gazetteer of the State of Michigan* . . . (Detroit, 1839), 55.
[567] *Detroit Gazette,* November 14, 1817.
[568] *Ibid.,* November 1, 1825.
[569] January, 1821.
[570] *Ibid.,* November 5, 12, 1824. Perhaps, it was said, because pork and beef sellers kept them out.
[571] *Ibid.,* November 1, 1825.
[572] Blois, *Gazetteer,* 56. The beginnings of American Fur Company enterprise in this business cannot be well traced because of loss of company papers prior to 1834 in the great New York fire of 1835.
[573] William Aitken (at Lapointe) to Ramsay Crooks, September 20, 1834, in *Calendar of the American Fur Company Papers* (2 volumes. *Annual Report of the American Historical Association,* 1944, Washington D. C., 1945), 1834. Crooks hoped to promote the fisheries, and shortly was writing to Gen. Charles Gratiot in Washington to find whether there was any honest way of avoiding the tariff on fish caught beyond the international line, but caught by Americans and cured with American salt on American boats.

rels with value of $125,000.[574] Although the American Fur Company and the Hudson's Bay Company were the chief exploiters of the fisheries, their monopoly was not complete.[575]

Salt as an article of commerce occupied a much more prominent place than it does today. Although it might be dispensed with for a while as an item of food for people and animals, it was indispensable for preservation and shipping of certain foodstuffs. Its perishable nature, weight, and variable quality made it difficult to handle and expensive to buy. Early salt licks played an important part in determining settlement. The saline lands were usually given the states of the Northwest, but under certain conditions.[576] Main salines were those on the Lower Wabash in Illinois, and on the Muskingum and Scioto in Ohio, but many lesser ones helped supply the local needs in earlier years. As early as 1812 the Scioto Salt Works, 16 furnaces, produced 70 to 80 barrels daily, which were marketed on horseback up to one hundred miles distance, until outside competition put it into decline. The Muskingum salines were one of the early commercial assets of Zanesville. The annual output of Muskingum County alone in 1826 was listed at 300,000 barrels, and in 1837 the main Muskingum River area was said to produce 500,000 bushels.[577] The Gallatin County, Illinois, output in 1827 was about 100,000 bushels; a thousand people were employed in the salines which were so important in early Shawneetown commerce.

With the coming of the steamboat and the canals these local salt manufactures were less important, for foreign salt could come in from the East or New Orleans, and domestic salt from New York and Virginia.[578] Failure of the New York supply to get to Pennsylvania and the West during the War of 1812 led to the rapid development of the Kanawha salt manufactures. In 1815 there were 52 furnaces in operation, each with 40 to 60

[574] Blois, *Gazetteer*, 57. Other estimates were 12,000 pounds from the Lakes, 7,000 in Superior. *Cleveland Herald and Gazette*, October 25, 1838. One column on the kinds of fish, where taken, etc., appears in this issue.

[575] A Cleveland company in 1839 built the 60-ton *Algonquin* to be used on the Canadian side of the Sault to try the Superior fisheries. *Cleveland Herald and Gazette*, November 6, 1839.

[576] See enabling act for Illinois, for instance. U. S. *Statutes at Large*, III, 430.

[577] Benjamin Drake and Edward D. Mansfield, *Cincinnati in 1826* (Cincinnati, 1827); Atwater, *History of Ohio*, 18.

[578] Ohio was permitted in 1824 to dispose of her salt lands, Illinois in 1828, and Indiana in 1832. Receipts usually went into the school fund.

kettles of 36-gallon capacity. Total daily output was 2,500 to 3,000 bushels.[579] By 1820 the Kanawha output surpassed that of all the other Ohio Valley salt works combined,[580] and in the next decade the Virginia salt industry tightened its hold on the interior salt trade to such an extent as to be accused of holding up the price on a monopoly basis.[581] In 1829, 73 works on the Kanawha produced 925,000 bushels, while 85 in Ohio produced only 426,-000, and Illinois but 138,000.

Indiana salines were relatively unimportant. Ohio production declined in 1840 to 297,000 bushels, but helped by the canals staged a comeback after 1840. At the same time Illinois produced 20,000 bushels and Indiana 6,400. The growth of meat packing and business in general after 1830 led to increased consumption of salt.[582] Improvements in drilling and cheap coal for fuel, as well as the stronger brine, left the Virginia works in strong position, regardless of the fact that Kanawha salt was charged with containing impurities, as did all the interior salts, which rendered them imperfect for use as a preservative for meats destined for southern markets.[583] As Michigan settled, imports of New York

---

[579] David Ruffner in *Niles' Weekly Register*, VIII, 135 (Apr. 22, 1815).

[580] Capital invested: $696,000. Isaac Lippincott, "The Early Salt Trade of the Ohio Valley," in *Journal of Political Economy*, XX (1912), 1048.

[581] Senator Thomas Hart Benton sought to have the duty on salt removed so as to relieve the Westerners from the Kanawha monopoly. Between 1817 and 1840 there were at least a half dozen combinations among the Kanawha salt producers. Price fixing, production regulation, "dead renting" (paying well owners to keep their wells idle), and other controls were arranged for. For the best account of the salt combines, see Louis C. Hunter, *Studies in the Economic History of the Ohio Valley . . .* (*Smith College Studies in History*, XIX, Nos. 1-2, 1933-34), 51 and following. Benton's first investigation was in 1830-31, the second 1839-40. This contest may be followed through Benton's speeches in the Senate, and in U. S. *House Documents*, 21 Congress, 1 session, No. 55, and in U. S. *Senate Documents*, 26 Congress, 1 session, No. 196. The subject is covered in Francis E. Andrew, "The Early Kanawha Salt Industry and Benton's Investigations of the 'Salt Monopoly,'" MS. M. A. thesis, Indiana University, 1936.

[582] Statistics may be found in U. S. Census reports, canal reports, etc. See Lippincott, "The Early Salt Trade of the Ohio Valley," 1029-52, for brief treatment of the subject.

[583] The best salt was sun-made salt, such as the Turk's Island salt, the most famous of the imported salt. Next best was rock or mineral salt. Boiled salt was the poorest, as in its crystallization it either did not oust the impurities or else they became mixed with the salt crystals. Chief impurities were "bittern" (minerals in the salt water), lime, tallow, lard, or other "aids" used to "cut the grain" or hasten granulation. A writer in the *American Farmer* in 1820 said the only difference between good salt and bad was in the size of the crystals, coarse salt being good, fine salt bad, and that good salt was the result of low temperature evaporation. But J. P. Hale, an early manufacturer of salt, said that the quality could be regulated by the temperature, 100 to 150° F. for coarse low grade, and near boiling for high grade. J. P. Hale, "Salt," in *Resources of West Virginia*, edited by M. F. Maury and W. M. Fontaine (Wheeling, 1876), 295.

salt increased. A party under Dr. Douglass Houghton, state geologist, in 1837 located the Saginaw Salt Springs, but this rich field was not developed until later.[584]

Salt weighed approximately 50 to 56 pounds the bushel,[585] and when not shipped by pack horse, was usually packed in barrels of five-bushel capacity. An interesting commentary on the relative importance of two important minerals at this time was the appearance of a notice that a Kentucky well had produced oil which flowed fourteen feet out of the hole. It was said this oil would make a brilliant flame when ignited, and was used in England for medicinal purposes.[586] Striking oil was considered a favorable sign, for it was understood that where oil was, by boring deeper, one could get salt water, which would prove highly beneficial to the surrounding country.[587]

The price of salt varied greatly. Salt sold at the Kanawha works at 62½ cents the bushel in 1812, about double that price in 1814, and at 50 to 62½ cents in 1815. In Ohio, the price was about $2.50. The first Kanawha agreement of 1817 tried to hold the price at $1.00 at the works, but ten years later the price had dropped to 25 cents. In 1831, it was 30 to 35 cents. Retail price at Cincinnati was 50 to 60 cents but Turk's Island salt was 80 cents. At Cleveland salt was $2.50 (probably New York or Turk's Island salt). Away from the rivers and roads salt sometimes sold at $5.00 to $8.00.

When Benton began his salt-tariff crusade the rate was 20 cents the bushel, on a false bushel of 56 pounds. Counting the

[584] Bela Hubbard, "A Michigan Geological Expedition in 1837," in *Michigan Pioneer and Historical Collections*, III (1879–80), 197.

[585] The salt bushel was almost as elastic a unit as the yard based upon the length of the King's arm. A bushel measure of Kanawha salt, packed damp at the lick, weighed 80 to 100 pounds, while a bushel of dry and pure salt weighed about 50 pounds. Benton stated that a measured bushel of alum salt (imported or natural salt) weighed 84 pounds. The Federal Government followed the British precedent and measured salt by the weight bushel of 56 pounds, but the salt manufacturers in their retail business sold it by weight bushel of 50 pounds. *Congressional Debates*, 21 Congress, 1 session, 428; *Documents Relating to the Trade in, and Manufacture and Uses of, Salt* (U. S. *Senate Documents*, 26 Congress, 1 session, IV, No. 196). Further, the Kanawha interests were said to have weighed this "lick weight," *i.e.* wet.

[586] *Edwardsville* (Ill.) *Spectator*, November 7, December 3, 1820; "Geology of Illinois," in *Illinois Monthly Magazine*, I (1830–31), 45; *De Bow's Commercial Review* (New Orleans, 1846–80), XXIII (1857), 133 ff.

[587] Louisville *Public Advertiser*, in *Hamilton Intelligencer*, April 28, 1829. For the "salt" argument used in winning the passage of Indiana's Wabash and Erie Canal law, see above, 502 n.

duty, merchants' profit on the duty, and the loss on the bushel, he figured the duty on alum salt to be about 400 per cent. Benton emphasized the fact that the high price of imported salt caused western farmers to drive stock to the East where they received 1½ to 2½ cents on the hoof and lost the use of hide, tallow and by-products which they could have realized by home butchering. Even the steamboat business suffered as a result. Various reductions in the duty were made from 1830 to 1840, until it was about 6 cents, but Benton failed in 1840, as he had in 1830, to get it abolished. Imports of salt into the West in 1835 were about 80,000 tons (50,000 through New Orleans, 25,000 through Buffalo, and 5,000 through Pittsburgh); five years later they were slightly less, with Buffalo gaining 5,000 tons and New Orleans losing 10,000.

Mineral or stone coal in the West was noticed by Father Hennepin as early as 1679. Christopher Gist took some as samples to the Ohio Company in 1751, Captain Hutchins marked Ohio coal lands on his London map of 1777, Manasseh Cutler located "coals" on his Ohio map of 1787, and Gilbert Imlay mentioned coal in his *Topographical Description* (1793). Jervis Cutler gave coal a prominent place in his book on Ohio in 1812, and John Kilbourn in the *Ohio Gazetteer* of 1821 considered the coal resources of each county.[588] Although generally known, there was no need for development of coal fields as long as wood had to be cleared off the land. Zanesville people were using coal, however, in 1810, and the first commercial mining began in Summit County about the same time.

Coal was referred to now and then in the newspapers as being, for steam engines, superior to wood.[589] Cincinnati citizens were told of its cheapness in an endeavor to overcome the general prejudice against coal because of its dirtiness. Pittsburgh coal at 12 cents the bushel, equal to a cord of good hickory wood, would cost $1.50 as against $2.87 for the wood.[590] In the earlier period coal was shipped in deep-draft barges, and low water sometimes ran up the price in the river towns. In 1836 coal was available in

---

[588] For a brief review of the interest in coal and iron ore, see Paul Wakelee Stoddard, "The Knowledge of Coal and Iron in Ohio before 1835," in *Ohio Archaeological and Historical Society Publications*, XXXVIII (1929), 219–30.

[589] "Observer" in a long article in *Cleaveland Herald*, July 16, 1829, talked up its advantages and said that it was easily available in a region 600 by 1,500 miles in extent.

[590] *Cincinnati Daily Gazette,* October 17, 1827.

Pittsburgh at $1.00 a ton, but in Cincinnati sold as high as $10, instead of the usual $3.00. Illinois coal was not so often mentioned. Wood was still cheap there, and only the poorer coals, mostly in the border counties, were exposed. Also transportation was a greater problem. Even so, Alton merchants' efforts were successful when they mined coal just below the mouth of the Illinois River in 1836.[591] In 1840 Ohio was credited with having "raised" 3,500,000 bushels of coal, Illinois 424,000 and Indiana 242,000.[592]

Iron ore deposits had not been so well noticed as coal, but an iron furnace was in operation on the Mahoning at the mouth of Yellow Creek in 1808,[593] and a forge and furnace were in use near the mouth of the Licking in 1810.[594] The three Ohio furnaces mentioned in the census report of 1820 were said to have had an annual output of 1,187 tons with value of 109,000. Thirty-four nail-making establishments were also listed with output of 39,000 tons.[595] During the next dozen years a number of furnaces and foundries were opened,[596] but not until the development of the famous Hanging Rock region, which centered largely in Jackson, Lawrence, Scioto, and Vinton counties, Ohio, did mining, smelting, and forging of iron, with the dependent charcoal and other industries, become important.[597] This area, including the region south of the Ohio, covered about 1,800 square miles,

---

[591] *Alton Telegraph* in *Detroit Daily Advertiser*, September 29, 1836.

[592] *Compendium of the . . . Sixth Census . . .* (Washington, D. C., 1841), 275, 287, 299.

[593] Charles Whittlesey, *History of the Coal and Iron Business* (Cincinnati, 1872), 5.

[594] Mills Day, "Travels in Virginia and Ohio in 1810" (MS.), cited in Stoddard, "Coal and Iron in Ohio," in *Ohio Archaeological and Historical Society Publications*, XXXVIII, 226.

[595] Fourth Census, cited in Stoddard, 226.

[596] Zanesville had an air foundry (1818) with capacity of making 150 tons of pig iron into castings annually, Columbus a cupola furnace with capacity of using 120 tons of pig iron, and Dayton one which turned out 3 tons of castings per week. The Phoenix foundry in Cincinnati (1825) produced 400 tons of castings annually and had a pay roll of $12,000. A number of other furnaces and foundries were operating. *Documents Relative to the Manufactures in the United States* (U. S. *House Executive Documents*, 22 Congress, 1 session, No. 308, 2 volumes. Washington, D. C., 1833), II, 862–72. In 1831 the Portsmouth Iron and Steel Company began producing bar iron, sheet iron, nails, etc. Vernon D. Keeler, "An Economic History of the Jackson County Iron Industry," in *Ohio Archaeological and Historical Society Publications*, XLII (1933), 148–49.

[597] For history of this region, see Eugene B. Willard (ed.), *A Standard History of the Hanging Rock Iron Region of Ohio . . .* (Chicago, 1916); Wilbur Stout, "The Charcoal Iron Industry of the Hanging Rock Iron District—Its Influence on the Early Development of the Ohio Valley," in *Ohio Archaeological and Historical Society Publications*, XLII (1933), 72–104; Keeler, "Jackson County Iron Industry," in *ibid.*, 133–238.

and in general the ores, though in thin veins, yielded 30 to 40 per cent iron. Between 1832 and 1834, with the opening of the Ohio Canal, fifteen furnaces were put in operation, but during the next decade only a few were added. Among the outstanding furnaces were Hecla, with its famous ironmaster, John Campbell, and Vesuvius (both in Lawrence County, 1833) where in 1836 hot-blast smelting was introduced.

The first manufacture of importance of crucible steel in America was begun at Cincinnati in 1832. English success in this type of steel, upon which the great Sheffield cutlery products depended, was based largely on a blend of three kinds of English pot clays. Dr. William Garrard, born in England, was a bricklayer in early life. When he set up his works in Cincinnati, he drew the plans and superintended the bricklaying himself. He overcame the handicap of lack of both proper clay and good local blister steel. He found a western Virginia clay which served his purpose for making the pots and discovered that charcoal iron from Missouri served as well as the high-grade Swedish iron for making cast steel. From Garrard's best cast steel, quoted at 18 cents to 25 cents per pound, were made saws, axes, and files, supposedly as good as Sheffield products. The blades of the first McCormick reaper were made from his steel. Reduction of import duties in the 1830's and the depression of 1837 closed his business.

Most of the iron was shipped by river. Cincinnati and Pittsburgh were the important markets, but Portsmouth, Maysville, Louisville, St. Louis, and New Orleans took their share. Local blacksmith shops, which made everything from pots to plows, no doubt consumed a large part of the output. Steamboats or keelboats carried small shipments; barges, flats, canalboats, even oxcarts were used for heavier lots. Since almost four cords of wood (137 bushels of charcoal), and more than 300 pounds of limestone were needed to produce a ton of pig iron from almost 5,000 pounds of ore, and since many furnaces averaged 2,500 tons annually, hundreds of timber cutters, colliers (charcoal makers), and haulers were employed. The iron manufactories provided a good market for local farmers and tradesmen who furnished grain, vegetables, molasses, oxen, tools, and work clothing.

Next to iron, coal, and salt, lead was the most important mineral product. Its production centered around the Galena-Mineral Point region, the development of which began in the early 1820's.[598] Mine output in 1823 was a little more than 300,000 pounds. From about a hundred miners the number jumped to 1,600 by 1827, when ore output was more than 11,000,000 pounds, from which 5,000,000 pounds of lead were produced.[599] Markets were reached by the Mississippi, and overland by wagon along the two trails to Chicago. The lead industry brought a rush of settlers, a cosmopolitan mining population, and attendant speculation and booming.

Limestone, which outcropped in the unglaciated region, particularly in southern Indiana, was used in iron smelting and burned in kilns at many places. Much of the lime was used locally for mortar, plaster, and for fertilizer, but some was shipped to New Orleans and elsewhere.

Ashes, though hardly a mineral product, were an important commodity, both for local uses and as a cash crop during the period of timber clearing. The farmer's wife used them for lye and soapmaking, but field ashes would bring 8 to 10 cents and fireplace ashes 12½ cents the bushel in goods or cash. Ashes brought $120 per ton (about 500 bushels) at Montreal in 1821. Black salts (potash or evaporated but unrefined lye) and pearlashes (potash with the carbon burned out in ovens) had a ready sale at $4.00 to $6.00 per hundredweight.[600] Local asheries developed to leach the ashes and burn down the lye. Along with the iron smelters, lime kilns, and steamboats, they consumed quantities of firewood. The only thing which prevented any settler in the timbered regions from paying for his land with the ash or black salts proceeds was lack of transportation. It seems that ashes were more likely saved and sold by the Yankee-New York settlers than the people from the South.[601]

[598] For the settlement and operations of the lead region, see Chapter X, 55–57.
[599] *Illinois Intelligencer* in Indianapolis *Indiana Journal*, March 27, 1828.
[600] Hamilton (Ohio) *Miami Herald,* September 26, 1817; *Cleaveland Register,* December 1, 1818; *Cleaveland Herald,* December 4, 1821; *Detroit Journal and Michigan Advertiser,* March 9, 1831, May 14, 1833, June 17, 1834. Potash manufacturing was of some importance in the colonial period. Thomas Stephens published in London in 1758 the *Rise and Fall of Pot-ash in America.*
[601] Ohio marketed 6,800 tons of pot- and pearlashes in 1840 of which more than 5,000 tons were from the two Reserve counties of Trumbull and Geauga. Michigan Territory listed 145 tons but Indiana and Illinois combined had only 2½ tons. *Compendium of the Sixth Census,* 278, 290, 302, 326.

A history of the development of manufacturing in the North-west is impossible at this point, but a few samples and general trends may be noted, as well as the relationship of industry to trade and transportation.[602] When Morgan Neville, of Cincinnati, reported to the Secretary of the Treasury of the United States on the condition of manufactures in the West in 1832, he said, "manufactories are but beginning to exist" and that factories were "few and far between." It was true that the great bulk of manufactured products was still produced on the farm, in the home, or in small "one-man" shops;[603] nevertheless, important beginnings had been made during the fifteen years following the second war with England. Even before the coming of steam navigation western industry had developed into a fairly self-sufficient local system, with its markets and distribution facilities. The gazetteers or emigrant guidebooks, travelers, and newspapers relate the rise of industry and are probably as reliable as any official figures.

At the end of the war manufacturing establishments were confined largely to the towns near the Ohio River. Steubenville in 1817 had a steam woolen mill, an iron foundry, a paper mill, a steam flour mill, a brewery, a cotton factory, nail factory, two earthenware factories, a wool carding machine, and a tobacco factory.[604] Besides these there were gunsmiths, blacksmiths, cabinetmakers, saddle makers, hatmakers, tanneries, and numerous other shops. Zanesville had a glass factory and a potash works in 1816, an air foundry two years later,[605] and within a decade had annual exhibits at the Muskingum Agricultural and Manufacturing Society fair, of broadcloth, carpeting, linen, fur hats, harness,

[602] For a general view, see Isaac Lippincott, "Pioneer Industry in the West," in *Journal of Political Economy*, XVIII (1910), 269, 293; Hall, *The West: Its Commerce and Navigation*.

[603] For domestic or household manufacturing processes, see Chapter IV.

[604] *Pittsburg Navigator* cited in *Ohio Archaeological and Historical Society Publications*, VI (1898), 239; Steubenville *Western Herald* in *Zanesville Express*, December 5, 1816. *Niles' Weekly Register*, XXI, 367 (Feb. 2, 1822) said, "The reflecting man will ponder not a little on the fact, that wool is transported from New-Jersey to be manufactured into cloth at Steubenville in the state of Ohio, and that such cloth is sent to the New-York, Philadelphia and Baltimore markets." By 1828 the Steubenville woolen mill was using 38,000 pounds of wool annually. Columbus *Ohio State Journal*, September 25, 1828.

[605] *Zanesville Express*, February 22, 1816; *Documents Relative to Manufactures*, II, 862.

and wheat fans.[606] Hamilton and vicinity had several carding mills, a fulling mill and a hatmaking establishment.[607]

Cincinnati by 1815 had in operation 23 cotton spinning mills, 71 roving and drawing heads, 14 cotton and 91 wool carding machines, and wool spinning machines with 130 spindles.[608] In 1815 there were 4 horsepower spinning mills with 1,200 spindles; a woolen mill operated by a 20-horsepower steam engine was advertised to open; its capacity was 60 yards of broadcloth per day. When this mill, commonly known as the Steam Mill, burned in 1823, the loss was placed at $100,000.[609]

In 1823, 55 of about 70 counties in Ohio reported to the Secretary of State of the United States manufactures aggregating more than $3,000,000 annually, and capital invested at nearly $4,000,000.[610] Muskingum, Hamilton, Montgomery, Jefferson, Warren and Ross counties led in order, in manufactured products. Only 8 of Indiana's 48 counties reported. Their total was 142,000 annual value of products and $150,000 capital invested. There was a small powder factory in Clark County, and a woolen mill in Dearborn with 75 spindles which employed three men, two women and two children. There were potteries in Dearborn, Fayette, Knox, and Scott. Distilleries in Clark, Knox, Dearborn, and Scott used 65,000 bushels of corn. There was a scattering of tobacco factories, and 65 pairs of millstones were in use in the mills.[611] Seven Illinois counties listed their output at $126,000, investment $74,000; for the five Michigan counties the figures were $34,000 and $60,000.[612] Most of the establishments were small, hardly distinguishable from household shops. Products listed ran from ashes and axes to wagons, wool, and whiskey. Hats, boots and shoes, furniture, candles, ropes, harness, saddlery, earthen- and tinware, cutlery, flour, meal, tools, and similar products were generally listed in all reporting counties.

Additional factories sprang up during the years following. By 1825 Cincinnati, with 16,000 population, had about 15 steam

---

[606] Cincinnati Daily Gazette, October 19, 1827.
[607] Hamilton Miami Intelligencer, July 13, 1814.
[608] Niles' Weekly Register, IX, 35 (Sep. 16, 1815).
[609] Cincinnati National Republican, November 7, 1823. It was also a flour mill, 87 by 62 feet; a 70-horsepower engine was used for grinding.
[610] American State Papers, Finance, IV, 447–55.
[611] Ibid., 215, 456.
[612] Ibid., 456–58.

engines in operation, and its industries amounted to about $1,800,000. The Colerain Cotton Mill Company, incorporated in 1823, capital $20,000, set up a combined water- and steam-powered mill, which by 1832 was turning out 60,000 pounds of cotton yarn. Men employees received $4.00 to $10 per week, women and children $1.00 to $1.75. The working day was twelve hours.[613] The Miami Cotton Mill, capitalized at $20,000, in 1830 built a water-powered mill which used 60,000 pounds of raw cotton annually; it employed 4 men at $1.00 per day and 16 women and children at 22 cents per day. There were 8 paper mills in the Miami country by 1832, including 2 steam mills in Cincinnati, which employed some 160 persons and produced annually $120,000 worth of printing and wrapping paper. This product was mostly used in Cincinnati.

Cincinnati by 1832 was the chief manufacturing center not only of Ohio, but of the West. Type foundries, book binderies, machine shops, tin-plate and sheet-iron works, machine carding establishments, rope walks, coachmaking shops, saddletree factories, tanneries, tobacco factories, and plow and ax shops were among the establishments.[614] The John Richards Steam Cooperage establishment employed 50 men and made annually 1,600 half barrels, 34,000 pork barrels, 2,000 beer barrels, 15,000 lard kegs, 4,000 hogsheads, and 1,000 tight hogsheads. A. Reuss's output was not so large for he made about four cabinet pianos per year, of bird's-eye and curly maple, and mahogany veneers at $350 to $700 each. Also harps. Small factories of this type were scattered from Cincinnati to St. Louis. Madison, New Albany, and Vincennes in Indiana, Shawneetown, Alton, and Vandalia in Illinois were leaders in their states.[615] When

---

[613] *Documents Relative to Manufactures,* II, 867.

[614] *Ibid.,* II, 868.

[615] The woolen mill of Thomas, John, and Levinus King at Richmond advertised carding, spinning, weaving, and fulling; it produced flannel, "cassinett, sattinett," and other types of cloth. Richmond *Public Leger,* May 7, 1825. Window glass manufactured in New Albany was marketed as far away as Rhode Island. *Brookville Inquirer,* May 11, 1825. Madison had a paper mill in 1828; Indianapolis expected to have a combined grinding, fulling, spring, and cotton mill and sawmill. *Indiana Journal,* January 31, February 14, 1828. In Orange County were quarried and milled the famous Hindostan "whet rocks" or sharpening stones. After Hindostan was wiped out by disease in 1822 the stones were marketed by way of Vincennes and other towns. (This small craftsman industry so important to the pioneer ax wielders and scythe swingers continues today, and ships stones all over the world.) John Hay, at Springfield, Illinois, announced a new cotton spinning factory in 1833 and advertised for a few boys and blind horses. *Sangamo*

Illinois took a state census of manufactories in 1835, 5 counties listed 16 or more.[616]

Morgan Neville considered the greatest obstacle to manufacturing in the West to be the want of capital. The few who had money to invest would not consider doing so unless there was a strong probability of earning 15 to 20 per cent on it.[617]

The opening of the canals and the general speculative activities and credit inflation of the 1830's naturally gave a considerable impetus to industrial development. Cincinnati in 1835, for instance, manufactured among other things more than 100 steam engines, about 240 cotton gins, 20 sugar mills, and 22 steamboats. It was the center of manufacture of drugs in the West; most of the "botanic" medicines were made here, the total annual value of which must have been in excess of the nominal figure of $101,000 (census of 1840) reported for the entire state of Ohio. Dayton in 1836 had 4 cotton factories, a carpet factory which employed 41 hands and had a daily capacity of 500 yards, a cast iron foundry, 2 gun barrel factories, 4 machine shops, a clock factory with annual output of 2,500, a paper mill, a carding and fulling mill, a last factory, and a soap and candle factory with 100,000 pound annual output. In the immediate vicinity were 7 gristmills, 7 sawmills, 5 distilleries, mills for laths, shingles, and the like.[618]

The mills and shops of the large towns from Pittsburgh and Cincinnati to St. Louis and Detroit had access to coal or other fuel and were far less dependent upon water power, and hence seasonal production, than those of the East. This was not true, of course, of the many mills in the country and small towns. These in return for their cheap power and simple machinery had to pay the price in the uncertainties of production based on rainfall.

In spite of the rise of industry, commerce outranked manufacturing in economic importance, and was second only to agricul-

---

Journal, August 3, 1833. Bakeries, hatmaking establishments, brick works, and cooperage and cabinetmaking establishments were numerous in the towns and villages.

[616] Madison 133, St. Clair 56, Randolph 53, Union 27, and Warren 16. Sangamon and Morgan had the most mills, 108 and 73 respectively. *Illinois Advocate and State Register,* February 17, 1836.

[617] *Documents Relative to Manufactures,* II, 861.

[618] *Dayton Democratic Herald* in *Cincinnati Daily Gazette,* January 17, 1837.

ture. A rough idea may be had from the fact that in 1840 total capital invested in manufactures in the four states and one territory of the Old Northwest was approximately twenty-eight millions, whereas investments in commission and retail establishments alone was about forty-three millions. If meat packing and lumber yards be included under commerce, as in the census compendium, total investments in commerce were nearly fifty million dollars. Only in Michigan did industrial investments exceed commercial, a condition which was the result of the high value of milling products and the absence of any towns of size.

During the years before the opening of roads or canals, fair stocks of merchandise were available only at the river towns, or those easily accessible to the lakes. At Zanesville in 1816 Eben Marian advertised: "GOODS—hardware, crockery, groceries, dye stuffs, paints, drugs, books, stationary and shoes." He would take in payment wheat, rye, corn, oats, whiskey, hogs, lard, butter, tallow, beeswax, country sugar, cheese, rags, ashes, black salts, furs, boards, clapboards, shingles, lime, and barrels.[619] At Hamilton, Sutherland and Ramsay, in an unusual quarter-page display, advertised cloths of many colors, coatings, blankets, assorted vestings, velvets, cords, Bombazines all colors, callicoes, muslins, cambric, white jean dimities, flag and silk bandanoes, ostrich feathers, crapes, silks, satin, elegant umbrellas and parasols, stationery, slippers, bonnets, chinaware, Liverpool and queens, cutlery, tools, groceries, indigo, bar iron, and leather.[620] A veritable department store.

The modest advertisements of Vincennes merchants in 1816 mentioned sundry merchandise, but soon began to list dry goods, hardware, fine boots and shoes, millinery and hats, saddlery, whiskey, salt, and other items.[621] Fifteen years later the market warranted specialization, for R. P. Price advertised only hats:

[619] *Zanesville Express,* February 22, 1816.
[620] *Miami Herald,* May 27, 1816.
[621] *Western Sun.* In 1817 Vincennes had 18 "stores of merchandise," as well as 6 taverns, 4 groceries, 4 blacksmith shops, 2 gunsmith shops, 3 shoemaker shops, 3 saddler shops, 4 tailor shops, 2 cabinetmakers, 3 hat factories, 2 printing offices, 2 market houses, several lawyers, doctors, a tinsmith, chairmaker, tobacconist, tanner, apothecary, and a livery stable. Sample prices of commodities: coffee 37½ to 50 cents, New Orleans sugar 25 cents, loaf sugar 50 cents, iron 16 cents per pound, ham 25 cents, brandy $6.00 per gallon, Madeira $8.00, rum $4.00, and Young Hyson $1.50 the pound. Wheat was $1.00, corn 50 cents, potatoes 37 to 50 cents, pork $4.50 cwt., and beef $3.00 to $4.00. David Thomas, *Travels,* 192.

beaver at $10, fine castor at $8.00, coarse beaver at $6.00, fine Rorame at $5.00, and coarse at $3.00. First-class workmanship, superior stuff, and "most fashioned style" were pledged.[622] Marron and Hunter announced a large assortment, just purchased in New York and Philadelphia, of "substantial and fancy dry goods, with hardware, cutlery, queensware, glassware, hats, shoes, and groceries &C &C." Wheat, corn, rye, pork, beeswax, cordwood, saw logs, feathers, dried apples, tallow, domestic linen, beans, deerskins, onions, and all merchantable products of home industry, were acceptable in barter.[623]

Indianapolis, where transportation was more of a problem, was, within two years of its founding, offering through Connor, Tyner and Company:

cloths, cassimeres, baize, cassinetts, flannels, blankets, bombazetts, robes, dress shawls, calicoes, cambrick, muslins, shirtings, vesting, hosiery, nankeens, handkerchiefs, umbrellas and parasols, plaids, stripes and chambrays, linen, hats, combs, bonnets, shoes,—black, coloured and morocco,—spoons, knives and forks, saws, files, saddlery, school books, butcher, shoe and pen knives, chissels, gouges and plane bitts, hammers and hatchets, hinges and screws, padlocks, latchets, spades, shovels, tongs, cotton and wool cards, augers &c. &c. Also, queensware and glassware, groceries, powder, lead and shot, iron, steel and nails, chalk and Spanish whiting, tinware &c. &c.[624]

Edward Cowles, of Kaskaskia, in 1818 offered superfine, fine, and coarse broadcloths, cassimeres, hosings, cambrics, linens, domestic, plaids, saddles, bridles, hats, shoes, and hardware.[625] John Brant, of Carmi, in addition to above items offered at either retail or wholesale, trimmings and ribbons, mantuas, sevantines, looking glasses, japaned trays, pit- and crosscut saws, window glass, English Crowley Mellington steel, Juneatta bar iron, and grindstones.[626]

Detroit shopkeepers, in addition to groceries, dry goods, and hardware, were offering drugs and medicines, stationery, and the works of Byron, Goldsmith, Cervantes, and Cooper.[627]

By the late 1820's specialization in merchandising was notice-

[622] Vincennes *Western Sun and General Advertiser*, May 15, 1830.

[623] *Ibid.*, April 17, 1830.

[624] Indianapolis *Western Censor and Emigrants' Guide*, cited in George S. Cottman, "Early Commerce in Indiana," in *Indiana Magazine of History*, IV (1908), 2.

[625] *Western Intelligencer*, January, 1818.

[626] Shawneetown *Illinois Emigrant*, January 23, 1819.

[627] *Detroit Gazette*, July 25, 1817.

able in Cincinnati. While J. L. Webb and Co., of Delaware, were listing dozens of items from broadcloth to tools,[628] many merchants in Cincinnati were emphasizing specialties such as imported Dutch bolting cloth, Du Pont's powder, coal grates, spermaceti oil, oatmeal, or books.[629] Gradually the little notices were carried in larger type, and besides the standardized cuts of boots for cobblers' ads, and pestle and mortar for the druggist, there began to appear cuts (wood engravings) of coal grate fenders, brooms, looking glasses, coffins and monuments, musical instruments, wagons, barouches, phaetons, chariottees, gigs, buggies, coaches, farm machinery, and the like.[630] A little later came cuts of drums (music store), umbrellas, pianofortes, pumps (plumbing), and horses (liniment ads). At Columbus special advertisements ran for peppermint and ginger lozenges, lemon drops and assorted candies; for drugs, axes, and vegetable oil.[631] Indianapolis papers carried notices and often cuts of beaver hats, tailored suits, and kegs of oysters.[632] Conspicuous by its absence in advertising was any mention whatsoever of Christmas. As a commercial institution it simply had not been discovered.

As pioneer society made the transition to a more specialized economy, the merchant, as well as the professional groups, became more important. Yet even in the earlier period his activities and functions were such that he can no more be omitted from the story than fur trader or soldier, boatman or doctor.[633]

The obvious function of the merchant was the retailing of food and manufactured goods. Even this, in the days of barter, absence of reliable money, credit, or transportation, was difficult enough, but he did much more. In smaller centers he acted as custodian for customers' funds (safety-box service), advanced credit, transferred money, wrote letters, ordered periodicals— perhaps through his eastern agents and thus avoided sending money through the mails. He aided travelers, sold books, acted

---

[628] *Delaware* (Ohio) *Patron*, October 27, 1825.
[629] *Cincinnati Daily Gazette*, November 2, 1827.
[630] *Ibid.*, 1832–33.
[631] *Ohio State Journal*, September, 1833.
[632] *Indiana Journal*, 1835.
[633] The best studies of the merchant are Lewis E. Atherton, *The Pioneer Merchant in Mid-America* (*University of Missouri Studies*, XIV, No. 2, 1939) and "The Services of the Frontier Merchant," in *Mississippi Valley Historical Review*, XXIV (1937–38), 153–70. Although these deal with a region a little farther west (Iowa and Missouri), the problem, practices, and methods are the same.

as postmaster, served as leader in community affairs, participated in politics, and helped satisfy (and stimulate) the aesthetic longings in the hearts of the women. In politics the merchants were preponderantly Whig. In general they did not consider their occupation particularly distinguished and left comparatively few records in the nature of journals or reminiscences. Judge James Hall, among whose many interests commerce ranked high, noted that merchants were often criticized or neglected by those in the seats of political power; he suggested that broader education and culture be emphasized as a means of overcoming prejudice against the merchants. He recognized their many services and believed that the prosperity of the West was created largely by the merchant class.[634]

Wholesale connections of western merchants were mainly with dealers in the cities of the Atlantic Coast. Philadelphia held her supremacy over both New York and Baltimore throughout most of the period.[635] Pittsburgh and to a lesser degree Cincinnati, Louisville, and St. Louis also served as wholesale centers. The merchant's wholesale market was determined by transportation costs, prices, and services offered. Modern hand-to-mouth buying and liquidity of stock depend upon a constant supply in the hands of jobber and manufacturer, and mail-like speed of delivery. In a day when the merchant had to order a year's stock in advance, not only was he more dependent upon the integrity of the shipper and longer term credit, but more severely penalized by errors of judgment.

Most merchants of importance found it best to make the eastern trip at least once each year and personally select their goods. Careful buyers accompanied their goods in transit west to avoid as much damage and spoilage as possible. These trips required about six weeks and no small expense outlay. Supplemental orders might be made by mail, but mail ordering was risky business. European houses might deal through an importer, but frequently, in the face of opposition of American importers, held their own auctions in eastern cities. These auctions were widely advertised.

[634] *The West: Its Commerce and Navigation*, 20 ff.
[635] In the spring of 1825 the *Buffalo Journal* pointed out to western merchants the advantages of traveling east by way of Lake Erie, canal packets, and stages instead of over the mountains by way of Philadelphia. Lawrenceburg *Indiana Spectator*, May 20, 1825.

Prices were usually below American wholesale prices. Terms varied from cash to six months or even a year. Western merchants sometimes complained that eastern merchants combined against their interests. In 1821, for instance, Boston, New York, Philadelphia, and Baltimore merchants agreed not to purchase auction goods except in the original package. This placed the western buyer at great disadvantage, for he could not make up an assortment of auction goods at less than package lots, and so had to buy from the city merchants. "Let trade regulate itself— let us alone," is all right for the other fellow, said the *Western Herald*, "but—"[636] Western merchants, however, made their little agreements, also. Farmers from several Ohio counties called a meeting at Middletown in 1836 to agree on a $7.00 price on pork, and resolved to give their business to buyers not in the pork combine.[637]

Eastern merchants did not rely entirely upon their newspaper advertisements, but usually advised western buyers by mail of the goods available. During the buying season displays were often arranged at the hotels patronized by the buyers, and "drummers or borers" were on hand to call attention to their merits.[638] Traveling salesmen, or drummers on the road in the West, were not common until after the railroad offered easier communications.

The country store has been described,[639] and samples of town store stocks listed, but the story of distribution is not complete without a reckoning with the traveling middlemen—the peddlers or hawkers and walkers of pioneer times. The peddler was almost a Yankee institution and dated back to early colonial days. Irish, Scotch-Irish, and Germans, mostly young men, also took up the business and followed the frontier west. So ubiquitous a character was the peddler that he was generally noticed by the traveler and became almost a necessary character in fiction.

These traveling gentry might be roughly divided into two types. First the peddler or retailer of goods, a peripatetic merchant who bought his goods and sold them at a profit. The

[636] *Western Herald and Steubenville Gazette* in *Piqua Gazette,* August 2, 1821.
[637] *Hamilton Intelligencer,* December 8, 1836.
[638] [John Beauchamp Jones], *The Western Merchant* . . . (Philadelphia, 1849), 167–68.
[639] *Ante,* 234-35.

chief interest of this type was in merchandising or selling. The other type was the artisan, whose chief interest was in his craft, but who made his wares and sold them where he could, and whose profit was essentially a manufacturer-to-consumer profit. Of course, many of this type became salesmen primarily, and bought other goods, or employed artisans to make goods for them. Many of the merchant peddlers were, as their prototype of earlier days had been, trunk peddlers of Yankee notions— pins, needles, buttons, scissors, knives, combs, lace, perfumes, trinkets, small hardware items, and the like—and carried their stock in trade on their backs. But as specialization developed, the horse and cart or wagon outfit was acquired, and up and down the countryside were carried stocks of shoes, tinware, clocks, dry goods, spices, essences and dyes, pottery, wooden ware, brooms, baskets, spinning wheels, or what not. There were "yarb and root" men, or drug peddlers, and peddlers of books. Bibles, spelling books, dictionaries, *Pilgrim's Progress,* Foxe's *Martyrs,* volumes on physic or domestic medicine, books of knowledge, almanacs, religious tracts, as well as scores of other items, were made available.

Wherever a crowd assembled, at auction sales, political meetings, court days, muster days, there was likely to be the peddler with his wares. In between times he covered the country, visiting from house to house. The farther removed the pioneer housewife was from local markets, the more likely was the peddler to have a hospitable reception. "Tin, tin. Come in," had a real meaning long before it became part of the routine of certain children's games. The shining tinware or the more elegant lacquer ware was always attractive to the housewife. Pies looked best when baked in the scalloped "tin" pan; a tin bucket was easier handled and cleaned than the wooden bucket. Handy also were the tin salt shaker or tea canister. With tea came the demand for queensware or "china." Tablecloths of bright design, and colored cotton prints for dress goods, as well as "warranted pure steel" knives, interested the women, as razors and clocks did the men, or jew's-harps the children. The peddler was a keen observer and psychologist as well as a shrewd trader. By many signs he judged the community and the individual, their wants and abilities to pay, and gauged his sales talk accordingly. His memory encompassed not only details of roads and trails, but faces, names, and previous sales. He remembered who was ill on the last visit, showed a solicitous interest in them, left some herbs which he had gathered in his tours. He dispensed advice, recipes, and gossip, and seemed more interested in the affairs of others than in his own. His bearing was insinuating; he knew no strangers.

The peddler had "dollar sense" as well. Although he always sold his goods at "ruinous prices" and "lost money with every sale," nevertheless the next season usually found him back again, "risen like the Phoenix from his own ashes, and ready to be ruined again—in the same way. He could never resist the pleading look of a pretty woman, and if she 'jewed' him twenty per cent (though his profits were only two hundred), the tenderness of his heart compelled him to yield. What wonder is it, then, if he was a prime favorite with all the women, or that his advent, to the children, made a day of jubilee?"[640] Since cash was so scarce, the peddler was often compelled to barter his wares for butter, eggs, yarn, ginseng, beeswax, or whatever was available, and found himself a middleman of produce, or "huckster." In fact the "huckster" wagon or traveling store often developed from the peddler's pack or cart. Many peddlers, having achieved a stake, established themselves as merchants and settled down to their counters and warehouses. Others found the appeal of the road too great to resist.

The artisan peddlers, or workmen of the road, were sometimes journeymen making their start in their trade. These men might locate in a likely situation to run their own shops, but many followed the road to the end. Traveling shoemakers, cobblers, weavers, tailors, cabinetmakers, clockmakers, tinsmiths, pewterers, mat, brush, broom, and basket makers filled a real need in the smaller settlements and rural regions. The pioneer housewife could weave a single coverlet, but not the much-desired double; could make the coat of linsey-woolsey but not of broadcloth. Her husband might make a churn or a cradle, but not a spinning wheel or a clock. In fact, as the family emerged from the simple existence, the greater became the demand for the article manufactured by the skilled worker, and the less likely was the head

[640] McConnel, *Western Characters,* 285.

of the family to have the time for, or necessity of, its manufacture in the home.

Steamboats, canals, better roads, and railroads eventually brought the consumer to the town and city markets, and in the end marked the decline of peddling. But not in our period. The peddler was as much a part of life as the doctor, the politician, or the preacher. Invasion of the field by sharp dealers was not yet noticeable. Reputable merchants dealt with these men, furnished them with goods, sometimes employed them as their agents. The itinerant merchant or artisan peddler was as "American" as anyone. In the country his visits were events, not only because of his display of wares, but because he brought news, gossip and stories. In this latter capacity he deserves to be thought of with the country doctor, the minister on circuit, and the traveler, rather than the mail-order catalogue which has so largely taken his place in the economic scheme of affairs.[641]

§ § § § § §

The hard times of 1819 to 1825 had slowly given way before the advance of settlement, the improved transportation facilities, and developing markets. In the late 1820's there was a brief period of dullness and monetary stringency. Newspapers all over the country complained of the slackness of trade and the businessman's fear that money was beginning to disappear.[642] Markets were slack in the West, but there was no sudden fall in prices as in the autumn of 1818. This proved to be but a minor setback and not a major depression.

In the early 1830's trade was brisk again and land booming going on at an unprecedented pace. Market prices were up and demand exceeded supply. "Ohio was never more prosperous or

[641] Richardson Little Wright, in *Hawkers & Walkers in Early America* . . . (Philadelphia, 1927), has written a charming account of all varieties of peddlers and pitchmen from early colonial times to the Civil War. Other interesting bits may be found in Marion Nicholl Rawson's *From Here to Yender*. One of the best firsthand descriptions of the peddler is in McConnel, *Western Characters*, 268 ff. John R. Commons, "American Shoemakers 1647–1895," in *Quarterly Journal of Economics*, XXIV (1909–10), 39–84, traces the development, organization, and marketing methods of this important craft. R. Malcolm Keir, "The Tin Peddler," in *Journal of Political Economy*, XXI (1913), 255–58, points out some interesting relationships between the peddler and industry.

[642] *Cincinnati Daily Gazette*, June 8, September 22, 1829.

increasing more rapidly than at present," said the *Hamilton Intelligencer* in 1834,[643] and none was enjoying it more than Cincinnati. The Queen City had noticeably benefited from improvements in steamboats, the new roads, and the Miami Canal. It was anticipating and, to a certain extent, discounting other improvements. Among these were the completion of the Miami Canal to the Maumee; a turnpike to Chillicothe; completion of turnpikes to Columbus, Springfield, Brookville, Lexington, and other points; the Whitewater Canal; the Lawrenceburg to Indianapolis railroad; a railroad to connect with the Mad River and Sandusky at Springfield on the one branch, and with Columbus and Cleveland on the other; and finally the Charleston and Cincinnati railroad to link up with the South. Warehouses were building, banks were moving into more pretentious quarters, business houses were going up, real estate was advancing. By 1839 merchants had organized a Chamber of Commerce.

In no way was Cincinnati's pre-eminence more apparent than in commerce, particularly in wholesaling and distributing facilities. Whereas Hamilton County's industrial investments in 1840 constituted less than half of the Ohio total, her commission-house investments were $5,200,000 of the state total of $5,928,000, and retail-store investments were almost thirteen million of a total of twenty-one million.[644]

Cleveland, with 6,000 population in 1835, was beginning to dream of the day when she might possibly rival Cincinnati with her 30,000 population and millions of dollars in business. Whole blocks of business buildings were being erected and river-front lots sold as high as $250 per front foot.[645] Among the needs of this rapidly developing commercial center were a breakwater for the harbor, increased hotel facilities, and a "Board of Trade" or Chamber of Commerce.[646]

Detroit was the only important mercantile center for Michigan. Merchants made their semiannual trips east for goods. Wholesale business was beginning. In 1837 a *Business Directory* was published and Detroit began to take on the airs of a city.

[643] September 28.
[644] *Compendium of the Sixth Census*, 277, 285.
[645] *Cleveland Herald*, August, 1835.
[646] *Cleveland Weekly Gazette*, March 7, 1837; *Cleveland Herald and Gazette* (weekly), March 25, April 1, 1837.

Indiana merchants bought largely from Cincinnati houses. Of the Indiana towns, Madison was the leading distributing center. Eastern Illinois, prior to the development of Chicago, bought mostly from Shawneetown, western Illinois from St. Louis. The more important merchants made trips to Cincinnati, Pittsburgh, Philadelphia, and New York.

By 1836 credit was easy and everyone seemed filled with ideas of manifest destiny and permanent prosperity. Accounts from various parts of the western country mentioned "unexampled rises in the value of landed property, and great speculation going on."[647] Portage County (Ohio) farms rose 50 to 100 per cent in value in one to two years. Town lots in Cleveland, Akron, and Cuyahoga Falls did as well, while those in Chicago and Milwaukee did even better.[648] At Cincinnati in April, 1835, market prices were beyond the highest known at that season of the year.[649] "The rage for speculation prevails in our provision market almost to a mania."[650] Fresh butter reached 50 cents, eggs 10 cents, and potatoes $1.50 the bushel.[651] Pork, bacon, flour, and beef were all up, and an immense business was done at the wharves. Wages, real estate, and rents were also advancing. Now is "an excellent time for capitalists to make investments," said Ohio's leading newspaper, but at the same time it added, "Let buyers and sellers take care."[652] As late as October, 1836, the *Gazette* said everyone was at a loss to account for the high prices.[653] With many idlers in the cities, it believed agriculture needed improvement. Parents should banish from the minds of their children the horror of having to earn their bread by the

[647] Ravenna *Western Courier*, March 24, 1836.
[648] See Chapter XII.
[649] *Cincinnati Daily Gazette*, April 23, 1835.
[650] *Ibid.*, April 3, 1835.
[651] *Ibid.*, April 23, 1835.
[652] *Ibid.*
[653] Some Cincinnati prices:

	May 1, 1833	May 1, 1834	March 3, 1835	March 1, 1837
Prime pork	$12	$10	$14	$20–$21
Mess pork	10.50	8.50	12.50	18– 19
Lard	7–7½ cents	4½–5 cents	7¼ cents	9½–10½ cents
Bacon—hams	7–7½ cents	6–6½ cents	8–9 cents	10 –12½ cents
Flour	3.75	2.62	4.12	7.50–7.87
Whiskey	.25½ cents	16–17 cents	.31	.35
Wheat				1.20–1.25
Potatoes				.25– .33
Corn				.33

Ibid., March 31, 1835, March 1, 1837.

sweat of their brows. A few months later, it decided that prices were not due to paper money or speculation, but to actual scarcity;[654] by September, 1837, however, it admitted that the markets were abundantly supplied, "but prices hold on, as if money was abundant."[655]

A writer from Michigan City, Indiana, in February, 1836, wrote, "I see by your prices current that you are 'in for it' as well as we are, in the way of all things eatable." He cited whole-sale prices in Chicago as follows: flour $12, corn $1.00, beans $2.50, potatoes $1.00, pork $5.00 to $6.00, and butter 25 to 40 cents. At Michigan City wheat was $1.50, flour $8.50, corn 75 cents to $1.00, pork $6.00 to $6.50, butter 25 to 37 cents, and groceries about 25 per cent above Cincinnati prices.[656] In Wisconsin Territory flour reached $20 to $25 the barrel.

"The United States have never known a period of more substantial prosperity than the present. The spirit of speculation, pernicious alike in its economic and moral influence, though it has raged to a mischievous extent in some places, leaves no permanent visible traces on Society; habits of steady industry appear in the main, to be but slightly disturbed by it."[657] Similar statements were plentiful, but a shadow of doubt crossed the minds of a few. "Throughout the whole country there is an apparent swell of prosperity. We have seen the like before and witnessed what followed. If this swell is now the enlargement of sound health, there is much reason to fear it soon will become distempered, and finally result in the bloating of enfeebling disease."[658] And in commenting on the high prices in 1835 the *Cincinnati Gazette* said: "Are we not beginning to swell again in a mode indicating another blow out in seven or eight years?" Although there was much mention of speculation, there was no apparent awareness of credit inflation in the papers of the day.

[654] *Cincinnati Daily Gazette*, March 1, 1837.
[655] *Ibid.*, September 6, 1837.
[656] *Ibid.*, February 24, 1837.
[657] *Detroit Journal and Michigan Advertiser* (triweekly), February 27, 1836.
[658] *Hamilton Intelligencer*, May 14, 1835, quoting *Cincinnati Gazette*.

VIII

Money, Banking, and State Finance, 1815–1836

The entire course of our lives is ordered by money. No single thing is more interwoven with human experience. Yet nothing seems so poorly understood by men as money. The most fantastic fallacies are, and long have been, current about it. For the great mass of people, the subject is shrouded in the densest and most pernicious ignorance; pernicious, because we allow persons in power, as ignorant as ourselves, often to take astonishingly stupid action about our money— without interference. Nor is this a modern phenomenon. For the approximately twenty-five hundred years that governments have had a close relation to money, the same confusion about it—both on the part of the masses of men who use it, and rulers who presume to do things about it—is clear and consistent in the records.

Harry Scherman, *The Promises Men Live By*

MONEY and credit play almost as important a part in the economic life of the people in modern society as does the circulation of the blood in the life of the individual. Unfortunately the people's knowledge of the laws which govern the former lags some centuries behind their knowledge of the latter. Possibly the very complexity of money, banking, and government finance makes an understanding of even the barest essentials impossible to the people, and thereby creates one of the most dangerous hazards upon which republics may founder.

It is impossible here to do more than outline the financial history of the states north of the Ohio prior to 1840 and to give a sample of contemporary opinion on the subject.[1]

---

[1] The literature of the subject is extensive and often confusing. The student who wishes to pursue it further is advised, after a review of some chapters in any standard text on money and banking, to read the chapter on "Frontier Finance" in Frederic L. Paxson, *History of the American Frontier,* and then proceed to the following special treatments: C. C. Huntington, "History of Banking and Currency in Ohio before the Civil War," in *Ohio Archaeological and Historical Society Publications,* XXIV (1915); Logan Esarey, *State Banking in Indiana (Indiana University Studies,* X, Bloomington, 1912); George William Dowrie, *The Development of Banking in Illinois, 1817–1868 (University of Illinois Studies in the Social Sciences,* II, No. 4, Dec., 1913). For Michigan see H. M. Utley, "The Wild Cat Banking System of Michigan," in *Michigan Pioneer and Historical Collections,* V (1882), 209–22; Charles Moore (ed. and comp.), "The Beginning of Territorial

If all business in the world could be transacted on a cash-and-carry, metallic-currency basis, not only students of history but financiers, businessmen, politicians, and the people would be relieved of much mental anguish and constant trouble. Unfortunately, there is not sufficient gold and silver (or other acceptable metals) with which to do this. Hence, means of expanding the currency by paper money, bank money, and credit have developed in modern times to such an extent that, generally speaking, nine tenths of our business is transacted by means other than specie and money based directly on specie.

When Alexander Hamilton induced Congress to charter the Bank of the United States in 1791, he was trying to furnish a circulating medium and a credit system adequate to the business needs of a country which had very little specie. In fact, Hamilton seemed to believe that banks actually created capital, that they bring about the "augmentation of the active or productive capital of a country. Gold and silver . . . when deposited in banks, to become the basis of a paper circulation, . . . acquire life, or in other words, an active and productive quality. . . . The additional employment given to money and the faculty of a bank to lend and circulate a greater sum than the amount of its stock in coin, are, to all the purposes of trade and industry, an absolute increase of capital."[2] Although the capital of the Bank was $10,000,000, only one fourth had to be paid in specie (the balance in government stock), and the Bank was permitted to open when only $400,000 of stock in specie was paid in. Apparently little more than the first installment of the specie requirement was ever paid to the Bank in specie. Furthermore, by a piece of financial magic, the government bought its share of

Government in Michigan," in *ibid.*, XXXI (1902), 510–612; Alpheus Felch, "Early Banks and Banking in Michigan," in *ibid.*, II (1880), 111–24; Friend Palmer, "The Old Bank of Michigan," in *ibid.*, XXX (1906), 410–23; and William L. Jenks, "The First Bank in Michigan," in *Michigan History Magazine*, I (1917), 41–62. Davis R. Dewey in *State Banking Before the Civil War (National Monetary Commission Report*, XXXIV, Washington, D. C., 1910), traces the evolution of banking theory and practice. Harry E. Miller, *Banking Theories in the United States Before 1860 (Harvard Economic Studies*, XXX, 1927) is excellent for theory and the bibliography lists many contemporary articles and pamphlets. Harlan Scott White, "Western Banking Ideas and Practices before 1840," MS. thesis, Indiana University, 1942, is a competent treatment of the subject. Most useful of the earlier works are Gouge, *Paper Money and Banking,* by an advocate of hard money, and George Tucker, *Theory of Money and Banks Investigated* (Boston, 1839), by a defender of the credit money system.
[2] Report on a National Bank, *American State Papers, Finance,* I, 67–68.

stock by a "simultaneous transaction" which did not require the payment of a single dollar in money.[3] It is also probable that the Bank in its early years discounted notes of its stockholders to enable them to pay subsequent installments on their stock subscription. As Daniel Webster said, Alexander Hamilton was the magician who "touched the dead corpse of the Public Credit, and it sprung upon its feet." The very success and profitableness of the first Bank of the United States no doubt gave banking in general a great boost in the minds of Americans.

The essential functions of a bank are: (1) to handle deposits, (2) make loans and discounts, (3) issue notes. The younger a country or region, the less specie and accumulated and lendable capital it has, and the more interested it is in the note-issue function, which makes possible liberal loans and discounts, or "easy money." There was also the "relief function." The pioneer demanded that banks create a money economy whether there was money or not. "A new country, poor in specie and loanable capital, is almost forced by the necessities of her situation to adopt monetary devices which would not be tolerated under better conditions. Some of these devices would be comparatively harmless if their true character were understood and they were used with moderation; but their tendency is misleading and intoxicating to the average mind and they are usually so abused as to offset the little benefit which might be derived from them."[4]

The first paper-issuing institution west of the mountains was not properly a bank, but the Lexington Insurance Company, incorporated in 1802 with capital of $150,000. Since the business was found to be profitable, in 1807 those engaged organized the Kentucky Bank, with nominal capital of $1,000,000.[5] In 1803 a number of enterprising Cincinnati merchants incorporated the Miami Exporting Company. Authorized capitalization was

[3] "Shorn of technicalities, the Government paid for its stock in bills of exchange in Amsterdam, then it borrowed these bills and gave its note for $2,000,000, payable in ten equal annual installments of $200,000 each, with interest at 6 per cent. The practice thus instituted by the Government itself of paying subscriptions with stock notes was followed widely and, in numerous instances, with disastrous effects, in the next fifty years." Holdsworth and Dewey, *First and Second Banks of the United States*, 33.

[4] Charles A. Conant, *History of Modern Banks of Issue* . . . (2 volumes. 6th ed., London and New York, 1927), I, 359.

[5] Gouge, *Paper Money and Banking*, part II, 127. Humphrey, Marshall, *History of Kentucky* . . . (2 volumes. Frankfort, 1824), II, 349, says that banking privileges were obtained "by some unaccountable means or other."

$500,000 but only about $200,000 was paid in. The charter was for forty years. Although ostensibly organized for trading purposes, the company did banking business from the beginning. This branch of the business became so profitable that in 1807 commercial activities were abandoned.[6]

The first regular bank in the Northwest, not counting the Detroit Bank mentioned below, was the Bank of Marietta, which was probably already doing business when chartered for ten years by the Ohio legislature in 1808. The same year the Bank of Chillicothe was chartered and the next year the Bank of Steubenville.[7]

When Congress failed to renew the charter of the Bank of the United States in 1811, the field was left open to the state banks. From 88 as of January 1, 1811, they increased to 208 by the end of 1814.[8] Ohio chartered two more banks in 1812 and one each in 1813 and 1814,[9] charters to extend until 1818. In addition there were a number of unauthorized banking concerns in operation at one time or other,[10] and the number so increased between 1811 and 1814 that the amount of notes issued was given attention by the legislature.

The Ohio banks during this period rendered useful services to business, state, and nation. Although note issues were large, with some inflationary results, a fair amount of specie existed and the banks maintained excellent credit. Whereas most banks of the country, except in New England, suspended specie payment in the summer of 1814, the Ohio banks continued until within a month or two of the close of the war.[11]

    [6] Gouge, *Paper Money and Banking*, part II, 127; C. C. Huntington, "Banking and Currency in Ohio," in *Ohio Archaeological and Historical Society Publications*, XXIV, 258–59; *Laws of Ohio*, 1803, pp. 126–36; Drake, *Natural and Statistical View, or Picture of Cincinnati*, 150.
    [7] C. C. Huntington, "Banking and Currency in Ohio," in *Ohio Archaeological and Historical Society Publications*, XXIV, 261–63.
    [8] Albert Gallatin, *Considerations on the Currency and Banking Systems of the United States* (Philadelphia, 1831), 45, 49, 53, quoted in Annual Report of the Comptroller of the Currency, 1876, U. S. *House Executive Documents*, 44 Congress, 2 session, No. 3, XL.
    [9] Western Reserve Bank, Warren; Bank of Muskingum, Zanesville; Farmers' and Mechanics' Bank, Cincinnati; Dayton Manufacturing Company, Dayton. C. C. Huntington, "Banking and Currency in Ohio," in *Ohio Archaeological and Historical Society Publications*, XXIV, 263–64.
    [10] Including the Alexandrian Society of Granville, which had been chartered in 1807 as a literary society. *Ibid.*, XXIV, 265.
    [11] Dayton *Ohio Republican*, February 6, 1815, cited in *ibid.*, XXIV, 268; Gouge, *Paper Money and Banking*, part II, 127.

Three other banks in the Northwest prior to 1815 should be noted. In 1806 the Governor and Judges of Michigan Territory chartered the Bank of Detroit. The simple economy of the frontier post probably had no great need for a bank; the project was that of a group of Boston capitalists who worked through Governor William Hull and Augustus B. Woodward, one of the territorial Judges.[12] In September, 1806, representatives of the Boston capitalists arrived in Detroit with about $20,000 in gold. After a compromise was arrived at among the Judges, a charter was granted September 19. The corporation's life was fixed at 101 years and capitalization at $1,000,000. "The President, Directors and Company of the Detroit Bank" might establish branches for discount and deposit, and its bills, payable on demand in specie, were made receivable for all payments in Michigan Territory. The Governor might subscribe for stock for the Territory. There were no provisions regarding the amount of capital to be paid in, nor restrictions on loans, debts, or amount of note issue.[13]

Within four days after the subscription books were opened, Boston interests had subscribed to 9,507 shares and the people and Territory of Michigan to 483. Judge Woodward was made president. Meanwhile John Gentle, a British subject resident in Detroit, who was opposing the policies of the Governor and Judges, had written an anonymous letter to the Philadelphia *Aurora*, a strong Jeffersonian paper. In an editorial, November 19, the *Aurora* said: "The establishment of a bank in Michigan merits some inquiry. What is the object? Who are concerned? Whence does the capital come? Under what circumstances? . . . What effect is it intended to produce? Is it calculated for mere speculation and the scheme of speculators, or is it connected with any *other* views? . . . Are the officers of the Government

[12] In 1806, when on a visit to Newton, Massachusetts, Governor Hull had been in contact with Boston merchants, among whom were Russel Sturgis, Nathaniel Parker, Dudley S. Bradstreet, and Henry Bass, Jr. These men drew up a petition to the Governor and Judges of Michigan Territory which requested the chartering of a bank. One of their arguments was that they had for some time been financially interested in the fur trade around Detroit, and needed banking facilities. This seems not to have been the fact. Jenks, "The First Bank in Michigan," in *Michigan History Magazine,* I, 42–43. Governor Hull gave such assurances that the petitioners went ahead to select the personnel of the bank, and to erect a building.

[13] *Ibid.,* I, 44–47. Governor and Judges were required by the Ordinance of 1787 and a law of 1805 to confine their lawmaking to selection from laws of the various states, but this charter, as a whole, was unique.

any wise concerned in it? These questions all afford ample subjects of inquiry."[14]

Michigan Territory, which in November, 1806, appropriated $20 for the first installment payment on its stock, sold its holdings the following year to Andrew Dexter, a Massachusetts promoter. The local stockholders did likewise. Dexter and others went East with $163,000 of the bank's notes which they hoped to lend on liberal terms and place in such a way that it would be difficult for them to be presented for redemption. All told it was said that more than $1,500,000 of notes were issued, all but a few thousand of which were taken East.[15] Conservative Massachusetts banks took action to protect their interests and Josiah Quincy brought up the subject in Congress. Secretary of Treasury Gallatin and Secretary of State Madison also became interested. Early in 1807 Congress passed a bill which disapproved of the Michigan Territory bank charter. Dexter endeavored to continue the bank as a private concern, and a new form of note was issued.[16] In December, 1808, in Judge Woodward's absence, Governor Hull and the two other Judges enacted a law which made it a crime for unauthorized persons to issue notes, or for anyone to pass them. Comparatively few of the notes had been in circulation in Michigan, and the bank's affairs were concluded early in 1809. Since the institution had received no deposits and discounted no notes, its demise little affected business in the Territory.[17] For a number of years the people of Michigan used specie, outside bank notes, or resorted to trade.

In 1814 the legislature of Indiana Territory chartered two banks, the Vincennes Bank and the Farmers' and Mechanics' Bank of Madison. The charters, which were to run for twenty years, provided for specie payment of all notes, that interest on loans should not exceed 6 per cent, and that loans be made to the territorial government on anticipation of taxes.[18] There were besides these banks at least two private banks of issue, the one

[14] Quoted in Jenks, "First Bank in Michigan," in *Michigan History Magazine,* I, 51.

[15] Documents relating to "The Beginnings of Territorial Government in Michigan," edited by Charles Moore, in *Michigan Pioneer and Historical Collections,* XXXI, Introduction, 520.

[16] It seems that the greatest portion of the note issue of the Detroit Bank was in this second form.

[17] Jenks, "First Bank in Michigan," in *Michigan History Magazine,* I, 51–60.

[18] Ewbank and Riker (eds.), *Laws, 1809–16,* pp. 747–63.

at Brookville and the Steam Mill Company at Vincennes. A territorial act of 1815 entitled "An Act to Prevent Swindling," and incorporated in the revised laws of 1818, recognized the right of individuals to issue notes, provided the names of the bankers were on the notes.[19]

When the speculative desires attendant upon the settlement of the West, increasing government land sales, and rapid increase in population and business called for more money, the banks were ever ready to fill the need. Ohio had sought by a law passed in February, 1815, to prevent the unauthorized issuance of bank notes, but with little success.[20] The following December, in his message to the legislature, Governor Thomas Worthington called attention to the great increase in bank currency and pointed out that the state was sharing no revenues from it. Early in 1816 the legislature passed another law against unauthorized note issues to go into effect January 1, 1817 and also the "bonus law" to control the number of banks and raise a revenue.[21] The charters of the incorporated banks (to expire in 1818) were extended to 1843, six new banks were incorporated, also six of the companies which had been engaging in banking activities without charter. Banks were empowered to capitalize up to $500,000 each, one share in each twenty-five was to be set off for the state, and the dividends in the state's shares were to accumulate until the state owned one sixth of the stock, after which the dividends were to be paid to the state. Books were to be open to inspection of the directors or state agents. All the previously chartered banks, except the Miami Exporting Company, complied with the provisions of the law. This law was regarded as a general banking law, but the day after its passage the Zanesville Canal and Manufacturing Company was incorporated by special act.[22]

---

[19] Ibid., pp. 605–8; Laws of Indiana, 1817–18 (general), p. 79; report on private banks, in Indiana House Journal, 1838–39, pp. 181–83. Said the report: "It is asserted then, that, under our constitution and laws, any man or set of men may set up a bank, and deal in specie and exchange, discount notes and issue bills."

[20] Laws of Ohio, 1814–15, p. 152. A tax of 4 per cent was levied on dividends. Penalty for unauthorized issue was a year's imprisonment and maximum fine of $5,000. It was not to apply until January 1, 1818, to banks in business before January 1, 1815.

[21] Liberty Hall and Cincinnati Gazette, January 8, 29, 1816, thought that the scheme to tax banks on the assumption that other taxes could be done away with was absurd, and contended that it placed despotic power in the hands of the legislature. A landowner would be submitted to double taxation.

[22] A list of the new banks chartered under the "bonus law" may be found in C. C. Huntington, "Banking and Currency in Ohio," in Ohio Archaeological and

In December, 1817, six new banks were incorporated and in January, 1818, one more. Five of these banks accepted the provisions of the "bonus law" but they were created by special acts and their charters differed in details. This made a total of twenty-six chartered banks and no more were created for eleven years.[23]

The Indiana Constitution of 1816 recognized the Vincennes and Madison banks as incorporated banks, and provided that either might be made the state bank.[24] Accordingly, the Vincennes Bank was made the State Bank in January, 1817,[25] by a law the intent of which was to create a banking monopoly in the state. The charter, for twenty-one years, provided capital increase to $1,500,000, of which $375,000 might be subscribed by the state. There were to be fourteen branches,[26] capitalized at from $10,000 to $35,000, each to accommodate three counties and to be constituent parts of the parent bank. Total debt was never to exceed twice the amount of paid-up stock, rate of discount was to be 6 per cent, and the bank was not to issue more notes than it could redeem.

This was an ambitious paper plan for the young state which with a scant 75,000 people was expected to absorb, all told, more than two millions of capital stock. Although the Farmers' and Mechanics' Bank of Madison was supposed to become a part of the system, its stockholders refused, and thus the most profitable banking area was largely cut off from the State Bank. Only three of the branches actually organized—Brookville, Corydon, and Vevay. The first State Bank of Indiana was sponsored largely by the propertied party of tradesmen and politicians of Vincennes, Corydon, and Brookville. They controlled the bank and the

---

Historical Society Publications, XXIV, 275. A complete list of incorporated Ohio banks at the end of 1816 is in *Liberty Hall and Cincinnati Gazette*, February 26, 1816; Hamilton (Ohio) *Philanthropist*, December 6, 1816; Chillicothe *Supporter*, December 17, 1816.

[23] The exact number of chartered banks in 1818 seems to be hard to arrive at. Huntington's list adds up to 25 or 26, the *Gazette* (February 26, 1816) list of 19 plus the 7 new ones makes 26. The *Supporter* list of 21 plus the 7 would make 28, as does the *Philanthropist* list and that of the *Portsmouth Gazette*, August 12, 1818 (23, omitting 5 of the ones created the preceding winter). Yet P. W. Huntington, "A History of Banking in Ohio," in *Ohio Archaeological and Historical Society Publications*, XXIII (1914), 312, says 20.

[24] Article X.

[25] *Laws of Indiana*, 1816–17, p. 185.

[26] (1) Centerville, (2) Brookville, (3) Lawrenceburg, (4) Vevay, (5) Madison, (6) Jeffersonville, (7) Brownstown, (8) Paoli, (9) Salem, (10) Corydon, (11) Troy, (12) Darlington, (13) some point in Posey County, (14) some point in Gibson County.

legislature, and were favorably connected, through the congress-men, with the Federal patronage. Opposition to the bank was led by Elihu Stout, founder of the Vincennes *Western Sun,* while warm support was given by the Vincennes *Indiana Centinel.*[27]

The Illinois territorial legislature yielded to the desire of the people to have banks, even as their neighbors, and from 1816 to 1818 chartered four banks: the Bank of Illinois (Shawneetown), the Bank of Edwardsville, the Bank of Kaskaskia, and the City and Bank of Cairo.

The Bank of Illinois was capitalized at $300,000, and char-tered for twenty years; the territory, or later the state, might purchase one third of the stock. On January 1, 1817, after $10,000 in stock subscription was paid in, in specie, the bank opened. It was to meet all its obligations in specie, but in event it should suspend specie payment, noteholders could collect 12 per cent interest. At the same session, however, the legislature enacted a stay of one year against any executions, unless the party desiring judgment would agree in writing to accept in payment the notes of the Bank of Illinois or other designated banks.[28] The defense of this evasion of the constitutional provision against a state making its notes legal tender was that the debtor class had to be protected against the sacrifices involved in specie pay-ment. This act made easier the circulation of the bank's notes. In the face of jealousy and opposition from Kaskaskia, and from the Bank of Missouri at St. Louis, the Bank of Illinois was able, through conservative management, to carry on successfully through a very difficult period, and to maintain specie payments until 1821.[29]

The Bank of Edwardsville began business in 1818 under more trying conditions. This bank, as well as the Bank of Illinois, was made a depository of United States funds. The Bank of Kas-kaskia and the fantastic scheme of the City and Bank of Cairo never got under way before the deflation of 1818. The former could not sell its stock and the latter apparently never even

---

[27] Esarey, *State Banking in Indiana,* 226–29.

[28] Banks of Cincinnati, Chillicothe, Vincennes, Missouri, and any of the banks of Tennessee or Kentucky. See Dowrie, *Development of Banking in Illinois,* 12.

[29] The land-office receiver at Kaskaskia would accept bills of the Bank of Illinois one day and the next refuse them. The Bank of Missouri would refuse its bills for a time, then accept them freely, collect a lot, and present them for specie all at once. Dowrie, *Banking in Illinois,* 13, and sources cited.

accepted its charter. The Illinois Constitution of 1818 provided that, except a state bank which might be created, no other banks or financial institutions should be permitted. It recognized the banks already created by law.[30]

The Bank of Michigan was chartered by the Governor and Judges, December 19, 1817, with an authorized capital of $100,000, charter to expire in June, 1839.[31] In January, 1818, with only $10,000 of paid-in capital, the bank opened for business. The charter permitted note issue equal to three times the capitalization, plus once the amount of specie on hand. The *Detroit Gazette* hoped that the organizers would proceed so as to create a feeling of confidence and "*profit by the thousand warning precedents* which they have before them, as well as their own experience."[32] By 1823, however, when notes of the Bank of Michigan were quoted at 20 per cent discount by an Ohio bank, the *Gazette* could not understand why "this Ohio shaving establishment" was quoting them below par, for, it said, the bank had always redeemed its notes and could still do so.[33] The following year David Stone, a Massachusetts capitalist, together with New York associates, took up the rest of the capital stock and the Bank of Michigan increased in importance. Although a cashier defaulted, the methods of transacting business were anything but careful, and discounts were frequently nearly up to the very liberal charter limit, this institution rendered valuable service to Detroit business. In 1832 the bank was made a government depository, although some of the officers thought this policy dangerous, and it continued to pay specie until caught in the general collapse of 1837.[34]

At the close of the War of 1812 the amount of paper issued

---

[30] Article VIII, Section 21.

[31] In 1831 the charter was extended twenty-five years. The original charter permitted capital increase by vote of the stockholders to $500,000, under certain conditions. Since the Governor and Judges by the Ordinance of 1787 were authorized "to adopt . . . such laws of the original states," and the bank charter was a composite of laws of New York, Massachusetts, and Ohio, the constitutionality of the charter of the Bank of Michigan was in 1830 contested in the courts of New York. It was held to be valid by the New York Supreme Court and later by the Supreme Courts of Michigan and the United States. For case references, see Felch, "Early Banks and Banking in Michigan," in *Michigan Pioneer and Historical Collections*, II, 112.

[32] *Detroit Gazette*, January 8, 1818.

[33] *Ibid.*, January 10, 1823.

[34] A brief sketch of this bank may be found in Palmer, "The Old Bank of Michigan," in *Michigan Pioneer and Historical Collections*, XXX, 410-23.

by the banks of the West was moderate in comparison with that of the eastern states. Only Kentucky and Ohio had set up the machinery for extensive banking operations. Specie was at a premium of about 6 per cent in the West, but 14 per cent in eastern cities.[35] The issues of the western banks increased considerably in the latter half of 1816 and still more the next year when Ohio and Indiana increased their banking facilities.[36]

The chaotic banking conditions and government finance of the war period had led to general suspension of specie payment on the part of the banks in all regions except New England. New Orleans banks suspended in April, 1814, and Philadelphia banks followed in August, after the Pennsylvania legislature incorporated forty-one banking institutions with $17,000,000 capital. The rest of the banks in the middle and southern states suspended also. Ohio and Kentucky banks held out until the end of the year and the Bank of Nashville until the summer of 1815. The eastern banks agreed to resume specie payment on termination of the war. "But, unhappily, the redemption of the pledge was not demanded by the public at the stipulated time, and the Banks, urged on by cupidity, and losing sight of moral obligations in their lust for profit, launched out into an extent of issues unexampled in the annals of folly."[37] Nor did the United States Government take action to compel the eastern banks to make good their pledge. Had it done so, the western country might have been but little affected by the suspension of specie payments in the East. But government is ever reluctant to disturb prosperity, no matter how artificial. Instead it "connived at the suspension of specie payments, sanctioned the use of incontrovertible paper, and by its fiscal manoeuvering encouraged the issue of additional amounts of such paper. . . ."[38] As a result the mania which had spread from New England and New York to Pennsylvania came west to Kentucky and Ohio. "The years 1815, 1816 may be well

---

[35] William Jones, president of the second Bank of the United States, in documents laid before Congress in 1819, cited in Gouge, *Paper Money and Banking*, part II, 128.

[36] There are no adequate banking statistics for this period. United States stamp duty applications from the banks to the Treasury Department throw some light on the situation. By Treasury figures the capital of Ohio chartered banks increased from $1,435,819 to $2,806,737 from 1815 to 1816, but fell to $2,003,000 in 1817. But the unauthorized banks were increasing their issues rapidly. Report of William H. Crawford, secretary of the treasury, February 12, 1820.

[37] Quoted in Gouge, *Paper Money and Banking*, part II, 65.

[38] *Ibid.*, part II, 127.

marked in the American calendar, as the jubilee of swindlers, and the Saturnalia of non-specie paying banks. Throughout the whole country, New England excepted, it required no capital to set up a bank."[39]

During the years of the Napoleonic wars and immediately following, there was nearly as much theorizing over the nature of money and the relation of bank notes, gold, and prices as during the period of the great depression of the 1930's. Over-issue of bank notes was the chief factor in placing gold at a premium, and in 1797 the Bank of England was forced off specie. The bankers refused to understand the cause, but it was clearly stated in the famous Bullion Report which was presented to Parliament in 1810.[40] Parliament was for the time won over by the opponents of the report,[41] who held that the pound sterling was an intangible thing, an abstract idea or standard of value, independent of the variable quantities and values of gold and silver. Fearing that an old statute of Edward VI would not suffice, Parliament passed Lord Stanhope's bill which made it a misdemeanor to make any difference in payment between guineas and bank notes.[42] The pound of the Bank of England was to be considered as good as gold, or even better. Naturally these ideas spread to the United States and the "antibullionists" aired their views.[43] The Secretary of the Treasury, George M. Dallas, however, was not converted. Whatever the outcome of the incon-

[39] Richard Hildreth, *Banks, Banking and Paper Currencies* (Boston, 1840), 67.

[40] Written by Francis Horner and others, and based upon hearings before the Parliamentary committee and in part upon Ricardo's "The High Price of Bullion." "The Bullion Report is remarkable not only for the clearness and precision with which it lays down the fundamental rules for regulating the volume of a paper currency, but for the discriminating judgment with which it discusses limitations of the then existing theories of prices and currency which only came to be generally accepted by political economists a generation later and have not been accepted by all of them today." Conant, *Modern Banks of Issue* (1927), 105. For summary of the Report, see Henry Dunning McLeod, *The Theory and Practice of Banking* (5th ed., 2 volumes. London, 1892), II, 29.

[41] Among others, Nicholas Vansettart, who said that "a standard in the sense used by these gentlemen, namely, a fixed and invariable weight of the precious metals as a measure of value, never existed in this country."

[42] That is, to offer more than 21 shillings in bank notes for a guinea in gold. Partial specie resumption was begun by the Bank of England in November, 1816. Gold again went to a premium and specie payment was stopped by law in April, 1819. A new committee was appointed to go into the whole subject. Sounder views prevailed than in 1810 and full resumption was permitted by law to take place May 1, 1821.

[43] Erick Bollman, *Plan of an Improved System of the Money-Concerns of the Union* (Philadelphia, January, 1816). Mathew Carey, *Letters to the Directors of the Banks of Philadelphia . . .* (Philadelphia, 1816), other pamphlets, and articles in *National Intelligencer*.

vertible paper experiment elsewhere, he believed it had no importance "as a precedent for the imitation of the United States."[44] Nor were there many open advocates of the idea in Congress.

In January, 1816, was reported another bill to establish a Bank of the United States. John C. Calhoun spoke of "an extraordinary revolution in the currency" whereby the power of Congress to regulate the currency had vanished, and believed that a "National Bank, paying specie itself, would have a tendency to make specie payments general, as well by its influence as its example." Accordingly was chartered the second Bank of the United States, and the burden of getting the banks of the country to resume specie payment was placed upon it. The Bank opened for business January 1, 1817, with $1,400,000 of capital paid for in specie, and $14,000,000 in United States stocks, out of the total charter capital of $35,000,000, $7,000,000 of which was to be paid for in specie. Later installments of specie capital were paid for, at least in part, with notes of the stockholders discounted by the bank.

The Treasury Department had tried in vain to get the state banks to resume specie payments on February 20, 1817, and Congress had done its part by resolving (April, 1816) that the United States should, after the above date, receive money payments only in gold, silver, treasury notes, notes of the Bank of the United States, or notes of specie-paying banks. Eastern bankers met and postponed the resumption date to July 1, by which time the Bank of the United States would be ready to help. Delegates of the Ohio chartered banks likewise met at Chillicothe in September, 1816. They declared that they had only suspended some months after eastern banks had gone off specie and begun to traffic in western specie, and that they were ready to resume, but did not think it safe to do so until the banks of the Atlantic cities did likewise.[45]

The second Bank of the United States was organized sooner than the eastern bankers had anticipated, and at a conference on February 1, 1817, it succeeded in getting the bankers of

[44] Report, December 7, 1815, quoted in Gouge, *Paper Money and Banking,* part II, 75.

[45] Hamilton (Ohio) *Philanthropist,* October 4, 1816; Dayton *Ohio Republican,* September 18, 1816; *Niles' Weekly Register,* XI, 57 (Sep. 21, 1816).

Philadelphia, New York, and Baltimore to promise to resume specie payment February 21. To do this it had to agree not to call for government balances in the banks—which were to be transferred to it—until July 1, and after that not to call for payment of balances against the banks which might arise from the ordinary course of business until it had made loans of $6,000,000. This was a one-sided agreement, by which the Bank assumed specie-payment responsibility for government drafts on its deposits, yet agreed not to draw specie from the banks. The banks on the other hand could draw upon it for specie. Furthermore, it forced the Bank to make large loans, under the assumption that the state banks would reduce their loans so as to be able to pay over the government deposits.

The Philadelphia, New York, and Baltimore banks resumed nominal specie payment February 20;[46] two of the Ohio banks and the Vincennes bank did likewise. A Cincinnati meeting of bankers of Ohio, Kentucky, and Indiana voted to resume April 20, but it was said had an understanding with the Treasury Department that they would be allowed until the ensuing season to make good on all their paper.[47] Notes of the Ohio banks were soon quoted in the East at 6 per cent discount, instead of 12 to 15 per cent.[48]

Cincinnati and Chillicothe had been eager to secure branches of the United States Bank; in January, 1817, the Cincinnati branch was established, to be followed by the Chillicothe branch in October.

Meanwhile, the number of banks and amount of bank currency had been increasing rapidly. "Wherever there is a 'church, a blacksmith's shop and a tavern' seems a proper site for one of them," said Niles in 1816. "Their evil has hardly yet begun, if they persevere in the courses they have generally adopted . . . and sacrifice of men and property will accumulate as the thing goes on like a snow-ball, to the making of immense fortunes for those who command the funds; though in the end, many of the banks must fail like individuals."[49] Banks were incorporated or

[46] Specie remained at a premium in Philadelphia.
[47] *Liberty Hall and Cincinnati Gazette*, February 2, 1819.
[48] Notes of the Ohio chartered banks were at 8 to 10 per cent discount in December, 1815, and 12 to 15 per cent a year later. Notes of the unauthorized banks were at 20 to 25 per cent discount. Ohio bank capital reached a total in 1816 not again equalled until the 1830's.

set up not because of capital seeking investment or the needs of commerce and industry but for purposes of speculation. In the West, Kentucky and Ohio were the main centers of over banking.[50] Borrowers were solicited and bank notes were put out at 6 to 10 per cent interest and, since the banks frequently paid neither interest nor principal, dividends were high.[51] Some of the banks were mere wildcats with the usual assets of a table, chair, or keg of nails with a few coins on top.[52]

"Why the high prices?" asked the Hamilton *Philanthropist*. Were they due to the late war? No, but to the use of old rags instead of honest Spanish dollars and American coin. Specie was escaping. It was gone. Nothing remained to cut up into sharp-shins. Also some can ride in fine coaches, eat huge dinners, speculate and get rich. "Remember the Continental Currency!" The Egyptians threw dust into the eyes of the crocodiles and led them as they pleased. So with the bankers. With notes issued equal to 20 times specie held, when one tried to get specie he was told half his notes were counterfeit. Institutions were springing up everywhere, without charter, respectability, responsibility, or capital, and circulating millions. Directors divided 10 to 17 per cent. "Remember the Continental Currency!"[53]

In disregard of the Ohio law which outlawed the notes of unauthorized banks after January 1, 1817,[54] many of these notes continued to circulate. Some were listed at Cincinnati at 17 to 20

[49] *Niles' Weekly Register*, XI, 130 (Oct. 26, 1816).

[50] Kentucky had 59 banks by 1818, Ohio 28.

[51] John Adams had foreseen the situation in 1810 when he wrote: "The Banking infatuation pervades All America. Our whole system of Banks is a violation of every honest Principle of Banks. . . . A Bank that issues paper at interest is a Pickpocket or a Robber. But the Delusion will have its Course. You may as well reason with a Hurricane. . . . The Number of Debtors who hope to pay their debts by this Paper united with the Creditors who build Pallaces in our Cities, and Castles for Country Seats, by issuing this Paper form too impregnable a Phalanx to be attacked by any Thing less disciplined than Roman Legions." *Old Family Letters* (Philadelphia, 1892), 272.

[52] The village of Salem, Ohio, had two of these. In 1818 when one of these went bankrupt, with assets of one table, a lawsuit resulted in an attack upon its president by the prosecutor. The president killed the prosecutor and was duly indicted, "not having the fear of God before his eyes, but being moved and seduced by instigation of the devil," and was acquitted. W. H. Hunter, "Pathfinders of Jefferson County, Ohio," in *Ohio Archaeological and Historical Society Publications*, VIII (1900), 195–96.

[53] Hamilton (Ohio) *Philanthropist*, June 21, July 5, 1816. Sharpshins were triangular bits of cut coin.

[54] It was made illegal to offer or receive such notes under a penalty of three times the amount of the note. Apparently the law was so worded that it could not be enforced. *Western Herald and Steubenville Gazette*, April 4, 1817.

per cent discount in the spring of that year. By the summer of 1818 they were worth little or nothing.[55] When the Bank of Michigan was being organized, the *Detroit Gazette* heartily congratulated "the citizens of Michigan on the prospect of this institution soon being able to relieve them from the trash of Ohio, which has so long impoverished the country by its uncertain value."[56] At Zanesville more than thirty kinds of paper money were circulating. In addition to bank notes of all sorts were the issues of scrip, "shinplasters," and "tickets" by business firms, contractors, bridge and turnpike companies, counties, and even individuals. These small bills were generally regarded a nuisance but in the absence of adequate small coinage were tolerated. Jealousies and impositions naturally arose to embarrass trade.[57] Paper money, the "Plenty of Money," was everywhere. "If the months of May, June, July, and August, 1815, were the 'golden age of Philadelphia,' the first months of the year 1818, were the golden age of the western country. Silver could hardly have been more plentiful at Jerusalem in the days of Solomon, than paper money was in Ohio, Kentucky, and the adjoining regions."[58]

The resultant inflation and high prices stimulated trade as well as speculation. Not only was money to be made at legitimate business, commodity speculation, and land booming, but at bank-note shaving as well. Luxury, extravagance, and waste accompanied the speculative fever.[59] Deflationary measures were resented by those who profited or hoped to profit. Many of the western banks opposed resumption if it meant contraction, and so did businessmen. Some of the latter protested against the condemnation of even the unchartered bank notes in Ohio.[60]

Nor were the United States Treasury and the Bank in agree-

[55] "The notes of all the unchartered banks in this state with the exception of John H. Piatt and Company's Bank, Cincinnati, which are in good credit, and the Bank of Xenia, which are still current in some places, are considered as good for nothing." *Portsmouth* (Ohio) *Gazette*, August 12, 1818, quoted in C. C. Huntington, "History of Banking and Currency in Ohio," in *Ohio Archaeological and Historical Society Publications*, XXIV, 286.

[56] June 12, 1818.

[57] There were frequent protests in the newspapers against the issue of small bills, but nothing seems to have been done about it. See, for instance, article in *Detroit Gazette*, September 5, 1817.

[58] Gouge, *Paper Money and Banking*, part II, 129.

[59] For land prices and sales, see Chapter III. For prices of commodities during the inflation period, see Chapter VII.

[60] *Western Herald and Steubenville Gazette*, May 9, 1817.

ment regarding policy concerning the state bank notes. Besides the controversy over transfer of government funds from the state banks was the problem of what bank notes would be acceptable for tax and land payments. While it was up to the Bank to force the state banks to resume and maintain specie payments, the government had no desire to lose revenue or create too much antagonism. By the agreement of April, 1817, between Treasury and Bank, the latter was left to determine what state bank notes were acceptable. Either intentionally or otherwise the Bank was made, as it were, the scapegoat or cat's-paw in both the matter of accepting responsibility for government funds deposited in state banks, and in determining what bank notes were acceptable for government receipts. While custom allowed the notes of nonspecie-paying state banks to circulate at a discount, the Bank of the United States could not enjoy any such privilege or accept the notes. It was certain to get into trouble when it presented these notes for redemption. When agents of the Pittsburgh branch presented a parcel of the notes of the Commercial Bank of Lake Erie (an Ohio chartered bank at Cleveland) to that institution for specie, they received specie, but before they removed it the directors changed their minds, took back the specie, and forced the agents to accept a post note payable twenty days later. The directors defended their actions in a two-column letter to the press,[61] and the trick was generally approved by the public. Many Westerners called the Bank a mere broker's concern and an unfair discriminator in its designation of what bank notes were acceptable for land-office payments.

"More oppression," said the *Steubenville Gazette*, when the land-office receiver had orders from the Treasury Department to accept only such money as the Bank would accept: specie, Bank of the United States notes, and Pittsburgh notes. No government measure since the first settlement has hurt the West more, continued the *Gazette*. What makes Pittsburgh paper better than Ohio paper? Ohio pays specie. It is a measure to enrich the few at the cost of the many. The government is taking away the means of livelihood. "All men are created equal." We separated from England because of such acts. The time has come not to be mealymouthed, but to do something.[62] Pressure of public

[61] In full in *ibid.*, June 27, 1818, and other Ohio papers.
[62] *Ibid.*, March 17, 1818, February 27, 1819.

opinion brought results, for soon the land-office receivers at Steubenville and Wooster were directed to accept notes of the Bank of Steubenville and the Farmers' and Mechanics' Bank of Steubenville. It was promised soon to include other Ohio banks on the acceptable list.[63]

The operations of the Bank of the United States also increased inflation in the West. The Bank lacked the courage to insist upon payment of balances owed it by the state banks, discounts and loans were overextended, and the notes of its western branches were issued in volume.[64] Since the trade balances were in favor of the North and East, these notes were not quickly returned to the branches but were redeemed in the eastern offices where the Bank's specie was further depleted. In May, 1817, Niles said: "Though our banks ostensibly pay specie, it is almost as rare as it was some months ago to see a dollar. 'Paper does the business' still."[65] By the beginning of 1818 he bewailed the speculative spirit and predicted ruin: "I feel it my duty to raise a full voice against it [speculative mania], and *to tell the people plainly, . . .* that the *most extensive and ruinous bankruptcies are about to take place amongst us that ever befell any people,* UNLESS A STAND IS TAKEN AGAINST THE BAND OF SPECULATORS, WHO FROM THE MISERY OF THE USEFUL CLASSES, WILL TAKE CARE TO BUILD UP PRINCELY FORTUNES FOR THEMSELVES. Without such a stand, *bank after bank will go by the board. . . .*" He advocated bringing the banks "before the bar of the public reason" to induce them to "abandon their present course, and cherish *productive industry,* rather than *speculation.*"[66]

Speculation and fraud, as well as mismanagement and circumstances, brought the affairs of the Bank of the United States to

[63] *Western Herald and Steubenville Gazette,* April 3, 1819.
[64] William Graham Sumner thought that except for the Bank of the United States the West would not have been drawn into the inflation. *History of Banking in the United States (History of Banking in all the Leading Nations,* I, New York, 1896), 109. In the spring of 1819, after considerable contraction had taken place, the Bank had nearly six and a half millions of its capital distributed among its interior western offices, as against less than one million among those north and east of Philadelphia. Gallatin, *Considerations on the Currency and Banking Systems of the United States,* 49.
[65] *Niles' Weekly Register,* XII, 185 (May 17, 1817).
[66] *Ibid.,* XIV, 1 (Feb. 28, 1818). Niles was strongly antibank and seemed never to realize that the people and their representatives were as much to blame as bankers.

a crisis in the midsummer of 1818. Since many of the state banks had refused to pay specie, the Bank had announced that all agreements with them would terminate on June 30 and ordered its cashiers to accept in deposit as cash only specie and its own notes.[67] By July immediate-demand liabilities of the Bank were $22,372,000 while the specie fund with which to meet them was reduced to $2,357,000. Strenuous measures were taken to save the institution. Discounts in the East were to be reduced $5,-000,000 and balances due from other banks were to be called for. The Cincinnati branch was ordered to call for the balances due it from the state banks at the rate of 20 per cent each month. The Cincinnati banks, which owed $720,000, tried to contract their debts and get the money, but borrowers had neither specie nor notes and could not pay. In October these banks owed more than they did in July. There had been constant suspicions regarding the condition of the Ohio banks; rumors and charges of not paying specie were circulated,[68] and by late June the Chillicothe branch of the Bank ordered the land-office agents to accept the notes of only ten of Ohio's banks.[69]

To make matters worse, the Bank in August ordered its branches to stop receiving each other's notes. The protests of the Cincinnati banks against the demands of the Bank availed not and, when the Bank refused their notes in payment, they suspended specie November 5 and appointed a committee to make a report.[70] Other Ohio banks were forced to follow; by January, 1819, only two or three were still paying specie.[71] The already depreciated notes began to drop further and some became practically worthless. In September the state treasurer had ordered tax collectors to accept only bank paper accepted by

[67] *American State Papers, Finance*, V, 69.

[68] Hamilton (Ohio) *Miami Herald*, May–June, 1818.

[69] *Ibid.*, July 1, 1818.

[70] *Liberty Hall and Cincinnati Gazette*, November 10, 1818; *Western Herald and Steubenville Gazette*, November 28, 1818. The report of the committee reviewed at length the period of war finance, the effects of the policy of the branch of the Bank of the United States at Cincinnati, and of the unfavorable balance of trade against the West.

[71] *Niles' Weekly Register*, XV, 361 (Jan. 9, 1819). "This state is a prey to Jew-brokers and bank directors, more, perhaps, than any other." The *Liberty Hall and Cincinnati Gazette* of May 7, 1819, states that the Bank of Steubenville, the Farmers' and Mechanics' Bank of Steubenville, and the Bank of Mount Pleasant had resumed specie some weeks since, but that it had not yet learned about the Cincinnati banks.

the United States land offices,[72] and by November the land office at Cincinnati was ordered to accept only specie and notes of the Bank of the United States.[73]

Other western banks were forced to follow suit. The Farmers' and Mechanics' Bank of Madison, recognized along with the Vincennes bank by the Constitution of 1816, could not keep its notes in circulation after the Bank refused to accept them, so suspended, although solvent.[74] The Vincennes bank did likewise, although it had but few notes in circulation and these mostly of larger denominations.[75] The Shawneetown and Edwardsville, Illinois, banks, however, paid specie until 1821.[76] "A glorious purgation is going on—'leprosy to the arm that would arrest it, by new modifications of fraud!' It is hard to bear and grievous, but it is wholesome; and the good effects will extend to posterity. . . . The effect . . . will be to bring us back to the state we were in about ten years ago, when a bank was considered as the *opposite* of bankrupt; though the terms now, of banking and bankruptcy, are so nearly synonymous!"[77]

A purgation it may have appeared to Niles, but it was panic and monetary chaos to the people. Prices underwent what was probably the most rapid and precipitate decline of our history.[78] Specie, always scarce in the West, was drained out; "$120,000 on the Wing," said the Hamilton *Miami Herald*, when two wagonloads of specie drawn from Ohio and neighboring banks was sent from the Chillicothe branch to the Bank at Philadelphia.[79] "So goes the specie of the West! How long will it be, at this

[72] This order was widely protested as exceeding the treasurer's powers. *Western Herald and Steubenville Gazette,* Chillicothe *Supporter,* etc., September, 1818.

[73] The December 28, 1818, Grotjans *Price Current* said that Ohio notes had no sale at Philadelphia. A little later Cincinnati, Chillicothe, Marietta, Steubenville, and Zanesville bank notes were quoted at 15 to 20 per cent discount. *Western Herald and Steubenville Gazette,* January 9, 30, 1819.

[74] Letter of cashier, *American State Papers, Finance,* IV, 725.

[75] By the report of December, 1820, only $13,000. The branches had out notes to the extent of $167,158. *Western Sun,* December 23, 1820, January 6, 27, 1821. Gouge, *Paper Money and Banking,* part II, 130, said the Vincennes bank issued notes payable at its Vevay branch and in small type printed "payable nine months after date."

[76] For a short time in 1819 the Shawneetown bank refused to accept the notes of the Edwardsville bank. The former claimed never to have refused to redeem a note on demand throughout this crisis. *Shawneetown Gazette* in *Edwardsville Spectator,* August 28, 1821.

[77] *Niles' Weekly Register,* XVII, 227 (Dec. 11, 1819).

[78] For land prices see Chapter III; for effects on trade, commodities, etc., Chapter VII.

[79] Hamilton (Ohio) *Miami Herald,* November 30, 1818. The *Cincinnati Gazette,* Chillicothe *Supporter,* Lancaster *Ohio Eagle,* and other papers took up the hue and cry against such "oppression."

rate, before the western country is exhausted of the precious metals? Such is the blessed tendency of the United States branches. We do not wish to add fuel to the flame that has already been kindled upon these institutions in this state and Kentucky; but we cannot, without the deepest regret, see the western states despoiled of their wealth, to supply the coffers of a corrupt aristocracy."[80] Niles estimated that $800,000 of specie was drawn from the Ohio banks from July, 1818, to June, 1819.[81]

Business was hard pressed for small change. A few Spanish dollars were still in circulation, but most of them were cut into quarters, bits (eighths), and fips (sixteenths). Often, however, a dollar was cut into ten bits and each passed as a shilling, or an eighteen pence piece was cut into five pieces and each passed as sixpence. Dimes, when available, usually passed at eight to the dollar.[82] Besides these "sharpshins" or "hobnail money," there were the multitudinous small bills, "shinplasters" or "tickets" issued by business firms, counties, and even individuals.

As for the flood of bank notes, it was impossible to know their value. Newspapers announced that they corrected their discount lists daily, but "What is good today may be bad tomorrow." Notes varied from day to day, but also from place to place. A laborer might be paid $2.00 a day wages in bank notes, and with a week's pay not be able to buy his tobacco ration in the next county. Since only a portion of the people had access even to the brief newspaper note lists, it became easy to cash in on their ignorance. Note shaving developed as a general practice, often more profitable than legitimate business. If the ordinary variations from time to time and place to place did not offer enough opportunity, rumors could be started on a bank and its notes bought at a much lower price than they were really worth. Banks became note shavers, even depreciating their own notes in order to buy them up cheap. It was said that agents of the Vincennes bank met unsuspecting emigrants at the eastern border of the state to trade them the much depreciated notes of its branches for eastern notes. The settlers discovered their loss when they tried their new money on the land offices.

[80] *Liberty Hall and Cincinnati Gazette,* in Chillicothe *Supporter,* March 3, 1819.
[81] *Niles' Weekly Register,* XVI, 298 (June 26, 1819).
[82] The *Detroit Gazette,* September 29, 1820, said that there was enough money for change, and that this practice should be prohibited.

Ohio, in January, 1819, enacted a law which made discounting a bank note a misdemeanor punishable with a $500 fine plus suit to recover face value.[83] Had the law been enforceable it would have prevented the people, the bulk of whose money was state bank notes, from getting any money at all acceptable at the land offices and elsewhere.[84]

By May, 1819, it was reported that several of the Ohio banks had resumed specie payment,[85] but it seemed very difficult to make certain. The Bank of Cincinnati was reported in August to have suspended specie payment again, and notices of other suspensions were printed.[86] The *Detroit Gazette* in September was asking its readers for information concerning the notes of the Farmers' and Mechanics' Bank and the John H. Piatt Company of Cincinnati.[87] A little later it classified the notes of a score of the Ohio banks as good, decent, middling, and good for nothing; in the last group it listed the notes of the two Cincinnati banks.[88] In December Detroit businessmen met and resolved to get and publish the facts concerning Ohio bank notes.[89] In May, 1820, Niles listed the banks of Chillicothe, Lancaster, Marietta, Belmont, Mount Pleasant, Western Reserve (Warren), and the two at Steubenville as paying specie.[90] He listed the notes of the rest of the 25 as at 70 to 75 per cent discount, but Gilmore in June listed the worst of the Ohio notes at only 50 per cent discount at Pittsburgh.[91]

[83] Chillicothe *Supporter,* February 24, 1819.

[84] Although there was considerable mention of this law in the papers of the day, it appears never to have been enforced. In 1820 a grand jury at Cincinnati refused to indict for its violation.

[85] The Bank of Steubenville, Farmers' and Mechanics' Bank of Steubenville, and the Bank of Mount Pleasant. The Western Reserve Bank and the banks of Marietta, Chillicothe, Lancaster, and St. Clairsville were said to "continue" specie payment. *Niles' Weekly Register,* XVI, 179 (May 8, 1819). By August was added the Belmont Bank and the Farmers' and Mechanics' Bank of Cincinnati. "The rest redeem their own notes with the notes of other banks, or do not trouble themselves about redeeming them at all." *Ibid.,* XVI, 405 (Aug. 14, 1819).

[86] *Western Herald and Steubenville Gazette,* August 14, 1819.

[87] September 10, 1819.

[88] In *Niles' Weekly Register,* XVII, 186 (Nov. 20, 1819).

[89] *Detroit Gazette,* December 17, 1819.

[90] *Niles' Weekly Register,* XVIII, 224 (May 20, 1820).

[91] J. & G. R. Gilmore, June 13, 1820, listed the notes of the above-mentioned banks and St. Clairsville at 1½ to 3 per cent discount, Canton at 12½, Columbus and West Union at 30 to 35, Dayton, Hamilton, Zanesville, Miami Exporting Company, Cleveland, etc., at 40 to 45, and John H. Piatt at 50 per cent. The Indiana State Bank at Vincennes was rated at 12½ to 15, as was the Bank of Illinois at Shawneetown, but the Indiana branches were at 40 to 45 per cent discount. *Western Herald and Steubenville Gazette,* June 17, 1820.

Depreciated notes did not prevent some of the banks from continuing to pay dividends. In northeastern Ohio one heard of "middle money," "wagon money," "Pitt-current," and "land-office money." The first was from the middle counties of Pennsylvania and Maryland, supposedly redeemable in coin, but not at par in the cities. Wagon money was any depreciated money still accepted by the freight haulers. Pitt-current and land-office money were notes accepted in Pittsburgh and by the government land offices. At Zanesville and elsewhere was "canal money," mostly from Pennsylvania, while at Cincinnati was "bankable money," that is, notes which the banks would accept as deposits on condition that depositors could be paid back the same kind.[92]

Then there were thousands of spurious or counterfeit notes in circulation. Citizens of Delaware, Ohio, were warned of a large number of $5.00 and $10.00 notes of the nonexistent "Scioto Exporting Company."[93] Counterfeiters were taken in Illinois in possession of more than $5,500, most of the notes being on the State Bank of Indiana.[94] At Corydon, Indiana, counterfeit notes were discovered in a cave.[95] Ohio in its misery sought to take comfort in the difficulties of her neighbor to the west. The *Cleaveland Herald* regretted to learn that the Indiana bank, recently established, "the capital stock of which consists of the skins of the various animals of that country, has sustained serious injury in its character and currency." Its principal issues consisted of raccoon skins of $1.00 denomination, opossum skins of 50 cents, mink of 25, and rabbit at 12½; it said that these notes were considered about the same as eastern paper by reason of the difficulty in counterfeiting them, but now it seemed that some had been transferring coontails to 'possum skins and the directors were offering rewards for detection.[96]

The suspension of specie by the Ohio banks in 1818 and the resulting depreciation, which followed the demand by the Cincinnati branch for balances due from the Cincinnati banks, called forth a legislative investigation. The committee made two reports

---

[92] Letter from Cincinnati to *National Gazette*, copied in *Detroit Gazette*, September 28, 1821.
[93] *Delaware Gazette* copied in Hamilton (Ohio) *Miami Herald*, October 28, 1818.
[94] *Western Sun and General Advertiser*, January 23, 1819.
[95] *Corydon Gazette*, July 13, 1820.
[96] *Cleaveland Herald*, November 21, 1822.

early in 1819[97] and came "inevitably to the conclusion, that the establishment and management of the United States Bank within this state, have very largely conduced to the present embarrassment of the circulating medium, and have had a direct effect in producing the recent suspension of specie payments by the state banks." Twenty of the twenty-five chartered banks of the state reported with data more or less complete. It appeared that paid-in capital—the capital of the five nonreporting banks was estimated—was $2,350,000, note issues $1,336,000, and specie held $460,000. Deposits of the twenty reporting banks were $268,000. These banks showed an average ratio of 67 cents circulation to each dollar of paid-in capital stock, $4.38 of paid-in capital stock to each dollar of specie in hand, and $2.92 of notes in circulation to each dollar of specie. Circulation and deposits combined equaled $3.59 to each dollar of specie.[98] On the whole the report considered the condition of the chartered banks as good as that of the Bank of the United States, and recommended a law to tax the two branches in Ohio $50,000 each, annually.[99]

Ohio was the only state in the Northwest in which the hatred against the second Bank of the United States manifested itself in open warfare. Indiana had in 1816 made constitutional provision against any branch within its borders, and Illinois did likewise in 1818.[100] In 1817 Maryland, Tennessee, and Georgia had levied taxes against the branches of the Bank,[101] North Carolina followed in 1818, and in January, 1819, Kentucky assessed a tax of $60,000 against each branch. Ohio had been considering a tax since the legislature met in December, 1817, and the House resolved (January, 1818) that it was both constitutional and

---

[97] Ohio *House Journal*, 1819–20, p. 415. The reports may also be found in leading Ohio newspapers, and the statistical tables are reprinted in C. C. Huntington, "Banking and Currency in Ohio," in *Ohio Archaeological and Historical Society Publications*, XXIV, 303 ff.

[98] *Ibid.*, XXIV, 306.

[99] Also for a law to provide for the appointment of an attorney general to enforce the law against unauthorized banking and to investigate the banks which did not report. The report rather exonerated the Ohio banks and blamed the war loans of eastern banks to the government, the drain of specie to the East, and the effects of the branches of the Bank of the United States in Ohio. Governor Ethan Allen Brown, in his message in December, 1818, said that since taxes on the state banks had failed to lighten the land tax burden, he saw no reason why the branches of the Bank of the United States should be exempt.

[100] Indiana Constitution, Article X, Section 1; Illinois Constitution, Article VIII, Section 21.

[101] Catterall, *Second Bank of the United States*, 64.

expedient to tax the Bank.[102] When final action was deferred until the next session, some insinuated it was because of influence of the Bank's friends in the legislature who were later accommodated at the Bank.[103]

Among the bitterest critics of the Bank in Ohio were the *Western Herald and Steubenville Gazette* and the *Cleaveland Register*. The former by September was declaring flatly against its constitutionality. The *Register* in December printed the following editorial:[104]

The evil arising out of banking institutions is felt, in a lesser or greater degree, by every person in the United States. The country is drained of the precious metals, and deluged with a paper currency, which will not pass at par twenty miles from the bank. The moneyed speculator is by this means enabled to purchase from the farmer (the paper he was obliged to receive in payment for his produce) at from 10 to 50% discount, and pay in paper, no better than what they have received. Thus have the honest and industrious farmers been compelled to dispose of their produce at a very low price, which was still rendered lower by the depreciated paper they have had to receive. Brokerage and swindling was never perhaps in any country, carried on with so high a hand, as it is at present in the United States. The hard earnings of the industrious farmer are arrested from his hands by a horde of swindlers employed by the banks.—Nor is this the only evil of banking—it holds out lures to the farmer to resign his plow and axe, for the more pleasing employment of measuring tape and selling pins—which but too often leads him to ruin and disgrace.

That luxury which is the bane of republics, and which threatens the speedy dissolution of our republican institutions, is owing in a great degree to the different monied aristocracies of our country. Within a few years we have witnessed the direful effects of banking, on the morals of our country, which appear to depreciate with bank paper. The seeds of aristocracy, so liberally scattered abroad in our land, by the 15th [14th?] Congress must be rooted out, or we are an undone people.

This monster of iniquity, was brought into existence under the administration of a short sighted chief magistrate, by a corrupt congress, who trampled on the constitution they had sworn to support in order to gratify their ambition for wealth. Had not the people become alarmed at this gross abuse of power, congress would at one more bold stroke, have arrested the last vestige of liberty out of the hands of the people—declared the presi-

---

[102] "It is therefore evident that the capital introduced into the country through these branches, is directly calculated to wither our agriculture and cramp our manufactures, and, of course, has no claim upon our indulgence; but is most unquestionably a proper subject of taxation." Ohio *House Journal*, 1817–18, p. 315.

[103] Three-column letter in the *Belmont Journal* copied in *Western Herald and Steubenville Gazette*, September 19, 1818.

[104] *Cleaveland Register*, December 1, 1818.

dency hereditary and themselves elect for life—the people not being prepared to part with their liberty, a bank was chartered with sufficient powers to bribe or terrify them into submission. How far this plan will succeed, and what will be its termination, God only knows.

Soon afterward the *Register* advocated a state bank for Ohio as the only way to rescue the banks from total ruin and "to save the last remnants of our precious metals from being dragged from the vaults of our State institutions into that vortex of iniquity, called the United States Bank."[105]

The report of the Congressional committee to investigate the Bank was made in January, 1819. Although it condemned the managers of the Bank for mismanagement, speculation, and charter violation, it was neither thorough, accurate, nor convincing. But it sufficed for the enemies of the Bank. Some papers published it in full and added editorials in italics. Said the *Western Herald,* "People of the West—debtors to the government—have we not repeatedly told you that you were imposed upon—that you were preyed upon by sharpers and speculators? What say you now?"[106]

Generally backed by public opinion in the state, the Ohio legislature in February enacted the law which placed a tax of $50,000 per annum upon each branch of the Bank within the state which should continue in business after September 15, 1819.[107] If the Bank refused to pay, the state auditor was authorized to seize money, notes, or property of the Bank. Early in March the decision of the United States Supreme Court in the case of *McCulloch* v. *Maryland* upheld the right of the Bank to establish branches without the state's consent and declared that the state had no right to tax them.[108] However, when the branches at Cincinnati and Chillicothe continued to operate, the state auditor, Ralph Osborn, determined to comply with the law. The Bank sought an injunction against the auditor in the United States Circuit Court at Chillicothe and, pending the issuance of the writ, on September 15 tried to restrain him by having served a copy of the petition in chancery and a subpoena

---

[105] *Cleaveland Register,* December 29, 1818.

[106] *Western Herald and Steubenville Gazette,* January 20, 1819.

[107] And a tax of $10,000 upon companies doing an unauthorized banking business within the state. *Laws of Ohio,* 1816–17, p. 190.

[108] The decision was published in full in leading Ohio newspapers by the end of March.

from the court.[109] These he ignored on advice of counsel and issued a warrant to the sheriff, John L. Harper, to enter the branch at Chillicothe and collect the tax. On September 17, Harper and assistants, equipped with a horse and wagon, entered the bank, took $100,000 in gold, silver, and notes to cover the tax on both branches, and carried them to the Bank of Chillicothe for overnight deposit. The next day the sheriff on his way to Columbus with the money was served with a writ to prevent paying over the money, and a like writ was served on the auditor. This writ was ignored, Harper took out $2,000 for fees, and obtained the state treasurer's receipt for $98,000.

The Bank of the United States brought action against Osborn and others for contempt, trespass, and carrying away $100,000 "under color and pretense of the law of Ohio." Harper and his assistant were arrested and imprisoned by a deputy United States marshal, but were released on a technicality. The court took proceedings against Osborn for contempt of court in disregarding the injunction and against the new state treasurer, Samuel Sullivan, for ignoring its stay on the $98,000 in the treasury; the latter was imprisoned until the case was appealed to the Supreme Court.[110]

These events caused a lot of excitement in Ohio and the West and called forth heated comment elsewhere. Long extracts from eastern papers, many of which accused Ohio of nullification, treason, and the like, were copied and debated.[111] In the autumn political campaign candidates for the legislature issued their "Declarations of Independence" against the Bank of the United States and indicted it on as many counts as was George III in 1776.[112] Newspaper comment and public sentiment supported

[109] The writ was finally issued September 18.

[110] For the details and citations of the writs, decisions, etc., see C. C. Huntington, "Banking and Currency in Ohio," in *Ohio Archaeological and Historical Society Publications*, XXIV, 318 ff., and Jean Dick Cheetham, "State Sovereignty in Ohio," in *ibid.*, IX (1901), 290-302. The controversy may be followed in brief in *Niles' Weekly Register* or in any of the leading Ohio newspapers.

[111] See *Inquisitor Cincinnati Advertiser*, October 19, 1819; *Western Herald and Steubenville Gazette*, October 2, 1819, etc., for copies of eastern comment. One of the most severe papers in its accusations was the *Detroit Gazette*.

[112] The Bank kept two branches in Ohio without the consent of the state, it combined with foreign speculators and banks, it quartered large bodies of armed brokers among us, etc. It was proclaimed that "all connection between the people of Ohio and the branch banks ought to be dissolved, and that as a free and independent state we have full power to levy a tax upon all banks within our jurisdiction of whatsoever denomination and by whomsoever established," etc. Letters

the legislature and state officers. The *Cincinnati Gazette* said that the bank episode "created as much consternation as if it had been an overt act of treason or rebellion." It believed that "If the general government can create a monied institution, in the very bosom of the states, paramount to their laws, then indeed is state sovereignty a mere name, 'full of sound and fury, signifying nothing.' "[113] In defending Ohio against the numerous reprobations from outside, the *Cleaveland Register* said: "We are Republican, attached to the general government and that glorious constitution which unites us into a federal compact, but when we observe our privileges taken from us, and feel the hand of oppression bearing on us heavily, we then assert the rights, guaranteed to us by the constitution of our happy country."[114] James Wilson, editor of the *Western Herald and Steubenville Gazette*, had been an uncompromising opponent of the Bank.[115] He stated that the arguments given in its defense were "those of interested men, rather than of correct politicians," and that for Ohio to submit to the Federal judiciary as "dispenser of justice between her and the U. S. bank" would but pave the way for some new attack upon state sovereignty.[116]

A few papers were more cautious. The *Cleaveland Herald*, for example, thought the question was a complicated one, but that it was apparent that nothing short of a strong conviction on the part of an enlightened legislature of the injurious tendency, if not the absolute unconstitutionality of the Bank, could have

---

to voters in Chillicothe *Supporter*, October 6, 1819. Gen. William Henry Harrison in his address to the voters of Hamilton County said that he would like to see every bank in the United States destroyed, if it were constitutionally possible, and a metallic currency substituted. He was most opposed to the Bank of the United States establishment, but was a director in one of the branches. As for the controversy between Ohio and the Bank, he thought it ought to be left to the courts. *Ibid.*, December 1, 1819. Harrison probably had no convictions on the money question, but such good Jacksonian doctrine is interesting from a man who was to be presidential candidate of the Whigs.

[113] *Liberty Hall and Cincinnati Gazette*, October 5, 1819.

[114] October 26, 1819. The anti-Marshall arguments are well covered in a four-column letter by "Ohio" in the *Columbus Gazette*, April 8, 1819. Rather ultra sentiments were expressed by "Dion" in the *Liberty Hall and Cincinnati Gazette*. Speaking of an English writer's prophecy that the United States would divide at the Alleghenies, the writer stated that, though it was a delicate subject, it must sometimes be publicly discussed. Copied in Chillicothe *Supporter*, June 2, 1819.

[115] For brief sketch of this outspoken Scotch-Irishman, see Chapter XV, 513–15, and Francis P. Weisenburger, "The Middle Western Antecedents of Woodrow Wilson," in *Mississippi Valley Historical Review*, XXIII (1936–37), 375–90.

[116] Wilson to Thomas Worthington, December 22, 1819, cited in *ibid.*, XXIII, 376.

resulted in such energetic measures.[117] The governor, Ethan Allen Brown, however, took a different view. He regretted the whole affair and was ashamed that it had happened in Ohio. And William Henry Harrison, candidate for the state Senate, although no friend of the Bank, felt the Ohio law had been "matured in the foul mind of the Hartford Convention."

The legislature which met in December, 1820, did not temporize. The auditor's report was referred to a joint committee which, under the chairmanship of Charles Hammond, distinguished lawyer-journalist,[118] brought forth a long condemnation of the idea that the Federal courts were sole expositors of the Constitution.[119] The committee cited instances to prove that a state did not of necessity have to accept Supreme Court decisions, and recommended that Ohio go on in defiance of the *McCulloch* v. *Maryland* decision until certain that the legislative and executive departments of the General Government intended to enforce the Court's doctrine. Resolutions were offered and passed which reaffirmed the doctrines of the Virginia and Kentucky Resolutions of 1798, and on January 29, 1821, an act was passed "to withdraw from the Bank of the United States the protection and aid of the laws of this state, in certain cases," unless it consented to a 4 per cent dividend tax to the state.[120] Another law, February 2, provided for the return of $90,000 of the money taken from the Bank, if it would promise to withdraw all suits and submit to a tax of $2,500 annually until the dividend tax could be calculated.[121] The Bank ignored these laws, obtained an injunction in the circuit court to prevent the auditor collecting the tax, and in September the court decided that the $100,000 plus interest on part of it should be returned to the Bank. Concerning this action the *Cincinnati Gazette* said, "The United States Judiciary is conducting a supremacy which, if not met boldly and decidedly by the press, will soon feel confidence enough to set public opinion at defiance."[122]

The law outlawing the Bank then went into effect. Sheriffs were forbidden to jail persons committed by actions of the

---

[117] November 2, 1819.
[118] After 1825 famous as the editor of the *Cincinnati Gazette*. See Chapter XV.
[119] Ohio *House Journal*, 1820–21, pp. 99–132.
[120] *Laws of Ohio*, 1820–21, p. 108.
[121] *Ibid.*, 1820–21, p. 173.
[122] *Liberty Hall and Cincinnati Gazette*, September 22, 1821.

Bank, judicial officers were not to acknowledge conveyances to which the Bank was a party, nor were the recorders to register them, and notaries were forbidden to protest notes held by and payable to the Bank. The Bank had no state protection for its property, even though burglary, robbery, or arson be committed, for justices and grand juries were forbidden to act.

Appeal was made from the decision of the United States Circuit Court of Ohio to the Supreme Court. Charles Hammond, John C. Wright, and others appeared for the Ohio officials and argued that in reality the case was a suit against the state. The arguments of Clay, Webster, and Sergeant prevailed, however, and the decision in *Osborn* v. *Bank of the United States*, 1824, sustained the circuit court. The opinion of the Court in *McCulloch* v. *Maryland* that a state could not tax a United States agency was reaffirmed and the law of Ohio declared "repugnant to the law of the United States, made in pursuance of the Constitution, and therefore void."[123] The $100,000 was ordered returned to the Bank.

Public opinion was not favorable to this decision, but accepted it. The legislature even curbed its outbursts, and in January, 1826, repealed the law which outlawed the Bank.

Indiana had no branches of the Bank of the United States upon which to wage war, but was having her troubles, neverthe-less. After some trouble with the Bank of the United States in 1817 regarding the Treasury Department's use of banks north of the Ohio as government depositories, a new arrangement was entered into whereby the Bank was relieved of responsibility for the depository banks.[124] In March, 1819, Secretary Craw-ford again made the Vincennes bank a public depository, on condition that that bank continue to pay specie and accept all money received by the land office as cash.[125] On the basis of the government deposits the Vincennes bank extended its loans, and when late in 1819 the Treasury presented several drafts for $20,000 to $50,000, the bank did not pay them. Secretary Craw-

[123] *Osborn and others* v. *Bank of the United States*, 9 *Wheaton*, 738 ff.

[124] Government deposits were credited to the Bank of the United States for use of the United States, and if the Secretary of the Treasury thought any bank unsafe, he might withdraw the deposits on two-months notice. *American State Papers, Finance*, IV, 571, 588, 590.

[125] President Nathaniel Ewing's argument regarding the benefits of government deposits to the Indiana merchants and settlers may be found in *ibid.*, III, 735.

ford protested in July, 1820, and warned that, unless the drafts were honored and all surplus (above the guaranteed minimum of $75,000) turned over within forty days, no more deposits would be made.[126] Since the bank did not meet these demands, government deposits were discontinued and the land-office receiver was ordered not to accept its notes.

The reputation of the Vincennes bank was being attacked. Most of its loans were said to have been to its directors and political friends. It had practiced all sorts of trickery to avoid having to redeem its notes, had been a notorious note shaver, and its affairs were all involved with the Steam Mill Company. Yet it had paid 8 per cent on its stock in 1819. Since the Vincennes bank was really the parent bank of the Indiana bank and branches, its condition was an issue in the state elections of 1820. A letter in the *Western Sun* stated that the bank was tottering, but this was refuted by the *Centinel*.[127] The bank's report to the legislature confirmed the worst suspicions, and soon thereafter, on January 2, 1821, the bank suspended specie payment. About a month later the great "Steam Mill," the bank's chief debtor, went up in flames. A legislative committee spent the session investigating banks, but accomplished nothing. In June the bank's president informed the directors that the institution was bankrupt. Managers of the "Steam Mill," also officers of the bank, were accused of embezzling $91,000 of the bank's money. It was decided to close up the affairs of the bank. Stockholders who owed the bank were permitted to pay with their stock, then worthless, at par value.

Indiana had borrowed $20,000 from the bank against which loan the bank held the same amount of state bonds. The state had accepted the bank's notes as tax payments, and the state treasury was unable to meet its expenses. Governor Jonathan Jennings called the legislature into session at an earlier time than usual in 1821, but it accomplished little. It did order the Knox County Circuit Court to bring a writ of *quo warranto* against the bank. Early in 1822 the directors of the bank declared a 40 per cent dividend for a part of the stockholders.[128] The bank settled with the United States Treasury by turning over to the Treasury's

---

[126] *Ibid.*, III, 737.
[127] December 23, 1820.
[128] *Western Sun and General Advertiser*, March 16, 1822.

agent its real estate and securities on hand, among which were $32,750 of state bonds. These the Treasury Department in 1822 permitted the state to buy back with the worthless bank notes taken as tax payments of which there were $21,000 face value in the state treasury. Included in the real estate was the property of the "Steam Mill," property of officers, and a number of town lots in Brookville.[129] The report of the bank to the state in 1822 stated that the nominal capital of the bank and branches was $129,363—$30,000 for each of the branches and $39,363 for the parent bank. Debts owing it were listed at $184,733, of which the "Steam Mill" owed $116,284 and bank directors $17,333. There was $30 in specie on hand and $3,218 in currency.

In 1822 the jury in the Knox County Circuit Court *quo warranto* suit found the bank guilty of charter violation.[130] The case was appealed to the Indiana Supreme Court where the decision as regards the charter was upheld, but the decision as to the bank's property was reversed. The bank's debtors were discharged and its creditors left without remedy.[131]

This was the end of the first State Bank of Indiana, so optimistically planned on paper and put into operation but a

[129] Senator James Noble was the agent who dealt with Secretary Crawford. The figures given in the account in the *Brookville Enquirer* copied in *Niles' Weekly Register*, XXIII, 167 (Nov. 16, 1822), vary somewhat from the above. Crawford was using the banks to build up a political machine and in 1824, when the Treasury still carried $168,511 on its books against the Vincennes bank, he wrote that what had looked fully secure might not be so safe. The Indiana Congressional delegation, especially Noble, had been friendly to Crawford and all had recommended the Indiana banks. As Noble reported it, Senator Ninian Edwards, of Illinois, expressed the idea when he said in 1824: "Now d—n it, you know we both live in States where there are many poor debtors to the Government for lands, together with a deranged currency. The notes on various banks being depreciated after the effect and operation of the war in that portion of the Union, and the banks, by attempting to call in their paper, having exhausted their specie, the notes that were then in circulation became of little or no value. Many men of influence in that country have united to induce the Secretary of the Treasury to select certain banks as banks of deposit, and to take the notes of certain banks in payment for public lands. Had he not done so . . . many of our inhabitants would have been turned out of doors and lost their lands and the people of that country would have had a universal disgust against Mr. Crawford. . . . No man in this Government could have conducted the fiscal and financial concerns of the Government with more integrity and propriety than Crawford did." *American State Papers, Finance*, V, 104. The documents concerning the bank were also printed in the Corydon *Indiana Gazette*, August 13, 20, 27, 1823.

[130] *Western Sun and General Advertiser*, July 13, 1822.

[131] The court held that the state could by *quo warranto* order the dissolution of a corporation which was violating its charter. The fact that the charter said that it was not to be dissolved until its debts were paid applied only to self-dissolution. *The President, Directors, and Company of the Bank of Vincennes, The State Bank of Indiana* v. *The State of Indiana*, I *Blackford*, 267 (November, 1823).

short half-dozen years before. In common with some of her neighboring states, Indiana had to pay the price for lack of understanding of the laws of economics, as well as corrupt politics and wholesale violation of the rules of common honesty. Some of the leading promoters were tricksters, others just plain embezzlers. At the same time most of them were the leaders in public life at the time and many were founders of respectable fortunes and families.

Neither of the two Illinois banks succeeded in weathering the difficulties of 1819–20. The Bank of Illinois (Shawneetown) made a brave struggle, but it was beset by a powerful neighbor (the Bank of Missouri) and domestic enemies, as well as by the conditions of the times. Specie payment was discontinued in 1821 and two years later the bank was forced to close its affairs. Outstanding notes were redeemed in so far as presented, but other liabilities, including a government deposit of $28,367, could not be paid.[132] The Bank of Edwardsville came to a more inglorious end. Senator Ninian Edwards, one of the directors, had been instrumental in getting government deposits for his bank, but on his return to Illinois in 1819 he found the bank in difficulties, resigned his directorship, and asked the president of the bank, who was also the local land-office agent, to withhold further government deposits until Secretary Crawford could better know conditions.[133] When Edwards announced in the newspapers his severance of connections with the bank, he assured the people that it was in sound condition and under good management. The failure of the Bank of Missouri, the largest bank in the West, in August, 1821, however, meant the beginning of the end.[134] A run of Missouri noteholders on the Edwardsville bank was met by keeping open extra hours and meeting all with specie, but after several days "temporary and partial" suspension was

[132] In 1837, when this bank was reorganized, a settlement was made with the United States. See Dowrie, *Banking in Illinois*, 13–14.

[133] This led to the Edwards-Crawford controversy regarding responsibility for continuance of the government deposits, the Congressional investigation, and political complications. See *Niles' Weekly Register*, XXVI, 140–49 (May 1, 8, 1824), and Chapter IX for political connections.

[134] Of a capital of $210,000 in the Bank of Missouri, stockholders had drawn out, on pledges of their stock, $186,335, leaving only $23,665 actual working capital. On this base its discounts were spread to $430,000, of which $297,000 were responsibilities of its directors. To such a bank Secretary Crawford allowed a permanent government deposit of $150,000. Ninian Edwards' address, in *Niles' Weekly Register*, XXVI, 141 (May 1, 1824).

necessary.[135] The bank continued to pay specie on notes under $10. The president assured Secretary Crawford that the United States funds were amply secured. The United States never recovered any part of the $46,800 deposit. Senator Edwards maintained that Crawford, for political reasons, delayed settlement until the securities placed in trust to cover the government deposit had become worthless.

A glance at the only financial report of the two Illinois banks shows that, as in Indiana and elsewhere, deposits played a negligible part in the banking of the day. The combined report issued by the Secretary of the Treasury in 1819 showed paid-in capital of $140,910, circulation $52,021, government deposits of $119,036, and individual deposits of $32,568. Yet loans and discounts amounted to $206,694, quite a bit more than capital stock and individual deposits combined.

After the demise of the State Bank of Indiana and the two Illinois banks, these states were left practically without banks. The Farmers' and Mechanics' Bank of Madison, which had refused to become a part of the State Bank of Indiana, had made an honest effort to carry on, but when the Bank of the United States in 1820 refused to include its notes among those acceptable for land payments and continued to draw on it at sight for large sums through the Louisville and Cincinnati branches, its directors decided to wind up its affairs. In 1824–25 all obligations were met in full and the bank ceased to be of importance.[136]

Illinois, in no wise made cautious by the experiences of her neighbors, in 1821 embarked upon one of the most fantastic experiments in state banking in the history of the West. It was more than a banking scheme—it was a combination of relief, philanthropy, and political-economic hocus-pocus.[137] Governor

---

[135] *Edwardsville Spectator*, August 21, September 11, 1821; Dowrie, *Banking in Illinois*, 17.

[136] Esarey, *State Banking in Indiana*, 225–26, states that this bank closed 1824–25. However, the Indianapolis *Indiana Democrat*, October 13, 1832, noted that it had "recommenced business" with a new issue of notes, and named its directors. And the Indianapolis *Indiana Journal*, September 26, 1834, quoted the Madison *Republican and Banner* to the effect that the Farmers' and Mechanics' Bank was destined to end its twenty-year career with the expiration of its charter January 1.

[137] The Vandalia *Illinois Advocate and State Register*, a strong advocate of chartering an Illinois State Bank in 1833, objected to its opponents making comparisons with the State Bank of 1821. "It is well known to every one, that the *old* Bank never had a share of *stock*, nor a dollar of *capital*, during its existence—

Shadrach Bond in his message to the legislature in December, 1820, straddled the question of a state bank. He had no doubt that the General Assembly would "do its utmost" to relieve embarrassed conditions. It was a subject of serious reflection whether this pressure in our money concerns should be left to correct itself or whether extraordinary measures were needed. "Temporary relief is sometimes afforded by an extraordinary effort, and as often followed by a state of things even more embarrassing."[138] Resolutions were presented from some groups to the effect that "the legitimate object of banking institutions is to afford a safe and convenient medium for the emission of loans founded on solid capital and not a project of needy individuals for the creation of funds."[139] A small number of representatives in each house argued against the bank as both unconstitutional and unsound. But the arguments that it was the duty of the state to afford relief and prevent the "unnecessary and wanton sacrifices of the property and possessions of the citizens of the state" prevailed.[140] The bill, passed by narrow majorities in both houses, met a unanimous veto by the council of revision com-

---

that it never was anything *more or less* than an establishment for the issuing of bills of credit." Issue of November 30, 1833. And in 1827 three prominent public men wrote: "When it is recollected that the establishment of the State Bank was a Measure of Relief—that its object was not to loan money on usury to the wealthy, for the purpose of gain, but to lighten the burden of our indigent and embarrassed citizens—and that, therefore, if any preference was to be shewn among applicants for loans, it was to be exercised in favor of those who were encumbered by debt— the only real matter of surprise is that loans made under provisions so liberal, would have been reduced with so much promptitude, and so little loss." William Kinney, Abraham Prickett, and Joseph A. Beaird, in Vandalia *Illinois Intelligencer*, February 3, 1827, quoted in Pease, *The Frontier State*, 58.

[138] The *Edwardsville Spectator*, December 5, 1820, printed a one-and-a-half-column petition for relief and advised voters to cut it out and get signatures. ". . . the sudden stagnation of business and commerce, growing out of combination of multifarious causes, has buried in oblivion and despair the infatuating prospects fabricated by a glowing spirit of speculation and enterprize; and the illusion has ensnared if not ruined thousands of worthy men, unless saved by legislative aid to redeem them from this enthraldom; to obtain which is the object of this petition." Petitions of this sort sought extended stay laws, assurance of sale of real and personal property at forced sales at at least two thirds its value, state loans to debtors, etc.

[139] A committee of Bond County voters to the legislature. *Edwardsville Spectator*, February 18, 1820. The resolutions further stated that, judging by the experience of other states, the bank notes would be sure to depreciate, but, since they would be accepted at face value for state taxes, either tax receipts would go down, taxes be raised, or a loan or further paper issue would be necessary. This prediction turned out to be quite accurate.

[140] Illinois *Senate Journal*, 1820–21, p. 10.

posed of the governor and supreme court judges, but was passed over the veto.[141]

The law established the State Bank of Illinois at Vandalia and provided for branches at Edwardsville, Shawneetown, Palmyra, and Brownsville. The capital stock, limited to $500,-000, was to be owned entirely by the state. The State Bank was made the sole depository of state funds. The issue of $500,000 of notes was permitted, $300,000 of which were authorized at the time, and the bank was to run for ten years.[142] The state was districted for loan-making purposes and the notes were distributed according to the population of the districts. Loans were limited to $1,000 to each person, to be secured by real estate equal to double the value of the loan.[143] These loans were to be renewable from year to year upon payment of 10 per cent of the principal. The state sought to avoid the provision of the United States Constitution against making state notes legal tender by making the bank notes legal tender for all public dues in the state and suspending the execution of judgments for three

[141] The bank charter may be found in *Laws of Illinois*, 1820–21. The discussion pro and con on the bank by way of voters' meetings and letters in the papers was more voluminous after passage of the bill than before. Some of these letters showed a pretty good understanding of banking and finance. Nearly all were long winded and verbose. "Curtius," in a series of a half-dozen articles, argued that the use of the state's credit would restore confidence between individuals, give relief, etc. *Edwardsville Spectator*, January—April, 1821. "Z" compared the law's opponents to the Hartford Conventionists. *Ibid.*, May 8. "Curtius" (December 26, 1820) had stated that the state had paid off its debts and would soon have a surplus, that the bank would not create temptations to overtrade, that it would not make any difference if it did, that its notes would not banish gold and silver, that they could be redeemed on time, and were not in violation of the United States Constitution. "Philo Curtius" argued on the other hand that the issuance of bank notes by the state was unconstitutional. "Will not this paper be land office money? Certainly, my good friends, when oranges grow in Greenland, and Symmes' hole [Captain Symmes' idea that the inhabitable interior of the earth could be reached via a hole near the North Pole] is made the penitentiary of the state." *Ibid.*, June 5, 1821. "XYZ" said all were familiar with private note shavers, "But for a state to prey upon itself, that is for the state of Illinois in its corporate capacity to shave the citizens of said state in their individual capacities, is an anomaly unknown since the fabled days of the vulture preying upon its own bowels." He pointed out that under the provisions of the $300,000 note issue on loans, payable in ten annual installments, there would be a shortage of state paper in the seventh year to pay the seventh installment and interest the eighth year; that farmers of the state would need $100,000 in specie to pay the bank, or else lose their farms. *Ibid.*, August 7, 1821.

[142] The state appropriated $2,000 for the purchase of plates for printing the notes.

[143] The president, branch presidents, and directors were permitted to borrow more.

years if the plaintiff would not accept the notes.[144] Members of
the legislature proclaimed their belief that the notes would pass
at par with gold, and by resolution asked the Treasury Department of the United States to accept them as specie.[145] Said a later
governor of Illinois:

The directors, it is believed, were all politicians; and either were then, or
expected to be, candidates for office. Lending to everybody, and refusing
none, was the surest road to popularity. Accordingly, three hundred thousand dollars of the new money was soon lent without much attention to
security or care for eventual payment. . . . And as the bills of Ohio and
Kentucky banks had driven all other money out of the State, so this new
issue effectually kept it out.[146]

In addition to the regular note issue, the State Bank, which
was made the place of deposit of the state's funds, was permitted
to issue notes double the amount of specie in the state's deposits.
These notes were to be redeemable in specie on demand.[147] Of
the regular issue, the state was to redeem and retire one tenth
each year.

The fond hopes of wishful thinkers were not to be realized.
Since there was no provision for redemption of the notes in
specie, the debtors, instead of taking seriously their obligations,
began to look upon them as a gift from the state and, as the
whole setup of relief legislation was conducive to this attitude,
the notes naturally began their decline. Within a few weeks after
the bank opened, they were circulating at 75 cents on the dollar,
a month later 62½ cents, and by 1823 were about 30 cents,
where they remained until 1825, in which year the state's finances
were further jeopardized by new legislation.[148]

[144] The United States Supreme Court, *Craig* v. *State of Missouri* (1830), decided
that bills of such banks, payable at a future date, were bills of credit and unconstitutional. 4 *Peters*, 410 ff. In December, 1833, in the case of *Linn* v. *the State Bank
of Illinois*, the Illinois Supreme Court decided that the bank's notes were bills
of credit and contrary to the Constitution of the United States. "It clearly appears
that our bank and the Missouri loan office, although called by different names,
were similar in their objects and both were established for the purpose of emitting
paper currency to circulate as money in their respective States."

[145] Ford, *History of Illinois*, 45–46. Ford says that when Lieutenant Governor
Pierre Menard, an uneducated but shrewd French pioneer, put the motion he said:
"Gentlemen of *de* Senate, it is moved and seconded *dat de* notes of *dis* bank be
made land office money. All in favor of *dat* motion say aye; all against it, say no.
It is decided in *de* affirmative. And now, gentlemen, *I bet you one hundred dollar
he never be made land office money.*"

[146] *Ibid.*, 47.

[147] This extra note issue privilege was repealed in 1823.

[148] In 1823 the principal bank at Vandalia was authorizing the cutting of its
notes below $5.00 denomination for the purpose of making change. At the same

A certain amount of recovery from the effects of the banking crisis of 1818–19 took place in the East in 1823–24, but the West was still suffering the consequences. Prices were at depression lows and business continued stagnant. Cincinnati pork sold as low as $1.00 to $2.00, corn at 8 cents, and wheat was frequently quoted at 20 to 25 cents in the interior. Emigration dwindled and land sales diminished. On the Miami and Scioto rivers in Ohio in 1823, 7,000 acres were offered at 90 cents per acre cash. Banking and currency troubles were certainly not the only cause for the continued depression. Most of the banks had been wiped out. Even in Ohio by 1826 there remained only ten banks whose notes were current throughout the state. The notes of the better Ohio banks which in 1820 had been listed at 15 to 25 per cent discount in the East gradually appreciated until in 1821 they were about 5 to 10 per cent, and by 1824–25 most were listed at 5 to 6 per cent.[149] The heavy debt burden, the tendency of stop laws, relief legislation, replevin acts, and the like to destroy confidence of men in each other and in their government, and lack of easy transportation and available markets were also important factors in retarding recovery.

The *Cleaveland Register* in 1819,[150] viewing the hard times, could see no way out. If Congress repealed the law chartering the Bank of the United States, many individuals would be ruined and the pressure for money would be more severely felt than before. If it did not, the members would bring down on their heads the curses of an incensed nation, the country banks would be ruined, and their debtors would be hard pressed. "The country will be injured, property must be sacrificed, and a general ruin ensue. It is idle to feast ourselves with hopes of better times. The mechanic, the merchant, the manufacturer, cannot do business, and must therefore turn their attention to something else. The agriculturist alone, who is not in debt will be able to stand the test in the worst of times." But in 1824 the *Cincinnati Ga-*

time the editor of the *Intelligencer* announced that he was compelled "from imperious necessity" to accept state paper from then on at what it was really worth. *Illinois Intelligencer*, March 15, 1823. Transylvania Medical College advertised student's board at $2.50 to $3.00 in specie, $5.50 to $6.00 in currency. *Ibid.*, November 29, 1823.

[149] C. C. Huntington, "Banking and Currency in Ohio," in *Ohio Archaeological and Historical Society Publications*, XXIV, 332, 333; Chillicothe *Supporter and Scioto Gazette*, November 29, December 13, 1823.

[150] March 9, 1819.

zette began to see one way out. It pointed out that, since most of the banks were gone, the prolongation of the depression was not owing to depreciated bank currency, but to a want of markets for the produce of the West.[151]

§

With the beginning of state internal improvement programs in the West, the problems of banking, currency, and state finance became more closely related and complicated. State finance in the early years was a relatively simple matter and involved mere arithmetic problems which both voter and politician could understand. With Jeffersonian Republican principles—"a light and simple government"—prevailing, the needs of the state governments were slight. A few thousand dollars annually took care of the main items—salaries of state officials, maintenance of the seat of government, a few office supplies, and an appropriation now and then for a road survey. Even the local governments, in the absence of real schools or roads, had few burdens. Road maintenance was a matter of labor rather than taxes. Poor relief was handled without much cost by binding out orphans and vagrants to the highest bidder who guaranteed maintenance.

From 1799 to 1825 Ohio derived its revenues mostly from a land tax. In addition were the Three Per Cent Fund[152] for roads, school-land funds, and the receipts from an occasional lottery.[153] There was no personal property tax. Land was divided into three classes according to quality, with a flat tax rate per hundred acres of 85 cents for first class, 60 cents for second, and 25 cents for third.[154] These rates were later raised to $2.00 for first-class land and others in proportion, and in 1816 the rates were $3.00, $2.25 and $1.50.[155] Such a simple tax system was intended largely to catch nonresident landowners, and was certain to lead to inequalities and loss of revenue as the population increased. For

[151] *Liberty Hall and Cincinnati Gazette,* May 18, 1824.
[152] Three per cent of the receipts from sales of public lands in the state provided in the enabling act. See Chapter II.
[153] The first Ohio legislature authorized a lottery for improving the Muskingum and Cuyahoga rivers.
[154] Theodore C. Pease (ed.), *Laws of the Northwest Territory 1788–1800 (Illinois Historical Collections,* XVII, Springfield, 1925), 471.
[155] *Liberty Hall and Cincinnati Gazette,* March 25, 1816.

instance, by 1825, 100 acres of first-class land near Cincinnati worth $3,000 and 100 acres in Portage County worth $400 paid the same tax.[156] The committee on finance of the legislature of 1824–25 pointed out this fact and indicated that the state should be getting more revenue.[157] The state treasurer's report for 1822 listed the year's expenditures at $78,994 and showed a balance of $33,217 in the general fund,[158] this, despite the fact that the auditor's lists of lands advertised for sale for delinquent taxes filled page after page of the *Ohio Monitor*.[159] In 1825 the state's revenue was $131,733,[160] but expenses were increasing rapidly. For additional revenue a tax law was enacted which made not only land but town and personal property also taxable for state purposes. This more than doubled the amount of value taxable by the state.[161] The state tax levy for 1826, including county, road, township, and school taxes, was $366,922; in 1828 it was $470,000.[162]

From the beginning of statehood Ohio had had no funded debt. Temporary deficits had been met from time to time by tax-anticipation warrants. Temporary loans from Ohio banks were made from 1813 to 1816 to meet the direct tax imposed by the United States for war purposes, but they were soon repaid from increased taxation. At the end of 1825 there was a balance of $34,325 in the treasury and the state's finances were in sound shape.[163] But they were not long to remain so for the state began building canals.[164] In entire disregard of the warning protest of Editor James Wilson and his *Steubenville Gazette*, who repeatedly asked, "Where is the money coming from?" the voices of

[156] A series of letters signed "Necker" in Ravenna *Western Courier*, August 13, 20, 27, points out the inequalities.
[157] From *Liberty Hall and Cincinnati Gazette*, January 21, 1825.
[158] *Ibid.*, December 21, 1822.
[159] May, June, 1822.
[160] Just slightly more than the $130,190 of 1818, regardless of the increase in population and basic wealth.
[161] In Hamilton County, for instance, in 1826, lands were listed at $1,489,922, town property, houses, horses, etc., at $3,210,886, and merchants' capital and carriages at $2,147,625. Under the old system only item one was taxed for state purposes, item two for county and township, and item three not at all. Under the new, the state tax was derived from almost seven-million valuation instead of one and a half.
[162] *Liberty Hall and Cincinnati Gazette*, December 22, 1826; Columbus *Ohio State Journal*, January 2, 1828. Land and dwellings were valued in 1828 at almost forty millions; horses were about equal in valuation to town lots and buildings and almost double the merchants' capital.
[163] Auditor's report, *Ohio State Journal*, February 2, 1826.
[164] See Chapter VII.

the majority prevailed: if present resources and credit were not sufficient, that problem could be taken up in time.

Governor Ethan Allen Brown had estimated the cost of the canals at $3,000,000. The law of 1825 authorized the canal commissioners to borrow $400,000 for that year, and not to exceed $600,000 in any year thereafter. This limit was soon raised to $1,200,000. State stock certificates, bearing interest not to exceed 6 per cent, redeemable after December 31, 1850, were advertised in eastern and European papers, and marketed largely through the Manhattan Bank of New York. Since the provisions as to interest and sinking fund appeared sound, the state was able to sell some of the issues at a fair premium. The state pledged all canal receipts, plus a sufficient annual tax increment, to pay interest and add $25,000 annually to a sinking fund for retirement of principal. As the canal receipts increased, the amount made up from taxes was expected to be reduced or wiped out altogether. But canal income proved inadequate to meet requirements of interest and sinking fund in the face of rapidly increasing loans for construction. Since the real and personal property values in 1825 were estimated at $59,000,000, adequate taxes would have met the bill.

But politicians were reluctant to see the taxpayer burdened or to have him realize the real cost of the canals. Financial legerdemain was easier. The commissioners and auditor, with legislative sanction, having used the proceeds of the sales of the Federal lands granted and borrowed the school funds credited to the counties, then "borrowed" the accumulated sinking-fund increments and spent them on construction. By bookkeeping transactions funds were transferred, "borrowed," and juggled, and the floating debt so kept on the move as to be almost impossible of exact location at any given time. By 1836 the state debt had been painlessly raised to $4,453,000—moderate enough considering the increased population and wealth. But the period of real Ohio high finance was yet to come.

The building of the canals did stimulate business. Thousands of laborers were employed, and there was a ready market for produce and supplies. Land values rose, emigration was encouraged, and the population of Ohio increased almost twice as rapidly as that of the United States as a whole. The general improvement in agriculture and business together with the state loans and public-works expenditures called for additional credit and money supplies.

In 1825 the bonus law of 1816, which proved satisfactory to neither the state nor the banks, was repealed and a tax on dividends substituted.[165] The state treasury by 1820 found itself in possession of more than $33,000 of uncurrent bank notes. Some of the banks had failed, and others were not paying specie. Suits on the part of the state resulted in favorable judgments, but led nowhere. A commission to look into these claims reported to the legislature in December, 1824, that some of the notes were sold at 33 to 37 cents on the dollar, and that others were worthless. The auditor's report of the same month made it plain that the state would derive no benefits from the provisions of the "bonus law." The accumulating 4 per cent of annual dividends which the law provided for was more than overbalanced by failures. Consequently, the legislature in 1825 provided for a 2 to 4 per cent tax on bank dividends.[166]

No further change in the banking law took place until 1831. By 1826 the notes of only ten of the twenty-five banks in operation in 1819[167] passed current throughout the state.[168] The banks whose notes were at 12 to 50 per cent discount in 1822 had disappeared and the notes of the 10 banks were current at 1 to 1½ per cent discount.[169] These surviving banks rendered valuable service to the state. The state auditor commended them in his report of January, 1829, and stated: "Their usefulness will not cease till they multiply so as to prey upon each other, or eagerness for gain leads to over-issues." Cincinnati, the leading commercial center of the West, had no bank except the branch of the

[165] The state auditor's report of January, 1819, showed that $79,930 of stock had been set aside for the state by the "bonus law" banks and $11,392 had been paid in taxes by the banks prior to acceptance of charters under that law. A legislative committee report of December, 1820, showed $84,385 of stock for the state of which $37,023 was in specie-paying banks. So the anticipated heavy revenues to the state had failed to materialize. Ohio *Senate Journal,* 1818–19, p. 207; *House Journal,* 1820–21, p. 195; C. C. Huntington, "Banking and Currency in Ohio," in *Ohio Archaeological and Historical Society Publications,* XXIV, 338–39.

[166] *Ibid.,* XXIV, 339–41; *Senate Journal,* 1824–25, p. 57.

[167] The twenty-five listed in the report of the legislative committee of 1818–19. Ohio *House Journal,* 1819–20, pp. 415 ff.

[168] John Kilbourn, *Ohio Gazetteer* (1826), 231. A list of the Ohio banks which failed, 1811–31, may be found in C. C. Huntington, "Banking and Currency in Ohio," in *Ohio Archaeological and Historical Society Publications,* XXIV, 346–47

[169] *Ibid.,* XXIV, 347–48; *Cincinnati Daily Gazette,* January 8, 1828.

Bank of the United States. The city was inadequately provided with money or credit. As business improved, 36 per cent interest was sometimes paid for small sums, and 10 to 20 per cent was not unusual for larger amounts. There was considerable discussion in 1826–27 regarding the need for another incorporated bank, but nothing was accomplished.[170] As the state began to market its stock for canal building ($3,800,000 between 1825 and 1828, most of which bore 6 per cent), and the money was spent, the supply of money in Ohio increased sufficiently to relieve the stringency. Said *Niles' Weekly Register* in 1827: "At present there is no section of the Union that has a better *circulating* medium, than Kentucky, Ohio, Indiana, Illinois, and Missouri—vexed as they have been with manufactories of paper money."[171]

Some sentiment in favor of chartering a state bank existed during this period. The legislature asked for information and the state auditor in his report of January, 1829, made comment on state banks but failed to recommend establishment of such an institution in Ohio. A legislative committee, however, reported in favor of a state bank with headquarters in Cincinnati. No action was taken, but early in 1829 the legislature chartered two new banks, the Bank of Geauga at Painesville, capital $100,000, and the Commercial Bank of Cincinnati, capital $500,000, of which $100,000 had to be paid for in specie before opening. This requirement was not met until two years later when outside capital came in. It is estimated that the circulation of the Ohio banks in 1831 was not materially greater than in 1819,[172] while the needs for money were much greater. In 1831, the same year that the Commercial Bank of Cincinnati opened, the Bank of Norwalk was chartered, and the Bank of Dayton, which several years before had liquidated and paid off its capital stock, was revived under a charter which still had a dozen years to run. The next year the Bank of Zanesville was incorporated and the Commercial Bank of Lake Erie, which had failed in 1820, was reorganized and reopened.

This banking expansion, however, did not keep pace with the

[170] *Liberty Hall and Cincinnati Gazette,* September 15, 1826; *Daily Gazette,* November 19, 1827.

[171] *Niles' Weekly Register,* XXXII, 37 (Mar. 17, 1827).

[172] It was about $1,300,000 in 1819. C. C. Huntington, "Banking and Currency in Ohio," in *Ohio Archaeological and Historical Society Publications,* XXIV, 359.

increasing demands for money and credit. Jackson's veto of the recharter of the Bank of the United States and the prospect of losing the two branches in Ohio, did not help the situation. A Cincinnati writer in the *Courier and New York Enquirer* described conditions:[173] "The distress for money here at present, is greater than can well be imagined, and the branch bank is, from necessity in prospect of winding up, curtailing. We have one other bank in the place, and its capital but $500,000. Money can be lent upon mortgage on good city property at from 12 to 15 per cent. when the security is unquestionable and worth at least one hundred per cent. more than the amount loaned. The brokers get readily one quarter per cent. per day." Early in the year the *Cincinnati Gazette* commented on the alarming scarcity of money, which it blamed upon the political action of the government against the Bank; it predicted that, if Jackson persisted in paying off the United States debt, half to three fourths of the large merchants of the country would be sacrificed to his vanity.[174] After the veto message the *Gazette* was prolific in its adverse criticism and quoted widely from eastern papers in support of its views. It said that the United States was strong enough to defy the whole power of Europe, but was helpless when its own government leagued against it.[175] The Bank and business were doomed to the buffetry of party spirit, and the whole force of the blow would fall upon the people.[176]

Obviously something should be done, and the sentiment for a state bank increased. Governor Duncan McArthur, a National Republican, had spoken in favor of recharter of the Bank of the United States in the autumn, but his successor, Robert Lucas, Democrat, in his message of December, 1832, favored the establishment of a state bank. He considered local banks controlled by different interests to be dangerous.[177] The Senate committee on finance reported that the actually useful banking capital of the Ohio banks was about $2,000,000, whereas four or five times that much was needed. It favored a state bank, with the state owning one fifth the stock and electing the same proportion of

[173] *Courier and New York Enquirer*, August 3, 1832, cited in *Niles' Weekly Register*, XLII, 436 (Aug. 18, 1832).

[174] *Liberty Hall and Cincinnati Gazette,* March 5, 1832, quoting the *New York Journal of Commerce* of February 2, 1832.

[175] September 12, 1832, quoting the Pittsburgh *Journal and Focus.*

[176] *Cincinnati Daily Gazette,* December 2, 1832.

[177] *Hamilton* (Ohio) *Intelligencer,* December 15, 1832.

directors, to meet the need of a sound and adequate currency.[178] Three bank bills were introduced, one of which provided for issue of $7,000,000 of state stock to provide funds for the creation of a state bank and branches which would have practically a monopoly of banking in the state. But there were also many bills introduced for chartering local banks, and the conflicting local interests and uncertainty regarding majority opinion in the state led to postponement of banking legislation until the next session.[179] The legislature did permit the increase of the capital stock of the Commercial Bank of Cincinnati from $500,000 to $1,000,000 and chartered the Franklin Bank of Cincinnati with capital stock of $1,000,000.

Still the shortage of money was noticed and in December, 1833, Governor Lucas again recommended a state bank. He attributed the deficiency in circulating medium in part to the decrease in the state's expenditures for improvements. One argument advanced in favor of a state bank with stock ownership restricted to Ohio citizens was that outsiders owned more than twice as much of Ohio's bank stock as did residents, and that at least $300,000 in dividends went out of the state annually.[180] Opposition of local bank charter seekers proved too strong, however, and the bill for a state bank was killed in the Senate in January, 1834.

The then current financial disturbance in the East was reflected in the West early in 1834 in tightening credit and fluctuating bank-note values. Drafts on New York were becoming difficult to get. "If matters continue long as they now are, the exchange will be *three or four per cent. on New York.*"[181] Some Ohio bank notes were at 2 per cent discount at Pittsburgh, Michigan notes at 3, Indiana at 5.[182] There were rumors in the East that some

---

[178] Ohio *Senate Journal*, 1832–33, p. 390.

[179] *Hamilton* (Ohio) *Intelligencer*, January 12, February 8, 19, 1833; *Dayton* (Ohio) *Journal*, March 5, 1833. The *Ohio State Journal*, February 2, 6, 1833, printed the main bank bill and amendments. The *Intelligencer*, February 19, said that another epidemic had broken out. Like the cholera, the state-banking mania was raging throughout the Union.

[180] Columbus *Ohio Monitor*, December 12, 19, 1833, cited in C. C. Huntington, "Banking and Currency in Ohio," in *Ohio Archaeological and Historical Society Publications*, XXIV, 365–66.

[181] Letter from Cleveland quoted in *Niles' Weekly Register*, XLV, 373 (Jan. 25, 1834).

[182] *Ibid.* In the summer of 1833 the notes of Ohio specie-paying banks were quoted at 1 per cent discount. T. H. Yeatman's table quoted in *Liberty Hall and Cincinnati Gazette*, August 14, 1833.

of the Ohio banks had stopped specie payment and that others were "tottering."[183] An Ohio businessman wrote that he was forced to sell 5,000 bushels of wheat at $850 loss "for no other reason than to gratify the ———— of persons in power; for no man of common sense can deny that this state of things has been brought about by the attacks of the government on the currency."[184] "The pressure is upon us: what was prediction a few weeks since is now history," said the *Cleveland Herald*.[185] It called attention to the fact that the Ohio legislature had said that the state of the country demanded this experiment (removal of the Bank deposits) and now it got ruin. And the *Detroit Journal and Michigan Advertiser*, in discussing the monetary policies of the Jackson administration, doubted whether gold could be made to replace paper money. It argued that if gold and silver exercised such an influence on prosperity that Spain should have become the most prosperous nation in the world. It believed that prosperity depended rather upon labor, industry, confidence, production, and resources, and that it could not be controlled by way of the price of gold.[186]

The threatened stringency and the defeat of the state bank bill led the Ohio legislature of 1834 to charter ten new banks with total authorized capital of $4,400,000.[187] One of these, the Clinton Bank of Columbus, was said to have been chartered by officeholders who had been instrumental in defeating the state bank bill. The capital stock of these banks was quickly oversubscribed. In addition, the Urbana Banking Company, which had failed some years previous, was revived, as was also the Miami Exporting Company. Many requests were received by the legislature of 1835, but no new banks were chartered. In 1835, then, there were 27 authorized banks in the state: 10 of the 11 old banks as of 1830, 13 new ones chartered between 1831 and 1834, and four revived institutions.[188]

---

[183] *Albany Daily Advertiser*, cited in *Niles' Weekly Register*, XLVI, 18 (Mar. 8, 1834).

[184] *Niles' Weekly Register*, XLVI, 84 (Apr. 5, 1834).

[185] April 5, 1834.

[186] August 5, 1834 (semiweekly).

[187] Ohio Life Insurance & Trust Company of Cincinnati; banks of Wooster, Massillon, Xenia, New Lisbon, Circleville, Cleveland, Sandusky, the Lafayette Bank of Cincinnati, and the Clinton Bank of Columbus.

[188] C. C. Huntington, "Banking and Currency in Ohio," in *Ohio Archaeological and Historical Society Publications*, XXIV, 372.

Adequate statistics for the condition of these banks are not available. The Ohio Senate Committee on Finance reported in January that, "The banks of Ohio are sound and conducted with prudence and security to the public, nor is there a suggestion of inability or want of disposition to fulfill their engagements."[189] When the state auditor's report was presented (January, 1835), the *Cincinnati Gazette* thought that much of the prejudice against Ohio banks, a result of a lack of knowledge of their true condition, would be removed and confidence inspired.[190] This report gave data on only 16 of the 27 authorized banks, however.[191] Levi Woodbury, secretary of the treasury, in a report to Congress in January, 1836, listed 31 local banks in Ohio, but the figures presented did not show the condition of all these banks at any one time.[192] It appears from these reports that the banks had specie equal to about one third of their note issues.

The legislature of 1835–36, which received petitions to charter thirty-four local banks, chartered only one. It believed that expansion of capital of the existing banks up to the authorized limit was preferable to the creation of new banks. The Democrats or antibank party was in power, and they began to show considerable anxiety regarding the issue of bills in small denominations. It was thought that notes smaller than $5.00 were less likely to be presented for specie, hence more likely to be overissued, and that they tended to drive out specie from the areas in which they were abundant. Several of the eastern states had passed, or were about to pass, laws restricting their issue. Governor Lucas in his message of December, 1834, had recommended such a law for Ohio. A Senate committee in December, 1835, canvassed the banks on this question but found most of the banks either noncommittal or opposed to restriction. The legislature went ahead, nevertheless, and in March, 1836, passed the law which subjected the dividends of all the banks (except the Commercial Bank of Cincinnati and the Franklin Bank of Cin-

---

[189] Ohio *Senate Journal*, 1834–35, p. 202, quoted in *ibid.*, XXIV, 373.
[190] *Cincinnati Daily Gazette*, March 5, 1835.
[191] These showed authorized capital stock of $12,200,000 of which $5,847,525 was paid in, discounts and loans of $6,799,247, note issue of $4,564,898, and specie, $2,489,912.
[192] Woodbury's data (*House Documents*, 24 Congress, 1 session, No. 42, pp. 82, 83) are reproduced in C. C. Huntington, "Banking and Currency in Ohio," in *Ohio Archaeological and Historical Society Publications*, XXIV, 375. Also a table which shows the distribution of Ohio banks by counties.

cinnati, which by charter were to pay 4 and 5 per cent tax on their dividends) to a tax of 20 per cent, unless by July 4, 1836, the banks gave up their right to issue bills smaller than $3.00 from that date, and smaller than $5.00 after July 4, 1837. If the banks complied, dividend taxes were to remain at 5 per cent.[193] All but five of the banks met the requirements of the law. Its effect was questionable, for in 1836 the circulation of the chartered banks in Ohio mounted $9,675,644.[194] Although circulation declined more than a million dollars by January, 1837, this fact may in part be accounted for by other reasons.

Indiana in the early years relied largely upon land taxes and poll taxes to meet the expenses of government. As in Ohio, land was divided into three classes and the tax in 1817 was $1.00 per hundred acres for first-class land, 87½ cents for second, and 50 cents for third.[195] In 1818 the tax on third-rate land was raised to 62½ cents. These rates were changed to $1.50, $1.25 and $1.00 by 1821, and revised to $1.50, $1.00, and 75 cents in 1822. In 1831 the rates were lowered to 80 cents, 60 cents, and 40 cents. The poll tax was fixed at 50 cents in 1822 and at 37½ cents in 1827.[196] The state prison, which was farmed out by law in 1824, netted the state $700 to $800 annually between 1831 and 1834; in 1835 it netted $5,492 above expenses. For county purposes maximum rates were fixed in 1817 as follows: horses 37½ cents each, stallions one cover charge, taverns $10 to $20, ferries $5.00 to $20, town lots not exceeding 50 cents per $100 valuation. In 1818 the state's tax receipts were $14,717, while expenses totaled $19,247, of which $17,000 was for salaries of state officials, $823 for wolf bounties, and $126 for the militia.[197] Although expenses were modest, taxes were difficult to collect. When, at the end of 1823, forty-four out of forty-eight counties were reported behind in their payments or half the taxes delinquent, the *Western Sun* stated that this was usually the case.[198]

---

[193] The bill passed the Senate, 20–15, and the House, 38–28, with almost a clear-cut party division. C. C. Huntington, "Banking and Currency in Ohio," in *Ohio Archaeological and Historical Society Publications*, XXIV, 382–83.

[194] U. S. Comptroller of the Currency, *Annual Report*, 1876, CXVII.

[195] *Laws of Indiana*, 1816–17, p. 133; 1817–18 (general), p. 259; 1820–21, p. 8; 1821–22, p. 106; *Revised Laws of Indiana*, 1830–31, pp. 126–27. A good brief summary of Indiana finance may be found in James E. Hagerty, *Early Financial History of Indiana* (Indiana History Bulletin, XIV, No. 10, Oct., 1937).

[196] *Laws of Indiana*, 1821–22, p. 106; 1826–27, p. 68.

[197] *Ibid.*, 1818–19, p. 147.

[198] January 26, 1824.

In 1827 tax receipts were about $33,000 and total receipts, including sale of lands, $46,500; total expenditures were $33,208. The balance in the treasury was $19,153 and the state debt was $18,700. The state debt, which during the first year of statehood was $18,557, had risen to $40,932 in 1822, and then declined to $18,700 in 1827.[199]

Roads, which were the largest item of expense, were financed largely from the Three Per Cent Fund (3 per cent of the sale of public lands in the state as granted by the enabling act). An act of 1821 appropriated $100,000 for road building and created an agent for this fund. Since the funds continued to accumulate, provision was made in 1831 for distribution among the counties. By the end of 1835 $224,464 had been received from the Three Per Cent Fund and $210,006 had been spent, mostly for roads. Roads were also financed in part from county treasuries and by corporations which were given toll rights.

Indiana's two most costly operations in this period were the Michigan Road (from the Ohio to the Lake) and the Wabash and Erie Canal.[200] Preliminary expenses on the road were paid from the state treasury. By act of 1830 the contract commissioner was to pay contractors in state certificates or scrip, pending sale of the road lands obtained in the treaty with the Potawatomi in 1826. By the end of 1835 total expenditures for construction and improvement were $200,371. More than 150,000 acres of the road lands had been sold for $222,904, with 16,561 acres remaining. A law of 1832 provided for the destruction of the scrip as it was paid into the state treasury.

On January 5, 1828, Indiana accepted the United States land grant for the Wabash and Erie Canal and created a board of canal commissioners. The legislative committee in that year estimated the cost at $1,000,000, which they thought could be borrowed and repaid from land-sale receipts.[201] Receipts from the land sales proved disappointing—only 42,000 acres at $75,000 out of 234,000 acres offered—and sales were stopped by the legislature in 1831. At the close of 1832 the fund commissioners (created in 1831) had $104,673 on hand, a large portion of

---

[199] Vincennes *Western Sun* in *Niles' Weekly Register*, XXVI, 326 (July 17, 1824); Indiana *House Journal*, 1827-28, p. 49.
[200] See Chapter VII.
[201] Vincennes *Western Sun and General Advertiser*, January 31, 1829.

which was on loan to personal friends. To remedy the decentralized management of funds the board employed a disbursing agent. In 1832 the legislature required the commissioners to borrow $200,000. Bond sales were advertised and J. D. Beers & Company, Merchants Bank of New York, took $100,000 of 6 per cent twenty-to-thirty-year bonds on an unfair bid[202] and half for credit, in violation of the law. Other loans were authorized which raised $605,247 at 5 per cent in 1835. By the report of the fund commissioners, January 26, 1836, $827,000 were issued or authorized,[203] and by the end of 1836 the total borrowed was $2,030,000.[204] The reports of the board were not complete or consistent. Although the commissioners kept an office and secretary in New York, apparently no books were kept and business was conducted as if it were a private affair.[205] The canal loans were not carried as part of the state debt, nor was the state's subscription to $1,390,000 capital stock of the second State Bank of Indiana. The state debt for 1836 was listed at $22,395, and the state's taxables at $82,163,687.[206]

"The establishment of the State Bank of Indiana was rather a matter of necessity than choice; and that necessity grew out of the discontinuance of the late National Bank," said Governor Noah Noble in 1836.[207] In his message of 1833 he had noted the general demand for a bank. The subject of a bank for Indiana had been under discussion in the state for some time. Although Indiana never had a branch of the second Bank of the United States, it had, after the demise of the first State Bank of Indiana, depended largely upon the Cincinnati and Louisville branches

---

[202] Which read, "one hundredth per cent. above any other bid."

[203] Report, January 26, 1836, in Indiana *Documentary Journal*, 1835–36, No. 22.

[204] Governor Noah Noble's message, December 5, 1836, in *ibid.*, 1836–37, No. 1.

[205] Esarey, *Internal Improvements in Early Indiana*, 117.

[206] Governor David Wallace's message, December 6, 1837, in *Documentary Journal*, 1836–37, No. 2.

[207] Message, December 5, 1836, in *ibid.*, No. 1. A letter from the *Wabash Courier*, copied in *Hamilton* (Ohio) *Intelligencer*, September 15, 1832, illustrates a common argument for banks. The writer said that the farmer slaved the year round, sold his crops, then got what? Specie? United States Bank notes? Oh no, only "Owl Creek" or "Steam Mill" paper under other names. When he went to pay the merchant, he heard of per cents, discounts, and got shaved of one fourth to one half. Big Cincinnati produce buyers were dependent upon banks for credit. No banks, no credit. No credit, no markets. So the farmer suffered. Other statements regarding the effect of the bank veto on the circulating medium may be found in Report of the President of the State Bank, December, 1835 in *Documentary Journal*, 1835–36, No. 3; *Indiana Journal*, December 31, 1831, February 18, 1832.

for credit and currency. The increase in population, business, and the needs for credit from 1825 to 1832, together with Jackson's veto of the recharter of the second Bank of the United States in the latter year, decided the state to act. Various plans were reported on and discussed in the legislative session of 1832–33, including petitioning Congress to recharter the Bank, to have Congress issue a national currency and distribute it among the states, issuance of a state currency based on the canal and school lands, and the organization of a bank with the state and people in partnership.[208]

The bank question occupied equal importance with internal improvements in the election of 1833.[209] The experience with the first State Bank (Vincennes bank) created doubts in the minds of some regarding a state bank, but the pressing need of banking facilities was so obvious that a majority of the people voted in favor of the idea. The idea and the general plan had been widely discussed and all that remained was for the legislature to act.

The charter, approved January 28, 1834,[210] was carefully drawn and was probably adapted from that of the second Bank of the United States. The State Bank of Indiana was capitalized at $1,600,000 (raised to $2,500,000 by law early in 1836), half of which was to be subscribed by the state. Provision was made for ten branches to be distributed over the state.[211] The head office was to be at Indianapolis but there was no parent bank; each branch was capitalized at $160,000 ($250,000 later) and could open when $30,000 in specie was paid in. The bank was forbidden to discount notes or other evidence of debt in payment of any installment due on the shares of stock to which a stockholder had subscribed. The state borrowed $1,300,000 to enable it to pay its share of the capital subscription and to lend the remainder to individuals on real estate, so the latter could finance their subscriptions. The bank itself was forbidden to deal in real estate, and was to forfeit its charter should it refuse to redeem

---

[208] Report of the Senate committee, John Ewing, chairman, with the arguments for and against the various plans, may be found in the *Indiana Journal*, January 2, 1833. See also Esarey, *State Banking in Indiana*, 247–48.

[209] For arguments in the election of 1833, see Chapter XI.

[210] *Laws of Indiana*, 1833–34, pp. 12–38.

[211] Another was to be created at the end of one year and a twelfth at the end of three years for the newer counties.

its notes in specie. Note issues in less than $5.00 denominations were forbidden, and the discount rate fixed at 6 per cent. In lieu of taxes the bank was to pay 12½ cents per share annually into the education fund.[212]

Although notes were made payable at the branch of issue,[213] it was provided that "each and every branch thereof [should] . . . mutually be responsible for all the debts, notes, and engagements of each other."[214] There was no division of profits, however, as each branch was entitled to what it earned. All notes were to be signed by the president of the bank and by the cashier of the branch of issue. Note issues of each branch were limited to double the amount of paid-in capital.[215] Each branch selected a representative on the bank board and the legislature elected four more. The board had authority to control note issues, inspect the condition of the branches, and close any if its condition was found to be bad. The president was elected by the legislature for a five-year term at a salary of $1,500. President and directors were bound to unlimited liability to creditors in case of fraudulent insolvency and, in case their assets did not meet all debts, stockholders were to be liable to the extent of their shares.

The bank was made the agent of the state in receiving and paying out state funds. Any earnings on the stock owned by the state, above the 5 per cent for interest on the bonds, were to be turned over to the commissioners of the sinking fund, who were empowered to lend such funds on freehold security. A sinking fund was created to meet maturity and interest on the stock [bonds] sold by the state to enable it to buy stock in the bank and to lend to individuals for the same purpose. Into this fund were to go unapplied balances from the sale of the stock, principal and interest on loans made to stockholders, and dividends on state-owned stock and the stock of individuals who had borrowed from the state to meet their installments and who had not repaid. This fund was reserved to meet the bond issue only. Any surplus beyond this need was to go to the common school fund. The bank's charter was for twenty-five years—to

[212] Both the note restriction and tax exemption were removed in 1841.
[213] Section 17.
[214] Section 9.
[215] Section 63.

January 1, 1859—but liquidation might not be undertaken until January 1, 1857.[216]

The bank board in February located the ten branches at Indianapolis, Lawrenceburg, Richmond, Madison, New Albany, Evansville, Vincennes, Bedford, Terre Haute, and Lafayette. The eleventh, at Fort Wayne, was located late in 1835 and the twelfth, at South Bend, in 1838.[217] Stock subscriptions were opened in March and early in May all the stock in the Indianapolis and Lawrenceburg branches was taken. The state fund commissioners had some difficulty in getting a loan for the state's share, but in August placed a half million.[218] The bank opened in November.

The organization of the bank was effectively and economically conducted.[219] Most stockholders bought on merit, not wild hope. The officer personnel selected was, on the whole, excellent. State officials—legislative, administrative, and judicial—were ineligible to be president or director of the bank or any of its parts, or be a cashier; nor could any president, cashier, or director of any branch at the same time hold office as director or president of the State Bank or any other branch. Samuel Merrill, the first president, had been state treasurer for a number of years and before that a member of the legislature. Among the officers who later distinguished themselves in national financial circles were J. F. D. Lanier, of Madison, and Hugh McCulloch, of Fort Wayne. The bank was conservatively managed and earned profits from the beginning. Early in 1837, before the panic, the bank showed specie reserve of about 26 per cent against notes and deposits.[220] Although essentially sound, the State Bank of Indiana was caught

[216] For brief study of the bank, see William F. Harding, "The State Bank of Indiana," in *Journal of Political Economy*, IV (1895–96), 1–36, 109–38; the charter act is printed in the appendix. See also Esarey, *State Banking in Indiana*. Hugh McCulloch, in *Men and Measures of Half a Century* (New York, 1888), 113 ff., discusses the bank during the period he was cashier at Fort Wayne and a member of the state board; the McCulloch papers, Indiana University Library, also contain information on the subject.

[217] Branches were later authorized at Michigan City, Logansport, Rushville, and Crawfordsville, but only the first of these ever opened.

[218] These were 5 per cent twenty-to-thirty-year bonds due in 1864. In 1835, $450,000 were sold, due in 1865, and the next year $440,000, due in 1866. Report of Commissioners of the Sinking Fund, December 31, 1856, in Indiana *Documentary Journal*, 1857, part I, No. 7, and Report of Ebenezer Dumont, president of the Bank, in *ibid.*, part I, 383.

[219] The cost of organizing was $614.45.

[220] April 29, 1837: Circulation $2,615,275, deposits of individuals $579,637, government deposits $1,435,300; specie $1,222,303.

in the financial troubles of 1837 along with its less well-founded and well-operated neighbors.[221]

One of the reasons the second State Bank of Indiana was created as an institution of equal members, instead of a parent bank with branches, may be found in the geography and resulting commercial divisions of the state. It may be noted that seven of the original branches were located around the edges of the state and only three in the interior. The seven were in the Whitewater region, the important market of which was Cincinnati, along the Ohio and Wabash, market New Orleans, and the Maumee-Great Lakes region which had eastern commercial connections. "Accordingly there is no point in the state calculated to command the business or extend its acquaintance over any considerable portion of its surface, and it is not a little singular that in locating the branches of our bank only three of them should be situated in the interior of the state, while the other seven are located on its very confines, and it is probable that the two hereafter to be established will be similarly situated. It would therefore have been extremely difficult, . . . to have constituted such a parent bank as could, satisfactorily and profitably, regulate all the movements of the branches." Thus wrote President Merrill when the bank was being organized.[222] He believed that the plan adopted would not be affected by local jealousies or influenced by political considerations.

Although the bank as a whole was forbidden to have more debts due than twice its paid-in capital, its credit facilities in any district at any particular time might be greater than this limit. The branches could accommodate each other. The pork season, which called for the largest amount of discounts, was seasonal and staggered in the different areas. The Ohio River region required most advances in November-December, the Wabash country in February-March, the interior (for purchase of hogs to fatten) in spring, and the northern region did not need heavy advances until the lake trade opened in late spring and early summer.

Illinois entered the Union with a small territorial debt, and in 1818 borrowed $25,000 to cover this debt and meet expenses

---

[221] See Chapter XII.
[222] *Indiana Journal*, February 22, 1834.

during the first year. This loan was paid by 1820,[223] and in January, 1823, the auditor's report showed a balance of $33,661 in the treasury. Receipts for the previous year were $62,226, a balance of $17,720 carried over, while expenditures were $46,285, most of which went for salaries.[224] Of the receipts during the early years, but a small portion came from taxes on residents. Although the enabling act forbade taxation of nonresident-owned lands at a higher rate, Illinois tried to get around this provision in its revenue act of 1819 by scheduling triple rates on landholders who did not list their lands and bank stocks before a certain date, and then setting the date early enough to make it impossible for outsiders to comply with the law. The law was soon changed to permit repossession of forfeited lands with a single year's tax plus interest; in 1821 nonresidents were given a year in which to redeem by paying the sale price plus 50 per cent and costs of sale. Even so, in 1821–22 the state received $38,437 from nonresidents' land taxes and only $7,121 from residents.[225] Other items of income were $10,763 from rental of salines and $5,659 from land speculation and sale of lots in Vandalia.

As in Ohio and Indiana, land was divided into three classes with a flat tax rate for each class. Land of the first class was valued at $4.00 per acre, second at $3.00, and third at $2.00. The tax was ½ of 1 per cent per annum. The same rate applied to slaves, indentured Negroes, or mulattoes.[226] By the law of 1819 the state took as its share the tax on bank stocks (½ of 1 per cent), the tax on nonresidents' land, and two thirds of the tax on residents' lands. Reliance on the land tax exclusively resulted in unequal taxation. A man under fifty years of age who had paid $80 down on 160 acres, his whole estate, was taxed $3.20, besides a road tax not to exceed $5.00 per year. Another, who owned 160 acres of improved land worth $4,000, a brick house ($3,000), and $3,000 worth of stock, would pay $8.20 taxes, or only three times as much as his neighbor, although his

[223] Receipts 1819–20 were $22,787 from resident taxes, $36,984 from nonresident taxes, $3,833 from the salines, and $2,282 from sale of lots in Vandalia. These left a balance of $17,725 after expenses of government. Auditor's report, January, 1821.

[224] Salaries of assembly, judiciary, and governor totaled $25,064, printing $2,976, saline expenses $5,776, militia $748, postage $234.

[225] Auditor's report, January, 1823.

[226] *Laws of Illinois*, 1819–20, p. 313.

estate was twenty-eight times as valuable. If over fifty he paid no road tax.[227] In 1821 the state reduced its share on residents' lands to one third. In 1823 a House committee on finance reported against any tax reduction despite the favorable condition of the treasury; it pointed out that three fourths of the revenue came from nonresidents and that when their lands were forfeited, the state frequently had to become the buyer.[228] In 1827 the counties were permitted to keep all the tax on residents' land. The counties in the Military Bounty Tract, since bounty lands could not be taxed for three years after the date of patent, were granted subsidies or gifts for local purposes.

In Illinois the saline lands granted the state by the enabling act were a more important source of revenue than in Ohio and Indiana. The private leaseholders offered the state $8,000 annually if they sold salt at $1.25 per bushel or $10,000 if permitted to sell at $1.50. The first legislature rejected these offers and its successor let the leases on a salt rental basis. Collecting the rent did not prove easy; the legislature, by compromising and passing relief legislation, as did Congress on the land debts, cultivated the idea that the debtors need not pay. Since the Illinois salt wells produced weak brine and salt of inferior quality which was not acceptable for packing meat for export, it was difficult to compete with the Kanawha and foreign product, and the revenue did not hold up to the estimates of those who expected the salines to produce one seventh of the state's revenues.[229]

Illinois had hardly got its state finances in good shape before the State Bank of Illinois was in difficulties. With its notes having depreciated two thirds in two years, not only were state officials who were paid in these notes embarrassed but each and every holder thereof had lost proportionately to the time he had held them. The only advantage was to nonresident taxpayers who could buy the notes at 50 cents or less and pay a dollar's

[227] Letter in *Edwardsville Spectator*, June 20, 1820. Some objected to the road tax as unreasonably oppressive and unconstitutional, as it applied equally to those who owned "not a hoof, or acre of land or a picq'un of property," and to those who possessed thousands. *Ibid.*, December 19, 1820.
[228] Vandalia *Illinois Intelligencer*, January 15, 1823.
[229] From the high of $10,763 of 1821–22, saline receipts dwindled rapidly. Total net revenues to the state from that source were only $24,105 up to 1833. Report of legislative committee cited in Vandalia *Illinois Advocate and State Register*, July 27, 1833.

worth of taxes with them.[230] Inadequate reports made it impossible to determine the condition of the branches. The legislature of 1822–23 went to the relief of the state officials by authorizing 50 per cent more pay (in the bank notes) than provided for in the constitution and by doubling the pay of legislators. Since the state treasury did not have enough of the notes to meet current expenses, treasury warrants bearing 6 per cent interest were authorized at the current value of the notes for the balance. That is, the warrant was paid by the state in exchange for services and goods measured not in specie or bank notes passing at par but in the depreciated state bank notes. Warrants and notes circulated side by side and both depreciated until in 1825 a legislative committee fixed their value at 33⅓ cents in specie.[231] The depreciated notes and warrants when used for payment of state taxes passed at face value, but when used by state officials for living expenses or state purchases passed at 33 cents. Since most of the taxes were paid with these 33-cent dollars, the result was that the state trebled its expenses without increasing its revenue. Or, to put it another way, the state was borrowing money at 200 per cent interest.

Governor Edward Coles in his message in December, 1824, blamed the legislature which created the bank (1820–21) for attempting to cure hard times brought on by excessive issue of paper money by issuing more of the same. An investigation of the bank's affairs was undertaken by the legislature but, although it was obvious that its condition was hopeless, the members of the legislature and their friends were so involved in the bank's affairs that no direct action was taken.[232] A law was passed to supplement the original provision which had required annual

[230] Even so delinquent taxes accumulated on nonresident-owned lands. The state auditor's list of August 1, 1823, of such lands to be sold for taxes filled thirty-seven two-column pages of the *Illinois Intelligencer* "extra" of September 13. This issue so flooded the mails that the regular issue of the paper could not be sent through for two weeks. *Ibid.*, October 13, 1823. In the military tract alone, where lands were tax-exempt for three years after purchase, upwards of 7,000 parcels were put up at auction in December. *Ibid.*, October 1, 1824. In 1825, 5,000 quarter sections were advertised for auditor's sale and about 1,500 sold. These might be redeemed within two years, however, by repayment of tax and costs, plus 100 per cent. *Ibid.*, February 9, 1826.

[231] *Laws of Illinois*, 1824–25, p. 182.

[232] The *Illinois Intelligencer*, August 20, 1824, had said that the embarrassments of the times called for rigid economy and industry, and hoped that the next legislature would not spend its time amusing itself and intriguing, but attend to its duties and go home in half the usual time in order to save the state many thousands of dollars.

retirement and burning of 10 per cent of the bank's notes. By this act the cashier of the main bank was to collect all notes on loans as soon as possible and all not yet signed, and burn them on the public square at Vandalia in the presence of the governor and judges of the supreme court.[233] Any notes paid out by the state treasurer were to be marked "re-issued" and bear no interest. The offices of president and directors of the branches were abolished and the branches made mere collecting agencies.

By December, 1825, repeated "purifications by fire" had reduced the note circulation of the bank to less than $200,000, and the following year the notes appreciated to about 70 cents.[234] Governor Coles in his farewell message, January, 1826, pointed out that a treasury deficit of $30,921 had accumulated in the past two years. This was the result of expansion of the judiciary, rebuilding of the state house, and the "*depreciation of currency*" in which taxes were paid. He condemned the law for issuing treasury warrants for the bank-note value of services to the state,[235] recommended they be issued on the specie value of services, and cautioned the legislature not to endanger the finances of the state further by more relief to the pampered debtor but to provide for settlement of its affairs. This sound advice was not to be followed.[236]

The House committee on finance in the session of 1825–26 listed warrants outstanding at $45,763 and estimated that there would be a balance of only $5,770 in the treasury at the end of the next year if the state continued to pay out warrants as before. If it would pay them out at the specie value of bills against the

---

[233] *Laws of Illinois,* 1824–25, p. 82.

[234] At the time of the second note burning the *Illinois Intelligencer* (June 24, 1825) said: "We hope that the time is not far distant, when our currency will not have to be paid out in defraying the expenses of our State Government, at so great a sacrifice as three to one."

[235] "This provision is most ruinous to the Treasury, and prejudicial to the financial credit of the state, and should be repealed. The effect of it is to issue the warrant, which is the obligation of the state, not for the real value of the service rendered, but for its appraised value in state paper; which warrant, in the nominal sum of this greatly depreciated currency, if retained until it recovers its value (which must be the case in a few years) will be paid by the Treasury, not in the same depreciated paper medium in which it was issued, but in the precious metals."

[236] The editor of the *Illinois Intelligencer,* November 18, 1825, in reply to arguments of Daniel Pope Cook in favor of the state taking over the Illinois and Michigan canal project, asked where interest on the borrowings would come from. All state revenue was pledged to redeem the state paper, "a pledge we are sorry to predict, the state may not so easily redeem."

state, as provided in a bill then pending in the legislature, the balance would be $16,000. But the law as passed continued the former policy of paying out the warrants at the value of state paper, such value to be determined quarterly.[237]

Governor Ninian Edwards, in his campaign for governor in 1826, bitterly attacked the bank, all connected with it, and the bungling policy of the legislature. In his inaugural address he reviewed the history of the bank and the harmful effects of relief legislation and hurled charges of "gross fraud and imposition, aggravated by the clearest moral perjury." He later laid specific charges against individuals connected with the bank, some of which he retracted, and the whole affair took on in part the character of a personal controversy. Since the legislature was not favorable to the Edwards policies, however, little was accomplished. The appreciation of the notes to about 70 cents in 1826–27, after about one third of the issue had been retired, led the legislature to believe that the discount on the notes could be regularly diminished until 1830 when the treasury notes might be issued on a par with gold.[238] The court practice of arbitrarily scaling down debts of individuals against whom the bank was given judgment was ordered discontinued. But the appreciation of the state paper led to more demands for relief and another relief law was passed.[239] Other relief laws gave further indulgence to debtors, and it became so difficult to collect from the debtors that Governor Edwards in 1829 proclaimed his intention of showing no further mercy in collecting the state's just dues.

In 1830 Judge John Reynolds ran for governor on an anti-bank platform, and pointed out to the people that they would have to pay heavily for the mistakes of the bank and legislature.[240] In his inaugural message Governor Reynolds recommended that the bank be liquidated since its charter was to expire in 1831. The state treasurer's report of December, 1830, showed $152,258 of bank notes still outstanding ($147,742 having been burned), which the state was pledged to redeem by

[237] *Ibid.*, January 25, February 2, 1826.
[238] *Laws of Illinois*, 1826–27, p. 82.
[239] Debtors to the bank who were in default, even though judgment had been rendered, were to be forgiven and permitted to renew their notes, provided they agreed to pay back installments. *Ibid.*, 1826–27, p. 377.
[240] As a legislator, however, Reynolds had supported the various relief laws.

July 1. In addition the state owed the bank $98,639 and there were school-fund warrants against the treasury for $28,283—money borrowed by the state.[241] To offset these obligations were $14,899 in cash to the bank's credit, the state had about $20,000, and the bank's buildings were estimated at $5,800. The December 1 balance against the treasury was $7,395, and the report pointed out that, were taxes paid in specie, there would be a surplus of $30,000 each biennium. Withdrawal of all state paper was recommended; also a loan of $40,000 to meet the immediate needs of the state.

The legislature approached its problem with no zest. "They feared to be denounced as a band of perjured and faithless men if they neglected their duty, and they dreaded to meet the deep roar of indignant disapprobation from their angry constituents, by performing it."[242] A considerable amount of courage as well as honesty was required to pass up the temptation to do the easy thing and repudiate. A law was enacted which authorized the governor to borrow $100,000 at 6 per cent for current expenses, to help pay off the bank notes and warrants, and to replace the money borrowed from the school funds.[243] The loan, payable after 1850 in specie or notes of the Bank of the United States, was made with Samuel Wiggins, of Cincinnati, and the honor of the state was saved.[244] But the reaction of public opinion to this sound solution was not entirely favorable.[245] Unprincipled demagogues stirred up the people to believe that dishonest legislators had sold out the state to the bankers. "The Wiggins' loan was long a bye-word in the mouths of the people. Many affected to believe that Wiggins had purchased the whole State, that the inhabitants, for generations to come, had been made over to him like cattle; and but few found favor in their sight who had

---

[241] No mention was made of the auditor's warrants issued in payment of salaries, etc. *Senate Journal*, 1830–31, p. 181.

[242] Ford, *History of Illinois*, 107.

[243] *Laws of Illinois*, 1830–31, pp. 130–31.

[244] Wiggins and associates contracted to pay $20,000 in specie or Bank of the United States notes by February 10, 1831, $30,000 by October 1, and $50,000 in specie, state paper, and auditor's warrants by October 1, 1832. Receipts from non-resident-owned lands were pledged by the state.

[245] A long article by "Civis" in the *Illinois Advocate* (May 20, 1831) in discussing the loan stated the law was passed without a dissenting voice. This was contested by the speaker of the House who said he had opposed the law as fraught with evils, as unnecessary, and as imposing an incubus on the people which would be fixed around their necks for twenty years. "Civis" replied to each of the speaker's eleven points and argued that the loan was the best solution.

anything to do with the loan."[246] Since many weak-kneed legislators had not the stuff to defend their action, denounce the demagogues and educate the voters in the essentials of honest finance, the political casualties ran high for a number of years.

Governor Reynolds staggered the borrowing so as to save interest. A commission composed of the governor, secretary of state, and the treasurer was created to count and destroy the bank notes. The treasurer was to use all specie not needed for current expenses to redeem notes and, when there was not enough, to issue a 6 per cent state bond, receivable for all state dues, for the remainder.[247] By January, 1832, all but $11,000 of the $300,000 original issue of bank notes had been redeemed; in 1835 only $6,554 were outstanding and not presented.

Governor Reynolds in his December, 1832, message called attention to the emergence of state finances "from that deranged and depressed condition," into which they had fallen. He listed the preceding two years' receipts at $102,000 and expenses at $91,000, but these figures did not include the disbursements and loans in payment of the debt created by the bank. The auditor's report showed a state debt of $266,642,[248] and the treasurer's report showed a $5,457 balance in the treasury, but there were $29,720 of warrants still outstanding.[249] The fact was that during the years 1831–36 expenditures from the state treasury were more than double receipts.[250] Although the state debt was approaching $300,000, the state had spent for "improvement" since 1818 only about $45,000. This was "truly a rapid state of improvement."[251]

At the same time the legislature was honestly facing the state's obligations, it enacted further relief for the debtors.[252] Another

---

[246] Ford, *History of Illinois*, 107. Two years later the *Illinois Advocate* (March 2, 1833) said the people will inquire, "How much money have *this* Legislature borrowed?" It could only reply that up to the present time, $32,000 from the school fund and $12,000 from the Wabash navigation fund, for current expenses.

[247] *Laws of Illinois*, 1830–31, p. 181.

[248] As follows:

State paper funded at treasury	$105,986
Wiggins loan	$100,000
Borrowed from school fund	$ 60,605

[249] *Sangamo Journal*, December 22, 1832.

[250] Auditor's summary, 1830–39, in *Illinois State Register and People's Advocate*, April 5, 1839.

[251] *Sangamo Journal*, February 9, 1833.

[252] Which allowed those who had not taken advantage of the law of 1829 to substitute a noninterest-bearing note due May 1, 1832, for their regular interest-bearing obligation and allowed 6 per cent rebate on this note if paid before December 1, 1831.

law in 1833 allowed any bank debtor who would settle before January 1, 1834, to deduct all interest and 10 per cent of the principal, provided the total reduction did not exceed 25 per cent of the obligation. Judgments which might distress widows and orphans could be set aside and the debts canceled.[253] In 1835 coercion and persuasion were combined in the law which canceled all past interest, 25 per cent of the principal, and allowed payment in three installments.[254] Such laws together with the hopeless bookkeeping on the part of some of the branches resulted in many loans never being repaid—perhaps $100,000.[255]

It is impossible to estimate the cost of this bank-relief scheme to the state of Illinois. Thomas Ford, who served as governor in the early 1840's, believed that the state lost more than $150,000 by receiving a depreciated currency, $150,000 more by paying it out, and $100,000 from loans defaulted by individuals which the state had to make good.[256] The *Alton Spectator* estimated the increase in the state debt for which the bank was responsible at $460,000.[257] The losses to individuals, the handicaps and penalties inflicted upon trade and agriculture, and the injury done the state's credit cannot be measured in dollars and cents.

The experience with the first State Bank of Illinois cooled enthusiasm for state banking for a brief interval. For two sessions of the legislature (1830–31, 1832–33) all banking projects were voted down. But Jackson's veto of the recharter of the second Bank of the United States, and the upward inclining cycle of trade and land speculation with the consequent need for currency and credit soon brought forth agitation for another state bank. Newspapers discussed the idea and on the whole were favorable.[258] Acting Governor W. L. D. Ewing, who finished Reynolds' term, favored the idea.

<hr />

[253] *Laws of Illinois*, 1832–33, p. 584.

[254] *Ibid.*, 1834–35, p. 67.

[255] The Shawneetown branch operated for six years before it kept any accounts against its debtors. Dowrie, *Banking in Illinois*, 55, 57; Ford, *History of Illinois*, 48.

[256] *History of Illinois*, 48.

[257] January 25, 1834.

[258] The strongly antiadministration *Sangamo Journal* (July 26, 1832) regretted the Bank veto and felt that the withdrawal of some nineteen millions of capital from the western country which had been enjoying a sound currency would lead to sacrifices and distresses unparalleled in its history, and that Illinois was more deeply concerned than any other western state. But after the removal of the deposits it took no stand on the question of a state bank. It admitted (October—November, 1833) that there was considerable discussion of the question and suggested meetings to ascertain the opinion of the people. The Democratic Vandalia *Illinois Advocate and State Register*, November 30, 1833, thought the fiscal con-

Joseph Duncan, the successful candidate for governor in 1834, had as one of his last acts in Congress introduced an amendment (June 24, 1834) to extend the charter of the Bank of the United States for twenty years. He feared a result of the demise of that bank would be another flock of wild banks as in the period from 1812 to 1818. He was opposed to making any such banks the treasury of the United States and pointed out that the West would be at a particular disadvantage, since it sold at New Orleans and took currency, which would always be at a discount where it bought. On the bank question, Joseph Duncan practically split with the Jackson party as then constituted. In his inaugural address as governor he advised the legislature to proceed with caution in creating a state bank. Although banks might be useful to society, a bank adapted to the needs of Illinois would be difficult to create.[259] In the legislative session of 1834–35 some Democrats, despite the general hostility of Jackson and their party to banks, combined with the Whigs to charter another state bank.[260] At the same session the lower house passed resolutions which heartily approved Jackson's action against the Bank of the United States and the removal of deposits. Meanwhile, the Bank of Illinois (Shawneetown), which had closed in

---

cerns of the country had been materially changed since the last legislature turned down a state bank by one vote. Indiana, Ohio, and Kentucky would establish state banks, and the important question was whether Illinois wanted to remain dependent on neighboring states or establish a state bank on sound principles with a *specie* capital. It thought comparisons of such a bank with the late "State Bank of Illinois" showed a complete lack of knowledge of the subject. A year later it said the state should act and not be "prey for surrounding nations. . . . We say, let the people awake to a sense of their real situation—let them say whether they will have a currency of their *own,* or will depend upon other states for one." January 21, 1835. The *Alton American* also favored a state bank as both expedient and constitutional. The *Alton Spectator* at first thought it was necessary to overcome popular prejudice against a state bank, but by March, 1834, it was against it.

[259] In his message of December, 1836, in which he recommended that the state subscribe to the bank stock reserved to it by the charter, Governor Duncan said: "Banks are to some extent monopolies, and, therefore, inconsistent with the true spirit of our free institutions. They have, however, grown up with our system and are so rapidly spreading their influence over the whole country, that it is extremely doubtful whether they can ever be entirely eradicated. Such is our attachment to a sound paper currency, that it is certain that Banks can only be superceded, if at all, by establishing a circulating medium of the same description, based upon capital invested in loans secured by bond and mortgage."

[260] The bill passed the House with a majority of one vote. Ford hints that the necessary majority was obtained by offering a state's attorneyship. *History of Illinois,* 172. In the council of revision Governor Duncan was opposed to the bill but was a minority of one and it became law on February 12, 1835. The *Sangamo Journal,* February 14, 1835, when it heard from travelers of the bill's passage, said, "Huzza for Internal Improvement and the State Bank!"

1823 but whose charter still had several years to run, had reopened in the autumn of 1834.[261]

The charter for the second State Bank of Illinois was to run until January 1, 1860. Capital stock authorized was $1,500,000, of which $100,000 was set aside for purchase by the state whenever the legislature should provide the money. Capital stock might be increased by another million if the need arose.[262] The bank was given full authority to discount bills and notes, buy and sell bullion, and issue notes, but was forbidden to own real estate, except for its buildings. Directors were forbidden to engage directly or indirectly in the purchase and sale of any goods or wares. The bank was given the power to use deposits or borrow up to a million dollars to reloan on Illinois real estate, for five-year loans, at 10 per cent interest. Ordinary short loans were to bear 6 per cent and other loans 8 per cent. Note issues were not to exceed two-and-a-half times paid-up capital, and total loans and discounts were not to exceed three times the paid-up capital. No notes smaller than $5.00 were to be issued. Stock subscribers were required to make a first payment of $10 in specie for each share and, when $250,000 in specie was paid in, the governor was to check up and announce the bank open for business. The main bank was located at Springfield, now nearer the center of population, but Vandalia, the seat of the first state bank, was guaranteed a branch.

When stock subscriptions were opened in April, 1835, the issue was promptly oversubscribed almost six times.[263] Small subscribers who were residents were given first preference, then larger resident subscribers (over $1,000 of stock), next corporations, and finally nonresidents. This procedure was to prevent out-of-state ownership and control. Out-of-state and local capitalists sought to get around this plan by having many small subscribers request stock, which would later be transferred to the big holders. John Tillson of Hillsboro, Thomas Mather of Kaskaskia, Godfrey, Gilman and Company of Alton, Samuel Wiggins of Cincinnati, and their business friends gained control.

[261] *Illinois Advocate and State Register,* November 26, 1834; *Sangamo Journal,* December 13, 1834.

[262] It was not stated whether the legislature or the bank had authority to do this.

[263] Total applications were $8,007,500. *Sangamo Journal,* May 23, 1835.

Mather was made president and a capable board of directors selected.[264]

The Springfield bank was opened for business in July, 1835. In addition to the Vandalia branch already designated by the legislature, other branches were located at Jacksonville, Alton, Galena, and Chicago. Early in 1836 three new branches were authorized by the legislature—and in time a fourth. They were located at Mt. Carmel, Danville, Belleville, and Quincy.

Loans were limited not only by charter provisions but by the practice of the United States depository at St. Louis of sending the Illinois bank notes back in quantities for specie for the United States treasury.[265] The managers of the Illinois bank sought to prevent depreciation of the notes and at the same time to conserve their specie. The St. Louis depository agreed to accept the notes for private business transactions. Another aid was the scheme which the bank used of printing separate notes for each branch, instead of a common note for the Illinois bank, and putting the notes of the various branches in circulation in districts other than that in which the branch was located. Since the notes were redeemable only at the branch of issue, this discouraged presentation for specie.

The favorable outlook for the bank resulted in appreciation of its shares to 113, and led the special legislative session of 1835 to attempt to take advantage of the charter provision for increase of the capital stock by another million dollars. Since the charter did not indicate whether the authority to create an increase in capital lay with the legislature or the directors of the bank, Governor Joseph Duncan hoped the state could create the new shares and sell them for its profit. Friends of the bank blocked this attempt, however, and by law of January, 1836, the right to issue additional stock was reserved to the directors of the bank.

The founders of the second Illinois State Bank had expected their institution to be made a depository for United States funds.

[264] Dowrie, *Banking in Illinois*, 65–66. Some people saw through the scheme and demanded exposure of the bank commissioners' actions. They asked how it was that bona fide citizens could get only two shares of stock and nonresidents five thousand shares. Letters in *Illinois Advocate and State Register*, June 10, 24, 1835.

[265] After the branch of the second Bank of the United States was closed, Missouri had no bank. The St. Louis agency of the Commercial Bank of Cincinnati was made the depository for United States funds.

President Thomas Mather and Theophilus W. Smith, one of the heavy stockholders, worked through Senator Elias Kent Kane and Secretary of the Treasury Levi Woodbury, respectively, to get a promise of deposits at the time the Bank was being organized. Woodbury would not commit the Treasury and still delayed action after the bank went into operation. When the Smith forces failed to get control of the bank, Smith warned the Treasury Department that it would be quite risky to put Federal funds into the keeping of the politicians who controlled the bank.[266] This was hardly necessary, however, as the Jackson administration was very dubious of the bank crowd who were mostly Whigs. The bank continued its efforts to get deposits but with slight success. In August, 1836, the Shawneetown branch was made a depository of the funds taken in by the land office at that place but, as the land sales fell rapidly soon thereafter, this privilege did not greatly aid the bank.

The State Bank of Illinois was not established on as sound and conservative principles as the State Bank of Indiana. It lacked such features as centralized control, provision for a surplus fund, restriction of note issues and loans, and mutual responsibility of all branches. In March, 1837, it was rendered even more speculative in character when by law the state was ordered to pay for its $100,000 share of the original capital stock and to buy $2,000,000 additional stock. By this increase the friends of internal improvements hoped to use dividends in lieu of taxes.

Michigan Territory got along for a decade with only the Bank of Michigan. In 1827 the territorial legislature issued a charter to the Merchants' and Mechanics' Bank of Michigan (Detroit), capital $200,000, and authorized it to issue fire and property insurance as well as conduct a banking business. The charter also contained a provision requiring the corporation to

---

[266] When R. M. Whitney, Treasury agent, in a letter in the Washington *Globe,* February 6, 1836, explained his position, the *Sangamo Journal* said it was an insult. March 5, 1836. It held the refusal to make the State Bank of Illinois a depository was purely politics, and that the administration hinted that, if the bank's friends did not keep quiet, it would ruin the bank. "Has it indeed come to this? Has the administration, with Reuben M. Whitney as its manager, so far obtained control of the moneyed operations of the country, as to be able to break down Banks, when it shall deem the measure advantageous to the party?" April 23, 1836. The *Register* halfheartedly defended Whitney on the ground that the bank's constitutionality was doubtful.

subscribe for and take $4,000 of the stock of a steam mill company, to be thereafter incorporated. The institution never went into operation under this charter. The same year the Bank of Monroe was chartered for twenty years, capital $100,000. In 1829 the Farmers' and Mechanics' Bank of Michigan was chartered, and five years later it was permitted to increase its capital stock and establish a branch at St. Joseph.[267] The Bank of the River Raisin was chartered in 1832 and permitted to establish a branch at Pontiac. In 1835 the legislature chartered five banks, the last to be created during the territorial period. The first was the Bank of Wisconsin, the charter of which provided that the total debts "by bond, bill and note," over and above the amount of specie actually on deposit, should not exceed three times the paid-in capital stock.[268] Stock subscriptions were opened at Mineral Point but only forty shares of $50 each were sold, and the commissioners returned to Navarino (Green Bay) discouraged. But the stock was well taken at Navarino[269] and the bank was ready to open in October, 1836.[270] The remaining four were chartered simultaneously: the Michigan State Bank (Detroit); the Bank of Washtenaw (Ann Arbor); the Bank of Pontiac; and the Erie and Kalamazoo Railroad Bank. The Michigan State Bank, the most important of these, was capitalized at $100,000, and 10 per cent of the stock was to be paid for at the time of subscribing. Its charter provisions were the same as those of the Bank of Wisconsin.

By 1836 then, Ohio had twenty-eight chartered banks with capital issues well below the authorized limits and capable of much further expansion of circulation. Indiana had a sound state bank with 26 per cent specie reserves against both circulation and deposits (including almost a million and a half of government deposits), but was not well protected against its "slow" loans or withdrawal of government deposits. Illinois had a state bank almost made to order for an internal-improve-

---

[267] For account of these Michigan banks, see Felch, "Early Banks and Banking in Michigan," in *Michigan Pioneer and Historical Collections*, II, 113.

[268] The Bank of Wisconsin was to be located in either Brown or Iowa counties as a majority of the stockholders might decide. *Green-Bay Intelligencer*, April 28, 1835.

[269] The *Green-Bay Intelligencer*, August 29, 1835, said 27,330 shares were pledged and it announced: "The Jumping Off Place," the "End of the West" has a bank.

[270] *Milwaukee Advertiser*, October 13, 1836.

ments, state-speculation splurge. Michigan Territory was still operating under the Bank of Michigan with its extremely liberal charter provisions regarding note issues, and had besides a number of chartered banks but was growing rather discontented, and getting ready to go into banking in a really large way.

The banking machinery was ready and the psychology of people and politicians right for the development of another boom which would, when it collapsed, drag down sound and unsound alike. Comparing conditions of 1836 with those of 1817–18 the *Cincinnati Gazette* wrote:

Now, as then, the State Banks that are the depositories of the public monies cannot pay their debt to the government, but upon a composition for time and other easements. Now, as then, the government fear to call for payments, upon account of the disasters such a call would bring upon the country. Now, as then, the tendency of the evil is to increase until it face an explosion. How long can that explosion be deferred? This is a question of high importance. We assume not to answer it, but we hesitate not to say IT MUST COME.[271]

[271] Copied in *Sangamo Journal*, April 30, 1836. For banking and state finance 1836 to 1840, see Chapter XII.